MW01519119

THE SEARCH FOR
THE ANCIENT ORDER

A History of The Restoration Movement
1849-1906

BY

EARL IRVIN WEST

Vol. 1
1849-1865
1953

We have heard with our ears, O God,
  Our fathers have told us,
What work thou didst in their days,
  In the days of old.
                    —Psalms 44: 1.

DEDICATION

*To my wife, Lois Louise,
and to the wives of all gospel
preachers who alone know the toils,
anxieties, and joys of their husbands,
this volume is affectionately dedicated.*

ALEXANDER CAMPBELL

CONTENTS

ACKNOWLEDGMENTS

The publication of a book of this size and nature necessarily demands the assistance of interested people to make it possible. Many have been a help to the author, whose assistance he wishes to acknowledge

Our appreciation is, therefore, expressed to the following: C. E W. Dorris of Nashville, Tennessee for the use of many valuable books, and for his assistance in reading the manuscript. B. C. Goodpasture for assistance on the manuscript. Enos Dowling, librarian for Butler University School of Religion, Indianapolis, Indiana, for use of the many valuable books in this library. Ada Mosher, librarian of the United Christian Missionary Society, Indianapolis, Indiana for use of the minutes of the early Society meetings Minnie Mae Corum of Winter Haven, Florida for original letters which have been used in this writing. Central Church of Christ, Nashville, Tennessee for use of valuable periodicals My father-in-law, Horace Hinds of Los Angeles, California, for assistance on the index.

FOREWORD

This work, "The Search for the Ancient Order," is monumental. It will take its place along with Richardson's "Memoirs of A Campbell" and Hayden's "Early History of the Disciples in the Western Reserve" as a "source book" for Restoration material. In the preparation of this work the author had at his command sources of valuable information not accessible to the average reader.

The author is a young man He was born in Indianapolis, Indiana on May 18, 1920 After finishing his high school work in Indianapolis, he entered Freed-Hardeman College, Henderson, Tennessee, in the fall of 1938, and was graduated from that institution two years later. In the fall of 1940 he entered Abilene Christian College, Abilene, Texas, with the purpose of receiving his B.A. degree from that institution But in the spring of 1941 the Broadway and Walnut Streets Church of Christ in Santa Ana, California, extended him an invitation to become its co-preacher. This invitation he accepted, and continued his college studies in George Pepperdine College, Los Angeles, California, receiving his B.A. in June, 1943. After being graduated from Pepperdine, he was invited by his home congregation, the Irvington Church of Christ, in Indianapolis, to "do local work." He accepted this invitation and still labors with this faithful congregation. During these years he has done graduate work in the School of Religion at Butler University where he received the M A. and B D. degrees, but he does not parade his degrees

Those who read this work will desire to read anything he may hereafter write

B. C. GOODPASTURE.

GENERAL INTRODUCTION

Shortly after the turn of the nineteenth century various forces were at work in American religious circles pointing toward a restoration of apostolic Christianity. Few religious groups escaped the plea for reformation within their ranks. Among the Methodists there was James O'Kelley; among the Baptists, Abner Jones and Elias Smith; among the Presbyterians, Barton W. Stone; and in both the Presbyterian and Baptist ranks a little later, there was Alexander Campbell. In the popular mind Stone and Campbell are much better known as leaders in the plea for the return to the ancient order of things.

This religious movement spread rapidly until the 1850 census showed it to be the fourth ranking church in the nation. In the decade from 1850 to 1860 its ranks increased far more rapidly than any other group. But after the Civil War an ominous note began to be sounded. The Missionary Society had been introduced as early as 1849 and sporadic opposition was engendered, but this warfare began to increase tremendously in that era following the Civil War. Too, the instrument of music began to be popularly used in the worship. From here on other practices and attitudes began to multiply, and as they did, the opposition grew. A division within the ranks of this religious movement began to be inevitable. Wherever the society was introduced and the organ came into the worship, groups who could not work and worship with these were forced out to start over again. For the most part these groups that had to leave were in the minority. But they went to work in earnest to rebuild upon what they considered to be the original plea for restoration:

The story of this restoration movement has many times been written, but the story, from the viewpoint of this minority, has never been told Yet it needs to be This minority in many parts of the nation is now the majority It is rapidly growing in many other localities Many are optimistic enough to believe that within the next quarter of a century not a city or town of any size will be without congregations knowing the plea for a return to New Testament Christianity.

The division within the ranks of those who began pleading for the primitive order was given its first census recognition in 1906.

The churches of Christ and the Disciples of Christ or Christian Church were for the first time listed separately. The report for the churches of Christ was compiled by J. W. Shepherd, and begins with a history of the churches followed by the statistics Because of the difficulty of getting congregations to report, this census was never regarded as being over a third of the total figures that should have been given. At any rate, the report states there were 2,649 congregations located in thirty-three states and territories 1,979 of these churches were located in the south central states with Tennessee leading, and Texas coming second Tennessee had six hundred and thirty-one congregations and Texas had six hundred and twenty-seven There were 159,658 members among the churches of Christ, according to the report. The church had 1,974 buildings with property valued at $2,555,372 Six hundred and ninety-three churches were using rented halls for meeting places. The report also shows that there were 2,100 preachers that year among the churches.

There were eight Christian colleges employing seventy-three teachers and having an enrollment of 1,024 students among the churches of Christ in 1906 Value of all school property was listed at $170,500. In addition, there was a normal and business college with ten teachers, three hundred and fifty students and property valued at $40,000. There was a classical institute employing six teachers and having eighty students enrolled The value of this property was listed at $20,000 Included was also an orphan school with six teachers and sixty pupils and property valued at $75,000 Of these, there were three schools in Tennessee, four in Texas, and one each in Kentucky, Alabama, Missouri and Oklahoma, according to the report.

The Disciples of Christ on the other hand had 8,293 local congregations. Missouri led that year with 1,424 churches The total report shows 982,701 members and 6,641 preachers

The significance of this year's report lies not in the numbers presented but in the fact that it is an outward expression of division which had been wrought within the ranks of those who were pleading for a return to New Testament Christianity. The fact that the religious periodicals of the two groups paid so little attention to the report can largely be explained on the ground that it came as no surprise to either group. For several years the division had been recognized. For at least twenty years before 1906 there had been little fellowship remaining between the two groups Down to the present day each has continued to go its own separate way.

To discover the underlying causes of this break which the census report then recognized after the turn of the century presents at once a complicated but most valuable study The study is complicated because these causes are at once varied Environmental and social causes are at work Personal or temperamental causes are at work In a measure political causes are at work. But, in the main, the causes, we think, narrow down to an interpretation of the plea, and a fundamental attitude toward the scriptures. On the other hand, the study is valuable because of the historical background it furnishes to present-day issues, and the inspiration it affords to those who are continuing at this late date the plea for a return to the ancient order.

The basic problem we face, then, is to seek to know the issues that caused this break in fellowship, and to try to go beneath them to discover the underlying philosophy of each group that made these outward issues so important. This, we realize, is a large order. But yet, this is the real problem which presents itself in a study of the restoration and without some conception, the movement is only partially understood. It would be useless to attempt any study which ignores the basic problem in it.

There are a number of factors to be taken into consideration in answering these problems First and foremost of these is the men in the movement. These issues were realized in the men who championed them The temperaments, dispositions, environmental background will be highly important Yet with this, we recognize at once a danger of drifting into a purely humanistic conception of the whole movement, and attribute everything to background and natural causes. This mistake we do not propose to make In view of that a second factor presents itself an analysis of the issues upon the basis of the scriptures themselves Whatever attitudes the men in the movement took, they did so because of convictions that here is what the Bible teaches. Our method, then, shall be to discover in the events and persons of the period what factors of environment, personal temperament and Bible teaching helped to bring these issues into the open and make them serious enough to have caused the division which came into the brotherhood

Every historical study must start somewhere and end somewhere. We have set the dates of our investigation for this study to begin with 1849, the year of the establishment of the American Christian Missionary Society, and to end with 1906, the year when the Religious Census for the first time gave recognition to a division. These dates we have purely arbitrarily set; maybe other dates would have suited the purpose just as well. We shall not be dogmatic in these dates, but they seem preferable to others which might be suggested.

The reader is, therefore, asked to remember that this is not intended to be a complete history of the restoration movement. By the year, 1849, the movement was well on its way. Its growth had been phenomenal Generally speaking, brethren were pretty much united. But over this period of growth, the reader may find any number of books which will give him a good conception of what took place. Robert Richardson's, "Memoirs of Alexander Campbell" is still unsurpassed. One may find in Barton W. Stone's autobiography or in the later "Barton Warren Stone" by C. C. Ware much material to give a general knowledge of the Stone movement Literature on the New England movement is, of course, much more scarce, but the reader will find M T. Morrill's "A History of The Christian Denomination in America" very helpful. On the other hand, there has been relatively little research done on the restoration movement from 1849 on down to the turn of the century It is during this time that the cause is at the crossroads. For the churches of Christ here is the really important part of the movement. It is upon this part that we propose to give the major portion of our attention.

Our first two chapters will deal in a general way with the early part of the restoration movement This material, we include for two reasons First, many of our readers will have little or no knowledge of this part of the restoration, and little or no opportunity to read the books which give it. This may supply in part their deficiency Second, a knowledge of the latter phase of the restoration will depend upon an understanding of the plea and principles which guided the movement in its earlier years. We shall hope to use this understanding of the earlier years as a platform from which to launch our investigation in a more critical and minute manner during the last half of the nineteenth century.

And so we begin.

CHAPTER I

EARLY BEGINNINGS

Although the political implications far overshadowed the religious, yet the revolt of the American colonies against the tyranny of George III was as much for religious freedom as for political It was only logical that England should bring her religion to the New World as well as her politics, and it was equally natural that these should partake of the same characteristics on this side of the Atlantic as on the other Consequently, in the pre-Revolutionary War days the most popular and well-known church was the Established Church, the Church of England All other groups were looked upon with disfavor, and persecution against them in one form or another was seldom absent.

The clergy of the Established Church ruled affairs in the colonies with an iron hand An assembly held in March, 1624, in Virginia provided that all must attend divine services on Sunday. Whoever missed once without an allowable excuse was fined one pound of coffee, a month's missing caused a fine of fifty pounds. Every person was told to conform to the "canons of England" and "to yield readie obedience to them under paine of censure." No man was allowed to sell his tobacco until the preacher gave permission. Each year at the tobacco harvest, a man was appointed to visit each plantation to collect the minister's portion "out of the first and best tobacco "[1] By 1632 the laws were revised to some extent but contained the same spirit. Non-attendance at services cost the guilty party one shilling instead of one pound of tobacco

In the main, however, one might conclude that these clergymen were kept busy hunting and punishing all types of heresy. The Act of Uniformity of 1642 enacted in order to preserve the "puritie of doctrine and the unitie of the church, that all ministers whatsoever, which shall reside in the colony are to be conformable to the orders and constitution of the Church of England, and the laws therein established, and not otherwise to be admitted to teach or preach publicly or privately."[2] The same act directed the Governor

[1] W. W. Bennett, *Memorials of Methodism in Virginia* (Richmond Published by author, 1871), pp 16, 17
[2] W W Bennett, *Memorials of Methodism in Virginia*, p 19

1

and counsel to enforce the law rigidly against "all non-conformists, compelling them to depart the colony with all convenience"

Particularly did the clergymen turn against the Quakers. The legislative authorities described them as an "unreasonable and turbulent sort of people, who contrary to the laws, daily gathered assemblies and congregations of people, teaching and publishing lies, miracles, false visions, prophecies, and doctrines tending to destroy religion, laws, communities, and all bonds of civil society."[3] Captains of ships were fined one hundred pounds of sterling for bringing Quakers into the state of Virginia All Quakers were imprisoned without bail

Persecution also raged against the Baptists The first Baptists came to Virginia in 1714 Fifty years later, on the eve of the Revolutionary War, they were relatively numerous But they would not be put down In January, 1768, John Waller, Lewis Craig, James Childs and some other Baptists were arrested. They appeared before three magistrates who charged "These men are great disturbers of the peace; they cannot meet a man on the road, but they must ram a text of scripture down his throat."[4] The magistrates offered to let them go if they would consent not to preach in that county for a year and a day. They refused and they sang as they marched down the streets of Fredericksburg to jail After serving some time, they were released They were later tried again At this trial the fiery Patrick Henry rode fifty miles to defend them He was sublime in his theme and dramatic in his actions "These men," he said, "are charged with—with—what?" In low, measured tones he continued, "preaching the gospel of the Son of God." He paused; waved the indictment above his head The silence was painful. Then lifting his head and hands to the sky, he exclaimed, "Great God!!" The men were immediately dismissed [5]

In spite of opposition from the English clergy the non-conformists continued to increase They grew more and more in favor with the colonists All the while the Established Church was becoming more distasteful By the time of the Revolutionary War two-thirds of the people favored the Dissenters, yet they were forced by law to pay the clergy. The people complained bitterly

---

[3] W W Bennett, *Memorials of Methodism in Virginia*, p 22
[4] W W Bennett, *Memorials of Methodism in Virginia*, p 38
[5] W W Bennett, *Memorials of Methodism in Virginia*, pp 38, 39

but to little avail   The Bill for Religious Freedom failed to pass
in the Assembly in 1779   It was seven years before Thomas
Jefferson's Bill for Religious Freedom passed, but it was 1801
before this final vestige of Church and State union was abolished [6]
.   One might get an additional view of the condition of the church
in New England in these days by a letter written by James
Madison, later president of the United States.   Madison writes.

Poverty and luxury prevailed among all sects, pride, ignorance
and knavery among the priesthood, and vice and wickedness among
the laity   That is bad enough, but it is not the worst I have to tell
you   That diabolical, hell-conceived principle of persecution rages
among some, and to their eternal infamy, the clergy furnish their
quota of imps for such purposes   There are at this time in the
adjacent counties, not less than five or six well-meaning persons
main, are very orthodox.
in close jail for publishing their religious sentiments, which, in the
. I have neither patience to hear, talk nor think of anything
relative to this matter, for I have squabbled, and scolded, abused
and ridiculed so long about it to no purpose, that I am without
common patience   So I must beg you to pity me and pray for
the liberty of conscience to all [7]

Meanwhile, a leaven was at work among the colonial churches
of the Established order   As early as 1729 this leaven had begun
working in England when John Wesley, noting the formality and
tyranny of the Church, proposed forming societies within the
church dedicated to the purifying of the corrupt elements   Wesleyan preachers were still Anglicans.   Wesley himself lived and
died a member of that church and was buried in his Anglican robes
"Wesleyan Societies" came to be established by persons demanding
a holier life on the part of the members of this church.   It was
natural that Wesleyan preachers should come to the New World
and should tirelessly preach   These Societies were formed throughout the colonies   It was also natural that the American clergymen
should look with disfavor upon the Wesleyan Societies and the
Wesleyan preachers   As the time of the Revolutionary War period
drew on, it was evident that these Wesleyan Societies were becoming a force with which to reckon.   The political upheaval
aggravated this situation.   The fires of liberty burned fiercely in
the hearts of the colonists   Meanwhile, the clergy looked to the

---

[6]W W .Bennett, *Memorials of Methodism in Virginia*, pp 42-46
[7]W E MacClenny, *The Life of Rev James O'Kelley* (Raleigh, N C.
Edwards & Broughton, 1910), pp 23, 24

English crown for orders and for protection. The clergy became the object of scorn, as their lot was cast among the Tories. On the other hand, the Wesleyan Societies in America were made up of colonists, crying for liberty. So the feeling of resentment continued to increase

The question of ordaining preachers was to be a great problem during these years. This was inescapable. The idea prevailed that a man could not preach funerals, administer the sacraments, baptize, or perform marriages unless he was duly ordained. The common belief of apostolic succession prevailed among Anglican clergymen in those days. No preacher could be ordained unless he was ordained by a duly ordained minister who himself was ordained by another duly ordained person on back to the apostolic era. The Wesleyan preachers were not ordained preachers. Not a single preacher in America could be found possessing the right to perform these functions. The Anglican clergymen who were ordained refused to ordain these preachers. The whole matter, then, became one of grave concern, for in time, the distinct existence of these Wesleyan Societies within the Anglican Church was threatened. The question of what could be done in such a crisis was raised on both sides of the Atlantic, and considerable anxiety prevailed.

By the close of the American Revolution, the English clergy in America had fled to their native country, and the colonies were left far short of preachers. The Wesleyan preachers stayed in the colonies but continued to raise questions about church government and the ordination of bishops. In Europe, John Wesley himself was no less concerned about the welfare of these American churches. In the fall of 1784 Wesley wrote in his *Journal*:

Wednesday September 1 —Being now clear in my own mind, I took a step which I had long weighed in my mind, and appointed Mr. Whatcoat and Mr. Vasey to go and serve the desolate sheep in America. *Thursday, September 2* —I added to them three more, which I verily believe, will be much to the glory of God.[8]

The next day Wesley ordained Thomas Coke as the superintendent in America and Richard Whatcoat and Thomas Vasey as presbyters to be sent with Coke

---

[8]John Wesley, *Wesley's Journal*, Vol II (New York· Hunt & Eaton, n d), p 602

Six weeks later, on November 3, 1784 these three men landed in New York. In the possession of Thomas Coke was a document, written by John Wesley, and destined to be known as the "Magna Charta of American Methodism" The document reads:

To all to whom these presents shall come, John Wesley, late Fellow of Lincoln College in Oxford, Presbyter of the Church of England, sendeth greetings:

Whereas, many of the people of the southern provinces of North America, who desire to continue under my care, and still adhere to the doctrine and discipline of the Church of England, are greatly distressed for want of ministers to administer the sacraments of baptism and the Lord's Supper, according to the usage of the same church: and, whereas, there does not appear to be any other way of supplying them with ministers ·

Know all men, that I, John Wesley, think myself to be providentially called at this time to set apart some persons for the work of ministry in America And, therefore, under the protection of Almighty God, and with a single eye to his glory, I have this day set apart as a Superintendent, by the imposition of my hands and prayers (being assisted by other ordained ministers), Thomas Coke, Doctor of Civil Law, a presbyter of the Church of England, and a man whom I judge to be well qualified for that great work And I do hereby recommend him to all whom it may concern, as a fit person to preside over the flock of Christ In testimony whereof I have hereunto set my hand and seal, this second day of September, in the year of our Lord, one thousand seven hundred and eighty-four. [9]

Two weeks after landing in New York, Coke and his company were at the famous Barrett's Chapel in Delaware. It was a Quarterly meeting and fifteen preachers were present, along with five hundred others. Here Coke and Asbury first met. Asbury at the time had been in America thirteen years and was now about forty years of age. Coke himself was prepared to use his powers of ordination to make Asbury a superintendent here in New England Asbury insisted, however, that a conference be called for the ordination. At the famous Christmas Conference in Baltimore in 1784, Asbury was ordained as Superintendent of the church in America It was at this conference that the discipline for the Methodist Episcopal Church was accepted, and here, too, for the first time, the title, Methodist Episcopal Church, was accepted as the name for the Wesleyan Societies The Societies were now trying to bridge the gap between being mere Societies and becoming a Church separate and distinct from the Church of England   The name chosen did not set well with many of the preachers   Nor did this type of government suit many.   Even John Wesley had admitted it was not apostolic, but most practical under the circumstances   A compromise was reached which denied the doctrine of apostolic succession   The Methodist Episcopal Church was now born

The government of this Church may be seen to owe its origin to natural causes rather than a view of doing what the scriptures taught   The background of Methodism was to be found in the Anglican church   But, whereas the Established Church in America grew into disfavor owing to its English leanings during the Revolutionary War days, it was natural that the Methodists should modify their government just enough to nullify this disadvantage   In consequence, its government became a mixture of monarchial and democratic principles   The democratic principles satisfied the freedom-loving colonies.   The monarchial phase was carried over from the Established Church.   Qualben says:

This final and permanent organization of the Methodist Episcopal Church was a mixture of monarchial and democratic principles   The bishops were given more administrative power than the bishops of England had enjoyed, yet, the legislative power was vested in regular conferences, which were soon almost completely controlled by the lay people   Thus the system was unlike that of any previously known system of church government.[10]

Scarcely had the Methodist Church started, until its first serious internal conflict began to rage   The cause was over a disagreement as to the type of government chosen for the church.   There were those who looked upon this government as contrary to the scriptures ˙ Too, they saw in it what they thought was the greed of Francis Asbury who wanted to place himself in the top position at the head of a new church   For a time the opposition was very intense.   Its interest to us lies in the fact that it presents the first major attempt of any people to go back to New Testament Christianity

Opposition to Asbury was mainly led by James O'Kelley.   O'Kelley as a leader was hardly second to Asbury.   He was said

---

[10]Lars P Qualben, *A History of the Christian Church* (New York Thomas Nelson & Sons, 1940), p 437

to be "laborious in the ministry, a man of zeal and usefulness, an advocate of holiness, given to prayer and fasting, an able defender of Methodist doctrine and faith, and hard against negro slavery, in private and from the press and pulpit "[11] Asbury and O'Kelley had first met in North Carolina in 1780. Asbury wrote in his journal. "James O'Kelley and myself enjoyed and comforted each other, this dear man rose at midnight and prayed very devoutly for me and himself He cries, 'Give me children or I die' "[12]

The date of O'Kelley's birth is not exactly known It is put anywhere from 1735 to 1757 The former date, however, has been generally accepted since O'Kelley's death was on October 16, 1826 at which time it was believed he was ninety-two years of age Records of O'Kelley's birth are not to be had It is generally agreed that he was born in Mecklenburg County, Virginia although some say, Wake County. MacClenny disagrees with both and puts his birth in Ireland At any rate, there is little question that he was of Irish descent. Shortly before 1760 O'Kelley married Elizabeth Meeks and to them two sons were born—John and William. After this the real story of James O'Kelley begins

O'Kelley's son, William, was twelve years old when the first Methodist preachers came into the Cedar Creek country of Virginia in 1775. William and his mother were converted, and William immediately began to seek the conversion of his father So zealous was he that William began thinking about being a preacher but his father discouraged him Shortly afterward, William left home and moved into the New Hope Valley in Chatam County In years to come he got into politics and was, for several years a member of the State Legislature of North Carolina

O'Kelley, however, was not long in getting interested in religion He listened to the preachers, and read the sermons they brought which had been delivered by Wesley. O'Kelley was struck by the fact that they gave all-sufficiency to the Bible. Wesley said, "We will be downright Christians," and this pleased O'Kelley. He writes

They (certain ministers) come to us under direction of John Wesley, whose name to me is of precious memory His writings magnified the Bible, and gave it preference and honor, he declared he regarded the authority of no writings but the inspired He

---

[11]W W Bennett, *Memorials of Methodism in Virginia*, p 315
[12]W. W. Bennett, *Memorials of Methodism in Virginia*, p 315

urged the sufficiency of the Scriptures for faith and practice, saying, "We will be downright Bible Christians "[13]

About the middle of the Revolutionary War O'Kelley began preaching He was continually traveling. The influence of Francis Asbury was everywhere seen, and in southern Virginia and North Carolina where O'Kelley traveled, the general impression was that Asbury was a religious tyrant. Fires of opposition were smouldering. His rule to "pay, pray, and obey" which he expected of all his laymen did not set well   As far as O'Kelley was concerned there was too much English in the system and too much Irish in the man to accept Asbury's rule   Tension then mounted.

A crisis was reached by the time the Virginia Conference met on May 18, 1779 at Brokenback Chapel, in Fluvanna County. O'Kelley that year was traveling the New Hope circuit. Preachers attended the conference expecting something to be done to end their servile dependence upon Episcopalian clergy. But Asbury fought the move   He insisted that Wesley was opposed to any such drastic move of separation from the Established Church. The Episcopacy as a form of church government such as the Anglicans had pleased Asbury very much. A deadlock ensued.

It was clear to Asbury that he must get the support of Northern preachers if he were to get over his ideas. Of the preachers south of the Potomac River almost all were opposed to Asbury   Asbury strengthened his position by an appeal to these Northern preachers.

O'Kelley might have gone further with some of his ideas except for the untenable positions he took at times   At this conference there came up the question of sprinkling or immersion for baptism   O'Kelley dogmatically maintained that sprinkling was baptism, and remained with this belief until his death   Moreover, a measure was passed through the Conference which said "All preachers were to make it a matter of conscience to rise at four or five in the morning, and it was declared a shame for a preacher to be in bed at six."[14] Preachers, being what they are, have never liked this, and it brought O'Kelley a measure of disrepute

For the next five years, O'Kelley found himself at odds with Asbury continually   By the time of the famous Christmas Conference in Baltimore, O'Kelley was generally recognized as against

[13]J Pressley Barrett, *The Centennial of Religious Journalism* (Dayton, Ohio   Christian Publishing Association, 1908), p 19
[14]W E MacClenny, *Life of Rev James O'Kelley,* p 36

Asbury's views. A week after this conference, O'Kelley and twelve others were ordained elders by Thomas Coke Returning from the Conference, O'Kelley began to marshal his forces for a show down battle with Asbury.

According to the Methodist government at this time, the power of appointing preachers rested in the hands of the superintendent, in this case, Francis Asbury. The preacher took the circuit appointed to him and had little he could do about it. The southern preachers didn't like the idea. In 1790 O'Kelley wrote Asbury, complaining that the latter had misused his episcopal powers and threatened Asbury with opposition if he didn't check his course In South Virginia O'Kelley turned most of the churches against Asbury But, Asbury was not of the disposition to change his actions and so the trouble mounted

Another crisis was reached when the General Conference met in Baltimore on November 1, 1792 O'Kelley introduced the motion that a preacher be given the right of appeal to the Conference if he didn't like his appointment This was a blow at Asbury, who immediately retired from the Conference, leaving the meeting in charge of Thomas Coke The debate that followed was intense and raged for three days. But finally O'Kelley lost. When this happened, O'Kelley and his followers served notice they were through with the Conference.

Standing by O'Kelley were Rice Haggard, John Allen, John Robertson and William McKendree McKendree later went back to the Methodists. Allen became a physician and gave up preaching. In the end, O'Kelley and Rice Haggard were the two to carry through with their principles of reform

Shortly after the General Conference was dismissed on November 14, O'Kelley and his followers met at Reese Chapel in Charlotte County, Virginia. Petitions were sent to the Methodists, asking for union, and stipulating certain amendments But the Methodists turned these down Another meeting was held at Piney Grove in Chesterfield County, Virginia on August 2, 1793 They petitioned Asbury to meet them in a Conference to examine the government of the Methodist Episcopal Church by the scriptures Asbury refused to meet. Another conference was held by the group at Manakintown in Powhaton County, Virginia on December 25, 1793. The group decided to officially sever all relations with the Methodist Episcopal Church. They took the name, "Republican Methodists "

"Theirs was to be a Republican—no slavery—glorious Church, free from all the evils of misgovernment."[15]

The next general meeting of the O'Kelley group was perhaps its most important   The meeting was held August 4, 1794 at Old Lebanon in Surry County, Virginia   A committee of seven had been appointed to devise a plan of church government. Finally, they decided to lay aside every manuscript and go by the Bible alone   Rice Haggard stood up and said:

Brethren, this is a sufficient rule of faith and practice   By it we are told that the disciples were called Christians, and I moved that henceforth and forever the followers of Christ be known as Christians simply [16]

Following Haggard's suggestion, a Brother Hafferty of North Carolina stood up and moved that they take the Bible itself as their only creed.[17]   From these two motions the O'Kelley movement devised what became known as the "Five Cardinal Principles of the Christian Church "

1. The Lord Jesus Christ as the only Head of the Church

2   The name Christian to the exclusion of all party and sectarian names.

3. The Holy Bible, or the Scriptures of The Old and New Testament our only creed, and a sufficient rule of faith and practice

4. Christian character, or vital piety, the only test of church fellowship and membership.

5. The right of private judgment, and the liberty of conscience, the privilege and duty of all [18]

In 1801 the "Republican Methodists" changed their name to the Christian Church

The significance of O'Kelley's action lies in the main, in the direction he was looking   Theirs was a movement to overthrow human elements in religion and go only by the scriptures. That weaknesses appear in their five cardinal principles is evident, but that they were on the high road back to the ancient order is equally evident

While the leaven of restoration was working among the Methodists in Virginia and North Carolina, it was also working among

---

[15]W E MacClenny, *Life of Rev James O'Kelley,* p 116
[16]J Pressley Barrett, *The Centennial of Religious Journalism,* p 264
[17]W E MacClenny, *Life of Rev James O'Kelley,* p 117
[18]W E MacClenny, *Life of Rev James O'Kelley,* pp 121, 122

the Baptists in Vermont and New Hampshire   Here the movement was led by Elias Smith and Abner Jones   So significant are
these two men that both must be given special attention.

Elias Smith was born June 17, 1769 at Lyme, Connecticut, in the
County of New London   His father was Stephen Smith and his
mother was Irene Ransom. His mother was the second wife of
Stephen Smith and thirteen years younger than he. She was only
nineteen years old when Elias was born   Of his parents Smith
writes: "Although my parents were never rich, yet they were industrious, and maintained by their righteous lives, the honorable
character of Christians "[19] Stephen was a Baptist until just one year
before his death when a church was formed at Woodstock, Vermont which "was called by the ancient name recorded in Acts 11
26, Christians "

The name, Elias, was given to Smith by his paternal grand-
mother. She had a son who died in the French and Indian War by
the name of Elias, and preferred the name for this reason. Smith
himself never did learn to like the name.

Smith was a boy while the Revolutionary War was going on
His family lived within sight of Long Island Sound. He could
see the cannons on the British warships belch their flames of death
He was six years old the day the Battle of Bunker Hill was fought
It was natural that as a child he should learn to have great dislike
for Tories, and that his heart should have a burning love for freedom. This desire for liberty soon extended itself to religion, and
compelled Smith to oppose the tyranny of human creeds

As a child Smith worried considerably over his sins   His spelling book had a form of prayer in it, and Smith would take this and
sneak off to the barn and weep and pray. His mother was a
"Newlight" Congregationalist, who believed in sprinkling   She
had her three children sprinkled, and Elias shared this fate, although he rebelled against it. His uncle chased him, threatened him,
and brought him back, and compelled him to receive the "seal of the
covenant."

In the spring of 1780, when Elias Smith was eleven years of age,
Stephen Smith moved his family to Hebron, thirty miles away.
Here, Smith got his last schooling. He could read the Bible some,

---

[19]Elias Smith, *The Life and Conversion of Elias Smith* (Portsmouth,
N H   Beck & Foster, 1816), p 14

and knew how to write a little   His youthful mind was fed on bad news from the war which gave him a feeling of the uncertainty of life   Groton Fort fell; the British burned New London, and Royalton, Vermont was taken by the Indians.

In May, 1779, while Smith was living in Connecticut, he became greatly concerned over the subject of baptism.   He gave himself to considerable study upon the subject, and finally convinced himself that believers were the only people to be baptized, and that immersion was the proper method.   The Baptist Church in Woodstock, Connecticut was holding a monthly meeting and William Grow was preaching   Having expressed his desire to be immersed, Smith was taken by Grow to Queechy River, near the house of Ichabod Churchill and was immersed in the name of the Father, Son and the Holy Spirit.

According to Baptist teaching, Smith was now a Christian although he wasn't a Baptist.   Four things were required of him to get into the Baptist Church   First, give a reason of his hope in Christ   Second, he must be baptized.   Third, he must give his consent to the articles of faith and the church covenant.   Fourth, he must be voted in   All of this Smith did and soon became a member of the Second Baptist Church in Woodstock, Connecticut   Yet Smith was not quite sure about his belief in the Articles of Faith.   Later he writes:

The articles of faith to which I then assented, contained what the Baptists call particular election; or that Christ died for the elect, and that such a number should be saved, etc.   These *articles* I did not understand for they had never been read to me before; and being read but once, it was not possible for me to remember much of them   I assented to them, because the minister and church thought they were true   Since that time, the minister and the members have rejected that abominable doctrine of partiality, and now stand in gospel liberty [20]

That summer of 1789 Smith began to think of becoming a preacher   He weighed the thought.   Meanwhile, he heard several Baptist preachers and turned away in disgust for they appeared to be men of little ability.   Smith said: "If I could not make out better than that, I would never try again "[21]   So, he made up his mind he would never speak without, first, having evidence of a call from

[20]Elias Smith, *The Life and Conversion of Elias Smith,* p 131
[21]Elias Smith, *The Life and Conversion of Elias Smith,* p 133

God, and second, doing all he could to adequately prepare himself
for the gospel ministry. He began, therefore, an intensive study of
the Bible. In November that year, he went to Elder William Grow
and asked for books that would help him learn to preach He was
given a book of sermons and a Cruden's concordance. It is thus
that Smith found himself gradually working his way into becoming
a preacher in the Baptist Church.

In the early fall of 1801 Smith moved to Salisbury, New Hampshire. By now he had begun to have some misgivings about certain doctrines in the Baptist church particularly that of Calvinism.
He had not hesitated to preach his views and before long found
himself in disrepute among many Baptists. In his reaction against
Calvinism, he for a time, almost went into Universalism. As was
his practice, he went into an intensive study of the scripture and
thus was prevented from going to the other extreme.

A man cannot study the Bible long intelligently and independently without coming to some definite convictions about the truth.
So, Smith writes:

When in my twenty-fourth year, I believed there would be a
people bearing a name different from all the denominations then in
this country; but what would they be called, I then could not tell.
In the spring of 1802, having rejected the doctrine of Calvin and
universalism, to search the scriptures to find the truth, I found the
name which the followers of Christ ought to wear; which was
Christians. (Acts 11 26) My mind being fixed upon this as the
right name, to the exclusion of all the popular names in the world,
in the month of May, at a man's house in Epping, N. H. by the
name of Laurence, where I held a meeting and spoke upon the text,
Acts 11 · 26, I ventured for the first time, softly to tell the people,
that the name, *Christian* was enough for the followers of Christ
without addition of the words, *Baptist, Methodist,* etc [22]

At this meeting Smith spoke against the catechism as being "an
invention of men " Opposition grew, and in the main, came from
the clergy. Smith gradually became convinced that the clergy were
not in agreement because they had a system of their own invention
contrary to the New Testament But, nevertheless, Smith was not
to be discouraged, and his work continued. At Portsmouth, New
Hampshire in October, 1802 the friends of Elias Smith rented a
hall called "Jefferson Hall" over the market and began holding
regular meetings here every Sunday morning. Arrangements were

[22]Elias Smith, *The Life and Conversion of Elias Smith,* p 298

made for Smith and his family to move there, which they did early the following December.

Unfortunately, the hall burned down on December 26, and the few people were left without a meeting house   There were only five members of the church, but they began meeting to discuss ways and means of organizing themselves into a church   These meetings were held in a school house. During them, the determination was expressed to follow the New Testament order and wear the name, Christian, "without any sectarian name added."   By the first of March the number had increased to ten   Smith writes:

> When our number was some short of twenty, we agreed to consider ourselves a church of Christ, owning him as our only Master, Lord, and Lawgiver, and we agreed to consider ourselves Christians, without the addition of any unscriptural name.[23]

And so the group grew   The last of March, 1803, they were holding meetings in the courthouse. On the first Sunday in April they held their first communion service.   By now there were twenty-two members   One year later, there were one hundred and fifty members   By this time the church purchased a lot with a small building on it, and here they continued to meet.

"In June, 1803, about the time of this difficulty, Elder Abner Jones, from Vermont, came to visit me, and was the first free man I had ever seen," writes Smith   In some ways, Smith admitted, Jones had gone beyond him in his thinking. At any rate, the meeting was heartening, for Smith up to this moment had the feeling he was alone.

The brethren, meanwhile, had been meeting to draw up church articles   This meeting, they referred to as a "Christian Conference"   But, in 1805 when this Conference met, it was agreed that their articles were useless and so they abandoned them, taking the New Testament as the "only and all-sufficient rule for Christians."

On September 1, 1808 Elias Smith issued from Portsmouth, New Hampshire the first issue of the *Herald of Gospel Liberty.* He had only two hundred and seventy-four subscribers   This was the first religious paper, according to Smith's claim, ever to be published in the world. The name, itself was significant. Smith writes in the first issue:

> It may be that some may wish to know why this paper should be named, *Herald of Gospel Liberty*   This kind of liberty is the

---

[23]Elias Smith, *The Life and Conversion of Elias Smith,* pp 313, 314

only one which can make us happy, being the glorious liberty of the sons of God which Christ proclaimed; and which all who have are exhorted to stand fast in, being that which is given and enjoyed by the law of liberty; which is the law of the spirit of life in Christ Jesus, which makes free from the law of sin and death.[24]

The *Herald of Gospel Liberty* was to have a stormy existence through the years ahead. The first issue came from the press dated Thursday evening, September 1, 1808. Thereafter, the paper was published every other Thursday from the home of Elias Smith on Jeffrey Street in Portsmouth, New Hampshire The cost was $1 00 a year. Each issue had four pages and each page was nine by eleven inches in size, three columns to a page On March 31, 1809, the time for publication was changed to Friday morning A year later Smith moved to Portland, Maine and from April, 1810 to July, 1811 the paper was published from here Early in the summer of 1811 Smith moved to Philadelphia and the issue of July 5 appears from there. Here Smith got hopelessly in debt, and to free himself he moved back to Portland. This was on February 4, 1814. By now the subscription list reached one thousand five hundred, a sizable number for those days

As the months bore on, Smith found his financial burdens unrelieved. In the spring of 1816 he moved to Boston. He began making appeals to his subscribers to send him money or else the paper would go under. As a desperation move, he changed it to a monthly. This helped but little Finally, in August, 1817 he announced that he would drop the paper immediately unless those who owed him would pay.

Meanwhile, Smith had more misgivings coming up about his beliefs His old problem of Calvinism still bothered him. In running from it once he had gone into universalism. There seemed to Smith for a time to be no other alternative—it was either Calvinism or universalism. This problem continued to bother him. On October 1, 1817 Smith published in his paper that he had gone into universalism, and this was the last number of the paper that he ever published.

In May, 1818 the *Christian Herald* succeeded the *Herald of Gospel Liberty*. The relationship between the two papers is not altogether clear, but one thing is certain: the *Christian Herald* did consider itself the successor of the *Herald of Gospel Liberty* But

---

[24]J Pressley Barrett, *The Centennial of Religious Journalism,* pp 33, 34

the new paper was not to last long   On January 15, 1835 the
Christian Herald announced that it was to become the property of
the Eastern Publishing Association.   Thereafter, the *Christian
Journal* became its successor.

In its own day the *Herald of Gospel Liberty* served well the
purpose of pointing men back to the New Testament.   On the
whole it followed well the motto which it carried across the top
of the first issue:

> From realms far distant, and from chimes unknown;
> We make the knowledge of our King your own.

But what were the convictions the *Herald* professed?   On the
whole they were about the same as those espoused by James
O'Kelley.   On December 18, 1808 William Guiry of Virginia
wrote:

After we became a separate people, three points were determined
on.   First.   No head over the church but Christ.   Second.   No
confession of faith, articles of religion, rubric, canons, creeds, etc.,
but the New Testament.   Third.   No religious name but Christians.[25]

On the question of fellowship the *Christian Journal* states:

They (the Christians) hold that the only proper test of Christian
fellowship is sincere piety, evidenced by an upright walk and meek
deportment.   Thus they extend the hand of fellowship to all who
have the "fellowship of the Father and the Son" They own all as
their brethren whom they have evidence that God owns as His
children   They are free to commune with all whom God communes
with.[26]

Of hardly less significance than Elias Smith was Abner Jones,
who has been accredited with the honor of establishing the "first
free Christian Church" in New England.[27]   Here the members
called themselves just Christians.

Jones was born at Royalton, Massachusetts on April 28, 1772.
When he was eight years old, his parents moved to Bridgewater,
Vermont.   Until he was twenty years old he lived an irreligious and
reckless life.   For a time he taught school in Granville, New York.
In the spring of 1793 he was converted and baptized into the Bap-
tist Church by Elder Elisha Ransom, a Baptist preacher.

---

[25] J Pressley Barrett, *The Centennial of Religious Journalism,* p. 46
[26] J Pressley Barrett, *The Centennial of Religious Journalism,* p. 60
[27] C C Ware, *Barton W Stone* (St Louis· The Bethany Press, 1932),
p 154

Shortly afterwards, Jones began to study and preach some. He became very much concerned with what to preach, and he determined to study the scriptures and find out. He was soon led to dissent from Calvinism and the result was the Baptist Church gave him the cold shoulder. He became more determined than ever to study the Bible and preach just what it taught.

Meanwhile, Jones had given much attention to medicine. In 1797 or 1798 he began to practice medicine in Lyndon, Vermont About this same time, he married Demaris Prior. Lyndon now became his permanent home. About this time too, a revival took place, and thoughts of the gospel ministry began to race through his mind. He ceased his practice of medicine and went entirely into preaching It was in the fall of 1801 that he organized this "free church" in Lyndon, which rejected human names, members insisting solely upon the name, Christian In 1802 he organized churches at Hanover and Piermont, New Hampshire. From here on, his life is connected with that of Elias Smith in establishing these "free" churches in New England.

This New England movement, as we have said, owes its primary significance to the fact that men and women were looking in the direction of the New Testament order of things, and away from sectarianism That they did not go far enough is only to be expected when one considers the natural tendency. For those days they were traveling an uncharted course. They were thinking their way along. It was to take time to get those thoughts developed, and for the most part, it remained for others to carry on with them from here.

CHAPTER II

THE STONE MOVEMENT

To Barton Warren Stone and Alexander Campbell has gone most of the credit for the restoration movement. Of the two, the latter has overshadowed the former in the popularity and recognition he has received for services rendered in the cause of the ancient order. Whether this popular opinion be justified or not is a mooted question, but that both Stone and Campbell deserve outstanding credit for the move to return to apostolic times is readily admitted. Each made his valuable contribution to the movement, and neither should be forgotten.

In 1772 Port Tobacco Creek wound through Charles County in Southern Maryland often with small boats carrying produce back and forth between towns. The Port Tobacco Creek of today is only a shadow of the former glory of this stream. The small town of Port Tobacco was in those early days of the American nation the chief port on the creek. Near this town on Thursday, December 24, 1772 Mary Warren Musgrave Stone, wife of John Stone, became the mother of a son whom she named Barton Warren, in honor of her father.

The first seven years of Stone's life were spent in this region of Maryland. His father died when he was only three years old, and his mother made the living after that. In 1779 the widow packed her belongings and with her children, moved over into the Dan River country on the border of North Carolina. The Revolutionary War was now on, and the youthful mind of Barton W. Stone began to pick up impressions that he was to carry on through life. In 1781 General Green and Lord Cornwallis met in a battle not far from Stone's home, at Guilford Courthouse. The British were making a strong bid to defeat the colonies. Stone could hear the distant roar of guns as the battle continued. Here as a lad he got to see war, and he learned to hate it. Fires of liberty were kindled in his soul that in years to come were to find expression in a violent dislike for creedalism in religion. Stone himself says·

From my earliest recollection I drank deeply into the spirit of liberty, and was so warmed by the soul-inspiring draughts, that

I could not hear the name of British or Tories, without feeling a rush of blood through the whole system [1]

Every person sooner or later faces the thought of religion and wonders what to do about it   Stone's interest was only slightly awakened in his earlier years   It was only natural that his mother should have had him sprinkled into the Church of England when he was an infant, for the Established Church had become the State Church of Maryland as early as 1692   But when the Revolutionary War was ended, the clergy's salaries were largely abolished owing to the fact that the church was no longer state supported from taxation, and most clergymen had gone back to England   The people then were left in spiritual destitution   The Lord's Day became a day of pleasure, and most meeting houses were deserted   Other preachers started coming, among these Samuel Harris and Dutton Lane, two Baptist preachers   Harris lived on Strawberry Creek, twenty-five miles north of Stone's home   Lane lived on Sandy Creek, a tributary of Bannister River, thirty miles from Stone's home in Virginia   From these men Stone first learned of immersion, but when he listened to the experiences which their converts showed, he couldn't quite fathom it   The Methodists came, and Stone liked them for their piety and sincerity, but he observed that both the Episcopalians and Baptists fought them for their doctrine of "salvation by works"   Stone listened to the religious controversies, got somewhat disgusted, and soon lapsed into total religious indifference

Not without some cause did the state of Virginia, where Stone now lived, come to be looked upon as the "Mother of Presidents"   Not far from Stone's home the fiery eloquence of Patrick Henry had helped to bring on the war   The very atmosphere was charged with themes on politics, and Stone naturally turned his attention to thinking of a career as a statesman   He was nearing eighteen years of age, when in 1790, his father's estate was divided up, and he got his share   Stone wisely decided to invest his share in an education.

Down in North Carolina, thirty miles southwest of Stone's home, was the famous school of David Caldwell   Twenty-three years before Caldwell had built himself a two story log cabin   He had

lived in the top and conducted school below   In 1790 the school
had about fifty students   When Stone came to the school on
February 1st that year, he found Caldwell to be a man in his
sixty-fifth year   Caldwell, born and reared in Lancaster, Pennsylvania, had graduated from Princeton in 1761, and four years later
was ordained to the Presbyterian ministry   In 1767 he had come
to preach at Buffalo and Alamance, North Carolina near Greens-
boro   He had opened his school soon after his coming, but made
his living by farming

When Stone arrived, he was not long in sensing that the domi-
nant influence in the school was religion.   Students were getting
religious, and Stone became concerned   James McGready, one
of the popular Presbyterian preachers of the day, came and thirty
students "got religion" and joined the Presbyterian Church   Stone
didn't want to get overly interested himself for fear he would
forget his career at the bar   He determined to go to Hampden-
Sidney over in Prince Edward County, Virginia   He set the time
for leaving North Carolina, and that day it stormed, and he
couldn't leave   What a difference there might have been in Stone's
life were it not for that storm!!

Shortly afterwards, Ben McReynolds, his roommate, asked him
to go with him to hear McGready   Stone went   The message was
enthusiastic and powerful and Stone was profoundly impressed
For a year he struggled, then he heard McGready again   He
began to have an intense interest in his soul   Meanwhile, his
mother wept over him   She sent for him and asked him to come
home and join the Methodists   Amidst this anxiety, Stone went
in the spring of 1791, to Alamance and heard William Hodge of
Hawfields, North Carolina, and joined the Presbyterian Church

Stone's associates in the school were all preachers, and before
long he cast his lot with them   He was given a text and told to
prepare a sermon to be delivered before the Orange Presbytery
which was to be a part of his examination to get license to preach
In addition, he was given the subject, "The Trinity," and told
to write a thesis   He had never heard or read a sermon on this subject, so he went to work studying Isaac Watts, "Glories of Christ,"
and devoured this   Through much effort he finally managed to
pass the course and received his license to preach from the Orange
Presbytery.

The license to preach, however, didn't come until the next session of the Presbytery. According to prevailing practice, a man was examined at one session, and given his license at the next. Sessions were held six months apart During this six months, Stone had time to think He began to doubt if the theology he had studied was really in harmony with the scriptures In the spring of 1796 there were three licentiates who were seeking licenses: Stone, Robert Foster and Robert Tate. Henry Patillo was the leader in the Presbytery He was a liberal Presbyterian who held, not the Westminster Confession of Faith, but the Bible before Stone to be accepted.

After getting his license, Stone went into eastern North Carolina to a very barren wilderness to do mission work Here he soon grew discouraged For a short time thoughts of ceasing to preach entered his mind, and while these were playing at his conscience, he decided on a move into Virginia On Reed's Creek, near Wytheville was located a Presbyterian meeting house called "Grimes Meeting House" Here on May 15, 1796 Stone spoke again, and the response was overwhelming He was persuaded to stay, but did so only until July that same year At that time he moved to Fort Chiswell. Fort Chiswell was right on the frontier Wagon trains moving into the west went through here, and before long, Stone got the fever to move west By the middle of August, he was in Knoxville and still headed west toward the Cumberland River. Fifteen miles west of Knoxville was Campbell's Station, and west of this was the badlands of the Cherokee Indians The route from Campbell's Station was through West Point, twenty-five miles from the Station, at the junction of Holston and Clinch Rivers, near the present Kingston From here, Bledsoe's Lick in Sumner County, Tennessee was one hundred and twenty miles Bledsoe's Lick is the present Castalian Springs, five miles east of Gallatin. Stone made this journey, often in danger of Indians, and approached Nashville, "a poor little village hardly worth notice," as Stone put it But Tennessee was not long to hold Barton Stone. A friend, John Anderson, told Stone of Kentucky, and the latter began to make plans to move near Lexington where a friend, John Blythe, was then living.

Robert Finlay, a Presbyterian preacher, had moved into the Lexington region of Kentucky a short time before Five miles

out of Paris, Kentucky Finlay had opened a log cabin seminary
at Cane Ridge, about a quarter of a mile east of the Cane Ridge
meeting house. Finlay here trained about ten or twelve Presbyterian preachers, among them Richard McNemar, John Dunlavy
and John Thompson But Finlay was a recalcitrant preacher for
his day, and on October 6, 1796 was deposed by the Synod for
"insubordination."

Ten miles northeast of Cane Ridge was the Concord meeting
house Here Barton W. Stone preached more or less regularly
for two years During this time, he was a licentiate, he had yet to
be ordained The thought of his ordination led him to re-examine
the Westminster Confession of Faith. He had some doubts and
misgivings, but was still in the process of thinking matters through
When the Transylvania Presbytery met in 1798 at Cane Ridge,
Stone was asked. "Do you receive and adopt the Confession
of Faith, as containing the system of doctrine as taught in the
Bible"? He replied: "I do, as far as I see it consistent with the
Word of God."[2] One might well judge that Stone's respect for the
Bible was increasing while his respect for human creeds was
decreasing. His face was turned in the right direction.

Kentucky at the turn of the century, was on the verge of a great
revival, and Stone felt it coming One thing which led to this
conviction was the work of James McGready in Logan County
McGready, who had powerfully influenced Stone while the latter
was a student in Caldwell's school in North Carolina, had come
to Logan County. He was a great evangelist. He had located
with the Gasper River, Red River and Muddy River churches—
all near Russellville, and great revivals had ensued McGready
could dangle people over the fires of hell, causing **great anxiety.**
But at such preaching, Stone was greatly concerned According
to Presbyterian doctrine, man was totally depraved, and had no
ability to believe. Yet, how could this doctrine be reconciled with
the persuading of men to repent and believe? Why preach to men
to believe if they were totally depraved and couldn't? For the
next few years this dilemma was to cause Stone no little anxiety.

In the fall of 1800 Stone left Kentucky to go to Virginia and
North Carolina Coming back, he began to show some concern

---

[2]C C Ware, *Barton W Stone* (St Louis The Bethany Press, 1932), p
74

for a general state of religious apathy around Cane Ridge   In the spring of 1801 he went to Logan County and saw one of McGready's great revivals out on a prairie   Stone was given the impetus to preach on the universality of the gospel and of faith as a condition of salvation   Plans of a great revival around Cane Ridge now began to come before him, but he had something else to do first   He hurried over to Virginia again and on July 2, 1801 married Elizabeth Campbell, daughter of Colonel William Campbell   As soon as the wedding was over, he headed back for Cane Ridge.

On Thursday or Friday before the third Lord's Day of August, 1801, the roads around Cane Ridge were crowded with carriages, horses and wagons with people hurrying to meeting   It has been estimated that from twenty to thirty thousand people were in attendance at this Great Revival at Cane Ridge   There were eighteen Presbyterian preachers plus some Methodist and Baptist preachers   Meetings were held on the Ridge at various spots and generally there were five or six preachers holding meetings at once

Today, looking back upon the Revival, there is a note of humor in the way it was conducted, but in those days, it was a serious affair   Conversion was quite literally a convulsion   Converts went through a series of bodily agitations   There were about five general types of these physical contortions · (1) the falling exercise, this was the most common   The subject would cry out in a piercing scream, then fall flat on the ground and lay for several minutes as though dead; (2) the jerks, in this exercise, various parts of the body would jerk violently to one side and then the other; (3) the dancing exercise, this would begin with the jerks and then pass on to dancing   Usually they would dance until they fell exhausted to the ground; (4) the barking exercise, this was really the jerks, but when a person's body jerked suddenly and violently, it caused a big grunt, which appeared to be barking to the observer , (5) the laughter and singing exercise was just what the terms signify.[3]

Stone's doctrine of the universality of the gospel and faith as a condition of salvation could not fail to get him in trouble with the Presbyterian Church as a whole   At first in Kentucky there

[3]Barton W Stone *Biography of Elder Barton Warren Stone*, pp 39-42

was only the Transylvanian Presbytery, but in 1799 two others
were added the West Lexington Presbytery and the Washington
Presbytery This latter covered northeast Kentucky and southwest Ohio It wasn't long until the Presbytery began opposing
the doctrines of the Cane Ridge Revival The orthodox Presbyterians considered Stone a heretic Their creed must be upheld
at all costs There were five men who came under their critical
eye, men who substantially agreed in Stone's teaching These were
Barton W. Stone, Robert Marshall, Richard McNemar, John
Dunlavy, and John Thompson

The first sign of trouble centered itself around Richard
McNemar The Washington Presbytery had condemned him for
his "Arminian views" The case then came before the Synod
of Kentucky which had been formed in 1802 and which held its
first meeting September 6-13, 1803 The Synod examined the
report of the Washington Presbytery and sustained it In the
midst of the proceedings, Stone and his colleagues retired to for-
mulate a proceeding of their own, knowing that McNemar's fate
would soon be theirs On Saturday, the tenth of September, they
submitted their objection to the Synod because of the treatment of
McNemar and declared themselves withdrawn from it The report
added that the Confession of Faith was an impediment to Revival

Thus came Stone's break with the Presbyterian Church Stone,
in his autobiography, commenting on the views which he and his
colleagues had, says ·

> The distinguished doctrine preached by us, was, that God loved
> the world—the whole world, and sent His Son to save them, on
> condition that they believed in him—that the gospel was the means
> of salvation—but that this means would never be effectual to this
> end, until believed and obeyed by us—that God required us to be-
> lieve in His Son, and had given us sufficient evidence in His word
> to produce faith in us, if attended by us—that sinners were capable
> of understanding and believing this testimony, and of acting upon
> it by coming to the Saviour and obeying him and from him obtain-
> ing salvation and the Holy Spirit [4]

The Calvinism of the day declared that a man was depraved and
man could do nothing to be saved, he had to wait and if God saw
fit to call him. He would do so, but if God didn't see fit, the man
was lost to the glory of God Stone and his group said that God

---

[4]Barton W Stone, *Biography of Elder Barton Warren Stone,* p 45

loved man, and wanted all men to be saved The gospel is God's power to save for it contains sufficient evidence to produce faith to the honest inquirer, and if the sinner will believe and obey this gospel he can be saved This, in 1804, was as far as Stone appears to have gone in his thinking, but it was far enough to make the Calvinistic Presbyterians consider Stone a heretic

When these five men withdrew themselves from the Synod of Kentucky, they set up a Presbytery of their own which they called the Springfield Presbytery Meanwhile, they sent letters to the churches, telling them of their views The document telling of their views became known as the "Apology of The Springfield Presbytery " It expressed their total abandonment of all authoritative creeds except the Bible Stone called the congregation together where he had been preaching and informed them he could no longer preach for the Presbyterian Church He stated that he would continue to preach among them, but not as a Presbyterian In taking this stand Stone sacrificed the friendship of two large congregations in addition to a large salary Under the new Presbytery, in less than a year, fifteen congregations were established—seven in Ohio and eight in Kentucky But it took also less than a year for them to see that this Presbytery "savored of a party spirit," and was a handicap to their work Plans were immediately begun to dissolve the organization, and on June 28, 1804 there was issued, "The Last Will and Testament of The Springfield Presbytery "

The Last Will and Testament contains less than eight hundred words, but it is one of the classical documents coming out of the restoration movement It showed the sincerity and honesty which characterized Stone in wanting to give up everything of human origin in religion and take only the Bible Once having planted their faith upon the Word of God they found themselves led farther and farther from human elements in religion Stone writes:

When we at first withdrew, we felt ourselves free from all creeds but the Bible, and since that time by constant application to it, we are led farther from the idea of adopting creeds and confessions as standards, than we were at first, consequently to come under the jurisdiction of that church now is entirely out of the question [5]

---

[5] C C Ware, *Barton W Stone*, p 145

Since the average reader of this book will not likely have the "Last Will and Testament of The Springfield Presbytery" easily accessible, we insert it at this point.

The Presbytery of Springfield, sitting at Cane Ridge, in the county of Bourbon, being, through a gracious Providence, in more than ordinary bodily health, growing in strength and size daily, and in perfect soundness and composure of mind, but knowing that it is appointed for all delegated bodies once to die and considering that the life of every such body is very uncertain, do make, and ordain this our last Will and Testament, in manner and form following, viz

Imprimis We *will*, that this body die, be dissolved, and sink into union with the Body of Christ at large, for there is but one Body, and one Spirit, even as we are called in one hope of our calling

Item We *will*, that our name of distinction, with its *Reverend* title, be forgotten, that there be but one Lord over God's heritage, and his name One

Item We *will*, that our power of making laws for the government of the church, and executing them by delegated authority, forever cease, that the people may have free course to the Bible, and adopt *the law of the Spirit of life in Christ Jesus*

Item We *will*, that candidates for the Gospel ministry henceforth study the Holy Scriptures with fervent prayer, and obtain license from God to preach the simple Gospel, *with the Holy Ghost sent down from heaven,* without any mixture of philosophy, vain deceit, traditions of men, or the rudiments of the world   And let none henceforth take *this honor to himself, but he that is called of God, as was Aaron*

Item We *will*, that the church of Christ resume her native right of internal government—try her candidates for the ministry, as to their soundness in the faith, acquaintance with experimental religion, gravity and aptness to teach, and admit no other proof of their authority but Christ speaking in them   We will, that the church of Christ look up to the Lord of the harvest to send forth laborers into his harvest, and that she resume her primitive right of trying those *who say they are apostles, and are not*

Item We *will*, that each particular church, as a body, actuated by the same spirit, choose her own preacher, and support him by a free will offering, without a written *call* or *subscription*—admit members—remove offences, and never henceforth *delegate* her right of government to any man or set of men whatever.

Item We *will*, that the people henceforth take the Bible as the only sure guide to heaven; and as many as are offended with other books, which stand in competition with it, may cast them into the fire if they choose, for it is better to enter into life having one book, than having many to be cast into hell

Item   We *will,* that preachers and people, cultivate a spirit of mutual forbearance; pray more and dispute less, and while they behold the signs of the times, look up, and confidently expect that redemption draweth nigh

Item   We *will,* that our weak brethren, who may have been wishing to make the Presbytery of Springfield their king, and wot not what is now become of it, betake themselves to the Rock of Ages, and follow Jesus for the future

Item   We *will,* that the Synod of Kentucky examine every member, who may be *suspected* of having departed from the Confession of Faith, and suspend every such suspected heretic immediately, in order that the oppressed may go free, and taste the swects of gospel liberty.

Item   We *will,* that Ja————, the author of two letters lately published in Lexington, be encouraged in his zeal to destroy *partyism.* We will, moreover, that our past conduct be examined into by all who may have correct information, but let foreigners beware of speaking evil of things which they know not

Item   Finally we *will,* that all our *sister bodies* read their Bibles carefully, that they may see their fate there determined, and prepare for death before it is too late.

Springfield Presbytery } L. S
June 28th, 1804

Robert Marshall \
John Dunlavy |
Richard M'Nemar {   Witnesses
B. W. Stone |
John Thompson /
David Purviance /

THE WITNESSES' ADDRESS

We, the above named witnesses of the Last Will and Testament of the Springfield Presbytery, knowing that there will be many conjectures respecting the causes which have occasioned the dissolution of that body, think proper to testify, that from its first existence it was knit together in love, lived in peace and concord, and died a voluntary and happy death

Their reasons for dissolving that body were the following · With deep concern they viewed the divisions, and party spirit among professing Christians, principally owing to the adoption of human creeds and forms of government   While they were united under the name of a Presbytery, they endeavored to cultivate a spirit of love and unity with all Christians, but found it extremely difficult to suppress the idea that they themselves were a party separate from others   This difficulty increased in proportion to their success in the ministry   Jealousies were excited in the minds of other denominations, and a temptation was laid before those who were connected with the various parties, to view them in the same light   At their last meeting they undertook to prepare for the press a piece entitled Observations on Church Government, in which the world will see the beautiful simplicity of Christian church government, stript of human inventions and lordly traditions   As they proceeded in the investigation of that subject, they soon found that there was neither precept nor example in the New Testament for such confederacies as modern Church Sessions, Presbyteries, Synods, General Assemblies, etc   Hence they concluded, that while they continued in the connection in which they then stood, they were off the foundation of the Apostles and Prophets, of which Christ himself is the chief corner stone   However just, therefore, their views of church government might have been, they would have gone out under the name and sanction of a self-constituted body   Therefore, from a principle of love to Christians of every name, the precious cause of Jesus, and dying sinners who are kept from the Lord by the existence of sects and parties in the church, they have cheerfully consented to retire from the din and fury of conflicting parties—sink out of the view of fleshly minds, and die the death   They believe their death will be great gain to the world   But though dead, as above, and stript of their mortal frame, which only served to keep them too near the confines of Egyptian bondage, they yet live and speak in the land of gospel liberty, they blow the trumpet of jubilee, and willingly devote themselves to the help of the Lord against the mighty   They will aid the brethren, by their counsel, when required, assist in ordaining elders, or pastors—seek the divine blessings—unite with all Christians—commune together, and strengthen each others' hands in the work of the Lord.

We design, by the grace of God, to continue in the exercise of those functions, which belong to us as ministers of the gospel, confidently trusting in the Lord, that he will be with us   We candidly acknowledge, that in some things we may err, through human infirmity, but he will correct our wanderings, and preserve his church   Let all Christians join with us, in crying to God day and night, to remove the obstacles which stand in the way of his work, and give him no rest till he make Jerusalem a praise in the earth   We heartily unite with our Christian brethren of every name, in thanksgiving to God for the display of his goodness in the glorious work he is carrying on in our Western country, which we hope will terminate in the universal spread of the gospel, and unity of the church [6]

[6]Charles A Young, *Historical Documents Advocating Christian Union* (Chicago   The Christian Century Co, 1904), pp 19-26

The noblest intentions are often perverted by enemies   Stone and his group were looking toward New Testament Christianity, but friends of orthodoxy could not tolerate this   Documents containing evil reports were scattered about them   The name, "New Lights" was hurled at them   This name was long used in religious circles at that time to denote any off-brand group in any religious sect   But the name stuck, and for years Stone's group was designated as the "New Light Christian Church."   Added to this trouble was that which soon came up from within the group and which was more grievous than any other.

Three missionaries from the Shakers soon made their appearance in the group—Bates, Mitchum and Young   They were neat, grave and very unassuming   They urged the people to confess their sins to them, taught marriage was wrong, and urged men to forsake the marriage state   About this time David Purviance began to notice the utmost pride in Richard McNemar and John Dunlavy   When the Shakers came, they stopped at Cane Ridge, but made no converts, and so they moved on into Ohio   John Thompson was at Springfield, but they could not move him   They went to Turtle Creek and here converted Richard McNemar, and at Eagle Creek, they converted John Dunlavy.   Stone labored night and day to save his ranks from these preachers, but to little avail   To make matters worse John Thompson and Robert Marshall went back to the Presbyterian Church and Stone found himself standing for a time practically alone

Meanwhile, the subject of baptism became agitated, and Stone found himself greatly unsettled.   Robert Marshall, who had been studying the question, became convinced that the Baptists were right on immersion.   Stone became concerned for fear Marshall would go to the Baptists, so he wrote Marshall, seeking to convince him of his error   Marshall's reply argued against pedobaptism and in favor of immersion   Stone, while not at first convinced on immersion, nevertheless, favored the view that pedobaptism was wrong   Very shortly the brethren came together and generally agreed that immersion was scriptural baptism   The preachers went to work and immersed each other   Many others also were immersed

Stone's investigation of the subject of baptism continued   Soon he convinced himself that immersion was for the remission of sins and should be administered to the penitent believer. At a great revival, about this time, when mourners were praying, Stone reflected upon Acts 2. 38   He got up and spoke his thoughts. However, he admitted, as he wrote about the occasion, "into the spirit of the doctrine I was never fully led, until it was revived by Brother Alexander Campbell, some years after."[7]   His reticence to press the point must be understood in the light of the times   He was greatly persecuted on every side, and being by nature a peaceful man, he would likely be hesitant about taking such an important step without slow, careful deliberation   Of the feelings at this time, Stone writes

The floods of earth and hell are let loose against us, but me in particular.   I am seriously threatened with imprisonment, and stripes I expect to receive for the testimony of Jesus   Kentucky is turning upside down   The truth pervades in spite of man   .   the scribes, the disputers of this world are gnashing upon us [8]

Again he says

God knows I am not fond of controversy   A sense of duty has impelled me to advance it.   In the simplicity of truth is all my delight.   To cultivate the benevolent affections of the gospel shall employ my future life [9]

For a number of years Stone's mind was unsettled on the whole subject of baptism   There seemed to be little question with him that the design of baptism was for the remission of sins, yet, he hardly feels sure enough to press the point too violently. Samuel Rogers, as late as 1821, attended a meeting which Stone conducted at Millersburg, Kentucky.   The audiences were large and interest at a high pitch.   After laboring with the mourners until late at night, Stone arose and said

Brethren, something must be wrong, we have been labouring with these mourners earnestly, and they are deeply penitent, why have they not found relief?   We all know that God is willing to pardon them, and certainly they are anxious to receive it.   The cause must be that we do not preach as the apostles did.   On the day of Pentecost those who were "pierced to the heart," were promptly told what to do for the remission of sins   And "they

---

[7]Barton W Stone, *Biography of Elder Barton Warren Stone*, p 61
[8]C C Ware, *Barton Warren Stone*, p 208
[9]C C Ware, *Barton Warren Stone*, p 210

gladly received the word and were baptized, and the same day about three thousand were added unto them"

Rogers admits that he thought Stone was beside himself.[10]

The questions of baptism were not alone in Stone's mind, but were found in the minds of brethren everywhere who were looking toward the ancient order. B. F. Hall, who was ordained to preach by Stone, on May 15, 1825, was one to have such a conflict During the summer of 1825, Hall held many camp meetings. Very often meetings would close, without the mourner's having found relief. Hall became dissatisfied and felt that something was wrong with the way of preaching. A year later, Hall found the conviction that he wanted. He went to the home of a Brother Guess on Line Creek, which divided Kentucky and Tennessee In the cabin he found the first copy of the Campbell-McCalla debate he had ever seen He read quickly, but took the time to follow carefully Campbell's speech on the design of baptism Suddenly he sprang to his feet, dropped the book to the floor, and cried "Eureka! Eureka! I have found it, I have found it!!" The whole plan of salvation now became clear to him. When he spoke of the matter to Stone that fall, Stone had replied that he had been preaching that, but found it chilled his audiences, and so had dropped it.[11]

Meanwhile, Stone had kept himself busy in the Lord's work. In 1819 he established the church at Georgetown, Kentucky, in 1823, he established the Union Church in Fayette County; and in 1828, he established the church at Cynthiana. During a part of this time, he kept himself busy teaching school. On November 2, 1819 he purchased a farm on the waters of North Elkhorn, near Georgetown, and began teaching in Rittenhouse Academy. A part of the time also, he spent in publishing his religious periodical, the *Christian Messenger* The *Messenger* began as a monthly in November, 1826 with twenty-four pages Its motto was· "Let the Unity of Christians Be Our Polar Star."

It was inevitable that Barton W Stone should come in contact with Alexander Campbell, for unquestionably the two were the foremost religious thinkers of their times. Stone and Campbell first met at Georgetown, Kentucky in 1824, and each received fav-

---

[10]John I Rogers, *Autobiography of Samuel Rogers* (Cincinnati Standard Publishing Co, 1880), pp 55, 56

[11]John I Rogers, *Autobiography of Samuel Rogers*, p 59

orably the views of the other   Stone was ever an admirer of Campbell   He writes of Campbell:

> I will not say there are no faults in Brother Campbell, but, that there are fewer, perhaps, in him, than any man I know on earth, and over these few my love would throw a veil, and hide them from view forever   I am constrained, and willingly constrained to acknowledge him the greatest promoter of this reformation of any man living   The Lord reward him![12]

As to the similarity of their views Stone writes

> The Reformed Baptists have received the doctrine taught by us many years ago   For nearly thirty years we have taught that sectarianism was anti-Christian, and that all Christians should be united in one body of Christ—the same they teach. We then and ever since, have taught that authoritative creeds and confessions were the strong props of sectarianism, and should be given to the moles and bats—they teach the same   We have from that time preached the gospel to every creature to whom we had access, and urged them to believe and obey it—that its own evidence was sufficient to produce faith in all that heard it, that the unrenewed sinner must, and could, believe it unto justification and salvation—and through the Holy Spirit of promise, and every other promise of the New Covenant was given   They proclaim the same doctrine. Many years ago some of us preached baptism as a means, in connection with faith and repentance, for the remission of sins and the gift of the Holy Spirit—they preach the same and extend it farther than we have done   We rejected all names but Christian—they acknowledge it most proper, but seem to prefer another [13]

Up to now Stone's group had insisted upon the name, Christian, to the exclusion of all others   Followers of Alexander Campbell took the name, Reformers or Reformed Baptists   The two groups would exist side by side in various towns, especially in Kentucky, and slowly understanding and agreement would be reached between them bringing about a union of forces. At Millersburg, Kentucky near Cane Ridge, the two groups were to be found   Occasionally they communed together   Finally, seeing there was little difference between them in faith and practice they united on April 24, 1831. But the union was soon to become larger in its scope

In 1831 Stone made the friendship of John T. Johnson   Each was fervently interested in unity. But there were others of great influence in Kentucky who were also as interested   There were

---

[12]Barton W Stone, *Biography of Elder Barton Warren Stone,* p 76
[13]Barton W Stone, "Union," *Millennial Harbinger,* Vol II, No 9 (September 5, 1831), p 385

men like John Rogers and "Raccoon" John Smith just as interested These men arranged a joint meeting of the "Christians" and "Reformers" for Christmas, 1831. This came on Sunday, so they arranged a series of meetings to last all week. This was the beginning of a series of joint meetings which lasted until 1835. The Oldham Cotton Factory, 168 N Broadway, was rented, swept and garnished for the meeting. Speeches were to be spontaneous. John Smith was the first to speak He concluded by saying·

Let us, then my brethren, be no longer Campbellites or Stoneites, New Lights or Old Lights, or any other kind of lights, but let us come to the Bible and to the Bible alone, as the only book in the world that can give us all the light we need [14]

Concerning the general spirit which prevailed at the meeting, John Rogers wrote in 1844, twelve years later

No one ever thought that the Reformers, so called, had come over to us, or that we had gone over to them, that they were required to relinquish their opinions or we ours We found ourselves contending for the same great principles of Christianity, and we resolved to unite our energies to harmonize the church, and save the world I entered into it upon principle I think immense good has grown out of it, that had it never taken place, our cause in Kentucky would be far in the rear of the position it now occupies [15]

How easy it is to forget the passing of time when discussing the events which come before us! Many important items of interest cry for attention while studying the life of Barton W. Stone Yet, with the passing of these events, we forget so easily that Stone is slowly reaching out for his three-score years and ten. Stone was in his sixty-second year when in 1834, he moved to Jacksonville, Illinois, the land of the Kickapoo Indians in the "far west." Here he gave his time to preaching tours But he was slowing down At his home out on the Diamond Grove Prairie near Jacksonville in the fall of 1836 he lay seriously ill Three years later, his hearing went bad, and two years after that, he suffered a stroke of paralysis, and almost died

Stone's death came on Saturday, November 9, 1844 at four o'clock in the morning He was at Hannibal, Missouri, at the home of his son-in-law, Captain Samuel Bowen, who had married his

[14] John Augustus Williams, *Life of Elder John Smith* (Cincinnati Christian Standard Publishing Co, 1904), p 454
[15] C C Ware, *Barton Warren Stone*, p 247

daughter, Amanda   Only a few days before Stone had attended
an annual meeting in Boone County near Columbia. At the meeting he had had an attack but presided anyway on Monday, and
delivered a discourse which he regarded as his last

On Thursday, Nov 7, he sent for Jacob Creath, Jr , but Creath
was sick and couldn't arrive until later. He and Stone sang a
song and had prayer   Creath asked Stone if he had any fear of
death   Stone's reply was, "O, no, Brother Creath, I know in whom
I have believed and in whom I have trusted, and I am persuaded
that he is able to keep that which I have committed to him.   I
know that my Redeemer lives.   All my dependence is in God and
in His Son Jesus Christ "   Then Stone quoted scripture, commenting upon them at the same time   Then he added, "But my strength
fails, but God is my strength and my portion forever."

Stone turned for a moment to his family and exhorted them to
be faithful   Turning back to Creath, he said, "Brother Creath, if
so great and so holy a man as Paul was afraid that he might be a
cast-away, may not so frail and poor a man as I fear too?   But my
God is good and merciful, and my Saviour is strong and mighty to
save me."   In a moment Creath had to leave   Stone called after
him, "God bless you, my brother   I hope to meet you in heaven "

Stone was put in a chair by his friends.   Dr David Morton
asked him what he thought of the doctrine he had been preaching
He replied that he believed it on the whole to be true although
some mistakes had been made   The rest of the time he spent
in smoking his pipe and conversing upon the love of God   Presently, he reclined his head upon the shoulder of his son, Barton,
and went to his eternal sleep.[16]

He was buried at Hannibal, but later his body was re-buried
at Cane Ridge   A monument today beside the old Cane Ridge
meeting house marks the place of burial of one of the greatest of
the pioneers—Barton Warren Stone

It is not likely that Tolbert Fanning overstated the case, when,
upon receiving news of Stone's death, he wrote:

The history of Brother Stone would be the history of the most
important religious movements in the United States, for nearly
half a century   To be sure his talent was not, perhaps, quite so
brilliant as some others, but his acquaintance with the Scriptures

---

[16]Jacob Creath, "Ob tuary," *Millennial Harbinger*, Third Series, Vol I.
No 12 (December, 1844), p 621

was extensive and critical, and a more humble, conscientious and pious man cannot be found If justice is ever done to his memory, he will be regarded as the first great American reformer,—the first man, who, to much purpose, pleaded the ground that the Bible, without note, commentary or creed, must destroy antichristian powers, and eventually conquer the world. Although I have heard Father Stone slandered, and his views grossly perverted, yet never did I hear mortal man utter a syllable derogatory to his moral worth. A man more devoted to Christianity, has not lived nor died, and many stars will adorn his crown in a coming day.[17]

---

[17]Tolbert Fanning, "A Good Man Has Fallen" *Christian Review*, Vol I, No 12 (December 1844) p 288

CHAPTER III

THE CAMPBELL MOVEMENT

In September, 1850, a young twenty-three year old man by the name of John F Rowe arrived for the first time in the little community called Bethany, Virginia to begin college under the tutorship of one of the most illustrious of religious leaders to live within the past century—Alexander Campbell In Rowe's pocket was a letter from J H Jones, preacher for the church in Wooster, Ohio, addressed to President Campbell on behalf of the youth. Accordingly, the first person Rowe wanted to see was Campbell, so out to Campbell's famous study he went. Stepping into the study, Rowe saw at once there were no other chairs besides the one Campbell occupied Campbell immediately piled up some books and pointing to them, said to Rowe "Please, Sir, take a literary seat '"[1] The words were spoken and the inward tension ceased, for Rowe had come with hero-worship in his heart for such a man whose reputation was known throughout the nation Throughout the rest of the conversation Rowe felt perfectly at ease

This unusual devotion which Rowe felt toward a man he had never seen, but about whom he had heard much, was a very common thing, for Alexander Campbell, president of Bethany College, was no usual man In personal appearance Campbell was tall, vigorous and athletic His hair was light and his complexion moderately fair His face had no straight lines, and his aquiline nose was arched as John Smith said, a "little to the north " Few ever saw him when his countenance was not cheerful Men came from miles to drink at this fountain of knowledge The saints of the age had beaten a path to his door.

Scarcely can a man be found who does not have some one trait more pronounced in his make-up than others While in Campbell there was a rare combination of many of the nobler traits, yet the outstanding quality seemed to be his power of concentration which gave to him a rich store-house of knowledge. His mind was keen and logical, and his arguments were generally well arranged Friend and foe alike spoke in praise of this man, and even the

---

[1]John F Rowe, "Reminiscences of the Restoration," *American Christian Review,* Vol XXIX, No 18 (April 29, 1886), p 141

worldly great recognized in Campbell no common man General Robert E Lee spoke of Campbell in the following words:

He was a man in whom were illustriously combined all the qualities that could adorn or elevate the nature to which he belonged Knowledge, the most various and extended virtue that never loitered in her career nor deviated from her course A man who if he had been delegated as the representative of his species to one of the superior worlds, would have suggested a grand idea of the human race. Such was President Campbell [2]

At the time of the debate with N L Rice in 1843 Alexander Campbell was at the height of his power Certainly in no period before or after was he any more active ‹ Tolbert Fanning, one of Campbell's great admirers, writes of Campbell at this period of his life in the following words

Alexander Campbell is about sixty years old, has been blessed by nature with a fine constitution, has led a most active life, and consequently enjoys remarkable good health for one of his age, and his intellect is as vigorous as it was at twenty-five In personal appearance, there is no man like him His scholarship is admired by both friends and foes, and in logical powers, the world, in my humble opinion, has not his equal As a declaimer, he is not generally admired by the multitude, but men of the best order of mind are always delighted with his addresses He is most chaste, pointed, and dignified, in all his public exhibitions, knows not how to take advantage of an opponent, and will not condescend to little tricks for the sake of applause His arguments are always well arranged, and are generally full and satisfactory on every point he touches It is scarcely probable any man has ever become truly distinguished, who has not attained his pre-eminence for some one particular trait, and evidently Alexander Campbell owes his greatness to his powers of *concentration,* and his habit of presenting the greatest subjects in a few *pointed* and *palpable propositions* His doctrine is that the universe is ruled by a few general laws, and to illustrate the most important truths, a few leading points only need be discussed For logic, scriptural knowledge. genuine criticisms, dignity of manner, fairness and Christian courtesy, it is barely probable Alexander Campbell has an equal living   [3]

These are strong words and one might well ask if it might be possible that Fanning overstated the case. Friends of Alexander Campbell do not think so There has never been a great question

---

[2] Robert E Lee, "The Late R E Lee's Letter," *Apostolic Times,* Vol III, No 4 (May 4, 1871), p 27

[3] Tolbert Fanning, "Campbell and Rice's Debate," *Christian Review,* Vol I, No 5 (May, 1844), pp 115, 116

to them but that Campbell was one of the foremost thinkers in
the nation, and that his religious influence has been on the whole
a precious enlightenment to those inquirers after the truth of God's
word.   Nevertheless, such strong testimonials of the greatness of
the man lead naturally into investigation of his life, his work, and
the secret of such a lasting influence.   Such a story takes us back
nearly two centuries and off to a country for its beginning far away
from America.

The story begins in Northern Ireland in the year 1786   A
better place to begin could not be found, for the people of Northern
Ireland are a people as distinct and different from the usual Irish
as are the Hindus from the Chinese.   Here in the northeastern
corner of the Emerald Isle where Alexander Campbell was born
the people were predominantly Anglo-Scottish in blood and
Protestant in religion.   Settled in the early seventeenth century by
Presbyterian Scots, this section of Ireland has long struggled with
Catholic Ireland to the south of them, but in their own independent
way they have declared their liberty even down to the present day.
Perhaps the geography has lent some to this fierce passion of independence, for northeast Ireland is a land of fertile valleys, stony
mountain moorland and bold rocky shores washed by the North
Channel and Irish Sea.   This section comprises the heart of the
commercial and industrial regions of Ireland today, and in Campbell's day those rich valleys were an agriculturalist's dreamland.
Here the people had their own living.   There was an air of financial
and economic independence, and so the people of northeastern Ireland lifted their proud heads in defiance of Catholic Ireland

The exact date of Alexander Campbell's birth will probably never
be settled to the satisfaction of every interested party.   Records of
this date were lost in a shipwreck, and so nothing authoritative remains by which to go.   From Campbell's day on down differences
of opinion have existed   Richardson places the date as September
12, 1788   W K Pendleton, twice the son-in-law of Campbell,
placed the date in June, 1786   Moses E Lard placed the date 1787
Tolbert Fanning thought Campbell to be older than any of these
men put it   In March or April 1835 Campbell and Fanning were
on an extended tour into the northeastern part of the United States
and on the way stopped in Georgetown, Kentucky to visit in the
home of John T Johnson   They were dining together and Richard

N. Johnson was present. Campbell and R. N. Johnson, in the course of their conversation, discussed their ages. There was, says Fanning, no doubt in the minds of either that they were the same age, and Johnson was fifty-four[4] In which case, the birth of Campbell is put back to 1781. Charles V. Segar, who wrote the biographical sketch of Campbell in the book, "Lectures on The Pentateuch," uses the date of Campbell's birth the same as W K Pendleton. Segar declares that this is the date Thomas Campbell gave to him in 1847 and the one which the family generally considered most correct[5] While it is well to recognize that the date can never be definitely set, yet the greater weight of evidence seems to point toward Segar's date, viz, that Alexander Campbell was born in June, 1786

As one looks northward on a map of Ireland, the rocky shores of Lough Neagh which border on County Antrim in northeastern Ireland suddenly take a sharp turn westward near the city of Antrim and continue so over into the county of Armagh before turning again southward to form the northern coast line for the Lough Here, only a few miles from where the Lough makes that first turn, on the north shores of the Lough, stands Shane's Castle Northward from here about a mile, over into County Antrim, stood a little village called Ballymena Only a short distance from this village was a little cottage, surrounded by a few acres of ground, where in 1786 there lived a preacher in the Seceder Church by the name of Thomas Campbell with a bride of less than a year, Jane Corneigle Campbell Here their first son, Alexander, was born.

Thomas, James, Archibald and Enos were the four sons of Archibald Campbell, Thomas being the elder He was born on February 1, 1763 in County Down Ireland Thomas had a bright intellect and determined to be a teacher. His first excursion into teaching took him into the south of Ireland, into the County of Connaught. But his father was dissatisfied, and summoned him back home He then settled down for a time to teach at Sheepbridge, near Newry in the southern part of County Down

Before many months Campbell had the customary experience which lead him to believe he was called of God to preach. He belonged to the Anti-Burgher group of the Seceders Through the

[4]Tolbert Fanning, "Sketches in the Life of Alexander Campbell, No 1," *Gospel Advocate,* Vol VIII, No 20 (May 15, 1866), pp 306, 307
[5]Charles V Segar, *Lectures on the Pentateuch* (Cincinnati Bosworth, Chase & Hall, Publishers, 1871), p 12

help of John Kinley who promised to pay his expenses, Campbell attended Glasgow University for three years, finishing the prescribed course, and then went to Whitburn where he studied under Professor A B Bruce in the Anti-Burgher School. Finishing his course, he took an examination, and was given a license to preach under the Synod   His first preaching was done near Sheepbridge   After his marriage to Jane Corneigle, he moved to Market Hill in the county adjoining Down on the west, County Armagh. He moved to Ahorey in 1798 in the same county, in a community called Rich Hill   It was near here that the youthful days of Alexander Campbell were spent

The greatness of Alexander Campbell can in no small measure be traced to his noble parents   Thomas Campbell was a severe critic, a kind disciplinarian, and a devoted scholar.   Alexander's mind was very early to be filled with large selections of literature. He read extensively, and memorized many choice items in literature and in scripture   It was the rule in the Campbell family that each child should sometime during the day, memorize a verse of scripture to recite at evening worship   Almost daily the boy studied the Bible along with Brown's catechism   He memorized rich passages in Greek, Roman, French and English literature   In later years many marvelled at the knowledge which Campbell possessed Fanning says of him

Hence, we never saw a man so perfectly familiar with the most important events recorded in the Sacred oracles, particularly the Old Testament, and also in Greek, Roman and English history. Singular as it may appear, Alexander Campbell could recite and fully appreciate more of the English poets, especially Milton, Shakespeare, Thompson and Young, than any one with whom we have had the satisfaction of associating [6]

Campbell, in his literary tastes, seems to have had little desire for the more modern productions   Everything from the Reformation movement on back to ancient history, he knew extensively.   But the more modern writings of his time did not challange his attention

Campbell's religious background is very interesting   Thomas Campbell had a high regard for the Bible, and this fact very early made an impression upon Alexander's mind   He would come into

---

[6]Tolbert Fanning, "Sketches in the Life of Alexander Campbell, No 1," *Gospel Advocate,* Vol VIII, No 20 (May 15, 1866), p 307

THOMAS CAMPBELL

his father's library and notice frequently the Bible and a Concordance upon the stand while many other books were in the library shelves untouched Gradually his father was turning more to the Bible as a pure fountain of living water and away from creeds and doctrines of men

The church to which the Campbells belonged, as previously stated, was the Seceder branch of the Presbyterian Church Its history is long and complicated, but the full story of the Campbells cannot be told without a brief sketch of it

There are often many strange ironies in history! In Scotland in 1559 there was a large class of insurgents, Calvinistic in belief, who opposed the regent Elizabeth, queen of England, hated them, yet politics makes strange bedfellows, and Elizabeth found herself fighting on their side. She won out and the Treaty of Edinburgh was signed in 1560 providing that the government of Scotland should be turned over to a council of Lords. In August that same year, the Scottish Parliament made Calvinistic Protestantism the Established Religion of Scotland.[7] But, for a few years, Calvinism was not to have an easy time. Much credit can be given to John Knox for withstanding Mary Stuart, regent of Scotland and an ardent Catholic, and thus preventing the nation from going into Catholicism. Before long Mary became unpopular, and was forced to abdicate the throne in 1566.

In 1578 the "Second Book of Discipline," embodying the full Presbyterian organization was drawn up. The General Assembly was made supreme. It worked through the provincial synods and presbyteries down to the local parish. The book of devotion which Knox had composed at Frankfort for use in the church at Geneva formed the substance for the "Book of Common Order" for the Scottish Church.

Notwithstanding these events it was not until 1690 that Presbyterianism in Scotland could sit on a more secure throne. Various attempts were made by the English to plant the Episcopalian religion in Scotland. In 1638 the Scots adopted the National Covenant of the Scots to defend the Presbyterian Church. The English king, Charles I, called shortly after, a parliament to handle the Scots. The result was a war which began in 1640. Eventually Scotland was subdued by Cromwell in 1640, but still little peace was found. It was not until the Westminster Confession of Faith was ratified in 1690 and Presbyterianism again reinstated in Scotland that peace was to be known.

Scottish Presbyterianism found a fundamental weakness in its close tie-up with the civil government. After the Presbyterian system had been established by the assembly, the old polity of the church was retained by law. In 1572 a compromise was reached between ecclesiastical and civil officers that old names and titles, such as bishops and abbotts should continue, but that the incumbents were subject to the General Assembly in spiritual things and to the king in temporal. By the turn of the eighteenth century, the General Assembly had begun to show a dictatorial spirit. This was

---

[7]George Park Fisher, *History of the Christian Church* (New York Charles Scribners Sons, 1946), p 365

in keeping with the general spirit of secularism which became characteristic of the times.

This secularism in Scotland began to assert itself after 1707 with the union of English and Scottish parliaments Deism began to assert itself in the country, and the church of Scotland became saturated with the secular spirit of the times Ultimately two parties came to the front—the Moderates and the Evangelicals The former fell in with the spirit of the times and the latter stayed loyal to the old orthodoxy.

The bulk of the people belonged to the Evangelical group, but the leadership in the church was going the way of the Moderates Dissension was fomenting, which was enhanced in 1712 when the Union Parliament took away the right of the people to select their preachers and restored patronage On the same issue the General Assembly took action in 1731 with an act declaring that when a vacancy was to be filled by a presbytery, the election should lie with the "heritors, being Protestants and the elders " The Evangelicals considered this a virtual surrender of their rights, and so, led by Ebenezer Erskine and three others, they strongly objected. Erskine was promptly expelled from the ministry of the church The next year he and others formed an Associate Presbytery and thus the Secession Church was born

The people were behind the new movement The Assembly announced in 1765 that the Seceders had one hundred and twenty meeting houses and a hundred thousand members who formerly belonged to the Established Church of Scotland By 1800 there were two hundred Seceder Congregations in Scotland But the good fortune of the Seceders was not to last long, for division was to be characteristic of them In 1789 the Seceders divided into Burghers and Anti-Burghers on the question of the burgesses taking an oath The burgesses of the towns required oaths binding the people to support the religion practiced in that realm Those who considered the oath unlawful were the Anti-burghers In 1799 both branches of the Seceder Church divided again into New Lights and Old Lights on the question of whether the Solemn League and Covenant should be made a term of communion Thomas Campbell was an Old Light Anti-Burgher in the Seceder Presbyterian Church Thus he was well acquainted with religious division

Amidst this religious division, Thomas Campbell worked for

unity and sought to bring himself and his family closer to God. He was led more and more to depend upon the Bible, and made firmer attempts to follow its leadings   Once the Governor-General of Ireland offered him a position as private tutor with a large salary and a luxurious home, but Campbell knew that to move there would place his family in an environment of worldly pride and fashion, and so he refused [8]   As a preacher, he worked hard, and before long developed a stomach trouble that gave him considerable pain The doctors could do him no good, so finally recommended a trip abroad

Several families around Rich-Hill had already come to America Thomas Hodgens had sold his land and come   His daughter had married James Foster, a Scotch Independent, and they, too, had come   Alexander had already told his father he was coming when he got old enough, so Thomas Campbell, when faced with the necessity of a trip overseas, naturally turned to America   For thirty-five days, then, in 1807 his ship plowed the waves of the Atlantic, finally to arrive in Philadelphia   It was early spring Fortunately, the Synod of North America was in conference at Philadelphia, and here, Campbell presented his credentials, only to be assigned to work under the Chartiers Presbytery in western Pennsylvania

The next two years of Thomas Campbell's life can be fairly easily traced through the records of the minutes of the Chartiers Presbytery, for often was Campbell's name before them   The minutes of Saturday, May 16, 1807 tell that Campbell was received for the first time into the fellowship of this group   At the session of June 30, and July 1, 1807, Thomas Campbell was given appointments at Buffalo on the second and third Sundays of July; at Mount Pleasant on the fourth, and on the first Sunday of August, at Pittsburgh Thus Campbell was kept busy, preaching Sunday after Sunday

A man who reads the Bible with an open and intelligent mind will sooner or later absorb much to make him dissatisfied with the human elements in religion   That man, if he has faith and courage, will dare to speak out sooner or later against what is wrong   As Campbell filled his appointments, he found himself teaching things contrary to the creed of the church, but things which he felt were

---

[8]Thomas W Grafton, *Life of Alexander Campbell* (St Louis   Christian Board of Publication, 1897), p 20

in harmony with the scriptures It was only a matter of time until earnest opposition would arise

The first sign of antagonism came at the regular meeting of the Chartiers Presbytery held at the Mt Hope meeting house on October 27, 1807 The order of business came around to the question of filling appointments, and it was found that a Mr John Anderson had not kept his appointment at Buffalo on one recent Sunday at which time he was to assist Thomas Campbell in administering the Lord's Supper When Anderson was called upon to give an account of his action, he replied that he knew Campbell to be a teacher of false doctrine in that he had heard him say before that there was nothing but human authority for creeds and confessions of faith The Presbytery asked if anyone else had known of Campbell teaching these doctrines, and a Mr William Wilson responded that he did

Both Anderson and Wilson were typical protectors of orthodoxy. Anderson was short and stocky in stature, having the appearance of having no neck His voice was weak, and his temper irascible, although he tried to appear humble and meek With the people as a whole he was a very unpopular preacher Anderson had become professor of theology for the Associate Churches in the Presbytery of Chartiers on April 21, 1794 Less is known of Wilson He was born in 1770, got his training at Glasgow University, came to America in 1791 or 1792, and was ordained a preacher in the Seceder church in 1800 [9]

Although Thomas Campbell objected to Anderson's charges, it did him little good The Presbytery promptly penalized him by taking away his appointments for the next two months Early in 1808, the Presbytery met again, but the matter only became worse On February 9 the meeting was at the Buffalo meeting house Charges were read against Campbell He was asked then to speak for himself Campbell replied

With regard to faith I believe that the soul of man is the subject of it, the Divine Spirit is the author of it, the Divine Word the rule and reason of it, Christ and Him crucified the object of it, the Divine pardon, acceptance and assistance, or grace here and glory hereafter, the direct, proper and formal end of it

With respect to Confessions of Faith and Testimonies I believe that the church has all the Divine warrant for such exhibitions of

---

[9] W H Hanna, *Thomas Campbell, Seceder, and Christian Union Advocate* (Cincinnati The Christian Standard Publishing Co, 1935), pp 38, 39

the truth, that our Confession and Testimony adduce for that purpose, and that it is lawful and warrantable to use them as terms of
communion insofar as our testimony requires, in which sense 1
have never opposed them.[10]

This meeting at Buffalo appears to have lasted down to Saturday,
February 11, 1808 It resulted in suspending Thomas Campbell
from the ministry in the Seceder Church Nevertheless, at their
next meeting at Mt Hope meeting house on March 8, Campbell
tried to get them to suspend their judgment, but they refused.
He was now ready to appeal his action to the Synod.

The Synod of the Associated Churches met on May 18, 1808 in
Philadelphia and Thomas Campbell was present. It was on Friday,
May 20 that it got to the case of Campbell Papers were read
containing the charges and Campbell's answer. Consideration of
the affair was postponed until the next day, and continued from
then on over to Monday, May 23 The result was that the Synod
upheld Thomas Campbell in many particulars but concluded by
saying his answers on the first two articles were "evasive," "unsatisfactory" and "highly equivocal "[11] And so, Campbell, much
against his will, was forced to submit.

Throughout June and July, 1808, Campbell preached by appointment in Philadelphia When the Chartiers Presbytery met again
on September 13, 1808 at Burgettstown, Campbell was there. He
found no assignment waiting for him, and asked the reason There
were sharp words of controversy, charges of falsehood, and Thomas
Campbell denounced the authority of the Presbytery, the Synod,
and all their courts The next day he was suspended from his
ministerial office This day, September 13, 1808, can be taken as
the day when Campbell formally made his separation from Seceder-
ism

Campbell saw the evils of division, and it became evident to him
that the trouble lay with human creeds. Nevertheless, he wanted
to be as charitable as possible. Alexander Campbell writes of his
father's attitude:

He objected not so much to the doctrines of the Secession creed
and platform, as a doctrinal basis, but to the assumption of any
formula of religious theories or opinions, as the foundation of the
church of Christ; alleging that the holy Scriptures, Divinely in-

---

[10]W H Hanna, *Thomas Campbell*, pp 45-47
[11]W H Hanna, *Thomas Campbell*, p 83

spired, were all sufficient and alone sufficient for all the purposes contemplated by their Author, in giving them [12]

Meanwhile, near Washington, Pennsylvania where Thomas Campbell lived, some friends from Scotland also lived. There was "General" Thomas Achesons, a Lieutenant-Colonel of the twenty-second Regiment of the Pennsylvania militia, James Foster and Thomas Hodgens, each of whom had come from Ireland. In the houses of these friends Campbell continued to preach. His voice was heard in Maple Groves where open air services were held. In due time it became evident that many of these hearers were in sympathy with Campbell's views. He proposed to some of the principal ones among them to have a meeting at some home to give more definite form to the movement. The House of Abraham Altars between Mt. Pleasant and Washington, Pennsylvania was chosen, and here, one of the most famous meetings of the restoration was held. Campbell's speech closed with the famous motto: "Where the Bible speaks; we speak, where the Bible is silent, we are silent."

The idea which Campbell embodied in this motto was not new. Many years before in 1659, Edward Stillingfleet, who later became Bishop of Worchester, had said: "For the church to require more than Christ himself did, or make the condition of her communion more than our Saviour did for discipleship, is wholly unwarranted "[13] Chillingworth had written his book, "The Religion of Protestants, a Safe Way to Salvation" in 1637, and had argued that the Bible was the sole authority in matters of salvation. His conclusion, "The Bible, I say, the Bible only, is the religion of Protestants" purported to be the claim of all Protestant bodies. Yet notwithstanding the idea Campbell presented in his motto was not new, it nevertheless was revolutionary in one phase · a few people now applied it to Protestant creeds and confessions of faith whereas, the Prostestant bodies had almost exclusively applied it to Roman Catholic traditions. For the first time there were some who realized that the motto struck with equal force against human creeds as it did against Catholic traditions.

Quite naturally then, when Campbell first spoke these words, and

---

[12]Alexander Campbell, *Memoirs of Elder Thomas Campbell* (Cincinnati H S. Bosworth, 1861), p 11
[13]A C. Watters, *History of British Churches of Christ* (Indianapolis Butler University, 1948), p 2

paused, there was a solemn hush that fell across the assembly that showed the intensity of the emotions of the hour Campbell sat down A Scottish bookseller, Andrew Munro, a rather sentimental person, was the first to break the silence "Mr Campbell," he said, "if we adopt *that* as a basis, then there is an end of infant baptism " Campbell replied "Of course, if infant baptism be not found in the scriptures, we can have nothing to do with it " Thomas Acheson then arose and cried: "I hope I may never see the day when my heart will renounce that blessed saying of the Scripture, 'Suffer little children to come unto me and forbid them not, for of such is the kingdom of heaven ' " Saying that he burst into tears James Foster, who even in Ireland had been opposed to infant baptism, arose and cried out "Mr Acheson, I would remark that in the portion of Scripture you have quoted, *there is no reference whatever to infant baptism.*"[14]

The anxiety which these men expressed must not be construed as division within their ranks On the contrary their various statements show an earnest seeking after the way of the Lord They were as men stepping out of intense darkness into light, and the light blinded them for a spell These men were coming out of the darkness of partyism and stepping forth into the glorious light of revealed truth, and they staggered for a moment to get their bearings But from here on, their activities were to be stepped up, and their ideas were taking on more definite form

At a meeting at the headwaters of the Buffalo held on August 17, 1809 this small band of men formed themselves into the "Christian Association of Washington " This Association was not to be recognized as a Church, but was a society for the promotion of Christian unity If the idea appears to be related more to denominationalism than apostolic Christianity, it can be explained on the ground that these men had not as yet fully come to a knowledge of the ancient order, but were step by step going in that direction Richardson explains:

Neither Thomas Campbell himself, however, nor those associated with him, had a full conception of all that was involved in these principles They only felt that the religious intolerance of the times had itself become intolerable, and that a reformation was imperiously demanded.[15]

[14]Robert Richardson, *Memoirs of Alexander Campbell* (Cincinnati · Standard Publishing Co, Vol I, 1897), p 238
[15]Robert Richardson, *Memoirs of Alexander Campbell,* Vol I, p 245

At any rate, as soon as the Association was formed, it was seen immediately that a building in which to meet was needed   Accordingly, a log cabin was erected on the Sinclair farm, three miles from Mt. Pleasant on the road to Washington   For a time this building was used for a school and Campbell renewed his teaching career here. Near this building was the residence of a Mr Welch, a man friendly to the views of the Association   Welch fixed up a room for Thomas Campbell and here Campbell spent much of his time in studying and writing   Here Campbell wrote the Declaration and Address   When it was finished, Campbell called a special meeting of the Association and read it before them   The document met their general acquiescence, and was ordered printed on September 7, 1809.

The Declaration and Address is another of the famous documents to come out of the movement to restore primitive Christianity   It is divided into three parts   The "Declaration" gives the purpose and plan of the Association   The "Address" goes more into detail, giving the forces at work in the religious world which necessitated a restoration movement   The third part is the "Appendix" which is designed to answer questions and refute arguments against the purpose of the Association   Campbell's plan for unity was, in brief, a re-statement in different words of Rupertus Meldinius famous maxim "In essentials unity, in non-essentials liberty, in all things charity"   Campbell uses the terms, faith and opinion   The former is based upon the expressed declarations of the Bible and the latter, upon things about which the Bible is silent   Unity, Campbell believed, could be realized upon the express teachings of the Bible, and in opinions, there should be liberty   The important and timely enunciations of the Declaration and Address have given it a deserved place among the classics in restoration literature

Meanwhile, back in Ireland, the family of Thomas Campbell waited patiently for news from Campbell that would call them to follow him to America   In March, 1808, the letter came, urging them to hurry to join him   So the family prepared to leave   But misfortune struck in the form of a smallpox epidemic which caused considerable delay   It was September 20 before they set out for Londonderry to get a ship to America. On September 28 the ship weighed anchor at Lough Foyle in her attempts to put out to sea   But the ship had a hard time, and didn't get started until

October 1. But hopes were short lived for the wind was bad and the ship didn't get out of the Lough. Finally the ship got into the sea.

In the calamities of the world sometimes the believer can see the hand of God at work It appears to have been an act of providence that the ship didn't go well, and before long was wrecked. Campbell used the time for meditation, and then and there decided to devote his life to preaching When youthful Alexander Campbell stepped from the sea on to the rugged coastland of Scotland after that wreck, he was a youth now determined to devote himself to God.

On November 8, Campbell entered Glasgow University where his father had gone many years before Campbell sat under Professor Young in Greek, Professor Jardin in Logic and Belles Lettres and Professor Ure in Experimental Philosophy The latter two had taught Thomas Campbell twenty-five years earlier.

Many students of Campbell have sought the answer to Campbell's thinking in those intellectual factors which influenced him during this time in Scotland. Just how far this influence went may be a hard matter to determine. That he came in contact with Scottish philosophy, and particularly the "Common Sense" School of Scottish philosophy is evident. That traces of this philosophy show in his thinking in later years is equally evident.

Thomas Reid, the founder of the Common Sense School of Scottish philosophy, died in 1796, twelve years before Campbell came to Glasgow. Since 1763 Reid had been professor of moral philosophy at Glasgow where for a century following him his teachings were followed. Intellectual centers like Aberdeen, Glasgow and Edinburgh were effected. Protestant thinkers both in Europe and America were influenced. Hamilton, Jefferson, Madison and many other leading figures in colonial America were philosophical disciples of Thomas Reid Reid had been educated at Aberdeen, and had followed Adam Smith, author of "The Wealth of Nations" as professor of Moral Philosophy at Glasgow in 1763. The honor probably came to him because of his rebuttal of the skepticism of David Hume. Hume was once the literary lion of Scotland, but Reid more than Immanuel Kant, calmed him down by the application of "Common Sense" or "Universal Reason". Reid in his philosophy did believe in God and did also believe that man had a soul. His was not the skepticism common in philosophical circles of that day.

While in Glasgow, Campbell also came in contact with the various independent movements in the church which doubtlessly influenced him profoundly Here he had met Grenville Ewing, formerly minister of Lady Glenorchy's in Edinburgh, who had founded the theological school at Glasgow Ewing was connected with the independent movement led by James and Robert Haldane The Haldane brothers had left the church of Scotland because of the cold formalism of the church Both were relatively wealthy, and Robert devoted his money to educating missionaries for work in India James was the preacher of the two who was more outstanding He was tireless in his efforts to preach In 1799 the Haldanes had organized an independent church in Edinburgh Within nine years they had organized eighty-five churches It was while Ewing was connected with their theological school that Campbell became acquainted with him, and the two became the closest of friends. An Independent Church had been established at Rich Hill in Ireland, and James Haldane had preached here while Thomas Campbell was yet there

Another movement, led by John Glas and Robert Sandeman also was prevalent in Scotland, and doubtlessly, Campbell learned extensively of these views John Glas, minister of Tealing, had been deposed from the Church of Scotland in 1730 and had organized independent churches in Dundee, Perth and Edinburgh These churches were congregational in government They denied that creeds or confessions of faith were worth anything Glas taught there were two classes of officers · the "extraordinary" consisting of Apostles, Prophets and Evangelists, and the "Ordinary" consisting of elders and deacons Robert Sandeman adopted Independent views in 1755. Sandeman believed that faith was a simple assent to the testimony of Christ. He advocated the weekly observance of the Lord's Supper and a plurality of elders in one local congregation. The Independent movement led by Glas and Sandeman differed from that led by the Haldanes by the spirit which characterized them Haldane was free from a controversial spirit, but Sandeman was of the opposite temperament. Alexander Campbell, much later, writes of Sandeman and Haldane

Concerning Sandeman and Haldane, how they can be associated under one species, is to me a matter of surprise. The former a Paido-baptist, the latter a Baptist; the former, as keen, as sharp, as censorious, as acrimonious as Juvenal, the latter as mild, as charitable, as condescending as any man this age has produced. As authors I know them well. The one is like the mountain storm that roars among the cliffs; the other like the balmy zephyrs that breathe upon banks of violets. . .[16]

From Grenville Ewing, Campbell's close friend, the latter borrowed an intensely independent spirit. At once, he began to examine for himself, the claims of the Seceder Church as a religious group. Slowly, he was led to doubt them. The crucial hour came at the semi-annual communion service, near the close of his stay in Glasgow. It was the custom to give all who were to partake of the Lord's Supper a metallic token to shut out the unworthies from partaking. As Campbell had come from Ireland without any letter or recommendation, it was necessary for him to take an examination before the elders on Saturday to determine his worthiness. He took the examination and passed. But the next day, his conscience hurt him. He put his token in the plate that morning and refused to partake of the communion.[17] Campbell had now crossed the rubicon; he was no longer with the Seceder Church.

On July 31, 1809 Campbell left Glasgow for Greenock. Four days later, he and his family were on the ship, *Latonia,* headed for America This time the trip went smoothly, and the ship landed at New York on Friday, September 29. The following Thursday, they left New York for Philadelphia where they arrived on Saturday. The following Monday, they started on that westward trek across Pennsylvania in the direction of Washington. Thomas Campbell, who had learned of their coming, had left his home in Washington, going toward Philadelphia. On the way, the two parties met. Thomas Campbell fondly embraced his family, and they, in return, had their spirits renewed within them by this reunion.

There was much to talk about—much that would leave its effect upon the future turn of events.

[16]Alexander Campbell, "Reply," *Christian Baptist,* Vol III, No 9 (April 3, 1826), p 228
[17]T W Grafton, *Life of Alexander Campbell,* pp 40, 41

CHAPTER IV

A MOVEMENT CRYSTALLIZES

It was early fall of 1809 that Thomas and Alexander Campbell met again in Pennsylvania. The Christian Association of Washington was a very young organization. The Declaration and Address had just been printed. The events of the previous two years had hurried by in the anxiety which Thomas Campbell had felt. So he had much to tell his son. The son listened patiently and thoughtfully, and then related to his father his own experiences which had led him out of the Seceder Church. Each was saddened with the conditions that prevailed in religious partyism, but each felt confident that the answer lay in a more complete return to the Scriptures. Thoughtfully did Alexander Campbell read the Declaration and Address through. Handing it back to his father, he expressed his approval of it, and his determination to devote his life to proclaiming the principles contained in it. He furthermore explained his determination to retire to his chamber, and spend six months in a careful study of the Bible. Then he announced that he would spend his life preaching the Divine Word, and for that preaching, he would never accept financial compensation. His father replied: "Upon these principles, my dear son, I fear you will have to wear many a ragged coat."[1]

It is said that soon after "Raccoon" John Smith of Kentucky began preaching, some of his friends came to him, advising him to cease preaching so strongly, or else his "Baptist brethren" would become angered, and not pay him, and he would never be able to get out of debt. To this Smith replied: "Conscience is an article that I have never yet brought into market; but should I offer it for sale, Montgomery County, with all its lands and houses, would not be enough to buy it, much less that farm of one hundred acres."[2] When John Calvin was studying at Strassburg one cold winter, his financial circumstances were so bad that he went days at a time without food, and was often without heat. A Cath-

---

[1]Richardson, *Memoirs of Alexander Campbell*, Vol I, p 275
[2]John Augustus Williams, *Life of Elder John Smith* (Cincinnati The Standard Publishing Co, 1904), pp 158, 159

olic offered him good financial means if he would cease his opposition to Catholicism, but Calvin refused. Such is the material of
which great men are made   It is the lot of great men to put the
cause of truth first and foremost in their hearts, then be loyal to
their conviction despite whatever else may be involved.

He who would seek to understand the greatness of Alexander
Campbell must study him in this light.   There was one object
always before the man. Truth   He wanted the Truth more than
he wanted anything else   He himself writes:

Often have I said, and often have I written, that *truth,* truth
eternal and divine, is now, and long has been with me the *pearl
of great price*   To her I will, with the blessing of God, sacrifice
everything   But on no altar will I offer her a victim   If I have
lost sight of her, God who searcheth the hearts knows I have not
done it intentionally. With my whole heart I have sought the
truth, and I know that I have found it.[3]

On another occasion he wrote:

Numbers with me count nothing   Let God be true, and every
man a liar. Let truth stand, though the heavens fall.   When
contending with thirty millions of Lutherans, I feel myself contending with but one man. In opposing seventy millions of Greek
and Eastern Professors, I am in conflict with but one leader
When one hundred millions of Baptists assail me, I feel myself in
a struggle with but one mind   In all the Methodists I see but
John Wesley, in all the Calvinists, John Calvin, and in all the
Episcopalians, one Cranmer   Names, numbers, circumstances
weigh nothing in the scales of justice, truth and holiness.[4]

When Campbell opened his debate with McCalla, he said

Men, Brethren and Fathers:

Through the goodness and mercy of God, I appear before you,
at this time and in this place, for the purpose of contending for
a part of that faith, and an item of that religious practice, once
delivered to the saints   My prayer to God is, that for the sake
of his Son Jesus Christ I may speak as I ought to speak; that in
the spirit of the Truth I may contend for the truth; that with
humility and love, with zeal according to knowledge and un-
feigned devotion, I may open my lips on every occasion when I
address my fellow mortal and immortal creatures on the subject

---

[3]Alexander Campbell, "A Demand for Justice from Editors in General,
and Mr Brantley in Particular," *Millennial Harbinger,* Vol 1, No 3
(March 1, 1830), p 97

[4]Alexander Campbell, "The Christian Organization—No XXV," *Millennial Harbinger,* New Series Vol VII, No 7 (July, 1843), p 307

of religion. Expecting that they and I will soon appear before the judgment seat of Christ, may I speak in such a way that I may not be ashamed nor afraid to meet them there. May I ever act under the influence of that "wisdom which cometh from above, which is first pure, then peaceable, then gentle, easy to be entreated, full of mercy and of good fruits, without partiality and without hypocrisy" And may you, my friends, examine and "prove all things and hold fast that which is good."[5]

In Campbell's search for Truth, he made the Bible the ultimate source of all his authority. He loved to study the Word itself, and it can be safely said that few men ever attained to the knowledge which he had of the Divine Word. Campbell expresses his attitude thus.

For the last ten years I have not looked into the works of these men, and have lost the taste which I once had for controversial reading of this sort, and during this period my inquiries into the Christian religion have been almost exclusively confined to the Holy Scriptures And I can assure you that the Scriptures, when made their own interpreter, and accompanied with earnest desires to the author of these writings, have become, to me, a book entirely new and unlike what they were when read and consulted as a book of reference— [6]

He who would undertake to put Truth first in his heart must find himself sooner or later facing the problem of what to do with the messages of other men who purport to be harbingers of truth It is all too easy to become slaves to other men's thinking. A man who can disregard the person of other men, and still pursue patiently the Truth is a rare commodity; his is the genius of greatness Campbell did read extensively from other men, but he thought independently, and took from other men what he conceived to be in harmony with the truth Time and again on this point he expresses his attitude In the article alluded to above, he also says:

I call no man master upon the earth; and although my own father has been a diligent student, and a teacher of the Christian religion since his youth; and, in my opinion, understands this book as well as any person with whom I am acquainted, yet there is no man with whom I have debated more, and reasoned more,

---

[5]Alexander Campbell, *A Debate on Christian Baptism* (Buffalo Published by Campbell & Sala, 1824), pp 41, 42

[6]Alexander Campbell, "Reply," *Christian Baptist,* Vol III, No 9, (April 3, 1826). p 229

on all subjects, than he—I have been so long disciplined in the school of free inquiry, that, if I know my own mind, there is not a man upon the earth whose authority can influence me, any farther than he comes with the authority of evidence, reason, and truth. To arrive at this state of mind is the result of many experiments and efforts; and to me has been arduous beyond expression. I have endeavored to read the Scriptures as though no one had read them before me; and I am as much on my guard against reading them today, through the medium of my own views yesterday, or a week ago, as I am against being influenced by any foreign name, authority or system whatever.

Yet, Campbell was always on the look-out for Truth. He never hesitated to read the writings of others for it, and to accept what Truth they had.

I was some fourteen years ago a great admirer of the works of John Newton. I read them with great delight, and I still love the author and admire many of his sentiments. He was not a staunch Episcopalian, though he died in that connexion. In an apology to a friend for his departure from the tenets of that sect in some instances, he said, "whenever he found a pretty feather in any bird, he endeavored to attach it to his own plummage, and although he had become a very speckled bird, so much so that no one of any species would altogether own him as belonging to them, he flattered himself that he was the prettiest bird among them." From that day to the present I have been looking for pretty feathers, and I have become more speckled than Newton of Olney; but whether I have as good a taste in the selection, must be decided by connoisseurs in ornithology.[7]

It was therefore Campbell's custom to take from the writings of men only what he conceived to be the truth, and to reject all else. This policy he followed unswervingly through his long life. Nowhere does this attitude come out more than in the great religious debates which he held As a debater, Campbell showed himself always interested in the cause of truth. He debated, not for the joy of polemics, but for the desire to know and dispense the Truth. His opponents, he insisted, must be the giants of the opposition. He would not lift his gun save at the champions of error, and when he did, he sought earnestly for the Truth. Campbell's attitude can thus be seen in his discussion with Rice in these words:

I care nothing for triumphing over Mr. Rice or any other mortal. It is no pleasure to expose human weakness or human folly,

[7]Alexander Campbell, "Reply," *Christian Baptist,* Vol III, No 9 (April 3, 1826), p 228

only in so far as the cause of the truth and mission of the Messiah, and the interests of humanity may require it. There is a higher tribunal in my eye, than human approbation, or the plaudits of my poor fellow-mortals.[8]

But aside from Campbell's independence of mind, another quality of his life contributed to his greatness: his tireless application of his energy to the work ahead. "An ounce of pluck," said James A. Garfield, "is worth a pound of luck." Beecher said: "The elect are 'whosoever will'; the non-elect are 'whosoever won't'." Alexander Campbell was a worker. Arising every morning at four o'clock, he worked steadily until ten at night. His health was excellent; his disposition cheerful. He was almost never sick. When not in his study, he was busy at some manual labor. He was rarely idle. Tolbert Fanning writes of him:

We do not deny that blood will always tell in man as well as in beast, but any one at all familiar with the every day life of this unequalled man, can but account satisfactorily for his great powers of endurance and his almost more than human executive abilities. In addition to his iron frame-work, his habits were studied, and, of course regular He was rarely sick, complained of few aches, was no dispeptic maintained a cheerful temper, and, of course, yielded to no melancholic temptations He rose at early dawn, ate and drank as a philosopher, and exercised in the open air as a man of common sense. When on journeys he exercised considerably in early walks, and at home, we have frequently seen him, and can almost see him now, with coat off and spade in hand, pitching about mother earth in a manner which seemed to say, "it is good for both soul and body." He was a farmer of a high order, an admirable mechanic, and loved dearly the shrubbery which he had planted with his own hands about his premises, and especially that upon which he could look from his own quiet little office, in which he did his best thinking. We never saw Alexander Campbell idle. This is the main key to his greatness. He worked with his hands to qualify himself for studying to advantage, and when not writing or preaching, he was busy in conversation with some one, as he often said he was no respecter of persons, but took men as they came, great and small, and he ardently labored to profit all. There was a work of physical majesty, self-possession and independence of appearance about Alexander Campbell, of which he was as unconscious and innocent

---

[8]Alexander Campbell, *Debate on Christian Baptism* (Lexington A T Skellman & Son, 1844). p 456

as a child, that said to the passer-by "this is one of nature's noblemen "⁹

And so Campbell, determined to independently study the Bible, and to work tirelessly in an effort to know the truth, began his long career which was destined to overshadow the influence of his father in years to come   Meanwhile, Thomas Campbell had been preaching in groves and in the houses of friends   But, it was seen that many members lived near Buffalo Creek, so it was decided to build a meeting house   A site was chosen on the farm of William Gilchrist, in the valley of the Brush Run, two miles above its junction with Buffalo Creek   Here, Alexander Campbell preached his first sermon on September 16, 1810

As a preacher, Campbell developed great power   In his delivery he had a decided Scotch brogue   He never moved about in the pulpit, and made few gestures   His voice never descended below a lofty conversational tone, or arose to strain his vocal cords [10]

Before long, the subject of infant baptism began to trouble Campbell   He read the third proposition in the Declaration and Address   "That (in order to church union and communion) nothing ought to be inculcated upon Christians as articles of faith, nor required of them as terms of communion, but what is expressly taught and enjoined upon them in the word of God   Nor ought anything to be admitted as of divine obligation, in their church constitution and management, but what is expressly enjoined by the authority of our Lord Jesus Christ and His apostles upon the New Testament Church; either in express terms, or by approved precedent "

"Upon reading this," says Alexander Campbell, "I asked my father in what passage or portion of the inspired oracles, he could find a precept or expressed precedent for the baptism or sprinkling of infants in the name of the Father, Son and the Holy Spirit "[11]

Campbell's thinking about infant baptism was also occasioned by another circumstance in his life   This was the birth of his

⁹Tolbert Fanning, "Sketches on the Life of Alexander Campbell—No 2," *Gospel Advocate,* Vol VIII, No 21 (May 22, 1866), pp 321-325
    ¹⁰W C Morro, *Brother McGarvey* (St Louis Bethany Press, 1940), pp 56, 57
    ¹¹Charles V Segar, *Lectures on the Pentateuch,* p 19

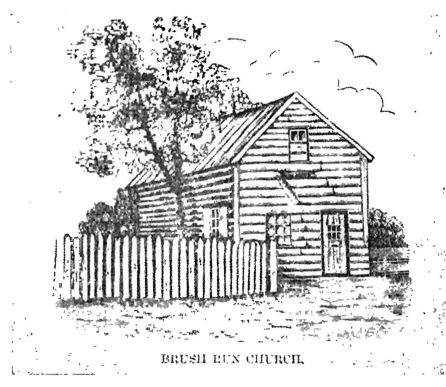

BRUSH RUN CHURCH.

first child, a tiny girl named Jane, who was born on March 13, 1812 Campbell's marriage had taken place a year earlier, almost to the day, March 12. His wife was Margaret Brown, daughter of John Brown, one of the most successful business men found in that region of Virginia. He lived eight miles from Charleston in the valley of the Buffalo on a rich farm He was a carpenter and millwright He owned a gristmill and a saw mill But, wherever Brown was known, he was spoken of as the man who lived in "The Mansion," a house to become famous for being the one that Alexander Campbell later lived in.

Most houses in Brooke County, Virginia were log stockades, built to serve the double purpose of furnishing a home and a fortress from Indian attacks But this one was different It was a pretentious thing three stories high, constructed of oak timbers and hand cut walnut weather boarding, painted dark red and put together with wooden pegs In the parlor on March 12. 1811 Alexander Campbell and Margaret Brown kneeled on two prayer benches of black walnut trimmed in gold and took their wedding vows.

So, after the birth of their first child, Campbell began to want to investigate the subject of baptism. He asked Andrew Munro to get him some books on the subject, and Munro did   Campbell studied the word baptize in Greek to see that it meant immersion. He concluded there was nothing in the scriptures favoring infant baptism, so he began making immediate plans to be immersed. He finally contacted a preacher by the name of Matthias Luse who agreed to immerse him. But Campbell by now found others that wanted immersion. His sister, Dorthea, also wanted to be immersed. On Wednesday, June 12, 1812, Campbell went to a deep pool in Buffalo Creek. Several were there. Before the baptizing was finished, Thomas Campbell, his wife, James and Sarah Henon and James Foster—in all, seven persons—were immersed. Before long, practically the whole Brush Run church had followed suit.

This bold venture of immersion immediately made the Baptists in the neighborhood lift an eyebrow. Campbell began to receive invitations to preach for them. Yet he was reluctant to accept. Alexander Campbell's opinion of the Baptist preachers of that day was not complimentary to them, for he thought of them as "little men in big offices." He writes:

> I had no idea of uniting with the Baptists more than with the Moravians or the mere Independents. I had unfortunately formed a very unfavorable opinion of the Baptist preachers as then introduced to my acquaintance, as narrow, contracted, illiberal, and uneducated men. This, indeed, I am sorry to say, is still my opinion of the ministry of that Association at that day; and whether they are yet much improved, I am without satisfactory evidence.[12]

Nevertheless, in the fall of 1812 Campbell learned that the Redstone Baptist Association was having a meeting at Uniontown, Pennsylvania, and Campbell determined to go as a spectator They insisted he preach, but he refused. He came home thoroughly

---

[12]Alexander Campbell, "Anecdotes, Incidents, and Facts," *Millennial Harbinger*, Third Series- Vol. V, No 6 (June, 1848), p 349

disgusted. He said later, "I returned home, not intending ever to visit another association."[13]

On his way home, however, he learned much to his surprise that the Baptist people themselves had no more use for their preachers than Campbell did. They too, looked upon them as defenders of partyism rather than proclaimers of the gospel. So Campbell decided to lay the matter before the members of the Brush Run Church.

East of Washington, Pennsylvania, along the Monongahela River, there were numerous Baptist Churches who had banded together in the Redstone Association. Redstone was the name of an old Indian fort on the river about sixty miles above Pittsburgh. Their doctrinal belief was found in the Philadelphia Confession of Faith, adopted by the Baptist Churches in 1742 The Philadelphia Confession was substantially the same as the Westminster Confession which the churches of Scotland had adopted in 1690. The Philadelphia Confession was, accordingly, thoroughly Calvinistic, and was changed only in those points that suited Baptist practices.

Campbell and the Brush Run Church had little confidence in creeds and confessions of faith. But the Baptists continued to insist that Brush Run join their association. When Campbell laid the matter before the church, it was decided that the church would draw up a statement of its beliefs and lay it before the association. This statement remonstrated against all human creeds and expressed a willingness to cooperate under the condition that the church could preach and teach what it believed the Bible taught. And so, the Brush Run Church was admitted in 1813 to the Redstone Association with only a small objection from a minority element.

In the long run, neither the Baptists nor Campbell were satisfied. The minority continued to work against Campbell for his heterodoxy. Campbell himself felt that he was a Baptist in name only. He writes to an uncle in Ireland in 1815:

For my own part I must say that, after long study and investigation of books, and more especially the Sacred Scriptures, I have through clear convictions of truth and duty, renounced much

---

[13]Alexander Campbell, "Anecdotes, Incidents, and Facts," *Millennial Harbinger*, Third Series, Vol. V, No 6 (June, 1848), p 346

of the traditions and errors of my early education. I am now an
Independent in church government, of that faith and view of the
gospel exhibited in John Walker's *Seven Letters to Alexander
Knox,* and a Baptist so far as regards baptism. What I am in
religion I am from examination, reflection, and conviction, not
from "ipse dixit" tradition or human authority [14]

The establishment of the church in Wellsburgh added little to
Campbell's favor among the Baptists. Campbell's father-in-law
John Brown and his family were converted from the Presbyterian
Church and became members of the Brush Run Church Soon it was
found that many members of this church were gradually moving
westward, so it was decided that the whole church should move
together to Zanesville, Ohio Brown didn't like the idea of
losing Alexander Campbell As an inducement to make him stay,
he gave to him his rich farm, together with the "mansion " Campbell changed his mind Meanwhile, Brown had moved to Wellsburgh and set himself up in business Campbell came occasionally and preached in the court house Two or three other families
lived here who were members of the church Out from Wellsburgh
was a Baptist Church of the Regular Baptist order on Cross Creek.
Here Brown went to church most of the time. Finally, it was
decided to put up a church building in Wellsburgh, and Campbell
volunteered to spend four months of his time, visiting the country
and raising money

When the Wellsburgh church was erected, Campbell, contrary
to his expectations, was in much disfavor. Elder Pritchard, who
preached for the regular Baptist Church out at Cross Creek, became extremely jealous He became bolder in his accusations as
to Campbell's heterodoxy, so the tension between Campbell and the
Baptists mounted It reached its height when Campbell delivered
his famous "Sermon On The Law" before the Redstone Association which met that year (1816) at Cross Creek.

For some time Campbell had been thinking upon the relation of
the two covenants in the Bible Baptists were accustomed to
disregard the covenants, and to quote one as freely as the other
to a sinner In 1812 Campbell had written to his father:

How many disciples of Moses are to be found in the professed
school of Jesus Christ! and how few among the teachers of the
New Testament seem to know that Christ's ministers are not

[14]Richardson, *Memoirs of Alexander Campbell,* Vol I, p 466

able ministers of the Old Testament, but of the New! Do they not, like scholars to their teacher, run to Moses to prove forms of worship, ordinances, discipline, and government in the Christian Church, when asked to account for their practices?[15]

Campbell had come to the conviction that much of the error in religious practice was due to the lack of understanding of the relation of the covenants. This idea was enveloping his mind at the time the Redstone Association met at Cross Creek on August 30, 1816.

Campbell came to the Association meeting as a messenger of the Brush Run Church There was a clamor among Baptist people to hear him But Elder Pritchard was the host, and he refused His excuse was that Campbell was too close, that someone farther should be the speaker. He accordingly arranged for Elder Stone of Ohio to speak. Providentially, Stone suddenly became ill. Pritchard was forced then, due to public desire, to ask Campbell to speak. Campbell, not having expected to speak, took only a few minutes to collect his thoughts, and then delivered his sermon Still, Pritchard would not give up A woman fainted in the audience, and Pritchard left with her. In the middle of the sermon, he called out many Baptist preachers, and a private council was taken against Campbell Pritchard wanted Campbell publicly condemned One of the Baptist preachers replied to Pritchard "Elder Pritchard, I am not yet prepared to say whether it be or be not Bible doctrine, but one thing I can say, were we to make such an annunciation, we would sacrifice ourselves and not Mr Campbell "[16]

The Sermon on The Law has become one of the most famous of Campbell's speeches In it Campbell showed that the law of Moses was abrogated, and therefore, not binding upon Christians The effect of the sermon was like a bombshell in the Baptist camps A movement started to charge Campbell with heresy and have him excluded from the Baptist fellowship. The next regular meeting of the Redstone Association at Peter's Creek in 1817 brought the subject up, but through the intervention of some friends, it was dropped. Nevertheless, for the next number of

[15]Richardson, *Memoirs of Alexander Campbell*, p 448
[16]Alexander Campbell, "Anecdotes, Incidents, and Facts," *Millennial Harbinger*, Third Series, Vol V, No 6 (June, 1848), p 349

years, the feelings which the Baptists entertained toward Campbell were never cordial.

Meanwhile, Campbell continued to study and to grow, and to use his influence to spread the cause of restoration. In accordance with this desire he made plans to open a seminary in his home which he called "Buffalo Seminary." This was in January, 1818. He wanted the school to instruct young men in religion, but here he felt a disappointment. Most students came from neighborhood farms and studied English and Language for professional services. Nor were these students inclined toward religion. Tuition was five dollars a quarter and board, one dollar and a half a week, so the price was attractive to this group. Campbell's disappointment caused the Seminary to be short-lived.

During this time, Campbell had never thought seriously of entering a religious debate. As a matter of fact, debates were particularly odious to him. They breathed the spirit of partyism, and Campbell noticed that in many cases the disputants strove for personal victory rather than a victory for the truth. Therefore, when, in the winter of 1819, Campbell began to receive letters from John Birch, a Baptist preacher in Mt. Pleasant, Ohio, to come and debate John Walker, a Presbyterian preacher on baptism, Campbell was reluctant to go. Birch had gone to Mt. Pleasant that fall and had succeeded in baptizing an unusual number of people. The ire of Walker was aroused, and he soon issued a challenge for a discussion. Birch wrote Campbell twice and received no reply. He wrote his third letter saying,

Dear Brother: I once more undertake to address you by letter; as we are commanded not to weary in well-doing, I am disposed to persevere. I am coming this third time unto you. I can not persuade myself that you will refuse to attend to the dispute with Mr Walker, therefore, I do not feel disposed to complain because you have sent me no answer. True, I have expected an answer, signifying your acceptance of the same. I am as yet disappointed, but am not offended nor discouraged. I can truly say it is the unanimous wish of all the church to which I belong, that you should be the disputant. It is Brother Nathaniel Skinner's desire; it is the wish of all the brethren with whom I have conversed, that you should be the man [17]

Campbell finally agreed and the debate took place near Mount Pleasant on June 19, 20, 1820. The debate was on the subject

[17]Richardson, *Memoirs of Alexander Campbell*, Vol II, p 15

and mode of baptism   Walker opened and Campbell closed it
Walker contended that baptism came in the room of circumcision,
and therefore, infants had a right to it   Campbell, who for the past
eight years had dwelt on the subject of the covenants, was thoroughly acquainted with his ground, and answered by a general reflection upon the place, purpose, and relationship of the two covenants.   The two contenders traversed the usual ground on the
mode of baptism, Campbell frequently going out of his way to state
the ground on which he proposed a restoration of the church

At the close of the debate, Campbell issued a challenge to "any
Pedobaptist minister of any denomination" to debate with him the
subject of infant baptism.   In May, 1823, he heard from his
challenge.   W. L. McCalla of Kentucky, a Presbyterian preacher,
responded that he was willing to accept the challenge.   A correspondence took place which lasted up into the summer.   Finally, it
was agreed that the debate should be held in a grove near Washington, Kentucky in October.

Campbell rode horseback to the debate, accompanied by Sidney
Rigdon, then a popular Baptist preacher in Ohio.   Jeremiah Vardeman, a well-known Kentucky Baptist preacher, was Campbell's
moderator.   The topic was the same as with Walker   the subject
and mode of baptism.   The two men went over the same ground on
the covenants, but when it came to infant baptism, Campbell injected the argument that baptism was for the remission of sins, and
therefore, could not be for infants since they had no sins.   This
thought was revolutionary for its day, and Campbell knew the
Baptists were against it   He says to them,

My Baptist brethren, as well as the Pedobaptist brotherhood, I
humbly conceive, require to be admonished on this point   You
have been, some of you, no doubt, too different in asserting this
grand import of baptism.[18]

Campbell had come to see that baptism was a way into the church,
and so declares "that baptism was never designed for, nor commanded to be administered to, a member of the church."[19]

By now Campbell was convinced that debating was really valuable.   Throngs of people had come to hear him   His reputation as

[18]Alexander Campbell, *Debate on Christian Baptism* (Buffalo   Published
by Campbell & Sala, 1824), p. 144
[19]Alexander Campbell, *Debate on Christian Baptism,* p 195

a speaker spread far and wide   Campbell could now see that debate
was worth while   He writes .

There are not a few who deprecate religious controversy as an
evil of no small magnitude   But these are either ill-informed, or
those conscious that their principles will not bear investigation
So long as there is good and evil, truth and error in this world,
so long will there be opposition , for it is in the nature of good and
evil, of truth and error, to oppose each other   We cheerfully confess that it is much to be regretted that controversy amongst
Christians should exist , but it is more to be regretted that error,
the professed cause of it should exist [20]

Indeed, these two debates convinced Campbell that "a week's debating is worth a year's preaching "

Meanwhile, Campbell's trouble with the Redstone Association
was continuing, and became increasing clear that something was
going to need to be done   Fortunately, in the summer of 1823,
while preparations were being made for the debate with McCalla,
an opportunity presented itself to do something   The opportunity
came from the Western Reserve, in northeastern Ohio, in the form
of an invitation for the Wellsburgh Church to join the Mahoning
Baptist Association   The leading spirit behind this Association
was Adamson Bentley, a Baptist preacher of Warren, Ohio who
had within more recent years found a decided similarity in his
views and those of Alexander Campbell

Bentley, after reading the Campbell-Walker debate in 1820, became a great admirer of Campbell's   At this time, he was using
his influence on the Western Reserve to hold annual "minister's
meetings" among the Baptist preachers to discuss the scriptures
At his suggestion, the Mahoning Baptist Association was born on
August 30, 1820 [21]   There was a noticeable difference between
this Association and others of that day.   Its general policy was less
tyranical, allowing more freedom among churches than was usual
for that day   Its constitution declared that it did not have authority
over the churches, but that it would recognize the independence
of the congregations   The association claimed to act in an advisory
capacity only, at the same time disclaiming any superiority, jurisdiction or coercive right

Fortunately, the original records of the Mahoning Baptist As-

---

[20] Alexander Campbell, *Debate on Christian Baptism,* p vi
[21] A S Hayden, *History of the Disciples in the Western Reserve* (Cincinnati Chase & Hall, 1875), p 25

sociation are still in existence. The original records were given by John Rudolph in the winter of 1875-76 to B. A Hinsdale, president of Hiram College Hinsdale turned them over to the college on September 17, 1888 where they are still kept. We give below the first six articles in the constitution that the general policy and character of the Association may be seen.

First Our object is to glorify God This we would endeavor to do by urging the importance of the doctrine And Precepts of the gospel in their Moral and evangelical nature commending ourselves to every man's conscience in the sight of God—not Pretending to Halve Atharity over any man nor over the churches whose representatives form this Association But we act as an advisory council only Disclaiming all Superiority, Jurisdiction, coersive Right and Infallibility and acknowledging the Independence of every church which has received Authority from Christ to Perform all Duties enjoined respecting the government of His Church in this world—

Second The utility of an Association Appears in many respects. as the obtaining a more general acquaintance with the State of the Churches and giving advice in cases of difficulty supply destitute churches; and guarding ourselves against innovations which the churches of Christ may expect always to be troubled with, by those who Ly-In Wait to deceive, Acts 15 2, 6 24—

Third The Messengers chosen, and sent to the Association by the Churches, should be judicious, well versed in the scriptures, prudent, men of integrity, and sound in the faith It is therefore expected that the churches will respect such qualifications, in order that they may be benefitted by the consultation of their Messengers No church is to send more than three Messengers

Fourth With the Messengers the churches are to send letters to the Association Those letters are to contain the Names of the Messengers from each church, the State of the churches respecting their continuance in the faith, their Number baptised, received by letter, Dismissed, Restored, Excommunicated, Deceised, and their latest number When any church wants council of the Association, they shall state their cases by Query in their letter by which they may expect the Judgment—

Fifth The Association to meet annually at such place, and times as shall be determined at their Preceding Session, and continue until the business is finished The Association to be opened with divine service, after which the letters are to be given in, and read, then a Moderator and Clerk selected Due care should be taken that a Person of a cool temper be chosen Moderator Then Business is to be attended to and Minutes thereof made, circular prepared and signed, and a coppy of it sent with the Minutes of the Association to each church in the Union

Sixth All matters are to be determined by a majority of the votes of the Messengers present.

Seventh. Churches are to be received into the Association by Petetion, setting forth their desire to be admitted, their faith order and willingness to be conformable to the rules of this associated Bobby When it is read and the matter ripened for note They being found to correspond to the faith and practice of this body of the petition the Moderator declares that such a church is received into the association. In token of which he gives the Messengers presenting the Petition the right hand of fellowship and bids them take his seat.

From here on, the constitution sets forth the beliefs of the Association. Article ten declares that baptism is by immersion and not sprinkling or pouring Article eleven shows that the proper subject of baptism is the believer. The thirteenth article shows the first day of the week to be the Lord's Day, the day of worship.

In the summer of 1821 Adamson Bentley and Sidney Rigdon, who at that time was the outstanding orator and preacher for the association, happened to go to Kentucky, and on the way back they stopped by to visit Campbell at Bethany. They discussed the scriptures all night and the next day Rigdon said that if he had within the last year taught and promulgated from the pulpit one error he had a thousand.[22]

During the summer of 1823, when Campbell saw that the Redstone Association was ready to take action, he became interested in going into the Mahoning Association. There was also the fact that the McCalla debate was soon coming up, and if Campbell allowed the Redstone Association to take action, it would hurt his influence in this coming discussion. Accordingly, Alexander Campbell, John Brown and George Young were appointed messengers from the Wellsburg Church to the Mahoning Association. A statement of belief was drawn up, peculiar in its independence and freedom from creedal verbiage. In August, 1823 the Association meeting was held at Hubbard in Trumbull County, Ohio. Bentley preached a sermon based upon John 3: 16, 17. Following this, the application of the Wellsburg Church was considered and Campbell's group was voted in

In the fall of 1822 Campbell began to think of giving up Buffalo Seminary. The published debate with Walker had taught him the

[22]A S Hayden, *History of the Disciples in the Western Reserve*, p 19

power of the press to disseminate his views. So he began thinking of printing a paper   About this time he made the acquaintance of a young preacher from Pittsburgh by the name of Walter Scott. Campbell, in discussing the idea of the paper with Scott, suggested that he wanted to name the paper, "The Christian," but Scott objected. He thought it would be a means of disarming prejudice to call it "The Christian Baptist." In the spring of 1823, Campbell published his "Prospectus" for the proposed paper. In this Campbell said:

"The Christian Baptist" shall espouse the cause of no religious sect, excepting the ancient sect, "called Christians first at antioch " Its sole object shall be the eviction of truth and the exposing of error in doctrine and practice. The editor, acknowledging no standard of religious faith or works other than the Old and New Testament, and the latter as the only standard of the religion of Jesus Christ, will, intentionally at least, oppose nothing which it contains and recommend nothing which it does not enjoin. Having no worldly interest at stake from the adoption or reprobation of any article of faith or religious practice, having no gift nor religious emolument to blind his eyes or to pervert his judgment, he hopes to manifest that he is an impartial advocate of truth.[23]

Campbell bought the type, presses, etc , and erected a building near the creek fording at the base of the cemetery hill. Here, he began publication of the *Christian Baptist,* the first issue of which appeared August 3, 1823.

For seven years the *Christian Baptist* breathed the spirit of iconoclasm. He was harsh and very often bitter in his denunciations of prevalent religious practices   Campbell sought to expose the pride, worldliness and paganism in the churches. He turned his attack against the "kingdom of the clergy," for he believed that the Protestant clergy was as guilty as the Romanish of deluding the people, and holding from them the words of life   Robert Semple, a Virginia Baptist preacher, wrote to Campbell under the title, "Robert Cautious," asking Campbell not be immoderate in his condemnation of evil and reminding him of the danger of "running past Jerusalem, as one hastens out of Babylon "

In spite of his extremities, Campbell's *Christian Baptist* exercised no small influence for good for the restoration   The pages of the paper vibrate with the call for a return to the "ancient order of things." Creeds, confessions of faith, and authoritative councils of

---

[23]Richardson, *Memoirs of Alexander Campbell,* Vol II, p 50

men are repudiated and the editor launches out alone in his quest for the way of truth   Many of his plans began to take more permanent and tangible form. He saw that partyism, creedalism, and the power of the clergy must fall. He pled for a return to the church of the New Testament, and for the destruction of denominationalism. He writes

I have no idea of adding to the catalogue of new sects   This game has been played too long   I labor to see sectarianism abolished, and all Christians of every name united upon the one foundation on which the apostolic church was founded   To bring Baptists and Paido-baptists to this is my supreme end   But to connect myself with any people who would require me to sacrifice one item of revealed truth, to subscribe any creed of human device, or to restrain me from publishing my sentiments as discretion and conscience direct, is now, and I hope ever shall be, the farthest from my desires, and the most incompatible with my views [24]

While Campbell did not intend to start a new sect, yet it was not his idea to bring all the sects together in one group   He writes

I have no idea of seeing, nor one wish to see, the sects unite in one grand army   This would be dangerous to our liberties and laws   For this the Saviour did not pray   It is only the disciples of Christ dispersed among them, that reason and benevolence would call out of them   Let them unite who love the Lord, and then we shall soon see the hireling priesthood and their worldly establishments prostrate in the dust [25]

If the question be asked just how Campbell proposed to restore the ancient order, it can be answered by saying that he advocated that men drop things of human origin in religion, and go by the sacred scriptures   Accordingly, Campbell writes ·

To make a move in the business of restoration, and in returning to the covenant is, I confess, quite a different thing from speculating or talking about it, and yet it only requires an intelligent mind and a willing heart   These will direct and embolden every effort   The people must abandon the language, customs and manners of Ashdod   For this purpose they will meet, and read, and examine the New Covenant writings   They will also look to Heaven for wisdom and courage, and as soon as any item of the will of Heaven is distinctly apprehended, it will be brought into their practice [26]

[24]Alexander Campbell, "Reply to 'T T ,' " *Christian Baptist,* Vol III, No . 7 (February 6, 1826), p 217

[25]Alexander Campbell, "A Restoration of the Ancient Order of Things—No III," *Christian Baptist,* Vol II, No 9 (April 4, 1825), p 140

[26]Alexander Campbell, "Reply to Faithful," *Christian Baptist,* Vol III, No 2 (September 5, 1825), p 185

Again Campbell says,

But a restoration of the ancient order of things, it appears, is all that is contemplated by the wise disciples of the Lord; as it is agreed that this is all that is wanting to the perfection, happiness, and glory of the Christian community. To contribute to this is our most ardent desire—our daily and diligent inquiry and pursuit. Now, in attempting to accomplish this, it must be observed that it belongs to every individual and to every congregation of individuals to discard from their faith and their practice everything that is not found written in the New Testament of the Lord and Saviour, and to believe and practice whatever is there enjoined. This done, and everything is done which ought to be done [27]

The *Christian Baptist,* in a few years made many friends, but also many enemies In spite of the fact Campbell did not want to be a sect his enemies continued to push every way possible to christen him and those of like mind as a sect   Campbell observes,

Some religious editors in Kentucky call those who are desirous of seeing the ancient order of things restored, "the Restorationers," "the Campbellites," and the most reproachful epithets are showered upon them because they have some conscientious regard for the Divine Author and the divine authority of the New Testament — This may go down very well with some, but all who fear God and keep his commandments will pity and deplore the weakness and folly of those who either think to convince or to persuade by such means [28]

By 1829, Campbell began to be concerned lest the name "Christian Baptist" be applied as a party name to those advocating restoration He determined at once to drop the paper, and put this name out of existence Moreover, his spirit had been bitter, and many of his friends had encouraged him to be more moderate in his condemnation of evil It was believed best to cease publication of the *Christian Baptist* at the close of 1829, and begin another paper So, on January 4, 1830 Campbell became the editor of the *Millennial Harbinger*

The name of this new periodical was particularly significant. Campbell believed in the millennium His view was that the millennium was a period of time when "the nations of this world are all to become the kingdoms of our King—they are all to submit to his government, and to feel the benign and blissful in-

---

[27]Alexander Campbell, "A Restoration of the Ancient Order of Things— No II," *Christian Baptist,* Vol II, No 8 (March 7, 1825), p 133
[28]Alexander Campbell, "A Good 'Christening,'" *Christian Baptist,* Vol IV, No 4 (November 6, 1826)), p 288

fluence of his sceptre "[29]   Campbell believed that **eventually** Christianity would triumph over the whole world and the influence of Christ would be preeminent.   But, Campbell also believed that "the sectarian establishments could not admit of this spread and triumph of Christianity."   Therefore, the only way to have the millennium was to restore the ancient order, and in addition, to destroy sectarianism in all its forms.   In view of this Campbell wrote in the "prospectus" for the *Harbinger:*

This work shall be devoted to the destruction of Sectarianism, Infidelity and Antichristian doctrine and practice.   It shall have for its object the development, and introduction of that political and religious order of society called THE MILLENNIUM, which will be the consummation of that ultimate amelioration of society proposed in the Christian scriptures. . .[30]

Campbell announced that each number of the *Millennial Harbinger* was to have forty-eight pages   It was to be printed on "super royal paper," and published on the first Monday of each month.   The cost was two dollars and fifty cents a year.

Meanwhile, step by step the advocates of restoration found themselves being driven farther and farther from Baptist ranks.   Some had begun to doubt the propriety of having such associations.   In Kentucky, the North District Association found Elder John Smith guilty of preaching "Campbellism."   At the meeting of 1827 three charges were veiled at Smith.   He was charged with using Alexander Campbell's translation called "Living Oracles," of saying, "I immerse you," instead of "I baptize you," and of administering the Lord's Supper in a way that he allowed the communicants to break the loaf for themselves.   Without waiting for himself to be singled out, Smith arose and said: "I plead guilty to them all."[31]   Much debating went on and the matter was tabled for another year, but at that time, the majority was favorable to Smith.   Finally, however, in 1830 the Association divided, and those advocating restoration soon dissolved themselves   J. A. Williams gives this account of the dissolution ·

But the main question, which had been held in reserve was now solemnly propounded: "Is there any authority in the Word of God

[29]Alexander Campbell, "Millennium—No I," *Millennial Harbinger,* Vol I, No 2 (February 1, 1830), pp 53-58
[30]Alexander Campbell, "Prospectus," *Millennial Harbinger,* Vol I, No 1 (January 4, 1830), p 3
[31]Errett Gates, *The Early Relation and Separation of Baptists and Disciples* (Chicago The Christian Century Co, 1904), pp 70, 71

for this Association to meet at all?" After some debate, in which nothing was said or done to give offense, they finally, and with much unanimity, resolved:

No church requesting the next Association to be appointed at any of their meeting houses, and this body not having authority to force it upon any; and every church which appeared here by her letter and messengers unanimously agreeing that the word of God is the only rule of faith and practice for Christians—on motion and second, that the Constitution of the North District Association of Baptists be dissolved—after consultation among the brethren, when the question was put, it was carried in the affirmative; and the said Association was thereby dissolved. Upon after consultation, the brethren agree to attend at Sharpsburg, at the request of her messengers in the name of the church, on Friday before the third Saturday, and the days following, in August, 1832, and there communicate with one another, either by letter or otherwise, such information respecting the progress and affairs of each church as they may think of sufficient importance of interest to communicate.[32]

Within the Bracken Association, the Licking Association and that of Boones' Creek, the story was the same: the Regular Baptists would become "corrupted" by the influence of the teachings of Campbell. The Association would divide, and that part made up of the Advocates of restoration would soon dissolve itself

In 1830 the Mahoning Association met in the church edifice in Austintown on the Western Reserve. The meeting opened with songs, exhortations, and prayers. John Henry, one of the preachers, stood up and said: "I charge you to look out what you are about to do here we want nothing here which the word of the Lord will not sanction." He sat down and in a moment suggested the resolution that the Association be dissolved, and it was carried. Commenting later, Campbell said:

Such a meeting was not witnessed in the memory of any present, as was the late meeting of churches in Austintown. The first day, Friday, was spent in declaring the wonders which God had wrought in various portions of the Western Reserve by the restoration of the ancient gospel. Songs of praise and tears of joy mingled with these reports, translated us nigher the regions of bliss than we had ever before approached. The next day, finding no business to transact, no inquiries to answer, nothing to do but "to love, and wonder, and adore," it was *unanimously* agreed that the Mahoning Association as "an advisory council," as "an ecclesiastical tribunal,"

---

[32]John A Williams, *Life of Elder John Smith* (Cincinnati Christian Standard Publishing Co, 1904), pp 416, 417

exercising any supervision or jurisdiction over particular congregations, should never meet again   This Association came to its end as tranquilly as ever did a good old man whose attenuated thread of life, worn to a hair's breadth, dropped asunder by its own imbecility

"Night dews fall not more gently to the ground,
    Nor weary worn out winds expire more soft,"
than did this Association give up the ghost [33]

Few men were capable of doing as much work as Campbell during his years of the prime of his life   He was constantly traveling, preaching and speaking before clubs and societies   His reputation as a speaker spread far and wide, and his services were in demand   Added to this is the activity which occasionally arose of engaging in debates upon his views

In February, 1828 Campbell received a letter from an individual in Canton, Ohio, bewailing the advances of infidelity   The man asked Campbell to come and meet a person who was spreading the tenets of Skepticism in that city   Campbell refused saying he would not draw a bow until he could shoot at the king of the skeptics himself.   That opportunity was soon to present itself, for Robert Owen, champion of Skepticism, had delivered a series of lectures in New Orleans, and challenged the clergy for a debate   Campbell published the challenge in the *Christian Baptist* and announced his acceptance of it   In a few weeks Owen came to Bethany to make plans for the discussion

Robert Owen was a brilliant man, born at New Wales in 1769. At the age of eighteen he had become a partner in a cotton mill   He was successful and arose rapidly in the business world.   He became head of the New Lanark Mills of Glasgow, employing over two thousand persons   He entered upon many benevolent projects to improve the working classes, and soon himself became quite wealthy   He began visiting foreign countries, delivering speeches. Unfortunately, the good he advocated was mixed with evil, for in addition to wanting to improve the social system, he fought Christianity, as standing opposed to all progress

Campbell met him in debate in the largest Methodist church house in the city of Cincinnati   Campbell's moderators were judge Jacob Burnet, former mayor of the city; Major Daniel Gano, and

---

[33] Alexander Campbell, "Mahoning Association," *Millennial Harbinger,* Vol I, No 9 (September 6, 1830), pp 414, 415

Col Samuel W. Davis The debate started on Monday, April 13, 1829, and with the exception of Sunday, continued over the twenty-first. The attendance was so large that many couldn't get in, and had to return home On the last day there were twelve hundred present

Eight years later Campbell spoke before the College of Teachers at Cincinnati This was really an association of those who either were teachers or had been. The group met on October 3, and Dr Joshua L Wilson spoke, recommending the Bible as a universal text-book In a subsequent lecture, Bishop Purcell of the Roman Catholic diocese in the city spoke and denied this Campbell spoke on "Moral Culture," connecting the rapid march of modern improvement with the Spirit of inquiry produced by the Protestant Reformation Purcell took exception, saying the Protestant Reformation was the cause of all the infidelity in the world Campbell told Purcell if he wished a discussion, that he, Campbell, was prepared At the same time he announced that he would speak on Monday evening at the Sycamore Street Church on the subject The evening following, he spoke at Wesley Chapel, and gave six propositions which he declared he would defend against Purcell. The debate began on Friday night, January 13, 1837.

The next of Campbell's great debates was with N. L Rice in the fall of 1843 While in Kentucky in 1842, the Presbyterians greeted Campbell, appearing to be favorable to a debate. A long correspondence was held, and, in August, 1843, final arrangements were made for the debate Campbell's opponent was to have been Professor Young of Centre College, but he became ill, and N L Rice of Paris, Kentucky was chosen Campbell, knowing something of Rice's bitter spirit, did not like the selection, but was forced to comply The debate began on Wednesday, November 15, 1843 in the Reformed Church at Lexington, and lasted for sixteen days

In the year, 1841, Campbell added to his busy program that of becoming president of a College Bethany College opened its doors that fall Campbell was president of a college, editor of a paper, preacher, lecturer, and in a short time, president of a missionary society.

Of Campbell's later activities there shall be occasion to give a more detailed account later. It is enough to get this brief background before launching into the details that will follow

CHAPTER V

EARLY PIONEER PREACHERS

Theatrical performances, dramas and plays must necessarily be preceded by an introduction to the characters who will perform. Across the stage of Time the drama of the restoration movement was enacted through most of the nineteenth century. The characters of this drama likewise need to be introduced to prepare our minds for the story they so well enacted. There is a romance about their lives and an inspiration gained from them. Their names adorn the pages of the history of the church and add a glorious lustre to the events of the previous century. One may well imagine that he is entering a great "Hall of Fame" of the restoration. All around the side there stands in imagination men like Walter Scott, W. K. Pendleton, David S. Burnet, Tolbert Fanning, Benjamin Franklin, Jacob Creath, Jr. Being dead, yet they speak, but their story can only be briefly told here.

Next to Thomas and Alexander Campbell the most celebrated leader of the restoration was Walter Scott, the announcer of the "Golden Oracle" whose eloquence stirred the Western Reserve in 1827 and 1828 as nothing else had ever done In personal appearance, in pulpit speaking, in type of mind Scott was the antithesis of Campbell, yet he supplemented Campbell in many ways. Campbell was tall, vigorous and athletic whereas Scott was of average height and slender. The disposition of Campbell was always cheerful, but Scott was meditative and sad very frequently. Campbell's face had no straight lines. His nose was arched a little to the right. His hair was light in color. Scott, on the other hand, had a straight nose, full lips, dark eyes and hair as black as a raven's wing. Campbell's mind loved to dwell upon great principles. Scott's mind was analytical It would take Scott's mind, not Campbell's, to think of the gospel as containing facts, commands, promises. But it would take Campbell's mind, not Scott's, to see in the promise of God to Abraham the germ of the two covenants with all their implications.

Walter Scott was a great preacher, but withal had many eccentricities, as the following account will show·

76

WALTER SCOTT

Brother Walter Scott took great care of his voice. His mind was greatly under its influence. If the instrument was in perfect tune, how admirably he could play upon it! When out of tune, he was as weak as Sampson when shorn of his hair Dear Walter! he was a great dyspeptic; and like all such persons, at times eccentric. He would change his diet to keep his voice, and consequently, his mind, in working order. Sometimes he would drink coffee, and then tea, and then water; and now and then milk. He was taking supper once with a good sister who had heard of his fondness for milk (he had just laid aside the lacteal diet and had gone back to coffee and tea), when she said, "Brother Scott, will you have a glass of milk?" "I thank you, sister. There is no music in a cow," said Walter, in his blandest way. Of course he thought that milk was injurious to his voice.[1]

---

[1] James Challen, "Memorabilia," *Christian Standard,* Vol V, No 15 (April 9, 1870), p 113

Robert Richardson, Campbell's biographer, compares Scott and Campbell in the following words

Thus, while Mr Campbell was fearless, self-reliant and firm, Mr. Scott was naturally timid, diffident and yielding, and, while the former was calm, steady and prudent, the latter was excitable, variable and precipitate. The one like the North Star was ever in position, unaffected by terrestrial influences, the other, like the magnetic needle, was often disturbed and trembling on its centre, yet ever returning or seeking to return to its true direction. Both were nobly endowed with the powers of higher reason—a delicate self-consciousness, a decided will and a clear perception of truth. But, as it regards the other departments of the inner nature, in Mr. Campbell the understanding predominated, in Mr Scott, the feelings; and, if the former excelled in imagination, the latter was superior in brilliancy of fancy. If the tendency of one was to generalize, to take wide and extended views and to group a multitude of particulars under a single head or principle, that of the other was to analyze, to divide subjects into their particulars and consider their details If the one was disposed to trace analogies and evolve the remotest correspondences of relations, the other delighted in comparisons and sought for the resemblancies of things If the one possessed the inducive power of the philosopher the other had in a more delicate musical faculty and more active ideality, a larger share of the attributes of the poet In a word, in almost all those qualities of mind and character which might be regarded differential or distinctive, they were singularly fitted to supply each other's wants and to form a rare and delightful companionship [2]

William Baxter, Scott's biographer, compares Campbell and Scott in the following words

Campbell was always great and self-possessed, Scott subject to great depression, and, consequently, unequal in his public efforts: but at times he knew a rapture, which seemed almost inspiration, to which the former was a stranger Campbell never fell below the expectations of his hearers, Scott frequently did, but there were times when he rose to a height of eloquence which the former never equalled If Campbell at times reminded his hearers of Paul on Mars Hill, commanding the attention of the assembled wisdom of Athens, Scott, in his happiest moments, seemed more like Peter on the Memorable Pentecost, with cloven tongue of flame on his head, and the inspiration of the Spirit of Truth in his heart, while from heart-pierced sinners on every side rose the agonizing cry, "Men and brethren, what shall we do?"[3]

[2]Robert Richardson, *Memoirs of Alexander Campbell* (Cincinnati Standard Publishing Co, 1897), Vol I, pp 510, 511 ·
[3]William Baxter, *Life of Elder Walter Scott* (Cincinnati Bosworth, Chase & Hall, 1874), pp 338, 339

On another occasion, Baxter made the following comparison

Scott's power, however, was over the hearts of men, of the masses, his dark eyes seemed to penetrate the secrets of the soul, and his voice was soothing or terrible as he gave utterance to the promises or threatenings of the word of God Multitudes were awakened under his preaching to the peril of their souls, and pointed successfully to the Lamb of God, and on some occasions bitter enemies and violent persecutors were changed, almost as suddenly as Saul of Tarsus, and became not only faithful Christains, but firm and life-long friends of the preacher whom they once had threatened and reviled.

Campbell's greatness and strength may in a great measure be realized by a careful study of his writings, but the noblest efforts of his worthy fellow-laborer, as far as the expression is concerned, perished almost at their birth, they could not be reproduced by either speaker or hearer, the impression made on the minds and hearts of those who heard him, will never fade until all things else shall fade But the tablets on which those memories dear and sweet are written, are perishable, and when the present generation passes, or rather when the remnant of those who heard him in his prime which yet lingers shall have passed away, the world will not know anything save by dim and imperfect tradition of the wonderful eloquency of this gifted, the princely man. I claim not to have set him faithfully as he seemed to me and the thousands who heard him, but these few fragments, imperfect as they are, will give some idea of the man; and while we can safely entrust the fame of Alexander Campbell to the proofs which his writings afford of his great, his eminent abilities, yet, at the same time, we cannot forbear laying this humble, heartfelt tribute upon the tomb of Walter Scott.[4]

Walter Scott was born in Moffat, Dumfriesshire, Scotland on October 31, 1796. His father was John Scott, a man of fine character, noble culture, whose occupation was that of a music teacher. His mother, Mary Innes Scott, was a gracious lady of great piety whose highest ambition for her son, Walter, was that he should be a minister in the Scotch Presbyterian Church of which she was a devoted member. She was a tender-hearted lady. In June, 1821 when her husband took a trip to Annan and suddenly died there, the grief of Mary Innes was so great that she followed him within a month in death

Mary Innes had a brother, George, who had left Scotland a few years before to seek his fortune in America. George was ambitious

---

[4]William Baxter, "Alexander Campbell and Walter Scott as Preachers," *Christian Standard,* Vol IV, No 24 (June 12, 1869), p 185

that all of his relatives should follow him, and to this end, he
worked and saved his money. One day, he wrote his sister to
send him one of her sons. The parents considered and decided to
send Walter. There was a reason for this decision. Walter Scott
had proved to be alert and capable, and accordingly had been sent to
the University of Edinburgh. He had the better education and was
more capable of making a success in America. So it was decided to
send Walter. George was working in New York City for the
government in the customs house. Walter prepared to go to his
uncle He sailed from Greenock in the late spring of 1818 and
landed in New York on July 7, 1818.

Soon after landing in New York, Scott secured a position as a
Latin teacher in a classical academy at Jamaica, Long Island. But
Scott was not destined to stay long in New York. The "West"
was beckoning, and immigrants were continually moving from
New York to the new lands and new opportunities out along the
Ohio River. Scott caught the fever, and before long he prepared
to go. He, with a companion, walked the distance from New York
to Pittsburgh in the spring of 1819 and arrived in the city on May
7, 1819.

After his arrival in Pittsburgh, Scott first turned his attention
toward a position for livelihood. Naturally he thought of teaching.
He learned of a George Forrester who was a preacher and a principal of an academy. Before long, he had secured a position teaching under Forrester. Both Forrester and Scott were devoutly
religious. Forrester, it appeared to Scott, was a peculiar person
in that he rejected all human creeds, and purported to take the
Bible alone for his religious guide This appealed to Scott. With
Forrester as his teacher Scott sat for hour after hour examining
the holy oracles to come to a fuller knowledge of the word of God.
Gradually the light dawned, and Scott began to see in some measure
the glory and beauty of the ancient religion of the New Testament
Church. He was convinced. But what should he do about baptism? He would study and see. It did not take him long to see
that infant baptism was unauthorized in the scriptures, and that
sprinkling or pouring were unknown to the Bible. Accordingly,
Scott was immersed by Forrester.

The church for which Forrester preached met in those days in
the courthouse. Most of the members were of Scotch descent and

carried with them much of the Scotch strictness. While the church wanted to hold fast the form of sound words, yet in many ways it went to extremes. The "holy kiss" was regularly practiced as well as feet washing. In matters of discipline, they were most strict. Any young lady who appeared in worship wearing costly apparel or jewelry and ornaments could expect a public rebuke. The elders of the church looked upon marriage outside of the church as a scandal If a man married a wife, no matter how good she might be morally; if she were not a member of the church, the man was rebuked in the presence of his wife and compelled to confess he was sorry for the marriage. It probably was some comfort to the wife to hear him say he would never do such a thing again.

At any rate, to this little church Scott went regularly to hear Forrester. This went on until Forrester drowned while bathing in the Allegheny River, and Scott had to take his place as public proclaimer Meanwhile, Scott had taken over the Academy. Robert Richardson and Samuel Church were two of his illustrious students. His rules for the classroom were obedience, order, accuracy. He believed in exercising as little discipline as possible, but continued to keep his rules ever before his students, trusting their honor to keep them.

Scott, in the meantime, had continued studying the Bible. His mind was toying with the subject of baptism. He felt there was a significance attached to it that he had not yet discovered. A tract on the subject came suddenly into his hands from a Scotch Baptist Church of New York City. Scott was impressed, so much so that he left Pittsburgh for New York to study the matter further But he was disappointed. In Pittsburgh, meanwhile, his absence was felt. The wealthy Richardson family wanted Scott back at the academy and sent letters urging him to return, and return he did.

His mind was yet unsettled on some points, so he continued to study. Soon after returning to Pittsburgh the idea took hold of him that the great central idea of the Christian religion was the Messiahship of Christ. Jesus is the Son of God! This idea Scott soon called the "Golden Oracle." He continued to study the Bible diligently, and made the vow that if God would give him a comprehensive view of the Bible, he would subordinate all other work to the preaching of the gospel.

The winter of 1821-22 Scott was still teaching in Pittsburgh.

It was at this time that Scott first met Alexander Campbell. He and Campbell soon began to discuss their religious views, and both were surprised to find they occupied very similar ground. Each recognized in the other qualities of superior nature Through Alexander Campbell Scott became acquainted with Thomas Campbell.

During this time, both Campbell and Scott were pondering the purpose of baptism as set forth in the Scriptures Both of them had arrived at a conclusion radical for the day that baptism, as set forth in the New Testament, was for the remission of sins. Campbell, in his debate with Walker in 1820, only hinted at the idea there. Scott could not help but have the same conclusion, but neither man was disposed to push the matter until it was necessary. That necessity was supplied in 1823 when Campbell received a challenge from W L . McCalla of Washington, Kentucky for a debate. Soon after getting the challenge, Campbell resolved to go over the whole subject again. But, at this time, Scott paid a visit to Bethany, and Thomas Campbell brought up the subject for them to discuss it. Alexander Campbell tells of the occasion in his own words:

Immediately on receiving a challenge from Mr Wm L M'Calla, of Kentucky, May 17, 1823, I resolved to settle the true meaning of baptism before I ever debated the subject again To examine this matter I went to my Testament with the zeal of a freshman Mr Thomas Campbell and myself discussed this matter at considerable length for some months It was not named to a third person till July or August following, when brother Walter Scott made his first visit to my residence During his stay my father informed him, in my presence, of the contemplated debate, and stated at considerable length the views of baptism which we had agreed to offer on the occasion As it had not been divulged to any other person, I was anxious for the judgment of one whom I so highly esteemed on account of his knowledge of the Holy Scriptures, and waited for his opinion with much interest He gave it upon the whole in favor of the views offered , and more than once during his stay recommended the importance of giving such a view in the approaching discussion [5]

By the spring of 1823 Campbell had determined to publish a paper He was prone to call it, "The Christian," but Scott convinced him of the lack of wisdom in this decision It was Scott's

---

[5]Alexander Campbell, "Events of 1823 and 1827," *Millennial Harbinger*, New Series, Vol II, No 10 (October. 1838), p 468

view that to call it "The Christian Baptist" would disarm prejudice among the Baptists. Campbell acquiesced, and the new periodical took this name. Scott himself agreed to present articles
for publication. He conceived of his relation to Alexander
Campbell as the same Philip Melanchthon bore to Martin Luther
in the Reformation. Under the title of "Philip" Scott wrote his
articles. The first one to appear was "A Divinely Authorized
Plan of Teaching the Christian Religion."

On January 3, 1823 Scott had married Miss Sarah Whitsett
who lived a few miles from Pittsburgh. Scott was now twenty-six
years old. He was rather handsome, but a meditative and melancholy youth Three years later, he determined to move his family
from Pittsburgh to Steubenville, Ohio. The purpose of this move
is uncertain, perhaps it was to get close to Bethany, the home of his
friend, Alexander Campbell. That same summer he attended the
meeting of the Mahoning Baptist Association held on the Western
Reserve. He went only as a visitor and an observer, but on
Lord's Day was invited to speak So eloquently did he present
his lesson that many thought he was Alexander Campbell Scott
probably did not imagine that in just one year he would be
chosen as Evangelist for the Association.

Soon after arriving in Steubenville Scott opened up an Academy.
In the summer of 1827 Alexander Campbell was on his way to
New Lisbon on the Western Reserve to attend the annual meeting of the Mahoning Association. He went by Steubenville on
the way to convince Scott to accompany him. Campbell, through
young Jacob Osborne, had an idea that an Evangelist was to be
appointed. To him Walter Scott was the logical man for that
work. Campbell writes:

In 1827 I had the pleasure of prevailing upon brother Scott,
then engaged in teaching a school in Steubenville, Ohio, to accompany me to the Western Reserve, where, by my frequent
visits in that direction, the Mahoning Association were almost to
a man on the side of going forward to the ancient and primitive
order of things. The churches had, however, as yet done nothing
but change their theory and resolve to go forward. A request
to have an Evangelist appointed, came, if I remember right, from
the before mentioned brother Osborne, then a resident in that
district, or from a church which he had induced to make such a

request　We all went to work in good earnest, and brother Scott was appointed and accepted of the work.[6]

After becoming the Association's Evangelist, Scott's first sermon was delivered in the Baptist Church at New Lisbon in Columbiana County.　When he arrived on Sunday, every seat in the meeting house was taken.　Soon many were standing and the aisles and the door were jammed with people　Scott preached on Matt. 16　16　A very peculiar circumstance occurred.　A devout man in the community, William Amend, had long before come to the conclusion that repentance and baptism were essential to salvation, as announced by Peter in Acts 2　38.　He had further declared his intention to obey the gospel the first time he heard a man teach that way　On the day Scott was preaching, Amend was late arriving　Outside the packed door, he suddenly heard Scott's first sentence which was a quotation of Acts 2: 38.　Amend pushed his way through the crowd and went down to the front and made known his intentions to obey the gospel　This was November 18, 1827.

Scott's work on the Western Reserve thus got off to a great start　Amend's conversion soon influenced more　Many heard the gospel for the first time and obeyed it.　Opposition was aroused　A woman requested baptism, but her son threatened to shoot Scott if he baptized her.　The sects were aroused, names were called, challenges were issued.　There was great excitement. Scott was in demand everywhere　New Lisbon, Deerfield, Austintown, Warren—Scott traveled and conversions were rapidly made　Scott, to get closer to his work, moved to Canfield Thomas Campbell came to observe Scott's work, and report on it to Alexander Campbell　For two years this work went on and the people were stirred up as nothing had stirred them before.

In 1831 Scott paid a visit to Cincinnati which was then the "Queen City" of the west.　James Challen was then the preacher for the church.　Challen was disposed to make a move, and it it was agreed that Scott should follow him　While in Cincinnati, Scott became ill with dyspepsia.　His pulpit efforts were on the whole very inferior.　The church didn't grow.　Scott grew discouraged.　He wrote to Louisiana asking Challen to come back.

------

[6]Alexander Campbell, "Events of 1823 and 1827," *Millennial Harbinger*, New Series, Vol II, No 10 (October, 1838)), p 469

Challen came back, and for a time, he and Scott worked together in Cincinnati.

January, 1832 Scott began the publication of a paper he called, "The Evangelist" About this time he moved to Carthage, Ohio, and began preaching for the small church There were few results, and Scott grew discouraged He blamed himself, and thought the people didn't like him. He determined to find out John T. Johnson, Benjamin Finnell, John O'Kane, Love H. Jameson, and B. U. Watkins were invited to come to Carthage and help out in a gospel meeting. They came Johnson and O'Kane did the preaching. For several days the meeting dragged on, and there were few responses Finally Scott stood up and spoke. He told the people that he had preached as best he could and there were no responses. Concluding it was his fault, he had gotten others to preach, and still they would not respond He wondered how they could sit back and listen to the preaching they had without being touched What was the matter with them? Some of the visiting preachers thought Scott had ruined the meeting, but he didn't Conversions started coming and there were thirty or forty before the meeting closed.

In 1835 Scott discontinued publishing the *Evangelist* in order to give himself time to write the book, the "Gospel Restored" which he published in 1836. In January, 1838 he resumed publishing the *Evangelist*.

Scott moved back to Pittsburgh in 1844 and found himself soon appointed an elder in the church. He set to work to publish another paper which he called the *Protestant Unionist*. A great fire swept through Pittsburgh on Thursday, April 10, 1845 and burned up his printing office. For the next few years, however, Scott continued his preaching in Pittsburgh

On April 28, 1849, Scott's wife died, and the next year he married Annie B. Allen of Mayslick, Kentucky About this time, the Baptists moved out of a school in Covington, Kentucky and Walter Scott started a Female Academy. This Academy he kept going for several years In July, 1855, Tolbert Fanning visited Cincinnati and with Benjamin Franklin went to see Scott at Covington College "of which he is at present proprietor "[7]

---

[7]Tolbert Fanning, "Tour North," *Gospel Advocate,* Vol I, No 3 (September, 1855), p 71

Scott's second wife died in 1854, and Scott married a rich widow, Eliza Sandige, of Mason County, Kentucky. This marriage was never congenial. Scott had no appreciation of money. He was so tender in heart that he gave away nearly all he ever made. Often he would go to a store for a basket of groceries, and give them all away before he got home. Once he had two cows and he gave a neighbor one cow, because the neighbor had none. Scott's third wife was not accustomed to such handling of funds. Overlooking the greatness in Scott's soul, she would storm at him and run him out of the house. Often he spent the night sitting on the door step of a neighbor. Once she ran him off from home. Several days later he was found walking the streets of Cincinnati in a daze.

About this time Scott began work on a new book which he was to call "The Messiahship, or Great Demonstration." This was his most elaborate effort at writing and was the last attempt he made. Scott explained the book in a letter addressed to Ben Franklin:

Dear Sir: Today I initiated the stereotyping of a volume to be entitled, "The Messiahship. or Great Demonstration." It will contain four hundred pages, more or less—the page containing 1705 ems which will give a great deal of reading in the whole book. It will be sold in retail at one dollar per copy.

The volume is intended to convey the reader into a field of thought and meditation lying somewhat beyond the domain of first principles, and I hope it has a freshness that will make it acceptable to him.

It can be brought out only at great expense, and as it is the fruit of much labor, much thought and some research—above all, as it has been got up for the particular benefit of my brethren, it would afford me unspeakable pleasure would they purchase it. . .[8]

While many widely praised the book, in reality it was a disappointment to both Scott and the brotherhood. Moses E. Lard's appraisal of Scott as a writer may appear to be harsh, but probably it is the most accurate appraisal of all. Lard wrote:

As a writer, we must in candor say we think Bro. Scott simply a failure. Such, at least, is the opinion we have felt compelled to form of the work which he evidently intended to be his masterpiece—The Great Demonstration As a book, it is too common

---

[8]Walter Scott, "A New Book," *American Christian Review,* Vol II, No 5 (February 1, 1859), p 18

for the learned reader, and too learned for the common reader. It clearly disappointed both its author and the brotherhood [9]

Walter Scott was now growing old. On October 31, 1860, he passed his sixty-fourth birthday. Since becoming a citizen of the United States, he had always had a great interest in his country's welfare. In politics he was a democrat yet he did not fail to see the good in men of the other party. With a heavy heart in the fall of 1860 Scott watched the trend toward Civil War. He had friends in both the North and the South that he knew would be affected. That summer he had written an essay called the "Crisis" which was an effort to check the feelings coming up between the states. Scott went to church, but the burden of a divided land and the hatred that existed between brethren was such that he refused to take the communion. What good was the Lord's Supper in a land torn by such strife? During the last quarter of 1860, Scott refused all efforts to get him to speak. Only once did he respond, and that was on Lord's Day, January 27, 1861. His few remarks were upon the state of the nation, and then he encouraged brethren to try to avoid the conflict He very quickly sat down. In the fall of 1860 he addressed a letter to his oldest son, John, then thirty-seven years of age and expressed his tremendous grief at the state of the nation When the news of the fall of Fort Sumter reached him, he wrote again of his terrible remorse at such a catastrophe

Broken badly in heart and soul with the country's evils, Scott, on Tuesday, April 16—three days after the fall of the federal fortress in 1861—became seriously ill The doctor called it typhoid pneumonia Quickly it grew worse, and by the next Sunday, Scott realized that the end was now in sight. Elder John Rogers was in the vicinity and stopped by to converse with his old friend. L. P. Streator, another of the preachers nearby, came to pay him a visit. Scott was dwelling in the land of memory, reliving the moments when he preached the gospel with such force and success on the Western Reserve. He spoke of the great honor which God had bestowed upon him to let him develop the kingdom of God among men. On Tuesday night at ten o'clock, he passed quietly away.

---

[9]Moses E Lard, "A Monument to Walter Scott," *Lard's Quarterly*, Vol. II, No 2 (January, 1865), p 133

John Rogers and L P Streator preached the funeral, and then Streator immediately wrote to Alexander Campbell the news His letter, dated April 25, two days after Scott's death, told of the severe attack of typhoid pneumonia which in seven days brought on the termination of Scott's life Campbell received the news with great sorrow and wrote

No death in my horizon, out of my own family, came more unexpectedly or more ungratefully to my ears than this of our much beloved and highly appreciated brother Walter Scott, and none awoke more tender sympathies and regrets Next to my Father, he was my most cordial and indefatigable fellow laborer in the origin and progress of the present reformation We often took counsel together in our efforts to plead and advocate the paramount claims of original and apostolic Christianity. His whole heart was in the work He was, indeed, truly eloquent in the whole import of that word in pleading the claims of the Author and Founder of the Christian faith and hope, and in disabusing the inquiring mind of all its prejudices, misapprehensions and errors He was, too, most successful in winning souls to the allegiance of the Divine Author and Founder of the Christian institution, and in putting to silence the cavilings and objections of the modern Pharisees and Sadducees of Sectariandom

He, indeed, possessed, upon the whole view of his character, a happy temperament It is true, though not a verb, he had his moods and tenses, as men of genius generally have. He was both logical and rhetorical in his conceptions and utterances. He could and he did simultaneously address and interest the understanding, the conscience, and the hearts of his hearers; and in his happiest seasons constrain their attention and their acquiescence . .

I knew him well I knew him long. I love him much We might not, indeed, agree in every opinion nor in every point of expediency. But we never loved each other less, because we did not acquiesce in every opinion, and in every measure. By the eye of faith and the eye of hope, methinks I see him in Abraham's bosom.[10]

But of all words written about Walter Scott by his contemporaries there perhaps was no encomium truer and more beautiful than that penned by Moses E. Lard. Lard writes:

We have not yet met the man of earth we loved more tenderly than gentle Walter Scott He was himself a poem, great and small, sublime and tame; but with a spirit as pure and aims as

---

[10]Alexander Campbell, "Elder Walter Scott's Demise," *Millennial Harbinger*, Series V, Vol IV, No 5 (May, 1861), p 296

high as ever fall to the lot of men With a mind singularly formed for large generalization, he yet combined traits strangely weak, while with an utterance rich even up to a gorgeousness, he would still mingle sayings insipid as those of a housemaid In two respects only did Walter Scott never become a common man—in profound, exhausting admiration for the Saviour, and in the love of truth Here he will never be excelled In thought he was strong, eccentric, and not always safe, in expression, antithetic and unnatural, but at times tender and sweet as the genius of Burns. As a preacher, he was generally to a high degree instructive and pleasing; at times positively enchanting, then again common-place as a plodding field-hand. He affected new modes of combining old truths, and new forms of speech for familiar thoughts, to an extent that lent a frequent charm to oratory, which, otherwise, would have been pronounced inelegant . . [11]

WILLIAM KIMBROUGH PENDLETON

One of the most influential of the pre-Civil War preachers and pioneer leaders was W. K Pendleton Certainly there were few more talented than he He had a broad cultural background and an educated mind that enjoyed to its fullest the finer productions in literature and learning. J. W. McGarvey once spoke of Pendleton as "one of the clearest headed men he had ever known "[12] McGarvey had met Pendleton when the former entered Bethany College in 1847 Very often did he have private counsels with his teacher Consequently, McGarvey said that on a great many of the important questions he had been forced to consider he had been influenced by Pendleton's private counsel more so than that of any man Pendleton, in his manners was always dignified, courteous and graceful He was rarely known to get unduly excited. His broad knowledge and calm, deliberate consideration of every issue made him a natural leader in the earlier days of the restoration.

Pendleton was born of the old Virginia aristocrats His father was Edmund Pendleton and his mother was Unity Yancey Kimbrough His ancestral history reads of heroic achievements and strong courageous leadership His mother was an Episcopalian, but his father claimed no religious affiliation until about 1833 when

---

[11]Moses E Lard, "A Monument to Walter Scott," *Lard's Quarterly*, Vol II, No 2 (January, 1865), p 133
[12]J W McGarvey, "W K Pendleton," *Christian Standard*, Vol XXXV, No 37 (September 16, 1899), p 1193

W K PENDLETON

he became intensely interested in the writings of Alexander Campbell. After being baptized, he continued to plead the cause of
restoration   When young Pendleton was an infant, his parents
moved from Yanceyville out to a home built by his great grandfather, Henry Pendleton   The name of this old home was, oddly
enough, "Cuckoo."

When W. K Pendleton was thirteen, he and his younger
brother entered the school of Jeremiah C. Harris who in those

days was looked upon as the "prince of the pedagogues." After finishing here, Pendleton went to a classical academy conducted by W. G. Nelson. After a few sessions here, he entered the school of David Richardson, a teacher of mathematics and astronomy. From here, Pendleton enrolled in the University of Virginia to put the finishing touches on his education.

Across the front of one of the stateliest buildings at the University of Virginia were printed these words: "You shall know the truth and the truth shall make you free." Pendleton was one of two hundred and sixty-five students who looked at these words in the fall of 1836 upon enrolling in school. He began a study of law as he dreamed of becoming one of Virginia's great statesmen.

Two years before Pendleton attended the University, his father and mother, and his older brother, Madison, all had become interested in the writings of Alexander Campbell and were baptized They formed the nucleus of a small congregation near Cuckoo called Mount Gilboa in Louisa County. It was only natural that while W. K Pendleton was in the University, he should devote some of his time to reading the *Millennial Harbinger* as well as some of the older copies of the *Christian Baptist* These, along with the Bible, gave him his religious instruction Until the spring of 1840, then Pendleton continued his study of law at the University, and his search for truth religiously

It was the custom of Alexander Campbell to travel extensively and preach in addition to editing the *Millennial Harbinger* His tours took him over a wide range of territory, and very frequently they took him to Virginia Quite often, Campbell would take one of his daughters with him on these trips Campbell's daughter, Lavina, was a young lady of great beauty and an unusual buoyant personality. She came with her father to Charlottesville, Virginia in 1838. Pendleton, while a student at the University there, lived with an aunt, Mrs. Lucy Pendleton Vowles. When Campbell and his daughter made their first public appearance in town, Pendleton was at home in bed sick. The boys at the University attended and saw Campbell's daughter. They came to Pendleton's bedside and joked with Pendleton and told him of her beauty. Pendleton joked back, assuring the boys he would get well, meet Lavina, and beat them all out yet. He lived to accomplish this feat

Pendleton left the University in the spring of 1840 and came back to Louisa County. In June that year he listened to Campbell preach, and was baptized by Campbell near the Mount Gilboa Church. Meanwhile, he had won Lavina's heart and the two were making plans to marry. On October 14, 1840, they were married. The ceremony took place in the Campbell mansion at Bethany—in the same room where Alexander Campbell later died. Warwick Martin performed the ceremony.

By now, Pendleton had reached a crisis in his life. All of his plans and his education pointed toward a career in politics. Too, he had bright prospects in that field. He belonged to the Whig party. In 1840 he acted as a delegate to the Young Men's National Ratification Convention in Baltimore. This convention followed the Whig Convention and was to endorse the nomination of Harrison and Tyler as leaders on the party ticket. Here, Pendleton met and heard Henry Clay and Daniel Webster who were both present. Yet, notwithstanding bright political prospects, Pendleton was feeling the pull from the Campbells. Alexander Campbell recognized the ability of Pendleton. Plans had already been announced that Campbell was to establish a college at Bethany, and Campbell was anxious to have his son-in-law associated with him in this work. And so for a time Pendleton pushed his political interests in the background although he never quite freed his soul from a desire for a place in the political world.

Bethany College opened its doors in the fall of 1841 and Pendleton, along with Robert Richardson, was elected as a teacher in physical sciences. Meanwhile, Pendleton and his wife had moved to their home in Bethany. On Sept. 2, 1841, their first daughter, Campbellina, was born. This is the daughter who in later years was affectionately known as "Miss Cammie." Around his house in Bethany Pendleton cared for his flowers, and in the college, taught his classes. His wife was of frail health, and undoubtedly brought many anxious hours to Pendleton. A few years passed, and she grew worse. On May 29, 1846 she died. The doctors called her trouble consumption. She was twenty-nine years old. Her body was borne to the cemetery at Bethany and laid to rest. On a slab over her remains were inscribed the words:

Beautiful in person, pure in heart, warm in her affections, ardent in her mind and ever ready to do good, her friends might well have prayed the good Lord to lend her a little longer to soothe and lighten the sorrows of earth, but He has taken her where there is fullness of joy, and though we raise this stone to her memory, we know she sleeps not here, but rejoices as an angel in the presence of God.[13]

The Trustees of the College met on August 13, 1845 and elected Pendleton to the office of vice-president. Campbell was gone frequently and the need of someone to take his place in his absence was evident. But during this time, Pendleton himself was sick often with dyspepsia. This, in addition to his wife's illness and his duties around the college, made the passing days more and more difficult. Early in 1846 Pendleton went to Philadelphia to consult a physican, and was advised to take an ocean voyage. Lavina's death that spring probably made the voyage seem more necessary so during that summer, Pendleton went to England. With him went Clarinda, another of Campbell's daughters, and a Mr. and Mrs. Semple of Pittsburgh. He returned from his trip somewhat refreshed.

Pendleton wanted to be released from some of his duties, but found more and more put upon him. In July, 1846, he offered his resignation to the Trustees of Bethany College, but it was promptly refused. Moreover, he was now acting as co-editor of the *Millennial Harbinger*, which position he began in January, 1846. During the months of May to October, 1847, Campbell was in England, and the editing of the *Harbinger* was left entirely to Pendleton. Pendleton now entered a period of intense activity. The paper and the college together allowed him little freedom. Moreover, plans were now developing for the establishment of the American Christian Missionary Society and Pendleton was to figure some in that. He attended the first convention in the fall of 1849 in the absence of Campbell who was sick.

In the summer of 1848 Pendleton had married his second wife. Again he chose a daughter of Campbell—Clarinda. In looks Clarinda was similiar to Lavina, but was quieter and more reserved. This marriage, too, did not last long for in 1850 Clarinda

---

[13]F. D. Power, *Life of W. K. Pendleton* (St. Louis: Christian Publishing Co., 1902), p. 78.

also died. Pendleton's third wife was Catherine Huntington King of Warren, Ohio, whom he married on September 19, 1855.

His work with the college and the paper continued and as Campbell grew more feeble, Pendleton stepped into his place. In 1864 Campbell turned the *Harbinger* over to Pendleton who continued its publication until 1870 when the press of college duties made it imperative to cease its publication. After Campbell's death in 1866, the Trustees elected Pendleton president of the college which position he held until he was too feeble to continue it. From 1869-1870 he served as associate editor with W. T. Moore of the *Christian Quarterly*. During a part of this time, at the request of Isaac Errett, he wrote some for the *Christian Standard*. About 1875 he became president of the General Christian Missionary Convention. In 1884, with advancing age making the proper fulfillment of his duties impossible, Pendleton resigned as president of Bethany College. He was asked, however, to allow his name to stand as president. This he did and B. C. Hagerman was appointed chairman of the faculty for a year At the end of the next year, however, he requested the Trustees to elect a president, which they did. W. H. Woolery was elected and thereafter, Pendleton was listed as president, *emeritus.*

Meanwhile, Pendleton's political interests never lagged. In 1855 he ran for Congress but was defeated. In the political campaigns of 1860 he supported Bell and Everett and ever after was a Democrat After the War between the States, when the state of West Virginia was formed, Pendleton was called upon for active political services. Both the Democratic and Republican conventions of his district nominated him to be their representative in the state's Constitution Convention in 1872. The following year he was State Superintendent of Public Schools, which office he held for years. While Pendleton was acting as State Superintendent of Public Schools, the Governor of West Virginia requested him to select and suitably inscribe the West Virginia Memorial Stone for the Washington Monument in Washington, D. C. This stone may be found at the two hundred foot landing of the monument.

Pendleton's last years were spent in Florida, although he continued to make trips to Bethany. In March, 1886, he moved to Deland. Shortly after this, he bought an orange grove and small farm near Eustis. Here he continued to enjoy his books and visit with friends who stopped by. It was while he was on a trip back to Bethany that he passed quietly and peacefully away   It was September 1, 1899.

DAVID STAATS BURNET

Another of the influential pre-Civil War preachers was D. S. Burnet   In personal appearance Burnet was a small man, but strong and healthful. His manners were very formal and stiff. He was really a humble man, but his aristocratic dignity often made many think he was proud and haughty. In nature, he was very sensitive. These qualities made him have many enemies that otherwise he might not have had   As a speaker, Burnet was outstanding   He was easy and graceful on the platform and his voice was rich and melodious. But as a writer, he was almost a failure   Although he was for a number of years in the editorial chair, he could not be considered greatly successful. It was as a speaker, and as an organizer that he gained his greatest reputation. In the latter ability he had few equals. He was the leading figure in organizing the Societies that sprang up among the brethren. On February 28, 1867—less than five months before his death—he wrote to W. T. Moore: "I consider the inauguration of our Society system, which I vowed to urge upon the brethren, if God raised me from my protracted illness of 1845, as one of the most important acts of my career."[14] Only a few years before his death he wrote the following: "From the time I urged the scheme of associated evangelical action upon the brethren, in 1845, to the present, the work has commanded my heart, my best energies, and my means."[15]

Burnet was born in Dayton, Ohio on July 6, 1808 When Burnet was eight years of age, however, his parents moved to Cincinnati. In these early days, Isaac G. Burnet, D. S. Burnet's father, was active in political circles. In 1821 he was elected mayor of Cincinnati, an office which he held for many years   D. S Burnet, although only thirteen years of age, became his father's clerk   Thus Burnet's background is to be found less among the common people of life and more in the political and aristocratic circles.

[14]W T Moore, *The Living Pulpit of the Christian Church* (St. Louis: Christian Publishing Co , 1867), p 45.
[15]D S Burnet, "Resignation of Brother D S Burnet," *Millennial Harbinger*, Fifth Series, Vol VII, No 4 (April, 1864), p 185

D S BURNET

From an early age Burnet was interested in religion. He had
been sprinkled and belonged to the Presbyterian Church in Cincinnati. When he was only sixteen, he was teaching a Sunday-
School class which compelled him to study scriptures   Before
long his investigations soon convinced him that sprinkling was
wrong On December 26, 1824, he was immersed into Christ and
became a member of the Enon Baptist Church. At this time the
cause of restoration was comparatively young. Aside from the
Campbells there were few who entirely embraced his views   In
Kentucky that number probably included only two—P. S. Fall
and Jeremiah Vardeman   Fall had gone to Cincinnati at the request of the Enon Baptist Church and had witnessed the immersion

of D S Burnet [16] Whether Fall baptized Burnet or not is not entirely clear   At any rate, shortly after being immersed, Burnet began preaching and became known as the "boy preacher "

In 1827 Burnet and William Montague of Kentucky established the Sycamore Street Baptist Church in Cincinnati with eighty members   A short time later, when Alexander Campbell's views became known in the congregation, the church divided into the Ninth Street Baptist Church and the famous Christian Chapel, located at the corner of Walnut and Eighth Streets

On March 30, 1830 Burnet was married to Mary Gano, the youngest daughter of Major-General John S Gano of Ohio   Mary had been immersed in 1827 by Jeremiah Vardeman, and was, therefore, already in sympathy with the views that Burnet entertained

Burnet's life was divided between writing, preaching, and teaching   During the year, 1833, he was busy in full-time evangelistic work   From 1836-40 he published the *Christian Preacher,* a monthly periodical   In 1846 he published the *Christian Family Magazine*   At various times he edited the following papers *Christian Age, The Reformer, The Monthly Age,* and the *Sunday School Journal*   Late in 1839 Burnet tried teaching. He purchased a farm from O M. Spencer on the Hamilton turnpike, eight miles northwest of Cincinnati   Here, he opened a "female" institution, as schools for girls then were popularly called   He named this institution "The Hygeia Female Atheneum "   Campbell seems to have doubted the wisdom of Burnet's running such a school, for upon the announcement of the opening of the institution, Campbell wrote ·

Brother Burnet's character, intellectual, literary, and moral, is so well and so favorably known, not only to our brethren, but very generally throughout the community of our widely extended readers, as to need no commendation. I am only sorry that one so eminently qualified to be useful on a large scale as an Evangelist, either in Europe or America, should be confined to the labors of either a public or a private Academy. [17]

In 1845 Burnet inaugurated the American Christian Bible Society, a Society which never was popular among any of the breth-

---

[16]Robert Richardson, *Memoirs of Alexander Campbell* (Cincinnati Standard Publishing Co , 1897), Vol II, p 122

[17]Alexander Campbell, "The Hygeia Female Atheneum," Near Cincinnati," *Millennial Harbinger,* New Series, Vol IV, No 1 (January, 1840), p 48

ren. Campbell was critical of Burnet. It seems that, while Campbell greatly admired the character and ability of D S Burnet, he frequently called in question the latter's judgment. Campbell believed the inauguration of this Society was premature. Campbell's attitude stung Burnet, but the whole matter eventually blew over. Burnet was present at the first convention of the Missionary Society in 1849, and was, until his death, one of the leading figures in it. For about a year in 1859 and 1860 Burnet was Corresponding Secretary. After the death of Campbell, Burnet was elected as the Missionary Society's president, but in this office he never served due to his own death.

Burnet's death came at 11:30 A. M on July 8, 1867 in Baltimore, Maryland. He had gone to Baltimore from Cincinnati in 1860, and was preparing to move to Louisville when his death came He possessed a very malignant form of dysentery which caused him much suffering, although his last few hours were quiet and peaceful. Tuesday morning before his death, although a sick man, Burnet went to the church building to baptize a person. The Sunday before he had preached his farewell sermon, and·had all his belongings packed when death came

His body was borne from Baltimore to Cincinnati for burial W T Moore, who then preached for the Walnut and Eighth Streets Church in Cincinnati for which Burnet had formerly preached, read an appropriate hymn at the funeral service. L. L. Pinkerton led the prayer Isaac Errett gave the address after which the body was taken to the cemetery at Spring Grove for burial

Thus did Burnet live and die His name shall appear often in this study of the restoration movement.

Chapter VI

OTHER EARLY PIONEER PREACHERS

It is not exaggerating in the least to say that after the death of Alexander Campbell in 1866 the most prominent man in the brotherhood was Benjamin Franklin When Franklin died, David Lipscomb wrote:

The cause loses its most able and indefatigable defender since the days of Alexander Campbell, and his loss is simply irreparable.[1]

Still the influence of Franklin goes back as early as 1845 Ten years prior to this Franklin had been preaching the gospel, but his influence then was limited to the places where he had labored His labors broadened in 1845 when he first came before the brotherhood in the capacity of an editor. From then until his death in 1878 his pen was seldom still. He was one of the greatest champions of truth since apostolic days

Joseph Franklin, the father of Benjamin Franklin, was born in Providence, Rhode Island in 1783 Early in life he moved into eastern Ohio and settled in Belmont County. About 1811 he married Isabella Devold, and to this union Ben Franklin, their eldest son, was born. The date of his birth was February 1, 1812 While Ben was still an infant, his parents moved on a stream called Salt Run in Noble County, Ohio, and here they lived until 1833. Seven children were born here—six sons and a daughter.

Joseph Franklin's brother, Calvin, had moved into Henry County, Indiana, and shortly afterward, in 1832, Ben Franklin, Calvin's nephew, came to live with his uncle. That year Calvin and a man by the name of William Stewart built the first mill south of Middletown on Deer Creek Ben Franklin was employed by his uncle. When Calvin decided to build a grist-mill of a better type, Ben digged the millrace. Middletown, where the Franklins now came, was located in the northwest corner of Henry County. The town was laid out in 1829 by Jacob Koontz, and the first sale of the lots took place on Christmas day of that year Deer Creek was south of the town in what was then a great wilderness. A part of the winter of 1832-33 Ben Franklin went to

---

[1]David Lipscomb, "The Death of Benjamin Franklin," *Gospel Advocate,* Vol XX, No 43 (October 31, 1878), p 677

BEN FRANKLIN

Knightstown to help construct the National Road which was then being built through Indiana. Ben Franklin bought an eighty acre tract of wilderness and spent a part of his time erecting a cabin and clearing the land Meanwhile, he "wooed and won" Mary Personett, a neighbor girl two and one-half years older than himself.

The Joseph Franklin family moved into Henry County in May, 1833. Up until this time, none of the family had shown the slightest interest in religion. As the manner of the community was, the boys drifted into profanity and general religious indifference. All of this was changed when, in 1833, Samuel Rogers moved with his family into Henry County.

Rogers set to work immediately and opened a school. All of the Franklin boys attended except Ben Meanwhile, Rogers also established a church by preaching in a school house   On one occasion when Rogers was forced to discipline and expel a member, the schoolhouse then was denied the church, so they met in houses and out in the groves when the weather permitted

Joseph Franklin, who was a neighbor of Samuel Rogers, had a Methodist background and did not believe in immersion.   Rogers went to work to convert him   Of Joseph Franklin Rogers wrote ·

Old Brother Franklin was not the best balanced man in the world, he was too much like myself in disposition, with a quick and impulsive nature, he was easily exasperated, easily excited. He suddenly became very happy, and as suddenly very unhappy. Sometimes he was lifted to the third heaven in transports of joy, and would then relapse into a state of despondency and gloom almost bordering on despair   We used to say he either lived in the garret or the cellar   Withal, however, he was a good and pure man; earnest in the advocacy of truth, and as far from making compromises with error as any living man · He stood upon principle, was ever ready to sacrifice personal interest and the praise of men for what he believed to be the truth [2]

Ben Franklin's mother had a different disposition, Rogers declared

She was always cheerful, and hoping for the best   While he was apt to look upon the dark side of things, she was always looking on the bright side; her sky was a cloudless one   There were very few women in her day who had a better acquaintance with the Bible than she, or who had so bright an intellect . . . When we consider the character of this woman, we are not surprised that four of her six sons became ministers of the gospel of Christ [3]

Samuel Rogers and Joseph Franklin agreed to meet in each other's cabins on Saturday afternoon and study the Bible through.   They studied honestly, agreeing to mark each passage on which they could not agree and come back to it   They avoided every sign of discussion or prejudice.   When they finished, they found that not a passage had been marked.   Before long the Franklin family, including Ben, had been baptized.

Ben Franklin went zealously to work studying his Bible and preparing himself to preach   To the average listener in those early days he doubtlessly appeared to have little prospects as a preacher. His education had been very limited, and consequently, his grammar was poor   His form of delivery showed his backwoods cul-

---

[2] John I. Rogers, *Autobiography of Samuel Rogers* (Cincinnati Standard Publishing Co , 1880), p 144
[3] John I Rogers, *Autobiography of Samuel Rogers,* pp 144, 145

SAMUEL ROGERS

ture   John Longley, one of Indiana's early pioneer preachers, often
went to hear Franklin, and was one of his severe critics   Franklin
had unconsciously formed the habit of saying, "My dear friends
and brethering" and he always had the "ing" on it.   Longley took
a piece of paper and a pin at one meeting and made a hole for
every time Franklin repeated this phrase.   At the conclusion of the
sermon, he counted one hundred and fifty holes.

Yet, despite this early handicap Ben Franklin developed into
one of the most powerful proclaimers of the ancient gospel ever
known on American soil   While Franklin gained wide fame as
an editor and a debater, yet in the pulpit he came as near repre-

senting perfection as a gospel preacher that could be found. He quoted scripture voluminously. He did not pretend to be a philosopher, a politician, a teller of stories, or anything of the kind. He was a *gospel preacher* in everything the term implies

In 1890 Joseph Franklin, son of Ben Franklin, was preaching for the church in Bedford, Indiana. One day Alfred Ellmore stopped at Bedford and spent some time with Joseph. During his stay, he on one occasion looked through the old family album. He came across a picture of Ben Franklin. Ellmore writes:

> While looking through the album, my eyes rested upon the picture of Benjamin Franklin which brought to my mind the scenes of other days, when I sat under the mighty ministrations of the greatest preacher I ever listened to. And even now, after having listened to many men of varied abilities, I am firm in the conviction that Benjamin Franklin was the greatest gospel preacher I ever heard.[4]

When Samuel Rogers grew old, and Ben Franklin had become famous as a preacher, Rogers found a great satisfaction in the knowledge of the fact that he had introduced Franklin to the gospel. Rogers writes:

> I have ever felt, in looking back over those times and considering that work, that, if I had done no more for my Master than to be instrumental in giving to the world Benjamin Franklin, I would have no reason to be ashamed; but would feel that I had by no means lived and labored in vain. Ben Franklin may, in common with his race, have faults and foibles but, to my mind, he is one of the most direct and powerful gospel preachers and writers of this age. He indulges very little, if any, in speculation, but lays down his proposition, and proceeds with proofs that carry conviction to the mind almost irresistibly. He is emphatically a gospel preacher. Christ is his theme, first, midst and last. We may have scores of men among us more learned, in the popular sense, and more refined and elegant in manners and address; but it is my judgment that we have not a man among us who can preach the gospel with less admixture of philosophy and speculation, and with greater force, than Ben Franklin.[5]

Shortly before Franklin's death, he visited Nashville on a tour into the South. Here, David Lipscomb heard him preach. Commenting on Ben Franklin's preaching, Lipscomb wrote:

---

[4]A. Ellmore, "Wheat and Chaff," *Christian Leader,* Vol IV, No. 16 (April 22, 1890), p 4

[5]John I. Rogers, *Autobiography of Samuel Rogers,* p 149

Earnestness, clearness, simplicity, with a strong reverence for and determination to know nothing in religion save what the Bible teaches, were the striking characteristics of his discourses [6]

J. W. McGarvey, commenting upon Franklin's power as a debator and preacher, said:

His power lies in two peculiarities. First His close and constant dependence upon the very words of the English Bible, which he has richly treasured up in his memory. Second. His earnest and vehement manner of pressing home upon the hearts of his audience any advantages which his position or his argument may have given him . . .
Brother Franklin has another peculiarity as a debatant of which I must speak, and which I cannot too highly commend to the imitation of all the brethren. He is preeminently an evangelist, and his whole soul seems to be wrapped up in the desire to convert souls to Christ This thought never forsakes him in discussion His speeches are therefore characterized by the same tender solicitude for his audience, the same solemnity of manner, and almost the same pathos, as when he is preaching for the conversion of sinners. It is not an uncommon occurrence for him to draw tears from the eyes of a large portion of his audience [7]

Daniel Sommer was preaching in Clark County, Kentucky in 1874 and was discussing Ben Franklin with an old elder in the church The old elder said that he was with Ben like Pat Caldwell was with the North Star at Newbern, North Carolina in 1833. That year, there was a great meteor shower, and stars were falling everywhere. Many thought the world had come to an end, and crowds of people were terror stricken But Pat Caldwell was calm. He cried out, "Be aisy, boys I've got my eye on the North Star, and if that don't fall, we are safe " The elder had his eye on Ben Franklin, and to him the cause of restoration was not lost as long as Franklin lived.[8]

It is not likely that a greater, nobler, truer, purer preacher of the gospel lived since apostolic times than Ben Franklin.

In 1835, shortly after his conversion, Franklin wrote his first article for the press It set forth the plan of salvation, and was published in the *Heretic Detector,* a paper published in Middleburg,

[6]David Lipscomb, "Benjamin Franklin," *Gospel Advocate,* Vol XX, No 48 (December 5, 1878)), p 758

[7]J. W McGarvey, "The Chillicothe Debate," *American Christian Review,* Vol III, No 23 (June 5, 1860), p 91

[8]Daniel Sommer, "A Neat Compliment," *American Christian Review,* Vol XVIII, No 24 (June 15, 1875), p 189

Ohio by Arthur Crihfield Meanwhile, Franklin earned a living by working at the mill which he owned and farming. In 1842 he moved to New Lisbon, ten miles southeast of Newcastle, Indiana He stayed here for two years A part of this time he preached for the church at Bethel, twelve miles north of Richmond. In 1844 he moved his family to Centerville, county seat of Wayne County, Indiana.

Daniel K. Winder had started a paper in 1843 which he called *The Reformer*. But a year later he dropped it Ben Franklin liked the name and beginning in 1845, started a paper by this same name. For a year Franklin's paper was published by Samuel C. Meredith, who also published a county paper in Centerville In the spring of 1846 Franklin obtained some printing material for himself *The Reformer* was a monthly and had three hundred subscribers the first year. In November, 1846 he enlarged the paper and put it out for $1 00 a year About 1847 Franklin moved to Milton, Indiana, and changed the name of the paper to *The Western Reformer*.

During this time, Franklin found himself getting into several religious discussions. In 1843 he debated George W McCune, a Universalist preacher. In October, 1847, he held a four days' discussion with Erasmus Manford, a Universalist preacher again This was his first published discussion A month later he debated a Methodist preacher by the name of Henry R. Pritchard

Alexander Wilford Hall, meanwhile, had begun publishing a paper which he called *The Gospel Proclamation* from Loydsville, Ohio. In January, 1850, Franklin negotiated with Hall to merge the two papers, and so *The Proclamation and Reformer* was born Alexander Hall and William Pinkerton were co-editors But Ben Franklin's editorial career through this period was rather uncertain. He was a popular editor and writer but appeared to lack the means to get himself as well established as he would like

The next of Franklin's editorial attempts came as a co-editor with D. S. Burnet on *The Christian Age* In 1844, shortly after he had moved back to Pittsburgh, Walter Scott began publishing *The Protestant Unionist*. In 1848 he moved it to Cincinnati At the close of this year George Campbell and others purchased the paper and emerged it with *The Christian Age*. At this time the *Age* was edited by Dr. Gatchell and T. J. Melish. Gatchell, shortly after, sold his interest to George Campbell and Melish sold his to

D. S. Burnet. In the spring of 1850 Campbell sold his interest to Ben Franklin and so, Franklin and Burnet came to be co-editors of *The Christian Age.* Meanwhile, Franklin attempted to publish both the *Age,* which was a weekly, and the *Proclamation and Reformer,* which was a monthly.

The five years between 1850-55 were years of disappointment and struggle for Ben Franklin. His publishing interests proved a financial loss, and often he was without sufficient money to buy the necessities for his family. Moreover, Franklin had moved his family near Cincinnati to Hygeia where he could be closer to his publishing interests and to his co-partner, D. S. Burnet, who operated the Female School at Hygeia. During this time, Franklin divided his time preaching for the Clinton Street Church in Cincinnati and the church in Covington, Kentucky. His family attended church at Mt. Healthy and most of his children there obeyed the gospel. Burnet was an aristocrat and Franklin was of little financial means. Franklin's wife was discontented. But perhaps Franklin's greatest disappointment came after 1853 when he and Burnet agreed to turn *The Christian Age* over to the American Christian Publication Society. Franklin saw himself pushed into the background. His independent spirit exerted itself and he broke all relations with the paper, giving his word to the Society that he would not publish another paper for at least two years.

Franklin, however, had fully determined to remain before the people as an editor. Immediate plans were made for a new periodical so on January 1, 1856 the first issue of the *American Christian Review* came off the press. At this time the paper was a monthly, but on January 5, 1858 the first issue of the weekly *American Christian Review* came off the press. Moses E. Lard, C. L. Loos, John Rogers, Isaac Errett and Elijah Goodwin were then listed as contributing editors. For many years the *Review* was to be the most influential paper in the brotherhood. It wielded an influence not equalled by any other.

The years between 1856 and 1878 found Franklin appearing in a diversity of ways. After the establishment of the American Christian Missionary Society in 1849, the influence of Ben Franklin went wholly behind that organization. For a short time in 1856 and 1857 he was the Corresponding Secretary. In his one speech before the Society Convention, he deplored the lack of interest in the Society, and urged men to get behind it. Yet, as time went on, his ardor for the Society cooled and by 1866, he turned solidly against it. Too, in 1869 when the Louisville Plan was accepted by the brethren, Franklin threw his influence behind that, but in slightly over a year, he had again turned against that plan. There is therefore an enigma about Franklin that is hard to explain. What is the explanation? Shortly after Franklin's death, David Lipscomb wrote an article evaluating his life and work Lipscomb writes that Franklin was ordinarily a man of great firmness, but at times was influenced by others against his own judgment. It would seem, then, that the great heart of Ben Franklin was torn between two great desires On the one hand he had a passion for unity among the brethren and on the other, he had a passion for an independent stand for the truth. It grieved Franklin deeply when his own passion for the truth conflicted with his desire for unity, but in the end, he was always faithful to his conviction. Lipscomb points out that Franklin was persuaded, even at times against his better judgment, that the adoption of societies would bring about better unity and activity. When he saw they failed, he returned to "always trust the primitive and divine methods " Back in the earlier days, while Franklin was advocating the societies, he had paid a visit to Franklin College, and spent a night with Tolbert Fanning They talked of the societies "that were then engulfing the brotherhood " Both of them agreed they were wrong. At the end of their conversation each gave the other his right hand as a pledge to "resist them and to walk in the good old ways."[9] About the same time, Franklin paid a visit to Jacob Creath, Jr., and Creath remembered Franklin's promise that he was going to get out of the societies and "wash his hands of them as soon as possible."[10] At heart Franklin was convicted that the societies were unscriptural, but he patiently waited to see if there was any way he could harmonize his convictions with the existence of the societies before he spoke out.

Franklin was bitterly opposed to the use of instrumental music in the worship. He regarded the instrument as an innovation and refused to preach where the instrument was used.

It will be unnecessary to detail here the chronicle of Franklin's

---

[9]David Lipscomb, "Benjamin Franklin," *Gospel Advocate,* Vol. XX, No 48 (December 5, 1878), p. 758
[10]Jacob Creath, "Brother Franklin's Death and Services," *American Christian Review,* Vol XXII, No 10 (March 4, 1879), p 73.

activity through the remainder of his life   That story is largely the story with which these further chapters shall deal.   Until that Tuesday afternoon of October 23, 1878, Franklin was a busy man in the kingdom of his Master   Even when that day dawned upon the home of James Plummer near Anderson, Indiana where Franklin was staying, the editor of the *Review* was in a jovial mood   All that morning he wrote his editorials for his paper   After lunch, he complained of a heavy load on his stomach and a severe pain around his heart   His daughter and wife tried to put him to bed, but he wouldn't go, for it was too painful to attempt to move.   They continued to insist but each time Franklin would stretch forth his hand and say, "Don't touch me, my time has come "   He remained seated in a chair.   The doctor was brought in, but he could do nothing   At four o'clock in the afternoon Franklin was unconscious   One hour later, he breathed his last—still sitting in the chair   W W. Witmer and M T. Hough preached the funeral for Franklin two days later in the Franklin home   The worn body of this sixty-seven year old gospel preacher was laid reverently in the grave near Anderson

Franklin's death was a severe blow to the aging Jacob Creath who looked upon Franklin as the saviour of the restoration.   Creath wrote ·

If our own brethren believed in canonizing men, he could soon be placed in the front ranks on the roll of canonization among our great men, and if their mantles ever fell upon any man, that man was Benjamin Franklin   His death is universally regarded by the readers of the *Review* as a great loss to our restoration   He has left no one who can fill his place, and we shall not see his like soon again.[11]

TOLBERT FANNING

Unquestionably, the most influential preacher in the Southland before the War Between the States was Tolbert Fanning.   There were other great men, of course   Among these were J. B. Ferguson, Sandy E Jones, J. K Speer, John Mulkey, J M. Barnes and W. H Wharton, but for lasting influence Tolbert Fanning towers above them all.

In personal appearance Fanning had much to his advantage.   Although he was far from being handsome, yet he was a giant of a

---

[11]Jacob Creath, "Brother Franklin's Death and Services," *American Christian Review,* Vol XXII, No 10 (March 4, 1879), p 73

TOLBERT FANNING

man, weighing between two hundred and two hundred and fifty at all times   Most of the time he weighed two hundred and forty. He was a tall man and in no sense of the term was he fat   This extremely good physical condition made it possible for Fanning to do as much work as most any two men would do   It was nothing unusual for him to spend all day at school or on the farm, and then write or study at night until 2 00 A.M   The next day he would continue his usual program   Fanning possessed a powerful brain, a strong will, an indomitable courage, great self-reliance and per- severance   He was of an intensely independent frame of mind and was absolutely unyielding in anything he set out to accomplish   It was Fanning's custom to decide slowly what was right and then to throw everything he had into what he believed   Some people considered him overbearing and selfish, and even his friends admitted this was one of his few weaknesses.

Fanning always maintained a great interest in the farm.   He loved good stock.   A large part of his time was devoted to the outdoors.   By hard work and the practice of economy Fanning managed to have a considerable amount of this world's goods on hand when he died.   Some of his critics claimed he had his heart too much on money   This was hardly true, although the best friends Fanning had thought that at times he devoted so much of his interest to the farm that he neglected his preaching.   The following letter, written by William Lipscomb, elder brother of David Lipscomb, and co-editor of the *Gospel Advocate* from 1855-1861, to W. C. Huffman, a preacher of Sumner County, Tennessee, will illustrate the point.

Franklin College
May 13, 1857

Dear Brother Huffman,

Your remittance came safe to hand and we can but return you our sincere thanks for your continued kindness.   Brother Fanning has been much engaged in stock business but I hope he is pretty well through.   I think an occasional word of admonition from abroad might be of service in calling his thoughts to more important matters   And I trust now he will labor abroad more than he has done.   The cause I know demands his service and I think the brethren ought to be more urgent upon him to devote his time to the work   All are well.

Yours in the truth,
W LIPSCOMB   '

Fanning himself was conscious of his great love for farm life. In another letter, preserved for us by Minnie Mae Corum, W. C. Huffman's granddaughter, now living in old age at Winter Haven, Florida, Fanning writes to Huffman:

Franklin College
May 25, 1868

Brother Huffman:

It is said "we are twice a child, but once a man "   I love fine animals, fine people, fine horses, fine cattle, fine sheep, fine dogs and fine hogs.   Now I am at the point.   Have you the growing birkshires that are all right in shape?   If so, I want some two sows and a boar if I can get them. I would like a young sow that will have pigs towards fall, and then a pair or two of pigs. Have you got them? Tell me exactly what you can spare, young or old and the prices. If you have not birkshires, who has the genuine? Health good. Would like to hold a meeting with you. Write.

Truly,

T. FANNING

Tolbert Fanning was born May 10, 1810 in Cannon County, Tennessee. His parents were William and Nancy Bromley Fanning, who had come to Tennessee a short time before from Virginia. William Fanning died in Texas in 1865. Around 1818 the family moved from Tennessee into Lauderdale County in northern Alabama. Here Fanning grew up amidst the poverties of pioneer life and early learned the value of hard work and economy.

Methodism was the predominant religion in Fanning's community although his mother was a Baptist and his father made no religious profession at all Nevertheless, Fanning himself had a deeply religious soul and always desired to do the will of God at all times. When he was a lad seventeen years old, he heard the gospel of Christ and obeyed its commandments It was September, 1827. B. F. Hall had gone from Kentucky into Lauderdale County to preach. On Lord's Day evening he preached on Cyprus Creek. Tolbert Fanning was present and heard the discourse. When the invitation was given, Fanning came forward and made the confession. The next morning, James E. Matthews, a Mississippi preacher, baptized him.*[12]

No sooner had Fanning been immersed, than he began to try to preach. He spoke in school houses and in groves, and for a short time, for the church at Cyprus Creek. There were few people who heard Fanning speak who believed he would ever make a preacher. He was a tall overgrown youth of six feet and six inches. His clothes were the homespun garments of the pioneers. Most of his early sermons lacked polish and organization. An elderly lady thought she would do Fanning a favor and so she

---

*In 1904 H. R. Moore of Huntland, Tennessee, delivered an address in memory of Tolbert Fanning and stated that Fanning was baptized by E D Moore The address is recorded in "Franklin College and Its Influences," p. 123. This is obviously an error. When James E. Matthews died, Fanning printed an account of it in the *Advocate,* stating at the time that Matthews had baptized him.

[12]John I Rogers, *Autobiography of Elder Samuel Rogers* (Cincinnati: Standard Publishing Co, 1880), p 60

said to him, "Brother Fanning, you never can preach, and will always run your legs too far through your breeches Do go home and go to plowing" Rees Jones, an early pioneer preacher, said to him, "I do not think you will ever make a preacher It might be well for you to go at something else." Both of these people lived to see the day when Fanning could address an audience for three hours and hold it in rapt attention Fanning developed into a powerful speaker. His utterances were clear and distinct and his voice was pleasant and clear. His English was always the purest.

Great respect was paid to the preaching of Fanning by T. B. Larimore, who was a student of Fanning's in 1867. Larimore writes

Tolbert Fanning was, in some respects, a preacher without a peer. His preaching possessed some strikingly strange peculiarities He evidently believed, without distressing, disturbing doubt or mental reservation, the gospel to be "the power of God unto salvation"; and he never tired of preaching it, in its peerless, primitive purity and sweet, sublime simplicity, without much variety or phraseology, but with a power and pathos that carried conviction to the hearts of those who diligently heard him.[13]

Fanning loved the gospel and believed with all his heart it was the power of God unto salvation. He would never tolerate any deviation from its precepts. While he was a man of great firmness, he was also humble and kind On one occasion Fanning was getting ready to hold a debate in Lebanon, Tennessee. His opponent was delivering his first speech and in the course of the speech quoted bombastically:

> "I'm monarch of all I survey,
>   My right there is none to dispute.
> From the center, all round to the sea,
>   I am lord of the fowl and the *brute*."

The speaker made the word, brute, defiantly point at Fanning. Without saying a word, Fanning got up and walked out. The debate ended then and there and to the thinking part of the audience Fanning won a quick and decisive victory.

Three years after his conversion Fanning left his home and crossed the Tennessee River to take up the work of preaching the

---

[13]T. B Larimore, *Franklin College and Its Influences* (Nashville Mc-Quiddy Printing Co, 1906), p 412

gospel The date was October 1, 1830 [14] For the next year Fanning preached in middle Tennessee In November, 1831 he entered the University of Nashville, and graduated in 1835. During this time he preached in and around Nashville In the spring of 1835 Fanning took an extended tour with Alexander Campbell, visiting points through Kentucky and the East During the time Fanning was in Nashville, Phillip S. Fall preached for the church there. In 1837 Fanning married Fall's sister, Charlotte The same year he opened a Female Seminary at Franklin, Tennessee For the next two years Fanning taught in this Seminary and preached in the vicinity. On January 1, 1840, Fanning moved to a farm five miles southeast of Nashville. He taught another Female Seminary here until 1842.

Tolbert Fanning was now making quite a reputation for himself His ability was everywhere recognized. At the time Fanning was with Campbell, Campbell wrote of him.

The church (in Nashville) now counts about six hundred members, and employs brother Fanning as its evangelist This devout, and ardent, and gifted brother, about finishing his academic studies in the University of Nashville, under the presidency of the justly celebrated Doctor *Lindsley,* one of the most talented, learned and liberal of American presidents, cannot make full proof of his ministry and therefore, only labors occasionally in the word and teaching. He expects to graduate next September, and is desirous of fitting himself for permanent and extensive usefulness [15]

On January 30, 1844, the legislature of the state of Tennessee granted the charter for the building of Franklin Collège The first session of the school began on January 1, 1845 Tolbert Fanning was president of the college In another chapter Franklin College will be more fully discussed, so further mention of it would be out of place here. Suffice it to say, Fanning continued as the president of the school through most of its existence and influenced profoundly many of the young men who later became some of the Southland's greatest preachers

Fanning never gained the reputation in religious polemics that many other preachers did Yet, occasionally he did debate. In 1842 he held a discussion at Perryville, Kentucky with N. L. Rice,

[14]Tolbert Fanning, "Notes on a Tour"—No 3," *Christian Review,* Vol I, No 11 (November, 1844), p 244

[15]Alexander Campbell, "Sketch of a Tour of Seventy-Five Days," *Millennial Harbinger,* Vol VI, No 6 (June, 1835), p 280

the man who, a year later, debated Alexander Campbell.* Fanning afterward regretted the debate for he feared Rice had used him for the purpose of getting ready for Campbell.

Another phase of Fanning's versatility needs to be mentioned In addition to being a preacher and teacher Fanning was an editor. One might well judge, however, that with Fanning, editing a religious periodical was purely a secondary matter. In January, 1844, he began publishing the *Christian Review.* Four years later, he turned this paper over to J. B. Ferguson, then a popular preacher in Nashville, who changed its name, and published it under the name, *Christian Magazine.* In the summer of 1855 Fanning, together with William Lipscomb began editing the *Gospel Advocate.* The War Between the States cut Fanning's editorial work short, but when the war ended, Fanning was again publishing the paper, using David Lipscomb as co-editor. After 1867 Fanning's name disappears from the *Advocate* editorial corps. For two years, beginning in 1872, he edited the *Religious Historian.*

From the first Fanning was a critic of the missionary society. However, his attitude toward the society shows the greatness of his mind. Fanning very early formed the conviction that the Society was an unscriptural institution. However, his objections were by and large held in abeyance The great men in the brotherhood promoted the Society. Alexander Campbell, D. S. Burnet, Benjamin Franklin, W. K. Pendleton, John T. Johnson and a host of others favored the Society. For a time Fanning appears to have assumed the attitude that he himself might be wrong. He gave himself every opportunity to discover his error. He went to the first convention of 1849 as an observer, thinking he might learn something to cause him to change his mind. In 1855 he started the *Gospel Advocate* intending to use its columns for open discussion on the question in the hope unity would be achieved. As he became more convinced that the Society was an evil, he spoke out more boldly against it. E. G. Sewell wrote of Fanning: "He never had much confidence in human plans and human schemes in

---

*A mistaken impression has cropped out regarding this debate H Leo Boles, *Biographical Sketches of Gospel Preachers,* p. 152, states that Fanning debated a Methodist preacher named Rice. Boles doubtlessly copied this from E. G Sewell's article written in the *Advocate* upon the death of Fanning Sewell's article shows, however, that it was written hastily and from memory Fanning informs us in the first volume of the *Christian Review* that it was N L. Rice, a Presbyterian

religion by which to do the work of the church, and as he advanced in life, and studied the scriptures more, he had less and less."[16]

For two years prior to his death Fanning had taken on the appearance to his friends of being a tired and rapidly-breaking man. His strong voice was weakening, and his body was beginning to stoop a little. The last week of April, 1874 began for Fanning with a bit of complaining about rheumatism and dyspepsia. But he went ahead working until Thursday evening, April 30th. He left home to walk to a shop not far from his house, and no sooner did he arrive until a terrible pain hit him in his side. He was assisted to the house, but found no relief there. A physician was called and he seemed to think the trouble was inflammation of the liver. Slowly, Fanning got worse until the next Lord's Day which was May 3rd. At the usual hour for worship, he asked the brethren to come to his room and break bread with him. He asked them also to sing, but such an effort on this occasion was difficult, but amidst tears, they did the best they could. At 12 30, shortly after noon of that Lord's Day, he breathed his last.

JACOB CREATH, JR

One of the most colorful characters of the entire restoration movement was Jacob Creath, Jr. He was fearlessly independent in his thinking and an oddity in almost all the deportments of his life. Typical of his idiosyncracies were the events surrounding his death. Two years before he died, he wrote out his own obituary. Since Jesus and the apostles all died without a funeral sermon being preached for them, there would be none for Jacob Creath, Jr., either. He requested that he be buried in a plain, cheap coffin, with his pocket Bible placed under his head and a copy of Campbell's *Living Oracles* under that. He had lived and fought with his Bible in one hand and the *Living Oracles* in the other. Nothing would suit him better than that they should be the pillow for his head until Time crumbled them to dust together. Jacob Creath, the "Iron Duke of the Restoration," as John F. Rowe called him, was quietly laid to rest on Monday morning, January 11, 1886. His death had taken place just two days before at seven o'clock in the morning at his old home in Palmyra, Missouri.[17]

---

[16]E. G. Sewell, "Brother T. Fanning," *Gospel Advocate*, Vol. XVI, No 21 (May 21, 1874), p. 493

[17]John F. Rowe, "Death of Jacob Creath," *American Christian Review*, Vol XXIX, No 5 (January 21, 1886), p 29

JACOB CREATH

Men like Jacob Creath are what make the restoration movement breathe the atmosphere of romance. Not often has the world known such men, and less often has it appreciated those few it has known "In the person of Jacob Creath we have stalwart Christian manhood, solidity of character, sternness of purpose, invincible will-power, a disposition that tolerates no wrong, a sense of justice that knows no relenting "[18] Rowe once called him the John Knox of the restoration.

---

[18]John F. Rowe, "Jacob Creath," *American Christian Review*, Vol XXI, No 49 (December 10, 1878), p 393

The father of Jacob Creath, Jr., was William Creath. He was born on December 23, 1768 while his parents were on a trip from Dublin, Ireland to Nova Scotia. William Creath's father, Samuel, declared himself in favor of the colonies during the Revolutionary War and was imprisoned for seven years by the British because of this. William was a Presbyterian, the same religion that his parents espoused, but in 1787 he was immersed by Elder Henry Lester and became a member of a Baptist congregation in Granville County, North Carolina. After his baptism, William studied theology under Elder John Williams, a Calvinistic Baptist. Very shortly he became an outstanding Baptist preacher. On one occasion a deist said there were only two things that could make him cry—shaving with a dull razor and hearing William Creath preach. A member of Congress once remarked that William Creath was the only man he ever heard preach who could deliver a three hours' sermon and not say something *not* worth hearing

William Creath married Lucretia Brame, a young lady of English descent. She gave birth to sixteen children. Since William Creath was away most of the time preaching, the care of the family fell almost entirely upon his wife. She was very devout and required her children to read the Bible and commit large portions of it to memory. Five of her nine sons became ministers. The home of William Creath was the home of Baptist preachers from Maine to Georgia.

When William Creath's second son was born, naming of the infant was left to William's younger brother, Jacob. Accordingly, Jacob gave the babe his own name. In years to come William's brother, Jacob was called Jacob Creath, Sr. William's son, Jacob, was called Jacob Creath, Jr. It was January 17, 1799 that Jacob Creath, Jr., was born. The place was a log cabin on Butcher's Creek, in Mecklenburg County, Virginia, six miles from Boydtown, the county seat. When Jacob Creath, Jr. was quite young, his parents moved on Taylor's Creek in the lower part of the county. Creath, Jr., went to a school taught by Joshua Stanley located three miles from his father's house. Later he went to school to Jones Gee under whom he learned the art of writing. He became thoroughly acquainted with his New Testament by reading it in the light of a blazing brush pile at night and in the day time, during brief periods when the horses were resting.

Since Creath's father was a Baptist preacher, it was only natural that he should think of the welfare of his soul and of conversion in terms of Baptist teaching. Baptists espoused the doctrine of "experimental religion."   A man could do nothing to be saved, but yet something had to happen before he could be saved, according to the doctrine   Creath tried to get an experience, and at times, thought he had one, but the emotion subsided, and he was left destitute of any hope   Soon he became disgusted and for a brief period tried to be an infidel, but found he couldn't honestly believe infidelity. Creath writes:

I never saw the day when I did not desire to be good and please God, my Maker. I often withdrew to retired places, and prayed to him that I might see a great light shining around me, like Saul of Tarsus; or hear a voice informing me that my sins were pardoned.   Under these circumstances nature sometimes gave way and I went to sleep on my knees, overwhelmed with the dreadful consideration that I was forever lost.[19]

In April, 1817 a meeting of the Meherrin Baptist Association was held at Ready Creek meeting house in Brunswick County, Virginia.   William Creath and some other prominent Baptist preachers were expected to be present. Jacob Creath decided to go.   After the last address, an invitation was given for all who wanted prayer on their behalf to come to the altar.   Creath thought this to be a good opportunity to be saved, so he went.   The preachers prayed, and Creath felt some temporary relief for his anxious soul. The Baptists readily declared him saved. Accordingly on the third Lord's Day of May, 1817 Creath was immersed by his father at the Baptist meeting house on Wilson's Creek.   When he came up from the water he felt a measure of peace

Creath by disposition was of a serious mind. He got more pleasure out of associating with the old than with the young. He boasted that he never read a novel.   In years to come this seriousness gave him a saturnine temperament. He had an irascible temper that he found it almost impossible to control. David Lipscomb once wrote of him:

He would rebuke and scold an audience on slight provocation, with severity, but present to them the gospel of the Son of God with the simplicity, and tenderness of child-like faith in the Saviour I have heard but few preachers that could present the gospel with more simplicity, tenderness and love than Brother Creath. He

[19]P Donan, *Memoirs of Jacob Creath, Jr* (Cincinnati: Chase & Hall, 1877), p 49.

had by nature an irritable temper to contend with. he made manful efforts to master it.[20]

Creath preached his first sermon on the third Lord's Day in June, 1817. The circumstances were rather peculiar. The Baptist preacher who was to do the preaching could not be present for the service at the meeting house because of high water. The Methodist preacher, James Nolly, was invited to speak. Nolly stood up and then spoke to Creath "Jacob, can't you preach for us today?" he asked. Jacob replied· "No sir, I can not. What led you to ask me that question?" "Oh," said Nolly, "I think you *will* preach and you had as well begin today." Creath refused to preach and Nolly delivered a sermon. At the conclusion of Nolly's address, he asked Creath to close the service. Creath preached a sermon on Gal. 3:10. After the service, an old lady told him that he could word a good prayer, but would never make a preacher.

Creath had a mind to agree with the old lady and so for two years he labored on a farm, not trying to preach. But the desire to preach the gospel got the better of him. In January, 1819 Creath went to see William Dossy at Society Hill to get some assistance through the Charleston Baptist Association for an education. He then attended the University of North Carolina at Chapel Hill and studied under Abner W. Clopton. He stayed in the university until the fall of 1820. Clopton moved to Caswell County and Creath went along. During this time he became an ordained minister in the Baptist Church. The ordination took place on September 23, 24, 1820 at the Mill Creek Meeting House in Caswell County. In November, 1821 Creath entered Columbia College in Washington, D. C. and worshiped with the First Baptist Church in Washington.

After leaving Washington, Creath went back to North Carolina, but stayed there only a short time, and moved to Kentucky. While he was in Kentucky, the churches in Louisville and Lexington offered him positions. Most of his time up to the late summer of 1826 was spent with the Baptist Church at Great Crossing in Scott County. In October, 1826 he moved from Kentucky to Natchez, Mississippi, and from there to New Orleans. All the while he continued to preach. On the way he spent several days at the Hermitage near Nashville, having letters of recommendation

---

[20]David Lipscomb, "Death of Jacob Creath," *Gospel Advocate,* Vol XXVIII, No 3 (January 20, 1886), p 38

from Col. Richard M. Johnson, brother of John T. Johnson, who was a prominent army official. Creath had as his companion Albert Gallatin Creath, son of Jacob Creath, Sr. In Nashville they visited Col. Robert Foster, lieutenant-governor of Tennessee At Natchez Creath so enraged the Methodists, Episcopalians and Presbyterians that they burned him in effigy.

In the fall of 1827 Creath contacted yellow fever. At times he almost died The disease caused him to leave the deep south, so early in 1828 he took a steamer from New Orleans and went to Louisville and from there to Bethany, Virginia. Before long, he was back in Kentucky and preached at Versailles, Cane Run and South Elkhorn

One of the most trying circumstances of his life came when the Great Crossings Baptist Church tried him for heresy. Creath, through reading the *Christian Baptist,* had become acquainted with restoration principles. He denounced creeds and taught that the word of God was the instrumentality through which conversion took place and that to be converted a man had simply to obey the word of God. Silas M. Noel, a strongly partisan Baptist, was then preaching at Great Crossings. The church sent Creath a letter dated May 17, 1829, demanding he give an account of himself Hearing of the letter, Creath's uncle, Jacob, Sr , came immediately to see him. Creath told his uncle he intended to stand by his convictions.

At the trial by the Great Crossings Church Creath read Paul's defense before Agrippa and Festus. John T. Johnson, who was later one of the leading pioneer preachers in Kentucky, was present. After the trial, Johnson said· "Absolutely, if they don't let that man alone the stones of the street will cry out against them."[21] Later Johnson told Creath that he would never have been connected with the restoration except for Creath

When the Elkhorn Baptist Association convened in August, 1829 in Lexington, an effort was made to adopt a resolution to exclude all of those from the Baptist Church who believed in taking the "Bible alone." Through the efforts of Johnson, the purpose was thwarted and for another year, the preachers remained free to preach.

At the close of the year 1829, Creath took a trip with Alexander Campbell to Nashville. On this trip Campbell encountered Oba-

---

[21]P. Donan, *Memoirs of Jacob Creath, Jr ,* p. 82

diah Jennings, a very biased Presbyterian preacher. Most of the controversy later appeared in the *Millennial Harbinger*.

As the time drew near for the annual meeting of the Elkhorn Association in 1830, Jacob Creath, Jr., and his uncle became anxious to know what would happen. The Baptist church at Lexington a year before had invited young Creath to be their preacher, a fact which estranged Creath and Jeremiah Vardeman. Vardeman thence used his influence against Creath. Indicative of what was to take place at the Elkhorn Association was the pronouncement of the Franklin Association which met a month earlier at Frankfort, Kentucky. This latter association prepared charges against Elkhorn for not having previously dismissed those in its number who held the heretical doctrine of the work of the Holy Spirit through the word in conversion. The Elkhorn Association, then, was "on the spot" when it did meet, for it had to do something or face criticism from other Baptist associations in Kentucky. At the meeting of the Elkhorn Association came Raccoon John Smith, Jacob Creath, Sr. and Jacob Creath, Jr. Charges were made and passed upon and not any of the three was allowed to speak in his own defense. Thus, these three men were expelled from Baptist fellowship in Kentucky

In September, 1831 Creath married Mrs. Susan Bedford, widow of Sidney Bedford of Bourbon County, Kentucky. For the next few years Creath farmed and then preached on Saturday and Sundays. In 1834 he held a debate with Lewis Green, professor of Ancient Languages in Danville College The debate was held in July in Lincoln County For the next three years Creath entered more extensively into preaching He and John T. Johnson were almost continual companions. In 1835 they held a meeting in Fayette County, Kentucky The same year they preached at Versailles and baptized a hundred and forty For the next three years they preached continuously until the sects became alarmed for fear the whole country was going to the "Campbellites"

The year 1838, marked the beginning of Creath's domestic troubles. His wife was thrown from her horse and permanently injured She was with child at the time The child was born but was always delicate and died early in life Creath's wife was now a permanent invalid. She felt she would die and so **requested** Creath to move to Missouri so she could die near her people. In 1839 Creath moved to Lewis County, Missouri. A year later he moved near Monticello on the Fabius River.

After the death of his wife on July 16, 1841, Creath had considerable trouble His wife, as has been mentioned, was the widow of Sidney Bedford. She had one son, Creath's stepson, Sidney Bedford, Jr. His wife's first husband had left considerable property and this had been willed to the stepson of Creath Creath had been appointed his guardian. Meanwhile, Sidney Bedford, Sr.'s sisters and brothers wanted the property They lured the boy away from Creath and they instituted proper court proceedings and secured the guardianship from Creath. The boy died underage in Washington, Pennsylvania, and the elder Bedford's relatives got the possessions Creath himself was ruined financially in the whole transaction.

In October, 1841, Creath moved to Palmyra, Missouri, where he lived until he died. In March, 1842, he married Mrs. Prudence Rogers of Bowling Green. Just what made Creath always prefer widows for wives has never been explained. Apparently he was always happy with them.

It is needless to follow through the next years of his life. The story would read more like a diary than a detailed history From Palmyra, Missouri, he traveled continually preaching the gospel and establishing congregations. His work took him over Illinois, Missouri, Louisiana, Kentucky, Indiana, Tennessee.

In Creath's many trips over Missouri in preaching, he rode an old horse he called Jack. He was very much attached to this horse. On one occasion he stopped with a brother in a village, and the man sent the horse to the tavern stable. The tavern was owned by a member of the church that knew Creath well Frequently, Creath would send someone over to see if Jack had been fed, then watered, and bedded. The lady became annoyed finally and sent word back to Creath: "Go tell Brother Creath that I have done everything for his horse I can think of, except to give him a cup of coffee, and I am getting that ready "

As the years slowly came upon Creath, his physical frame began to gradually give way, but his mind remained active In 1877 John A. Brooks held a meeting in Palmyra Creath was then seventy-eight. Brooks writes:

In his person and carriage, he reminds me much of Brother Campbell He is a man of magnificient proportions, and under the weight of nearly eighty years, stands as erect as an Indian. His physical frame is wearing out, but his mental faculties know no failure yet [22]

In 1884 John F. Rowe was on a trip west and at seven o'clock one evening stopped by Palmyra to see Creath. Creath was just going to bed but upon seeing Rowe for the first time stayed up and talked with him for three hours Creath did almost all of the talking. The cause of Zion was heavy on his heart. It must have been a touching scene to listen to such a man talk. Rowe writes of this meeting :

But he has about finished his course, he has fought the good fight, and, with his beloved companion, he soon expects to pass the shores of mortality, and receive his crown of righteousness. He fully comprehends the present crisis of the churches, many of which he was instrumental in bringing into life; and though cheered by the prospect of a home in heaven, he mourned over the desolation of Zion, as Jesus lamented the desolation of Jerusalem We assured him that all was not lost, but that the heart of the great brotherhood, when not misdirected by the "kingdom of the clergy" rising up in our midst, still beats responsive to the loud call of the gospel, and still throbs with pulsations of renewed life and vigor.[23]

When Rowe stood up to leave, both he and Creath recognized that this was probably their last meeting together on earth. Creath stood up to walk to the doorway with Rowe. He was a large man —at least six feet tall. He had a large high forehead, a sharp aquiline nose, penetrating blue-grey eyes, a firmly set mouth, and a deep sonorous voice. In general appearance Creath looked a great deal like Alexander Campbell. But, as Rowe and Creath moved to the door, Creath smothered the younger man in his large arms. They stood in the doorway like that, and Creath lifted his wrinkled face to the darkened skies, and there prayed fervently and deeply as only Creath could pray that God would guide and bless this godly brother.

When Creath prayed, it was as though one was standing in the presence of someone divine. One Saturday in June, 1854, L B Wilkes went to Lagrange, Missouri to preach. His appointment was to preach on Saturday night, Sunday morning and Sunday evening. When he arrived and had gone to the home of a Brother

---

[22]John A Brooks, "Jacob Creath," *Gospel Advocate,* Vol XIX, No 5 (February 1, 1877), p 67
[23]John F Rowe, "Beyond the Mississippi," *American Christian Review,* Vol XXVII, No 7 (February 14, 1884), p 52

Gill, he found Jacob Creath there   About eight o'clock that evening
it started raining, and it rained almost all night   But the next
morning was the Lord's Day   The rain had stopped, the sun
was shining brightly, and from the distant trees the birds were
warbling merrily   Creath and Wilkes came down to breakfast.
Creath was very meditative and silent.   After breakfast he said to
Wilkes, "Let us take a walk"

They walked for a quarter of a mile.   Not a word was spoken.
Finally Creath pointed to the right and said, "This way."   They
walked two hundred yards further into a woods.   There was no
path or road, and Creath was so silent that Wilkes was afraid to
speak   "Yonder is a good place" said Creath in a moment.   They
walked over beside a fallen tree, and here both bowed down while
Creath prayed.

Here beneath the tall trees, the air full of the music of glad birds
and redolent with the odors of thousands of flowers, all praising
God, Brother Creath said. "Let us pray" We fell on our knees and
O such a prayer!   The earth had drunk up the rain and all nature
seemed to be refreshed and happy   Every leaf and flower and bird
and being in nature around us seemed to be striving its utmost to
magnify God   All this Brother Creath mentioned in his prayer, and
then called upon his soul and all that was within him to bless the
Lord   My soul trembled with excitement   Brother Creath talked
so to God that I voluntarily felt for the moment that if I should
open my eyes I should certainly see him upon whom no one can
look and live   I never heard such a prayer before, and now
thirty years have passed since that remarkable experience, and
yet I have heard no such prayer since   At the close of his
lengthy prayer, he asked me to pray   I did   During the
second prayer, he would every few moments break forth
in expressions of thanksgiving and praise   "Oh bless the Lord, my
soul   Give thanks unto his name   His mercy endureth forever."[24]

On one occasion, during the War Between the States, a company
of troops was encamped near Palmyra, intending to capture the
city   Creath went out to the grove to pray and the leader of the
troops happened to be near   He edged closer to the grove and
listened as Creath prayed for his neighbors, his town and for peace.
The next day the troops withdrew without any attempt to capture
the town

Creath was of the firm conviction that around 1849 a great

[24]L B Wilkes, "no title," *American Christian Review,* Vol XXVII, No
17 (April 24, 1884), p 131

change came over the restoration movement, and over Alexander Campbell. The *Millennial Harbinger* of these years was not the same paper that it was before. He believed that Campbell was easing out of the picture, and that his corps of younger teachers and friends were influencing him in the wrong direction. In 1857 Dr. Robert Richardson published in the *Harbinger* some articles on "German Neology and French Philosophy." Neither Creath nor Tolbert Fanning liked it. Both wrote Campbell a protest. Creath wrote that if what Richardson was printing was the gospel, ninety-nine out of one hundred readers of the *Harbinger* did not know what the gospel was, and he added, "I am one of that number." Creath believed that Richardson would kill the *Harbinger* if that were allowed to go on. Campbell soon stopped Richardson, but it made the latter look with great disfavor upon Creath Consequently, when Richardson wrote his "Memoirs of Alexander Campbell," he mentioned every other pioneer with whom Campbell had been connected, but brought in Creath's name only when it was unavoidable, and then stated only points to his disfavor. After publication of the "Memoirs," Creath wrote to Richardson, asking why this was done His letter received no answer

Creath avowed that in the last fifteen years of the life of the *Millennial Harbinger,* it was as different from the earlier *Harbinger* as day and night When Campbell died, Creath wrote to W. K. Pendleton, asking that his subscription to the paper be discontinued Pendleton wrote back urging that he continue, and Creath did for one more year. But after that, he wrote to have it discontinued Pendleton wanted his reasons Creath's reply was that he disagreed with the attitude of the *Harbinger* toward the South in those days of the War Between the States. The *Harbinger* had spoken of "justice" being on the side of the North, and of the South's being "conquered" Such expressions were not right in a paper devoted to the spread of the gospel, Creath thought and so expressed himself The effect was that now he was looked upon with disfavor both by Richardson and Pendleton.

I mention this fact to show that my discontinuance of the *Harbinger* after Bro. Campbell's death was another cause why I was treated as I was by the author of the last years of the Harbinger, and by the author of his Memoirs, and that the brethren and posterity may know the reasons of the treatment I received that whosoever writes the history of this Reformation may do me more justice than did the author of the Memoirs [25]

No one more bitterly opposed missionary societies and other human organizations to supplant the church than Jacob Creath, Jr He was the first great opponent of human organizations. By nature he could not refrain from speaking out against practices he believed to be wrong Likewise he was an opponent to the use of instrumental music in the worship. Throughout most of this study the work of Jacob Creath will be further noted Truly he was a mighty prince in Israel.

---

[25]Jacob Creath, "The Bible Alone Rejected by the Conventions," *Gospel Advocate,* Vol. XIX, No. 47 (November 22, 1877), p. 724.

CHAPTER VII

THE PROGRESS OF THE CAUSE

Before launching directly into the historical events of the years to be covered in this study, it would be well to get a general view of the progress of the cause up to the pre-Civil War days. To what extent had the church grown? What were the problems that it met? What was its general condition? To see this general condition will furnish a background on which to paint the events that are soon to be pictured, and will add interest and enchantment to the intensely thrilling story of the restoration movement.

The "reformation" first attracted men of the middle class These men were not highly cultured but they were men for the most part of 'fair education. Moreover, most of them were men of independent turn of mind and of great courage. They loved liberty and were willing to sacrifice everything for what they believed to be true To be sure there were many men of prominence in politics, medicine and business who accepted the views of pioneers. At first their views were peculiar to most hearers. Consequently, they invoked study. Moreover, with the clergy of the day they were greatly abhorred. Nobody accepted then, the gospel message because it was popular, for it wasn't There was that courageous love for the liberty of the gospel, free from human creeds and from the authority of council that gave the impetus for men to submit to the living oracles. Once converted, they worked intensely to convert others They were convinced they were right and would have others to be. The whole restoration movement soon took on the color of beligerency and aggressiveness. These pioneers believed in their cause, and they pressed on, wilting before no tribunal, but with the profound conviction they had the truth and that the truth, under God, would triumph.

Referring to these pioneer preachers, Champ Clark, one-time Speaker of the House of Representatives in Congress, said in a centennial address delivered at Pittsburgh, Pennsylvania:

First in the field, they set the compass and fixed the chart by which our ship has sailed, and by which it will sail till Gabriel's trumpet summons the quick and dead to the judgment-bar of God.

Their names live forevermore and their works do follow them. If the spirits of just men made perfect on high take cognizance of the affairs of this world, as I have no doubt they do, the souls of these masterful pioneers must be filled with amazement and delight as they contemplate the results of the first hundred years of the movement which they started

As these early preachers went out, they relied solely upon their Bibles. Most of them knew little about philosophy, although there were exceptions to this rule. Their preaching was almost entirely expository and any other kind was tabooed. They freely underwent sacrifices, satisfying themselves with the conviction that at their worst, they had more material prosperity and ease than their Lord. In their presentation of the gospel, their phraseology was charged with scripture quotations or references. Oratory was the order of the day, and sermons less than an hour long were never head of—most of them running two and a half hours. Concerning the preaching of these days Morrill says:

This preaching was powerfully emotional and thoroughly spontaneous. A single text-book, the Bible, provided preachers with their whole stock in trade. It must be confessed that in these latter days we have very superficial ideas about the sermon preparation of a hundred years ago. Given a man dead in earnest, with a book like the Bible, viewed as it was in those days, a book read and re-read and largely committed to memory, and given a man whose mind, thoroughly awakened, was charged to the brim with scripture, and solemnized by prayer vigil and lonely meditation; and given the motion and fire of delivery prevalent in those days, and you have a generator of tremendous sensations and impressions. The sermon might be fanciful and extemporaneous, but it could not be unprepared. The exegesis was faulty no doubt, but the application was direct and pointed. Many a sermon abounded in oratorical grace and fascination, and contained a residium of homely truth that was wholesome and palatable Notes were tabooed and regarded as a stigma. . . .[1]

Down to the year 1827, the Campbells had established only two churches—Brush Run and Wellsburgh The years from 1809 to 1827 were for the most part formative ones. Step by step, the Campbells were thinking their way along, trusting to the revealed word for guidance. By 1823 when Campbell started the *Christian Baptist,* his mind on all essential points of doctrine was made up.

---

[1]Milo True Morrill, *A History of the Christian Denomination in Amer ica* (Dayton: Christian Publishing Co, 1912), pp 103, 104.

Creeds and Confessions of Faith had kept men away from the word of God. Consequently, Campbell pointed his guns toward the ramparts of the clergy and let loose with an unrelenting barrage that shook the kingdom of the clergy as it had never been shaken. Such teaching had its effect, but it was not strongly evangelistic. Campbell was planting the seed, but up to 1827, he saw little evidence of a harvest. That year when Walter Scott was sent as evangelist to the Western Reserve and kept the baptismal waters stirring, Campbell grew concerned for he had never known the cause to prosper in such a way before. The evangelistic fever took hold, and the restoration was on its way

By 1836 D. S. Burnet remarked that the disciples numbered over one hundred thousand and ranked as the fourth largest body of religious people in the nation[2] Ten years later Campbell wrote:

We little expected, some thirty years ago, that the principles of Christian union and a restoration of primitive Christianity in letter and spirit, in theory and practice, could have been plead with such success, or have taken such deep hold of the consciences and of the hearts of multitudes of all creeds and parties, of all castes and conditions of society, as we have already lived to witness. We must say that it is, "the Lord's doing, and marvelous in our eyes'"[3]

By 1850 a writer in the *Ecclesiastical Reformer* reports the total number of disciples to be over two hundred thousand, but others put the number as high as three hundred thousand A year later, Campbell writes:

The territory over which the doctrine of the reformation has been more or less diffused, within one quarter of a century, is unprecedented in any age known in history and to me. It is preached or read in books, not only in all the United States of America, and in all the British provinces of North America, from St. Johns to San Francisco, and from Oregon to the Neuces it has also been preached or read in England, Scotland, Ireland, Wales, and the Isle of Man It has crossed the Pacific to Australia and New Zealand, and visited Liberia, on the coast of Africa. At some of these points it has, indeed, touched but slightly but even there, like a little leaven hid in a large measure of meal, it must work, as the Messiah said, until the mass be leavened[4]

---

[2]D S. Burnet, "Progress of the Present Reformation," *Christian Preacher,* Vol I, No. 1 (January, 1836), p 21.

[3]Alexander Campbell, "Preface," *Millennial Harbinger,* Third Series, Vol III, No. 1 (January, 1846), p. 1

[4]Alexander Campbell, "The Cause of Reformation," *Millennial Harbinger,* Series IV, Vol. I, No. 10 (October, 1851), p 590

Some years later, Isaac Errett reports that based upon the rate of increase, the disciples were first in the decade from 1850 to 1860. By 1870 it was the fifth largest religious body in the United States [5]

Although this picture is somewhat bright, there is a darker side to it The strong evangelistic appeal, with its emphasis upon first principles, naturally left the church in need of some teaching that it was not getting What was the nature of the New Testament church? How was it to be organized? Because there was a lack of the proper conception of the church, Tolbert Fanning undertook to write many articles on "Church Organization." As early as 1845 Fanning wrote of the glorious progress of the cause, yet he paints a darker picture, citing examples to show that in many cases the church was degenerating into a sect. Was this church about which the pioneers preached to be the New Testament Church, and would its leaven work effectively throughout Babylon to call men back to Jerusalem, or would the product of their efforts be the erection of another sect in Christendom? To men of vision and foresight this question was of grave concern A few warnings begin to appear. Fanning wrote:

No other proof is necessary to establish the fact, that an apostacy has commenced The preachers and churches in many places, have evidently stopped at first principles, and have, from ignorance of the spiritual organization, practices and enjoyments of God's empire, and from an ambition to have a name amongst men, grown weary, and desire peace with the conflicting parties   .
There are tens of thousands, who will sacrifice all that is earthly, before they will "strike hands" with the drunken captives of Babylon. Indeed, while we profess, a belief of the scriptures, and obedience thereto, are essential to Christianity, and compromise with factions is yielding the whole apostolic ground .
The crisis has come. . . The churches are not generally walking blamelessly, and some of the leading preachers begin to talk of their clerical *"brethren"* amongst the sects, and are really taking more pleasure in seeking popularity amongst parties, and worldly gain and honor, than in teaching the disciples the whole truth [6]

In 1846 *The Reformer*, edited by Benjamin Franklin, came out with a picture of this darker side Franklin was then a young editor, but his influence was already being felt. He bemoans the

---

[5] Isaac Errett, "How We Stand in the Last Census," *Christian Standard,* Vol VIII, No 2 (January 11, 1873), p 12
[6] Tolbert Fanning, "The Crisis," *Christian Review,* Vol II, No 10 (October, 1845), pp 217, 218

fact that the restoration has come to a dead halt, an observation
which doubtlessly was overstated. Franklin gave five reasons for
this lack of progress (1) Great political excitement. (2) Second
advent excitement. (3) Lack of faith among disciples. (4) Many
good preachers had left the field. (5) Preaching lacked zeal,
scriptural argument, as in the former years   But, what was the
answer?

Under these circumstances, what is to be done? We answer,
let every Disciple of our blessed Lord determine to read the
Scriptures some every day, with the most devout and prayerful
attention possible. . . . That the cause in which we are engaged
is emphatically the cause of God, whether our actions are always
the best calculated to promote it or not, we have never entertained one doubt since we first acknowledged the authority of the
great King. . . . Let us, then, brethren, make one mighty effort
to save the church from corruption, lukewarmness, speculation,
and sin of every kind, that it finally may be presented to the Lord,
"a glorious church, without spot, or wrinkle, or any such thing,"
and ascribe all the glory to God and the Lamb forever and ever.[7]

Franklin had the utmost faith in the cause he espoused. He
believed thoroughly it was from God   As long as men were true
to this cause, God would bless them, and the cause would triumph.
Upon the inauguration of the *American Christian Review* in 1856,
Franklin states in his "Introductory Address"

We have seen the workings of this cause during the last twenty
years and have carefully considered its history since the first effort
in the United States, to call the attention of the people to original
Christianity, as well as the rise of Christianity in Jerusalem at
the beginning. We have also carefully considered the means
employed to oppose it, and impede its progress, and we are well
prepared to say that it is the cause of God, and that it can be
successfully maintained, defended, and extended, in defiance of
all opposition   There is no cause on earth that can stand before
it.[8]

Only a short while before his death, John T. Johnson views the
cause of Christ and expresses his amazement.

Taking a bird's-eye view of the field before us, what most
prominently strikes the eye? Congregations have sprung up as
by enchantment; the land has been dotted over with houses of

---

[7]Joseph Franklin and J A Headington, *The Life and Times of Benjamin
Franklin* (St. Louis Christian Board of Publication, 1879), pp 91, 92
[8]Benjamin Franklin, "Introductory Address," *American Christian Review*,
Vol I, No 1 (January, 1856), p 4

worship, evangelists have been sustained in the field beyond any former example, schools, male and female, and colleges, are rising in every direction. . . .[9]

If one were to step into the worship service of one of these churches in the early restoration movement, what would he find? How were the services conducted? One might find himself well able to understand this picture by considering the description given of the church at Noah Springs in Kentucky. The church was established in 1828 with twenty-eight members. Two years later there were ninety They met at first only monthly, and generally connected a meeting on Saturday with that of the Lord's Day. In 1830 their service is described as follows:

They have done away their monthly Saturday meetings, and now meet every first day of the week. Their order is as follows: After meeting early, say between nine and ten o'clock, they engage in singing hymns of praise to their exalted King Next, as appropriate prayer is offered by one of the Elders or Bishops (for they have four selected from among themselves), an opportunity is then afforded to anyone who wishes to make a profession of their faith in Jesus as the Messiah. If any come forward upon such profession, they are immersed into the name of the Father, Son, and Holy Spirit, and then they are received into the congregation as fellow disciples. One of the elders then instructs the congregation from some portion of the Holy Oracles, afterwards an exhortation by one of the others is delivered. The Deacons then prepare and furnish the table One of the Elders, after singing an appropriate hymn, prays and then breaks the bread In like manner the wine is poured; and all who have been legally naturalized, and deport themselves as disciples, are authorized to participate, without regard to any human *theory* or *ism,* to commemorate and show forth the Lord's death A hymn is then sung, and the brethren greet each other as fellow disciples, by a shake of the hand, and then retire.[10]

With this statement of the general condition of the church before the War Between the States a more detailed description of the advancement of the cause in the various states now must come before us Yet, this picture must necessarily be brief. Large books have been written on the church in various states, so it cannot be expected that more than a brief outline of brother-

[9]John T Johnson, "Communication from Elder J T Johnson," *American Christian Review,* Vol. II, No 1 (January, 1857), p 27.

[10]Stephen, "News from Kentucky," *Millennial Harbinger,* Vol I, No 9 (September, 1830), p 425

hood activities can be given in a single chapter. No attempt, then, can be undertaken to describe the state of the church in the various sections of the country in anything like completeness, but a briefer sketch will at least portray the extent to which the plea for a return to the ancient order of things had gone

One finds in New York City in 1842 a congregation with one hundred and thirty members meeting on Green Street. The church had Silas E. Shepherd as its preacher. Another congregation in New York City met on Lawrence Street with seventy-five members Both churches were predominantly made up of Scotchmen, and both had had considerable trouble. A new congregation was established in Brooklyn in 1842, but apparently was never successful By 1845 one finds congregations at Manchester, Amsterdam, Pittstown and Troy in the state of New York By 1850 the church in New York City was meeting on Seventeenth Street about thirty yards from Sixtieth Avenue. By 1855 there were four congregations in the one county of Onandoga

In Philadelphia before the war the church was small and hard pressed to grow In 1848 Dr B F Hall moved to Philadelphia He reports that there were a few members meeting in a poor building which itself was poorly located. Hall writes:

Almost everything flourishes here, but pure, primitive Christianity; it has a hard struggle to keep its holy head above the proud waves of sin, sectarianism, and infidelity "

When Alexander Campbell visited Philadelphia in 1842, he found the church had one hundred and thirty members and met on Fifth and Gaskill Streets. There was another small congregation meeting on Race Street. After B. F. Hall left Philadelphia, James Challen moved there from Cincinnati, and the church perhaps had her greatest growth under Challen.

The first statistics for the state of Pennsylvania were compiled in 1851 At that time it was discovered there were fifty-five congregations in the state with a little over two thousand members. The largest congregation met at Allegheny City Here, Samuel Church, "the walking Bible," lived and preached

The church in Baltimore, Maryland, fared better. When Alexander Campbell visited here in 1842, he found the church in

"B F Hall, "Letter from Dr B F Hall," *Christian Magazine*, Vol I, No 7 (July, 1848), p 204

a healthful condition and meeting on St Paul's Street. Seven years later, a meetinghouse was put up at the cost of six thousand dollars It was here D. S Burnet preached later and here that he died

The church in the nation's capital was established in 1843 by Dr. James T. Barclay, who later was the first missionary sent out by the new society to Jerusalem. The church at first met in his home, but after Barclay went to Jerusalem, it met in the home of R G Campbell, one of the deacons In the spring of 1850 it had only eighteen members Until after the war, the church was kicked about from one place to another, never securing a permanent building of its own until the war had ended.

In Virginia the church fared well. One could find thriving congregations in Antioch, Jerusalem, Newton, Smyrna, and Richmond as early as 1845 At Fredericksburg the church had serious internal conflicts that prevented a large growth and influence. James Henshall and R. L. Coleman were perhaps the two outstanding Virginia preachers before the war.

In the Carolinas the churches were few and far between. Joshua K. Speer established a church in Dobson, Surry County, North Carolina, in 1856. There were some churches of the O'Kelley movement there much earlier in the restoration movement In South Carolina, the most famous congregation was at Erwintown Dr Erwin pioneered the cause here Erwintown was not really a town but a "Christian neighborhood " It consisted of a post office, a male and female academy, and a congregation [12] There was a church at Evergreen in Anderson district and one at Union in Barnesville district

Perhaps no state, however, enjoyed greater growth of the church before the war than Ohio. By 1852 the state had over twenty thousand members The southwest district of the state had sixty-seven congregations with over five thousand members. There were ten thousand members on the Western Reserve and five thousand more in the remainder of the state. Yet, by 1852, there were in Ohio twelve cities with over six thousand population, and churches in only four of these There were eighty-seven county-seat towns, and only twenty-one had congregations [13] One of the

[12] J J Trott, "Evangelizing in the South," *Christian Review,* Vol IV, No 4 (April, 1847), pp 133-136

[13] T J Melish, "Our Cause in Ohio," *The Disciple,* Vol I No 9 (April, 1852), pp 272, 273

oldest churches in the state was the Antioch Church in Clinton County, established by Samuel Rogers. The churches on the Western Reserve were largely established by Walter Scott when he preached under the direction of the Mahoning Association in 1827. In Cincinnati, the church came over from the Baptists very early in the restoration.

In Michigan, one finds congregations to be less numerous than in Ohio. A church met in Detroit early in the 1850's, and by 1856 one reads of plans to erect a building. Isaac Errett moved to Lyons, in Ionia County, that year and organized a church with twenty-four members. Thereafter, the churches in Michigan seemed to grow much faster.

No state enjoyed greater growth than Indiana. Very early did the cause reach this state, and the progress was phenomenal. The cause began in southern Indiana very early after the turn of the nineteenth century. The city of Vincennes on the Wabash River in Indian Territory fell to the small army of George Rogers Clark on February 24, 1779. The legislature of Virginia, in recognition of his victory, gave him nearly one hundred and fifty thousand acres of land in what is now southern Indiana which was called "Clark's Grant," afterwards known as Clark County. Toward this plot of ground in the summer of 1799 came the family of Absolem Littell. He had two sons, Absolem, Jr., aged eleven, and John T., aged nine.

At that time Clark's Grant knew but one church, a small Baptist Church having been organized the year before by Isaac Edwards of Kentucky. A few years passed, and by 1819 John T. Littell was recognized as the pastor of the church For thirty years this little church grew, and in 1829 it numbered a membership of two hundred and fifty. On July 24, 1812, it led in the formation of the Silver Creek Baptist Association. When the first issues of the *Christian Baptist* began to be read, it profoundly influenced the members. By 1828 the majority in the church had adopted the views of Alexander Campbell. The next year the Baptist Articles of Faith were voted out, and a division in the church resulted. Of this history, James M. Mathes writes·

Before the Reformation was preached in Indiana, a very large and respectable Baptist Association called the "Silver Creek Association" held its annual meetings in this county Elders Absolem Littell, Mordecai Cole, and J. T. Littell were the leading men in this body, but these beloved brethren, together with others, embraced the reformation at an early period and boldly contended for union upon the Bible alone. The result of their self-denying and zealous efforts in favor of the ancient gospel was that a large majority of the "Silver Creek Association" also embraced the reformation. And if I am not mistaken, as early as 1827 or 1828 they had exchanged the name "Regular Baptist" for CHRISTIAN, and the "Confession of Faith" and "Rules of Decorum" for the Bible alone, and accordingly the churches were reorganized upon the ONE FOUNDATION.[14]

Among the early pioneer Indiana preachers were such men as John Wright, Joseph Hostetler, Elijah Goodwin, Benjamin Franklin, James M. Mathes, John P. Thompson, Beverly Vawter, Ovid Butler, John O'Kane, S K. Hoshour, and John Longley, John O'Kane established the first church in Indianapolis as early as 1833 in the home of Benjamin Roberts, who lived in a log cabin on the northeast corner of Illinois and Market Streets. The first state-wide meeting of the churches was held in 1839, a full report of which was sent to the *Millennial Harbinger*. The report showed that Indiana then had a total of one hundred and fifteen churches with seven thousand, seven hundred and one congregations identified with the restoration[15] Four years later, the *Christian Record* reports more than twenty thousand members in the entire state

With the establishment of Northwestern Christian University in 1855 in Indianapolis, this city took on greater importance as a radiating center for the gospel Famous preachers over the brotherhood found their way to the city, and in no place was the cause more prosperous in the days before the war Yet, despite this fact, there was a temptation to ease the struggle, as Benjamin Franklin observed when he visited the city in 1856:

In Indianapolis, there are some fifteen or eighteen preachers— some of them old and experienced men, some in the prime of life, and others young—aiming to perfect their education and knowledge for a more useful life In a place like this, where the professors in the college are all preachers, where there are other able and eminent men, and where the characters of young men are forming for the ministry, those from abroad will expect to find a model church. . . Such an expectation is natural and right. In

[14]James M Mathes, "Notes on a Tour to the South Part of the State," *Christian Record*, Vol II, No 4 (October, 1844), p 84
[15]F W Emmons, "Statistics of Indiana," *Millennial Harbinger,* New Series, Vol III, No 7 (July, 1839), pp 355-357

view of it, there should be an effort, as far as possible, to show forth Christianity in this church   At present, the church has no preacher whose business it is to look after its interests and take the special oversight   It certainly cannot succeed in this way.[16]

The church likewise got an early start in Illinois   The first congregation appeared to have started in Wabash County.   Seth Gard and James Pool organized Barney's Prairie Christian Church on July 17, 1819   Gard, who was a member of the Convention that framed the State Constitution, was an elder in this church The second congregation in the state was established a month later on Coffee Creek in Wabash County   Small country congregations multiplied for the next ten years   In 1832 a congregation was established in Jacksonville by people who moved in from Kentucky   At Old Union, ten miles west of Clinton, a church was organized October 13, 1832, under a white oak tree. Hughes Bowles preached here   His son, Walter P Bowles, was perhaps the best known preacher in Illinois at this time   Young Bowles and Abraham Lincoln were the closest of chums   One day Lincoln said to Bowles "Wat, if I could preach like you, I would rather do that than be president "

Kentucky, too, saw the advancement of the restoration movement.   Perhaps no state was in the heart of the movement more Men like Jeremiah Vardeman, P. S. Fall, and Raccoon John Smith were the early advocates in the state   John T. Johnson, John Rogers, and Jacob Creath were among the later preachers   Kentucky received its first impetus toward restoration from the Barton W. Stone movement which has already been recounted   After the appearance of the *Christian Baptist,* many Kentucky Baptists started the return trip to Jerusalem, and so the movement went forward at a rapid pace   Big meetings were the order of the day. John Allen Gano had forty-one additions in December, 1848, at Paris, Kentucky.   By 1844 the *Christian Journal* reports fifty thousand members in the state, although it is likely that this number is somewhat exaggerated   Twenty-five to seventy-five additions, however, were frequent in meetings especially under such preaching as that done by John T. Johnson and Raccoon-John Smith

Some idea of the size of the church in Kentucky can be gotten by the report of S M Scott, who was sent to visit all the congre-

[16]Benjamin Franklin, "Affairs About Indianapolis," *American Christian Review,* Vol I, No 3 (March, 1856), pp 90, 91

gations in the state in 1845. He reports three hundred and eighty congregations with a membership of thirty-three thousand, eight hundred and thirty. This number is much more likely than the fifty thousand previously mentioned   There were one hundred and ninety-five preachers in the state. One hundred and thirty-six congregations had been established in the past year." By 1858 it was estimated that there were fifty thousand in the state, which is probably an accurate estimate

From Kentucky and the North our attention now turns toward the Southland with a view to a sketch of the extent to which the churches had grown here. General reports coming from the South before the war indicate that the church had known only a slow growth, much slower than in the North. The reports indicate a general wave of religious indifference that swept the whole Southland. A. Paden reports ·

I should be glad were it in my power to give quite an extended history of the church in the South, but at present I cannot. I can say, however, as far as I can learn, that our members are very few, and are almost destitute of proclaimers   In all my travels I do not think that I have seen so great a field for evangelical labor as South Mississippi and Louisiana. . . .[18]

On another occasion J. A Butler reports:

There is an onward steadfastness in the brethren here, which shows strength. And if the spirit of the world could be cooled down, and the spirit of Christ increased, I think our vessels, cargoed with the waves of eternal life, would sooner outride the storm of sectarianism and safely anchor on the shores of everlasting deliverance   The energy is here, but we lack concentrated effort. But we make fair promises; if we *fail of compliance,* we will do better in the future [19]

In 1838 and 1839 Alexander Campbell made an extended tour into the South. He writes to R. L. Coleman of the conditions he found in the following words:

Disciples of Christ are not numerous in the South. . . We are disabusing the public mind of false impressions and presenting definite views of first principles. The Baptists are exceedingly

---

[17]S. M Scott, "Christian Statistics of Kentucky," *Christian Review*, Vol. II, No 11 (November, 1845), p 238
[18]A. Paden, "Religious Intelligence," *Christian Magazine*, Vol. I, No. 3 (March, 1848), p 96
[19]J. A. Butler, "Prospects in Mississippi," *Christian Review*, Vol II, No. 5 (May, 1845), p 118

opposed through the decrees of their Associations, who have forbid the opening of their meetinghouses to me and the brethren . . . Favourable impressions have been made in all places, and a few converted. But our population in the South is much more ignorant than in Virginia. We have a few educated, intelligent men, as we have a few rich and powerful; but the majority are poor, ignorant, and uneducated. . . . The brethren are of the best class of citizens and of very respectable attainments But it will require many sermons and labors, or much reading, to achieve much in these regions.[29]

It can be dangerous to speak too broadly in terms of generalizations, for these can be easily misunderstood. Yet there are values which must not be overlooked. To say that a general wave of indifference swept the South before the war is not to say that there were not religious people there, for there were. Some of the most devoted people in the nation were there, but the general picture of the Southland as a whole is that of indifference toward religion During this time, the cause of the restoration progressed slowly But in the North the picture was different, and here the church became deeply implanted The war left the people of the South in poverty and desolation so that, when the war ended, a general wave of religious enthusiasm came across the people, which made the South a fertile field in which to plant the seed of the New Testament Christianity. By the war's end, the issues of the society and the instrument of music had been frequently discussed. Through the influence of men like Tolbert Fanning and David Lipscomb, together with Franklin College and the *Gospel Advocate,* this seed began to be sown in what was almost virgin soil These men had already been convicted that societies and instruments were wrong New churches that were planted soon were indoctrinated against all innovations Consequently in the matter of time the churches of the South stood rigidly against these innovations. In the North where the bulk of the brotherhood resided, there were enough teachers who believed in societies and instruments to swing the churches in line. Perhaps the South in particular, and the present-day churches of Christ in general, owe much to these prewar conditions.

In another chapter a lengthy discussion will be found on the church in Tennessee Nothing comprehensive will be attempted

_____

[29] Robert Richardson, *Memoirs of Alexander Campbell,* Vol II, pp 453, 454.

at this point   In East Tennessee the churches were very scarce.
G C Metcalf wrote Fanning in 1846 saying that next to "midnight darkness reigns in this section of the country "[21]   J. J. Trott
held a meeting at Hamilton in 1845 in the home of a Brother Price
and established the "church of God in Hickory Valley."   In 1844
there were eleven congregations in East Tennessee   As late as
1855 there was no church in Chattanooga.   The most influential
church in middle Tennessee, if not in the whole South, was in
Nashville   This congregation had been formed in 1828 from the
Baptist Church in the city   In West Tennessee the picture is
somewhat optimistic   John R Howard resided at Paris, and was
undoubtedly a very influential preacher.   In Obion County there
were three congregations as late as 1855.   That year a church of
ten members was established at Dyersburg   At Memphis there
was a thriving congregation before the war.

Likewise were there few members in Alabama, although many
congregations were being established   The strongest church in
Alabama before the war was at Marion where Alexander Graham
resided   Marion, in Perry County, was often referred to as the
"Eden of the South" and by others as the "Athens of the South "
"It is the cradle of science, and the home of scholars."   Here was
located Howard College, Judson Institute, and Marion Female
Seminary   This congregation took the lead in spreading the gospel throughout the state

Another strong Alabama church before the war was located at
Russellville   This congregation was established in 1842 under
unusual circumstances   Tolbert Fanning left Nashville on January
20, 1842, on a tour to the South.   He visited Franklin and Columbia
in Tennessee and found these churches nearly dead.   He went on
to Florence and Tuscumbia, Alabama, and from here to Russellville   At the latter place he met Dr Sevier, son of a former
governor of Tennessee, who was the only member of the church
then in the city.   Fanning spent a night in the city and preached
on the importance of searching the scriptures.   The next morning
he started to leave town.   About a mile from the city the slender
carriage gave way.   He was informed that it would take several
days to repair it   He and his wife walked back to town through
the mud, and here again he began an extended gospel meeting

---

[21]Tolbert Fanning, "Church Intelligence," *Christian Review,* Vol. III, No.
1 (January, 1846), p 22

He preached a week, and twenty were baptized But Fanning was tired. He went to Tuscumbia, and W. H. Wharton came down to help. Before the meeting ended, Fanning baptized two doctors, one lawyer, the clerks of the county, circuit, and chancery courts with their families, the wife of the postmaster, the jailer and his household, and the wife and daughter of the sheriff. The meeting ended with seventy-four additions [22] Later, Fanning reported one hundred and five additions, indicating that others soon came in as a result of the meeting. [23]

Before the war one finds churches at Lafayette, Clinton, Bluff Creek, Fayetteville, Cedar Plains, Florence, Moulton, in addition to the other places already mentioned

The strongest church in Mississippi before the war appeared to be at Columbus This church was established in 1842. They built a new brick building in 1845, and by that time had ninety members. By 1847 the church had one hundred and fifty members, most of whom were young people. At Jackson there was no church in 1844, but five years later one reads of T. W. Caskey baptizing twelve persons there. When Fanning visited Jackson in 1847, he found but few members A brother, General Clark, lived there. So did James E. Matthews, who was an outstanding preacher of the gospel in Mississippi before the war Fanning preached in the Baptist meetinghouse and then in the state house. He immersed three persons, and from this beginning, it appears, the church in Jackson, Mississippi, started [24]

On this tour to Mississippi, Fanning makes the following observation regarding the church generally throughout the South:

Through all parts of Alabama, Mississippi, and Tennessee we passed, there is a great lack of godly intelligence and godly piety The people are generally intelligent on other matters, and friendly disposed, but the blessings of the pure and spiritual religion of the Bible are but imperfectly enjoyed A hundred able and humble preachers are needed where there is one to be found at present. [25]

---

[22]Tolbert Fanning, "News from the Churches," *Millennial Harbinger,* New Series, Vol VI, No 4 (April, 1842), p 186

[23]Tolbert Fanning, "The Church at Russellville, Alabama," *Christian Review,* Vol II, No 1 (January, 1844), p. 47

[24]Tolbert Fanning, "Observations on a Tour to the South," *Christian Review,* Vol IV, No 2 (February, 1847), pp 37-45.

[25]Tolbert Fanning, "Notes on a Tour—No 4," *Christian Review,* Vol I, No. 12 (December, 1844), p 269.

P. B. Lawson was another Mississippi preacher   In 1855 he resided at Crawfordsville, a city renowned for "wealth, wickedness, and mud." He complains that people are so completely engrossed in politics that they care nothing for spiritual interests [26]

The restoration movement in Georgia in some ways antedates that led by the Campbells in other states.   There were men in Georgia pleading for restoration who had never heard of Alexander Campbell or Barton W. Stone.   Christian Herman Dasher was one such man   Dasher's parents had fled Salzburg, Germany, to escape persecution by the Roman Catholics.   They were Lutherans religiously   Dasher himself was very much dissatisfied with religious division and began to search the scriptures on all subjects, but especially upon the subject of baptism.   While studying the Bible, he chanced to meet a Mrs. Threadcraft of Savannah, who told him of a preacher in her city by the name of S C. Dunning, who had formerly been a Baptist but who was now pleading for the Bible religion   Dasher went to Savannah, talked to Dunning, and was baptized   After returning home, Dasher baptized his wife, his wife's sister and her husband.   This group began holding services as early as 1819.   Later Dasher moved from Effingham County, where he had been residing, to Lowndes, near where Valdosta now stands   Most of the little congregation went with him   Dasher died in 1866, but the congregation, though small, lived on.[27]

The most influential church in the state of Georgia before the war appears to have been at Augusta   No preacher traveling through the state would have wanted to miss this congregation. Most of the wealth and talent in the church was found here   A rich widow, Sister Tubman, lived here.   She at one time donated ten thousand dollars to endow a chair at Bethany College.   Frequently she gave money to the erection of meetinghouses in the brotherhood   She gave eight thousand dollars to erect a house of worship in Augusta.   When Alexander Campbell visited Georgia in 1845, he stayed with Sister Tubman   He found in the church men like Dr D Hook, former mayor of the city, and an influential worker pressing the cause of Christ.   While in Augusta, Campbell

---

[26] P B Lawson, "Report from P B Lawson," *Gospel Advocate*, Vol I, No 4 (October, 1855), p 126

[27] James A Harding, "The Church of God at Valdosta, Georgia," *Gospel Advocate*, Vol XXV, No 7 (February 15, 1883), p 102

visited with Ex-Governor Schley. Schley almost became a Christian and expressed to Campbell after their conversation that all doubt had now been dispelled from his mind. Unfortunately we have no way of knowing whether this man ever acted upon his convictions or not After Campbell left, Dr. Hook decided to devote his time to being an evangelist. For the next few years he and N. W. Smith planted small congregations in Georgia.

Late in 1848 Samuel J Pinkerton went to Augusta to preach. J. S. Lamar also came shortly after. A. G. Thomas and P. F. Lamar became prominent in the work. But in 1855 Pinkerton left the church and joined the Episcopalians, and this did the church no small amount of harm. The next year J. S. Lamar and A. G Thomas began publishing a paper called *The Christian Union*. It is doubtful if this paper ever had a wide influence, but it probably did much to stabilize the church in those early, critical days.

In the western side of the Mississippi River the cause of restoration moved forward, although, in the case of Louisiana, its progress was much slower. Few congregations were to be found in the state before the war. At Baton Rouge, John T. Johnson held a meeting in 1849 and baptized thirty-eight In New Orleans the church fared well until the speculations of J B. Ferguson set it back. In 1845 the New Orleans congregation met at 82½ Julia Street Five years later a new house of worship was built at the corner of Camp and Melpomere Streets, and J. B Ferguson delivered the dedication sermon. Shortly before the war the theories of Ferguson crept into the church and divided it.

The plea for restoration made its inroads into Arkansas very early. At Little Rock, the state capital, this was particularly true, and, like Nashville, the church owed its origin to the Baptists. In 1824 Silas T. Toucray established the Baptist Church in the city. This congregation was strongly Calvinistic. On July 4, 1832, led by B F. Hall, this church renounced its creed and took its stand upon the Bible alone Less than three weeks later, W. W. Stevenson, a preacher for the Cumberland Presbyterian Church, renounced denominationalism and took his stand for the truth His preaching and work with the congregation in Little Rock helped it tremendously. In 1845 John T. Johnson and R C. Ricketts came to the city and conducted a five weeks' evangelistic meeting, baptizing eighty-three and having ninety-seven additions in all.[28]

There were other smaller congregations in the state, but their progress for the most part was slow   Stephen Strickland, a Baptist preacher, was converted by reading the *Christian Baptist* and the *Millennial Harbinger*   He founded one of the first congregations in the state at West Fork in Washington County in June, 1836   By 1847 one finds David S   Pyle laboring in Carroll County where he organized a congregation of thirty-one members in August, 1847   Nathan Polly and William H. Stewart were among the other early Arkansas preachers.

But, undoubtedly, the most influential congregation in the state was found at Fayetteville, and was largely the work of Robert Graham.   Graham had graduated from Bethany College in July, 1847, and by December that year was in Arkansas.   He held a week's meeting in Little Rock, and was urged to locate there.   Refusing, he went on to Fayetteville.   He arrived at the latter place February 2, 1848.   At this time John T. Johnson was in Arkansas, so Johnson and Graham preached in a two weeks' meeting.   The usual order was, Graham preaching and Johnson exhorting.   Their services were held in the Methodist church building on West Center Street.   Before the meeting closed they had converted a preacher, a doctor, and four lawyers.   Among the lawyers converted was Lafayette Gregg, who, in 1886, was a candidate for governor of the state on the Republican ticket.   The preacher converted was William T   Larimore of the Cumberland Presbyterian Church.   When Graham and Johnson arrived in Fayetteville, they found seven members of the church already there, among whom were Dr. Thomas J. Pollard and Judge Jonas M. Tebbetts, who were the pillars of the church.

Graham's main purpose in going to Arkansas had been to act as an agent for Bethany College and the *Millennial Harbinger*. After his meetings at Fayetteville, he continued on his itinerary, later coming back to Fayetteville to locate with the church.   For a while the church met in the courthouse and then in the Masonic Hall.   It enjoyed a steady growth.   But Graham had visions of a school   On December 14, 1852, a charter was granted for a college   The school opened at the corner of Dickson and St

---

[28]W   W   Stevenson, "News from the Churches," *Christian Review*, Vol. II, No 5 (May, 1845), p 119

Charles Street, and the first class to graduate was on July 4, 1854. Meanwhile a lot was purchased on the southwest corner of the public square. By 1859 a commodious building of brick and cut stone had been erected   The war affected the church seriously in Fayetteville, but this will be shown in more detail in another chapter.

The state of Missouri was hardly behind any when it came to the progress of the restoration. Soon after being admitted as a state in 1821 people from Kentucky and Tennessee began over-flowing the land in quest for cheap farms and a more stable finan-cial security. With these people came the story of the restoration plea, and churches were planted rapidly in Missouri before the war. Randolph County was early settled by people coming from Fayette County, Kentucky   They were mostly Baptists, but some had rejected denominational creeds for the Bible alone before coming   A meetinghouse was erected, and Allen Wright came to hold a meeting. The result was the establishment of the Antioch Church, the first in the county. From this congregation came Alexander Proctor, later a famous pioneer preacher

The most influential preacher in Missouri was undoubtedly T. M. Allen   Allen was born in Virginia in 1797 and moved to Boone County, Missouri, when he was thirty-nine, in the year 1836   Allen had a crippled arm and hand. He had settled on a nice farm, owned several slaves, and was quite wealthy financially for those days. He held meetings throughout Missouri and planted churches over the state.

The church in St. Louis was established February 18, 1837, and at first worshiped in the Sheppard School on Fourth Street. R. B Fife was the leading spirit that kept the church going before the war. Fife was born in Edinburgh, Scotland, in 1792, and by trade was a gunsmith. He came to Missouri sometime shortly after 1830. When W. H. Hopson's father died, Fife married Hopson's mother. W. G. Fife, his son, also was a leading influ-ence in the St. Louis church. By 1844 the church in St. Louis had one hundred members but no house of worship. They met in the third story of a house at the corner of Vine and Third Streets, but the next year had moved to Sixth Street and Franklin Avenue.

State meetings were held very early in Missouri. Some knowl-edge of the spread of the restoration can be gained by the reports

T M ALLEN

of these meetings   In 1845 it was reported that there were eighteen thousand members in the state   By the war this number had reached hardly less than twenty-five thousand

As the American frontier pushed westward the plea for restoration moved with it   Pardee Butler went to Kansas, and largely through his efforts the cause began to be preached there   The gold rush to California in 1849 opened up the far west   By 1852 there were three congregations in that state—Stockton, Santa Clara, and San Jose   But by far the cause knew its greatest advancement in the west in the state of Texas

Congress granted statehood to Texas in December, 1845   Al-

ready there were some pleading restoration in the state E. H.
East writes.

It affords me pleasure to be able to say there are a few even
in Texas who reject all human creeds and take up the New Testament alone for their rule of faith and practice [29]

But there were few preachers in Texas. S. B. Giles hád moved
there in 1837, and was one of the few who devoted his time to
preaching A few school teachers and lawyers preached occasionally Churches were begging for preachers to move there A
small congregation had been established at Brenham and another
at Travis, and both agreed to pay a preacher three hundred dollars a year to move out. From Huntsville, Texas, Robert T.
Walker wrote in 1845:

There are but few disciples in this country, and there are no
evangelists in this county (Montgomery); there is no church, and
I firmly believe, never will be until we are succored by the brethren
of the United States Brethren, help us, *help* us, or many, I fear,
will perish! Imagine our situation, bring your Christian minds
to bear on our *deplorable situation!* We are here, scattered like
lost sheep, tossed to and fro by many melancholy breezes, and
are susceptible of many sensual impulses . . [30]

B F Hall went to the state in 1849 on business and preached as
often as he could, although he was sick most of the time. He writes
back·

The people of Texas, among whom I have traveled and preached,
are hospitable, intelligent, independent, every man claiming the
right to believe and act for himself in religion I have never seen
a people more ready to hear and obey the gospel I know of no
country which presents so fine a prospect for usefulness as Texas
just now The people are not yet sectarianized [31]

With such encouragements preachers did slowly migrate to
Texas Hall went back to Kentucky and then returned to Texas
to live the rest of his days Carroll Kendrick, editor of the
Ecclesiastical Reformer, moved to Crockett in January, 1851.
That year Kendrick reported to the *Reformer* that there were
one hundred preachers in the state.

---

[29]Tolbert Fanning, "From Texas," *Christian Review,* Vol II, No 8
(August, 1846), p 191
[30]Robert T Walker, "A Call from Texas," *Christian Review,* Vol II, No
8 (August, 1845), p 191
[31]B F Hall, "Things in Texas," *Millennial Harbinger,* Third Series, Vol
VII, No 2 (February, 1850), p 103

There were seven counties in the general vicinity of San Augustine which had no preachers at all during these years. In Austin, S. B. Giles labored with a congregation of thirty members. But the cause grew rapidly. In March, 1852, Kendrick reported that nineteen had been added in the previous two months. Giles went to West Texas in 1855 and in a meeting baptized one hundred and seven persons in five months. This same year the church in Dallas was planted.

The *Gospel Advocate* very early in its existence made much headway in the state Kendrick, soon after arriving in the state, began publishing a paper which he called the *Christian Philanthropist* This paper was short-lived, and the subscription list was turned over to the *Advocate* Tolbert Fanning then requested Kendrick to edit a "Texas Department" in the paper, which he did The *Advocate* very early became a popular paper in the state, a fact that was to later influence the direction of the cause in the coming struggle over innovations.

With this picture before us of the extent of the spread of the cause before the Civil War, we are prepared to launch directly into the major events of the period Again it is emphasized that this picture is necessarily far from being complete, the only purpose being in giving it to recount to the neophyte in restoration history the broad extent to which the cause had grown so there may be a more tangible platform from which to observe the coming **events.**

CHAPTER VIII

EARLY EFFORTS AT ORGANIZATION

In the northeastern part of Ohio is one of the most interesting geographical areas of the restoration movement It was here that the first real problem of organization among the brethren began to exert itself. So important to a study of restoration history is this area that a few observations about it are not out of order.

The Western Reserve, as it was called, was bounded on the north by Lake Erie, on the east by the state of Pennsylvania, on the south by the forty-first parallel of north latitude, and on the west by Sandusky and Seneca Counties It stretched one hundred and twenty miles each and west and fifty miles north and south, in all occupying some three million acres of land. The name, Western Reserve, is of interesting derivation. King Charles II had granted to the colony of Connecticut in 1662 all lands in the new world stretching within certain specified boundaries to the far west. It must be remembered that at this time the knowledge of the lands of America was very imperfect It was generally supposed that the "South Seas" or Pacific Ocean was but a few miles west of the Appalachian Mountains, so Connecticut was granted all land between the forty-first and forty-second latitude to the Pacific Ocean. After the colonies united themselves into a federal government, these land-grants became a source of conflict. However, in September, 1786, Connecticut ceded to the new federal government her right to all the land she had been granted, except that three million acres between Sandusky and Seneca Counties, Ohio, and the Pennsylvania state line. These lands she reserved for herself. Before long this territory was known as the Connecticut Western Reserve, and finally the Western Reserve

It has already been recounted that on Western Reserve in 1820 the Baptists formed the Mahoning Association on very liberal terms. The Wellsburgh Church, of which the Campbells were members, applied for membership in the association and was received Walter Scott became in 1827 the evangelist for the association and through his preaching the apostolic gospel was announced for the first time generally on the Reserve For three years churches were planted by magic on the Western Reserve, and converts were made by the scores. So singular was Scott's success that Alexander Campbell became anxious whether the truth and the truth alone could convert men that rapidly. Later Campbell wrote:

I was so doubtful of these conversions that, when I visited the Mahoning Association last August, I was asking every person who could inform me both of the means employed in the great conversions in that quarter, and also of the behaviour of the converts   I also was particular in inquiring about the apostasies, and found that they were free from these exceptions, and that in about one thousand conversions in one year, not more than six or seven individuals had turned away from the holy commandment.[1]

Even though the cause was apparently prospering under the work of the Mahoning Association, some brethren became anxious as to whether or not such an organization could be defended by the scriptures   As a vital part of the message of these men was the plea for a return to original ground, it was asked by inquiring minds, "Was there scriptural authority for the existence of such an organization?"   Although some were not convinced that such an organization violated any teaching of the word of God, yet there was a general feeling among members that the association ought to be permanently dissolved   Accordingly plans were made to accomplish this at the meeting in Austintown in August, 1830

This particular historic meeting of the Mahoning Association opened as usual with its songs, exhortations, and prayers   John Henry, one of the preachers, stood up and said: "I charge you to look out what you are about to do here; we want nothing here which the word of the Lord will not sanction "[2]   He sat down and in a few moments arose and suggested a resolution to dissolve the association   This resolution was passed and the association was dissolved.

The death of the Mahoning Association indicates that a spirit of unrest was being felt regarding ecclesiasticisms unknown to the scriptures as early as 1830.   Many of these early brethren, too, had come to the restoration principles from the Baptists where they had seen the extremes of creedalism and human societies

---

[1] Alexander Campbell, "Dialogue Between the Editor of the Christian Baptist and Adelphos," *Christian Baptist,* Vol VI, No 8 (March 2, 1829), p 526

[2] Alexander Campbell, "Mahoning Association," *Millennial Harbinger,* Vol 1, No 9 (September, 1830), p 415

Many had been ostracized, denounced, and rejected by the various associations, and there was, therefore, an inward fear of such ecclesiasticisms. Yet many others were quick to realize that the danger of a thing does not argue against its existence There was an attitude of fear and restraint that made it apparent that if ecclesiasticisms were ever to gain much headway among the brethren, they would need to be sold on the idea. Proponents of institutionalism must pursue cautiously or else run the danger of a division within their own ranks The next twenty years were to find the subject up many times for discussion.

Alexander Campbell was not pleased with the dissolving of the Mahoning Association, but sensing the intense desire on the part of the majority, he silently acquiesced After the resolution for dissolving the association was passed, Campbell arose and said: "Brethren, what now are you going to do? Are you never going to meet again?" A hush fell over the audience, and then Campbell suggested that the brethren meet annually hereafter for preaching the gospel, mutual edification, and for hearing reports on the progress of the cause Accordingly, the next meeting of the brethren was held at New Lisbon on Friday, August 26, 1831. William Hayden presided at this meeting, and Walter Scott delivered a sermon on the reason of the Christian's hope.[3] After these discussions, the topic of "Cooperation" was discussed, the beginning of a long discussion of this subject which was to last for years ahead.

The term, cooperation, obviously indicates a working together for some specific purpose The great question among the pioneers was, how and in what manner can the various congregations work together to convert the world? The scope of this question at first limited itself to districts, then to states, and then to the entire brotherhood. Consequently, district cooperation meetings were among the earliest held, but one soon reads of state meetings and then finally of brotherhood attempts at cooperation which were realized in the formation of the American Christian Bible Society and the American Christian Missionary Society, the latter being the greater of the two.

Brethren who favored the cooperation efforts feared that the nature of their cooperation meetings were much misunderstood.

---

[3]Alexander Campbell, "General Meeting in New Lisbon," *Millennial Harbinger,* Vol II, No 9 (September, 1831), pp 445, 446

Consequently, frequent articles inform the readers of the various publications of the real purpose and design of these meetings. In Kentucky the brethren who had been under the influence of Barton W. Stone had very early shrunk back from any kind of organized effort between brethren. While Stone's followers looked with some suspicion upon Campbell and the "reformers," still the two groups found themselves coming slowly together. The publication of the *Christian Messenger,* which began in 1826, had something to do with this. It was not long before the subject of cooperation made its appearance in the *Messenger.* Walter Scott, writing under his usual name, "Philip," presented an article to the *Messenger* early in 1827 favoring conferences and cooperation meetings. Scott wrote:

Brother Stone:

As the subject of conference is considerably agitated at present, in the religious community, on the propriety of which there is (as upon almost every other subject) a variety of opinions; and as it certainly is a matter of no small importance, I beg leave to invite your attention to the subject, with a single view of eliciting information and ascertaining, if possible, what is propriety.

The very considerable hostility of many of our good brethren to every convocation in the shape of conference, together with the importance of the subject, renders it necessary that something should be said. For my own part, I have really thought that the most of the opposition to our annual meetings, from the brethren of the Christian Connection, arises from a want of correct information as to the objects of our association. For names I wish not to contend; I care not whether a religious convocation be termed conference, association, or annual meeting; but as to the propriety of the brethren occasionally meeting for religious edification, instruction, and information, from different parts of the community, within proper and limited bounds, there should exist no doubts whatever, particularly when the innocent as well as the useful objects of our meeting are ascertained.

Many are under the impression that we associate for the purpose of legislating or making laws for the rule and government of our churches. Nothing is more foreign from our views. I acknowledge one lawgiver and believe the great Head of the church has left a perfect code of laws for the government of his people; therefore, we stand not in need of human lawmaking to facilitate the prosperity of the Redeemer's cause . . .

It may then be inquired, what propriety is there in your conference or annual meeting? I answer, simply to worship together and strengthen the bonds of union; to receive and obtain infor-

mation from the different churches, either from their letters or
messengers, and attend to their suggestions, and as far as in our
power, comply with their requests; attend to ordination, if thought
proper, when required by the brethren, to arrange our appointments so as to supply the destitute churches with preaching, and
imitate the primitive church by making such requests only as may
be proper to set things in order [4]

To this article Stone replied that he appreciated the views set
forth and agreed with them in the main Nevertheless, the brethren of the Christian connection had been led away from conferences
and cooperation meetings because they saw in them too much
similarity to the Baptist Associations which they felt were tremendously despotic

J. Eichbaum, one of the editors of the *Christian Magazine,*
found himself in 1850 trying to put down a rising tide of opposition to cooperation meetings in Tennessee In answering the
question, "What is the design of cooperation meetings," Eichbaum
wrote:

1. They are *not* designed to interfere with the perfect and
untrammeled independence of any congregation of Christ whatever, whether rich or poor, influential or obscure

2. They are *not* designed to frame or devise a creed, church
covenant, or articles of faith, or in any degree to infringe upon
the fullest exercise of the divine right of private interpretation.

3 They do *not* claim the slightest authority to legislate as to any
ordinance, custom or usage, that must or must not be observed by
he churches of Christ.

4 They do *not* claim any right to excommunicate or in any
legree disfellowship any congregation that may think proper to
refuse participation in their measures or recommendations.

5 They are *not* designed to establish any tests of Christian
character, nor to decide who or who are not evangelists, bishops,
or deacons, nor in any sense to interfere with the action of any
congregation with reference to sending forth preachers of the
word.

6 They do *not* claim any authority to arbitrate the differences
that may exist between different members of the same congregation or between distinct congregations.

7 They have *not* authority to enforce any recommendation or
plan of expediency, and their resolutions must be regarded, not as
decrees or laws, but as simply *propositions* to the churches, with
whom resides all power.

---

[4]Walter Scott, *For the Christian Messenger,* Vol. II, No. 3 (January 25,
1827), p 49

8. They are not designed to permanently concentrate power and money in the hands of a few. As a matter of fact they have never done so, nor is it possible that they ever can.

9. They are not intended to give a separate and independent existence to any body ecclesiastic.

10 They are *not* designed to divert the means of the brotherhood from necessary and beneficial local operations, but rather to encourage and build up these local efforts

On the other hand—

1   They *are* intended to ascertain the true condition of the various congregations cooperating, and show the state of the cause in any given section   Without true, reliable knowledge on these matters, it is impossible to know either what *ought* to be done, or what can be done.

2 They *are* designed to secure the training and organization of those brethren who are scattered throughout the country, who do not enjoy Christian instruction, and who are unable to provide for it.

3. They *are* intended to bring the small means of individual congregations together, and to accomplish with these united means what no one congregation could effect.

4. They *are* intended to secure, as far as possible, the accomplishment of the church's mission   "Go ye into all the world, and preach the gospel to every creature."

5. They *are* designed to secure system and efficacy of action in place of irregularity and inefficacy.

6.   They *are* designed to be instrumental in setting on foot the best ways and means of carrying out what are confessedly the duties of the church of Christ.

7. They *are* designed, by congregating the talents of the churches, to elicit the truth on such subjects as come up for action, and then to disseminate this truth.

8. They *are* designed to unite the brotherhood, not by a system of consolidation, but by the influence of truth, love, and harmony.

9. They *are* designed to refresh the spirits of the holy brethren, to give words of encouragement to the weary, wisdom to the inexperienced, strength to the weak, humility to the proud, and to shed over all the genial influences of fraternal love.[5]

The only apology needed for such lengthy quotations is that they convey to the reader the purpose and nature of the cooperation meetings. These meetings were but assemblies of the delegated messengers of the congregations, who, when they came together, organized themselves with their presidents, secretaries and

---

[5]J Eichbaum, "Cooperation Meetings," *Christian Magazine*, Vol. III, No. 9 (September, 1850), pp 277, 278

treasurers. They made it clear that their purpose was not to, in any way, infringe upon the local autonomy of a congregation, or to legislate laws for the churches, but to discuss the progress of the cause and suggest ways and means of evangelizing the particular community where the member-congregations in the co-operation were located. Congregations through their messengers to the cooperation pledged certain specified amounts to finance the preaching of the gospel Cooperations selected evangelists and assured them their pay and authorized them to preach within a certain area.

Thus cooperation meetings were logical forerunners of the organizations and societies, both state and national, later to be found in the brotherhood Any defense that could be made for them was the same that could be made for later Missionary and Bible Societies Cooperations, from all practical intents and purposes, were innocent-looking organizations. They left the churches free and independent. Their resolutions were only recommendations and not laws and legislation For this reason they found wide acceptance in the brotherhood. On the other hand another group of brethren looked with suspicion upon them. The opposition was spotted, unorganized, and sometimes senseless, and all in all, accomplished little Campbell, writing of some of these opposers, said:

I have found a large class of men, professors, too, who will sit for a year rather than rise up crooked They are conscientious men; but they do nothing right lest they should do something wrong.[6]

Nevertheless, the general frame of mind in the brotherhood made it evident that the subject had to have free discussion. The year 1831 found Campbell presenting a series of five essays on the subject through the *Harbinger*. The second and third essays were written by Walter Scott in the absence of Campbell and do not materially affect the issue The articles were somewhat exhaustive of the theme and pursued the entire subject slowly. Campbell started the series by laying down the general thesis that Jesus left the conversion of the world up to the church, a fact which no one was ready to deny. Next Campbell proceeded to

---

[6]Alexander Campbell, "Cooperation," *Millennial Harbinger*, New Series, Vol II, No 6 (June, 1838), p 269

another plank in his platform viz., that the agency for this conversion was the word of God. With these as the beginning points
Campbell went on to point out that each member of church was
to do the preaching of the word, and, at times where the task
was too great for individual members the local congregations
must take over   From here Campbell proceeded to point out that
where the task was too great for a local congregation, many
congregations should go together to perform it   So he wrote "A
church can do what an individual disciple cannot, and so can a
district of churches do what a single congregation cannot "[7]
Coming then directly to the point Campbell urged that the churches
of his day begin taking active steps toward cooperation among
themselves.

Agreeably to the reason and nature of things, which must
never be lost sight of, and to all that is said or implied in the
New Testament, upon this subject, it behooves the churches at
this time, to regard their location, as respects states and counties,
in their efforts to convert the world .

The only question is, how shall this be done to the best
advantage? The New Testament furnishes the principles which
call forth our energies, but suggests no plan .   The churches
in every country, have from scripture and reason, all authority to
bring their combined energies home, they may, and ought to cooperate with their weaker neighbors, in the same state, and so
on increasing the circle of their cooperations, as they fill up the
interior, with all light and goodness, until the knowledge of the
glory of the Lord cover the whole earth [8]

From this one may well see Campbell's viewpoint toward these
organizations for cooperation   He believed the New Testament
Church was to preach the word to convert the world   But, he
believed the New Testament was not a code of laws, and therefore,
while it was up to the church to preach the word, since the New
Testament offered no plan, any plan within the bounds of reason
was permissible on the ground of expediency. On this ground
Campbell was ever wont to defend organizations outside of the
local congregations doing the work of the church.

Scarcely had Campbell's articles reached the public until opposition came up A Mr. "A. B G " replied immediately to the

---

[7]Alexander Campbell, "The Cooperation of Churches—No I," *Millennial
Harbinger,* Vol II, No 5 (May, 1831), p 237
[8]Alexander Campbell, "Cooperation of Churches—No IV," *Millennial
Harbinger,* Vol II, No 10 (October, 1831), pp 437, 438

Harbinger that "there never was, and there never can be, any occasion for such a combination of the churches to build up the Redeemer's kingdom "[9] This, of course, was striking directly at the root of the problem. That the church was God's agency to convert the world was evident to all, and that the instrumentality to do the converting was the word of God, was equally evident. That the churches could and should cooperate was also evident. But, did the churches have scriptural authority to organization institutions and ecclesiasticisms separate and apart from the local church to do the work of the church? This was the real problem. Campbell's reply was in the affirmative and was defended on the ground of expediency.

After the discussion of 1831 and 1832 in the *Harbinger* on cooperation, little was written on the subject for a decade When, in the spring of 1838 Barton W. Stone wrote Campbell informing him that many preachers were going into worldly positions to make enough to live on, Campbell replied with an article urging better cooperation to prevent this [10] But aside from this little was said until 1841. By this time Campbell was thoroughly convinced that the brethren were not taking full advantage of their opportunities and therefore, better organization was needed Accordingly, at the close of 1841 Campbell wrote that "our organization and discipline are greatly defective, and essentially inadequate to the present condition and wants of Society." From this Campbell reopens the whole field of study on cooperation He writes:

From my spiritual observatory, and by means of the telescope of faith in history sacred, ecclesiastic, and political; aided, too, by the accumulating lights of experience, observation and biblical developments, I am so deeply penetrated with the necessity of a more intimate organization, union and cooperation than at present existing among us, that I feel myself in duty bound again to invite the attention of the brotherhood, especially of those who are in heart and life devoted to the honor, dignity and influence of Christianity in the world, to a more thorough and profound consideration of the subject than they have ever yet given to it [11]

Campbell continues and bemoans the fact that there is no general

---

[9] A B G, "Cooperation of Churches—No V," *Millennial Harbinger,* Vol III, No 5 (May, 1832), p 201
[10] Alexander Campbell, "Cooperation," *Millennial Harbinger,* New Series, Vol II, No 6 (June, 1838), pp 267-271
[11] Alexander Campbell, "The Nature of the Christian Organization," *Millennial Harbinger,* New Series, Vol V, No 11 (November, 1841), p 533

cooperation, no general organization, no coming together for the support of the gospel He states the reason that he holds ; viz., such meetings in the past have been converted into legislative halls, and therefore, brethren had rejected them.

The whole field of cooperation had been opened up again. Campbell's purpose is now clear : he believes the church stands in need of a "general organization," a brotherhood-wide organization, through which the churches might cooperate to convert the world After hurling the challenge to the brethren to investigate the subject anew, he proceeds to lay down again certain principles to which he holds This time Campbell begins with the conception of the church as à kingdom. He lays down the fact that a kingdom must have a constitution, organization, joint and common, interests, and a community organization. Campbell writes :

Now if Christ's kingdom consists of ten thousand families, or churches—particular, distinct, and independent communities—how are they to act in concert, maintain unity or interests, or cooperate in any system of conservation or enlargement, unless by consultation and systematic cooperation? I affirm it to be, in my humble opinion, and from years of observation and experience impossible.[12]

It will be necessary to notice at this point a particular concept which Campbell held which clashed with that held by many others. Over these concepts considerable division was yet to come. The church of the New Testament is spoken of in two different senses— the universal and local. The church universal consisted of all baptized believers. The church in this sense is spoken of in the scriptures as the body of Christ, the kingdom of Christ, the house of God, temple of God, etc. The church universal has but one officer—Christ who is the Head of the body, the King plenipotentiary over the kingdom. In New Testament times this King appointed his special ambassadors to establish the church and indoctrinate it in its infancy. The apostles, strictly speaking, were not officers of the church. They existed before the church did, and were appointed by Christ, not by the church They were officers *pro tempore* and with the close of the first century left the church in the form of individual congregations overseen by bishops or elders to accomplish the work of converting the world

[12]Alexander Campbell, "The Nature of the Christian Organization—No II," *Millennial Harbinger*, New Series, Vol VI, No 2 (February, 1842), p 60

to Christ The church universal, as such, was not left with any specific work to do, but all work to be done was left up to the local congregations. Hence, in New Testament times, the only organization of Christians to exist was a local church. It is obvious, then, that the plan of the New Testament by which the world was to be converted was the establishing of local churches in every community of the world, and these local churches, in turn, under Christ, convert those within its reach. From Jerusalem to Judea, thence to Samaria and finally to the uttermost parts of the earth, churches were planted in New Testament times without the aid of any other organization than the local church, and souls were thus converted to Christ.

Ecclessiasticisms unknown to the church owe their origin directly or indirectly to beginning with the church universal. This has been carried to the farthest extreme in Roman Catholicism. Beginning with the consideration of the church universal, they reasoned that an earthly pope must reign in the place of Christ. The apostles must have their successors, and so the bishops became this On these two major assumptions, both starting with the concept of the church universal, Roman Catholicism has built its structure. The Synods, Conferences of Protestantism all have started from the same premise, but have not gone to the extreme of Romanism. For the brethren of a century ago to begin at this point and work toward general organizations was likewise to start on a false premise, and in these concepts the differences arose.

In 1842 Campbell began a series of essays on "Church Organization" which lasted up through 1848. In his first article on this subject he sets forth five arguments for Church Organization. Actually, there are six, the last two being numbered five each, and in all probability because of a typographical error.

1. We can do comparatively nothing in distributing the Bible abroad without cooperation.

2 We can do comparatively but little in the great missionary field of the world either at home or abroad with cooperation

3. We can do little or nothing to improve and elevate the Christian ministry without cooperation.

4. We can do but little to check, restrain, and remove the flood of imposture and fraud committed upon the benevolence of the brethren by irresponsible, plausible, and deceptious persons, without cooperation.

5 We cannot concentrate the action of the tens of thousands of Israel, in any great Christian effort, but by cooperation

5. We can have no thorough cooperation without a more ample, extensive, and thorough church organization.[13]

The next year, 1843, Campbell presents his views on Church Organization by presenting a hypothetical case of a group of evangelists who go to an island called Guernsey. In five years they establish congregations which Campbell calls A, B, C, D, etc. After a while, Campbell says, these churches discover they cannot work efficiently without pooling their resources. A meeting is called at congregation A, and here the churches decided to band together and act in all matters just as one church.[14]

To this hypothetical case there was strong objection, at least from one anonymous individual. He replies:

We do not misapprehend Brother Campbell, then, when we say seven separate churches in the island of Guernsey are in his plan of organizing, to form one "whole church"—the church of Guernsey. Here then, I affirm, is a new organization, a new church, and a new name—a district church—a district name. I call it new, because no such use of the word church is found in the scriptures.[15]

The writer of these words goes on to point out that Campbell has in mind a political embodiment of Christians that has no foundation in scriptures. He furthermore argues that in no way could this superimposed organization find it necessary to govern itself and the churches but by the iron grasp of a pope or an emperor He looks upon this suggestion from Campbell as embodying a complete abandonment of New Testament Christianity. Accordingly, he continues:

For instance, some persons, Brother Campbell informs us, wrote to him for an organization, and he propounded the Guernsey case for an answer. I will say of all such applicants that if they are not duped and led astray from the simple organization of the New Testament, they will owe their safety, not to their own prudence, but to the discretion of others totally, for in that they sought an organization at his hands, they gave to all men the most animated demonstration of a disposition lurking in them to associate the fortunes of original Christianity, which we have been these twenty-

---

[13]Alexander Campbell, "Five Arguments for Church Organization," *Millennial Harbinger*, New Series, Vol VI, No 11 (November, 1842), p 523

[14]Alexander Campbell, "The Nature of the Christian Organization," *Millennial Harbinger*, New Series, Vol VII, No 2 (February, 1843), p 78ff

[15]Anonymous, "Organization," *Millennial Harbinger*, Third Series, Vol I, No 1 (January, 1844), p 42

five years seeking to restore, with the wisdom of a human organization. Can it be that such brethren do not know that most of our churches already possess an organization, and neither require nor demand another at the hand of any man? What does our church at Carthage want of Brother Campbell? If he encourages the brethren to play their part well on the present organization, he does well.

In November of that year, 1843, the Campbell-Rice debate was held in Lexington, Kentucky. The subject of cooperation was being by now considered so much that few brethren could get together for long without its being discussed. In between sessions of the debate several brethren got together and discussed cooperation along with the possibility of forming a missionary society. Jacob Creath, Sr. "by his tears, his prayers and his arguments" got the brethren to abandon their plan temporarily.

In October, 1844 a meeting was held at Steubenville, Ohio to exchange views on the subject of cooperation. At the conclusion a committee of five was appointed to draft some propositions for a more general meeting at Wellsburg on December 26, 1844. At this meeting the propositions were discussed, but only a few congregations were represented. Another meeting at Wellsburg was held on April 1, 1845. Campbell made it plain that these meetings were only for the purpose of getting discussion.

No individual or set of individuals has any authority to dictate to their brethren or enforce upon them any views or rules of action on any subject connected with their spiritual relations to the Lord and to one another [16]

The purpose was to get a discussion on the subject in order that some recommendations could be made to the brethren as a whole. The whole procedure was to be democratic, so far as Campbell was concerned.

If then they prefer disorder to order, no general organization, to a general organization; if they can prefer what now is, to any thing that can be substituted for it, of course they must have it.

That year, 1845, Campbell was able to write·

Much has been written, and a great deal said, and little done, on the whole subject of Christian organization. But there is a growing interest in the subject manifested, and there is a growing

[16]Alexander Campbell, "Church Organization," *Millennial Harbinger*, Third Series, Vol II, No 2 (February, 1845), p 60

need felt for a more scriptural and efficient organization and co-operation [17]

The very fact that the cause for greater cooperation and for organized institutions outside the church had Alexander Campbell behind it, was enough to put it over.   Yet, there was some scattered opposition, as we have already seen   T. M. Henley criticized the prevailing trend toward organizations and suggested a plan of his own.

It does appear to me there is a falling off in some measure from what we set out with—"a restoration of the ancient gospel and order of things, and a pure apostolic speech " If I am mistaken in this, it will give me pleasure to find it to be so   But it seems to me like a departure from the simplicity of the Christian institution to have cooperation meetings with *Presidents* and *Secretaries,* calling for the *Messengers* of churches, and laying off districts.   This was nearly the principle upon which the Baptists began in Old Virginia (except their creed) and it has now become the scourge and curse to the peace of society   I am for cooperation too; but cooperation, if I understand the term, implies *weakness* When any one church wishes to send out an Evangelist, and is unable to sustain him in the field, she may invite her sister congregations to cooperate with her.   If the invitation is accepted, when the members visit those inviting them on a set day, they ought to act as if in the *house of another family.*   The elders of this congregation preside and state the object for which they were invited and their inability to perform the work themselves, and ask their assistance and the sum of money wanting   This being agreed on, then all concerned can unite in selecting their evangelist or pointing out the most suitable ground to be occupied by him—for one year or the time agreed on   The congregation proposing to cooperate appoints one of its members or elders to receive all moneys and pay over quarterly to their evangelist what they may judge necessary to sustain him in the field   This broth- er's account to be presented to the churches cooperating annually. Such is our course, and I think there is not the same danger of running into the popish principles and practices of the sects as when we have Presidents and Secretaries—with their anathemas following [18]

For a number of years Tolbert Fanning watched the efforts at cooperation with grave doubts in his mind   Fanning on all points

---

[17] Alexander Campbell, "Church Organization," *Millennial Harbinger,* Third Series, Vol II, No 2 (February, 1845), p 59

[18] T M Henley, "Cooperation of Churches," *Millennial Harbinger,* Vol VII, No 7 (July, 1836), pp 333, 334

"hastened slowly." He generally thought a thing through, but in the end came to an independent conclusion and stayed there. In 1855 Fanning wrote:

It is well understood that for many years I have doubted the practical results of the cooperations in Tennessee, and indeed in other states, but I have yielded to my brethren of age and experience, and I should be willing to yield longer, could I conclude it would be to the honor of God [19]

That year Fanning established the *Gospel Advocate* One of his chief purposes in doing so was to give the whole subject of cooperation a thorough examination. So he continues:

In establishing *The Gospel Advocate,* I determined, by the help of the Lord, to give the subject of cooperation a thorough examination I do not pretend to say how it has been wrought about, but I have for years believed that a change must take place in our views of cooperation before we can labor to each other's advantage, or to the honor of God

The church in Nashville, Tennessee, very early had its own misgivings about these cooperative organizations. A number of brethren met in the church house in January, 1842, to discuss cooperation. They studied the Bible as though they had never seen it before. At the end they reached the following conclusions

1 That there is positive scriptural authority for every religious work that is well pleasing to God.

2. That the church of Christ is the only divinely consecrated organization on earth for Christian labor

3. All other organizations through which men propose to perform spiritual labor tend but to obscure, discredit, and subvert the reign of the Messiah [20]

Encouragements in cooperative efforts were not long in having their effect Organized efforts sprang up like magic over the nation. In Virginia, around Wellsburgh, district cooperations were begun as early as 1831 At the close of a protracted meeting in Jacksonville, Illinois, in 1834, it was decided to start a cooperation meeting. The Illinois State Meeting was held for the first time two years later. In 1839 a Cooperation Meeting was held in Richmond, Virginia, representing twenty-five congregations The same year, the first state meeting of the churches in Indiana was

[19]Tolbert Fanning, "Cooperation," *Gospel Advocate,* Vol I, No 4 (October, 1855), p 110

[20]Tolbert Fanning, "The Path of Safety," *Gospel Advocate,* Vol VIII, No 6 (February 6, 1866), p 82

organized   A convention of South Kentucky churches was organized in 1842   The same year a convention in northern Missouri was organized, and also the same year an organization was
formed at Warrensville, Ohio. By 1844 one reads of the General
Cooperation of Disciples in Virginia. By 1850 the Kentucky State
Missionary Society was organized with John T. Johnson as president. Two years later the Ohio Christian Missionary Society
was organized at Wooster. The list could be extended to great
length, but these are enough to convey the thought that the general
trend in the brotherhood was more and more toward organizations
outside the church to do the work of the church

One major step in this direction needs special attention—viz. ·
the American Christian Bible Society   It was the first attempt
at anything similar to a brotherhood-wide organization yet promoted. It was founded by D. S. Burnet in Cincinnati, Ohio, on
January 27, 1845   Soon after its establishment, its constitution
was widely published in brotherhood periodicals along with articles
urging the support of the brotherhood to this society.

No sooner was the Bible Society organized than opposition
poured down upon it.   Aylette Raines, editor of the *Christian
Teacher,* a Kentucky publication, doubted the practicability of the
enterprise. J. J. Goss, editor of the *Christian Intelligencer* of
Virginia, thought it would be wiser to cooperate with the American
and Foreign Bible Society, a Baptist organization, than to establish
another   Campbell himself thought the Bible Society to be premature, thinking the brethren were not yet ready for it   Campbell
also felt that the colleges—Bethany, Bacon, and Franklin—should
be put on a more substantial financial basis before trying something
like a Bible Society.

Burnet seemed to have been stunned by the opposition   For
several issues of the *Harbinger* after 1845 he and Campbell defended themselves over the society.   Burnet wanted to know if
the brotherhood had been sufficiently consulted when Campbell
established Bethany College   Campbell's reply was that the nature
of the two institutions was entirely different. Bethany College
was a private institution, established from the funds of himself
and his friends, whereas the Bible Society purported to be a brotherhood organization   Very little of the opposition to the Society
came because brethren thought it was an organization, but only
because it was inexpedient at that time to start it.

For eleven years the Bible Society existed with very little interest displayed in it It was off to a bad start and never got much sympathy behind it In 1856 the Ohio State Convention met and agreed to terminate the Bible Society and turn its funds over to the American Bible Union. This was done, and so ended the first general brotherhood attempt at organization.

Of course that which far overshadowed the Bible Society was the American Christian Missionary Society It is toward this society that we turn our attention in the chapter that follows

CHAPTER IX

THE AMERICAN CHRISTIAN MISSIONARY SOCIETY

"The most important event in the history of the Disciples, next to the founding of Bethany College, was the organization of the American Christian Missionary Society."[1] D. S. Burnet wrote to W. T. Moore in a letter dated February 28, 1867· "I consider the inauguration of our society system which I vowed to urge upon the brethren, if God raised me from my protracted illness of 1845, as one of the most important acts of my career."[2] These strictures, stating the importance of the founding of the American Christian Missionary Society, are not overdrawn The establishment of this society marked the climax of years of intense effort on the part of Alexander Campbell to urge the brotherhood to found some kind of a general organization through which the entire brotherhood could cooperate to evangelize the world. The society's establishment also was the first real test to which the unity of the brotherhood had been put Likewise was it the first real occasion for the airing of internal differences with the church—differences which in the course of time were to create a widening breach within the ranks of those advocating a return to the primitve order of things.

1849!! This is a year when a rather youthful nation and an equally youthful religious movement were afflicted with "growing pains" The nation was going through its most critical period. Zachary Taylor was the president, and with the exception of Abraham Lincoln, never was a president faced with such grave problems The question of slavery was before the nation, and violent debates were thundering from the halls of Congress Gold had been discovered in the Lower Sacramento Valley in 1848 During the next year, eighty thousand immigrants swarmed into the new El Dorado. The government found itself with laws inadequate to meet the controversies arising. National expansion

---

[1]Frederick D Power, *Life of William Kimbrough Pendleton, LL D* (St Louis Christian Publishing Co, 1902), p 128
[2]F M Greene, *Christian Missions and Historical Sketches of Missionary Societies Among the Disciples of Christ* (St Louis· John Burns Publishing Co, 1884), p 172

key-noted the times. At the very time the Convention of 1849 was meeting to decide the wisdom of establishing a missionary society, California was seeking entrance into the new-born Union. These were the days when Webster, Clay, Calhoun, and Benton were thrilling the people with their glowing eloquence. But their language painted a horizon of gloom behind the glowing sunrise, for slavery told the most thoughtful that darker days were yet ahead. Side by side the nation and the church were headed for internal chaos whose results would not soon be lost by either

Campbell's frequent essays on Church Organization between 1841 and 1848 were producing their effects, although in some cases these effects were not altogether desired The magic name of Alexander Campbell behind any idea usually was enough to discourage any opposition from becoming too effective. On the other hand, his name frequently caused too ready acquiesence from many The articles in opposition to Campbell's essays on Church Organization did not discourage him, for Campbell felt his way along slowly enough to know that he had the bulk of the brotherhood behind him. Consequently, the opening of the year 1849 gave Campbell the feeling that the groundwork had been sufficiently laid that some more difinite action should now be taken to form a general organization for cooperation. He was encouraged, too, by the fact that brethren who agreed with him were urging him on

There is now heard from the East and from the West, from the North and from the South, one general, if not universal, call for a more efficient organization of our churches Experience, than which there is not a more efficient teacher, decides and promulgates that our present cooperative system is comparatively inefficient and inadequate to the exigencies of the times and the cause we plead . . [3]

Sensing a wide demand for a general organization, Campbell urges that some definite attention be given to it Still, he urges calm and deliberate action and warns against extremes

There are extreme views on all subjects as well as moderate and rational ones I have always been a pleader for organization, still organization is not faith, nor humility nor liberality [4]

---

[3]Alexander Campbell, "Church Organization—No I," *Millennial Harbinger*, Third Series, Vol VI, No 2 (February, 1849), p 90
[4]Alexander Campbell, "Church Organization—No I," *Millennial Harbinger*, Third Series, Vol VI, No 2 (February, 1849), p 92

Campbell went on to point out that the principles for which he had pleaded were as firmly established as those of the Protestant Reformation   Throughout the land he believed there were a thousand or more local congregations vehemently crying for some means of cooperating their efforts.   Many people appeared to believe that if they had such an organization as would unite their combined efforts, they would carry everything before them   While Campbell shared this optimism, he also believed that some sort of organization was necessary to prevent the restoration movement from going into retrograde

Two questions presented themselves for consideration   First, Campbell asked· "What shall be the form or character of our organization?"   The second was: "How shall it be established?" Campbell suggested that a committee be appointed and investigate the subject and make some report to the brotherhood

Have we, then, no scriptural model, no divine precedent or authority for any form of church organization and cooperation? and if so, what is it?   We must appoint a committee to examine the subject, and to report in our next number [5]

Two months later Campbell reports that the committee had been able to meet only once, and, therefore, was not ready at that time to give a report.   In view of that he decided to set forth again his views on the subject of a general organization for the benefit of those who might yet be unconvinced   After recognizing the independent character of the congregations, he asserts that this independence did not forbid their working together on any great accomplishment   In his next article, Campbell shows that the New Testament usage of the term. church, embodied single congregations, and the church of Christ in the aggregate or the whole is the entire Christian community on earth   That being true, he suggested that the church knows two classes of officers—officers who belong to a local community such as bishops, elders, and deacons, and those who belong to the whole Christian community —the apostles, prophets, and evangelists   Campbell then struck with a very forceful conclusion:

In all things pertaining to public interest, not of Christian faith, piety, or morality, the church of Jesus Christ in its aggregate character, is left free and unshackled by any apostolic authority

---

[5] Alexander Campbell, "Church Organization—No II," *Millennial Harbinger*, Third Series, Vol VI, No 4 (April 1849), p 221

This is the great point which I assert as of capital importance in any great conventional movement or cooperation in advancing the public interests of a common Christianity and a common salvation My strong proof for this conclusion is that, while faith, piety, and morality are all divinely established and enacted by special agents —apostles and prophets possessed of plenary inspiration, matters of prudential arrangement for the evangelizing of the world, for · the better application of our means and resources, according to the exigencies of society and the ever-varying complexion of things around us—are left without a single law, statute, ordinance, or enactment in the New Testament [6]

This is the heart of Campbell's reasoning on Church Organization He insists upon beginning with the church in the aggregate or universal sense of the term It is vital to his viewpoint to ignore, at least for the time being, the local character of the church It is with the church universal that he begins Reasoning from the point that the church in the aggregate has the responsibility of converting the world, and that since Christ has given no divine plan for the church, in this sense, to function, therefore, the church is left free to devise its own plan, according to its own wisdom, with only the law of expediency applying To be sure, any plan the church would devise would be unauthorized in the New Testament, and it would be the height of folly to look for a New Testament example for it To Campbell, it was expediency pure and simple and on that ground could be defended.

The weakness in Campbell's reasoning was to be found in his beginning point—the church universal The church universal had but one set of officers—the apostles, and these were the personal ambassadors of Christ sent on a special mission to supervise the work for Christ in the infancy of His Church Through the apostles the divine word was spoken by Christ, and through the apostles Christ established and confirmed His Messiahship. At the close of the apostolic age, when the last apostle had died, the church was known only by the individual congregations scattered over the world The work of Christ through the church to evangelize the world was carried on through the influence of the local church in its community Even in apostolic times the churches felt no need of an organization, devised by human planning, through which the church could cooperate to evangelize the world They had a

[6]Alexander Campbell, "Church Organization—No III," *Millennial Harbinger*, Third Series, Vol VI, No 5 (May, 1849), p 270

fervency and zeal, and the history of the church has well shown that the less zeal and devotion there is in the church, the more institutionalism and human organizations are needed.

By the late spring of 1849 Campbell urges his readers to write to him any criticisms, objections, or suggestions they may have. Then Campbell suggested that if his views were agreed upon, "we will dispatch the matter with all speed and concur with them in the call of a general meeting in Cincinnati, Lexington, Louisville, or Pittsburgh "[7]

The Christian Intelligencer, published in Virginia, took up Campbell's plan and suggested the calling of a general convention to meet in Baltimore, but rather in Cincinnati   There were a number of reasons for this, but the main one was that Baltimore was out of reach of the main bulk of the brethren who lived in the "west." (Indiana, Illinois, Missouri, Arkansas, and all territory in the Mississippi Valley was then the west.)   Another point of consideration not to be overlooked was that the church had probably had a greater growth by this time in Cincinnati than any other city   Moreover, it was easily accessible by steamboat, the main method of travel in those days.

The time for this general convention was generally suggested to be the month of October   The *Christian Magazine* wrote:

We believe in the necessity and propriety of such a meeting. We think Cincinnati the most eligible point for such a meeting, and would make an effort to have the churches of our state represented there. We would be gratified that the meeting should take place so as to include the fourth Lord's Day in October next   We are confident our State Meeting, which will convene some ten days prior to that time, will make arrangements to be represented[8]

Campbell, however, opposed October as the time for the meeting and suggested it be called the first Monday of November. His reason for this suggestion grew out of the fact that an epidemic of cholera was then sweeping the city, and he felt there might be a possibility that it would subside by November. Needless to say, Campbell's insistence on November was overridden and the meeting was set for October.

---

[7]Alexander Campbell, "Church Organization—No IV," *Millennial Harbinger,* Third Series, Vol VI, No 5 (May, 1849), p 273
[8]Tolbert Fanning, W H Wharton, J J Trott, J B Ferguson, "Meeting for General Consultation," *Christian Magazine,* Vol II, No 8 (August, 1849), p 311.

As the summer of 1849 bore on, Campbell continued to press the urgency of "a more efficient and scriptural organization." He writes·

I am of opinion that a convention, or general meeting, of the churches of the Reformation is a very great desideratum. Nay, I will say, further, that it is all important to the cause of reformation. I am also of the opinion that Cincinnati is the proper place for holding such convention But the questions are: *How shall such convention be obtained, when shall it be held, and for what purposes?* These I cannot more than *moot,* or propound. I must, however, to suggest considerations to our brethren, say that it should not be a convention of bookmakers, or of editors, to concoct a great book concern, but a convention of messengers of churches, selected and constituted such by the churches—one from every church, if possible—or if impossible, one from a district, or some definite number of churches It is not to be composed of a few self-appointed messengers, or of messengers from one, two, or three districts, or states, but a *general* convention. I know that neither wisdom nor piety are rated by numbers, still in the multitude of counselors there is more general safety, and more confidence than in a few. The purposes of such a primary convention are already indicated by the general demand for a more general and efficient cooperation in the Bible cause, in the missionary cause, in the education cause [9]

Up to this time the character of the proposed convention had been very little discussed. By this time Campbell insists that the convention should not be one of bookmakers or of editors, but truly a representative body of the brotherhood at large. He did not use the term, delegate, but messenger, insisting that messengers be sent if possible from all the churches Moreover, in Campbell's insistence upon a "more general and scriptural organization," he does not use the term, missionary society, as an equivalent of this The missionary society was but one phase of the organization in which he was interested He wanted an organization that would be missionary, educational, and benevolent, taking care of all the interests of the church and not limited to any one interest.

Alexander Campbell, because of sickness, was unable to attend the convention when it did meet in October that year This is a simple statement of fact, and yet there are matters to raise questions in one's mind. There is no evidence of any sickness which

---

[9]Alexander Campbell, "Convention," *Millennial Harbinger,* Third Series, Vol VI, No 8 (August, 1849), pp 475, 476

Campbell had that was at all serious. Apparently he was not sick enough to stay away from his regular duties. One cannot help but feel—although it is just a feeling—that there were other matters that prevented Campbell from attending the convention. Was it because he feared that his ideas would be rejected and that he himself might possibly be placed in a false light? The question cannot be answered with any degree of certainty, and yet there are indications pointing in that direction.

By the year 1849 there was at least a mild rumble of opposition to Campbell running through many places in the brotherhood. While it is true that these might possibly be caused by misunderstanding, yet they were there By this time there were not less than twenty to twenty-five publications in the brotherhood, and yet Campbell had, at various times, insisted that these were not needed, but were a waste of money, of time, and of ink He had opposed a tract society at Cincinnati, and had looked with displeasure upon other schools aside from Bethany College with the feeling they were not needed. It was only natural that Campbell should be accused of being jealous for his own interests. Did he want all other publications to cease being printed merely that the *Harbinger* might enjoy wider reading? Was he jealous of the tract society at Cincinnati for fear that Cincinnati and not Bethany would be the Jerusalem of the restoration? Did he look with disfavor upon other schools than Bethany merely that Bethany might enjoy greater prominence? There were many brethren who thought so, and some seemed to fear that the "general organization" Campbell had in mind was to be an ecclesiasticism to exercise controls over the brotherhood that would favor Campbell. Campbell doubtlessly sensed that many were looking upon him as a dictator, and resolved not to attend the convention, that the organization be the work of the brethren and not of himself While it is true that no quotation can be given to substantiate the views expressed above in the writings of the day, yet by dipping back into the past and sensing the general feeling, the explanation seems to be highly plausible, and we doubt not, correct

The Convention met, according to announcement, on Tuesday. October 23, 1849, at Christian Chapel, corner of Walnut and Eighth Streets, in Cincinnati In Campbell's place came W. K Pendleton. Writing later of the entire meeting, Pendleton says

We met, not for the purpose of enacting ecclesiastic laws, not to interfere with the true and scriptural independence of the churches, but to consult about the best ways for giving efficiency to our power, and to devise such methods of cooperation, in the great work of converting and sanctifying the world, as our combined counsels, under the guidance of Providence, might suggest and approve. There are some duties of the church which a single congregation cannot, by her unaided strength, discharge . A primary object being to devise some scheme for a more effectual proclamation of the gospel in destitute places, both at home and abroad, the Convention took under consideration the organization of a Missionary Society.[10]

We are assured that many wild schemes were suggested during the meeting, but that Pendleton headed them off and guided the entire course of the way on "safe" grounds.

He found many prepared to push some wild scheme or another, involving publications, etc., such as some already well-established organization might afford to carry on He seems to have been the clear-headed, cool-headed one to check the exuberant and speculative, and prove helpful on the side of the more practical; to have been the wise and careful one in counsel, and strong and safe in argument, favoring the adoption of feasible propositions [11]

The first meeting of the convention in the Walnut and Eighth Streets church building was hardly more than a preliminary one. L. L Pinkerton was called to the chair, and John M. Bramwell of Indiana was appointed secretary. A group of permanent officers had to be selected. Even though he was absent, Alexander Campbell was elected president. There were four vice-presidents These were David S. Burnet, John O'Kane, John T. Johnson, and Walter Scott. James Challen, who had labored so long in Cincinnati, was chosen corresponding secretary A committee was appointed to define the order in which the business should be taken up, and was required to make a report the next morning. With this work completed, the first session of this historic convention closed.

The next morning at nine o'clock the convention held its second meeting. In the absence of Campbell, D. S Burnet took the chair and presided He also led the morning's prayer. The first order of business was brought forth from James Challen, who the day

---

[10]W. K. Pendleton, "The Convention of Christian Churches," *Millennial Harbinger,* Third Series, Vol VI, No 12 (December, 1849), pp 689, 690
[11]F D Power, *Life of W K Pendleton,* p 131

before had been selected as corresponding secretary. Challen now declined the invitation. Two men—Thomas J. Melish and John W Bramwell—were then appointed to fill the position.

It would be interesting to follow the business procedures in each of the sessions, but yet this would involve many details which would contribute very little to this total study. A knowledge, however, of the general procedure might well give one an idea of how such meetings were ordinarily conducted   When the morning session of Wednesday, October 24, finally got into full swing by settling the men for the office of corresponding secretary, J. J. Moss wanted to know, at the outset, what constituted a delegate, and then followed by suggesting that the name *delegate* be dropped and the word *messenger* used instead. Moss' motion was over-ridden, but for what purpose is not explained. Some discussion then followed as to who should be allowed a member of the organization   J. Young of Kentucky moved that all members of the Christian Churches in North America be invited to participate with the Convention. W. K Pendleton moved, as an amendment, that each church represented be given one vote. He pointed out that the independence of the churches should be recognized   Elijah Goodwin wanted the convention to be regarded as an experiment, and thought that the largest liberty should be allowed until some future meeting when a definite principle could be adopted. William Begg of Indiana then offered the following resolution: "Resolved, That every properly accredited Christian evangelist and elder of a Christian church present, or that may be present, be, by virtue of their office, invited to a seat with us, as members of this convention." R. G. Fife, of St. Louis, Missouri, strongly objected. He had fears that the adoption of such a resolution would be the beginning of clericalism in the church, and would eventually destroy the equality of the churches. The resolution, then, was tabled   By now the morning session was ready to be closed, so John T. Johnson worded a benedictory prayer.

The afternoon session, which met at two o'clock, was very brief, but yet, was a definite step in the progress of the convention. After a reading of the forty-fifth Psalm by D S Burnet and a prayer led by W K Pendleton, John T Johnson offered the following resolution to the convocation: "Resolved, That a missionary society as a means to concentrate and dispense the wealth and benevolence of the brethren of this Reformation, in an effort to convert the world, is both scriptural and expedient." One cannot help but wonder as to the propriety of such a resolution, for certainly the fact that it was passed or declined would effect the issue of whether or not the society was scriptural in no way. A committee was selected to draft a constitution, and with this the afternoon session closed. Those included on the committee were John O'Kane, John T. Johnson, H. D Palmer, Walter Scott, John T Powell, and L. L. Pinkerton.

When the convention met that evening at seven o'clock, the scripture was read by D. S. Burnet, who read from the twelfth chapter of Isaiah, and the prayer was led by W. Davenport of Illinois. Nothing of great importance was forthcoming from this sesson. L. L. Pinkerton very tersely remarked that "our existence as a people is involved in some general cooperation for the conversion of the world " Then followed another resolution which recommended the society to the cordial support of the brethren This particular resolution was introduced by W. K. Pendleton and read "Resolved, That the Missionary Society contemplated by this action be presented to the brethren as the chief object of importance among our benevolent enterprises " And so ended the three sessions of Wednesday, October 24, 1849.

The meeting the next morning seemed to concern itself with the interests of the Bible Society. As was customary, the meeting opened with a scripture reading and a prayer The one hundred and twenty-seventh Psalm was read, and the prayer was led by William Begg H Van Tuyl of Ohio recommended a resolution that the American Christian Bible Society arrange her constitution so as to make a missionary department The motion was laid on the table. T. J. Melish of Ohio made the motion that the Bible Society be resolved into an Evangelical Society for the promotion of both Bible and missionary objects and that the convention drop the Missionary Society idea altogether. He contended that a union of the two would both harmonize the brotherhood and avoid bringing into existence cumbrous machinery S S. Church then moved that the American Christian Bible Society change her constitution to read, American Christian Bible and Missionary Society The question was argued considerably W. K. Pendleton opposed the union of the two on the ground that this union would prejudice the brethren against both societies. Pendleton's motion that the Missionary Society be considered by the brethren as the chief work was put to a committee of seven that a resolution might be prepared for it. The committee immediately adjourned and came back in a few minutes with the resolution formed that the Missionary Society be recommended to the support of the brethren, and that the managers of the American Christian Bible Society were requested to furnish the Missionary Society with Bibles. It was a good compromise move, but probably not too well pleasing to the managers of the Bible Society.

By the time of the afternoon session at two o'clock on this Thursday, October 25, the committee which had been appointed to draw up a constitution was ready to report They read their constitution slowly article by article and discussed each point. The name, upon which they had settled was, Christian Missionary Society Walter Scott wasn't particularly fond of the name, and suggested a more up to date name by recommending the word, American, be placed in front of the name. Scott's motion was carried, and the name now became, American Christian Missionary Society Before the session had been dismissed, E. B. Howels of Cincinnati gave one hundred dollars to make Alexander Campbell a life member of the Society.

The next morning, Friday morning, October 26, business was resumed as usual at nine o'clock. A motion was suggested whereby the Convention was asked to recommend to the churches that they not countenance as a preacher any man who was not approved and acknowledged by two or more churches. Another recommendation was suggested to the churches that they call in other men when ordaining their evangelists Carroll Kendrick objected on the ground this was an unscriptural move. John O'Kane didn't agree He argued that an evangelist was an officer of several congregations and not of one. Walter Scott agreed, and so went the meeting.

The entire convention lasted four days There were one hundred and fifty-six delegates who met in all The constitution which they accepted contained thirteen articles which are here given:

Article 1st. This Society shall be called the American Christian Missionary Society.

Article 2d. The object of this Society shall be to promote the spread of the gospel in destitute places of our own and foreign lands

Article 3d The Society shall be composed of annual delegates,

Life Members and Life Directors. Any church may appoint a delegate for an annual contribution of ten dollars. Twenty dollars paid at one time shall be requisite to constitute a member for life, and one hundred dollars paid at one time, or a sum which in addition to any previous contribution shall amount to one hundred dollars, shall be required to constitute a director for life.

Article 4th. The officers of the Society shall consist of a president, twenty vice-presidents, a treasurer, a corresponding secretary, and a recording secretary, who shall be elected by the members of the Society at its annual meeting.

Article 5th. The Society shall also annually elect twenty-five managers, who together with the officers and life directors of this Society, shall constitute an executive board, to conduct the business of the Society, and shall continue in office until their successors are elected, seven of whom shall constitute a quorum for the transaction of business.

Article 6th. Two of the vice-presidents, the treasurer, the secretaries, and at least fifteen of the managers shall reside in Cincinnati or its vicinity.

Article 7th The executive board shall have power to appoint its own meetings, elect its own chairman, enact its own by-laws and rules of order, provided always that they be not inconsistent with the Constitution; fill any vacancies which may occur in their own body, or in the offices of the Society during the year, and if deemed necessary by two-thirds of the members present at a regular meeting, convene special meetings of the Society. They shall establish such agencies as the interest of the Society may require, appoint agents and missionaries, fix their compensation, direct and instruct them concerning their particular fields and labors, make all appropriations to be paid out of the Treasury, and present to the Society at each annual meeting a full report of their proceedings during the past year.

Article 8th All moneys or other property contributed and designated for any particular missionary field, shall be so appropriated or returned to the donors, or their lawful agents.

Article 9th. The treasurer shall give bonds to such an amount as the executive board shall think proper.

Article 10th. All the officers, managers, missionaries and agents of the Society, shall be members in good standing in the churches of God.

Article 11th. The Society shall meet annually at Cincinnati on the first Wednesday after the third Lord's Day of October, or at such time and place as shall have been designated at the previous annual meeting.

Article 12th No person shall receive an appointment from the executive board, unless he shall give satisfactory evidence of his Christian character and qualifications.

Article 13th. No alteration of this constitution shall be made, without a vote of two-thirds of the members present at an annual meeting, nor unless the same shall have been proposed at a previous annual meeting, or recommended by the executive board

The chief weakness which later caused so much consternation in the restoration was to be found in Article 3d. This article made membership in the Society dependent upon the payment of money, which many looked upon as definitely a weakness. This will later come to our attention as this study proceeds.

Before closing the Convention, it was necessary to fill in all of the officers required by the Constitution. Alexander Campbell was already elected the president. Twenty vice-presidents had to be found. These were D. S. Burnet, Dr. Irwin, Walter Scott, T. M. Allen, W. K. Pendleton, John T. Johnson, John T. Jones, John O'Kane, Tolbert Fanning, Daniel Hook, E. Parmley, Francis Dungan, Richard Hawley, James T. Barclay, Francis Palmer, J. J. Moss, M. Moberley, William Rowzee, Alexander Graham, and William Clark. The corresponding secretary finally resolved itself upon James Challen. Recording secretary was George S. Jenkins and treasurer was Jesse B. Ferguson.

The managers selected included T. J. Melish, Gerge Tait, S. S. Clark, B. S. Lawson, T. J. Murdock, S. H. Hathway, Andrew Leslie, Lewis Wells, Thurston Crane, C. A. Gould, N. T. Marshall, R J Latimer, James Leslie, and W. A. Trowbridge The foreign managers were Samuel Church, George McMannus, R. L. Coleman, William Morton, P. S Fall, Elijah Goodwin, S. S. Church, A. Gould, Alexander Hall and Jesse B Ferguson

Before the convention closed, a motion was made which would allow each person an opportunity to become Life Members and Life Directors of the Society, according to the terms of the constitution. The brethren promptly responded and in a few minutes fifty-two persons were entered as Life Members by paying twenty dollars each Eleven were entered as Life Directors by paying one hundred dollars each All totaled there was $2,140 subscribed, and enough promised to make the finances of the first convention amount to over five thousand dollars.

After the Convention was over, D. S Burnet addressed a letter to Campbell, informing him that he had been elected as president. Burnet wrote ·

When Bro. Pendleton appeared in the convention and informed us that your absence occurred in consequence of illness, we doubly sympathized with you in an affliction, which was also a disaster to us, as it deprived the convention of your society and counsel. The convention over which you were elected president has requested me to assure you of their sympathy and prayers—a duty most genial to my feelings, the more especially as I can, in the same communication, contribute to your joy by announcing a happy issue of our meeting   About five thousand dollars was raised in money and pledges for our various enterprises but especially for the Bible and Missionary Societies, which shared about equally in the munificence   I never knew so fine a meeting   It lasted one week and filled us full of joy and love.   The representatives of the churches from abroad amounted to about two hundred [12]

Campbell himself seemed to be very much pleased with the results of the convention.   He wrote.

Denied the pleasure of having been present on this interesting occasion by an unusually severe indisposition.   I am peculiarly gratified with the great issues of deliberation.   Our expectations from the Convention have been more than realized.   We are much pleased with the result, and regard it as a very happy pledge of good things to come   The unanimity, cordiality, and the generous concurrence of the brethren in all the important subjects before them, was worthy of themselves and the great cause in which they were enlisted   Enough was done at one session, and enough to occupy our best energies for some time to come.   Bible distribution and evangelical labor—two transcendent objects of Christian effort most essential to the conversion of the world—deserve at our hand a very cordial and generous support [13]

Whether or not Alexander Campbell was entirely pleased with the results cannot be for certain told.   That the American Christian Missionary Society does not appear to coincide in every detail with what he wanted appears evident   Campbell had plead for more of an ecclesiasticism, organized on truly democratic principles, to devise ways and means of operation for the churches in all points of expediency   The Missionary Society was but one phase of the idea, and yet its organizers tried to steer it clear of any ecclesiasticism to direct the churches in order to avoid criticism   C L Loos wrote:

In all the discussions and acts of the convention, the strictest and most jealous care was taken never in the least degree to assume

[12]F M Greene, *Christian Missions and Historical Sketches,* p 67
[13]Alexander Campbell, "The Convention of Christian Churches," *Millennial Harbinger,* Third Series, Vol VI, No 12 (December, 1849), p 694

any ecclesiastical privileges   That assembly—composed of men who were in heart and soul 'revolutionary soldiers' in the good, early war against all ecclesiastical assumptions, and who were yet fresh and brave as ever in the defence of the cherished principles of freedom from the old fetters of ecclesiastical bondage—would have sprung to their feet to a man at the first attempt to usurp any ecclesiastical authority   Again and again, from the beginning to the end, clear voices were heard repudiating the very thought of such unauthorized purpose or action   This is a most noteworthy fact in the history of this assembly.[14]

Loos, throughout his life, was intimately connected with the Society, and bore a certain bias in favor of it.   It is not likely that the Society was ever as completely free from ecclesiasticism as the strength of his words would indicate.

Throughout the year, 1850, Campbell had much to say about the Missionary Society.   Early in the year he wrote

We have an organized Missionary Society—a committee of ways and means—and desire no more, at present, than to notice the foundation laid, on which we may build a glorious superstructure. In our next, we shall consider the field of labor, with our views of the ways and means by which it is to be cultivated.[15]

While in these articles that followed, Campbell appeared to be interested in pushing aside all criticism, yet some was to come, and with the passing of years was to increase.   The chief work of 1849 now had been done, the rubicon was crossed; the crisis had come.   A glance at the horizon ahead showed the gathering of dark clouds, but to escape them was impossible.   Straight toward them the course of events was moving.

---

[14]Charles L Loos, *First General Convention* (Guide Printing & Publishing Co, 1891), p 71.
[15]Alexander Campbell, "The Christian Missionary Society," *Millennial Harbinger,* Third Series, Vol VII, No 2 (February, 1850), p. 76.

CHAPTER X

ALEXANDER CAMPBELL AND THE
MISSIONARY SOCIETY

One of the most mooted questions coming out of this period of the restoration movement relates itself to the attitudes of Alexander Campbell toward the American Christian Missionary Society. The subject forms a great part of the controversy which, in years to come, was to be before the brotherhood. No study of the origin and early activities of the Society can be complete without a discussion of this controversial point.

The heat of such a controversy can be attributed to the high veneration in which Campbell has been held by all adherents to restoration principles. While such veneration is commendable, yet it has its dangers for too frequently is there a temptation to ascribe to Campbell a greatness of which he was not worthy. Indeed, it is the danger of the study of the whole restoration movement, for with many there seems to be a fundamental interest in restoring the restoration rather than the New Testament Church. In the restoration movement no authority of any kind is to be found. No man is qualified to intelligently approach the study unless he recognizes that those who played the important roles were just men, and liable to errors. We lose nothing in admitting that at times they were wrong, for there is only one authority—the New Testament scriptures. This study of the restoration movement is approached, not with the idea of attempting to fit any pioneer leader into a mold, but to study as objectively as possible what they did teach. Where they were wrong, we shall frankly state it, where they were right ,we shall gladly uphold it.

But those who favored and those who opposed the society back in the restoration movement held Campbell in the highest esteem. It was only natural that each should want to feel that Campbell favored his position. But what are the facts? While it is admitted that Campbell, in the period immediately preceding and following the establishment of the Society, favored this organization; yet, opposers of the Society feel that Campbell was then in old age, and was under the influence of younger men who swayed

181

him in favor of the Society   It was only natural that these younger men should deny this charge, and should stoutly defend Campbell as being in favor of Societies. To say the least of it, the problem is great, but yet not an impossible one. To get at all the facts the heart of the controversy which followed these earlier years is laid before us, and from these we draw what we believe are logical conclusions.

Perhaps the leading champion of the view that Campbell changed his position was David Lipscomb, who for years, following 1866, was editor of the *Gospel Advocate*. Lipscomb built this conviction upon two or three facts, the first of which was a statement made by Charles V. Segar that after 1847 Campbell was never again himself. It may be recalled that W. T. Moore undertook the work of gathering up some of Campbell's "Lectures on The Pentateuch" delivered at Bethany College in 1859 for publication. Moore assigned the task of introducing the book with a biography of Campbell to Mr. Segar of Cincinnati. Segar was not a member of the church, and to get his information paid a visit to Bethany to speak to the wife of Campbell. Segar, having Campbell's family as his authority, then wrote:

In 1847, Mr. Campbell made a tour to Europe, partly for his health, and partly to visit the congregations of his church in Great Britain. On reaching London he was the honored guest of our Minister at the Court of St James, Mr. Bancroft, and through him and through letters from the first men of this country, was the recipient of honors and attentions from the great leaders and molders of political opinion in England. Only in Scotland, in the city of Edinburgh, did any thing occur to mar the influence and pleasure of his trip   His position on the slavery question had been grossly misrepresented by a clergyman who was desirous to engage him in debate, but with whom Mr Campbell refused to hold any intercourse on account of his questionable character. The refusal, for the cause assigned, led to a recourse before the civil tribunals, on the part of the clergyman, in an action for libel, the final result of which was a verdict in Mr Campbell's favor. The labors and events of this tour, added to the burden of the college, seemed to have materially affected his mind and general health; but the deadliest portion mingled in his cup of baleful care and sorrow was the sad news which awaited his touching the shores of his adopted country. The son of his old age, the child of his prayers and hopes, was no more! Wyckliffe Campbell had been drowned at his father's mill! It is said by those who were near him, that Alexander Campbell never was equal to himself after this stroke; but it was long before the admiring world perceived any change.[1]

The closing statement, "It is said by those that were near him, that Alexander Campbell was never equal to himself after this shock," particularly impressed Lipscomb and was often used by him.

Still another fact that helped Lipscomb form the conviction that Campbell had changed was a statement made by Tolbert Fanning a few years after the Society was formed. Lipscomb was then a young man, an admirer of Fanning who had tutored him Fanning grew distressed at the course Campbell was taking in favor of the Society, and made a visit to him at Bethany. Speaking of Fanning's return, Lipscomb years later wrote:

I remember well, on his return he stated that he was shocked to find his (Campbell's) mind was so shaken that he could, with difficulty, keep it on one subject; that he could converse in general terms on things he had studied in the past, but that all power of close, connected reasoning was gone; that he had to be continually prompted to keep up an ordinary conversation.[2]

Thus Fanning helped mold Lipscomb's conviction.

Frequently in years to come advocates of the Society quoted Campbell as favorable to their position. When it happened, Lipscomb usually met the challenge and answered it The *Old Path Guide* in 1884 began running a series of articles showing Campbell's support of the Society. The *Guide* was edited by F. G. Allen, who took the position popular for many years in central Kentucky, that instrumental music was unscriptural but that the Society was scriptural. When the *Old Path Guide* first showed Campbell favorable to the Society, Lipscomb replied with a number of quotations from the *Christian Baptist*, showing Campbell to be apparently against Societies then. After these quotations, Lipscomb writes:

We might greatly multiply quotations showing his conviction of the unlawfulness of all associations or conventions or representative connections of the church, that they, inimical to the pure character and destruction of the work of the churches, were robbery of both God and the church of God This reaches over seventy years of his most effective advocacy of the supreme authority and supremacy of the word of God for all religious ends. That he afterward

[1]Charles V. Segar, *Familiar Lectures on the Pentateuch* (Cincinnati: Bosworth, Chase & Hall, Publishers, 1871), pp. 37, 38.
[2]David Lipscomb, "A Campbell and the Societies," *Gospel Advocate*, Vol XXVI, No 23 (June 4, 1884), p. 358.

worked in Societies we have no disposition to conceal, that in doing it, he violated his own principles, built again the society he destroyed and destroyed that supreme and undivided respect for the word of God, and his appointments which he had vindicated is beyond doubt, true It represents another case, so pregnant in the history of the church, opposing others, substituting the appointments of the institution of God, yet doing them himself [3]

Lipscomb goes on to point out that in later years Campbell's mind and will power lost much of their force and that his friends convinced him that these organizations were harmless, so he submitted

F. D Srygley, who in later years became a strong opponent of the Society, was in his earlier life in favor of it   Srygley wrote articles in the *Old Path Guide* in 1884 favoring the Society, and frequently answered Lipscomb's charges of Campbell   Srygley accused Lipscomb of saying that Campbell in 1849 was a "fool," and defended Campbell by showing he was an editor, college president, lecturer, and preacher. Lipscomb, however, was not to be shaken from his conviction. He asserted that Campbell still was a great preacher, but that in some respects he had declined.

Until the end, he could make speeches abounding in the general truths and principles he learned in his early manhood, but his power of applying them to present facts and theories, was gone. Srygley, at this time, followed the practice generally followed by advocates of the Society, compiling the names of great pioneer preachers who favored the society. But the weight of great names did not sway Lipscomb   He continued:

That appeal is a setting aside the authority of God by the wisdom and numbers of men   I am constrained to believe that no man ever made it except from a consciousness that the position could not be maintained by Divine authority. At what period of the world's history, have the learned, the institutions of learning, the wise, the scholars, the big preachers, the great popular crowds and currents, even in the church, been on the side of maintaining in its purity the word of God? Was it in the days of the Saviour? The doctors, they learned, the wise were against him.   . The learning and wisdom of the world. the educational centers, the professors, the preachers of earth, the great papers, are all against the whole movement back toward the apostolic ways [4]

On May 4, 1887 J W. Higbee of Mexico, Missouri began a

---

[3]David Lipscomb, "Solid Thoughts by Earnest Men," *Gospel Advocate,* Vol XXVI, No 17 (April 23, 1884), p 262
[4]David Lipscomb, "A Campbell and Missionary Society," *Gospel Advocate,* Vol XXVI, No 24 (June 11, 1884), p 374

series of articles on "Christian Unity." Higbee stressed three kinds of unity: (1) Unity of fellowship which is the recognizing of one as a member of the church. (2) Unity of thought and purpose. (3) Unity of plan or of method Under the third head he advocated the principle of liberty, and went on to gently upbraid those who stood in opposition to the society. In Lipscomb's answer there were many things said about the society and especially of the attitude men favorable to the society took. Lipscomb wrote:

Bro. Higbee never makes a protest against division, to those who introduce the occasion of this strife, so far as we can see, this impresses us all that the protest is more in the interest of building up the society than in peace So it destroys the force of the appeal for peace with us

Then again these Society brethren have always said they would be glad to see us at work without the Society. We have a long while doubted this We have been at work all the time, but as it has been at home, it has not been open to view. Since we have begun work by sustaining the Indian mission, and are making preparations to do other work at a distance, the bitterness toward us seems greatly increased—Brothers Garrison and Spencer —the two 'sweet-tempered' men, compare us to the hypocritical Pharisees who crucified the Saviour They can assign no reason for this charge than that we are trying to work in the way approved by God, and insist to depart from his way is to reject his authority. Hence, Brother Garrison says we are legalists, we dishonorably represent the brotherhood, remind him of the hypocritical Pharisees who persecuted the Saviour.

Accept God, Brother Higbee, as the only legislator in the church of God, and discussion and division will cease. Till then God demands the battle shall go on . [5]

Higbee was surprised to see his article answered. In his reply he politely accused Lipscomb of being old and of being reared in those dark and gloomy years of the 1840 decade, and therefore, blamed those years for giving to Lipscomb the attitude of seeing controversy in everything. In those early days the pioneers were fighting sectarianism so hard that they didn't have time to teach on missions. Higbee was thankful that he was a young man and therefore filled with the spirit of optimism. All who opposed the society were to Higbee skeptical and covetous. Lipscomb replied to Higbee by saying:

---

[5]David Lipscomb, "Brother Higbee's Article," *Gospel Advocate*, Vol XXIX, No 18 (May 4, 1887), pp 278, 279

Any society that takes from the churches of God, the work committed to them, or that transfers the control from the earnest, devoted elders to the young, the rich, who chiefly give their money to be seen of men, and disfranchises the poor from a voice in the work of spreading the gospel, is sinful in all shapes, principles and works [6]

Before long, in these articles, the subject of Alexander Campbell's change came up. Reference was made to W. K. Pendleton's speeches on this subject, which shall later be studied, and Lipscomb replies that he can see but two explanations to Pendleton's denial that Campbell had changed:

First, Mr Campbell denounced these societies when used by others in all their shapes and forms "as the man of sin, the son of perdition." When managed by him and his friends, they were all right. That is, he was so intoxicated by the idea he was president of one and it promoted his glory, that it blinded him to his life-long work and he from selfish motives approved what he had all of his life condemned, and he had not the candor to acknowledge this, but denied it   This is discreditable to his moral character. I am unwilling to believe it is true [7]

There were others who shared Lipscomb's conviction that Campbell had changed his conviction on the Society. L. F. Bittle for about fifteen years was one of the most forceful writers in the *American Christian Review.* He wrote considerably when Ben Franklin edited this journal and received the highest commendation from Franklin   Bittle wrote under the name B. F. Leonard, and at times contended for the view that Campbell changed. John F. Rowe, who followed Franklin as editor of the *Review,* likewise believed Campbell had changed   Rowe wrote:

Alexander Campbell favored the Society as simply representing the cooperation of the congregations, but he never went beyond that, as his writings in the *Harbinger* show   He was opposed to missionary societies composed exclusively of the clergy. He was opposed to complicated machinery. He was absolutely opposed to societies which assumed to dictate to congregations; which assumed to assess them; which assumed to try preachers and pronounce upon their fitness to preach; which assumed to take the control of colleges and other secular institutions, which assumed to read out preachers and congregations who would refuse to acquiesce in the measures and policies of the societies, which assumed to the as-

---

[6] David Lipscomb, "Brother Higbee's Article," *Gospel Advocate,* Vol. XXIX, No 23 (June 8, 1887), p 359
[7] David Lipscomb, "Higbee Reviewed," *Gospel Advocate,* Vol XXIX, No 33 (August 17, 1887), p 518

senting editors; which assumed to sequestrate church property, and to appoint courts of inquiry.   Alexander Campbell, while he had complete possession of his mental faculties, never wrote a syllable in favor of such ecclesiasticism.   He was in favor of the absolute equality of the brethren, and opposed to a system of things that would estimate the moral standing of a Christian in proportion to the amount of money he contributes to the society [8]

With these quotations one side of this great controversy has been unveiled.   Led by David Lipscomb, in the main, there was a group of brethren thoroughly convinced that Campbell had, from the days of the *Christian Baptist,* changed his views on the Society.   He was, in his older days, less the mental giant of his former and was therefore, an easy victim of younger men who influenced him in favor of the Societies, according to their point of view.   The other side, of course, had its champions who vigorously held to the conviction that Campbell had not changed.   On this side were many men, but the leader of the group was doubtlessly W. K. Pendleton. Pendleton was called upon to defend the Society and Campbell's position at two periods of crisis   In 1866 Ben Franklin threw the *American Christian Review* for the first time against the Society. The *Review* was at this time the most popular paper in the brotherhood, and its weight against the Society all but annihilated it The following year Pendleton was called upon to deliver an address before the Society in its defense, which address was printed in the *Harbinger.*   In 1869, as an appeasement policy to stop the opposition of the *Review,* the Society adopted the *Louisville Plan*   The *Review* backed the Society then for about a year under this plan, but then again opposed it.   By 1874 the Society had reached another low point, and Pendleton was called upon again to defend it.   Pendleton's speeches, especially that of 1866, give considerable attention to the subject of Campbell's so-called change.   It will be right to notice some of his remarks at this point.

There is a class among us, who have a sort of bibliolatry toward the Christian Baptist, and, as is usual in such cases, they imagine that it has uttered many oracles, which upon a more careful study it will be found, are not to be discovered on its pages.   This is especially the case, with reference to this subject of missions.   Early in the issue of this work, in the second number, the Editor declared that he did not intend to dwell much on this topic—and every one

---

[8]John F. Rowe, "Reminiscences of the Restoration," *American Christian Review,* Vol XXIX, No. 19 (May 6, 1886), p. 148

familiar with its pages, knows that this purpose was strictly ad-
hered to   Not only is the measure of interest which was given to
this subject greatly exaggerated, but the spring and main motive
of it, are almost universally misunderstood.   It must be remembered that in his early writings, he was engaged almost inces-
santly in the fiercest and closest conflicts with the various forms of
sectarianism, which surrounded him, and was as organizations,
both in their theory and their practice, he was deeply convinced,
were injurious to the highest interests of the church, and incum-
brances upon the primitive power of the Gospel   As such he
attacked them. 'Their missionary *plans*' was but one feature of
many, and this, as a *plan,* not as legitimate *purpose,* he criticised,
with a moderation and caution, however, which showed that he
desired to touch it but gently   His arrows were directed against
the *scheme'. . . .*[9]

It will be seen at once that Pendleton asserts that Campbell did
not change his views from the days of the *Christian Baptist.*
Campbell's objection to the missionary society, as voiced in this
early publication, Pendleton says, must be understood in the light
of the fact he was attacking the *abuse* and not the institution   This
appears to be the thought Pendleton was driving at, for his use of
the words, "plan," "purpose," and "scheme" might be misleading
Nobody ever accused Campbell of opposing missionary *work,* but
only the *plan* of doing it through the society.

Pendleton proceeds in the speech to which reference has been
made to point out Campbell's part in the early society. He says

When this Society was first formed, he was made its President,
and in this relation he continued, by the partiality of its members
and with his own consent, till he was called to join the congregation of the first-born in Heaven. From the first, he threw his
mighty influence in its favor   During the earlier months of 1849, in
the autumn of which year it was organized, he gave his pen and
the pages of the *Harbinger* liberally to prepare the way for its
adoption.

Having now the testimony of W. K. Pendleton before us, that of
Charles L Loos also is worthy of some consideration. Loos, for
several years was president of the Missionary Society as well as the
College of the Bible at Lexington, Kentucky. In 1891 Loos printed
a series of articles in the *Apostolic Guide* on the general theme of
the first missionary society, which articles were later compiled

---

[9]W K Pendleton, "Address by W K Pendleton," *Millennial Harbinger,*
Vol XXXVII, No 11 (November, 1866), pp 497, 498

into a book entitled, "Our First General Convention." Speaking of Alexander Campbell's part in the Society, Loos writes:

For years preceding the convention of 1849, this eminent man had been impressed with the urgent need of such national meetings, representative of the churches, their desires, their best intelligence and piety He felt that the time had come for the church to enter, in full cooperation, on such enterprises as were necessary to ex- ecute its great mission of extending the kingdom of the Messiah to the ends of the earth He held, in deepest conviction, that any enterprise of importance, which concerned the entire brotherhood and required and solicited their support—such, for example, as the gospel mission for the whole world at home and abroad—should only be established and directed by the combined will and wisdom of this same brotherhood, as far as such united action was possible and practicable This man of far-seeing judgment, whose heart was filled with the purest and deepest concern for the triumphant success of the great cause to which he had given his life, was in- tensely troubled when he saw, here and there, the lack of a spirit of union and cooperation among us in matters of vital moment The manifestations of a tendency to separate action, where unity was wisdom and was absolutely necessary for large success, to distrust, where generous confidence only was right and only could be blessed, the revelation of a morbid, narrow prejudice that hin- dered and resisted the free, legitimate development and action of the power of the church in great undertakings—a prejudice based upon ignorance of the law of liberty with which Christ has endowed his church—all this brought sorrow to his great heart, and stirred him up at times to strong remonstrance . .[10]

Loos proceeds to quote lengthy passages from the *Harbinger,* many of which are the same as the reader may find in the preceding chapter of this work

In the long debate which lay ahead over whether or not Campbell had changed his position, there were many others to enter into the discussion on both sides Pendleton and Loos have been sided on the one side and Lipscomb and Rowe on the other. Neither to be sure, ever seriously influenced the other Pendleton and Loos considered Lipscomb and Rowe as ignorant and prejudiced, while Lipscomb states his views on Pendleton's speech as follows:

But what of President Pendleton's assertion? During the years 1842-44 A Campbell wrote sixteen articles on 'Christian Organi- zation' In them are found the sentences quoted by President Pendleton, referred to be the *Old Path Guide* We read the

---

[10]C L Loos, *Our First General Convention,* pp 17-19

speech of President Pendleton when it was delivered; and we now say that speech was intended to convince the world that A. Campbell had changed his position on the subject, before the shock to his mental and will power came; and the investigation to which it led me, satisfied me of the very opposite.

... I esteem President Pendleton as a scholarly and conscientious man, but on this subject a prejudiced juror. I accept all he states as a witness. His conclusions, drawn from the facts I doubt.[11]

Having set forth the views of representative men pro and con as to Campbell's attitude toward the society, it is in order now to turn to some of the writings of Campbell, as found in the *Christian Baptist,* and other sources, to see if there is a discrepancy in his attitude Campbell says; speaking of the apostolic church:

The *order* of their assemblies was uniformly the same. It did not vary with moons and with seasons. It did not change as dress nor fluctuate as the manners of the times. Their devotion did not diversify itself into the endless forms of modern times. They had no monthly concerts for prayer; no solemn convocations, no great fasts, nor preparation, nor thanksgiving days. Their churches were not fractured into missionary societies, bible societies, education societies, nor did they dream of organizing such in the world. The head of a believing household was not in those days a president or manager of a board of foreign missions; his wife, the president of some female education society, his eldest son, the recording secretary of some domestic Bible society; his eldest daughter, the corresponding secretary of a mite society; his servant maid, the vice-president of a rag society; and his little daughter, a tutoress of a Sunday school They knew nothing of the hobbies of modern times. In their church capacity alone they moved. They neither transferred themselves into any other kind of association, nor did they fracture and sever themselves into divers societies. They viewed the church of Jesus Christ as the scheme of heaven to ameliorate the world, as members of it, they considered themselves bound to do all they could for the glory of God and the good of men. They dare not transfer to a missionary society, or bible society, or education society, a cent or a prayer, lest in so doing they should rob the church of its glory, and exalt the inventions of men above the wisdom of God. In their church capacity alone they moved Their church they considered 'the pillar and ground of the truth', they viewed it as the temple of the Holy Spirit, and the house of the living God. They considered if they did all they

---

[11]David Lipscomb, "Alexander Campbell and Missionary Societies," *Gospel Advocate,* Vol XXVI, No 31 (July 30, 1884), p. 487.

could in this capacity, they had nothing left for any other object of a religious nature [12]

The above article is a part of the first article written in the *Christian Baptist,* and is one which Lipscomb frequently quoted on the subject. The second issue of the *Christian Baptist* reveals, in part, the following:

The New Testament is the only source of information on this topic. It teaches us that the association called the church of Jesus Christ is, in *propria forma,* the only institution of God left on earth to illuminate and reform the world. That is, to speak in the most definitive and intelligible manner, a society of men and women, having in their hands the oracles of God; believing in their hearts the gospel of Jesus Christ; confessing the truth of Christ with their lips; exhibiting in their lives the morality of the gospel, and walking in all the commandments and ordinances of the Lord, blamelessly, in the sight of all men When spiritual man, i.e., men having spiritual gifts, or, as now termed, miraculous gifts, were withdrawn, this institution was left on earth, as the grand scheme of heaven, to enlighten and inform the world. An organized society of this kind, modelled after the plan taught in the New Testament, is the consummation of the manifold wisdom of God to exhibit to the world the civilizing, the moralizing, the saving light, which renovates the human heart, which elevates human character, and which prostrates in the dust, all the boasted expedients of ancient and modern times. The church of the living God is therefore styled the pillar and ground of the truth; or, as Macknight more correctly renders it, the pillar and support of the truth.[13]

Robert Richardson, Campbell's biographer, quotes Campbell's definition of the church, and those definitions bear directly upon the theme. Richardson quotes Campbell as having said:

I am taught from the Record itself to describe a church of Christ in the following words. It is a Society of disciples professing to believe the one grand fact, the Messiahship of Jesus, voluntarily submitting to his authority and guidance, having all of them in their baptism expressed their faith in him and allegiance to him, and statedly meeting together in one place to walk in all his commandments and ordinances This society, with its bishop or bishops, and its deacon or deacons, as the case may require, is perfectly independent of any tribunal on earth called ecclesiastical.[14]

---

[12]Alexander Campbell, "The Christian Religion," *Christian Baptist,* Vol I, No 1 (August 3, 1823), pp 6, 7

[13]Alexander Campbell, "How, Then, Is the Gospel to Spread Through the World?" *Christian Baptist,* Vol I, No 2 (September 1, 1823), pp 15, 16

[14]Robert Richardson, *Memoirs of Alexander Campbell,* Vol II, p 58

Campbell saw in ecclesiastical tribunals a transferring of the glory of the church to human organizations. So he wrote.

' Every Christian who understands the nature and design, the excellence and glory, of the institution called the *church of Jesus Christ,* will lament to see its glory transferred to a human corporation. The church is robbed of its character by every institution, merely human, that would ape its excellence and substitute itself in its place.[15]

Thus Campbell speaks out against human organizations which rob the church of its glory.

Great pains have been taken to compile the many quotations which bear on the subject of Campbell's proposed change Lipscomb and Rowe, with a host of others, on one side claimed he had changed his views since the days of the *Christian Baptist.* Pendleton and Loos, with another group on the other side, denied he had changed. From their remarks on the subject we have gone directly to see what Campbell did say in the *Christian Baptist.* These are the tools that are now before us. What conclusion shall we reach? Did Campbell change his position? What was the attitude of Campbell toward the Missionary Society?

Fortunately the student of restoration history can afford to be entirely objective in his approach Members of the churches of Christ are creed-bound to no man's views Strong and weak points held by her pioneer preachers in no sense alter the convictions which members hold, nor does the fact a weakness is admitted in any pioneer reflect upon the intelligence, honesty or character of that individual. The objective historian must be always in search of Truth Truth, to him, must be the Pearl of Great Price. The Truth cannot be dishonored in our quest to honor great pioneers. As honestly and objectively as we can, we shall seek only after the Truth.

In seeking to determine Campbell's attitude toward the Society, let us itemize some irrefutable facts that our conclusions may be drawn from these

(1) *Alexander Campbell was active in the Society and defended its existence* This fact is denied by no one. It is a matter of historical record that Campbell was the Society's first president, ' and that he defended the society until his death as a scriptural in-

---

[15] Cf Alexander Campbell, "Mr Robert Cautious," *Christian Baptist,* Vol I (1823), p 33

stitution. On September 12, 1849, six weeks before the convention met, Campbell was sixty-two (perhaps sixty-one) years old It is admitted by all that from this time to his death Campbell was a firm believer in the Society.

(2) *Alexander Campbell never himself believed that he had changed his conviction on the Missionary Society* This fact must certainly bear some weight A man sixty-two years old is not ordinarily in his dotage It is most reasonable to expect that if he had changed Campbell would have been aware of it If Campbell had been aware of it, he would have doubtlessly admitted it

The first person to accuse Campbell of having changed his views from the days of the *Christian Baptist* was Jacob Creath, Jr In 1850 Creath wrote to Campbell·

Now, permit me, my dear brother, to say to you in all kindness and candor, that your brethren who now oppose conventions, and who have opposed them since they entered this Reformation, are equally sorry to find you and others opposing conventions in the great platform you laid down for us in the *Christian Baptist,* and now to find you and them, advocating conventions as zealously as you then opposed them If you were right in the *Christian Baptist,* you are wrong now. If you are right now, you were wrong then.[16]

Campbell, however, remarks:

This objection, and all this alleged antagonism between the *Christian Baptist* and the *Millennial Harbinger,* are disposed of, or, rather, annihilated, by one remark, viz.· *convention* indicates merely a coming together for any purpose Such is its established meaning. Hence, a convention may be either scriptural or unscriptural, consistent or inconsistent with Christian law and precedent, good or evil, just as the end or object for which it is constituted, or for which it assembles [17]

It is clear, then, that Campbell was not conscious of having changed his position His statement above indicates that his opposition to conventions was not intended to be an opposition to any and all conventions, but to those that were improperly run and were abusing their own existence

Yet, it must be admitted, that the reasoning of Creath, and later, of Lipscomb and others was certainly not far-fetched A careful reading of Campbell's remarks in the *Christian Baptist* certainly indicates that he was opposing conventions, missionary

---

[16]Jacob Creath, "Conventions—No V," *Millennial Harbinger,* Third Series, Vol VII, No 11 (November, 1850), p 637

[17]Alexander Campbell, *ibid ,* p 638

societies, etc. as such. If lurked away in Campbell's own mind was the thought that he was only opposed to their abuses, it may be fairly said that probably few of his readers got that idea   Nevertheless, it is fair to Campbell to understand his former statements in the light of his own explanation, and admit that he was only fighting their abuses.

(3) *Alexander Campbell favored the principle of the missionary society before 1847.* David Lipscomb, borrowing from Charles V. Segar, alleged that in 1847 Campbell's mind was affected so that he could never reason as closely after that as before. This was caused by his imprisonment in Scotland and the drowning of his son, Wycliffe. Yet, it must be admitted that before this time, Alexander Campbell favored the principle of human organizations such as underlay the missionary society. Campbell admits that he was displeased with the abandonment of the Mahoning Baptist Association in 1830. Beginning the following year, he wrote much favoring cooperation meetings which were but missionary societies on a smaller basis. Throughout his life Campbell showed himself to be a friend and advocate of organizations. He attended state and district cooperation meetings and at times held offices in them.

References in the preceding chapter will show that Campbell advocated a general organization for the churches. It is true that he did not use general organization as synonymous with missionary societies. Campbell thought that the general organizations should include more than missionary societies, and in fact that every phase of the interests of the church as a whole which could not be handled by local congregations should be handled by the general organization. Missionary societies were but one phase of this total organization   Nevertheless, the *principle* involved in a missionary society and the *principle* in the general organization were the same. This being true, it is unlikely that the happenings of 1847 influenced Campbell's thinking on missionary societies especially when the principle undergirding the society was a definite part of his conviction before this year

(4) *Alexander Campbell did not criticize brotherhood organizations before 1847.* If Alexander Campbell had been against human organizations before the year 1847, it would be logically expected that he should lift his voice against them. Yet, with the exception of his articles in the *Christian Baptist,* Campbell did not

lift his voice against the human organizations arising all about him in the church.   State organizations were being formed very early, yet Campbell failed to criticize these organizations.   Almost his only criticism came against the American Christian Bible Society, but it is noticeable that this opposition was only on the ground that Burnet had not sufficiently consulted the brotherhood, not because Campbell thought the Society, as such, was unscriptural in its existence.

As fairly and honestly, as we can read Campbell's writings on the subject of human organizations, we are convinced that Campbell favored them even before 1847.   His writings in the *Christian Baptist* are somewhat mystifying.   Taken at their face value and for what they say on the surface they most certainly seem to oppose the missionary societies as unscriptural in their existence. Our only recourse is to take Campbell's own explanation as the answer, and if we err, let it be on the side of charity.   However, the many articles which appear from his pen in the *Millennial Harbinger* from 1830 on down show a particular bias in favor of all human organizations in the church, and on this testimony, we base our conviction that Campbell did favor these organizations. Nevertheless, as previously stated, we feel no particular embarrassment for taking this position.   Campbell is not our authority. He was a great man, but withal, a man, with the same tendency to err as others   That he was wrong in advocating these organizations, we believe most deeply, but that he nevertheless was friendly to them is a fact against which we cannot argue.

Campbell believed in them, but Campbell was wrong.   This is our conviction.

CHAPTER XI

GROWING OPPOSITION

Scarcely had the American Christian Missionary Society been organized when a wave of opposition began sweeping over the brotherhood. This opposition came from various localities and for various reasons, but many, it seemed, looked upon the establishment of the society as a dangerous trend in the restoration, some avowing that it was definitely unscriptural. Some viewed with mild alarm the establishment of the Society and issued gentle warnings against it J. B Ferguson of Nashville, Tennessee, editor of the *Christian Magazine* comments at the close of 1849 that "the mails of the past week have brought to us letters from some of almost every class of laborers in the Lord's vineyard, and of every variety of talent and acquirement, urging us, by appeals to the highest and purest motives, to lift our voice against the *present dangerous tendency of the Reformation !*"[1] One brother wrote to Ferguson

I consider our recent movements contrary to the teaching and usages of the Primitive Disciples; and so far as they are carried into operation, a trespass upon the free privileges of every Disciple of Christ; tending to a most hateful assumption of power, and that it is now the imperative duty of every sincere Disciple of Christ to throw himself in the breach if he would not lose everything that has been gained by our severest struggles[2]

There were some during the early years who looked with suspicious eye upon the Society, who were not thoroughly convinced that it was scriptural, but who for the sake of peace gave in to the majority of brethren. James M. Mathes, one of Indiana's leading pioneer preachers, was editor of the *Christian Record* Soon after the establishment of the Society, Mathes wrote:

A Missionary Society was formed for the spread of the gospel in our own and foreign lands. This is quite an important measure We have always been in favor of sending the gospel to the destitute at home and abroad, but our own plan was to do all this through the church, as such But as the brethren of the Indiana State

---

[1] J B Ferguson, "Fear of Consolidation—Independence of Individual Churches," *Christian Magazine*, Vol III, No 7 (July, 1850), p. 207.
[2] J B Ferguson, "Fear of Consolidation—Independence of Individual Churches," *Christian Magazine*, Vol III, No 7 (July, 1850), p 207.

Meeting, and those composing the general Convention, have thought proper to organize a Society for this object, we acquiesce [3]

There were many brethren in the church who took the attitude of Mathes. They would not be the cause of contention or division, so they reasoned, and therefore, would not press their opposition. In years to come David Lipscomb declared that he believed that Ben Franklin would never have thrown his influence at first behind the Society except for the fact that he lived in the part of the nation where the Society was popular and therefore, acquiesced against his better judgment. That Franklin at first defended the Society is evident. In the years, 1858-59 Franklin conducted a discussion in the columns of the *American Christian Review* with D. Oliphant of Brighton, Canada West. Oliphant edited a paper called the *Christian Banner*. In years to come Franklin adopted many of the arguments of Oliphant and used against the Society, but during these years, he defended the Society's existence

Nevertheless, it is plain that the core of Franklin's reasoning in these early years was sound. In years to come Franklin admits that he tried for the sake of peace to defend the Society even when in his own mind he was not sure of his position. Franklin shows that he is thinking along the right line when, shortly after establishing the *American Christian Review*, he writes·

We are perfectly aware that if we wish to put the Christian communities into the power of men, to control them, wield them, and make them engines to honor man, we need some kind of an organization, beyond the simple organization of the New Testament, but the simple, independent church, for keeping the ordinances, religious instruction, and saving the world, is all-sufficient for the good of the saints and the glory of God. Indeed, one of the principal reasons why this question of organization has perplexed the minds of so many is, that they are looking for, and trying to make out of something unknown to the whole New Testament They overlook the simple, easy and common-sense arrangement of the New Testament, and complain that we have no arrangement. It is amusing to see the different routes by which brethren have attempted to arrive at the same conclusion, on this point One brother sets out gravely to show scripture authority for such an organization as is desirable, and claims that he finds abundant authority for it. Another looks over the matter, and is satisfied that he has failed. He throws all that plan aside, and claims that the whole matter is left to human prudence and descretion, and that

---

[3]James M Mathes, "The Great Convention," *Christian Record,* Vol VII, No 6 (December, 1849), p 178.

we need no authority for it, any more than to build a house of worship, or send out a missionary to a certain field of labor.[4]

The last idea—that no more authority is needed than that to build a house of worship—is reminiscent of the attitude of Campbell, who placed such human organizations on the par of expediency. Consequently, Campbell wrote:

I do not place meeting-houses, pews or hymn books, on a footing with civil government or the church of God! The building of a meeting house is as conventional as a Bible Society or a missionary society; and he that opposes the one, should, on all his premises and logic, oppose the other.[5]

When the news of the establishment of the Missionary Society reached the churches, most of them concurred with the action, but some read carefully the constitution to see whether or not the Society was worth their backing. At once there was opposition from a few congregations on various grounds. Some did not agree that membership should be contingent upon the payment of money. Others thought the establishment of the society was, to say the least of it, a dangerous thing because of its possibility of disrobing the churches of their independence, and of its danger of becoming an ecclesiastical tribunal. Some considered these societies a departure from the earlier restoration principles, and the very existence of them as sinful. The church at Connelsville, Pennsylvania seems to have objected on all three counts. A list of ten resolutions was sent by the Connelsville church to the various periodicals, declaring the congregation's convictions on the Society. Of the ten resolutions, articles four, five and six are especially significant.

4th. That, conscientiously, we can neither aid nor sanction any society, for this or other purposes, apart from the church, much less one which would exclude from its membership many of our brethren, and all of the apostles, if now upon the earth, because silver and gold they had not.

5th That we consider the introduction of all such societies a dangerous precedent—a departure from the principles for which we have always contended as sanctioning the chapter of expediency —the evil and pernicious effects of which the past history of the church fully proves.

---

[4]Benjamin Franklin, "Clerical Organization," *American Christian Review,* Vol I, No 4 (April, 1856), p 116

[5]Alexander Campbell, "Conventions—No III," *Millennial Harbinger,* Third Series, Vol. VII, No. 9 (September, 1850), p. 501

6th That we also consider them necessarily heretical and schismatical, as much so as human creeds and confessions of faith, when made the bonds of union and communion.[6]

In commenting upon their resolutions the Connelsville church agrees "that the church of Jesus Christ is; in constitution and design, essentially missionary, we conceive to be an axiomatic truth. Not *a* missionary society, but emphatically and preeminently *the* missionary society—the only one authorized by Jesus Christ or sanctioned by the apostles " In anticipating certain arguments the congregation further said:

We know it is thought by some, that these Societies are not separate and apart from the church, but part and parcel of her. But by a little reflection, it will be seen, that although they may be entirely composed of members of the church, (which is not often the case,) yet they are separate and distinct from her; as much so as any Free Mason or Temperance Society composed of church members Her president is not the president of any of them; her constitution is not the constitution of any of them; her laws are not their laws, she has an initiatory *rite*—*they* have initiatory *fees;* and but comparatively few of her members are members of any or all of them. Hence, it follows that they are distinct organizations, separate and apart from the church.[7]

After the report of the convention of 1849 reached the ears of the churches in Detroit, a very similar action was taken there. Their report, signed by a committee, was dated January 6, 1850 and was forwarded to the *Ecclesiastical Reformer*. The report said in part:

That while we thus approve of the Preamble to the Bible Society, its objects and the objects of the Missionary Societies, yet we are sorry that we cannot also approve of the constitutions themselves, inasmuch as they create new organizations, distinct from, and in some respects, independent of the churches; which we believe to be contrary to the teaching of God's holy word, and also to the example of the churches under the guidance of the apostles; a returning to these being the express object, and avowed intention of those calling themselves the Disciples of Christ, in

---

[6]A. Shallenberger, L L Norton, E Holliday, "The Christian Missionary Society," *Millennial Harbinger,* Third Series, Vol. VII, No. 5 (May, 1850), p. 282.

[7]Colin Campbell, Alexander Linn, John E Dixon, "Action of the Church in Detroit, Michigan, Respecting Our Bible and Missionary Societies," *Ecclesiastical Reformer,* Vol III, No 2 (January 19, 1850), pp 139, 140

these latter days, the accomplishment of which is our heart's desire and prayer to God [8]

Meanwhile in Virginia, a meeting was held May 4, 1850 at Emmaus in Caroline County to discuss cooperating with this new society. This general meeting of the churches found several objections to the Society   Their opposition was worded as follows:

. . . the principle of membership recognized by them, which admits members by virtue of *pecuniary consideration,* (the sum of one dollar,) and not by virtue of any appointment by, or authority from their respective churches, and secondly, on the ground that they admit Christians, Jews and Infidels, as members—thereby amalgamating the church and the world   We further object to the provisions for life-membership, which makes an invidious and unchristian distinction between the rich and the poor in the kingdom of our Lord; . . .

It may be seen that one of the strongest objections, voiced from many quarters to the Society, was the fact that membership was made contingent upon the payment of specified amounts of money. Some argued that this would immediately make it impossible for either the Lord or His apostles to have belonged to the Society since "silver and gold had they none." Anything that would exclude the Lord would exclude them, they argued   This particular objection to the Society was to be a source of worry to the Society for many years to come

Advocates of the Society, however, did not take the objections without some struggle   D S Burnet accepts the challenge which the church ot Connelsville seemed to be hurling out by a strongly-worded answer.   Burnet says:

I was born into the missionary spirit, and did not relinquish it when I associated myself with my present brethren   Before I was eighteen years of age, I was one of the Secretaries at the first session and at the formation of the Ohio Baptist Convention for missionary purposes, and the Bible and missionary causes have lain near my heart from before that time to the present [9]

It was not without some foundation that in future years brethren who opposed societyism complained that the Society was born in the heart of D S. Burnet, who, when he left the Baptist Church, was not thoroughly converted to the cause of restoration but

[8] P Woolfolk, R Y Henley, "Missionary and Bible Societies," *Millennial Harbinger,* Third Series, Vol VII, No 7 (July, 1850), p 415
[9] D S Burnet, "Reply to the Connelsville Letter," *Christian Magazine,* Vol III, No 6 (June, 1850), p 173

brought with him a part of his Baptist practices. To the charge that the preaching of the gospel must not be left to an organization separate and apart from the church, Burnet says that this is a lack of understanding of the *direct* and *indirect* influences of the church   Burnet contended that Christians had an influence outside the local church, and therefore, could work through such societies. He proceeds to lay down the charge, as others after him were so often wont to do, that those who oppose the Societies were those who wanted to do-nothing in the church   This charge, although often made, was generally recognized by the more thinking brethren to be a stronger appeal to prejudice than to reason   No group of men established more churches, baptized more people, than those who commonly objected to the societies   Their work was generally of a less sensational nature, and consequently, got less publicity   But they were anything else but men who did nothing.

Even though objections were raised by these congregations, yet, the chief war against the Missionary Society was fought by Jacob Creath, Jr   in the months immediately following the society's establishment   At first Creath was evidently trying to be diplomatic   His early articles were but lengthy quotations from Dr. W E Channing of Boston, who had written much against Conventions   These articles in addition to Creath's comments, furnished his first objections   As time went on Creath become bolder and laid the charges directly down himself   Creath's first quotations from Channing served to point out the dangers and disadvantages of conventions   It was charged that the few did everything, and soon had the tendency of becoming despotic. Campbell's reply was that the abuse of a thing did not argue against the thing itself   By this rule, Campbell reasoned, the church itself should be opposed since it is a convention   Conventions, he pointed out, may err, but do not necessarily do so [10]

It has already been seen that some brethren who really in sentiment were opposed to the society, acquiesced because this was the course the majority of the brethren took.   Such an attitude did James M Mathes have, as already has been seen   Yet, Creath was an independent thinker and actor   To sustain such societies be-

---

[10]Alexander Campbell, "Dr William E Channing's Opinions of Conventions," *Millennial Harbinger,* Third Series, Vol VII, No 7 (July, 1850), pp 408-412.

cause the brethren agreed to them meant little to Creath. Consequently, he writes:

As to the argument offered to sustain these associations— that they are acceptable to our brethren—we would say, that they have been *unacceptable* to them until recently What has produced this change in them? What new light is this which has sprung up so recently upon this subject? I confess I have no more light now, upon the subject of associations, than I had twenty-five years ago. Will these brethren, who have been so recently and suddenly converted from their former faith upon this subject, furnish us with a small portion of this new light, that **we** may be converted too? I suppose the golden calf was acceptable to all the Jews, *except Moses.* I believe the calves set up at Dan and Bethel were popular with Jereboam and the ten tribes. The report of the spies was acceptable to all the Jews, *except Caleb and Joshua.* The pope is very acceptable to the Catholics; so are creeds and clerical conventions to all the Protestant parties. But does all of this prove that they are acceptable to God?[11]

Campbell had argued that the abuse of a thing does not argue against the thing itself. Creath says this is the same argument that the liquor traffic and that opium eaters have always put up. He writes:

Your saying that conventions have not *always erred,* is a tacit admission that they have *generally erred,* that they have done more injury than good to truth; that good men ought not to use them; that they are dangerous weapons, that safety is on the side of abstinence.[12]

Campbell had said that the church itself was a convention and therefore to argue against conventions was to argue against the church. Creath answers:

You place conventions on a level with the church of God and civil governments From the Acts of the Apostles, we have authority for the organization of all the early Christian churches. Paul says the governments that exist are ordained of God—Rom. ch. 13. Now, if you will produce as good authority for conventions as I have for the congregations of God and civil governments, *I will yield* the controversy to you.

Creath is forceful in demanding of Campbell apostolic authority that authorized the use of conventions

---

[11]Jacob Creath, Jr, "Dr William E Channing's Opinions of Conventions —No. II," *Millennial Harbinger,* Third Series, Vol VII, No. 8 (August, 1850), pp. 470, 471.

[12]Jacob Creath, "Conventions—No III," *Millennial Harbinger,* Third Series, Vol VII, No 9 (September, 1850), p 496

You say that our Saviour and the apostles did not denounce conventions, as such. Did they denounce Popery or corrupt Protestantism, as such? Did they denounce infant baptism, or creed making, or auricular confession, as such? It is for you to show where they *authorized* conventions.

The heart of Creath's argument lay in his insistence that there was no scripture authorizing the use of conventions. He writes again:

. . . it will be seen that, in this discussion, the advocates of conventions have *totally abandoned* the rule on which we and all Protestants set out—that the Bible alone is the religion of Protestants. They have not produced one passage of scripture, to countenance these assemblies from the New Testament [13]

Again Creath argues in the same article:

Because God our Father *divinely commissioned* his Son to our world, and his Son sent the apostles as missionaries to the world, and they *divinely organized* individual congregations all over the Roman empire, in the first century, does it, therefore, follow, that we in the nineteenth century, without any *divine warrant,* and contrary to our own rule of faith, have the right to call conventions, from Bible, missionary, and tract societies, elect popes, and do all other things we wish? My logic does not run that way. They had divine credentials for what they did. We have none for what we are doing That is the difference between them and us

Society advocates had long argued that their idea of a society was not one that would disrobe the church of its own independent right of action. Societies were not to be legislative tribunals, but mere organizations through which the churches could work to do their missionary work John T. Johnson had early favored the Society and had even introduced the resolution at the first convention saying the society was scriptural. Yet, Johnson was careful to oppose any type of organization that would be over the churches. Shortly before his death, Johnson wrote:

The congregation plan is the divine arrangement It works best It accomplishes most good, by calling forth all the energies and resources of each congregation, and the least injury is the result . . .

I am yet to learn that an ecclesiastical establishment, by its messengers, has the divine right to select and ordain evangelists, to sit in judgment on evangelists, on congregations and their difficulties; to try heresies, to declare fellowship, non-fellowship, etc, etc.[14]

---

[13]Jacob Creath, "Conventions—No IV," *Millennial Harbinger,* Third Series, Vol VII, No 11 (November, 1850), p 615.

[14]John T. Johnson, "Communication from Elder J. T. Johnson," *American Christian Review,* Vol. II, No 1 (January, 1857), p. 28.

When Tolbert Fanning found himself in conflict with George W.
Elley of Kentucky over the Society in 1857, Elley was quick to point
out that the Kentucky State Society had no ecclesiastical powers
whatever   Elley wrote:

The State Meeting of Ky claims no authority over any congregation, nor do they exercise any control over any evangelist farther
than to direct him to the proper field of labor, connected with
such other objects as belong exclusively to the work of their voluntary agents   No church is bound either to send money or messengers, and consequently it can have no existence or executive rule
only as they are pleased to give it [15]

When, therefore, Jacob Creath argues that the Society possessed
the potential danger to the church of becoming an ecclesiastical and
legislative body, Campbell was quick to defend the independence
of the church.   He answered Creath by saying:

I have indeed, since I became a writer, always opposed, do now
oppose, and I presume so far as to say, that I am likely always to
oppose, all ecclesiastic, associational, conventional, or synodic meetings, to legislate for the church, or any form of sound words or
sound doctrine, enacting new formulas of church ethics, church
politics, or church enactments, or anything called morality or
church polity.   But because other men, in other times, have, in
running out of Babylon, run past Jerusalem, I have endeavored
till now, and will always, I presume, simply endeavor to run into
Jerusalem   I am glad to opine and hope that our good, gifted, and
well informed Brother Creath, will not, with Dr. Channing or any
other popular and gifted man, run off into an extreme, or into
inappreciable tangents, or into mere metaphysical disquisitions [16]

The weight of Alexander Campbell's name served the purpose
to subdue very great opposition to the Society for a time, and
was a powerful recommendation for it to many people.   The objections of Jacob Creath in addition to those of the Connelsville
church and the Detroit church were about the only voiced for
some time.   The minutes of the Society's annual meetings and the
addresses of the correspondent secretaries show that the Society
was not receiving the financial backing that it needed.   Several of
the major addresses during the decade of the 1850's breathe an
atmosphere of depression   To bolster its influence the Society tried

[15]G W Elley, "no title," *Gospel Advocate,* Vol III, No 7 (July, 1857),
p 213
[16]Alexander Campbell, "Response to Dr Channing—No II," *Millennial
Harbinger,* Third Series, Vol VII, No 9 (September, 1850), p 495

discarding the article from the constitution, making membership dependent upon the payment of stipulated amounts of money, but this availed little It is evident, then, that much of the opposition to the Society made itself known, not by public remonstrance but through indifference and refusal to support it on the part of the churches

Tolbert Fanning had for a number of years doubted the wisdom and scripturalness of human organizations. But while the doubt was, still rolling in his mind, and before it settled down to a stern conviction, Fanning gave at least lip devotion to these organizations At times he even strongly defended them as he did in the case of the American Christian Bible Society. Fanning frequently attended the Cooperation Meetings in Tennessee, and apparently encouraged them There is no question that Fanning wanted to be convinced that human organizations were right if he could be convinced conscientiously He attended the great convention of 1849 in Cincinnati in the hope that he might see or hear something to settle his doubts in favor of the Society, but he came away as great a doubter as ever His troubles in Nashville over the speculations of J B. Ferguson occupied almost all his thought from 1852 to 1855, and he doubtless had little time to give the subject as thorough an examination as he intended When, in July, 1855, he and William Lipscomb established the *Gospel Advocate,* he had hopes that the *Advocate* might be used for a free discussion of the subject of human organizations pro and con Fanning had hopes that through this means the truth might be unveiled so that brethren might become settled either for or against and thus go forward on a united front Consequently he writes

In establishing 'The Gospel Advocate,' I determined by the help of the Lord, to give the subject of cooperation a thorough examination I do not pretend to say how it has been brought about, but I have for years believed that a change must take place in our views of cooperation, before we can labor to each other's advantage, or to the honor of God [17]

The *Gospel Advocate* began as a monthly in July, 1855 Throughout the first year and a half of its publication Fanning found nothing at all to ease his doubts as to human organizations

---

[17]Tolbert Fanning, "Cooperation," *Gospel Advocate,* Vol I, No 4 (October, 1855), p 110

His observations upon the conduct of the brethren and the influence of the Society but more and more convinced him that the church was being pushed in the background for the Society and that advocates of the Society were depending and exalting more and more human wisdom in the place of divine revelation. His convictions were moulded and more and more he presented them through the columns of the *Advocate* to see if they would stand the test of critical analysis and argumentation. In February, 1857 he writes:

We regard the church of Christ as the only divinely authorized Bible, Missionary and Temperance Society on earth; and furthermore, we believe that it is in and by means of the church the world is to be converted, and Christians are to labor for the Lord   . In all the efforts to do the service of the Lord through human institutions, it has seemed to us that the church is degraded, and rendered indeed useless.[18]

Three months later he wrote again:

We believe and teach that the Church of Christ is fully competent to most profitably employ all of our powers, physical, intellectual, and spiritual; that she is the only divinely authorized Missionary, Bible, Sunday School, Temperance and Cooperation Society on earth. It is, has been, and we suppose always will be our honest conviction, that the true and genuine service of God can be properly performed only in and through the church. Hence, we have questioned the propriety of the brethren's efforts to work most successfully by means of State, district, and county organizations, 'Missionary,' 'Publication,' and 'Bible Societies' or 'Bible Unions,' 'Temperance Societies, Free-Mason and Odd-Fellowship Societies' to 'visit' the fatherless and widows in their affliction, or any other human organization for accomplishing the legitimate labor of the church.[19]

Still again Fanning goes on to say:

The church, as we have often said, is Heaven's missionary society to a suffering world, and the ministers commissioned, sent out and supported by the church, are God's missionaries to call sinners to life   We have not been able to see the necessity of a missionary society beyond the church   We ask the brethren, in all kindness, if it would not be better even to send our beloved, Brother, Dr Barclay and his most amiable, intelligent and really accomplished family, to Jerusalem, by the agreement and cooperation of the churches than by another and strange body.

[18]Tolbert Fanning, "The American Christian Missionary Society at Cincinnati, Ohio," *Gospel Advocate*, Vol III, No 2 (February, 1857), p. 43
[19]Tolbert Fanning, "Missions and Missionaries," *Gospel Advocate*, Vol III, No 5 (May, 1857), p 130.

Fanning's purpose was to glorify the church instead of human organizations and to glorify divine revelation instead of human wisdom. It was only to be expected that he should have an influence far and wide, especially among the readers of the *Advocate.* One evidence of this was to be found in Tennessee itself. Up to this time the churches in the state had followed the general practice of organizations such as was characteristic of other states. Tennessee churches had their cooperation meetings, and finally, their State Meetings much as other states. By 1857 these meetings were beginning to lose some ground as brethren became filled with doubts as to their use. That year William Lipscomb attended the Mountain District Cooperation Meeting. After the meeting, he wrote:

While there was no special discussion of church cooperation, still we think that the disposition manifested by many of the brethren was clearly for the supremacy of the church of Christ in opposition to all other organizations. There are some few of the brethren I think who do not yet see exactly how they can get along without a little human machinery, but we hope that these will soon see the way clearly.[20]

Some were looking with less and less favor upon the usual arguments of society advocates stressing the need of better organization. S B. Giles of Austin, Texas wrote in the *Advocate* in 1857:

Throughout the length and breadth of the land, there seems be a manifest desire for a better organization. All the delinquencies of churches and individuals, are charged to bad organization, or the want of organization. While I admit our organization is not perfect, still I think there are some other causes that retard our progress. . . I think I see a manifest disposition with some, to adopt a system of organization that will create hireling priests and a clerical dominion I venture the assertion that those who are loudest in their complaints and clamor most for organization, are those who have made the least sacrifices in support of Christianity, and would be the first to accept the gown and salary. Such are always deploring our lukewarmness and inefficiency, and lauding the order, zeal, and progress of some of the sects That there is some departure from Gospel purity and relaxation in devotion by the brotherhood, I think requires but little sagacity to discover.[21]

---

[20]William Lipscomb, "Mountain District Cooperation," *Gospel Advocate,* Vol III, No 1 (January, 1857), pp 26, 27

[21]S B Giles, "Signs of the Times," *Gospel Advocate,* Vol III, No 1 (January, 1857), pp 17, 18

The *Gospel Advocate* during these early years of its existence very frequently discussed the issue of human organizations Sometimes the issue dealt with the Society, sometimes with Cooperation Meetings,'and at least once with an Educational Society. In all cases the very principle was the same . does a human organization have the right to usurp the work of the church? Fanning was answering, no. Early in the year, 1856, Fanning found himself in a controversy with George W. Elley, a popular Kentucky preacher. The churches in Kentucky had organized the Kentucky Christian Education Society. This society was to select worthy young men, pay their tuition, and send them to one of the colleges. To this Fanning objected saying, "Our experience is unfavorable to educating men in the schools with the view of making preachers of them."[22] It must be made clear that what Fanning was opposing was the existence of theological seminaries. He believed in the education of youth, and in teaching the Bible in educational institutions, but theological seminaries with him were different. At any rate, an unnamed Kentucky correspondent, noting the move on the part of the Education Society, saw a danger and wrote, saying

We move in Kentucky with a steady step toward a hierarchy as unscriptural as that of Rome, or England, and the preachers who seek to make themselves the Church, appear to think all is well It seems that some are endeavoring to degrade the Church into an auxiliary to the more than foolish societies of our age and country. [23]

This statement—which later was shown to be written by W. G. Roulhac of Hickman, Kentucky—drew the ire of Elley Elley defended the organization by admitting it was a human organization and had the right to exist on the grounds of expediency. To this Fanning replied and went to the core of the trouble.

Bro. George W Elley admits that the Kentucky State Cooperation is a human organization It would be well for the brethren to decide the question as to the utility of such organizations to keep the church alive Can she perform her mission on earth without the aid of human legislation? Can the churches of

---

[22]Tolbert Fanning, "The Kentucky C M Education Society," *Gospel Advocate*, Vol II, No 6 (June, 1856), p 168

[23]G W Elley, "Reply to Certain Remarks in Reference to Real or Supposed Errors in the Managements of Brethren in Kentucky by a Kentuckian," *Gospel Advocate*, Vol II, No 10 (October, 1856), p 316

Christ cooperate as churches without converting them into human establishments? This embraces all the controversies of the age Settle this point and all sincere religionists will become one [24]

This series of discussions between Fanning and Elley continued through the columns of the *Advocate* for some time. To Fanning's criticism that human organizations had no authority to assume to do the work of the church Elley replied by asking for scriptural authority for two or more congregations uniting their efforts to send the gospel to destitute places. Fanning cited such scriptures as 2 Cor. 8: 19, and Phil. 4. 16 On the whole Elley's articles show that he could not conceive of cooperative work taking place without the forming of a human organization.

The controversy over human organizations in the restoration movement shows the development of an attitude on the part of the advocates of these organizations that became a thorn in their side. Oddly enough those who favored human organizations generally managed to generate more enthusiasm and energy on behalf of these organizations than they ever had for the church. Of human organizations Elley had written: "They have been advocated as necessary to the increase of the number to be saved."[25] This led Fanning to make the charge that some men believed these organizations were necessary to keep the church alive. This is an error into which the over-zealous advocates of these enterprises have fallen into, not once but many times Robert Milligan defended Societies as "institutions of necessity," and W. K. Pendleton, in the hope of subduing opposition, asked Fanning to suspend his judgment until some further time But Fanning concluded by saying:

. . but we say to these good brethren, and all others concerned, that we made up our mind long ago, and unless better reasons are shown, we shall consider all religious expedients unnecessary, and in opposition to the reign of Christ.[26]

As already noted by the year, 1857, Fanning had crossed the Rubicon Beginning with the first edition of the *Advocate* in 1855, he stated his doubts on societies and was willing for his ideas to be

---

[24]Tolbert Fanning, "Notice of Brother Elley's Essay," *Gospel Advocate,* Vol III, No 2 (February, 1857), p 54

[25]Tolbert Fanning, "Notes on Brother G W Elley's Essay Regarding Cooperation," *Gospel Advocate,* Vol III, No 7 (July, 1857), p 214

[26]Tolbert Fanning, "Missions and Missionaries," *Gospel Advocate,* Vol. III, No 5 (May, 1857), p 131.

put to the test. More and more did he become convinced that there was no ground on which these societies could be defended. Consequently, in the spring of 1857 he states his position more boldly .

We think it due to ourselves, to the cause we plead, and to the brethren especially who seem to differ widely from us, to state our teaching in reference to cooperative labor—embracing missions and missionaries—in very plain terms. It was with much hesitation we brought ourselves to the conclusion, in 1855, to commence the publication of the Gospel Advocate. As expressed to our intimate friends, we were satisfied that we would be forced to attack existing institutions among the brethren, and we felt unwilling to have their opposition. But we have freely spoken, and now all we ask of our brethren is a fair discussion [27]

In the year 1859 at the regular meeting of the Society in October, Fanning was invited to be present. He went and delivered a discourse. Later Fanning explains that his purpose in presenting this particular address was to elicit some discussion on the subject of human organization. Fanning complained that Isaac Errett, the corresponding secretary that year, carefully squelched any possibility of a discussion by directing the line of thought to something else, and thus defeated Fanning's purpose.

Fanning, in this address, directed attention to the way he believed missionary work, and cooperation work, should be conducted. He cited the example of the way they were then doing it. The church which met at Franklin College in Tennessee had sent out J J Trott as missionary to the Cherokee Indians Two or three other congregations were assisting in the support of this work This, Fanning defended as being scriptural and right As to human institutions, Fanning remarked:

Touching, however, institutions not recognized in the Scriptures, as agencies to carry forward the good work of saving the world, many of us have staggered, and still entertain serious doubts as to the expediency of taking any part in them Not that we doubt for a moment that there is something good in them all, but we have been impressed with the idea that the church of God, which is represented as 'the pillar and support of the truth,' fully covers all the ground which Christians should occupy in their labors of love.[28]

[27]Tolbert Fanning, "Missions and Missionaries," *Gospel Advocate,* Vol III, No 5 (May, 1857), p 131
[28]Tolbert Fanning, "Brother Fanning's Remarks," *Gospel Advocate,* Vol VI, No 1 (Jan, 1860), p 8

During these years, the position of the *American Christian Review* was somewhat dubious. Ben Franklin had founded and begun editing this periodical as a monthly in January, 1856. While Franklin, as already pointed out, was defending human organizations, especially the Missionary Society; yet, there were times when his articles completely condemned the principle upon which these Societies were founded. It should have been clear to readers of the *Review* that Franklin was headed for a crisis when he would swing one way or the other. A man with Franklin's independence of mind and fearlessness of spirit could not long try to defend two irreconcilable principles. Two years before, while editing the *Christian Age,* Franklin had written a series of articles on "Church Organization." In these he deplored the weakened condition of the brotherhood. He took note that many were blaming this upon the lack of organization. He challanged the men who favored a better organization to produce one. In the latter part of 1855, as an attempt to improve upon the organization, the "Central (Kentucky) Christian Union" was formed with H. T. Anderson as president Some brethren, particularly Franklin, looked somewhat aghast upon this institution. One statement in its constitution said:

If there shall at any time arise any who shall teach things tending to the injury of the churches and the cause which we plead, such person or persons shall be subject to the discipline of the Union.

The nine churches which made up the Union seemed truly to have formed an organization that was synodical and denominational in its entirety. Franklin felt convicted to say something against it. As a result he writes:

We are truly sorry that this controversy has come up It appears that schism among men is becoming so rife, that no great and good work can be prosecuted with general unanimity Our power must constantly be weakened by jarring and opposing elements I am truly sorry these brethren have made the move they have; because I esteem them, love them, and desire the most fraternal feeling between us; and I fear I cannot make the objections I solemnly entertain without producing unpleasantness [29]

Franklin proceeds to sum up his objections in the following words:

We object to the organization formed by our brethren in Danville, not merely because it is not done to suit us, but because the

---

[29]Ben Franklin, "Organization II," *American Christian Review,* Vol I, No 2 (February, 1856), p 79

entire move is uncalled for, unwise, and wholly unauthorized The thing is unknown to the New Testament. The New Testament records inform us of the organization or rather the institution of individual communities, or churches, and the appointment of officers in them. But these records know nothing of any organization of the churches in any given district into one body, under a new set of officers, who are officers not of the churches but of the district.[30]

Later, Franklin attempted to get at the very root of the weakened condition of the brotherhood. The most commonly-expressed cause of this weakness was the lack of organization, but Franklin took direct issue here. If the cause was languishing, it was so only because the preachers were not as fervent as they once were He says, "If preachers lament that the cause languishes, let them cease scheming about some organization unknown to the New Testament, and go into the field and labor for the Lord's sake, and for the Lord's name, as brethren did years ago, and as we are doing now; and as certain as God is the author of the Bible, we shall prosper." The thing needed was better preaching, so Franklin adds: "Preaching is what is needed, fervent, soul-stirring preaching, exhortations, entreaties and impressive persuasions with the people to turn to God, and be saved." Unquestionably, Franklin was hitting at the real cause. The history of the restoration movement shows that the less devotion men have to Christ the more they stand in need of human organizations.

Thus we bring to a close the early objections raised against the American Christian Missionary Society and all human organizations. It will be noticed that these objections fell into three classifications. The first of these was based upon the Society's method of membership, viz., making membership depend upon the payment of stipulated amounts of money The second of these stemmed from the potential danger the Society maintained of infringing upon the independence of a local congregation The third objection came from the conviction that human organizations were unauthorized in the scriptures, and therefore, were unscriptural The Society found it could overcome the first of these by changing its constitution, the second could be overcome by suggesting that the danger of a thing did not argue against the thing itself The third ob-

[30]Ben Franklin, "Clerical Organization," *American Christian Review*, Vol I, No 3 (March, 1856), p 115

jection, the Society sought to answer by saying that human institutions were matters of expediency. Eventually this last objection became the core of the issue, although in years to come many churches who believed in societies found that the Society very little respected their local independence. But all of that is by way of anticipation; we shall leave it until later.

CHAPTER XII

ORGANIZED MISSIONARY EFFORTS

The activities of the American Christian Missionary Society forms an intrical part of the historical data on the restoration movement for those years before and during the war. It is of little concern whether one agrees with the existence of the Society or not; still it is a historical fact that the Society did exist and that it carried on certain activities which activities form a vital part of the study of the restoration. Certainly then, no investigation into the period can be complete without some comprehensive analysis of the activities of these years.

Scarcely had the Society been established until a matter of business came up relative to the sending out of foreign missionaries. But who should be sent and where? Early in the year 1850 Campbell began the publication of a series of articles on the American Christian Missionary Society After a discussion on the Society, its place and purpose, Campbell came directly to this point.

But where shall we begin? Charity begins at home, as the old adage goes; but, as someone has said, 'it does not continue at home' . . . But whither shall we send our missionaries abroad? I am anticipated in the judgment and good sense of some of our brethren. They have named Jerusalem as especially worthy of a concentrated and protracted effort. The claims of Jerusalem are, with me, paramount to those of any other spot on the green earth.[1]

At the same time, Carroll Kendrick, editor of the *Ecclesiastical Reformer,* wrote · "How grateful the thought, that Jerusalem, which at the beginning gave us the gospel, should from our hands receive it back again "[2] Thus there was a sentimental cause for the selection of Jerusalem as the first place for a missionary. Few in the brotherhood needed to be convinced of this for there was a ready concurrence that the first site should be Jerusalem, the city of the Great King.

Moreover, there needed to be little argument as to who would go.

---

[1]Alexander Campbell, "The Christian Missionary Society—No II," *Millennial Harbinger,* Third Series, Vol VII, No 2 (February, 1850), p 86
[2]Carroll Kendrick "Jerusalem Mission," *Ecclesiastical Reformer,* Vol III, No 2 (January 19, 1850), p 50

As early as October 5, 1848 Dr. James T. Barclay had written to James Challen, offering his services as a missionary if the society were to be organized Furthermore, he had the backing of Alexander Campbell who was vitally interested in his going abroad as a missionary. So significant is this first missionary of the American Christian Missionary Society that it might be of interest to note more about him.

Thomas Barclay, grandfather of Jane T. Barclay, was one of the very earliest settlers in this country. The Continental Congress appointed him in 1781 as the first American consul to France. Robert Barclay, son of Thomas Barclay and father of James T., was a moderately wealthy business man, who drowned, however, in 1809 as he crossed a swollen river in King and Queen County, Virginia James T. was born on May 22, 1807 at Hanover Courthouse, Virginia His early education was received at Staunton Academy, Virginia Upon graduation from the school of chemistry in 1826, he entered the medical school of the University of Pennsylvania and stayed there for two years At the end of this time he married Julia Ann Sowers of Staunton, Va.

Six years after the death of Thomas Jefferson, Barclay purchased the famous Monticello home from Jefferson's grandson, Jefferson Randolph, for $7,500 Barclay at that time lived in Charlottesville in a home valued at $4,500. He traded this and gave three thousand dollars extra for the Monticello home. Monticello, it will be recalled, was designed by Thomas Jefferson himself when he was but twenty-one years old He completed the building of it in 1802 at a cost of $7,200 Bricks for the home were made on the ground, and the nails were made by Jefferson's own negro boys. The home was run down when Barclay got it, and he repaired it to make it look very much like a mansion He was once offered twenty thousand dollars for Monticello, but turned down the offer Later, when he finally did sell it, he lost over two thousand dollars on the sale

The Barclays were Presbyterians, and James T was very religiously inclined His early ambition was to be a missionary to China, but his mother would never hear to it About 1839, after the death of his mother, James T and his wife heard the preaching of R. L Coleman, one of Virginia's early gospel preachers,

and were baptized by him in the James River near Scottsville
Barclay immediately used his influence-to establish a church in
Scottsville. Shortly afterward, he went to Washington, D. C.,
where in 1843, he succeeded in establishing the first congregation
in this city. This congregation met first in his home, then in the
fire station, and then in the city hall.

His decision to go to Jerusalem as a missionary came about in
an interesting manner. One evening he returned from taking
care of a patient. He was sitting on the front lawn of his
Scottsville home. His daughter was sitting on a lawn stool by his
side with her head on his knee. Mrs. Barclay was reading from
the eleventh chapter of Romans. The two boys were some distance
away, putting up a beehive. Barclay himself sat in a reflective
mood as he listened to the scripture reading. The boys soon
came to him. Then Barclay spoke thoughtfully to his family.
"Our constant prayer is for the fulfillment of the promises contained in that chapter. I have been reflecting on the question
whether we can pray with confidence for anything which we are
not willing to lend our aid for the accomplishment of   . We
have all been praying for the conversion of the Jews; yet no one
has stepped forward to engage in the work. If the end is to be
gained, someone must commence the undertaking. Shall I, if I obtain the cheerful cooperation of my family?" Thereupon the family
agreed to abide by his wishes.

Early in 1850 Barclay was selected to go to Jerusalem. John
Boggs acted as a representative for the Society in collecting funds
for the Jerusalem Mission. He met considerable opposition some
of which came as a criticism of Barclay's attitude toward slavery.
It was known that he had been a slaveholder, and northern churches
were reluctant to back him. Nevertheless in time, the money was
raised, and Barclay prepared to depart. On September 14, 1850
the Barclay family boarded the Devonshire, and sailed for Europe.
The sea was rough, and Barclay was ill most of the way. He
landed in London in twenty-one days. After some difficulty, he
finally left London on board the Hebe, and sailed for Malta. From
Malta the Barclays took a steamer to Beirut, and from there they
went horseback through Tyre, Sidon, Ptolemais, and Joppa to
Jerusalem where they arrived on February 10, 1851.

The Convention of 1850 met in Christian Chapel, corner Walnut

& Eighth in Cincinnati on Wednesday, October 23, at 2 00 P. M. Campbell was absent again and so D. S. Burnet took the chair. G. R. Hand was appointed secretary, *pro tem.* James Challen delivered an address, reviewing the year's activity. Since the first annual convention the year before, the Board had been meeting once a month. They were chiefly engaged in surveying the field, gathering resources and selecting men for the fields. The corresponding secretary in his report stated that they had much prejudice to all, much opposition to overcome, and much apathy and lukewarmness to encounter. The report complains of the lack of preachers to go. One thousand preachers were needed to preach along the states bordering on the Mississippi River. In Illinois alone, the report stated, there were thirty to forty towns on the river without preachers. Indiana had then a population of over a million, and yet preachers were sorely needed. The Society that year had in contemplation missions in New Orleans, Boston, Michigan, California, Oregan and Texas in addition to the mission already established in Jerusalem

The opposition to Life Directorships and Life Memberships being contingent upon the payment of money came in for some consideration. As a result the constitution was changed so that any church in North America was entitled to one representative or member for the year. However, by giving twenty-five dollars any congregation or organization could have another representative. The proposal was made by James Challen and was incorporated into Article Three which now read:

Every Christian Church in North America, cooperating with this Society, and all associations of churches, shall be entitled to representations equally at the annual meetings.

Just what real change this meant is hard to see in view of the fact that by payment of the extra twenty-five dollars, increased representation could be had.

So went the Convention of 1850 The next year the Convention met on Wednesday, October 22, in Cincinnati. Alexander Campbell was present now for the first time and delivered an address which he got up on the impulse of the moment. The report of the Corresponding Secretary showed the progress within the past year. The Barclays had been paid $881 88 to start their trip and then, had been sent another five hundred dollars, making $1,351 88 for the Jerusalem Mission. The Secretary's report showed that little had been done for home missions, since the most of the funds had been going to the Barclays. The report likewise showed that the previous year's change in the constitution regarding Life Directors and Life Members was still a source of trouble The controversy and dissatisfaction with them had not abated John Shackleford decided that the controversy was useless and moved that the article be restored to its original reading which was done. Still there were two other items of business that were interesting. J J Moss moved that a paper be published by the Societies, both Missionary and Bible, to promote their cause, but this suggestion was not acted upon James Challen proposed a mission on the Pacific coast in view of the rapid growth of California, but in view of the hard financial circumstances that the Society was feeling, no action was taken upon this proposal

Meanwhile, in Jerusalem James T Barclay was not idle although the results of his work were not sensational His first year in the city had resulted in twelve baptisms. His reports home showed that the general conditions of the so-called Christian section of the city were so deplorable that not one Mohammedan had been converted to Christianity but many Christians had been converted to Mohammedanism. By Christian as Barclay used the term here, he meant all types of sectarianism in opposition to Mohammedanism Barclay not only preached in the city but acted also as physician His report home showed that two thousand cases of sickness had come before him that first year

In December, 1852 Barclay received word from Bethlehem that six hundred people wished to become Christians They were prepared to come over "en masse" to the cause of New Testament Christianity Barclay strongly objected on the ground that they hadn't been sufficiently taught He went to Bethlehem, rented a room, and started a small school to thoroughly teach these people. Opposition soon grew against his school, and many of the people refused to attend Miss Mary Williams, whom Barclay had met after his arrival over there, was placed in charge of the school while Barclay established a hospital over which he placed his son, Robert The school did not last long because of enticements and threats from Jews and Catholics The hospital for a time was successful, but the Catholics soon placed a trained doctor in the city with a hospital and threatened those who dared patronize Barclay. Soon the hospital closed.

Shortly after this, Barclay bought a piece of land from some Sheiks in the valley of the Wady Farah When he went to take over the land, he found that the Sheiks had no title, so he had lost in the deal. His intention had been to erect a place of refuge for the poor among his converts. It seemed, then, that every effort of Barclays went wrong In three years he had baptized only twenty-two persons and on every hand was checked in his advancement In a letter to Alexander Campbell, dated August 27, 1853, he expressed his disappointment that results were not greater. Trouble also came on the home front for funds did not come to the Society fast enough for them to support Barclay. Not only so but Barclay's general physical condition was gradually getting worse. The shapening up of events pointed toward Barclay's coming home, and so during the summer of 1854, the Jerusalem Mission was closed, and Barcley was on his way home.

Meanwhile, as interest had waned in this mission, another way was in the making, which was to prove to be equally as much a failure D S. Burnet, through the columns of the *Christian Age* had encouraged the brethren to think of sending a missionary to Africa Campbell took up the plea, and in his address before the convention of 1853 said·

That we should have an African mission as well as an Asiatic mission—a station in Liberia as well as in Jerusalem—missionaries peregrinating accessible portions of the land of Ham as well as of the land of Shem, appears to me like a duty, a privilege and an honor We are abundant in means, and wanting, if wanting at all, only in will, in purpose or in liberality.[3]

In this speech Campbell told the convention of the fact that a certain Ephraim A. Smith had volunteered to visit Africa and survey Liberia and return and report conditions there. His going was to be no financial cost at all to the Society With him was to go Alexander Cross, an emancipated slave, from Christian County, Kentucky

Early in the spring of 1853 D S Burnet had started pleading for a mission in Africa through the columns of the *Christian Age* A member of the church in Christian County, Kentucky wrote to

---

[3]Alexander Campbell, "An Address," *Millennial Harbinger,* Fourth Series, Vol III, No 11 (November. 1854), p 614

Burnet that he had the man for the task. He had overheard a certain negro addressing his slaves sometime before on the subject of temperance. This negro showed an unusual amount of intelligence. Burnet wrote back to the brethren in that county, recommending that the freedom of Cross be purchased at once. This was quickly done. The church at Hopkinsville began putting the negro through a training course to help him to become more familiar with the scriptures. Meanwhile, a session of the Kentucky State Convention willingly turned Cross over to the Society, and along with him came four hundred and seven dollars from G. W. Elley and John G. Allen for his support   Besides this the church at Hopkinsville sent twenty-eight dollars.

Cross sailed from Baltimore on November 5, 1853 accompanied by his wife and his eight-year-old son.   Early in January, 1854 he landed at Monrovia.   Two months were spent in getting prepared to do this mission work, but during this time Cross showed little prudence relative to his own physical condition   In his zeal he went too far. He was warned to be careful of the hot tropical sun, and not expose himself too frequently or too long in the direct rays   But Cross was indifferent to the warning   In an effort to build himself a house at a certain point on the St Paul's River, Cross poled a canoe fourteen miles up the river under the hot African sun.   In a few days he fell down with a fever, and died. His little boy, James, who was along, also took the fever and he too, soon died.   With this tragic episode the African mission came to an abrupt close.

There were other missions readily proposed   An Indian Mission was under consultation, awaiting the proper moment to send a man to the Cherokee tribe.   A China Mission was proposed but delayed during this time for lack of funds and a missionary to go Missions to Germany and France were also under consideration. Home Missions were in demand with the Society especially looking toward Chicago where a few members had more recently moved.

Attention during this time was also being given by the convention to the American Christian Publication Society.   This Society was first called the Cincinnati Tract Society, having been founded through the joint efforts of D. S. Burnet and Ben Franklin. When the Convention first met in 1849, J. J. Moss recommended that the Sunday School Library, organized by certain brethren on the

Western Reserve be amalgamated with the Cincinnati Tract Society and the whole be the property of the brethren at large There was a ready agreement by the Convention, and the constitution of the Cincinnati Tract Society was changed to read, Christian Tract and Sunday School Society The objects of it were confined to tracts and Sunday School books The next year, the title was changed to read, American Christian Publication Society.

This Society in the year, 1853 took over the publication of the *Christian Age* which was then being edited by Ben Franklin The Publication Society also was publishing the *Sunday School Journal* The circulation of the *Age* at this time was admitted to be over six thousand, and that of the *Journal,* eight thousand. During the year, 1854 the Publication Society published D. S. Burnet's "Jerusalem Mission" and a new edition of the biography of Barton W. Stone

As has already been mentioned, James T Barclay left Jerusalem during the summer of 1854 to come back to America. Soon after his arrival at home, he began gathering material for his book, "The City of The Great King," which was published in 1858. During the summer of 1856 Barclay approached Alexander Campbell with the suggestion of reopening the Jerusalem Mission He found Campbell favorably impressed with the idea This gave Barclay the encouragement to try further The annual meeting of the American Christian Missionary Society met that year of 1856 in Christian Chapel, corner Walnut and Eighth in Cincinnati on October 21 Barclay attended and delivered an address before the convention suggesting the reopening of the mission The measure was favorably received, and Barclay prepared for a return trip It was not, however, until 1858 that he could find passage abroad, so on May 26, 1858 Barclay left Boston to finally arrive in Joppa in August. He found all of his converts except two gone, and living conditions deplorable By December, he found a home, and also found it difficult to get around for he had contracted rheumatism. The next May a malaria epidemic hit Jerusalem, so Barclay left to make his home in Joppa From here on, he had his hands full. His daughter married at this time and gave birth to twins The twins died Early in 1860 a revolt broke out between two tribes on Mt Lebanon and, as a medical doctor, Barclay was again very busy. Then the Civil War in America broke out, and the Jerusa-

lem missionary was forced to return because of low funds. Thus
ended permanently the Jerusalem Mission.

The report of the Convention was read in 1856 by D. S. Burnet,
who was then acting as Corresponding Secretary. His words were
filled with discouragement. He remarked that during the past year
little had been done in the way of mission work. He complained
of a general want of concerted action, stating that he had received
only two hundred and fifty-six dollars and seventy-five cents during
the entire year. Burnet himself laid the cause of this to worldliness
in the church and a general state of apathy regarding the salvation
of men.

The next year the report to the convention was read by Ben
Franklin, then the Corresponding Secretary. Franklin held this
position through the following circumstances · in 1856 Charles L.
Loos left Somerset, Pennsylvania to become the preacher for
the church at Walnut and Eighth Streets in Cincinnati, and shortly
afterwards, was appointed corresponding secretary of the Society.
But hardly had he arrived in Cincinnati until he was offered the
position as President of Eureka College in Illinois, so Loos accepted
and the job of Corresponding Secretary was turned over to Franklin   Franklin's report before the convention of 1857 stated that
the Society was yet in a deplorable condition, although it had some
improvement over the previous report. Its interests had been
hindered by the deaths of such men as John T. Johnson, S. W.
Irwin and H W Parrish who had died since the previous convention. Moreover, a severe drouth had hit the nation the previous
year, producing a minor depression, which reflected in less money
coming in to the Society. The trouble also lay, Franklin pointed
out, in the fact that brethren were showing more of an interest
in State Missionary Societies, and local missionary work, than in
the foreign   Not one single man had been found who would devote
all of his time to the Society. But Franklin thought he found
some encouragement that the opposition to the Society was not
having the effect as it formerly had   He reported that $1,752.45
had been given in the previous year.

Meanwhile, other missions were opening up. The Jerusalem
Mission this year—1857—was not ready to be opened due to the
lack of funds, but plans were made for another mission   J O
Beardslee of Collamar, Ohio visited Cincinnati and talked to Ben
Franklin about going to Jamaica. The Society agreed to send

him, and so on January 20, 1858 Beardslee and his wife left New York harbor for the island of Jamaica where they arrived on the twenty-seventh of the same month   Ten months later Beardslee reported that eighteen had been baptized   When the Convention met in October, 1858, there was high enthusiasm over the Jamaica Mission, for it was looked upon as a stepping stone to the continent of Africa   David Livingstone was just opening the dark continent and the Society had visions of future work there themselves.

Still another mission was opened by 1858 in Nova Scotia. W W. Eaton was the missionary there, and his written report sent to the convention indicates considerable progress   Forty-seven had been baptized there in fifteen weeks. But more encouraging to the Society perhaps in its days of financial stress, was the fact that the Nova Scotia mission was self-sustaining.

Isaac Errett became Corresponding Secretary for the Society in 1858   The next year his report to the Convention showed some reason for optimism by the Society. The church in Jamaica now had thirty-seven members. As to Nova Scotia, W. W. Eaton had been forced to return early in 1859 but William Patterson was sent in his place   Patterson by the first of October had baptized thirty-five persons. The Kansas Mission had opened up and John O'Kane had been sent there with a view of doing half-time work in Kansas and the other half with the church in Independence, Missouri   The Jerusalem Mission already by now had Barclay back, but the progress was almost non-existent.

The Convention of 1860 met admidst troublesome times. In national affairs there was high political excitement over the election which was less than two weeks off.   The Convention met, nevertheless, in Cincinnati, and for the first time met in the church located between Smith and Mound Streets and not in the building at Walnut and Eighth Streets   The general color of mission reports was about the same. Jamaica was encouraging, and Jerusalem was getting worse due to the intolerance of Turkish rule   John I Rogers was preaching under the Society's supervision at Leavenworth, Kansas having C. G Bartholomew as his helper.

This year of 1860 the Convention was the largest in point of attendance the Society had yet witnessed. Fifteen states were represented when the Convention met on Tuesday afternoon, October 23.   The report of the Corresponding Secretary informed the

Society that over fifteen thousand dollars had been raised since the previous year's meeting and a total of one thousand three hundred and forty-four additions to the church had been made   D S Burnet was this year elected to be the Corresponding Secretary

When the Convention met on Tuesday, October 22, 1861, at the Walnut and Eighth Streets church in Cincinnati, it probably had its most trying circumstances of it   The war had begun the previous spring, and in view of this attendance was off considerably The report on mission work was not encouraging to the Society in any realm.   The subject of the war was so much on the minds of the attendants that it was impossible to keep it from coming up The sympathy of most men was decidedly toward the North, so it was difficult to keep northern bias away from the Society's activities   This fact was later to cause considerable criticism to the Society and probably helped southern churches considerably in their opposition in the years ahead   J P. Robison of Ohio suggested the following resolution:

Resolved, That we deeply sympathize with the loyal and patriotic in our country, in the present efforts to sustain the Government of the United States.   And we feel it our duty as Christians, to ask our brethren everywhere to do all in their power to sustain the proper and constitutional authorities of the Union.

When the Resolution was suggested, D S Burnet immediately questioned whether such a resolution was not contrary to the second article in the Society's constitution   The Chair, however, upheld the resolution.   John Smith was present and asked that the decision pass from the Chair to the entire house for a vote.   This was done and the decision to pass the Resolution was defeated.   L. L Pinkerton, who had ardently seconded the motion, suggested a recess of ten minutes.   During this recess, D S. Burnet was called to the Chair, and the resolution re-read.   James A. Garfield, a Colonel at this time in the Forty-Second Regiment of the Ohio Infantry, was present, and made a few remarks.   After which another vote was taken, and the resolution was passed with only one negative vote cast.   This entire procedure was to prove a precedent for another similar action two years later.

When the Convention met the next year, 1862, Alexander Campbell was present for the last time   His presence at these meetings for the past several years had hardly accomplished much, for Campbell was old, and most action was taken by others   R. M. Bishop, one of the vice-presidents was present and leading a portion of the time Burnet's report for this year indicated that $6,773 09 had been received As to the Missionary work, the only report of encouragement to the Society came from Jamaica where J. O. Beardslee reported that he had immersed one hundred and seventy-two The previous year, on October 11, 1861, Barclay had resigned the Jerusalem mission, and had already arrived back in the United States For all practical intents and purposes the mission to Jerusalem had been a failure

The Convention of 1863 might be termed the War Convention. Because of its resolutions in favor of the Northern position, considerable criticism, especially from the South, but from other sources as well were later cast against it In the absence of Campbell, Isaac Errett, first vice-president, sat in the chair The report of the Corresponding Secretary announced that Beardslee was planning to return from Jamaica the next spring As to the funds received, the announcement was made that over eight thousand dollars—nearly nine thousand—had been received since the previous convention. The work in Kansas, Nebraska, and other Home Mission fields continued with about the same degree of success

The report had apparently gotten around that the Society was indifferent toward the war R Faurot, accordingly, suggested three resolutions, placing the Society definitely behind the cause of the Northern army. Only the second resolution need be mentioned

Resolved, That we tender our sympathies to our brave and noble soldiers in the field, who are defending us from the attempts of armed traitors to overthrow our Government, and also to those bereaved, and rendered desolate by the ravages of war

Immediately the question was raised whether these resolutions were in order. Errett, who was on the Chair, replied that two years ago, the house had voted against adopting a similar resolution, and that he would be forced to uphold their decision, although such a decision was contrary to his own convictions. A vote was taken of the house, after considerable discussion, and the resolution was adopted

W K Pendleton, because of sickness, was unable to attend this particular convention The passing of Faurot's resolutions was,

to him, a source of great displeasure as he learned about it later.
He writes:

We have deeply regretted the unpleasant excitement which has
been occasioned by the forced innovation in the last anniversary
upon a long cherished principle among us, concerning the introduction of resolutions foreign to the objects of the organization [4]

Still, while Pendleton regretted the lack of wisdom in writing up
these resolutions, he nevertheless did not agree to abandon the
Society because of them. He says,

Our Missionary Society must not be abandoned because of a
single imprudence or unwarranted innovation upon its sacred
principles. These things are human, and we must deal with them
as such.

The passing of such Resolutions made some brethren realize
what a dangerous instrument a Missionary Society could be. The
confidence of many was shaken, and the Society entered into one
of its black eras of unpopularity. Pendleton admits this by saying,

It ought not to be disguised, that the fortunes of the Am. Ch M.
Society have for a year or two been under a cloud. The confidence
of many of her oldest and most liberal supporters has been in good
measure withdrawn from her, and she has not been repaid for
this loss by any correspondent accession of new friends.[5]

During the spring of 1864, D. S. Burnet resigned as Corresponding Secretary. Burnet's wife had been ill and besides, Burnet's
own health had been gradually getting worse. H S. Bosworth,
the Recording Secretary, began immediately acting as Corresponding Secretary. B. W. Johnson then took the position but acted as
secretary only a few months. O. A. Burgess then took it over,
but one reads a year later that W. C. Rogers had the position.

Pendleton was doubtlessly right in saying that the attitude of
brethren toward the Society had changed considerably. Truly, the
Society was making enemies and few friends. Neither of the
Conventions of 1864 or 1865, both of which were held in Cin-
cinnati, displayed anything spectacular in the way of progress.
The latter Convention had a note of optimism about it in that

---

[4] W K Pendleton, "Monthly Summary," *Millennial Harbinger*, Fifth
Series, Vol VII, No 3 (March, 1864), p. 190

[5] W K Pendleton, "American Christian Missionary Society," *Millennial
Harbinger*, Fifth Series, Vol VII, No 9 (September, 1864), p 419

the war had ended, and there were great prospects of preaching facing them

In accordance with the design of this first volume, we shall leave the Society here at 1865. We note, however, its condition. With the cessation of hostilities, the Society faced the world with a wave of unpopularity sweeping against it. The next ten years were to be crucial ones, but we leave these for a later time.

Chapter XIII

IMPRESSIVE LEADERS

While the Missionary Society must often come before us in our survey of the restoration movement, yet we must not linger too long on it. The drama that was the restoration movement had many impressive actors, men whose names today are revered as great pioneer proclaimers of the ancient order. As we move from step to step in recording events and analyzing discussions and controversies, we must first pause long enough to familiarize ourselves with the men behind the movements. In this chapter, therefore, we turn our attention to three impressive leaders of the pre-war years of the restoration—John T. Johnson, P. S Fall, and "Raccoon" John Smith.

Exclusive of Alexander Campbell, there was probably no preacher in the days before the war so widely loved, highly admired, and so exuberantly eulogized as John T Johnson He was a man of great power and ability who succeeded in baptizing many hundreds in the twenty-six years he preached the word. He had not the wit of John Smith, and accordingly, was not the controversalist that Smith was He was reserved, strongly emotional, progressive and active at all times. Still he had not the timidity of P. S Fall He had a lawyer's mind and a poet's heart and he preached with strong appeals both to logic and to emotions

John T. Johnson at times was an editor. He never held a debate, in the popular sense of that term. It was preeminently as an evangelist that Johnson was known It is as an evangelist that he is most widely remembered, and as an evangelist he gained his great reputation To know John T. Johnson in the two-fold aspect of an evangelist and a man is to go a long way toward becoming acquainted with him as he lived in those early years.

W K. Pendleton once called John T. Johnson the "Chevalier Bayard of the pulpit in Kentucky'" Truly he was one of the few preeminently great preachers in that state in these earlier years Alexander Campbell wrote of him,

The boldness, cheerfulness, vivacity, fluency, and perseverance of brother Johnson eminently qualify him for great usefulness. I wish Kentucky had a few persons equally gifted for taking care

JOHN T JOHNSON

of the sheep, as brother Johnson is for marking them and putting them into the green pastures.[1]

Indeed, Johnson's ability to mark the sheep and put them into the pasture was almost incomparable. In the pulpit he was dignified, and yet simple in his presentation   Samuel Rogers, who heard him often, says of him:

As an evangelist, I have thought John T. Johnson the best model I have ever known. ' Perhaps, I ought not to speak of him as a model at all, for no man could imitate him. His style beggars all

---

[1]Alexander Campbell, "Incidents on a Tour," *Millennial Harbinger,* New Series, Vol III, No 6 (June 1839), p 265

attempts at description   I have read descriptions of him as a preacher, from the pens of those who are masters in the art of composition; but the best of them were tame in comparison with the real John T. Johnson as you saw and heard him for yourself.
.   He stood like a lord before the people, and yet no one was awed in his presence, for his dignity was blended with the sweet simplicity of a child. He did not wear the dignity of the world, but it was that of conscious rectitude and goodness   In coming before his audience, he had the appearance of a bold, fearless, and defiant champion, every nerve being fully strung, and his dark eye flashing fire.[2]

It was said of Johnson that he had the ability to make every theme something that lived in the present. In speaking on hell, his hearers were often made to think they were looking into the very abyss of torment. It was only natural that he could move people with such preaching.

A little boy sat beside his mother, listening to Charles H. Spurgeon speak   In a moment the boy looked to his mother and asked, "Mother, why does he keep preaching at me?"   Spurgeon could make his sermons *personal*.   Here was one phase of the power of Johnson as an evangelist.   Accordingly, Jesse B. Ferguson once wrote of him:

Brother Johnson is known to our readers as one of the first, most zealous, indefatigable and successful advocates of Primitive Christianity. It has called him from the bar and from the halls of Congress, to plead the cause of life and salvation with his fellow-men.
Twenty years of unremitting labor has he devoted to this cause, and when we last saw him, although he had some of the marks of a war-worn soldier of the cross, we thought him as fresh and vigorous as many of the younger recruits . . .

The cause of his unexampled success in inducing his fellow-men to bow to the Sceptre of Prince Emanuel, has often been inquired into   No reflecting man would long be in doubt after hearing him address the world of the ungodly. His personal appearance and address are those of an honest, courageous man   His discourses are discursive in their character and marked by great vitality and energy; whilst his appeals are so various and happy that scarcely a man who hears him who does not feel that he is directing his address to his peculiar state. His manner is affectionate, earnest, intrepid and scriptural. And, well furnished with facts and truths drawn from every source and rendered tributary to the great themes of the gospel proclamation, he grapples with his audience,

---

[2]Samuel Rogers, *Autobiography of Elder Samuel Rogers* (Cincinnati: Standard Publishing Co, 1880), p 200

and that man must be pertinacious and obstinate indeed, who will not yield in the athlete struggle [3]

The encomiums to John T. Johnson by brethren who knew him were characteristically superlative. He was a preacher without a peer; an evangelist incomparably successful W. K. Pendleton found many things about Johnson analogous to those in the saintly apostle Paul himself. Pendleton writes:

The qualities which made Paul colossal in the world, were many of them shared in a pre-eminent degree by John T. Johnson Unflagging zeal, golden purity, Christian charity, dauntless courage, indomitable energy, care for the churches, confidence in the power of the gospel, singleness of purpose, fidelity to Christ, reverence for his authority, trust in his sustaining aid, a restless ambition to be useful in his service, an unclouded vision of the things not seen, and an earnestness in all, that almost consumed his heart—these were some of the elements that made up his noble life, and put upon his brow the stamp of its nobility.[4]

In personal appearance Johnson was slightly under six feet tall. He was erect and slender. Early in life his hair had been the color of Walter Scott's—black as a raven's wing, but later it became very thin and sprinkled here and there with silver. He had a bilious temperament although he was never discouraged and even buoyant under the most adverse of circumstances. He had little time for clownishness. In his conversation, he was easy and somewhat familiar although always chaste, dignified and almost exclusively he dealt with things concerning the kingdom of God In his speaking—whether public or private—he was always in earnest

The birth of John T Johnson takes us back to Scott County, Kentucky in the year, 1788 About three miles west of Georgetown, on the Owenton Road was a place called Great Crossings It got its name from the fact that in the earlier days a main buffalo path had here intersected North Elkhorn Creek Here on October 5, 1788 Johnson was born. He was the eighth of eleven children

Johnson's family connections were very much related to the military which doubtlessly influenced him much in his earlier life. His father, Robert Johnson, was a colonel in the army. The name of his brother, Richard Mentor Johnson, became very familiar in

---

[3] J B Ferguson, "Encouragement—J T Johnson," *Christian Magazine,* Vol I, No 2 (February, 1848), p 64

[4] W K Pendleton, "Life of J T Johnson," *Millennial Harbinger,* Fifth Series, Vol VI, No 4 (April, 1863), p 181

military circles.   Richard was a colonel in the army during the War of 1812.   Later he became the ninth vice-president of the United States.   Another brother, James, was a lieutenant-colonel in the Battle of Thames, and for several years, a member of Congress.

It was only natural that the mind of John T Johnson should also turn toward the military, and that he should accept the first call that came his way.   During the War of 1812 General William Henry Harrison commanded the North-western army at Fort Meigs.   Harrison invited Johnson to become a volunteer aid. Johnson accepted, and joined the forces at the fort   During the spring of 1813, many of the volunteers found their time of enlistment was up, so they began returning to their homes   The Indians, sensing that the Fort was undermanned, began planning an attack. Harrison, unmindful of the planning, left for a visit to Cincinnati with his family   The battle with the Indians, fought at Fort Meigs on May 5, 1813, was very fierce.   Johnson escaped the battle unhurt, although he had a fine gray horse shot from under him. After the battle, Harrison sent Johnson to join the forces of his brother, Richard M , but on the way, John T. got down with a fever and barely managed to get home alive.   He was sick for some time but finally recovered.

Considering the educational opportunities of the times, John T. Johnson was a well educated man   He went to school at first to Malcolmb Worley who ran an acadamy near his home   Worley was a devout Presbyterian.   Later he followed Barton W. Stone out of Presbyterianism, and after that, when Stone's followers were badly shaken by Shakerism, Worley was one to abandon the cause.   At any rate, after finishing his schooling with Worley, Johnson entered Transylvania when this school was under Dr. James Blythe.   Here he studied law.   Upon graduation, he applied for and received his license to practice even though he was under twenty-one.

While Johnson was a student at Transylvania, he boarded with a family by the name of Lewis.   Mrs. Lewis took a particular liking to John T.   When the subject of girls would come up. she often commented to Johnson that he needn't worry about a wife, for she was rearing a daughter especially for him   The statement was truer than Johnson realized.   On October 9, 1811, he married

Sophia Lewis, the fifteen year old daughter of the Lewis family. Johnson himself was now twenty-one, six years her elder.

Soon after marriage, Johnson settled on a one hundred and fifty acre farm on South Elkhorn, near Georgetown. He and his younger brother, Joel, built a mill and went into business They continued this business for many years. In 1815 Johnson went into politics, running for the legislature of the state. He was elected each year for the next four. Meanwhile, with his farm, his business, and his politics, he managed to build up quite a wealthy position for one who lived in the backwoods of Kentucky as he did. But all of this was to be short-lived. In 1819 a severe panic swept the country. Johnson's tender heart had compelled him to sign many promissory notes for his friends and neighbors When the panic hit, they couldn't pay, so the obligation fell upon him Johnson gave up about fifty thousand dollars worth of his real estate to pay these notes.

In 1820 Johnson turned his attention toward national politics, and ran for Congressman. He was elected that year, and also, re-elected several times In 1825 in the hotly contested election of Andrew Jackson, which finally had to be decided by Congress, Johnson voted for Jackson In 1828 he was reelected to Congress, and immediately announced that he would retire from politics after this term. His busy life had caused him to neglect his family, and in deference to their wishes, he was determined to quit public life.

Johnson, even though busy with his thinking about politics, never entirely forgot thinking about religion. He was only a boy when the Great Revival of Cane Ridge took place in 1801, but he long remembered this event. In 1821 he joined the Baptist Church at Great Crossings. Of this, Johnson says, "Oh, it was a most glorious thing for me It preserved me from a thousand temptations, and kept me a pure man "[5] In 1823 Alexander Campbell began publishing the *Christian Baptist* but Johnson was so busy thinking of politics that he had no time to seriously investigate it But around 1830, while he was preparing to retire, Johnson found that he had more leisure to examine it. Moreover, there was a compelling urgency since the whole community around him was aroused over what it vulgarly called "Campbellism " He determined in his own mind that he would examine this teaching in the light of the

---

[5]John Rogers, *The Biography of Elder J. T. Johnson* (Cincinnati 1861), p 21

Bible, and determine for himself what the truth was. And so, he began an earnest investigation of the scriptures, and gradually the light began to dawn   Of this he later says,

My eyes were opened, and I was made perfectly free by the truth. And the debt of gratitude I owe to that man of God, A Campbell, no language can tell [6]

Immediately after his conversion, Johnson set his goal to converting the Baptist Church at Great Crossings where he was a member   In his innocency he did not take into account the power of religious prejudice   They scorned him until he became convinced that they were beyond the realm of possible conversion   On the second Saturday in February, 1831 he, together with B S Chambers, and W Johnson, formed a separate congregation at Great Crossings worshipping after the ancient order   Before long he had baptized his wife, his brother, Joel, and his wife   In one year's time the number in this church increased to seventy

It will be seen that Johnson's life had undergone a radical shifting of emphasis   If his wife found him too busy in politics to give his time to his family, it is not likely that she found him less so in his preaching of the gospel   In addition to his preaching, Johnson was soon called upon to do considerable writing   In 1831 Barton W Stone lived near Georgetown, and was editing the *Christian Messenger*   He urged Johnson to become co-editor   Johnson continued this until Stone moved to Illinois in 1834   The next year, Johnson, feeling that a paper was needed in Kentucky, collaborated with B F. Hall in publishing a paper they called the *Gospel Advocate*   This paper, however, continued only for a short time

By and large the life of John T Johnson, from his conversion to the principles of restoration in 1831 until his death in 1856 is connected with his preaching work   Seldom was he away from it   In 1832 he led the forces of Barton W Stone and Alexander Campbell into a union   In 1836 he gave some assistance toward establishing Bacon College. He attended the conventions of the American Christian Missionary Society and was an ardent support of it   But withal, he spent the most of his time in preaching   He traveled extensively, all over the south, and into the west—Arkansas and Missouri   It is not necessary, nor would it be of great

---

[6]John Rogers, *The Biography of Elder J T Johnson*, p 21

profit, to list these excursions and preaching engagements. Needless to say, if it were done, the biography of John T Johnson would read very much like a diary.

The death of Johnson came on December 18, 1856, and came as a sudden shock to the whole brotherhood His health apparently had been good. No one suspected that death, even for one his age, was as close by as it was. Johnson had attended the annual convention of the Society in October, 1856, but had stayed only two days. During these two days, he was with Ben Franklin a good deal, and even spoke for the church at Covington, Kentucky, across the river, where Franklin then preached. He left Cincinnati early in order to take an extended tour into Missouri. After arriving in Missouri, he preached at Columbia, Fayette and Rocheport. Then he went on to Lexington, arriving there on the fourth Lord's Day of November, this day being the twenty-third. His arrival at this particular time was unexpected. It was Sunday morning when the steamer docked, and the church services were already under way. Johnson headed for the building to find Allen Wright already up preaching. Wright stopped in the middle of his sermon, and insisted that Johnson speak. Thus began a meeting in which Johnson preached twice a day, and which was destined to be his last such meeting.

On Sunday evening of the first Lord's Day in December, Johnson preached his last sermon. The night was cold, and the building was unusually warm. The sermon was entitled, "The Word." After the discourse was over, Johnson left the building, walked a little way, and pulled his coat up over his throat, complaining that he was cold. The next morning he slept late, but was still feeling ill. That afternoon, he was suddenly struck with a severe pain in his side, and had to be helped back to bed He was staying in the home of Thomas C. Bledsoe, and from this bed, never walked away again.

He had an attack of pneumonia which was followed by other attacks bringing severe pain and suffering to him Most of the time he was delirious. Five days before his death he had a severe hemorrhage of the bowels. It was seen that he could not live long. Bledsoe informed him of the news he was going to die. Johnson's reply was, "I did not think that death was so near, but let it come." Asked if he had any fears in dying, Johnson replied: "None, none whatever, I have lived upon Christianity, and can die upon it." In his delirious moments, Johnson would quote scripture or preach, his preaching consisting of thoughts on the sacrifice of Jesus for sin. A few hours before his death he asked Allen Wright and a Brother Duval to sing, "O Land of Rest For Thee I Sigh," a favorite song. Johnson tried to sing along, too, as they in their feeble way, sang the hymn   Only a few minutes after sunset on the evening of December 18, 1856 did John T. Johnson close his eyes in death. The time was 6:15 P.M.

PHILLIP S. FALL

The life of Phillip Sydney Fall was largely limited to three localities—Frankfort and Louisville, Kentucky and Nashville, Tennessee   P S. Fall was not a controversalist, but by temperament was quiet and reserved. Yet, he was a man of strong conviction, pure and lofty ideals, and a deep and pure love for Christ. Consequently, his influence upon those around him was definite and uplifting. While his part in the restoration was not so public as that of others, yet, in his quiet and reserved manner, he served the Lord. Particularly is he important in a study of the restoration movement for two things: his early connection with Campbell's principles, and the progress of the church in Nashville, Tennessee.

Fall was born in Keloedon, England in September, 1798   His parents seemed to lean a little toward the Episcopalian beliefs. His maternal grandfather was an Episcopalian, while his paternal grandfather was a Baptist. Fall himself was educated religiously in the Episcopalian belief until he came to America   This trip to the United States occurred in 1817   His parents stopped for a short time in Pittsburgh, and then came on to settle near Russellville, Kentucky. But they had only been in their new home for about a year when they both died, leaving P S Fall to look out for himself.

The year, 1818, the year that his parents died, Fall established an academy near Louisville, Kentucky. That same year he united with the Baptist Church, and began to give his attention toward preaching. The next year, in December, 1819, he was licensed to preach in the Baptist Church.

In 1821 Fall married Miss Annie Bacon, who came from one of the illustrious families of the state   She was of great assistance to her husband in his preaching, and stood faithfully by him. That same year Fall was invited to visit Louisville once a month

o

P S FALL

and preach for a newly organized Baptist Church here   This church was meeting in the courthouse and stood badly in need of a preacher.   Through Fall's monthly preaching, it grew until in 1823, he was invited to move to the city, and devote more of his time to the church.   It was while here preaching for this church, most members of which he had converted, that P. S. Fall began to give his attention to the cause of the restoration movement.

After Alexander Campbell's debate with John Walker in 1820, considerable excitement was raised among the Baptists of Kentucky.   It was easily apparent that Campbell was no ordinary man.   In learning, in piety, and independence of thought he was already standing above the other preachers in the denominations. Yet, Baptists generally had mixed emotions over Campbell. They liked his emphasis upon immersion, but they questioned seriously his view of the two covenants, with his emphasis upon the abrogation of the old. Up to the time of the McCalla debate, Campbell had hinted very little as to his conviction upon the purpose of immersion. But when his debate with McCalla occurred, he was ready to declare his belief that immersion was for the remission of sins Baptists now cocked an eyebrow. Accusations of heterodoxy began to rumble from various quarters. One of P. S. Fall's temperament,—who sincerely loved the truth for truth's sake, could not bring himself to defend party beliefs just for party's sake. He would examine the matter fairly in the light of the scripture, and determine the truth for himself

In 1822, while still preaching monthly in Louisville, Fall read Campbell's sermon on the Law. He followed closely Campbell's reasoning The next winter he openly preached these ideas himself, and received considerable criticism. The Baptist Church in Louisville was convinced and joined the principles of restoration. P. S Fall himself became the first resident Baptist preacher in the state to accept the ancient order of things He was not long in being cast into disfavor by most Baptists He was secretary of the Long Run Baptist Association, and in 1824 was invited to write the circular letter to the churches. Fall did so, explaining that the New Testament was the only rule of faith and practice But of course, the letter was finally rejected

The Nashville Female Academy of Nashville, Tennessee issued an invitation for Fall to teach there Accordingly, he moved to the city in 1825, and in addition to teaching, began preaching for the Baptist Church. He explained to the church his conviction, however, that he must be left free to preach only the Bible, and that he would reject all human creeds The church acquiesced, and Fall began preaching The Baptist Church in Nashville was a member of the Concord Baptist Association Fall's insistence that the church take only the New Testament for its rule of faith and practice soon put it into disfavor with the Baptist Association The minutes of the Concord Baptist Association for 1827 refer to P. S Fall as "a thorough dyed Campbellite under a Baptist cloak." It is small wonder they thought so

Fall and Alexander Campbell became the very closest of friends.

In November, 1824, while Fall was still in Louisville, Campbell paid a visit to the city. On a Friday night he spoke to the church. He spoke for two hours from the book of Hebrews. The house was crowded, and five Presbyterian preachers were present Meanwhile, Fall was being invited to speak in those Baptist churches that leaned toward the restoration In Cincinnati the Aenon Baptist Church was such a congregation. Its influence was extending far and wide. Jacob Burnet, one of its members, was mayor of the city. Fall went to preach for this congregation late in 1824. He visited in the home of Mayor Burnet, and had the privilege of seeing the latter's son, David S., a boy then only fifteen years of age, immersed into Christ.

Fall stayed in Nashville until 1831, and because of ill health was forced to move back near Frankfort, Kentucky. During his stay in the city, he had succeeded in getting the church to leave the Baptists and standing solely upon the Bible. Through his influence, too, Alexander Campbell first visited the city, and made many friends there which occasioned his return many times in the future. At Frankfort, Fall established the Female Eclectic Institute where many of the daughters of Kentucky's great families received their education. For twenty-six years Fall conducted this school. Meanwhile, Fall preached around the state, very frequently having skirmishes with the Baptists Silas M. Noel was a prominent Baptist preacher. Through the *Christian Examiner*, Fall addressed a letter to Noel, criticizing certain attitudes Noel took Noel replied by a sarcastic poem directed at P ,S. Fall

> Our little Phill, can ne'er be still,
> From nestling and from hatching,
> 'Tis point look up, to Cam'mell'sville,
> 'Tis point no point, with little Phill,
> And yet he will be scratching
> Chorus—Twittle twattle, etc [7]

Probably nobody took such remarks seriously, especially not P S. Fall.

In 1852 the church in Nashville began having serious trouble over the teaching of J. B. Ferguson, which shall be recorded in our next chapter Suffice it to say, the church was badly divided.

---

[7]Alexander Campbell, "The Holy Spirit, for Which Silas M Noel Contends," *Millennial Harbinger*, Vol II, No 3 (March, 1831), p 143

The feeling generally was that only one man could remedy the unpleasant condition and that was P. S Fall. They appealed to Fall to return to Nashville. In 1858 Fall came back, and preached here until 1877, when he felt that the work should be turned over to men younger than himself. Accordingly, he turned his attention again toward Frankfort, and here spent the remainder of his life.

In the fall of 1889 the Missionary Society held its annual meeting in Louisville. Fall attended. He by this time was quite feeble and very deaf. Fall went to the Convention, not because he agreed with the Society, for he never did. He was against human societies to do the work of the church. Fall had the feeling he would soon be dying, and he wanted this last opportunity to see some of his old friends. The *Louisville Times* on the occasion, gave Fall quite a write-up. But yet, time was about to catch up with him. On December 3, 1890 Fall died He was ninety-two years old. His body was laid to rest near Frankfort where he had spent so many years.

"RACCOON" JOHN SMITH

Perhaps the most colorful character of the restoration movement was John Smith of Kentucky. More frequently he was referred to as "Raccoon" John Smith, this backwoods sobriquet being given to him after a sermon he delivered at the Tate's Creek Baptist Association at Crab Orchard, Kentucky around 1815. A vast audience, seeing his unkept appearance, started to leave as he stood up He then called aloud

'Stay, friends, and hear what the great Augustine said!' and they all stopped to listen.

'Augustine wished to see three things before he died,' continued Smith. 'Rome in her glory and purity, Paul on Mars Hill; and Jesus in the flesh' A few now sat down, but many smiled, and started off again

'Will you not stay,' he cried, in a still louder voice, 'and hear what the great Cato said?' Many returned and took their seats, and seemed willing to be amused.

'Cato,' he continued, 'repented of three things before his death: first, that he had ever spent an idle day, secondly, that he had ever gone on a voyage by water, when he might have made the same journey on land; and thirdly, that he had ever told the secrets of his bosom to a woman.'

The people continued to come back, and began to crowd close to the stand. A few acquaintances, who had not seen him for a long time, now recognized him, and passed the word among the crowd—'It is John Smith, from the Little South Fork!' Seeing groups of persons still standing in the distance, he called again with all the strength of his heavy voice

'Come, friends, and hear what the great Thales thanked the gods for.'

'Let us go and hear the fellow', said one, 'there may be more in him than we suppose.' And they all, at last, sat down near by to listen.

'Thales thanked the gods for three things first, that he was endowed with reason, and was not a brute; secondly, that he was a Greek, and not a Barbarian; and thirdly, that he was a man, and not a woman.'

'And now, friends, I know you are ready to ask. 'And pray, sir, who are you? What have you to say for yourself?'

'I am John Smith, from Stockton's Valley. In more recent years, I have lived in Wayne, among the rocks and hills of the Cumberland. Down there, saltpeter caves abound, and raccoons make their homes. On that wild frontier we never had good schools, nor many books; consequently, I stand before you today a man without an education.'[8]

In a little while a man went to Jacob Creath, Sr., begging him to come and hear the sermon. "Sir," he said, "the fellow with the striped coat on, that was raised among the 'coons is up, come and hear him preach. His name is Smith." Reared among the 'coons of Stockton Valley and in Wayne County, Smith soon acquired the epitaph of "Raccoon" which has always stayed with him.

Kentucky had many great pioneer preachers. Jacob Creath, John T. Johnson and John Smith were among the more famous. Of these three John Smith's name is probably more familiar to the neophyte in restoration history. Who has not loved to tell— and to listen—to the countless stories of wit and humor coming out of Smith's life? Yet, who among those who have studied his life have failed to walk with Smith through the valley of despair? His life is one of humorous incidents on the one side and one of pathos and drama on the other. We laugh with him in the sunlight of his days, and weep bitterly with him in the many tragedies that marred his life, and darkened the sunless days. We stand in awe at his fearless independence, and watch with profound ad-

---

[8] J A Williams, *Life of Elder John Smith* (Cincinnati The Standard Publishing Co, 1904), pp 89, 90

miration his unbounded zeal at work in bringing stubborn wills
in subjection to the King of Kings. Smith was without education,
knew little of human philosophy, never heard of modern comforts of
life, but he loved the Lord and the cause of truth and everything
else good and noble and pure with a heart that had no limitations
for such love. Rustic, uncouth, and unlearned though he was, he
was a good man, a noble man, a courageous man. His life reads
like a legend of the sacrifices the early pioneers made for the
cause of truth.

Smith was born on October 15, 1784 in what later became
Sullivan County, East Tennessee, although at the time of his
birth, it was called by the people the state of Franklin, in honor
of Benjamin Franklin, the great American statesman. His father
was George Smith, and was of German descent His mother was
Irish, and named, Rebecca Bowen. His father fought in the
colonial struggle for independence, and then came back to his
wife and eight children to provide a living on their farm But
the west was beckoning. Land was cheap, opportunities unbounded, so in this direction he turned his attention. With his
large family he moved into the Valley of the Holston early in
the year 1784. On the banks of this river, he erected a log
cabin, and here in the middle of October, John Smith, the ninth
of thirteen children was born

The parents of John Smith were hardy pioneers quite capable
of meeting the rigors of wilderness life Smith's mother had none
of the luxuries that wealthier women possessed, and toiled long
hours each day for her family George Smith, his father, worked
equally as hard. By disposition he was quiet, grave and somewhat diffident. But his children loved his presence. Smith's
parents held firmly to the teaching of the Philadelphia Confession
of Faith, and accordingly, were members of the Baptist Church.
They were thorough-going Calvinists in belief and felt that no one
could be saved until a mysterious call came from the Holy Spirit.
Smith's father sat in the log cabin on Sundays, while the farm
work remained idle, and read aloud to his family from the Bible.
In this kind of a home atmosphere characterized by godliness, and
rigorous toil, the children of George and Rebecca Smith grew up.

Educational advantages in those early years didn't exist Occasionally a schoolmaster would journey through the wilderness,

visiting each log cabin and trying to convince the parents to release their children from the hard work to attend school. When John Smith was about eight years old, he managed in this manner to secure about four months' education, but in that time, he learned to read sufficiently that he could read with comparative ease the New Testament. Soon Smith's father was asking him to read the scripture to the family every Sunday.

In the fall of 1795 George Smith began to get restless to move his family into a different locality. He sold his farm on the Holston, and moved into the Powell valley. Here he erected a cabin and made suitable preparations for his family to live. Taking with him two of his sons, John and Joseph, he said goodbye to the rest of his family, and started across the mountains into Kentucky. He followed the trail to Crab Orchard and from there proceeded to the valley of the Cumberland River. He stopped in a valley at the foot of Poplar mountain, in what later became Clinton County. The little valley was called Stockton valley in honor of a pioneer who had preceded him. Here George Smith purchased two hundred acres of forest land and began immediately to build a home.

Before going back for his family, George Smith desired that the farm work be largely done. To plant the crops in the spring seed corn was needed, and yet the nearest place to buy this corn was in Danville, nearly one hundred miles away. John was now twelve. His father called him to his side and told him he was old enough to take this journey alone. Getting his horse, John set out. He crossed swollen rivers, traveled through thick wilderness trails, and spent the nights in log cabins along the way. He made the trip safely, returning with the corn. The spring crop was planted, and Joseph and John were left to tend it while George Smith returned to Powell's valley for his family By midsummer the family was reunited in their new home in Stockton's valley.

The only religion John Smith knew during his childhood days in this valley home was the Baptist. Issac Denton, a Calvinistic Baptist preacher, moved to the valley, and Smith was often in his companionship. Calvinistic ideas were more heavily implanted in the young boy's mind, and he began to listen to every movement in the forest, every happening of his life, for some voice to speak to him, declaring that he was among the regenerated.

The older children in the Smith household began to marry and provide homes of their own. William moved into Wayne County, and George into the Green River country. Others settled down nearer their father. John paid occasional visits to see his brother, George. The first visit occurred when the rumor reached home that George had been captured by an outlaw band of murderers by the name of Harpes. George was safe, it was discovered, although he had a narrow brush with death. On Smith's second trip to see George, he witnessed for the first time the religious excitement led by James McGready such as occurred at Cane Ridge. Smith turned from these scenes in disgust, although he still held to his youthful impressions of Calvinism.

Smith began to think more and more seriously of his own salvation and waited more anxiously than ever the divine call. He tried to convince himself that he was totally depraved—worse than the Harpes brothers who had murdered so many He underwent an inward struggle that was intense, but could feel nothing more than concern because he couldn't realize a call. After one such intense struggle to feel converted, he relaxed. The rolling sea of emotions gradually subsided and a calm swept over his soul. Then Smith told himself that this might be the sign that he was saved. His friends told him so, and urged him to go before the church with this personal experience. Finally he agreed and so on Saturday, December 26, 1804 he told the story to the Baptist Church in Stockton valley. He was voted in, and was immersed the next day in Clear Fork by Isaac Denton.

Denton felt that John Smith would be a preacher He urged him to lead public prayer, and to read the scripture publicly. But yet, Smith awaited the call. In the meantime, he bought a farm near his brother, William, in Wayne County, and began to build it up He attended social meetings in cabins and led in a study of the Bible, but still he felt no call to preach. At one of these meetings, he saw a beautiful young lady by the name of Anna Townsend. Smith had rarely noticed the opposite sex before, but now felt attracted to this one. He paid occasional visits to the Townsend household, and on December 9, 1806 was married to the first and only girl he ever loved. The next morning he and his new wife moved to Wayne County, to settle on Smith's farm.

But Smith continued to look for a call to preach. In everyday events he thought he saw a call that he wanted. He side-stepped a rattlesnake, and was prone to think this meant he had been spared to preach. But finally, in a struggle with an ox in which it looked for a moment that he might be killed, he suddenly vowed that if he got away alive, he would preach. He did escape, and this was interpreted as a divine call. In May, 1808 he took an examination for his ordination to preach, and passed. He was now a full-fledged Baptist preacher.

Two years went by, and Smith became convinced that a move would do him good. He had made the acquaintance of Jeremiah Vardeman, who was perhaps the most famous Baptist preacher in Kentucky, and Vardeman urged him to move into the Blue Grass region. Smith went up there, but didn't like it. The war with England came on, and Smith heard of land selling for $1 25 an acre near Huntsville, Alabama He had visions of selling his Kentucky farm, and buying this in Alabama, and coming out ahead financially in a matter of time Still he was undecided. The year, 1814, came, and he definitely decided to go. He sold his farm, and in the fall of that year, settled on a new farm in northern Alabama.

Misfortune frequently followed Smith, and the first of any serious consequence met him here He was off preaching. His wife left the cabin to care for a sick neighbor. The children were left at home with Hiram Townsend, brother to Smith's wife. Suddenly, the cabin caught afire, and quickly burned to the ground. Two of the children were burned alive The terror and horror that struck Smith's wife can only be dimly imagined. The sad news reached Smith, and he returned home as quickly as possible His wife, like Rachel, would not be comforted. The days passed by and she sank lower and lower only finally to be planted beneath the soil beside the ashes of her two departed children Smith himself got sick He contracted a fever, and for days hovered near death Slowly he improved.

In a matter of months he sold his farm, and started retracing his steps back to Kentucky. He headed back for Wayne County to talk to his brother, William, and get advice. When he arrived, he found a note from Vardeman, urging him to attend the Association meeting at Crab Orchard, and it was on this occasion that he spoke, as we have already narrated, of being reared among the 'coons' of Wayne County.

The meeting at Crab Orchard together with the kindness of so many friends seemed to inspire Smith to greater work He continued his preaching tours. Before long he married Nancy Hurt and settled down again on a farm, trying to start anew with a heavy indebtedness hanging over him. Meanwhile, as he continued preaching, and studying his Bible, questions began to be raised in his mind. There was something wrong somewhere in their teaching that didn't match the teachings of the scripture, but he didn't know where. In March, 1822, he was preaching at Spencer's Creek, urging sinners to repent and believe the gospel. He got confused. Suppose the elect didn't believe, would they be saved? Suppose the non-elect did believe, would they be saved? He closed his address abruptly saying:

Brethren, something is wrong—I am in the dark,—we are all in the dark; but how to lead you to the light, or to find the way myself, before God, I know not.[9]

While Smith was thus pondering the subject of salvation, and of Calvinism's teaching, Alexander Campbell began publishing the *Christian Baptist*. Smith became a subscriber, and read eagerly every word. Campbell's reputation had followed his debates with Walker and McCalla, and many Baptist preachers looked upon him with great disfavor. Smith studied and waited. Meanwhile, news came that Campbell was going to visit Flemingsburg and Mt. Sterling. As an act of courtesy, Smith proposed that a delegation of Baptist preachers meet and accompany Campbell. The preachers turned it down, so Smith went alone. He arrived in Flemingsburg ahead of Campbell, and spoke to William Vaughn, a Baptist preacher. He inquired of Vaughn, who had heard Campbell, whether Campbell was a Calvinist, an Arminian, an Arian or a Trinitarian. Vaughn replied that Campbell had nothing to do with any of these things When Smith inquired if Campbell knew anything about Christian experience, Vaughn replied that he knew everything.

Before meeting, Smith met Campbell, and desired just to sit

---

[9]John A Williams. *Life of Elder John Smith,* pp 115, 116

and look at him. At the service, Campbell spoke on the allegory of Hagar and Sarah. When the meeting ended, Smith turned to Vaughn and said:

"Is it not hard, brother Billy, to ride twenty miles, as I have done, just to hear a man preach thirty minutes?"

"You are mistaken, brother John; look at your watch. It has surely been longer than that."

When Smith looked, he found Campbell ·had preached two hours and thirty minutes. Two hours were gone, and he knew not where.

During the months that followed, Smith continued to read articles from the *Christian Baptist,* comparing them to the Bible. He was sure there was something wrong with his own teachings, but still he remained unsure that Campbell was right. Gradually he became convinced that human creeds were wrong, and by 1825 was asking the churches to reject them. Soon he began to see that Calvinism was the great evil in the doctrine of Kentucky Baptists, and he began to urge that people be Christians by believing upon Christ as the Messiah and obeying Him in baptism. In taking such positions Smith was turning squarely against his early teachings He had to turn down the influence of his aged mother in addition to a host of friends including Isaac Denton. But Smith could not preach a thing that he conscientiously believed to be wrong He could not refrain from opposing something that he thought was standing in the way of the salvation of numerous souls, such as he believed Calvinism was doing By the year 1826 Smith had joined the other preachers of Kentucky in proclaiming a return to the ancient order.

It was to be expected that Smith's preaching would excite the Baptists a great deal. When the North District Association held its annual meeting at Cane Spring on the fourth Saturday of July, 1827, Smith went, expecting the Association to take action against him A letter was read before the Association, directed at Smith, although not calling him by name. It charged that certain ones were guilty of the following three heresies: (1) Of reading from Campbell's translation of the Bible instead of the King James version (2) Of saying "I immerse you" instead of "I baptize you" when administering baptism. (3) Of allowing the communicants to break their own bread when partaking of the Lord's

Supper instead of having the preacher do it for them in advance.
When Smith heard the charges, he jumped up and cried, "I plead
guilty to them all " After considerable altercation, the Association
decided that no action should be taken against Smith, but that
such action should be postponed for another year. Smith's replies
to the Association on the charges gained for him the sympathy
of the people while securing the dislike of the clergy.

But Smith found himself with plenty of company. Jacob Creath,
Sr., Jacob Creath, Jr., and John T. Johnson had joined the host
of those pleading for a return to the apostolic order, and often
stood beside Smith before the Elkhorn, Franklin, and North
District Association. Together with him they received their
anathema, and like him they counted it a joy to suffer for the
name of Christ and for the cause of truth The years that lay
ahead were years that these men together planted the seed of
the kingdom over the state of Kentucky They saw hundreds immersed, and witnessed the establishment of congregations throughout the state.

During these years of experience as a gospel preacher, Smith
found frequent use of his witticisms, but all of them were used to
illustrate a point. Smith was never without an answer, no matter
the unexpectancy of the occasion. Once when he had baptized
several members of a certain family, he afterwards met the father,
who had always been a close personal friend.

"Good morning, my brother," said Smith to him kindly.

But the old man fixed a scornful look upon him and said · "Don't
call me brother, sir! I would rather claim kin with the devil himself."

"Go then," said Smith, "and honor thy father !"

Smith, in his preaching was hard on the false doctrines of his
time, and especially was this true with Calvinism His wife felt
that at times he was too severe, and urged him to let up. One
day Smith held up a glass of water before her and said, "Nancy,
can I fill this tumbler with wine, till I have first emptied it of water?
Neither can I get the truth into the minds and hearts of the
people till I have first emptied it of water Neither can I get the
truth into the minds and hearts of the people till I have first dis-
abused them of error."

Such illustrations but show the natural turn of Smith's mind

He was fearless, positive, humorous and uncompromising in his presentation of the truth. He had strong convictions that money, position or prestige could not buy. These he continued to declare until those last hours of the year 1867 and early 1868 when the faint gallop of the pale horse and his rider could be heard approaching off in the distance.

In the fall of 1867 Smith went to Mexico, Missouri to spend the winter with his son-in-law and daughter. Although then in his eighty-fourth year, his mind seemed to have suffered little. His memory was yet clear and his wit remained undiminished. On Lord's Day February 9, 1868, while at the home of his daughter, Mrs. Emma S. Ringer, Smith stated that he would go to church and preach as usual. It was an unusually cold day, and Smith remarked to his daughter that he had never seen such a cold day before. Nevertheless, against the wishes of his daughter, he walked from her home to the church house. His discourse on this day was the last that he ever gave. He walked home again, his aging frame shivering in the cold. After a cup of hot coffee and a meal, he went to his room and went to sleep. He awakened in the afternoon and would have gone to meeting that night but his family was insistent that he stay home, so he complied with their wishes. The next morning he was suffering from inflammation. For nearly three weeks Smith lay in bed before passing to his reward at half-past eight in the evening on Friday, February 28, 1868 Three days earlier Smith had sent word by W. J. Mason to Elder Wright, editor of the *Christian Pioneer.* "Tell Bro. Wright," he said, "I am better and most home."[10]

Smith had already made plans for the body to be shipped back to Lexington, Kentucky for burial. It arrived at the depot at eleven o'clock in the morning on the next Wednesday, March 4th. J W McGarvey and a delegation of brethren with a hearse and carriages met the body when it came in, and reverently escorted it to the church building. Some of the brethren were asked to give short discourses and did so John A. Williams, the biographer of Smith, and a very close friend, could not be present He was especially wanted to deliver the funeral address, but since that could not be, on the third Lord's Day of May, Williams did

---

[10]W J Mason, "Elder John Smith," *Christian Standard,* Vol III, No 11 (March 14, 1868), p 85

preach a memorial discourse at Somerset, Kentucky. Following the short messages over the body at the church in Lexington which were delivered by J. W. McGarvey, Robert Graham, and George W. Elley among others, the body of Smith was borne to the cemetery and carefully laid away in the grave.

The next Sunday afternoon, George W. Elley wrote a letter to W C. Huffman, his good friend, of Sumner County, Tennessee. This letter we now have in our possession. It is an interesting letter in the light of the events just recorded.

Lexington, March 8th, 1868

Dear Bro Huffman,

This is the 'Lord's Day,' and a soft bright beautiful day it is. I have just returned from town and from hearing a discourse from Moses Lard, upon "As in Adam all die, so in the Christ shall all be made alive." His mind seemed to be unsettled and wandering, as are the mental visions of us poor preachers at times, and he did not show his usual clearness but said much that was good and cheering to us pilgrims. Generally he is instructive and profitable.

Last week our venerable John Smith was brought here from Mexico, Missouri and planted in our cemetery, a beautiful spot there to lay until our Lord comes. He was with one of his daughters in Mexico. He was in his 84th year and was seriously ill for only a few days He was not only a good but an extraordinary man What he knew to be truth he would teach anywhere and insist upon it. No man in Kentucky or the West has been more efficient for Christ than John Smith In 1827 he immersed 700 persons. God has greatly blessed his ministry since he became an advocate for the whole truth.

I feel that my days are rapidly coming to an end, altho my health is better than for years. And as my time is short I feel more anxious to be at work and owing to my present situation I am unable to give myself to the work. We live one mile out from the city on a small farm, and no white person here but wife and myself Consequently, it is difficult for me to leave home so as to do any good. . . .

G. W. Elley

The Lord had blessed the labors of Smith. To him largely the success of the church in Kentucky can be attributed.

CHAPTER XIV

TENNESSEE TROUBLES

It is not known for certain when the plea for a return to apostolic Christianity first entered the state of Tennessee. The Bethlehem church in Wilson County took its stand for the truth in 1816, and seems to have been the first in the state to do so. One reads of the old Liberty congregation in Marshall County separating from the Richland Association of United Baptists to take an independent stand for the Bible alone as early as 1823. By 1827 the church at Nashville had left the Baptists. By 1840 there were a large number of congregations standing on apostolic ground in the state. It can be stated for certain that by the time of the war between the states the cause in Tennessee had made great progress and was resting upon a substantial basis.

For a time before the war brethren took great pains to collect statistics about the church. Due to this effort, the strength of the church in the state can be fairly accurately known, as well as, in many cases, the origin of the various churches. An analysis of the information at hand may prove, not only interesting but profitable to our investigation of the progress of the cause of restoration.

In east Tennessee in the year 1844 there were but eleven congregations. The largest of these churches seems to have been at Boone's Creek in Washington County with two hundred and fifty members. In the same county were three other churches: Kibber's, with thirty-nine members: Limestone with fifteen and Buffalo with one hundred and twenty-one members Four congregations were found that year in Carter County—Buffalo, Mt. Pleasant, Turkey Town, and Crab Orchard. Buffalo was the largest of these churches with one hundred and twenty-one members. There were two congregations—Liberty and Roan's Creek—in Johnson County, and the Concord and Fork churches in Sullivan County.

In 1846 A. G Branham visited the churches in Wilson County to gather statistics of their strength. He found a number of congregations although in many cases, they were meeting only once a month. At Rutland's meeting house, where John Scobey was a deacon, the church was having only monthly meetings. This

251

congregation separated from the Baptists in June, 1832, and by
1845 had forty-seven members. The church in Lebanon had a
difficult time getting on a substantial basis during these early
years. It was organized in October, 1836 with nineteen members,
but many moved, and the church reorganized in December, 1842.
By 1845 it had only forty-two members. As already mentioned,
the oldest congregation in Wilson County, if not in the state, was
the old Bethlehem church. Its first building was made of hewn
logs and was located six miles from Lebanon on the old Trousdale
Ferry turnpike. Calvin Curlee and John Bonner were among the
first preachers at the Bethlehem church. Alvin Hobbs is said to
have preached the first full gospel sermon at this congregation.
Sandy E Jones held the first meeting here, baptizing forty persons.
Barton W Stone, Jesse L. Sewell, Tolbert Fanning, J M Kidwell
and E G. Sewell did much of the first preaching here. W. C.
Huffman preached for this church after the war. When the war
broke out, Turner Goodall, a young preacher enrolled in Franklin
College, visited the church regularly. When the war started,
however, he joined the Confederate ranks and lost his life   Many
years after the war C. M. Pullias and F. B. Srygley preached here [1]
Wilson County had another congregation called the Big Spring
church which was organized in September, 1839

At least ten congregations were found in Jackson County
before the war. The church at Liberty was organized by John
Mulkey as early as 1826   Ten years later a congregation was
formed at Bagdad. Between 1840 and 1846 the following congregations were formed   Trace Creek, Salt Lick, Ridge Meetinghouse, Pleasant Hill, Buckeye on Flynn's Creek and Meigsville.

A small congregation existed in Marshall County that shared
the distinction with the Bethlehem church of being the oldest in
the state. Wilson Hill on Globe Creek was also formed in 1816.
The new church in the county was organized in 1828 by Joshua K.
Speer. Soon there came along other congregations. Cedar Creek
church was organized in 1831. The Long's House congregation
was formed in 1840   Two years earlier the church at Lewisburg
had been formed, and met in the Court House. There were

---

[1] John M Hill, "History of Bethlehem Church, Wilson County, Tennessee," *Gospel Advocate*, Vol XLV, No 18 (April 30, 1903), p 279

churches formed on Richland Creek·and Cane Creek in the year 1843.

In Warren County, there were three hundred and fifty members in 1848 divided among the following congregations. Ivy Bluff, Fountain Spring, Philadelphia, Irving College, Rocky River, and McMinnville. In Rutherford County the churches appeared to be rather numerous by 1850. There were congregations at Cripple Creek, Millersburg, Rock Spring, Murfreesboro, Fall Creek, Fayetteville, Woodbury. At Millersburg a large camp meeting was held in September, 1847. In Bedford County there were churches at New Hermon, Big Flat and Richmond. In Lincoln County there were congregations at Cane Creek and Lynchburg, and in Cannon County, the Brawley's Fork church had one hundred and twenty-eight members by 1850. A congregation with twenty-five members was organized at Dresden in Weakley County that same year.

The first congregation in Sumner County, Tennessee was organized at Sylvan Academy on March 30, 1834 by Professor Peter Hubbard. There were only nine members of the church. On the evening of April 22, 1837 W C. Huffman was baptized here by John Mulkey Sylvan Academy was the school house, owned and used by Peter Hubbard Later, in 1838 there was a church organized at Electa Cyria After this building burned, the name was changed to Union, and soon became known as "Old Union." Huffman worked with this church for several years. Through his efforts John T. Johnson and George W Elley came from Kentucky on various occasions to hold meetings here

At Chattanooga the church was late being established J J Trott and J Eichbaum visited here in the summer of 1848 and preached in the Presbyterian church house When Fanning visited here in 1855, he says, "We found no church of the disciples, and heard of but few members in the vicinity."[2]

Turning briefly to the western side of the state, one finds the cause less flourishing The church in Memphis was established in 1847 by B W Stone. (This was not Barton Warren Stone.) By the following summer, the congregation had about seventy members. There was a congregation at Union in Shelby County

---

[2]Tolbert Fanning, "A Tour Through Georgia, Alabama, and Mississippi," *Gospel Advocate*, Vol I, No 1 (July, 1855), p 11

which was organized in 1839. At Fayette there was a church with thirty-seven members. In Henry County there were about seven hundred members, the church at Paris, being organized in 1833, had by 1850 over a hundred members.

In middle Tennessee the church was not outstandingly strong. Fanning and Absalom Adams established the church in Franklin, in Williamson County, in 1832 with twenty members. Between the years, 1837 and 1839, Fanning conducted a Female Academy here and his influence helped the church to grow considerably. In 1846 W. J. Barbee, who was a physician, did the preaching for this church. At Columbia the church met in the court house in 1848. J. K. Speer conducted a meeting here that year with thirteen additions. There was considerable complaint that the church had poor leadership and many worldly and disorderly members. In Davidson County there were several other congregations besides the one in Nashville. The church at Franklin College was organized in 1846 with fifty members. The church at Sam's Creek, eighteen miles west of Nashville, had nineteen members. South Harpeth, twenty miles southwest of the city began in 1834, and the following year, a congregation was organized at Sycamore, twenty-five miles northwest of Nashville.

In other sections of the state a few congregations could be found. We have failed up to now to mention that a congregation of thirty-five members existed at Clarksville in 1844, but the church had no meeting house of its own At Pikeville in Bledsoe County there was a church. W. D Carnes in the year, 1848, ran "Pikeville Academy" in this vicinity There was a church also at Athens, and at Lavergne, in Rutherford County.

The work of planting all of these churches fell on the great evangelists of the church who were so willing to sacrifice for the advancement of the cause. One of the earliest of these preachers was John Mulkey. He was the son of Jonathon Mulkey, a Baptist preacher. Mulkey was born in South Carolina on January 14, 1773, and began preaching in East Tennessee during his twentieth year. He had a brother by the name of Phillip, the two being among the strongest Baptist preachers in the community. In 1809 John Mulkey changed his mind on "unconditional election," and as a result, Baptist ire was aroused against him. On the 2nd Saturday of November of that year he and a few others decided to leave off creeds and take only the Bible. This was the same year that Thomas Campbell wrote his Declaration and Address. How significant that so many people, in widely separated areas, were thinking along the same line! Mulkey continued to preach until in 1841 he became too old and feeble. He died on December 13, 1844 at 12:45 A.M. In fifty-one years of preaching, he had delivered ten thousand sermons.[3]

Another of Tennessee's early preachers was Joshua Kennerly Speer. Speer was born in 1794 in Yadkin County, North Carolina. He was reared a Baptist. At the age of twenty-four he moved to Williamson County, Tennessee to live near Franklin. He was religious by nature and wanted to do the will of God. J. J. Trott, who was in those days a Baptist, taught him Baptist doctrine. On the fourth Lord's Day of November, 1823 Speer began preaching. But he wasn't satisfied with his beliefs. He studied his Bible, and also read the *Christian Baptist*. Before long he was converted to the restoration plea, and discarding all creeds and confessions of faith, he began to urge men to come back to the Bible. For thirty-five years Speer preached the gospel. He held meetings all over Tennessee, and baptized hundreds of people. He died at his home in New Hermon on May 27, 1858.

Jesse Londerman Sewell was another of Tennessee's leading preachers. He was an older brother to E. G. Sewell. He was born on Wolf River in Overton County on May 25, 1818 of Stephen and Annie Sewell. There were fourteen children in all, twelve of which lived to be grown. Jesse L. Sewell had but little education, although his younger brothers, Isaac, Caleb, and Elisha, got more after they were grown. He was religiously inclined and very early learned to read the Bible. Consequently, he became a member of the Wolf River Baptist Church at an extremely early age. He was not yet ten years old when he became a member on the third Sunday of December, 1827. Of him, David Lipscomb writes:

Jesse, when young, was small of stature and slender. He became fleshly as he grew older, but his bones and feet and hands were always small. His head was large, well balanced and full; his arms were awkwardly hung upon his body, he never learned what to do with his hands while preaching.[4]

---

[3]Isaac T. Renau, "Obituary," *Christian Review*, Vol. II, No 5 (May, 1845), p. 120.

[4]David Lipscomb, *Life and Sermons of Jesse L. Sewell* (Nashville: Gospel Advocate Publishing Company, 1891), p 49

On July 21, 1839 he married Elizabeth A. Speer. Two years later he began devoting his life to preaching, although he was, at this time, still a member of the Baptist church. Jesse Sewell's older brother, W. B. Sewell, married a member of the church of Christ in 1840. Consequently, W B. Sewell often attended these meetings. Finally, he was led to see the truth, and obey it. The Baptists turned him out of the church. Jesse L. Sewell was disappointed in his older brother, and so, began to search the scripture to convince him of his error. Instead of finding something to convict his brother of, Jesse Sewell himself was converted. He spent many years after this preaching the word, and died at his home at Viola, Tennessee while seated upon his front porch on June 29, 1890.

Still another Tennessee preacher was W. C. Huffman. He was born of German parents in Central Kentucky on May 4, 1802. Early in his life he became a blacksmith. He had a powerful physical constitution and an extremely quick mind. Religiously, he was nothing in his early years. He reacted to the religious divisions by going into Universalism. He moved to Cairo, Tennessee on the Cumberland River in Sumner County in 1825. Two years later he married Lucy A Goodall, daughter of Charles Goodall. Meanwhile, he maintained his belief in Universalism until 1836 when he read the language of Jesus in Matt. 25 · 46. His father-in-law was a Cumberland Presbyterian. Huffman went to their meetings and turned away in disgust He decided to study the Bible for himself to see if it were true. He concentrated upon the study of the Messiahship of Jesus He concluded the Bible was true, and went back to the meetings determined to take nothing the preachers said unless it was read from the Bible He went to the mourner's bench, but found no consolation for his soul. At night, he couldn't sleep. Once he got up, put on a light, and read his Bible, and resolved to be immersed The next morning early he went to an old man by the name of Wiseman, a Baptist preacher. The preacher asked Huffman for a personal experience, so it could be told to the church the next Sunday, but Huffman insisted that he wanted to be baptized for the remission of his sins. Wiseman refused but told Huffman that a man would be preaching that kind of doctrine the next week at Peter Hubbard's school house. Huffman went and heard John Mulkey. He was immersed on April 22, 1837. Huffman labored with the churches in Sumner County until after

W C HUFFMAN

the war. The last two years of his life he preached at Union City in West Tennessee He died on February 19, 1880.[5]

With this background of the Tennessee churches our attention now turns to the city of Nashville where excitement and misfortune were frequently known in those early days before the war In 1780 a party of forty families traversed the wilderness led by General James Robertson and came to the Cumberland River where they established what later became the city of Nashville The

[5]A Alsup, "Wilkinson C Huffman," *Gospel Advocate*, Vol XXII, No 21 (May 20, 1880), pp 328, 329

church in Nashville was established in July, 1820 by Jeremiah Vardeman and James Whitsett. It wore the name of "Baptist Church of Nashville." The membership at that time included: R. C. Foster, Sr., H. Ewing, Dr. John O Ewing, S Whitsett, M. Fly. The women members were Sarah Ewing, A. Foster, Phereby White, H. Temple, S. Robertson, E. Boyd, P. McIntosh, L. Gibbs, S Hays, P. Taylor, A. Goodwin, and L. Garner.

In December, 1820 Elder Richard Dobbs was installed as the first preacher for this congregation. Soon after its establishment, the church had applied for and received membership in the Concord Baptist Association. This Association had been formed in 1810 in Wilson County with twenty-one Baptist churches. But, while Dobbs was preaching for the church, the congregation withdrew from the Association. Dobbs died on May 21, 1825. The next year, the Nashville Female Seminary invited P S. Fall to the city, and he accepted. Arrangements were made and Fall became the preacher for the church on May 20, 1826. The next year the church reunited with the Concord Association. A letter was addressed to the Association, written by R. C. Foster and P. S Fall. The letter said:

Dear Brethren: When the church of Jesus Christ in Nashville sent us up to meet you, she vested us with authority to request to be dismissed from the Association, should circumstances render it proper. Our only object in uniting with you, has been to promote the welfare of the Christian cause, and the harmony of the disciples, and although we cannot approve the course some individuals have pursued in the present controversy, yet we do not wish to be considered as taking a part therein. We do not think there is authority in the New Testament for Association, at any rate, and much less is there any ground for supposing that it authorizes their existence for the purposes to which they generally apply. If we can meet you at any future time, merely for the purpose of worship and general edification, we will cheerfully attend   But until we think those ends can be gained, we request the privilege of continuing to ourselves.[6]

At this time the church in Nashville had one hundred and thirty-one members   It will be seen that the church went back into the Association thinking it was advancing the Christian cause. When it very readily became apparent that they were not, they withdrew. Of the membership, all except five went with the reformation

---

[6]John Bond, *History of the Baptist Concord Association* (Nashville Groves, Marks & Co, 1860), pp 40, 41

In December, 1830 Alexander Campbell, with Jacob Creath, Jr., came to Nashville. On Friday, the tenth, he spoke on the apostasy, and announced that the next night he would speak again Questions were passed to him. It was during this time that Obadiah Jennings, a Presbyterian preacher, arose and disputed with Campbell. For the moment Campbell paid little attention to him. On Christmas Day, after returning from a trip to Franklin and Columbia, Campbell debated Jennings, after which thirty persons were baptized. Following this meeting in Nashville, Campbell wrote:

This Christian congregation is so far advanced in the reformation as to meet every Lord's Day, to remember the Lord's death and resurrection, to continue in the apostle's doctrine, in the fellowship, breaking of bread, and in prayers and praises. From its location, in the capital of the state, this society has already exerted, and is likely still to exert, a happy influence over the whole state.[7]

As we have already seen, P. S. Fall left Nashville in June, 1831 because of ill health. At this time the church had two hundred and fifty members, having enjoyed a remarkable growth during Fall's stay. For the next ten years the church was without a regular preacher. Tolbert Fanning came to the city in 1832 to enter the university, and helped to serve the church on various occasions. Early in 1835 Alexander Campbell returned to the city with his daughter, Lavina. During his stay, there were twenty additions, and by now the church was said to number six hundred members, although it is not unlikely that this figure is a little high, for in 1849 the church is said to have numbered five hundred and forty-three members, and in 1852, five hundred and fifty members. It is very probable that in 1835 the church had nearer three hundred than six hundred members. At any rate, it may be at once seen that the church during these years, up to 1852 enjoyed a remarkable growth.

From the time that P. S. Fall left in 1831 up to 1842 the church appears to have been without a regular preacher. The feeling began to be widespread in the church that a preacher should be secured to labor full-time with the congregation. As a means of talking over the work in general, and of discussing the issues then facing the church, in Nashville several leading brethren met. The subject of cooperation was discussed and then the matter of secur-

---

[7]Alexander Campbell, "The Church in Nashville," *Millennial Harbinger*, Vol II, No. 3 (March, 1831), pp 121, 122

ing a preacher. Tolbert Fanning was present at the meeting. As for himself Fanning was always opposed to the idea of a preacher locating with a congregation. The woes which later came upon the church Fanning could not help but lay to the fact that it had a regular preacher Of this meeting, Fanning remarks ·

It was taught that the labor of an evangelist consisted in preaching the gospel to the lost, in planting churches and enabling the members to do their work—to keep house for God. It was understood that the pastor's office devolved, of right, upon the older members of the church, and upon no others. Then the idea of beardless lads, flippant, and impertinent orators, taking the oversight of venerable sages and matrons, was regarded highly ludicrous [8]

Despite Fanning's objections, the church secured the services of W. H Wharton, then a popular southern preacher. But as time went on, Fanning noted that Wharton got himself busy with other things until his sermons grew stale. By the year, 1846, there was a general feeling that a younger man was needed, and so in May, that year, J. B. Ferguson cast his lot with this church as its proclaimer of the word

In the meantime, other events had taken place around Nashville that will bear some notice. Franklin College was organized in 1843, but more will be said of this in our next chapter. In January 1844 Fanning began the publication of a paper which he called the *Christian Review* His purpose for establishing this publication he outlines in the first issue. Basically there were four reasons for beginning. First, the sentiments and beliefs of the church, Fanning believed, were woefully misrepresented and the truth needed to be taught. While he conceded that there were other papers doing this, yet, none of them enjoyed a very extensive circulation in the "southwest" The second reason was that the Christian religion was not being practiced by any party of the age, so Fanning felt a responsibility to call men back to the word of God. In the third place, Fanning felt that the churches of Christ were not yet fully and scripturally organized, and consequently the disciples of Christ were not as intelligent, spiritual and zealous as they needed to be Lastly, Fanning believed the *Review* would be in a better position

---

[8]Tolbert Fanning, "The Church in Nashville," *Gospel Advocate*, Vol III, No 3 (March, 1857), p 72

to get brethren acquainted in different parts of the country, because it had reporting editors in many of the different states [9]

With high hopes, then, Fanning started the *Review* Its motto was "Union and Peace On the Bible Alone." For four years it continued its publication, and doubtlessly did much to advance the cause in the southland during those years. Yet, Fanning was always busy, and most of the time, too busy. He could not do the paper justice, so made plans to turn it over to someone else. In casting around for a new editor, his attention immediately centered upon J. B. Ferguson, who at this time had been in Nashville less than two years. He had arisen constantly in popularity with the people, and had all the appearance of being a man with great ability, soundness and judgment. So Ferguson was selected to be Fanning's successor.

Of Jesse Babcock Ferguson, H. Leo Boles has well said,

Like a meteor which flashes across the horizon, making a trail of glorious light behind it, and then suddenly disappearing and leaving nothing but darkness in its wake, so Jesse B. Ferguson came above the horizon and shone as a great pulpit orator in the church of Christ at Nashville, Tenn., and then as suddenly disappeared and dropped into obscurity. Perhaps no preacher of the gospel ever stood so high in the estimation of the people and received the plaudits of the populace and then dropped so low as did this man.[10]

Ferguson was born in Philadelphia, Pennsylvania on January 19, 1819. His father was Robert French Ferguson, who soon after Jesse B's birth moved into the Shenandoah valley in Virginia. When he was eleven years old, Ferguson attended Fair View Academy. He failed to get to attend William and Mary College and so turned his attention toward an apprenticeship in printing. When he was twenty-one years of age, he moved to Ohio, but stayed here only a short time, later moving to southern Kentucky.

In 1838 Ferguson began preaching the gospel. His fame spread far and wide in Kentucky. He was both eloquent and brilliant, and he knew it Flattery fell abundantly upon his head, and he grew vain and proud, losing at the same time, his spirituality. His popularity reached Nashville, and in May, 1842, he was invited to con-

---

[9]Tolbert Fanning, "The Christian Review," *Christian Review*, Vol I, No ' (January, 1844), p 1
[10]H Leo Boles, *Biographical Sketches of Gospel Preachers* (Nashville pel Advocate Co. 1932), p. 186.

duct a gospel meeting. The meeting was a huge success, and he was urged to locate with the church. He declined the offer. Two years later he conducted another meeting, and again was begged to locate with the church, but he declined. He began regular wrok with the church in the spring of 1846 and continued this for several years.

Therefore, in 1847, when Fanning was looking for an editor for his paper, decided upon Ferguson. Ferguson accepted the invitation. He decided, however, to change the paper. The name of it now became *Christian Magazine*. It was somewhat larger, and a little more attractive. Ferguson introduced this new publication by saying:

We need a work suited to the times in size, spirit and matter. We have been often and earnestly solicited to commence such a work; but until recently, owing to the fact that we have so many publications, but meagerly sustained, we have hesitated and declined. But in our present enterprise this difficulty is removed; we enlarge and seek to improve an existing periodical, while we have thrown around us increased facilities for making a paper such as we desire . . .

To our friends in the South and South-west, especially, we look for support. Theirs is a somewhat new and uncultivated field of labor.[11]

The *Christian Magazine* continued publication until the end of 1853 At first B. F. Hall and Tolbert Fanning were associate editors, but this arrangement was brief. In 1850 John Eichbaum was chosen associate editor, but he continued in the capacity for only about two years. The Society belief was sweeping all the churches, and the Tennessee churches for a few years fell in line. In 1849 at a State Meeting, it was decided to start a Publication Society, and turn the *Christian Magazine* over to it. But Jesse B. Ferguson continued as the editor, and stipulated the policy of the paper.

The real woes for Jesse B. Ferguson and for the Nashville church began in April, 1852. At this time, in the issue of the *Christian Magazine* for that month and year, Ferguson set forth his views upon 1 Pet. 3: 18-20. He suggested that he had been requested to write on this, and, although he had held this view for eight years, he had refrained from saying so because he knew he

---

[11] J B Ferguson, "Introduction," *Christian Magazine,* Vol I, No 1 (January, 1848), p 1

differed radically from his brethren upon it. Then, in commenting upon this scripture, Ferguson wrote:

It is clear to our mind that the language of the apostle conveys the idea that Christ by his spiritual nature, or by the Spirit, did preach to the Spirits of the invisible world. And as if to include all, the apostle refers to those who died in disobedience in the days of Noah, which would make his language equivalent to all the dead; which he afterwards confirms by declaring that in order that Jesus Christ might be the judge of the dead and living, the 'gospel was preached to the dead'—to those now dead—not 'in the flesh,' 'now in prison.'[12]

When Alexander Campbell read the above article, he was somewhat stunned and took an immediate issue. To Ferguson's idea that when Christ died, he went to Hades and preached the gospel to those that had been disobedient, Campbell answered by calling it a "posthumous gospel." He pointed out that this interpretation contradicted the plain teaching of the scripture that "it is appointed unto man once to die and after this the judgment." Certainly, it would have been successful preaching to preach to the dead, for it would take little argument and no urging to get lost men out of Hades. But what did the passage mean? Campbell says,

The passage fairly construed is this—He warned the spirits in prison that once were disobedient, while the ark was preparing, in which few (that is, eight) persons were saved through the flood, or through the water, that unless they would repent they should all perish.

These spirits, then, were Noah's contemporaries, and were addressed by Noah, speaking through the Holy Spirit, which emphatically is, and ever was, dispensed officially by the WORD, which became flesh and dwelt among us. So that during one hundred and twenty years this great preacher of righteousness, through the Spirit which was in Christ, announced repentance, or ruin, to his contemporaries, then confined, or in prison bounds, during the time the ark was in building and furnishing.[13]

Ferguson's reply to Campbell was entitled, "The Rewards and Punishments of The Life." It was a vague answer, if any at all. Campbell later complains that he read this article five times and was never able to determine whether Ferguson believed in a punishment after death. Meanwhile, the brethren as a whole, were somewhat

---

[12] J. B. Ferguson, "Exposition of Scripture," *Christian Magazine*, Vol. V, No 4 (April, 1852), p 113

[13] Alexander Campbell, "A New Discovery," *Millennial Harbinger*, Fourth Series, Vol I, No 5 (May, 1852), pp 322, 323

excited. Samuel Church of Pittsburgh complained that Ferguson had a "maggot in his brain." John Rogers wailed, "O, if I could blot out the lines he has written on this subject with my tears, most gladly would I do it "[14]

In line with Campbell's suspicions Ferguson soon let it be known that he did not believe in punishment after death Heaven and hell, he argues, are not places but states. Ferguson exclaims:

Is Hell a dungeon dug by Almighty hands before man was born, into which the wicked are to be plunged? And is the salvation upon the preacher's lips a salvation from such a Hell? For ourself, we rejoice to say it, we never believed, and upon the evidence so far offered, never can believe it [15]

From these beliefs Ferguson went farther and farther from the truth. Before long he began to teach that men could have communications with the spirit world, and thus went off into Spiritualism. The influence of these teachings around Nashville was disastrous to the church. Almost all of the church followed him in the belief. Many congregations went off with him. In Nashville there were some who tried to save the church from such teaching. In November, 1854, W H. Wharton read a letter publicly to the church, objecting to Ferguson, but a large body of the brethren stood with Ferguson, so about fifty left to worship somewhere else. Late that same year, Campbell was called in to preach on this doctrine publicly. Meanwhile, Ferguson had had a spirit communication from Dr. William E. Channing, advising him to have nothing to do with Campbell, so he failed to show up at the meetings. Nevertheless, the meetings did, however, do some good, and a year later, Ferguson's popularity had declined some.

On the last Lord's Day in 1855 Ferguson read a letter, signed by five men, asking him to stay on as a preacher Significantly, none of the five were members of the church. When the matter was put to a vote, only a third of the people now wanted him to remain. Bitter division now ensued, and the question of the legal right to the property came up. A lawsuit was planned. but on June 1, 1856 Ferguson resigned, and the brethren settled the difference without such legal procedures. The next February the elders of the church—James H. Foster, J. D. March, Frank

---

[14]Alexander Campbell, "The Spirits in Prison," *Millennial Harbinger,* Fourth Series, Vol I, No 7 (July, 1852), p 414
[15]J B Ferguson, "The Punishments and Rewards of the Future Life," *Christian Magazine,* Vol V, No 7 (July, 1852), p 202

McGavock—announced the property matter cleared up and back in the right hands. By this time, Ferguson had shown, even to many friends, his true color. He left the church completely and went off with a denomination.

It was to take a little time to completely revive the congregation after these disastrous events The church had sold its old building and moved into a newer, much nicer one, on Cherry Street. But, on April 8, 1857 this building mysteriously caught fire, and burned to the ground. The church managed to rent its old building, and in a few months had repurchased it. Meantime, the church had been casting around for another preacher. Old timers remembered P. S. Fall and his good work twenty-five years before They needed now an older man, one in whom they had confidence, and so Fall was urged to come In 1858 he arrived, and then began collecting together the scattered flock. Forty-two white people and fourteen colored were snatched from Ferguson's influence By 1860 the church numbered two hundred members, and was at peace once again.[16]

Fanning, in the meantime, watched the Ferguson fiasco with a heavy heart. He fought bravely and furiously to save the church from the wreck Ferguson had brought upon it. To make matters worse, so far as his own conscience was concerned, he felt he had helped Ferguson by giving him the *Christian Review*. But that mistake was past, and he could do nothing about it, save to make what amends he could He resolved to try to off-set Ferguson's harm by again establishing another paper. Ferguson had closed the *Christian Magazine* in 1853, which was fortunate By the spring of 1855 Fanning had fully determined to start another paper, and to have another partner in his work. This time he selected William Lipscomb to serve with him as co-editor of his new paper.

William Lipscomb was, by seventeen months, the older brother of David Lipscomb. He was born on June 20, 1829. His parents were Granville and Ann Lipscomb Physically, William was a sickly child, lacking in physical vigor and activity common to youth. A great portion of his life he was semi-invalid, suffering from asthma and bronchial troubles The sight of blood severly sickened him, and so weak was he that frequently during his life, he would bleed at the lungs, so that friends would never have been

---

[16]James Challen, "The Church in Nashville, Tennessee," *Millennial Harbinger*, Fifth Series, Vol III, No 4 (April, 1860), pp 214-216

surprised at his death at any time. Yet, William lived a good long life   There were twelve in his graduating class at Franklin College, yet he outlived them all except one. He was the weakest member, physically, of the Franklin College faculty, but he outlived all of his fellow teachers. Very often he was too weak to walk two hundred yards to his school room, and would ride the distance.

William Lipscomb was fond of school books, of reading and studying. Studies never seemed difficult to him. He entered Franklin College in January, 1846 and graduated at the top of his class two years later. His proficiency in his studies made Fanning interested in making him a full time professor at the school. Here he taught Greek and Latin. Both teachers and students recognized him to be the most thorough scholar in the college, and no man exercised a greater influence   He was at once an outstanding mathematician, a master of the English language, and unexcelled in Botany.

William confessed Christ in the summer of 1846 and was baptized by Tolbert Fanning. He preached some, but his physical disabilities made it impossible for him to be a great preacher. When he was twenty-two, he married Anna Fulgham. They lived together twenty-four years and had seven children. When· she died, William married Allie Hudson and they lived together for thirty years   He died in East Nashville at the home of his daughter, Mrs G. A Davis, on February 7, 1908.

Self-assertion and aggressiveness were not traits that belonged to William Lipscomb, and consequently, he was never an outstanding leader. He did, however, have his own convictions and never hesitated to stand for them. He had a great, kind and good Christian soul, and his friends loved him greatly.

In July, 1855 William Lipscomb and Tolbert Fanning began publication of the *Gospel Advocate,* a monthly periodical   As already mentioned, a chief purpose in starting this work was to make amends for the harm done through the *Christian Magazine,* which Fanning felt that his lack of proper foresight had partly caused. So, Fanning writes at the outset:

The history of the work substituted for 'The Review' is well known and bitterly regretted. The error committed cannot be corrected—'there is no place for repentance.' But we would gladly shroud the past in impenetrable night. We once more appear before our brethren and the world as a religious journalist, and whilst we ask the indulgence of all, we are happy in the belief that our labor in the 'Gospel Advocate' will prove a blessing to many.[17]

As to the course the *Gospel Advocate* was to pursue, the editors wrote:

The 'Gospel Advocate' will be devoted to the interests of the church of Jesus Christ, and especially to the maintenance of the doctrine of salvation through 'the gospel of the grace of God.' It will be the careful study of the conductors to present, in an intelligible form, the great and distinguishing principles of the Christian institution, and affectionately enforce the observance of its heavenly practices; to give such reviews and notices of religious systems, speculations, books, publications, and sayings and doing of men, as may to them seem proper and useful, and to keep the reader advised of religious and educational progress. Their motto shall be, 'Open columns and free discussion of all questions calculated to advance the spiritual interest of society.'

While they feel not at liberty to compromise the least 'jot or tittle' of truth, they will regard it an honor to fraternize with all who fear God and respect His institutions, as developed in the Divine Oracles.[18]

Scarcely had the prospectus gone out until letters began to come in expressing best wishes for the undertaking. Campbell wrote·

We are of opinion that such a periodical is needed in Nashville, and in Tennessee. The condition of things in the city and state call for not only oral, but written and printed materials of thought and action The press, well furnished and guided, is a powerful auxiliary of truth or of error. If evil spirits use it in the projects of evil, why should not good spirits use it against fraud and imposture? Under the editorialship of Elders Fanning and Lipscomb, we anticipate for it a large circulation and a liberal patronage.[19]

Ben Franklin wrote: "Respecting your proposal to publish a newspaper, I can say that I think the move a good one. I trust you will meet the new phases of unbelief in such a manner as to do great good. I will furnish you a few short pieces, and everything I can do to encourage your enterprise, I will cheerfully do. May you have abundant success."[20]

---

[17]Tolbert Fanning, "Reminiscences," *Gospel Advocate*, Vol I, No 2 (August, 1855), p. 27.

[18]Tolbert Fanning and William Lipscomb, "Prospectus for the Gospel Advocate," *Millennial Harbinger*, Fourth Series, Vol. V, No 6 (June, 1855), p 358

[19]Tolbert Fanning, "Friendly Expressions in Regard to the Success of the Gospel Advocate," *Gospel Advocate*, Vol I, No 2 (August, 1855), p. 25.

[20]*Ibid*, p 25.

The name, *Gospel Advocate,* was not particularly new. A Baptist periodical in Virginia some ten years before had worn this name. In addition, as we have seen, John T. Johnson and B. F. Hall had published a paper in Kentucky with this name in 1835-36. Neither of these facts seemed to have influenced the name which Fanning and Lipscomb decided to give to their paper. Since it was the gospel that was to save the world, the paper should take that title. Moreover, since the avowed purpose of the editors was to advocate the gospel, and not the opinions of any man or party, it seemed fitting to call it, the *Gospel Advocate.*

The *Advocate* continued publication until the War Between the States began in 1861. During the war, when the mails were closed, the paper was discontinued. It started again in 1866 as a weekly and not a monthly.

Thus we bring to a close our survey of troubles in Tennessee before the war, and the influences resulting which deserve a place in a study of the restoration.

CHAPTER XV

EDUCATIONAL ENTERPRISES

The brotherhood has had from its very beginning a major interest in two types of work—the press and the classroom. As early as 1818 Alexander Campbell was running Buffalo Seminary in his own home at Bethany, and by 1823 was editing an influential religious periodical. Walter Scott, while running his academy at Pittsburgh, did not fail to teach the Bible along with teaching other subjects P. S. Fall was running a female academy as early as 1831 near Frankfort, Kentucky, and Tolbert Fanning was running one at Franklin, Tennessee. Many members of the church had disinguished themselves in the classroom, and it was only natural that they should want to incorporate the teachings of the Bible in their curriculum as time went on. More and more, then, the minds of many turned in the direction of the school where the Bible could be taught.

This emphasis was occasioned largely by the need for the Bible and its teaching which was not and could not be given in the colleges and universities over the country. In addition to intellectual training, it was thought that an emphasis had to be placed upon "moral culture", the teaching of the principles of Christian living as outlined in the Bible. From 1835 until his death this great need was constantly upon the mind of Alexander Campbell. The *Millennial Harbinger* is replete with articles, emphasizing the need of a knowledge of the Bible, or spiritual teaching as well as intellectual. Campbell's long series entitled, "Conversations at the Carrollton House," which were purely fictitious conversations, were for the purpose of stressing the need of Bible teaching as well as other kinds.

Campbell's mind thought in terms of great principles. One of his favorite lines of thought was to divide his study of man into three important phases or states—the natural, preternatural, and supernatural—man as he was, as he is, and as he will be. Man is a physical, spiritual, and intellectual being, and no education can be complete that does not train man for all three To train man to be a physical and intellectual giant while overlooking the spiritual is like putting a high-powered gun in the hands of a savage He becomes a potential threat to the safety and progress of the community.

The many controversies which were later to arise over colleges were never thought of in these early years. Men who taught in these schools were for the most part school teachers by education and training   They desired to take their Christianity with them in their business, and while teaching other subjects, they would not neglect the greatest book of all—the Bible. Theological seminaries were for the most part tabooed. The idea was to give a general education, and along with it teach the Bible, for it was just as necessary to a complete education as any other phases of study. So, accordingly, Campbell writes to Tolbert Fanning, in answer to a query:

Colleges are not instituted especially for the benefit of qualifying men for preaching the gospel   Sacred history, and the Bible in colleges as a textbook, with regular systematic lectures thereon, are just as necessary to properly educate school teachers, lawyers, doctors of medicine, farmers, merchants, mechanics, etc., as to educate preachers. This question insinuates a doubt whether colleges are not primarily, in our esteem, got up exclusively for theological purposes. I judge not the intention of its propounder, but its relevancy to the question of moral culture in colleges   Colleges, as far as religion is concerned, must be a blight to any community, if irreligious , if conducted without religion and the Bible [1]

No attempt is going to be made to trace the history of all the schools which the brotherhood had before the war, for if all of these are considered, large and small alike, it would occupy a large volume in itself. There were three schools that were destined to play a decided role in the future of the restoration movement. These were Bacon College, Bethany College and Franklin College. A more detailed consideration of these is to be given, but before closing the chapter some less detailed study of others will be included.

Bacon College was the first of the colleges established in the brotherhood. Its first session began on November 14, 1836 and was held at Georgetown, Kentucky, then the home of the school. The school owed its origin to dissention with the Baptists in that town, and to a man who otherwise played a very small role in future events in the restoration movement.

---

[1]Alexander Campbell, "The Bible a Textbook in Colleges," *Millennial Harbinger*, Third Series, Vol. VII, No. 9 (September, 1850), p 511.

Thornton F. Johnson, a graduate of West Point, and a teacher of civil engineering by vocation, had gone to Georgetown, Kentucky in 1829 to become one of the faculty members for the Baptist college. Barton W. Stone lived near Georgetown, and soon became a close friend of Johnson's. In 1832 Stone was seriously considering a move to Jacksonville, Illinois and urged Johnson to accompany him and start a college in this vicinity. Johnson decided to go and view the possibilities. In 1834, while he was in Jacksonville, the Baptist college at Georgetown reorganized its faculty, leaving all teachers who were not sympathetic to their doctrine. Johnson then went about his plans of establishing the school in Jacksonville, but another reorganization at Georgetown took place, and Johnson was urged to return. Finally, he agreed to do so, and so for the next two years worked hard to build up the college.

In 1836 the Baptist college again began to tighten its grip on the school, and Johnson felt himself being pushed out   Nothing but a separation would do, so Johnson began planning for another school. Preferably, he wanted a Female Academy, and so urged P. S. Fall to move his school from Frankfort to Georgetown. Fall refused. Johnson built a large brick house on Clinton Street. He waited until after the opening of the Baptist college before opening his own to avoid the criticism of taking other students   On November 10, 1836 he met with the students, but because many faculty members had not yet arrived, the formal opening of the college was delayed until November 14. Nearly sixty students were present for the occasion, and so the college opened with high hopes.

The name attached to the school was Bacon College in honor of Sir Francis Bacon, the great philosopher. The first president of the school was Walter Scott, although, for some reason not stated, Scott never served beyond delivering an inauguration address. Scott was scheduled to teach Hebrew Literature. Besides him the faculty consisted of S. Knight, professor of moral and mental sciences; T. F. Johnson, professor of mathematics and civil engineering; S. G. Mullins, professor of ancient languages; C. R. Przriminski, professor of modern languages and topographical drawing; Tolbert Fanning, professor of natural history; J. Crenshaw, teacher in preparatory department.

The first board of trustees consisted of Walter Scott, John T. Johnson, S Hatch, John Curd, Henry Johnson, James Challen,

Samuel Mickolls, Asa R. Runyoun, J. H. Daviess, T. C. Flourney, George W. Williams H. M Bledsoe, John Duncan, P. S. Fall, S. W. Muckolls, Thomas Smith and John Bowman.

In Scott's place D. S Burnet was elected as president   John T. Johnson was vice-president.   T. F. Johnson resigned in 1837 to carry out his original design to establish a female school   Thus, the school carried on until 1839.   A problem, not peculiar to Bacon College, had arisen relative to securing enough financial aid to run the school.   Considerable opposition had been incurred in Georgetown.   This opposition had been manifested even in getting the State Legislature to grant the charter.   It was finally obtained with a vote of nineteen to thirteen in the senate, and sixty-one to thirty in the house of representatives. Now this opposition made the securing of the school financially even more difficult.   By 1839 the situation for the school had entered a stage where something had to be done.

The trustees of the school made it publicly known that they would move the college from Georgetown to any town that would promise financial subscriptions equal to at least fifty thousand dollars.   Major James Taylor, a lawyer of Harrodsburg, saw an advantage in having the school there   He went to work and raised one hundred subscriptions of five hundred dollars each, besides another ten thousand dollars for a building site.   On May 2, 1839 the trustees of Bacon College agreed to move the school

Although Alexander Campbell complimented the move, all of the problems were by no means settled   D. S Burnet resigned as president and Samuel Hatch began to serve *pro tempore*.   Meanwhile, the school moved in on the residence of James Curry in Harrodsburg, and opened its first session on September 2, 1839.

The need of a permanent president was seen.   The next year the College had secured James Shannon to fill this office.   Shannon was a prominent educator, a man of high qualities and noble bearings.   He was born on April 22, 1799 in Ireland.   In 1815 he entered the Royal University at Belfast and graduated three years later.   A position was soon opened to him as rector of an academy at Sunbury, Georgia, and he accepted.   Here he was immersed and became a member of the Baptist church.   In January, 1830 he was professor of languages at the state university at Athens, Georgia. Five years later he became president of the College of Louisana at Jackson.   He went from here to Harrodsburg.

In 1843 Bacon College moved into a building put on a ten acre tract which Major Taylor had purchased for this purpose in 1839. But now, the attendance began to decline, and again the school entered a financial distress. Shannon handed in his resignation in 1845. Immediately friends of the school got busy and raised some more money, so Shannon took back his resignation and agreed to stay for another five-year period. The College now had twenty thousand dollars worth of property and a fifteen thousand dollar endowment. But the income got worse. All of the scheming, begging and planning could not raise enough funds to keep the school going. What was wrong?

Carrol Kendrick, during this time, was editing the *Ecclesiastical Reformer* in Kentucky. Kendrick took up the battle, and for several months he and Shannon debated the issue before the brethren of the state. Kendrick charged that the brethren of Kentucky were refusing to support the school because Bacon College was not serving its cause. Shannon revealed to the brethren for the first time the utter misconception which he had of the restoration plea. Yet, Shannon's position was one that in later years was freely adopted by many of the schools. Shannon declared that their charter, which was borrowed from Centre College at Danville, had stipulated that the peculiar doctrines of no sect should be preached. Shannon defended the school by insisting they were teaching the Bible, but that they had consistently refused to teach the peculiar doctrines of the churches of Christ. For the first time, in all probability, many brethren learned that they belonged to a "sect," according to Shannon. It is not at all unlikely that Kendrick had struck at the basic trouble with the College, although there were many who agreed with Shannon in his viewpoint.

Nevertheless, matters continued to get worse for the school. When his time expired, Shannon resigned. This was in 1850. That year he became the president of the University of Missouri. On June 14, 1850 the trustees voted to close the college. Apparently, Bacon College had failed, but things were not as bad as they appeared, so far as the future of the school was concerned.

The buildings of the college continued to be used for a high school, conducted by Samuel Hatch. This prevented many legal technicalities from occurring. In 1852 at a state meeting of the churches it was voted to reopen the college, but to amend the chaiter so that the school would belong to the "Christians in the state of Kentucky." No action, however, came from this. Meanwhile, Hatch continued to teach here until 1855 when he closed down the high school. It was now urgent that something be done with the College, but what?

The solution was offered by John B. Bowman. At a meeting of the brethren held at Harrodsburg on October 22, 1855, Bowman suggested that a university be established upon the ruins of Bacon College. It doubtlessly occured to Bowman that the state needed such a university and the people would more likely support it if this could be done. The Board of Trustees approved the idea, and some plans went immediately ahead to raise the money Thirty thousand dollars was immediately raised in Mercer County. By Nov. 7, 1856 Bowman was able to announce that a hundred thousand dollars had been raised, and soon after this, that number was one hundred and fifty thousand. On the first Wednesday of May, 1857 the donors to the project met to decide upon definite action John Allen Gano was present and acted as chairman. A committee of seven was appointed to draw up another charter to be presented to the State Legislature.

The new charter was soon drawn up. It called for a self-perpetuating board of thirty curators, two-thirds of whom were to be members of the church in Kentucky. The Board of Trustees approved the charter and submitted it to the state legislature where it met approval on January 16, 1858. A Board of Curators was appointed and on September 19, 1859 the school began operation under the new name, Kentucky University.

The new president of the University was Robert Milligan, a man whose name was destined to be among the immortals of the church. Milligan was predominantly an educator, and as an educator, always was best known He was born in Tyrone, Ireland on July 25, 1814, and the next year, came as a baby with his parents to settle in Trumbull County, Ohio. In 1831 he entered Zelienople Academy in Beaver County, Pennsylvania and two years later, entered the Classical Institute at Jamestown in Crawford County, Pennsylvania. His father had been an elder in the Associate Reformed Presbyterian Church, so in 1835 Milligan became a member of the same denomination Milligan opened his first school at Flat Rock in Bourbon County, Kentucky While

ROBERT MILLIGAN

he was teaching here, some of the students asked the meaning of
certain passages in the Greek New Testament. Milligan set out
to re-examine the New Testament and ended up by being immersed
into the New Testament church at Cane Ridge by John Irvine in
March, 1838 The next year, he entered Washington College in
Pennsylvania, and by 1843 had received both his Bachelor of Arts
and Master of Arts degrees. He taught English literature at this
college, as well as chemistry and natural history In 1852 he
resigned this position and moved to Bloomington, Indiana where

he taught mathematics in Indiana University for two years   In 1854 he taught mathematics at Bethany College and became co-editor of the *Millennial Harbinger*. He also served as an elder of the church in Bethany.   He was serving in these positions until he went to Harrodsburg to become president of Kentucky University.

There were one hundred and ninety-four students at the opening session of the university, but this number rapidly decreased   The political excitement of the elections, and finally, the war, hurt the attendance considerably.   School continued, however, during the war except for a brief time after the battle of Perryville which was fought October 8, 1862 when the Confederate army took over the university's buildings for a hospital

On the night of February 16, 1864 a tragedy occurred to the school which affected its future course. The main building burned to the ground. Would it be more profitable to put up this build-ing, or, since it is down, would it be wiser to move to a better location? There was the question   The trustees decided to move, and appointed a committee to investigate the possibilities   Four years earlier—in June, 1860, the trustees of Transylvania University in Lexington had made a proposition to turn over their property to Kentucky University if it would move there. Besides the citizens offered thirty thousand dollars. At the time the Trustees had turned down the offer. However, in 1864 when the offer was again made, it was readily accepted. The state legislature approved the move on February 28, 1865, and the University opened its doors in Lexington on October 2, 1865.

BETHANY COLLEGE

The opening of Bacon College in 1836 caused a delay in the plans of Alexander Campbell to establish a college at Bethany. Campbell had been planning such a school, and had made those plans known only to D S. Burnet   For fear that he might be accused of working against Bacon College's interests, he had de-cided to wait until this school was well re-established before going ahead with his own plans   After three years of waiting, Camp-bell divulged to the public his plan for the first time in the October, 1839 issue of the Harbinger. He writes:

' I am now about to divulge to this community, to philanthropists, to lovers of good order, to the Disciples of Christ a favorite scheme deeply impressed upon my mind; long cherished, and in the establishment and supervision of it, it is probable, *if the Lord will,* I shall close all my earthly project.[2]

With this announcement, Campbell proceeds with his statement of the establishment of Bethany College. With Campbell, keeping the Bible foremost, was a paramount interest. He continues.

We want no scholastic or traditional theology. We desire, however, a much more intimate, critical, and thorough knowledge of the Bible, the whole Bible as the Book of God—the Book of Life and of human destiny, than is usually or indeed can be, obtained in what are called theological schools.

Campbell announced that the College would have the following buildings. (1) Stewart's Inn for the boarding and lodging of students. (2) The Family House where children, ages seven to fourteen, could live in a parental atmosphere. (3) Three Professor's Mansions or private dwellings for the faculty. (4) Primary School Rooms where children, ages seven to fourteen attend classes. (5) The College Proper for classes (6) The church edifice.

With these announcements, the plans were formulated and action was brought to bear as quickly as possible. The charter for the College was procured by John C. Campbell for the Virginia State Legislature in the winter of 1840 The Board of Trustees consisted of the following men: Alexander Campbell, Albert G. Ewing, Samuel Church, Henry Longley, James T. McVey, Robert Y. Henley, Samuel Grafton, William Stewart, Josiah Crumbacker, Adamson Bentley, Robert Nicholls, Campbell Tarr, Matthew McKeever, John Andrews, Robert H. Forrester, Jacob Creath, Robert Richardson and John C. Campbell. The first donation was for a thousand dollars and came from Phillip B. Pendleton.

The first meeting of the trustees was held at Bethany on Monday May 11, 1840 Thomas Campbell was called to the chair. W. F. M. Arny was chosen secretary, and Alexander Campbell treasurer. A building committee was appointed consisting of William Stewart, Robert Richardson, Matthew McKeever, and Alexander Campbell.

---

[2]Alexander Campbell, "A New Institution," *Millenial Harbinger,* New Series, Vol III, No 10 (October, 1839, p 446

The second meeting of the board was held Friday, September 18, 1840. At this meeting Campbell turned over to the Board a deed for ten acres of land. The trustees authorized the building committee to erect any buildings they deemed necessary for the school. At this meeting, Alexander Campbell was elected president of the college. The third meeting of the Board was held on Monday, May 10, 1841. A report was read stipulating that $11,045 had been promised to the school, but ten thousand of that was only promised, not yet received. At this meeting other faculty members were selected   W. K. Pendleton, who had recently married Campbell's daughter, Lavina, was selected.   Robert Richardson, Andrew F. Ross, and Charles Stewart were the others selected

By the following October only Stewart's Inn was ready, but school opened nevertheless on the 21st of the month.   Edwin W. Bakewell was the steward.   There was considerable confusion getting started as both students and professors crowded into the same building.   There were one hundred and two students that enrolled, coming from nine states and Canada   Twenty classes were formed, the first one meeting at 6 30 every morning.   Alexander Campbell met this class and walked each morning to it from his home, three quarters of a mile away.

Regulations for the students were rather strict, and for our day a little unusual, but they were rigidly maintained in Campbell's day. Each student, upon entering the college, must submit testimonials of his good moral character that were at least ten years old. All students dressed alike in either dark gray or black color with cloth at a price not to exceed six dollars a yard   The Trustees recommended that each student wear Kentucky bluejeans   The college bell was rung every morning at dawn, and each student was compelled to arise at that time   "Early to bed, early to rise . . . ," and they dare not forget it

With the students as a whole Campbell was well pleased   Nevertheless, he found one disappointment, which doubtlessly every college official has seen   Campbell says,

Some it would seem, have either wholly mistaken the character of their sons or the character and intentions of our institution They seem to have regarded it as a sort of pentitentiary institution, to which youth of either doubtful or desperate character may be sent in the hope of reformation [3]

---
[3] F D Powers, *Life of W K Pendleton,* p 63

Campbell, therefore, had to make it clear that he was running a college, not a reform school. Many a parent has decided to send her wayward child to a "Christian College" with the hope he would be changed. When this child arrived at the school, he found many other parents with many other wayward children had the same idea. These soon got together in their wayward acts and the result has been that the college received a bad reputation over it. Even modern-day college presidents can sympathize with Campbell's problem.

The second year of the college started with more hopeful prospects for the future. There were one hundred and fifty-six students enrolled. Besides, Campbell had announced during the summer that over seventeen thousand dollars had been promised to the school. More buildings had gone up. The College Proper, four stories high, had been finished. So had Stewart's Inn. One wing of a mansion house had been completed. John Mendel, John Atkinson, Basil Wells, Samuel Muckols, and Joseph Wasson had been added to the Board of Trustees.

College commencements at Bethany were gala affairs. They were always held on July 4th, and lasted for hours at a time. The one held in 1843 may serve as an illustration. It was attended by one thousand, five hundred people. It opened by prayer and music at 9:30 in the morning. This was followed by a reading of the Declaration of Independence. Then followed seven speeches, among them a valedictory by Alexander Campbell and a Latin and Greek ode. The program continued without interruption for five hours.

The selection of a college emblem was left up to Robert Richardson. Richardson selected a tripod supporting two volumes— Truth and Science. Upon this was placed a quiver of arrows, and a bow with the motto inscribed above in Latin: *Pharetram Veritas, sed arcum Scientia donat*. The tripod was to indicate they were divine oracles. Truth was using the arrows to pierce her enemies.[4]

At the regular meeting of the Board of Trustees, which met August 13, 1845, a motion was made by John C. Campbell that

---

[4] Robert Richardson, "Seal of Bethany College," *Millennial Harbinger*, New Series, Vol VII, No 6 (June, 1843), p 281

"for the ensuing year it is expedient that there should be added to the offices of the Institution a Vice-Presidency. . ."[5]

Accordingly, W. K. Pendleton was appointed to fill this office.

Alexander Campbell wanted Bethany College to keep the Bible always first. He wrote:

Bethany College is the only College known to us in the civilized world, founded upon the Bible. It is not a theological school, founded upon human theology, nor a school of divinity, founded upon the Bible; but a literary and scientific institution, founded upon the Bible as the basis of all true science and true learning.[6]

Concerning the ideas he had in mind in establishing the college, Campbell also said:

Not a feeling or thought of State pride or glory, of northern or southern, eastern or western interest, spirit or character, had anything to do with its conception, incipiency or design. It was the cause of education—intellectual, moral, religious education— the cause of Reformation, in its connection with literature, science and art—the conviction that educated minds must govern the world and the church—that God had made men of learning, talent and character, his great instruments of human redemption, from the days of Moses and Aaron to the days of Paul and Apollos—that originated the idea of Bethany College   It was emphatically the conviction, that pagan mythology, that Grecian and Roman idolatry, fable and fiction, had supplanted the Bible, that college education, now-a-days, was more skeptical than Christian, more secular than moral or religious, that induced me to add its burden to more than enough before.[7]

Bethany College had many advantages over Bacon and never had many of the problems of the other school. The best talent in the brotherhood constituted its faculty. The dream of every young man was to have the opportunity to sit under Campbell's feet and be taught by this great man. Campbell's great reputation, wide acquaintance among the wealthier people, made the securing of finances with him less of a problem than with Bacon. Moreover, Bethany's location among the hills of northern Virginia, in a comparatively out-of-the-way place, gave it seclusion and protection during the war, and the school continued without interruption.

[5]Alexander Campbell, "Bethany College," Third Series, *Millennial Harbinger*, Vol II, No 9 (September, 1845), pp 417, 418
[6]Alexander Campbell, "Bethany College," *Millennial Harbinger*, Third Series, Vol VII, No 5 (May, 1850), p 291
[7]Alexander Campbell, "The Northwestern Christian University," *Millennial Harbinger*, Third Series, Vol VII, No 6 (June, 1850), p 333.

Occasionally, a disaster struck such as it did on the night of December 10, 1857. A golden glow played across the windows of the professor's mansions and Stewart's Inn with its hideous message of fire. Before anything could be done, the college proper had burned to the ground costing the school nearly sixty thousand dollars. The library with its many valuable collections was gone But classes were interrupted for only one day, and work immediately began on rebuilding the structure But, aside from these rare occurrences, Bethany College continued right on through the war, and sent from her halls many of the greatest of the pioneer preachers.

FRANKLIN COLLEGE

Franklin College, near Nashville, Tennessee, was largely the product of Fanning's mind. Like Campbell, he believed that the educational institutions of the world had overlooked the need of the Bible and so, he proposed changing this. It was in devoting his life to this work that Fanning felt he was doing the most good. He once wrote:

Years since, I think I can say with a good conscience, I saw the folly of Christians toiling to heap together earthly dust, and although I had prepared myself in the profession of law, for practice, my final determination was to devote myself, with what ability I might possess, to the good of man Many sincere friends advised me to give myself to the proclamation of the gospel; but with a hope of greater usefulness, I determined to spend my life, and be spent, in the education of youth. With a full knowledge of the difficulties of the profession, I was induced to attempt the establishment of a high school of learning.[8]

In the spring of 1844 Fanning gave considerable attention to establishing the college. By late spring, he was ready to make the following announcement in the *Christian Review·*

Perhaps it is not known to the readers of the Christian Review, that arrangements are in progress to establish by the beginning of another year, Franklin College, at Elm Crag, the residence of the writer. A charter was granted at the last session of the Legislature. . . .[9]

A farm belonging to Tolbert Fanning and B. Embry called Elm Crag, and located about six miles southeast of Nashville, was to

---

[8]Tolbert Fanning, "Education and Franklin College," *Christian Magazine,* Vol II, No 6 (June, 1849), p. 211

[9]Tolbert Fanning, "Franklin College," *Christian Review,* Vol I, No 6 (June, 1844), p 130

be used for the college   By the summer of 1844 they had invested about fifteen thousand dollars, and needed about four thousand more   Their plans called for the erection of suitable buildings by the end of the year

A Board of Trustees was selected consisting of the following . David G Ligon, Moulton, Ala , Dr M W Phillips, Edwards Depot, Gen Patrick Henry, Hinds Co Mo , Hon J. A Gardner Dresden, Tenn , Col Samuel Martin, Campbell's Station, Tenn ; Dr. John Shelby, Dr John W. Richardson, Stewartsborough, Tenn , W. G Roulhac, J J Trott, Turner Vaughn, Ladoga, Tenn ; Tolbert Fanning, George W Martin, W H Wharton, John Simpson, Thomas Martin, David King, Andrew Ewing, Beverly Nelson, John R Wilson, Frank M'Gavock, B Embry, James H Foster, and Edward Trabue.

Franklin College opened its first session on Wednesday, January 1, 1845   The school was divided into three departments Juvenile, Preparatory, and College Proper   The following constituted the first faculty Tolbert Fanning, President, J N Loomis, professor of mathematics and chemistry, John Eichbaum, professor of languages, E S Chandler, professor of Music, A J Fanning, Principal of Preparatory Department, P R Runnels Principal of Juvenile Department, and B Embry, Steward of the Boarding House   When school opened, Loomis couldn't fill his position, so J. Smith Fowler of Ohio took his place   School opened with forty-five students, and this number soon increased to seventy

In certain respects Franklin College was unlike any other school. Fanning divided education into physical, moral and intellectual His ideal was to combine all three   For the intellectual the regular college courses gave this education   The Bible furnished the moral, and so the word of God was regularly studied   But, in addition, every boy who attended the College spent a portion of each day working on a farm, which was run in connection with the school   This supplied the physical education   Still in another respect was the college different   It had no endowment, wanted none and argued against them Alexander Campbell had something to say about both of these unusual features   Concerning the first, Campbell wrote

There is Franklin College, not far from Nashville, Tennessee, under the presidency of Elder Fanning, also rising into notoriety and increasing in the number of its students. The energy and enthusiasm of brother Fanning are equal to almost any undertaking, and by his industry and perseverance this institution has been built up within a few years to a respectable seminary of learning, combining some of the useful arts of social life, usually called trades, with a literary and scientific education thus putting it in the power of young men to work their passage aboard the ship trade into a liberal and practical education [10]

Concerning the endowment feature, Campbell had some other ideas. He writes

The Franklin College asks for no endowment, and argues against endowment   It asks for aid to get up its buildings, and will have no fund   In this, it is our opinion, and in the history of all Colleges, decidedly in error   Not a College in the world has existed one century without endowment, nor can they.   This fact is worth a thousand lectures   Can any one name a college that has seen one century without other funds than the fees of tuition?   [11]

The average number of students in Franklin College for the first four years was one hundred and thirty   The faculty consisted of the president, four regular professors, and a teacher in the juvenile department.   Around Tennessee, people were slow to come to the rescue of the school financially, for many were under the impression that it was a money-making scheme   In reality Embry and Fanning sank fifteen thousand dollars of their own money in it, and obligated themselves for a debt of five thousand more.   With no endowment, and an extremely low tuition price, they were dependent upon the contributions of brethren   Fanning was a man of great faith, fully determining to do the will of God and depending upon God to look after him.   With Franklin College he would undertake to please God and do good   He wrote

Colleges and schools have sprung up with remarkable rapidity, amongst the disciples, within a past few years. . . . In a Christian point of view, there are few things more vain and corrupting than the idea that colleges give denominational respectability, and it is not altogether clear, that the kind of training most popular is, at the same time, most favorable to true piety   If personal aggrandizement, or sectional and sectarian pride, have influence with us, our colleges will prove a curse instead of a blessing to the world.

[10] Alexander Campbell, "Our Colleges," *Millennial Harbinger,* Third Series, Vol III, No 6 (June, 1846), pp 386, 387
[11] Alexander Campbell, "Our Colleges," *Millennial Harbinger,* Third Series, Vol II, No 9 (September, 1845), p 420

The honor of God, and good of man should be our exclusive study.[12]

From its humble beginning in 1845 until the opening of the war Franklin College continued to exercise considerable influence in the south. Her roll of graduates includes many of the southland's outstanding preachers in later years. Fanning continued to act as its president. No great changes were made in the school until the summer of 1857. Fanning had by now concluded that he was too busy and absent too much from the college. He proposed a reorganization of the Board of Trustees together with the faculty to give the school added strength. When college opened that fall, there was a new board. One now finds on the board for the first time David Lipscomb, who that year resided at McMinnville, Tennessee; James E Scobey of Lebanon, Tennessee and Joshua K. Speer of Lavergne, Tenn.

A change also was made in the general administration of the faculty. Before this, smaller children in the preparatory department had been forced to be thrown with the older students of the college, making teaching extremely difficult. A separate department was created and F M. Carmack was placed in charge The business management of the college was also changed so to relieve Fanning from this burden.

Fanning, however, apparently found the work too arduous even yet. After serving sixteen years as president, he proposed that he step down W D Carnes, president of East Tennessee University became the next president. That year, 1860, the college was bought by an association of friends who did so with a view to establishing two colleges—one male and one female. A Board of Managers, with David Lipscomb as secretary was selected to look after the school The buildings were repaired and put in first class condition and by the fall of 1860, the future of Franklin College looked brighter than it had ever been.

Then came the political election of 1860 followed by its rumbles of war War came upon the south, and the boys from Franklin College quit school to bear arms W D Carnes went back to his home, and Franklin College closed its classrooms. For the next months the soldiers of first the south and then the north used it for barracks.

---

[12]Tolbert Fanning, "Colleges Under Christian Influence," *Christian Record,* Vol III, No 2 (February, 1846), p 48

There were other schools to be established during those years before the war but anything like a complete history of all of them would make almost an endless volume. On the Western Reserve, the Western Reserve Eclectic Institute was born on November 27, 1850. This school was established through the joint labors of many Ohio brethren. In the fall of 1844 A. S. Hayden was conducting a school in Callamer, Ohio in a copper shop. At a yearly meeting of brethren in June, 1849 in Russell, Ohio, Hayden suggested to the brethren that some consideration be given to establishing a school among them Another meeting was held at Ravenna on October 3 Then another followed in November at Aurora where thirty-one churches were represented. At this meeting it was agreed to establish a college and that it should be located at Hiram in Portage County. Another meeting was held in December at which a board of trustees was selected. The name, Western Reserve Eclectic Institute, was suggested by Isaac Errett. Shares of stock were sold at twenty-five dollars each to raise five thousand dollars. A farm of fifty-six acres was purchased, and by the summer of 1850, construction of buildings was well on its way. The school opened that fall with A S Hayden as president. There were one hundred and two students

At Indianapolis there was yet another school that began during these years. At a state meeting of brethren held in Greensburg in October, 1847 the business committee reported "that the brotherhood in this state ought to make some special effort in the cause of education " During the discussion that followed, brethren from Lawrence County promised to raise eight to ten thousand dollars if the school would be located in their county. George Campbell made a similar proposal for Rush County. A committee was appointed to meet in Indianapolis in December to hear proposals from other places The committee met and heard that Lawrence County would raise five thousand dollars if the school would be located at Bedford But the committee decided to submit the matter to the brotherhood of the state The next May another committee was held at which there was reluctance to agree upon locating the school in Bedford despite the insistence of Elijah Goodwin. However, they pushed the decision of location upon the next state meeting which was to be held in October, 1848.

At this meeting the Lawrence County brethren went up in arms, severely reprimanding the committee for a strong sectional bias against locating the school in Bedford. Nothing could be done except to appoint a group to visit every church in the state to get their views. At the next meeting the following year, it was decided to establish North Western Christian University at Indianapolis, and a committee of seven was appointed to take the steps necessary to found and endow the college.

The charter, which was granted by the state legislature in January, 1850 stipulated that the college was to be a joint-stock company with a capital of seventy-five thousand dollars in shares of one hundred dollars each One-third of the capital was to be used on the erection of buildings and the rest was to go into a permanent endowment Accordingly, the college opened in 1855 for classes.

There were many other schools In Missouri was to be found Christian University at Canton, and the Female Academy which was run by L B Wilkes and W H. Hopson at Palmyra In Tennessee there were Minerva College, Burritt College and Hope Institute In Kentucky there was Popular Hill Academy; in Indiana Fairview Academy So it was all over the brotherhood, a multitude of academies and schools all of which did good in many respects but which can only be mentioned here in passing along

CHAPTER XVI

LARD AND McGARVEY

We are gradually approaching the period of the restoration when the names of two individuals stand out prominently before us. These men are Moses E Lard and John W. McGarvey Both men were scholarly, pure men, and good preachers They stood together on the major issues which came to face the brotherhood, although in temperament and disposition were different Our attention turns first of all to Lard

The full story of Moses E Lard is yet to be written One rarely reads a biography of this man from anybody who seemed really to understand him, and probably there is a reason for this Lard was a difficult person to understand He was a man of extreme nervous temperament, and of extreme moods His blood circulated vigorously, causing his face always to be aglow His mind worked rapidly; his feelings were always intense After great mental exertion, he would have times of deep despondency. He was very often of a melancholy nature, and brooded for days over matters that no one could help.

Lard passed through life from one mood to another As he grew older, he tended to reflect upon his past, and hard days were there, too He found himself losing faith in humanity His restless intellect made him search into things he could not possibly understand He would labor at great ends to understand those scriptures which deal with life after death He had a hard time reconciling eternal punishment with the nature of God And so, he brooded frequently over the mysteries of the future He was given much to speculation about the future, and one of the few just criticisms given to him, even by his friends, was on this point

Never could Lard do anything he conscientiously thought was wrong He found it impossible to cooperate with brethren who were using the instrument of music This fact added to his despondecy In the whole affair about Kentucky University, which shall be recounted in our next volume, Lard found himself placed in a false light before the brethren, and he could do little about it More than anything else he wanted the College of the Bible to

MOSES E LARD

serve the brotherhood   During the last year that John Bowman
was regent of the University, Lard served as president of the
College of the Bible   The brotherhood thought Lard had sold out
to Regent Bowman, for whom they had little confidence   But
Lard had taken the position only with the understanding that Bowman would resign after a year. But this fact, he could not tell to the
brotherhood   His position and influence in his last days became
narrowed   He became a lonely man, and out of sympathy with most
of the brethren.

Too, Lard's family contributed considerably to this despondency
which he had in his last days   His wife and children were continually afflicted   This was a continual drain on both his time and

energy, while at the same time, his own health was gradually getting worse He moved about in silence, seldom in contact with the brotherhood All the while he continued to study the mysteries of the scriptures and ponder the whole thought of life and of death.

Yet this was but one side of Moses E Lard, a side which is necessary to be known if Lard is to be understood. To ignore this side might be more charitable, but certainly less truthful, for a partial picture is only partially the truth. But Lard had many, many noble qualities about himself. There was in the man a sense of loyalty that seemed to be unlimited. Woe to the man that assailed one of his friends! Woe to that man who proved a traitor to to the truth of God! Lard seemed to be able to dip his pen into the fires of hell and belch out anathemas that would melt the whole field before him. Lard loved a good debate. He loved to get into a discussion, and the hotter the better. He once wrote:

I am so sorry Bro. Shepherd is averse to controversy Were he not, what a nice time he and I could now have I like controversy. I like it all the better the hotter it grows I like to see it leap up even to a white heat Give me a foeman over on the other side deeply entrenched in great banks of error Only let the truth be with me; and then let the battle rage I like sharp practice at short range. What if error shoots up high, and hisses and blazes like rockets? There is no cause for alarm. The rainbow with its soft, blending colors, lifts its arch high over the storm that rages below So with truth Gentle and bright as the star that hung over the cradle of the infant Saviour, it will still shine on, and bring the feet of the weary to the fountain of life But two conditions are essential to make even controversy lovely · Let the end sought be truth, and the Spirit shown be Christian [1]

It is as a preacher of the gospel that Lard is especially remembered. Unquestionably, he was one of the most eloquent speakers to come out of the whole restoration. Yet, there were times when Lard did not measure up to expectations In this respect he was similar to Walter Scott. Lard, as we have said, was a man of mighty emotions When those emotions were aroused, he would pour forth a stream of eloquence that would sweep an audience away. Once when he finished an eloquent discourse, he called suddenly on the audience to stand and sing Not a word was uttered It took several minutes for that great sea of emotion to

---

[1] Moses E Lard "Church Independence." *Apostolic Times,* Vol III, No 49 (March 14, 1872), p 388

calm down enough that the people could sing On another occasion, Lard was preaching near Winchester, Kentucky shortly after the war. Two old men sat in the front listening. One was William Azbill, and the other was "Uncle Si" Collins. "Uncle Si" was an eccentric but devoted old man. He loved to hear Lard preach On this occasion Lard was at his best The music of his eloquence floated out like enchanted whispers. Higher and higher in a heavenly crescendo swept his eloquence until finally it seemed that the whole host of heaven had broken loose in one grand anthem of praise Collins sat nodding his approval, clapping his hands, and slapping his knees Finally when he could hold himself no longer, he jumped up in the air, slapped old William Azbill on the back and shouted: "Brother Bill, isn't he a sugar stick?"

Yet, Lard was not always at his best. Much of the time he was in evangelistic work He had some thirty or forty sermons that were incomparable The labor which he put on this was colossal Such thoroughness of preparation and complete mastery of material few preachers ever knew Beyond these sermons, he was sometimes disappointing Dr Winthrop H Hopson was perhaps Lard's closest rival for pulpit supremacy When someone asked him which was the greater preacher, himself or Moses E Lard, Hopson replied· "Up to thirty sermons Lard can beat anybody, after that, up to two hundred and fifty, I can beat him " Sometimes Lard entered the pulpit moody and despondent, and his sermons were below par, but Lard at his best had no equal in his day Concerning Lard as a preacher, a close friend of his once wrote·

The flashing activities of his intellect and imagination opened the fountain of his soul, gave it strong and daring wings, and it soared away to other worlds and into the light of other suns, and how often it brought back to the heavy atmosphere and dull days of earth dust of gold and gleaming splendors of celestial jewelry on its starring wings, ten thousands of living men and women can proudly testify I have heard him form word pictures in his ecstatic moments that were unutterably grand, and at the same time clothed with a shimmering robe of beauty which seemed to have been woven in the looms of heaven by angelic fingers [2]

The life of Moses E Lard began at Shelbyville, in Bedford County, Tennessee on October 29, 1818. His Scotch parents

---

[2] J W Cox, "Moses E Lard," *Christian Standard,* Vol XV, No 31 (July 31, 1880), p 241

joined in the migration westward in 1829 toward Missouri. His father, Leaven Lard, went to Missouri because of the plentifulness of game. He was poor. When therefore in a few years he died of smallpox, his widow found the burden too great for her She had six children and no means of support. At a very early age, then, Moses E Lard and a brother had to leave home to make their own way His mother gave to each her blessing and a New Testament Of this 'scene Lard in later years wrote

As my brother and myself stood beneath the little cabin eaves, just ready to take leave of the only objects on earth dear to us, and thus close the saddest scene of our lives, my mother said: 'My dear boys, I have nothing to give you but my blessing and these two little books' Her soul was breaking, and she could say no more She then drew from her bosom two small testaments, and as her tears were streaming, and lips quivering, she screamed as if it were her last, and placed them in our hands We all said good-by, and that family was forever broken on earth To that little book and the memory of that scene my future life owes its shaping I never neglected the one, thank Heaven, nor forgot the other.[3]

By 1835, when Lard was seventeen years of age, he could not read or write. During these years he lived in Clinton County He had taken up the trade of being a tailor, but he determined to learn to write. Around the village where he lived, he tore down the advertising and used the letters to learn to read and write. Thus Lard became what might be called a "self-educated" man

During the next few years, Lard's mind experienced the vagaries common to youth with only imperfect knowledge on the subject of religion He listened to denominationalism, and heard the pleas of Calvinistic preachers, urging sinners to get an experience From these Lard turned away in disgust Feeling that there was nothing to religion, he finally turned toward infidelity Finally, however, he began to hear of preachers who were advocating a return to the ancient order Into his hands there was placed a copy of Walter Scott's *Gospel Restored,* and Lard literally devoured it A number of years after this, Walter Scott made a trip to Missouri, and for the first time met Lard Immediately Lard threw his arms around Scott and said· "Bro Scott, you are the man who first taught me the gospel "

[3]W T Moore. *The Living Pulpit of the Christian Church* (Cincinnati R W Carroll & Co, 1868), p 229

"How so?" asked Scott.

"It was by your Gospel Restored," answered Lard.[4]

But Lard was twenty-three years old in 1841 when the first proclaimer of the ancient gospel came his way. This man was Jerry
P. Lancaster. Lancaster had at one time been a Methodist
preacher. His life later proved to be unfortunate in some respects.
He migrated to Missouri from Kentucky, and began to preach the
true gospel. Most of his preaching was done in the upper counties
of the state. Lard went to hear Lancaster, and accepted the gospel,
later being immersed by this same man. In years to come
Lancaster fell away from the truth, and consequently, his name is
little known today   In 1849 rumors flew in Missouri that he was
a Universalist. That same year Lancaster moved west to
California in the gold rush   In California he made shipwreck of
the faith and became a very bad man in many ways. There is a
happier end to the story in that several years later, when the war
was over, Lancaster came back to Missouri, friendless, penniless,
and in need of assistance   He went to a meeting being conducted
by T M. Allen, one of Missouri's oldest pioneers. Allen had
talked to him privately before   During the meeting, Lancaster
came forward and back to the Lord   He was always faithful
afterwards   Though Lancaster was criticized heavily by other
preachers, yet Lard always had a tender feeling toward him, and
spoke kindly of this man who had immersed him.

It was in Clay County that Lard was immersed. It was in this
county also that he preached his first sermon. Soon he was
doing some preaching in Richmond and Lexington, also practicing his trade as a tailor at the same time   At Lexington, he made
the acquaintance of Jacob and Ruth Riffe, who had a daughter,
Mary, in whom Lard was interested   Very shortly Lard married
her   By 1845 he was a married man with two children

For Lard to think seriously of going to school at this time was
almost out of the question   He had little education, was married,
and the father of two children   Education was costly   To go to
school, and support a family at the same time, was something Lard
could only dream about   Nevertheless, circumstances were paving
the way in his favor   At Richmond Lard had become the good

---

[4]William Baxter, *Life of Elder Walter Scott* (Cincinnati   Bosworth,
Chase & Hall, 1874), p 314

friend of General Alexander W. Doniphan, one of Missouri's leading citizens, and an ardent and faithful Christian. Doniphan saw the potentialities in Lard and encouraged him to make the sacrifice to go to Bethany College. Lard determined to try and on March 4, 1845 enrolled in the school.

In its organization Bethany College had one feature that particularly proved advantageous to Lard. Students in the college, one discovers, "are not restricted to a fixed routine of classes requiring attendance at College a certain number of years, without regard to age or proficiency."[5] The classes were so arranged that the more mature minds could make the most rapid progress without being held longer because of class organization. In other words, a man who entered college late in life, could by proper application of his time, take a full four-year course in much less time, the time being determined only by how much he might apply himself and advance This arrangement helped Lard. He completed a four years' course in three years. Even though he worked at physical labor while going to school, he graduated as valedictorian in his class.

Out of the gratitude of his heart, Lard wrote to Alexander Campbell, expressing his appreciation for what was done for him·

Four years and four months ago, strange, homeless, penniless, and untaught, I landed a stranger at Bethany College. It was my fixed purpose, though encumbered with the responsibilities of of a family, to qualify myself for more extended and enlightened usefulness. This object, the first and nearest to my heart, I wanted the means to accomplish.[6]

Lard goes on to tell of the letter from Campbell that brought him out to Bethany. "For which, and for the disinterested and cordial manner in which you have so often aided me when want bore heavy on me, I owe you the feelings of gratitude which I have no power to express " He continues

To my tried friends and brethren in Christ, W K Pendleton and J. O. Ewing, I am under the strongest obligations Friends, they proved themselves to me when I needed friends. They have untied their purse-strings and tendered me their gentlemanly aid at times and in ways of which I cannot think without the tear of grateful remembrance starting in my eye [7]

[5]Anonymous, "Circular—Bethany College," *Christian Review*, Vol. II, No 3 (September, 1844), pp 69-72
[6]F W Powers, *Life of W K. Pendleton*, p 135
[7]F. W. Powers, *Life of W. K Pendleton*, p 135

Upon graduation from Benthany College on July 4, 1848, Lard took his family and moved back to Missouri, locating at Independence   For the next few years only occasional notices tell us of Lard's activities   From Independence he moved to Liberty. From Liberty he moved to Camden Point where for a short time he was president of a Female College   From Camden Point he later moved to St Joseph   In the spring of 1850 the church at Lexington divided, and one finds Lard taking an active part in trying to bring about peace.

Meanwhile, Lard was developing as a preacher   At first, like all young preachers, he had made many blunders, received many criticisms   Jacob Warrinner had often proved a tried friend   Warrinner would pat him on the shoulder and say, "Go on, my son, you have done well, be thoughful and persevere, and when 1 am gone, you will be a man "[8]   Almost every preacher can contribute a part of his success, no matter how great or small it may be, to the encouragement of older preachers   No man had farther to go than Lard, yet he traveled the road with the help of the Lord, the determination of his own spirit, and the encouragement of those who saw in him great possibilities for the Lord

Lard's first gospel meeting was held at Hainesville church in Clinton County   Perhaps his most famous meeting was held at South Point, where through the influence of Dick, a colored slave he baptized the boy Thomas, Dick's master   Lard was a masterful story teller   This story he tells in his first issue of *Lard's Quarterly,* and those who have access to it would find it interesting reading   The South Point Church was located five miles above Camden on the road to Liberty. It was established in the summer of 1853 by Lard with eighty-four members   Three years later a new meeting house was constructed here.

In 1857 J B Jeter, a Virginia Baptist preacher, decided to examine "Campbellism " Campbell, although giving the examination some notice in the *Millennial Harbinger,* decided that a more thorough notice should be given to it   He himself was too busy, and Moses E. Lard was selected for the work   This indicates the high opinion that Campbell had of Lard by this time

There is no record of a great number of debates that Lard ever held. If he ever held many, they must have been too insignificant

[8]Moses E. Lard, "Dick and South Point," *Lard's Quarterly,* Vol I, No 1 (September, 1863), p 17

to be recounted   The one public discussion that he did have was conducted at Brunswick, Missouri in October, 1860 with W. G. Caples, presiding Elder of the Methodist Church   It was a lengthy discussion, beginning on Monday, October 8 and closing on October 18, Thursday   There was no debate on Saturday or Sunday.   The audiences ranged from one thousand and five hundred to three thousand   Many outstanding preachers were present, among the number being, John Smith, W H Hopson, T. M. Allen and J. W McGarvey, and John R Howard   Howard, reporting on the discussion, said of Lard's part ·

Such were the purity and chasteness of his language and diction, and his great earnestness, seeming ever to be properly impressed with his subject and with the importance of the great and solemn topics of the Christian religion, throwing his whole soul into what he was uttering, that he came nearer possessing the character of the real orator, the true Christian orator than almost any man I ever heard.   His words generally fell from his lips, like coins from the mint, correctly struck and properly impressed by the organs of speech, and seemed to be ready for the press without any correcting or revision [9]

Just exactly when Lard conceived of the idea of publishing a Quarterly may never be exactly determined   Nevertheless, by the year 1859 his plans were beginning to materialize themselves into action.   In the spring of this year Lard announced to the brotherhood his intentions of publishing a periodical to be called *The Christian Quarterly,* from St. Joseph, Missouri.   The first issue was to be sent out on the first Monday in January, 1860 provided two thousand paid-up subscriptions could be received by this date.[10]   A month before Lard made this announcement the Central Pennsylvania Cooperation Meeting, on February 18, 1859 passed the following resolution:

Resolved, That the issuing of a quarterly, edited by Brother M. E. Lard, meets our hearty approbation [11]

After making the announcement of his intentions to publish the *Quarterly,* Lard waited for the response.   Two thousand sub-

---

[9]J R Howard, "Debate Between Lard and Caples," *Gospel Advocate,* Vol VI, No 11 (November, 1860), p 338

[10]Moses E Lard, "Prospectus of the Christian Quarterly," *American Christian Review,* Vol II, No 14 (April 5, 1859), p 55

[11]Jesse H Berry, "Central Pennsylvania Cooperation Meeting," *American Christian Review,* Vol II, No 10 (March 8, 1859), p 39

scriptions didn't come in On January 10, 1860 Lard wrote to
W. K. Pendleton:

Allow me to say that as the required number of Subscribers for
the Quarterly has not been obtained the work will not be published.[12]

Probably many brethren, as well as Lard himself, were disappointed
that the subscribers didn't respond. The reason may be hard to
give. The uncertainty of political affairs at this time probably
influenced the people. If they subscribed, could the paper continue? In addition, the brotherhood has shown over a number of
years a general reluctance to accept *Quarterlies*. People with a
limited supply of money would rather receive a weekly than a
Quarterly or even a monthly. The *American Christian Review*,
a weekly, was the most popular paper in the brotherhood, exceed-
ing even the *Millennial Harbinger,* a monthly But, up to this
time no one had tried to publish a *Quarterly,* and someone had to,
by bitter and disappointing experience, discover this fact. It
was left up to Lard to do so.

Lard, although disappointed, was not inclined to give up He
still believed in a quarterly periodical, and the fact that there was
a war on, with mail service limited, and a large portion of the
brotherhood cut off from him, didn't discourage him. Perhaps, for
his own good, he was overanxious. In the spring of 1863 Lard
wrote:

To our brethren especially in Kentucky and Missouri, I have a
word to say. You frequently write me to inquire whether I have
wholly abandoned my purpose to publish the Christian Quarterly.
Be patient, brethren, and if God will spare my life and open for
me a door in the future, you shall yet look in the pages of the
Quarterly. I have four numbers of it lying in my drawer awaiting
the favorable moment to visit you Again I say, be patient and you
shall not be disappointed.[13]

On August 5, 1863 Lard wrote to Ben Franklin:

I have this day placed in the hands of the printer the manuscript
of the first number of my Quarterly, now so long delayed. The
work will be printed in Frankfort, Kentucky; and each number
will contain 112 pages Cost of the work per year, $2 *in advance.*

---

[12]Moses E Lard, "The Quarterly Not to Be Published," *Millennial Harbinger,* Fifth Series, Vol III, No 2 (February, 1860), p 103

[13]Moses E Lard, "Correspondence," *American Christian Review,* Vol. VI,
No 18 (May 5, 1863), p 71

The first number will be ready for delivery by the first of September following.

These are perilous times in which to commence the Quarterly. But now, more than ever before in this country, should the whole strength of every true man be exerted, and every legitimate means be used, to unite the hearts of Christians and spread the truth. A deep desire to work for these grand ends is both my reason and apology for commencing the work now [14]

The name of the new periodical was not *Christian Quarterly,* as apparently had been the intention up to the very last, but *Lard's Quarterly* On the opening page Lard states the purpose of the paper.

The chief of these certainly was the strong desire felt to increase our facilities as much as possible, for laying before the age in which we live, the claims of *Primitive Christianity* With us these claims were paramount; hence the desire to give them the widest possible circulation swayed us in our decision, more than every other consideration besides. The highest distinction, then, to which the QUARTERLY aspires, is to contain a clear, true statement, and just defense of Christianity as taught in God's holy word. Should it, even in a small degree, prove to be successful in this, its highest aim will have been realized On its opening page, then, we dedicate it to the uncorrupted Gospel of Christ, and to that noble body of saints who, for the last forty years, have been laboring for its restoration to the world.[15]

Into the *Quarterly* Lard put some of his greatest works. Despite this fact, the periodical was not widely received. At the close of the year, 1866, it had only one thousand five hundred subscribers —not enough to pay for its publication The editor, because of the lack of funds, was preaching out of Lexington, Kentucky, very frequently which caused the paper to appear irregularly. Lard continued to beg for subscribers Finally, in the summer of 1868, unable to go farther, he announced that publication would cease. Earlier in the year, February 23, 1868, Lard had written the following letter to the brotherhood:

Dear Brethren: Up to this date I have not felt sufficiently encouraged to place another number in the hands of the printer, nor even now am I sure that it is right to do so. Still hoping better things

[14]Moses E Lard, "M. E Lard's Quarterly," *Millennial Harbinger,* Fifth Series, Vol VI, No 8 (August, 1863), p 378
[15]Moses E. Lard, "Preface," *Lard's Quarterly,* Vol I, No 1 (September, 1863), p 1

for the future, I at once place No. 1 in the press   You may, therefore, expect it as soon as it can be printed   How far I can proceed with the work will depend on you [16]

The *Gospel Advocate* printed the above letter, and urged the brethren to subscribe   While David Lipscomb admitted there were many things in the *Quarterly* with which he could not agree, he says, " . . we have long since learned that it is a very narrow and selfish bigotry that refuses to sustain a paper because every thing in it does not suit ourselves "   Lipscomb had on other occasions complimented the paper.

It is conducted with marked ability   Brother Lard, as a writer, in his own peculiar style, has not a superior among us, for point, pungency and force   His sentences are always pointed, not unfrequently barbed.   There is a piquancy and an air of independent thought, that in this age of tame, sterotype styles and matters of thought in religion, are refreshing.   There is an earnestness of thought and feeling manifested that exhibits hearty faith and decided convictions of truth, that stand in marked contrast with the almost universal time-serving, policy-ruling spirit of even the Church of Christ.[17]

But why, it may be inquired, did the *Quarterly* fail to get subscribers?   Two reasons have already been suggested.   There was a marked uncertainty about national life during these days of the war   People living as close as most of them did to the conflict, were thinking of it more than of trying to help a religious periodical live.   Secondly, people with limited supplies of money would much prefer to spend it upon weekly papers like the *Review* or a monthly like the *Harbinger,* than upon a Quarterly.   There was yet a third factor that entered in   The editorial policy of the *Quarterly* on the major issues was a middle-of-the-road one.   Lard was strictly against the use of instrumental music and advocated that preachers refuse to preach where it was being used   It was, in and of itself, sinful.   With regard to the Missionary Society, Lard took the belief, then so popular around Lexington, that it was a matter of expediency.   There was nothing wrong or unscriptural about it, in and of itself   Yet, he went farther and admitted that while it was an expedient, it was an unnecessary expedient.   Lard wrote:

---

[16]Moses E Lard, "Lard's Quarterly," *Gospel Advocate,* Vol X, No 12 (March 19, 1868, page 276

[17]David Lipscomb, "Lard's Quarterly," *Gospel Advocate,* Vol VIII, No 21 (May 22, 1866), p 326

The right of Christian men to have them is a right we by no means call in question; but a claim to have them based on any really necessary ground is a claim the force of which we must in candor say we have not felt.[18]

The general policy of the paper pleased but very few in the brotherhood Friends of the Society, who were by far in the majority, did not appear anxious to support a paper that condemned them as this one did. The opposers of the Society did not altogether agree with the ground on which Lard objected These, then, are the chief reasons why, in our opinion, the *Quarterly* was not supported, and why, in the summer of 1868, it had to come to a close

After the close of the *Quarterly*, Lard threw his editorial fortunes in with the *Apostolic Times*. More about this shall be noted in our next volume Suffice it to say, the *Times* likewise, proved not to be successful Lard found himself among that number occupying positions which made him stand quite alone in the brotherhood Although Lard was not an old man when he died in 1880, yet he had been sickly, disappointed, and was growing despondent Physically, he was a large man, six feet and three inches, with a bony frame, black hair and small piercing eyes That body began to give way under the strain, and Lard died His body was borne from Lexington back to St Joseph, Missouri where he had labored and preached so long, and was laid to rest in the Mount Mora cemetery.

JOHN W. McGARVEY

David Walk attended the convention of the American Christian Missionary Society in October, 1862 as an observer. John William McGarvey was there and spoke Walk thus describes him:

He is probably three-and-thirty years of age, about 5 ft 6 inches in height, has light brown hair and hazel eyes; head disproportioned to the size of his body, being very large and striking in appearance, countenance of the most radiant and innocent expression; with as pleasant and agreeable a contour generally as one would be likely to meet with in a day's travel It will be seen from this description that he is not a man whose person would attract attention in a crowd The plain, simple truth is, Brother McGarvey is a ten-fold greater man, intellectually, than any one would be led to suspect on merely seeing him. . . . We hail him

---

[18]Moses E Lard, "Missionary Societies and Our Hymn Book," *Lard's Quarterly*, Vol II, No 2 (January, 1865), p 136

J W McGARVEY

as one of the 'coming men' of the age   Nay, more, *he is even now here.*[19]

It is highly interesting to note that one like David Walk would describe the J. W. McGarvey of 1862 as one of the coming men of the age, and then say, "nay, more, he is even now here."   How absolutely right Walk was probably he himself did not fully realize.

[19]David Walk, "Brief Sketches of Noticeable Characters at the Late Missionary Meeting in Cincinnati," *American Christian Review,* Vol VI, No 3 (January 20, 1863), p 1

For in the years to come the name of J. W. McGarvey was to be household wherever the cause of the ancient order had gone.

There are yet a few older persons who sat at the feet of McGarvey in the College of the Bible at Lexington, who can appreciate to some extent Walk's description of McGarvey. In later years, however, some changes, brought out with time and labor, occurred. McGarvey was five feet, seven inches tall, of medium weight, with blue-gray eyes. Those who remember him now will recall that he was a little round-shouldered, although this was not true in his youth. When Walk saw McGarvey, his hair was a dark brown, but those now who will remember him, will remember it as sprinkled heavily with silver He wore a beard all of his adult life, and in later years was rarely seen without a long ear trumpet in his hand, for McGarvey was very deaf. In personal appearance he was always neat. In disposition his most outstanding attribute seemed to be his kindness. He was rarely angry, never known to lose control of himself. In the presence of women he was always chaste and chivalrous and that made him many friends among them.

J W. McGarvey was a man of deep convictions for truth, and kindly feeling for men He believed the Bible most implicitly and could not tolerate men who cast a reproach upon it or rejected any part of it. His enemies called him a "legalist" and a "conservative" When he noted a man forsaking the scriptures, McGarvey would attack with a relentless barrage of criticism and argument, often becoming very bitter Yet, personally he felt no bitterness In a measure this was characteristic of the age During the last half of the previous century, men fought furiously for their ideals They took no offense at criticism and expected no one else to Men born of a more modern spirit have often found this hard to understand. McGarvey loved the truth, and spoke accordingly. Men always knew where to find him

The life of McGarvey is, in itself, an inspiration. He was born at Hopkinsville, Kentucky on March 1, 1829 His father was an Irishman who had migrated to Hopkinsville a short time before Here, he had made the acquaintance of Miss Sarah Ann Thomson, daughter of John Thomson, and married her They were married only four years when he died, but during this time, he ran a dry goods store in Hopkinsville. John W. was the second child of four born to this union. He was thus four years old when his father died

The child life of J. W McGarvey was, therefore, spent under his step-father, Gurdon F. Saltonsall. Saltonsall's father had died when he was a young man, and he lived with an uncle in Connecticut. He fled his uncle's home and came to Georgetown, Kentucky where he secured a job working for John Thomson. Later he married Polly Thomson, McGarvey's aunt, who was the sister to his mother. Polly died leaving Saltonsall with nine children. Saltonsall then married McGarvey's mother and this made them have thirteen children. To this new union six more children were born, making a nice, quiet little family of nineteen children, quite a sizeable congregation in itself

In 1839 Saltonsall moved his family to Tremont, Illinois. He had scruples against slavery, and thought this would benefit his family to move   Here, McGarvey's young manhood was spent He was now ten years old and lived here until he was seventeen. He worked on the farm, and learned the fine arts of manufacturing hemp   Meanwhile, he had an unusual opportunity for going to school under James K Kellogg   Kellogg was far in advance of most teachers of that day, and under him McGarvey got a good start in the fundamentals

Saltonsall himself had been converted to the cause of restoration He was a successful business man, and therefore, was a donor and a trustee for Bethany College   He had by 1848 given $2,500 to the College with but one stipulation and that was that any son or sons that he might send there would be educated off the income received from this money   Later, when he died, Saltonsall made Bethany College the twentieth child in his will, and it shared equally with the rest ° McGarvey by his own choice determined to enroll in Bethany   Consequently in March, 1847 he entered school. He himself tells us that it was on March 17, 1847 that he first took his seat in chapel at Bethany College [20]

While he was enrolled at Bethany, McGarvey determined to become a Christian   He made up his mind that at the first opportunity, he would confess Christ and be immersed   He listened to Campbell preach much, but it was not Campbell's custom to extend an invitation after each sermon, so McGarvey waited two weeks after he made up his mind before he had the opportunity of stepping forward and making the confession   It was, as Mc-

[20] J W McGarvey, "W K Pendleton," *Christian Standard*, Vol XXXV, No 37 (September 16, 1899), p 1193

Garvey would describe it, "an ordinary service" McGarvey confessed Christ, and was baptized in Buffalo Greek at Bethany by W. K Pendleton.

School ended for McGarvey on July 4, 1850. He was graduating with honors, and was selected to give the Greek oration. As yet, he had not fully decided his future life He wanted to preach, but by temperament, he was naturally diffident, and lacked, therefore, the full confidence in himself he needed So McGarvey turned his attention toward home, not yet fully decided upon what to do.

His family had moved from Illinois to Fayette, Missouri They wrote to their son, not to come down the Ohio River, as was generally done, for fear of cholera, but to come by the Great Lakes. McGarvey had quite an excursion on this trip, but he finally arrived at his new home in Missouri. His fortunes for the next twelve years were to be cast here. He did nothing great or outstanding, but McGarvey took full advantage of these years to use them for his own advancement and strengthening

Soon he had fully decided that he wanted to preach Yet he realized that he was not ready, for he needed more knowledge of the scriptures. He opened a private school for boys at Fayette, and on the side, studied the Bible as he found time He reviewed his Greek, and became very adept at this subject He continued this way until September, 1852 when the church at Fayette invited him to preach for them. He was ordained, according to the custom of the day, by the laying on of the hands of T M. Allen and Alexander Proctor.

Young preachers frequently need the help of old preachers. T. M. Allen proved to be a counsellor and helper for young J. W. McGarvey in these early days. Allen himself was a great preacher. His one strong point was McGarvey's weak point Allen's exhortation to sinners was mighty, eloquent and moving McGarvey never possessed this power Once when Allen and McGarvey were together in a protracted meeting, it was understood that Allen should preach in the morning and McGarvey in the afternoon. Just before McGarvey got up, Allen reached over and whispered one day, "Now John, come out and under whip and spur, head and tail up" McGarvey did his best to oblige.

In 1853, about this time, Alexander Campbell visited Missouri. G. F. Saltonsall had died recently and Campbell visited one evening with his widow, McGarvey's mother. James T. Saltonsall,

McGarvey's half-brother had attended Bethany a year before Mc-
Garvey, and was now a prominent lawyer in Fayette. But, concerning, McGarvey, Campbell wrote:

His brother, J. W. M'Garvey, is, however, as we are assured,
devoting his life to a higher usefulness, and a more honorable rank
in the Christian army. He was also one of our best and most gifted
students, and no one left the College, during his years there, with
a higher or more enviable reputation, for all the elements essential
to a learned, useful, and exemplary man He has not disappointed
the expectations of his *alma mater* or his friends, but is yearly
growing in favor with the church and all the people of his acquaintance.[21]

In the fall of 1852 McGarvey, together with Proctor, held a
meeting at the church in Dover. McGarvey received an invitation
to locate. In January, 1853 he began his lengthy ministry for this
church While here, McGarvey married Otwayana Frances Hix
on March 23, 1853. Alexander Proctor officiated at this wedding.
Their first child was born in April of the following year.

McGarvey was preaching at Dover when the war broke out.
As was customary with him on all points, he was positive and
straightforward. He believed it was wrong for Christians to go to
war, and maintained this idea throughout his life. The church at
Dover became divided in sentiment, and many criticisms were made
of him Moreover, McGarvey met once a month with a large
gathering of negroes to teach them the Bible, and opposition came
because of this. His work at Dover therefore, was not as pleasant
as before. McGarvey was, therefore, prepared for a move when
the right invitation should come.

That invitation came in the spring of 1862. W. H. Hopson was
the preacher for the Main Street Church in Lexington. Because of
his pronouncedly sympathizing viewpoint for the South, several in
the Lexington church were antagonized Hopson saw that he
needed to move. He recommended J. W. McGarvey of Dover,
Missouri as the proper man for the place Hopson showed great
wisdom McGarvey was neither northern or southern politically.
He taught both sides to lay down arms and settle their troubles
without bloodshed He could antagonize neither When therefore,
McGarvey arrived in Lexington, the church ranked fourth in size

---

[21]Alexander Campbell, "Notes of Incidents in a Tour Through Illinois and
Missouri—No III," *Millennial Harbinger,* Fourth Series, Vol. III, No 3
(March, 1853), pp 130, 131

of all churches in the city, but in a short while, it was first. His work was relatively uninterrupted by the war, except during the battle at Richmond, at which time the Main Street church building was used for a hospital.

Very soon McGarvey's fortunes were being cast with the College of the Bible. McGarvey had received invitations on two different occasions to teach mathematics at Bethany College and he refused both times When he arrived in Lexington, Robert Milligan, president of Kentucky University offered him a position as teacher of English literature. Again he refused. McGarvey wanted to study the Bible. If he ever taught, he would teach the Bible, and he stayed dogmatically with this determination.

In 1865 Kentucky University moved to Lexington. McGarvey helped plan the curriculum for the College of the Bible. He himself agreed to teach two hours a day a class in Sacred History, which was a survey of the Bible. In a year, however, he was devoting too much of his time to the school to be able to do adequate work for the church, so he resigned to work entirely for the school

In the years that lay ahead McGarvey found himself in the very center of most of the brotherhood activities. Upon the death of Alexander Campbell, Bethany College virtually surrendered the sceptre to Lexington, and here the center of activities was to be found. McGarvey then played the central role. In the regrettable conflicts over the College of the Bible which occurred between 1872-1875, McGarvey was in the middle Later, when liberalism began sweeping the brotherhood, and frequent denials were heard of the inspiration of the Bible, McGarvey wrote prolifically in the *Christian Standard*. In sentiment, McGarvey was bitterly opposed to instrumental music, and refused to worship where one was used He was, however, an ardent supporter of Missionary Societies.

It is not necessary for our present purpose and object to go into detail with McGarvey's life with his activities from 1865 to his death on September 12, 1912. We shall find frequent occasion to do this in our next volume, and therefore, we leave our analysis at this point, anticipating a closer analysis of his future activities in our next.

CHAPTER XVII

INSTRUMENTAL MUSIC

Destined to play an important role in the future struggle over instrumental music was the *American Christian Review* edited by Ben Franklin   The recognition of this importance is at once the apology for introducting this chapter with a brief analysis of the origin of this periodical

The first issue of the *American Christian Review* was sent out in January, 1856, just six months later than the first issue of the *Gospel Advocate*   It appeared as a monthly for the first two years of its existence   Reference to the biography of Ben Franklin will show that this was by no means the first paper he published. He had either edited or partially edited the following papers: *The Reformer, Western Reformer, Proclamation and Reformer,* and the *Christian Age*   This last periodical he was publishing with D. S. Burnet when it was turned over to the ownership of the American Christian Publication Society   This arrangement did not meet with Franklin's approval at all, and in 1854 he resigned as editor with but one stipulation, viz , he would not edit another paper for at least two years   By January, 1856 that two-year agreement was up, and Franklin launched out again as an editor with an entirely new periodical, the *American Christian Review.*

In his introduction Franklin wrote:

Dear Reader · In the good providence of our most gracious and heavenly Father, we are again before you in the capacity of an editor , and desire to introduce to your acquaintance 'The American Christian Review' . . . In looking over our history for the last six years, the reader may conclude we are addicted to change, and that our operations are not as reliable as could be wished .   [1]

Franklin goes on to state that these changes were beyond his control, and that they could not be fully explained or understood "till all the works of the children of men are manifest."   He states that any failure now would be entirely his fault since the *Review* is now entirely under his control   Franklin is anxious too, to get the cooperation of the brotherhood at large:

---

[1]Benjamin Franklin, "Introductory Address," *American Christian Review,* Vol I, No 1 (January, 1856), p 1

In entering the field again, we wish the friendship, the fellowship and cooperation of all those great and good brethren of the same calling We enter the list, not as a competitor or rival, of any one of them, but a cooperator with them in the same great work, and we wish them all possible success.

Franklin's ability was widely recognized and compelled the brethren to entertain great hopes for the future of the paper. After the January issue was off the press, reactions from various readers began to pour in   Aylette Raines of Paris, Kentucky wrote:

I have read, I think, nearly all that you have written, from the beginning, and I am glad to see you again on the arena, with a broad space, within which to battle it for the truth, and I trust a good supply of ammunition.   You are, in my estimation, one of the few suited to the editorial chair.   Clear, cool, strong, dis criminating, balanced!—without these characteristics a writer cannot succeed, to any great extent in the advocacy of apostolic Christianity.   Hence, many have made such havoc, both of themselves and of the cause of truth.[2]

Carroll Kendrick, now in Texas, writes:

Most heartily do I unite with brethren Raines, Rogers and others, in rejoicing that you are again at the helm of so good a vessel.   The times demand such men.   I mean not to praise you; but you have given evidence of good common sense strong, and so intelligent that you can afford to speak in God so strong, and so intelligent that you can afford to speak 'the truth, the whole truth, and nothing but the truth,' without fearing what man can do to you. You seem, too, to look all around a question, and from one end to the other of it, before speaking; to consider its bearings, general and special, in connection with its comparative or its absolute importance.   Hence you are not a *hobby rider* . . .[3]

When the Prospectus of the *Review* was sent out, Tolbert Fanning wrote:

We call attention to the Prospectus of Brother B. Franklin's paper under the caption. Without the least disposition to flatter, we assure the brethren that Brother F. is one of our best thinkers on all matters connected with the Christian economy.[4]

With the January 5, 1858 issue, the *American Christian Review* became a greatly enlarged paper published now weekly.   The

---

[2]Aylette Raines, "Letter," *American Christian Review,* Vol I, No 2 (February 1856) p 83
[3]Carroll Kendrick, "Letter from Texas," *American Christian Review,* p 189
[4]Tolbert Fanning, "The American Christian Review," *Gospel Advocate,* Vol I, No 4 (October, 1855), p. 128

editorial corps reached out to gather in the greatest name in the brotherhood Those included were, Moses E. Lard, John Rogers, C L Loos, Isaac Errett, and Elijah Goodwin. Alexander Campbell now wrote:

Brother Franklin is an eminently *practical* man. He discards all metaphysical speculation in matters of religion and pleads able and earnestly for the Bible as the only infallible rule of faith and practice among all Christians.[5]

It was only natural that the *Review* should become the brotherhood's leading paper. It was a large weekly with an eminent man at its head. Franklin was a man of the people, he spoke their language, knew their problems, and moreover, was unsurpassed in his knowledge of the scriptures and his ability to apply it Even the veteran paper of all, the *Millennial Harbinger,* gave evidences of yielding the sceptre to it The paper was edited from Cincinnati, in those days the very heart of the brotherhood. It had easy access to Kentucky, Ohio and Indiana where a large bulk of the disciples lived. The resolution passed by the Central Pennsylvania Christian Cooperation in February, 1859 was perfectly in line with the feelings of a vast number of brethren. The resolution read:

Resolved, That we recognize the *American Christian Review* the paper for the times—that we regard it all sufficient as a weekly for the brotherhood, and that we urge upon the brethren of the "Keystone State" to lend it their patronage.[6]

Many of the more liberal preachers to arise in the future found the *Review* very much against their liking, and because the paper was so popular with the people, they found it difficult to wean the people away from it to their more liberal ideas.

The origin of the controversy over instrumental music, however, really antedates the origin of the *Review* There was a brief flare-up of the issue in Kentucky as early as 1851. This affair, while it was brief, yet it was intense. Thoughtful men might have taken it as an omen of things to come, but most men were too glad to see it die down to raise the question for at least eight years after that On February 22, 1851 a man who signed his name "W" wrote to

[5]Alexander Campbell, "The American Christian Review," *Millennial Harbinger,* Fifth Series, Vol I, No. 2 (February, 1858), p 92
[6]Jesse H Berry, "Central Pennsylvania Cooperation Meeting," *American Christian Review,* Vol II, No 10 (March 8, 1859), p 39

J. B Henshall, associate editor of the *Ecclesiastical Reformer,* the following letter :

Brother Henshall—What say you of instrumental music in our churches? Should not the Christian Church have organs or Bass Viols that the great object of Psalmody might be consummated? Would not such instruments add greatly to the solemnity of worship, and cause the hearts of the saints to be raised to a higher state of devotion while the deep toned organ would swell its notes of "awful sound"? I think it is high time that we awaken to the importance of this subject. We are far in the rear of Protestants on the subject of church music I hope, therefore, that you will give your views in extenso, on this much neglected subject.

Henshall replied by saying,

In proportion as men become worldly minded, provided they have not entirely lost the fear of God, do they begin to require *helps* to their devotion. That they could require such helps under a dark dispensation where they were rather lead into the use of symbolic rites, than inwardly illuminated by God's word and spirit, is not at all astonishing ; but to say that we need them who live in the full light of the gospel privileges, and enjoy God's mercies and providence over us, is to say that we have no gratitude in our hearts, and that we are every way unworthy of these benefits.[7]

While these were not the only articles to appear in the *Ecclesiastical Reformer* on the subject of instrumental music, they are enough to show the drift. On the one side, there were those who felt that the denominations were using them, and that the brethren were allowing themselves to get arrears of them by not using the instrument. Others felt that instruments in worship belonged only to those destitute of real spirituality

John Rogers read with great disappointment the articles in the *Reformer,* advocating the use of the instruments. Rogers was a devotee of the old paths. He was baptized by Barton W. Stone at the age of eighteen in Wilmington, Ohio in the year, 1818. Most of his preaching career was spent around Carlisle, Kentucky. He baptized over a thousand people here in the twenty-five years from 1823 to 1848. When he read of the use of instruments in the churches of Kentucky, he wrote to Alexander Campbell · "But my brother, (would you believe it?) a popular ·preacher has come out in two numbers in the 'E. Reformer,' in favor of instrumental

---

[7] J B Henshall, "Instrumental Music," *Ecclesiastical Reformer,* Vol IV, No 6 (March 15, 1851), p 171

music in churches and social dancing in our families!"[8]   Rogers
begged Campbell to make a statement on the subject at this early
date. `After some delay, Campbell wrote a short essay on the
subject. He says·

The argument drawn from the Psalms in favor of instrumental
music, is exceedingly apposite to the Roman Catholic, English
Protestant, and Scotch Presbyterian churches, and even to the
Methodist communities.   Their church having all the world in
them—that is, all the fleshly progeny of all the communicants, and
being founded on the Jewish pattern of things—baptism being given
to all born into the world of these politico-ecclesiastic communities—I wonder not, then, that an organ, a fiddle, or a Jews-harp,
should be requisite to stir up their carnal hearts, and work into
ecstasy their animal souls, else 'hosannahs languish on their tongues
and their devotions die.'   And that all persons who have no spiritual discernment, taste or relish for their spiritual meditations,
consolations and sympathies of renewed hearts, should call
for such aid, is but natural.   Pure water from the flintly rock
has no attractions for the mere toper or wine-bibber.   A
little alcohol, or genuine Cognac brandy, or good old Madeira,
is essential to the beverage to make it truly refreshing.   So to
those who have no real devotion or spirituality in them, and whose
animal nature flags under the oppression of church service, I think
with Mr. G., that instrumental music would be not only a desideratum, but an essential prerequisite to fire up their souls to even
animal devotion.   But I presume, to all spiritually-minded Christians such aids would be as a cow bell in a concert.[9]

Aylette Raines, in 1851, was preaching at Millersburg, Kentucky.
Raines was in a habit of keeping a diary, and on April 27, 1851
made the following entry: "Brother S(aunders) wishes to introduce the melodeon into the church."[10]   Raines, however, bitterly
opposed it, and it did not get in at Millersburg at this time.

The subject of instrumental music did not come up again before
the brotherhood until 1860.   At this time, a letter was sent to Ben
Franklin, asking him to express his views on the use of the instrument.   Franklin's opposition was worded in an ironical vein
He said there might be occasions when the instrument would be
permissible, such as the following:

---

[8]John Rogers, "Dancing," *Millennial Harbinger,* Fourth Series, Vol I,
No 8 (August, 1851), p 467
[9]Alexander Campbell, "Instrumental Music," *Millennial Harbinger,* Fourth
Series, Vol. I, No. 10 (October, 1851), pp 581, 582
[10]A W Fortune, *The Disciples in Kentucky* (Published by Convention of
Christian Churches in Kentucky, 1932), p 373

1. Where a church never had or has lost the Spirit of Christ. . .

2. If a church has a preacher who never had, or has lost the Spirit of Christ, who has become a dry, prosing and lifeless speaker, so as to be entirely incapable of commanding and interesting an audience, it is thought that instrumental music would draw out and interest the people . . .

3. If a church only intends being a *fashionable society,* a mere place of amusement and secular entertainment, and abandoning all idea of *religion* and *worship,* instrumental music would be a very pleasant and agreeable part of such entertainment.[11]

After the appearance of the above article, Franklin heard from L. L. Pinkerton of Midway, Kentucky. Pinkerton was the preacher at Midway. His whole life had been spent in central Kentucky. At Midway he had been instrumental in establishing the Female Orphan School.

Pinkerton replied:

So far as known to me, or, I presume, to you, I am the only 'preacher' in Kentucky of our brotherhood who has publicly advocated the propriety of employing instrumental music in *some* churches, and that the church of God in Midway is the only church that has yet made a decided effort to introduce it   The calls for your opinion, it is probable, came from these regions.[12]

Thus the use of instrumental music and the church at Midway have been connected in the thinking of persons acquainted with restoration history from that day to the present. The facts about the introduction of the instrument at Midway may be gleaned from various sources which, when collected together, reveal an interesting story. The suggestion to use the instrument did not come from Pinkerton himself, although the persons responsible undoubtedly knew his opinion and that he would not oppose its introduction even before it was brought in.

The introduction of the instrument owed its inception to the deplorable singing the congregation did   This singing had degenerated into screeching and brawling that would, as Pinkerton said, "scare even the rats from worship." At first it was suggested that a meeting be held on Saturday night to practice the songs. Shortly afterwards, someone brought in a melodeon to be used in getting the right pitch   Before long, one of the sisters was ac-

---

[11]Ben Franklin, "Instrumental Music in Churches," *American Christian Review,* Vol III, No 5 (January 31, 1860), p 19

[12]L L Pinkerton, "Instrumental Music in Churches," *American Christian Review,* Vol III, No 9 (February 28, 1860), p. 34

companying the singing with her playing on the melodeon. The group observed that the effect of the use of the melodeon was good on the singing, and so it was decided to try to use the instrument on the Lord's Day worship. Thompson Parrish, son of James Ware Parrish, one of the founders of the Midway Female Orphan School, played the instrument at the worship.

The presence of the instrument caused considerable friction. The most effective opposition came from Adam Hibler, one of the elders   Late one night Hibler pushed one of his colored slaves by the name of Reuben through a window. Reuben passed the melodeon through, and Hibler took it home with him. But another instrument was afterwards brought in, and continued in use by the church.

The church at Midway is the first congregation *on record* to use the instrument. It is not entirely accurate, however, to say that it was the first congregation among the pioneers to do so. It is evident that as early as 1851 some churches had put in the instrument to cause the flare-up to which allusion has already been made. Just which congregations these were remains unknown. To the church at Midway, then, must go the distinction—if it is a distinction—of being the first of the congregations on record to adopt the use of the instrument.

After the 1860 episode the subject of instrumental music again died down for about four years. The occurrence of the war immediately turned the attention of the brotherhood to other more immediate problems. In 1864 the question was renewed, and this time it was raised in the *Millennial Harbinger.* Early that year a brother, signing his name "Ancient Order," sent W. K Pendleton the following question:

Will you inform me whether it is in accordance with the Scriptures to use in the churches organ or other instrumental music connected with the worship?

To this question Pendleton replied by giving a lengthy history of the use of instruments, and then setting forth his own ideas.

With respect to instrumental music, I presume that no one at all acquainted with ecclesiastical history will pretend to claim for its introduction in the church any pretence of primitive authority or warrant. . . The best authorities seem agreed that the first introduction of the organ, or any other instrumental music, (for the organ was the first form used,) was after the time of Thomas Acquinas, for this eminent man himself declares, (A D. 1250)

'Our church does not use musical instruments as harps and psalteries, in the praise of God, lest she should seem to Judaize . . .

We confess to a fondness for good music of all kinds; and find it no offense to our own feelings of piety or praise to hear the grand and majestic swell of the organ rolling forth, laden with the strains of our sacred music; yet like Paul with respect to meats, I would rather never hear one again, than to have them interfering with the free, full, grateful, heartfelt singing of the whole congregation . . .

But this does not settle the question after all—for there are many things established and right, in the practical affairs of the church in this 19th century, that were not introduced in the days, nor by the authority of the apostles—questions of mere expediency, that involve neither moral nor spiritual principle or teaching . . . We have no evidence that in the apostolic days, the disciples owned houses, such as we would now call churches, at all . . .[13]

This lengthy quotation is given because of the gist of the argument it presents In sum substance this was to be the apology that advocates of the instrument were to use in the years to come. It will be observed that Pendleton admitted that the early church, the apostolic church, did not use the instrument. As we have already seen in the case of the missionary society, so now in the case of the instrument, Pendleton did not consider the *silence* of the scripture on these points a sufficient reason not to use them. In both cases the silence is admitted.

The apology then for the instrument, Pendleton places on the plain of expediency, such as the eating of meats. To Pendleton it fell in the same classification as using meeting houses in which to worship. The scripture said nothing about a meeting house just as it said nothing about the instrument. That there was a fallacy in Pendleton's reasoning is easily apparent, but, lest we anticipate too much from the great controversy over this point which we shall notice in our next volume, we pass with only a review of Pendleton's argument.

Late that year, 1864, the controversy over the instrument gained momentum when J. W. McGarvey entered the battle. He writes:

In the earlier years of the present Reformation, there was entire unanimity in the rejection of instrumental music from our public worship. It was declared unscriptural, inharmonious with the Christian institution, and a source of corruption. In the course

---

[13]W K Pendleton, "Pew-Renting and Organ Music," *Millennial Harbinger,* Fifth Series, Vol VII, No. 3 (March, 1864), pp 126-128

of time, individuals here and there called in question the correctness of this decision, and an attempt was occasionally made to introduce instruments in some churches [14]

McGarvey went on to say that at first the newness of the thing caused the brethren to shrink from it, so men would refrain from pushing it on the ground that it was offensive. Now brethren had gotten to the point where they didn't care   McGarvey pled that brethren would lay aside all feeling pro and con, and start anew with the inquiry. Ought we to make use of musical instruments in public worship? He asked brethren to come out with their views on it, concluding, "Let us, then, have the question fully discussed and finally settled."

McGarvey himself began this discussion by an examination of the ground instrumental music apologists generally covered   If instrumental music were in the Bible, and if God by his written word approved it then, let us have the scriptures, McGarvey would say. If it is not in the Bible, McGarvey pled that the whole ground of expediency be given a thorough examination. He proceeded then to discuss the first question by examining the scriptures commonly used by those declaring the word of God favored it

The first to answer McGarvey was A. S. Hayden. Hayden lived and preached on the Western Reserve, formerly being the president of the Western Reserve Eclectic Institute   Hayden made it clear that he was not advocating the use of the instrument, which meant, as such statements have always meant, that with him it was on the plain of expediency. He replied only because he thought he saw weaknesses in McGarvey's argument, Hayden maintaining that the silence of the scripture was not sufficient ground for rejecting it.

Advocates of the instrument frequently, when and if they believed the written word upheld the instrument, referred to the Old Testament scriptures   McGarvey, as well as many other pioneers, saw that the very fact that the church, when established, rejected the use of the Jewish worship of the Old Testament, was proof enough that the instrument was not suited to the worship in the church   The worship of the Jews was particularly fitted for the economy under which-they lived   Their worship consisted of offering sacrifices, ceremonial washings burning of incense, and

---

[14] J W McGarvey, "Instrumental Music in Churches," *Millennial Harbinger*, Fifth Series, Vol. VII, No 11 (November, 1864), p 510

the use of instruments of music, among other things. The church on the other hand is the realization of an entirely different economy, fully spiritual in scope. Here God chose a worship where the worshipper, directly from his heart worshipped the Lord without the aid of incense, animal sacrifice or mechanical instruments. McGarvey then, after reasoning upon the differences in the two economies and of musical instruments being out of place under the Christian dispensation, closed by saying,

Now, Brother Hayden, if this argument is valid, I again repeat, that every man who bows to the authority of God's word, must oppose the use of instrumental music in the church. If it contains any fallacy, please to point it out, for I declare to you, I am unable to see it.[15]

This same argument had been substantially made earlier in the *American Christian Review* by Z F. Smith. He wrote:

It is very clear that musical instruments were used by the Jews in their praises to God. It is equally clear, to every one familiar to the New Testament, that not one evidence, either in precept or example, of such practice, is found in the appointed orders of Christian worship. This omission must be esteemed a consideration of great importance in solving the question of its right, and especially when viewed in the light of those circumstances which marked the change from one dispensation to another. Whatever was peculiar to the genus and character of both, was preserved, what was peculiar to the former alone, was omitted. Paul says of the Tabernacle services, that they 'stood only in meats and drinks, and divers washings, and *carnal ordinances,* imposed on them until the time of reformation' While the types and shadows of the Temple service were *carnal* (addressed to the senses) in some respects, such is not the case with the appointments of Christian worship. While the magnificence of the temple-building and the costly splendor of its furnishings, the rich odors of incense, the official trappings of the priesthood, etc, entranced and gratified the senses of the worshiper, enjoined by the Saviour, *there is not the least shadow of an effort made to gratify carnal man!* What is it? The religion of Jesus Christ is purely spiritual, as such, its genius and character forbade the introduction of a carnal element[16]

Early in 1865 S Salisbury of Mumford, New York wrote, advocating the use of the instrument He pointed to the fact that it was used both in the Old Testament, and, according to the book

---

[15]J W McGarvey, "Instrumental Music," *Millennial Harbinger,* Vol. XXXVI, No 2 (February, 1865), p 94
[16]Z F. Smith, "Instrumental Music in Worship," *American Christian Review,* Vol I, No 5 (February 2, 1858), p 17

of Revelation, in heaven   McGarvey seems to have paid little attention to these arguments, as the answers should have been self-evident.

In the main, the discussion on the subject through 1865 took place between McGarvey and A. S Hayden.   Moses E. Lard was not long in getting into the discussion either   Early in 1864 he wrote

. . . what defense can be urged for the introduction into some of our congregations of instrumental music?   The answer which thunders into my ear from every page of the New Testament, is none.   Did Christ ever appoint it?   did the apostles ever sanction it? or did any one of the primitive churches ever use it?   Never. In what light then must we view him who attempts to introduce it into the churches of Christ of the present day?   I answer, as an insulter of the authority of Christ, and as a defiant and impious innovator in the simplicity and purity of the ancient worship [17]

It could be denied that the churches were in isolated places putting in the instrument at this time   What action should those who opposed its use take?   Lard raises the same question

But what shall be done with such churches?   Of course, nothing If they see fit to mortify the feelings of their brethren, to forsake the example of the primitive churches, to condemn the authority of Christ by resorting to will worship, to excite dissension, and give rise to general scandal, they must do it   As a body we can do nothing. Still we have three partial remedies left us to which we should at once resort.

1. Let every preacher in our ranks resolve at once that he will never, under any circumstances or on any account, enter a meeting house belonging to our brethren in which an organ stands   We beg and entreat our preaching brethren to adopt this as an unalterable rule of conduct.   This and like evils must be checked, and the very speediest way to effect it is the one here suggested   2 Let no brother who takes a letter from one church ever unite with another using an organ.   Rather let him live out of a church than go into such a den. 3. Let those brethren who oppose the introduction of an organ first remonstrate in gentle, kind and decided terms.   If their remonstrance is unheeded, and the organ is brought in, then let them at once, and without even the formality of asking for a letter, abandon the church so acting; and let all such members unite elsewhere.   Thus these organ-grinding churches will in the lapse

---

[17]Moses E Lard, "Instrumental Music in Churches and Dancing," *Lard's Quarterly,* Vol 1, No 3 (March, 1864), p 331

of time be broken down, or wholly apostatize, and the sooner they are in fragments the better for the cause of Christ [18]

Of course, both McGarvey and Lard were beginning to be looked upon by some brethren as extremists, but they were men of firm and deep conviction as it respects this issue.

It will be easily apparent that the issue of instrumental music did not occupy as large a role in the thought of the time as it came to much later. After the war, the instrument began to be used more and more and the issue became more warmly contested. We shall see a little later a greater conflict over the use of the instrument. °

[18]Moses E Lard, "Instrumental Music in Churches and Dancing," *Lard's Quarterly,* Vol 1, No 3 (March, 1864), pp 332, 333

CHAPTER XVIII

THE CHURCH DURING THE WAR

Never had the nation faced greater peril than it did through that decade from 1855 to 1865. A political upheaval had been fomenting for some time, and was now reaching its climax. The passing of the Kansas-Nebraska Act by Congress dealt a death blow to the Whig party and provided the way for establishment of the new Republican party. In the election of 1856 James Buchanan of Pennsylvania, a Democrat, was able to defeat the first Republican presidential nominee, John C. Fremont of California. But his four years in office served to prove to many people that the Democratic party was not prepared to settle the national strife. The Supreme Court, on March 6, 1857, announced that Dred Scott, a Missouri slave, was not considered a citizen for that honor belonged only to the white race. Chief Justice Roger B. Taney and his associates went on to announce that the Missouri Compromise "had all along been void for Congress lacked the constitutional right to enact a law which arbitrarily deprived persons of their property, slave or otherwise, in the territories of the United States."[1] Democratic efforts at compromise were availing little Stephen A Douglas of Illinois, in his debates with Abraham Lincoln, found himself in dilemmas from which he sought escape by the famous Freeport Doctrine, which was so obnoxious to southern Democrats that they called it the "Freeport Heresy." Meantime, the nation looked forward to the crucial election of 1860.

Early that year the political parties began to prepare for the fall presidential election The Democrats met at Charleston, South Carolina, on April 23rd, and chose Stephen A. Douglas as their champion Southern Democrats were not satisfied and so elected John C. Breckinridge of Kentucky as their candidate. In May the Republican party met in Chicago, declaring that "the union of the States must and shall be preserved." Abraham Lincoln was chosen as their standard-bearer The Constitutional Union party which met that same month nominated John Bell of Tennessee as their

---

[1]Homer Carey Hockett, *Political and Social Growth of the American People, 1492-1865* (Macmillan Company, New York, 1940), Third Edition, p 699

318

presidential candidate, and so, after the customary campaigning, the nation waited tensely to see the outcome of the November balloting.

The electoral count showed that Lincoln had received 180 votes, and all of these came from free states. Breckinridge had received 72 votes and these had come from the south. Douglas received 39 votes and Bell, 12, both of the latter receiving all votes from the border states. The popular vote showed that Lincoln had received only forty percent, Douglas, twenty-nine percent, Breckinridge, eighteen, and Bell, nearly thirteen. After the vote was known, tenseness in the nation only increased No one hardly knew what the next step would be.

Southern statesmen for the most part were reluctant to be too hasty. They now wanted to wait and see what the new president would do, most apparently feeling that he would take some definite action shortly against the south which would give them justifiable reason to take further steps. There were extremists, however, who were found mostly in the seaboard states from South Carolina to Texas that were ready for secession The state of South Carolina took the lead. Having received the news of Lincoln's election, the legislature called a special state convention. The convention met and on December 20, 1860, formally announced a dissolving of the union and the state of South Carolina. Six weeks later Mississippi, Florida, Alabama, Georgia, Louisiana and Texas had followed suit. On the fourth of February, 1861, delegates of the several seceding states met at Montgomery, Alabama, and organized a new federal government, electing Jefferson Davis as president. The new name chosen was Confederate States of America. Optimism and enthusiasm was in a gradual crescendo arising to a higher pitch. Excitement was everywhere

In the closing days of his office, President James Buchanan was at a loss to know what to do. Again, as was customary, he chose a compromise position He denied emphatically the constitutionality of secession, but at the same time declared that the nation had no right to force a state to stay in the union if it didn't want in. He placed the blame almost entirely with the north. While his intentions were good, yet numerous questions were demanding an answer, one of which was: "What shall become of Federal property, such as forts, which resided within the Confederate States?" In the harbor at Charleston, South Carolina, Major Robert Anderson and a small body of men occupied the Federal Fort Sumter on the small island in the middle of the harbor.   Early in January Buchanan sent an armed steamer, *Star of the West,* to the fort with military supplies   Confederate batteries on the shore opened fire and drove her off.   While this was really an act of war, Buchanan ignored it   Other forts in Confederate territory with the exception of Fort Pickens at Pensacola, Florida, capitulated without bloodshed to the South.

Adding greatly to the perplexity of the days was the arrival of the new president in Washington for the inauguration.   To the vast majority of the nation he was an uncouth backwoodsman, certainly unfit for the White House.   Homely to the verge of ugliness, awkward in manner, his actions often shocked the dignified statesmen of his time   His jokes were not always in good taste and often led to his being accused of being flippant on grave occasions.   A neophyte in politics, the nation at first felt a little apprehensive under his leadership.   He was the butt of many cartoons, but the plain people, one of whom he was, loved him dearly.   As events proved, he was providentially the man of the hour.

No sooner had Lincoln taken office than word came from Major Anderson that he would have to surrender unless help was forthcoming immediately.   All the members of his cabinet except two —Chase and Blair—recommended that Anderson evacuate the fort. Lincoln very much disagreed   To evacuate looked to him like recognizing the Confederate government   Besides it would seriously impair the morale in the North   He pitted his judgment against his cabinet and ordered supplies to be sent to the garrison At the same time he notified the Confederates that he was sending provisions without adding to the garrison or supplying it with ammunition   His move proved to be a show of superior judgment, for he avoided a warlike move and left that decision up to the South.   If the Confederates now fired, they would immediately gain the reputation of being the aggressors   Upon receipt of the information, the Confederates ordered Major Anderson to surrender, but the latter refused.   Southern batteries opened up on the 12th day of April, firing those first shots of the war   From their blazing guns thundered in fire and smoke, in death and devastation, a declaration of war more dramatic than any ritual in Washington could make it.   North and South now pitted their respective strength against each other, and for four long, weary years Mars was to rule America.

The attempt to reconstruct the story of what took place among the churches of the restoration movement during this period can only be summarily told, for the reason that our sources are too inadequate. How, in a material way, did the war affect the members of the church? To what extent did they take part, and to what extent did they suffer? What were the issues raised by the war and what position did the brethren take on them?

From the time of Lincoln's election in November, 1860, until the guns sounded at Fort Sumter in April, 1861, there was intense excitement the like of which was never seen in the land before During this period Tolbert Fanning was on a journey through Mississippi, Louisiana, Alabama and Georgia. Leaving. Nashville at six o'clock on the evening of November 27th, he went to Corinth, Mississippi, and then on down to Jackson, the capital of the state The Mississippi state legislature was then in session and Fanning confesses that while he thought on other occasions that he had seen political excitement, now he knew that he really hadn't. He went into the legislative halls and heard the speeches of Mississippi's southern orators. The only question before them was, "When, and how, shall Mississippi secede from the Union?" Significantly enough, the veteran preacher of the South, T. W. Caskey, was among the number chosen to draw up the document of secession and present it to the legislature. What a difference this spirit of war made in the church! Fourteen years before, Fanning had preached in Jackson to audiences that nearly filled the chamber of the House of Representatives in the State House. Now he preached for two days, and the audiences were very small.

From Jackson, Fanning went to Vicksburg and then on down to New Orleans. His searches revealed only two or three Christians worshipping after the New Testament order. From New Orleans, Fanning went on to Mobile, Alabama, and from there visited brethren throughout the state Arriving in Montgomery, the capital of the state, he found the city in such a turmoil that no one had time or thought about the Lord No brethren could be found, so Fanning went on to Atlanta, Georgia He arrived here December 21st. He visited in the home of Dr A G Thomas, but was disappointed. Fanning says, "Dr A. G. Thomas is a brother of fine address, superior talents and learning, but we saw him with a feather in his hat and a glittering sword in his right hand, and doubted if he would be able to hold the sword of Georgia in one hand and the sword of the Spirit in the other."[2]   The impressions made upon Fanning's mind were very solemn.   He expresses regret that so many brethren had gotten excited over political affairs, and mildly castigated his brethren who were forgetting the Lord over affairs in the state.

During this period of excitement Alexander Campbell was on a tour of the North.   As the 21st of December had found Fanning in Atlanta, it found Campbell in Indianapolis.   Here he met with his most recently appointed associate-editor of the *Millennial Harbinger*, Isaac Errett, whose work with the *Harbinger* was really to begin with the January issue of 1861.   Errett had turned down the offer to teach at Bethany College but had accepted the invitation to be traveling agent for the school to raise funds   It was in this capacity that he and Alexander Campbell were now visiting the churches in the North, especially in Indiana.   Their journey began among the cities and churches of the state, New Year's day finding them in Crawfordsville, visiting in the home of S. M. Huston, who was then faithfully serving the cause here.   Campbell spoke here before a large audience, a member of which was former Indiana Governor Lane, who was then a United States Senator from Indiana   Lane was a Methodist, although both his parents were connected with the restoration.   This journey took Campbell and Errett on to Greencastle, Terre Haute, Washington, Vincennes. Bedford, Bloomington, New Albany, Madison, and then via Columbus back to Indianapolis   At Vincennes they met D S. Burnet, who accompanied them on the rest of the journey   At Indianapolis Campbell preached to a large crowd on Lord's Day morning, and Burnet spoke at night   Burnet also spoke before the assembled student body of Northwest Christian University that afternoon   Scholarly S K Hoshour was then its president. By the middle of February, 1861, Campbell and Errett had arrived back at Bethany College [3]

Errett was at this time preaching in Detroit, Michigan   After returning from his Indiana tour, he held a short meeting at Ionia

---

[2]Tolbert Fanning, "Tour Through Mississippi, Louisiana, Alabama, and Georgia," *Gospel Advocate*, Vol VII, No 2 (February, 1861), p 39
[3]P S Fall, "Letter from Elder Phillip Fall," *Millennial Harbinger*, Fifth Series, Vol IV, No 9 (September, 1861), p 530

which proved very successful in spite of the political turmoil He
went next to Monmouth, Illinois, for a short meeting and then
prepared for an extended tour into Virginia in the interests of
Bethany College But Errett had little success. The excitement
of war was too great Dispatches were passing between
Washington and Fort Sumter, and hourly men were expecting the
worst Then came the news of Anderson's surrender. Madness
ruled the hour as men in the South feverishly cursed the North, and
those in the North did the same to the South Errett prepared to
leave Virginia at once, and on his return trip to Detroit, passed
through Washington, D. C., Wheeling, Cleveland, before getting
home Every town, large and small, was filled with shouting,
milling people. Flags were unfurled in the breeze, banners were
streamed across public places; shouting, hurrahing, screaming were
heard everywhere. No man could possibly describe the excitement
then heard over the nation.

On April 5, 1861 W. H. Hopson began a very hopeful gospel
meeting for the church at Walnut & Eighth Streets in Cincinnati.
During the meeting news of the fall of Fort Sumter came across
the wires Streets were filled with crowding, milling, shouting
people. The music of fife and drum whipped the excitement up
to near frenzy R. M Bishop, one of the elders of the church
was mayor of Cincinnati. Only a month before he had entertained
Abraham Lincoln who was on his way to Washington for the
inauguration. On this day Bishop drove Hopson through the
streets in his carriage. They talked of the meeting and the war,
and both agreed to close the meeting abruptly that night

In both the North and the South members of the church joined
in with the excitement Preachers of the restoration stepped down
out of the pulpit and joined the cause of both sections Young
men in "our colleges" left school to join with the army of their respective sections James A. Garfield at the opening of the war
was president of Western Reserve Eclectic Institute at Hiram,
Ohio When news of the struggle came to him, he petitioned
Governor Dennison to give him an appointment He was soon
commissioned a Lieutenant-Colonel, and given permission to raise a
regiment Garfield went back to Hiram, and among the young men
Ohio Volunteer Infantry Garfield was soon made a full colonel.
in the student body, he formed the forty-second Regiment of the

and placed in full command of the regiment. By November 26, its eleven companies were fully outfitted at Camp Chase near Columbus, Ohio On December 14, they moved toward Louisville. Early in January, the next year, they fought their first battle near Paintsville, Kentucky and proved the victors They joined the Union army of General Grant at Shiloh, Tennessee, and fought there. They drove on to Corinth, driving the Confederate army out. They proceeded across northern Mississippi and Alabama, stopping to make temporary headquarters at Huntsville Garfield's fame was recognized by the Union. He was recalled to Washington, then committed as aid to General Rosecrans at Murfreesboro. Rosecrans pushed from Murfreesboro to Chattanooga, and led the Union army to its defeat at Chickamauga Here Garfield was made a Brigadier-General, but soon resigned to enter into Congress as representative from **Ohio.**

There were two hundred and fifty boys from Hiram College in the Union army, most of whom fought under Garfield in Co A of the 42nd Ohio Regiment. J. S Ross led this company in the last campaign as a captain. Major F A Williams, a very faithful member of the church, was killed early in the war. Charles P. Bowler, another member, was killed at Cedar Mountain Wallace Coburn, also a member of the church, was killed at Winchester, Kentucky in 1862. Both belonged to the 7th Ohio Regiment. Major Delos R. Northway, a faithful Christian, was killed in the Wilderness in 1864.

The opposite of Garfield in some of these struggles was a young man doing scout duty who was destined to become one of the foremost proclaimers of the ancient order. T. B. Larimore joined the Confederate army the first year of the war and reported for duty to Colonel McClellan at Knoxville. At the battle of Fishing Creek in Kentucky, he was present on special duty. With General Buckner under a flag of truce he went to get the body of General Zollicoffer, his commanding general who fell in the battle. After the battle, Larimore rejoined his command at Murfreesboro, and from here went to Shiloh. He was in charge of a group of guards above Pittsburg Landing, whose duty was to watch for a possible Federal landing higher up the point. Larimore wrote the dispatch that went to Albert Sidney Johnson, notifying him of the passage of the first Federal gun-boat up the river. Larimore

was in the retreat to Corinth, and from here fell back with the
. Confederate army along the south bank of the Tennessee river
He was on scout duty in the Sequatchie valley and was captured at
McLemore's Cove

At Franklin College W D Carnes fought frantically to keep
the issue of war out of the classroom. When, however, Lincoln
issued his first call for volunteers, almost the whole student body
left school to join the Confederates, many of whom never came
back. Carnes closed the school and went back to Pikeville.

Meanwhile, the brethren in what was then the west—Arkansas
and Missouri—were severely influenced by the conflict Missouri
was at first southern in sentiment. But her southern governor
was dismissed and the state legislature voted to go with the Union.
Not so with Arkansas for she, like Texas, voted to go with the
South. Most of the people of these states felt that since they
were out of reach of the North and East, that little warfare would
ever reach her borders, but in this, they were badly mistaken.
War came and when it did, it hit the church there as much as
anywhere.

William Baxter was at this time president of the college at
Fayetteville, Arkansas. Robert Graham, who had founded the
school, resigned a position he was holding at Kentucky University
at the request of the brethren in Arkansas and returned to work
among them.

The fall of 1860 opened at Arkansas College, looking to be
the most prosperous yet. Almost all of the students were members
of the church. Baxter kept down the political discussions, although among the student body there were persons of both
sentiments. As the spring semester wore out and Fort Sumter
fell, the call of Lincoln was issued for volunteers and several of
the young men came to Baxter to announce the fact that they
were to enlist. Baxter, seeing it was of little use to try to persuade
them not to, got them together and talked with them kindly before
leaving Some of the boys fought for the Union and some for the
South When the last gun of the war was fired, many of this same
group were sleeping silently on the battlefields from Gettysburg to
Prairie Grove.

The battle of Pea Ridge and the battle of Prairie Grove were
both fought at the outskirts of Fayetteville, Arkansas The college

was occupied at different times by Southern and Northern troops,
but once, on retreat by the Confederate army, was burned to the
ground   Fayetteville was overrun frequently by the armies of
both sides. After the long battle of Prairie Grove, the city became one large hospital where Confederate and Union soldiers
cried in agony   Graham had been forced to escape the city secretly
because of too pronounced Union sentiments but Baxter remained.
He went to the buildings where the sick were, saw the doctors
cutting off legs and arms without the use of antiseptic, heard the
terrifying screams of soldiers in pain, viewed the dead and bloated
bodies of soldiers placed in the streets until workers could bury
them   This was a part of the aftermath of war. The sadder part
came when the bodies of young men, members of the church in
Fayetteville, were brought in from the battlefield and placed in
the church building. It was terrible to watch the mothers cry over
them and kiss so fondly the lifeless lips of their boys whose bullet-
ridden bodies now lay before them.

Many members of the church fought in the war on both sides.
The names of some who did can be known, but most will remain
to us unknown. Several lost their lives. Nothing would be gained by
recounting all of the names of boys who went to war, for to most
of us they would be just names without much meaning. On the
other hand, there are some whose names are more or less familiar
who might well be noticed. At the battle of Pea Ridge in Arkansas
a regiment of the Texas Rangers joined the ranks of General
M'Culloch   This regiment was led by Barton Stone, a son of
the renowned Barton W Stone Chaplain in the regiment was B F.
Hall of whom we have made previous mention. Hall, it will be
recalled, moved from Kentucky, his native state, to Texas, preaching for a short while in Memphis, Tennessee, on his way. The
influence of B. F. Hall was never so great after the war as before it and the reason can be well seen

Before the battle of Pea Ridge, when the Confederate army was
encamped at Fayetteville, Arkansas, William Baxter and Robert
Graham decided to pay a visit to Hall and talk to him   Never
was any visit regretted so much. Hall had changed completely
He was advocating strongly the Southern cause and, all in all,
acted more like a fiend than a Christian gentleman   He rode a
fine mule, had a splendid rifle, and expressly requested of all

friends that if a "Yankee" appeared, please let him get his share. During the conversation with Graham and Baxter, Hall mentioned not one word about the church, about the gospel, or what one might ordinarily expect of a preacher, but spoke only of his rifle and how many Yankees he hoped to kill. Graham had never met Hall before and he sat speechless at the violence of Hall's attacks against the North. The Texas chaplain told of a friend, Alf Johnson, who had gone over the battlefield after the battle of William's Creek and who, when seeing a wounded Federal soldier begging for medical assistance, instead ruthlessly shot him. Hall would tell this story and then laugh as though he thoroughly enjoyed and approved of such conduct. Graham, ordinarily an even tempered man, struggled to keep from expressing his views. Hall advocated catching every Yankee soldier, cutting off their right hands and sending them back home with the hand tied to the saddle. Graham asked Hall how he could feel this way toward his brethren in the North, and Hall replied that he had no brethren in the North, they were all infidels.

Going outside, Graham asked Baxter how he liked Hall and what he thought of the conversation. Baxter replied that he felt as though he had been in the presence of a highwayman instead of a Christian. Human nature being what it is, men who brag the most of doing something great will seldom do much. When the battle of Pea Ridge came off, B. F. Hall went to the front as chaplain for the Texas Rangers. About the only activity he ever saw was running, when the shattered columns of General M'Culloch's army poured back through Fayetteville on their way south. Baxter and Graham stood by and watched B. F. Hall, looking tired and worn, head back in retreat.[4]

The feeling in both the South and North reached great heights and dark deeds were done. Members of the church did not altogether escape disaster. Andrew Allsman, a member of the church in Palmyra, Missouri, was taken out and shot by Confederate General Porter. As members of the church go, he wasn't much, but yet the killing of him was wholly unwarranted. When news of the deed reached General McNiel, Union general in the same area, he selected ten men of his Confederate prisoners who would

[4]William Baxter. *Pea Ridge and Prairie Grove* (Cincinnati. Poe & Hitchcock, 1864), pp 113-123

be shot in retaliation. These men were placed in a cell and the
day for their execution set. Jacob Creath, Jr, was called in to
speak to them   As he stepped into their cell, he saw ten different
men.   One or two were silent, others were crying bitterly, begging for pardon   One tall youth with blond hair was a lieutenant.
He was brave but despondent.   His girl back home was waiting
for his return so they could marry.   Creath could do nothing to
cancel their execution but begged them to have their heart right
before God and be prepared   The morning came and all ten fell
before a firing squad [5]

When the army of General John Sherman swept across the
South toward Atlanta, pillage, rapacity, plunder followed in its
wake The South suffered much because of this.   In this army was
the fourth Kentucky Regiment and in this regiment was one John
B. Vawter, later to become one of the great preachers of the restoration in Iowa While camped outside of Atlanta, General Sherman sent two thousand men around the city to cut off the supplies
and cut the rail and telegraph lines Vawter was among the number
to go But his regiment was attacked and almost all of the men were
either destroyed or captured.   Vawter was captured and sent to the
Andersonville prison where misery and suffering reached its height [6]

In Missouri, A H. F. Payne was one of the first located
preachers in the state   He spent most of his life in Clay County
He was born in Mason County, Kentucky on April 14, 1807   He
moved from Lexington, Kentucky to Missouri in 1836 and
preached in Clay County until 1854 when he moved to Plattsburg.
He was strongly for the north in his political sentiment   He was
ruthlessly murdered by a group of bush-whackers who came to
capture him under the pretense of an order from a commanding
general.

And so went the war! Men everywhere were affected by it.
Churches in some places divided; others became discouraged and
ceased to meet   The condition of the churches in Kentucky may
be best seen in a report sent to the general convention of the
Missionary Society in October, 1862 by J. W McGarvey.
McGarvey wrote:

---

[5] P Donan, *Memoirs of Jacob Creath, Jr* (Cincinnati Chase & Hall,
1877), p 179
[6] Sergeant Oats, *Prison Life in Dixie* (Chicago · Central Book Concern,
1880), p 1ff

But a storm of human passion, seldom equaled in the history of our sinful world, is raging around us, and we have caught the infection. The results are such as human passion must always produce. Many brethren have been swept into hopeless apostasy, the zeal of many has been chilled, distrust prevails among many who were once bosom friends; the evangelical labors of nearly all have been much contracted; churches languish, congregations dwindle, and there is a fear that such divisions as have distracted the religious sects of the day, may yet disgrace our history

The above report is taken from the original minutes of the Society for their meeting of 1862.

Our sources are inadequate to present anything like a complete picture of the activities of brethren in and during the war, so therefore, our minds must be contented with a partial picture In this case a partial picture is better than none for it at least gives some information as to what was happening to the churches during those dark and dreadful days.

Yet there is another side of the whole picture at which we must now look and this side concerns itself with the issues that were raised by the war. Fundamentally, there were two The first antedated the war. It was the issue of slavery—of whether or not a Christian could scripturally own slaves The second issue was raised during the war. It asked, Does a Christian have a right to go to war and kill his fellowman? Both of these were highly important. Our attention now turns to the first one

The question of Christians holding slaves was first raised among the brethren early in 1845. Both Thomas and Alexander Campbell expressed their views upon the subject and dropped it The first article to appear came from Thomas Campbell in January of that year. He determined to thoroughly examine the Bible on it. Taking up all the scriptures on the subject one by one, he then drew certain conclusions He decided, first, that God has allowed slavery at certain times as a punishment for sin The descendents of Ham, therefore, were being punished by those of Japheth and Shem down to this day. Second, to hold slaves was divinely permitted Slavery, while an evil, was one which God at times permitted.[7]

---

[7]Thomas Campbell, "Elder Thomas Campbell's Views of Slavery," *Millennial Harbinger*, Third Series, Vol II, No 1 (January, 1845), pp 1-8

Alexander Campbell spoke on the subject in the next issue. He stressed the need of such a discussion by saying,

Any one of much sagacity must see that the controversy between the North and the South has commenced. . . . Already, indeed, has it come into our American ecclesiastical courts, and distracted the councils of one of the most imposing communities in our Protestant ranks.[8]

But Campbell had the greatest confidence in his brethren in that he believed the principles to which they held would never allow a division in their ranks over slavery. Significantly enough, Campbell proved to be a true prophet, for the churches of Christ were among one of the very few that did not, in the war, divide over the question of slavery. At any rate, Campbell wrote that "we are the only religious community in the civilized world whose principles (unless we abandon them) can preserve us" from a division.

The position Alexander Campbell took toward slavery showed his deep knowledge of the scriptures. In a day when there were fanatical extremists on every side, Campbell taught that the issue was not a moral one, but a political one. That is to say, slavery was neither right nor wrong in and of itself so far as the scriptures taught, but that the settlement of it was to be left up to political discretion. He found many passages in the scriptures *regulating* slavery, but none prohibiting it. There was Biblical teaching to tell a slave how to conduct himself toward his master, and the same for the master toward the slavery. The scriptures neither condemned nor upheld slavery, therefore, it must be left to the political government as their peculiar issue. Campbell then concludes:

To preserve unity of spirit among Christians of the South and of the North is my grand object, and for that purpose I am endeavoring to show that the New Testament does not authorize any interference or legislation upon the relation of master and slave, nor does it either in letter or spirit authorize Christians to make it a term of communion . . . .

Every man who loves the American Union, as well as every man who desires a constitutional end of American slavery, is

---

[8]Alexander Campbell, "Our Position to American Slavery," *Millennial Harbinger*, Third Series, Vol II, No 2 (February, 1845), p 51

bound to prevent, as far as possible, any breach of communion between Christians at the South and at the North.[9]

Campbell had struck boldly at the heart of the issue. While there were those in the church who took both extremes, Campbell's influence and his stand prevented anything like serious conflict ever arising over slavery.

In 1850 the question of slavery arose again. Congress passed that year the Fugitive Slave Law, making it compulsory by law for a person who captured a fugitive slave to return him to his owner. A heavy fine was imposed upon any who refused. The law caused tremendous excitement Those brethren in the North who held it was sinful to own slaves, believed it violated the scriptures for them to return a slave Campbell, however, disagreed He pointed out that the government was ordained of God, and that therefore, any Christian who disobeyed the Fugitive Slave Law was disobeying this stricture from God. As to his position Campbell declared:

So far, then, as editors in general are presumed to act, I stand on neutral ground. But, as I judge, I owe it to myself and to my readers, North and South, to place myself before them in my true and real position on this very interesting and exciting subject.[10]

Samuel Church substantially agreed with Campbell. Church preached in Allegheny City, and was one of the most highly respected preachers in his day. He wrote:

Slavery, be it good or bad, is not the voluntary choice of the present generation in the South They inherit it, and all their established habits of thinking and acting, individually and socially—morally, politically and religiously—are, more or less, identified with it. If its existence be sinful, they are not conscious of it, and are unlikely to be enlightened by calling them thieves and villains.[11]

In the main, these positions were recognized as logical although a few disagreed. Occasionally a man was found like John Kirk of Palestine, Ohio who wrote to Campbell:

I have come to the conclusion that I will neither patronize

---

[9] Alexander Campbell, "Our Position to American Slavery—No V," *Millennial Harbinger*, Third Series, Vol II, No 5 (May, 1845), p 195

[10] Alexander Campbell, "Slavery and the Fugitive Slave Law," *Millennial Harbinger*, Fourth Series, Vol I, No 3 (March, 1851), p 171

[11] Samuel Church, "Our Position on American Slavery," *Millennial Harbinger*, Fourth Series, Vol I, No 2 (February, 1851), p 106

priest nor paper that is not strictly anti-slavery. Your position to American slavery I very much dislike [12]

Another extreme abolitionist in the church was Nathaniel Field. When Campbell visited Louisville, Kentucky in April, 1835, he met Field whom Campbell described as "body, soul, and spirit opposed to American slavery." At that time Campbell wrote:

There is, indeed, a healthy, rational, and scriptural reform of this great and growing evil much wanted, and which I am of the opinion would be satisfactory to the Doctor and many other good men, which as an incipient measure, is certainly practicable, and absolutely necessary to our pleading of reformation. No Christian can, on the principle of humanity or the gospel, sell a wife from a husband, or a husband from a wife; an infant from its parents, or parents from their infant offspring, under any pretense whatever. And no laws of any state can justify any Christian man in keeping his servants ignorant of God, of Jesus Christ, or of the Bible facts, any more than the laws of Greece or Rome could have compelled the first Christians to have worshipped idols, or to have called Jesus anathema, or sanctioned them in so doing Of all this I have no more doubt than I have that Jesus is the Messiah [13]

Tolbert Fanning in the meantime, plead that warfare was not the way to handle slavery, but peaceful means should be pursued. He says:

I regret exceedingly that the brethren of the North or South should be suspicious of each other. True, many of the north look upon slavery as a great evil; but as to the abstract question of good or evil, ninety-nine hundredths of the disciples of the south will have no controversy. If it be a destructive sin, it is our misfortune in the south,—we could not prevent the state of affairs, and now we must make the best of the subject we can. [14]

Some, like Walter Scott, were perplexed upon the subject. They did not know what to say, and thought silence in this case the lesser of two evils. Scott wrote:

The manumission of our slave population can be accomplished now only by a means which heaven only knows—I know it not . . . I am no friend of slavery, I deprecate its commencement I deplore its continuance, and tremble for its issue, but I am silent because I

---

[12]John Kirk, "Our Position on American Slavery," *Millennial Harbinger,* Fourth Series, Vol I, No 1 (January, 1851), p 49
[13]Alexander Campbell, "Sketch of a Tour of Seventy-Five Days," *Millennial Harbinger,* Vol VI, No 7 (July, 1835), pp 331, 332
[14]Tolbert Fanning, "Christian Bible Society," *Christian Review,* Vol II, No 11 (November, 1845), p 234

think to speak would be folly. What ought to be said I cannot say, and what ought not to be said I will not say [15]

Ben Franklin took substantially the same position as Alexander Campbell. Franklin, as an editor, learned what many an editor soon learns, viz , he receives many inquiries to answer certain questions which the querist asks, not because he wants to find out anything, but because he wants to agitate an issue, and would use the editor as a tool Franklin received inquiries on the slavery question, and for the most part paid little attention to them. However, in the spring of 1859 he brushed the question aside by answering that neither Jesus nor Paul had ever stated whether slavery was right or wrong. Who, then, was he to do something they didn't?

Did the Lord and the apostles do right in never deciding the question, whether slavery is right or wrong, discussing and never saying one word about that question in any form? If they did, we do right when we treat it in the same way. If they did wrong, we do wrong when we treat it the same way.[16]

We turn now from the question of slavery to one that far outweighed it in importance, the question of the Christian's right to take arms for his government Early in 1861, when it became obvious that a war was seriously threatening, Tolbert Fanning began to answer these questions. After admitting that there had never been a time when the nation had suffered so much or was threatened so much as then, Fanning went on to say that it was not his duty to tell politicians what to do, but since the church of Christ was innocently involved, he must needs speak plainly to his brethren. He expressed the belief that the religion of Jesus Christ could prosper under any form of government and reminded the brethren that the kingdom of Christ was not of this world. He referred to the fact that Jesus was the Prince of Peace and His preachers, messengers of peace. He pled that it was only right for North and South to settle their differences, not on the field of battle, but through discussion. The politicians of both sides did not fear the Lord and should not be followed in this matter He laid the blame for the agitation of war at the

[15]William Baxter, *Life of Elder Walter Scott* (Cincinnati Bosworth Chase & Hall, 1874), p 360

[16]Ben Franklin, "Our Position Called For," *American Christian Review.* Vol II No 11 (March 15, 1859), p 42

feet of such men as Theodore Parker, Wendell Philips, Ralph Waldo Emerson and Henry Ward Beecher. He called the policy of southern preachers unchristian who were trying to excite the Southland to action.[17]

Later, getting more to the point, he argued that wars all came from the passions of men and did not meet the approval of God. He stated his firm conviction that Christians have no business fighting in them. He says:

Our conclusion of the whole matter is, that the wars of heaven, are moral conflicts between the church of Christ and the opposing world powers, and the wars of earth are struggles in the world without by men of the world, inaugurated by wicked men for wicked purposes, but which God may overrule for good. The history of the world sustains us in these conclusions, but the church of Christ is composed of "a peculiar people," separate from others, are not of the world, engage not in its bloody conflicts, and yet the Lord has promised to sustain them to the end [18]

Some years earlier Fanning had expressed himself on the same question. Franklin College was reputed to have "military exercises," which were nothing but physical exercises, but someone had carelessly used the wrong word, and the school was receiving some criticism Some thought training for war was being given. After explaining the exercises, Fanning wrote·

This was far from my view, for I have long been satisfied war, in every shape, is unsuited to civilized governments and opposed in all its bearings, to the Christian religion The grand distinguishing characteristic of Christianity is, men shall not return evil for evil [19]

The brotherhood had been divided into two different camps respecting the issue of war. There were those who favored a Christian's participation, and those who opposed it We shall set before ourselves first of all the attitude of those opposing war and their reasons and then, the same for those who felt Christian participation was permissible.

Alexander Campbell had been opposed from very early to a

[17]Tolbert Fanning, "Duty of Christians in Reference to the Political Crisis of 1861," *Gospel Advocate*, Vol VII, No. 2 (February, 1861), p 33

[18]Tolbert Fanning, "Wars of Heaven and Earth," *Gospel Advocate*, Vol. VII, No 7 (July, 1861), p 205

[19]Tolbert Fanning, "Gymnastic Exercises in College," *Christian Review*, Vol II, No 6 (June, 1845), p 127

Christian's participating in war.   In the first issue of the *Christian Baptist,* Campbell said:

And, stranger still, see that Christian general, with his ten thousand soldiers, and his chaplain at his elbow, preaching, as he says, the gospel of good will among men; and hear him exhort his general and his Christian warriors to go forth with the Bible in one hand and the sword in the other, to fight the battles of God and their country, praying that the Lord will cause them to fight valiantly, and render their efforts successful in making as many widows and orphans as will afford sufficient opportunity for others to manifest the purity of their religion by taking care of them!!! If any thing is wanting to finish a picture of the most glaring inconsistencies, add to this those Christians who are daily extolling the blessings of civil and religious liberty, and at the same time, by a system of the most cruel oppression, separating the wife from the embraces of her husband, and the mother from her tender offspring; violating every principle, and rending every tie that endears life and reconciles man to his lot, and that, forsooth, because '*might gives right,*' and a man is held guilty because his skin is a shade darker than the standard color of the times, adverting to these signs of the times, and many others to which these reflections necessarily lead, will you not say that this prophecy is now fulfilled—2 Tim. 4: 3, 4—'There will be a time when they will not endure wholesome teaching, but having itching ears, they will, according to their own lusts, heap up to themselves teachers.   And from the truth, indeed, they will turn away their ears and be turned aside to fables!" Chap. iii. 1-5.   'This also know, that in latter days perilous times *will* come.   For men will be *self-lovers, money-lovers,* boasters, proud, blasphemers, disobedient to parents, ungrateful, unholy, without *natural affection.* covenant-breakers, slanderers—*having a form of godliness but denying the power of it.* NOW FROM THESE TURN AWAY.'   Christian reader, remember this command and 'from such turn away.'[20]

In 1846 when it looked as though war would come again, Campbell to set forth his position reprinted the above article, and expressed that from these views he had "subtracted nothing," but that his convictions were then even stronger.

Shortly after the first guns were fired in the war, Campbell wrote:

Civilized America! Civilized UNITED STATES! Boasting of a humane and Christian paternity and fraternity, unsheathing your swords, discharging your cannon, boasting of your heathen bru-

---

[20]Alexander Campbell, "Christian Religion," *Christian Baptist,* Vol I, No 1 (August 3, 1823), p 8

taltty, gluttonously satiating your furious appetites for fraternal blood, caps the climax of all human inconsistencies inscribed on the blurred and moth eaten pages of time in all its records [21]

Shortly after war broke out, W. K. Pendleton pled with brethren to have no part in it. He wrote:

O, my Christian brother think of it! When you shoulder your musket and equip yourself with all the instruments of death, ask yourself have you the right thus to take the life of your fellow? Who gave you the right? What has your brother done that you may shoot him?—Has he stolen your property? Can you murder him for that? Has he differed with you about political governments? Can you not part in peace?. . . .

I am anxious for the peace of Zion. Let not brother meet brother in battle. Let not two Christian souls perishing by mutual violence, going down to death, frantic with the rage of mortal combat, hope to rise to the climes of celestial peace from such a struggle.[22]

T. M. Allen, the veteran of Missouri, expressed himself tersely in these words: ". . . . I would sooner go to the grave being killed for not killing my brother, than to go to the tomb with my brother's blood on my hands."[23]

At the outset of the war, Benjamin Franklin, editor of the *American Christian Review,* took a decided stand against the Christian's participation in it. He wrote:

We cannot always tell what we *will,* or *will not do.* There is one thing, however things may turn, or whatever may come, that *we will not do,* and that is, *we will not take up arms against, fight and kill the brethren we have labored for twenty-one years to bring into the kingdom of God.* Property may be destroyed, and safety may be endangered, or life lost; but we are under Christ, and we will not kill or encourage others to kill, or fight the brethren.[24]

Again Franklin wrote:

We have never felt the value of our position, since we have been a people, as we have done during the political excitement that has swept over our country, and as we do now while such exciting things are occurring. We have been actively engaged every day

[21]Alexander Campbell, "Wars and Rumors of Wars," *Millennial Harbinger,* Fifth Series, Vol IV, No 6 (June, 1861), p 348
    [22]W K Pendleton, "A Plea for Peace," *Millennial Harbinger,* Fifth Series, Vol IV, No 7 (July, 1861), p 410
    [23]T M Allen, "Progress of Reform," *Millennial Harbinger,* Fifth Series, Vol IV, No 8 (August, 1861), p 478
    [24]Joseph Franklin and J A Headington, *The Life and Times of Benjamin Franklin* (St Louis Christian Board of Publication, 1879), p. 287

during this long political conflict, in directing the attention of the people to the one great center of attraction—the Lord of life and glory. We have had no time to turn to the right or to the left, to discuss the merits or demerits of exciting political issues of the times. We have left them to the men of the world—to the statesmen . . .

While the eyes of the men of the world are red with political strife and rage, and while their feet are swift to shed blood—while rapine and violence are stalking abroad in open day and threatening to destroy the peace and safety of the country, the children of God are assembling to hear the gospel of peace and to worship the God of their fathers. While sectarian preachers are haranguing their audiences on the question of political strife, and thus adding fuel to the flame, the preachers of the Cross are preaching peace by Jesus Christ, He is Lord of all.[25]

Benjamin Franklin goes on to say that not a preacher in the brotherhood had preached politics but had continued to preach Christ.

Seeing that war was inevitable, J. W. McGarvey, just a few days before Fort Sumter was fired upon, wrote his views:

I know not what course other preachers are going to pursue, for they have not spoken, but my own duty is now clear, and my policy is fixed. I shall vote, when called upon, according to my views of political policy, and whether I remain a citizen of this Union, or become a citizen of a Southern Confederacy, my feelings toward my brethren everywhere shall know no change. In the meantime, if the demon of **war is let loose** in the land, I shall proclaim to my brethren the peaceable commandments of my Saviour, and strain every nerve to prevent them from joining any sort of military company, or making any warlike preparations at all. I know that this course will be unpopular with men of the world, and especially with political and military leaders; and there are some who might style it treason. But I would rather, ten thousand times, be killed for refusing to fight, than to fall in battle, or to come home victorious with the blood of my brethren on my hands.[26]

McGarvey, furthermore, worked to get the leading preachers to use their influence to prevent other brethren from participating in the war. He wrote to Isaac Errett, whose Union sentiments were very pronounced, and tried to get his support.

It is absolutely necessary in a time like this, that our leading men —preachers, professors, and editors—should take no active partisan

[25]Benjamin Franklin, "Our Position in These Troublesome Times," *American Christian Review,* Vol III, No 49 (December 4, 1860), p 196

[26]Ben Franklin, "Our Position in These Troublesome Times," *American Christian Review,* Vol III, No 49 (December 4, 1860), p 287

position   The more prudent brethren ought to speak out plainly for
the benefit of the more rash.[27]

Errett's answer to McGarvey on this point is not accessible.   However, there can be little doubt as to the way his sentiments went,
for McGarvey wrote again to him, saying:

Your favor is received and carefully perused, and although we
differ as widely as ever, I am glad to be assured that you have no
disposition to push your views forward in such way as to injure the
cause. I have no doubt that you could easily produce a serious division in the churches of the North [28]

McGarvey was tireless in getting the support of brethren to the
neutral position in the war. He got up a large circular on the duty
of the Christian to stay out of war and sent it to the *American
Christian Review* signed by many of the outstanding preachers of
the state of Missouri.

On the side of those who felt Christian participation permissible,
there were a few leading brethren. B. W. Johnson was one, although he preferred to pursue a cautious course. His article on the
subject was printed in the June 25th issue, 1861, of the *Review*.
It was generally misunderstood and even McGarvey wrote Johnson,
congratulating him on his anti-war stand. Johnson came back,
expressing regret that he had been misunderstood. His belief was
that the issue should not in such times of stress be argued in the
pulpit. He tended toward the belief that the question was political,
not religious   While deploring war, he yet held that the government was ordained of God and that it was the Christian's right to
belong to that government   He argued that if government was
right, the means to sustain that government is also right. He cites
scriptures in the New Testament where men belonged to or held
political offices   He furthermore declared that there is no proof
that the soldiers of the New Testament times ever were told to
cease being soldiers after becoming Christians. Relative to a
Christian's duty to his government, Johnson concluded:

Either he can sustain it, or he is an incubus to his country; a
State is weak in proportion to its Christian element and the conversion of a majority of the people would result in national ruin.[29]

---

[27] J S LaMarr, *Memoirs of Isaac Errett* (Cincinnati · The Standard Publishing Co, 1893), Vol 1, p 242

[28] *Ibid*, p 243.

[29] B W Johnson, "Should Christians Go to War?" *Millennial Harbinger*,
Fifth Series, Vol IV, No 10 (October, 1861), p 586

On the same side, the *Harbinger* presented a letter from Jacob Creath, Jr . on the subject which had been addressed to Benjamin Franklin   Creath suggested that he had been asked on various occasions to preach on the subject but had declined   He had nothing to do with the war and wanted nothing   Yet, if a Christian did go to war and did kill, Creath could only see that the guilt would fall upon the rulers of the country, not upon the individual   In the final analysis, he left the decision up to the individual to make for himself

Thus we see two sides of an issue   Both sides admitted that war was an evil. The question of whether a Christian could engage in this evil practice was seen differently   Those who felt that it was allowable for a Christian to participate in carnal struggles based their conclusions on the fact that government was ordained of God, and that the God-ordained government had a right to protect, by bloodshed if necessary, its interests   The only question was, did a Christian have a right to consider himself a part of this government?   If so, the Christian was not held *individually* responsible for killing, but he was acting as an official of his government, doing what the government was ordained of God to do   Johnson says,

My kingdom is not of this world, *if it were,* then would my servants fight

Johnson reasons that since the kingdom of Caesar *is* of this world, and since it is right for a Christian to be a part of this kingdom, then it is right for him to fight for the kingdoms of this world

On the other hand there were others who believed that warfare was intended for the kingdoms of man, and not for the kingdom of Christ   If the world would kill and murder, it must do so, but let the Christian maintain his allegiance to a higher kingdom   They looked upon war as basically conflicting with the Christian economy, maintaining that the Christian was to do good to his enemies, love those that despitefully used him, and return good for good instead of evil for evil

Suffice it to say the problem has always been the occasion of much strife among brethren, especially during times of war   It is not likely that all men in the church will ever see eye to eye   Good men, consecrated men see differently, and at times, in the heat of passion, express themselves unkindly toward the other. For our part we admit that there are many angles to the whole question we have been unable to answer. But that a Christian can take up arms, kill his fellowman, make widows and orphans and cripples of innocent people, is in our opinion wholly incompatable and irreconcilable with the very genius and nature of the Christian economy.

Chapter XIX

TRENDS OF THE TIMES

When Phillip Henry, father of the famous author of the set of Bible commentaries, was thinking of marriage, he asked the hand of a certain young lady from her father. The father was unwilling, and later remarked to his daughter that this man, who had proposed to her was but a poor preacher. He was young, had little guarantee of a large-enough income to support her, and withal had some particular weaknesses which he singled out. She replied that she knew all of this but still she had confidence in him for she knew "the direction he was going."

What direction was the restoration movement going up to 1865? Can we say we like this direction? Was the church drifting away from her mooring or standing more solidly for the earlier principles? Generally speaking what was the state of the church as we find it at the end of the war?

In one sense of the term this is the most important chapter of all and yet it undoubtedly is the most difficult. The physician looks at the symptoms, carefully analyzing these, before applying the remedy for the disease. We are here looking at symptoms, carefully analyzing them to see if we can discover the disease. In the science of physics we are told that every action must have a reaction We are studying reactions, trying to discover the actions that produced it. We are watching the movement of the windmill to determine the direction of the wind There is something intangible, yet dangerous, about it all The doctor can view the symptoms and mistakenly doctor the wrong disease. We are taking the events of the time and analyzing them, not for their significance as events, but in the fact that they show the direction in which the restoration movement was traveling.

In the late summer of 1856 Robert Milligan began setting forth a series of articles in the *Millennial Harbinger* on the "Permanent Christian Ministry." Tolbert Fanning took exception to this, and printed his reply in the *Gospel Advocate* For several issues in both periodicals the discussion was carried on Respecting the subject for discussion, there is very little that needs to attract our attention. Fanning was tremendously interested in the subject of

"Church Organization " In fact upon no subject did he write more often Fanning's view of "Church Organization" was briefly this: The logical teachers, and overseers of the church were the elders. The elders were but the elderly men in the church. They "kept house for the Lord," and edified the saints. All the teaching was done by this group. They had no office, but each elder (old man) in accordance with his ability, taught and edified the church The evangelists went from place to place, preaching the gospel, establishing churches, and encouraging them to meet regularly With Fanning located preachers were but pastors and were taboo So with salaried ministers Milligan's articles as they respect this subject were accordingly much nearer the truth than Fanning, although Fanning was ready always to defend himself on this issue Yet, out of the discussion, Milligan presents an attitude, a symptom of a disease that was creeping over a large portion of the brotherhood

In the course of the discussions Milligan wrote:

In our present independent, weak, and distracted condition, we can, *as a church,* do but little for the salvation of the world. If we want to supply our own country with Bibles, or to send out a missionary to Jerusalem, or Liberia, we cannot do it *as a church,* in this capacity we have no means of cooperating: but we must form a Bible society, and a missionary society, to deprive the church of the glory of converting the world.[1]

Fanning missed no opportunity to pick this up and note it to be a symptom of a certain type of thinking. It is little wonder that Fanning saw in this a reflection upon the church, upon the wisdom of God, as well as upon the Bible. God had ordained that the church should preach the gospel to save souls. But, according to Milligan, the church could not do this, and must form itself into human societies before the work can be accomplished Not only so, but the wisdom of God declared and instituted the church for the purpose of saving the world; but since the church couldn't do this, and since human societies had to be formed, man in his wisdom was wiser than the wisdom of God.

Here, then, was a strong objection that more and more came to be raised against missionary societies. Their very existence was a reflection upon the wisdom of God, the adequacy of the church, and

---

[1] Robert Milligan, "The Permanent Orders of the Christian Ministry," *Millennial Harbinger,* Fourth Series, Vol VI, No 9 (September, 1856), p 499

the Bible as the necessary guide Their origin came, not from divine revelation, but from human planning, therefore, there was a subtle implication that the Bible was not a sufficient guide, but that something beyond it was needed. In years to come this was to be a forceful argument, especially with David Lipscomb. The whole program, he would point out, upon which the societies worked was a setting aside of the scriptures It was not strange to him that in the years to come friends of the society became the most ardent advocates of liberalism and modernism, for they *began* by setting aside the word. How else could they *end?*

In the earlier days of the restoration movement Thomas Campbell had voiced the famous motto. "Where the Bible speaks, we speak, where the Bible is silent, we are silent" Milligan also pointed out in the discussion that a "thus saith the Lord" could not be found in the New Testament for all things regarding the church, its work and organization, for the New Testament was not a code of specific precepts Milligan asserted that God made the New Testament to furnish us with a book of motives, and so the church is governed today by generic laws, examples, and motives. This was the forerunner of the viewpoint which later came up that the Bible was not to be obeyed in the *letter,* but only in the *spirit.* If man had the *spirit* of obedience in his heart, although he didn't obey the letter of the law, he was acceptable to God

Fanning viewed Milligan's assertion with alarm. To him such a program deprecated the entire New Testament, not to mention the earlier platform of the restoration Fanning referred to such commands as to believe, repent, be baptized, observe the Lord's Supper, etc. These were specific, not general. Milligan's position, Fanning asserted, was the next-door neighbor to the one Protestant bodies and infidels alike took, viz, if a man's *motives* were good, if he were sincere, nothing else mattered

In fairness to Milligan it must be admitted that he did not mean to go this far, nor would he have been among the number to deny the necessity of any of these. Milligan admitted these specific commands, but cited other commands, as, "Honor thy father and thy mother," "whatever you do in word or deed, do all in the name of Christ," etc, as general commands. Fanning, however, was not wrong in seeing a danger to such assertions from Milligan, for led to the logical end, they would have said what Fanning argued they did. It was only a question of a very short time that they did lead this far.

Fanning's discussion with Milligan probably did not accomplish the aim Fanning had for it. There was some general prejudice against Fanning's idea on Church Organization to begin with. Many doubtlessly thought he was seeing symptoms of a disease that didn't exist. But with Fanning this was far too serious to be taken lightly. He was confident that friends of the society were leading the church in a general departure from the Bible. This was the disease, and the symptoms became more and more numerous as he watched anxiously the passing of time.

Less than a year after his discussion with Robert Milligan, Fanning found himself at odds with Robert Richardson. Richardson was one of the favorite teachers at Bethany College. He was a very pious and deeply spiritual man. His greatest fame, perhaps, was gained a few years after this when he wrote the Memoirs of Alexander Campbell. In the March, 1857 number of the *Harbinger* Richardson began a series of articles on "Faith versus Philosophy." The gist of the articles was this: The restoration movement had been launched upon some great principles that had been tried and tested. Yet, Richardson went on to assert, it had not gone on to perfection. The movement had fallen down as it respects true spirituality and the real practice of the teachings of Christ. The reason for this Richardson ascribed to an introduction of human philosophy into the fundamental teachings of the restoration. This philosophy is oftentimes held without the person holding it, knowing it, he went on. Here, in his third number, he introduced the example of Tolbert Fanning, who had only recently run articles against human philosophy. Fanning had, in those articles, denounced Natural Theology, and made the claim that man could not know God from the works of nature, but only through the revealed word. Furthermore, the popular philosophy of intuitive knowledge, or a knowledge of God *a priori*, that man was born with certain intuitive capabilities to know God, Fanning also rejected. Richardson went out of his way to show that Fanning, while deriding philosophy, yet held a philosophy, for this was his own

About the whole discussion, there is an atmosphere of misunderstanding and mystery. Jacob Creath, Jr, was no doubt right when he wrote to Alexander Campbell complaining against Richardson's articles. He said if what Richardson was writing were the gospel, he himself had been preaching for years, and had been ignorant of it. He went on to beg Campbell to stop Richardson or he would ruin the *Harbinger*. Richardson's essays on this subject were lengthy and extremely wordy. Surely he was capable of clearer writing. At times he had a venomous pen, hardly characteristic of one with the reputation of piousness that he had. One finds himself disappointed with these articles from Richardson's pens · Again some allowance must be made for Fanning's position, for few today would hold today as tenaciously as he did that there was not, in the works of nature, some evidence of the existence of God. Nevertheless, there was a symptom apparent that Fanning was quick to see.

Fanning had the utmost confidence in the Bible, and would strongly object to those who indicated a lack of such confidence. He was undoubtedly right that Richardson, perhaps unconsciously, was putting too much confidence in philosophy himself, and too little upon the Bible. There was definitely a tendency in this direction, and the Bible was being partially shelved in favor of the more learned theology and philosophy of the times.

It has been remarked on various occasions that Ben Franklin up to the war days was following pretty much with the general drift of the brotherhood. He supported missionary societies, and meanwhile, watched anxiously the passing of the years, with the apparent refusal to believe that a drift from the truth could ever come. But by 1859 he began to have a definite feeling that all was not right within the walls of Zion. Unknowingly, the Trojan horse had been rolled into the mighty fortress, and now Zion was beginning to boil with internal dissention. There were enemies on the inside, and he was just awakening to the fact. Consequently, he writes:

We have tried to construe things we have seen among us in a favorable light, and to keep up the conviction that no evil was intended But it was all in vain; the conviction is *there, deep* and *strong,* and though we desire to remove it, have tried to have it removed, it only becomes deeper and still deeper, that *evil, most ruinous and mischievous evil is intended.*

Franklin goes on,

It is now wisely discovered that the terms of pardon laid down in the New Testament, as advocated, propagated, and defended with such unprecedented success by the Disciples, for the last thirty years, as one man expressed it, 'have rendered us ridiculous in the eyes of the world,' and that we must 'go on to perfection.' But where have these men gone to, in 'going on to perfection'? Some of them have gone so far as to reach the silly, the anti-evangelical practice of praying for the conversion of sinners at the mourner's bench! Others of them have progressed so far as to make the remarkable discovery that the voice of conscience is the voice of God. Again, it has been discovered, that man can not believe the testimony of God till the Spirit quickens him and gives him life. It is again maintained that men in our time speak by inspiration, and that miracles should be performed in the church! What use. have such men as these for the Bible?"[2]

Tolbert Fanning copied the above from the *American Christian Review,* and inserted it into the *Gospel Advocate* with the following additional note.

Fear not Brother Franklin, the cause we are advocating is the Lord's   We have felt confident for years that you have seen the storm cloud rising   The trifling matter with J B. Ferguson, in Tennessee, is not to be compared with the evils still threatening the brethren, particularly in your latitude.[3]

Particularly should the student of restoration history ponder well those last words from Fanning. The battle was coming, "particularly in your latitude"—particularly in the North where the *Review* was being published. What a marvelously accurate prophecy of things to come!

Fanning's outspoken remarks against the symptoms that were rapidly increasing around him got for him the reputation from his enemies of being "ambitious," and of desiring to "lead a party" On many of the particular points that Fanning emphasized, he was not always right. Some of his very closest friends recognized this Yet, in the main, Fanning was on the right track, and men closest to him knew it. Ben Franklin, therefore, came to his defense against such attacks by saying,

We have some personal acquaintance with Brother Fanning, and have read nearly everything he has written, and, while we do not precisely agree with him in everything, we do not believe there is a fairer man in investigation in the Christian ranks than he, one freer from misrepresentation, or less ambitious, or one who has less intention of heading a party.   There is no man in our ranks possessing a higher sense of honor, a stricter respect for and devotion to

---

[2]Ben Franklin, "The Defection Again," *American Christian Review,* Vol II, No 15 (April 12, 1859), p 58
[3]Tolbert Fanning, "The Defection," *Gospel Advocate,* Vol V, No 6 (June, 1859), p 169

the oracles of God than he   He is unquestionably, in the main issues he has had with brethren, maintaining the very soul of what we have, as a body, struggled for from the beginning, and the brethren are with him   He is a full-grown man, now of mature years, deliberate, decided, and determined, and is not to shrink, nor to be put down by the charge of 'ambition' and the desire to 'head a party,' on the part of those who can never answer him.[4]

In December, 1861 in the *Millennial Harbinger* and the *American Christian Review* there arose another controversy that might be taken as a symptom. This particular discussion more than anyone up to date, showed particularly the different attitudes that brethren had toward the Bible. The subject matter under discussion was, "Communion With The Sects," but the basic attitude the whole discussion revealed was the underlying conception which various men had of the church, and toward the Bible as the proper guide in matters of faith and practice. We, at the present time, are more interested in this attitude than in the issue, although a brief notice of this seems necessary.

Richard Hawley, one of the leading members in the church at Detroit, Michigan, wrote to W. K Pendleton, deploring the rise of Phariseeism and exclusiveness in the church with relation to the sects Actually, what he called "phariseeism" and "exclusiveness" had been there, but there, was arising a liberalism of which he apparently was unaware. At any rate, his letter caused W. K. Pendleton to invite various leading men to express themselves on the question of having communion with the sects.

Isaac Errett was one to accept the invitation to express his views upon the subject. Errett laid down four propositions as follows:

(1) In primitive times all who partook of the Lord's Supper were immersed believers

(2) Corruptions have crept into the church because of Popery and have scattered the people of God into various sects.

(3) Our plea is for a reunion of the people of God. While our plea does not recognize these sects as of divine origin, yet it recognizes a people of God among them

(4) "We are compelled, therefore, to recognize as Christians many who have been in error on baptism, but who in the *spirit* of obedience are Christians indeed "

[4]Ben Franklin, "President Fanning," *American Christian Review,* Vol II, No 22 (May 31, 1859), p 86

As to whether or not it was right to invite the sects to a communion around the Lord's table when they attend on Lord's Day, Errett's reply was: "Our practice, therefore, is, *neither to invite nor reject* particular classes of persons, but to spread the table in the name of the Lord, for the Lord's people, and allow all to come who will, each on his own responsibility."[5]   On the same point, Robert Richardson replied, "We simply leave each individual to determine it for himself."[6]

W. K. Pendleton's answer was,

We have ever most cordially approved the general, I may say almost universal, custom of our churches, in disclaiming all authority to exclude from the Lord's Supper any who, by their walk and conversation, and in their own hearts, approve themselves as the Lord's people We have never known any evil to result from the practice, but on the contrary, much good.   Such is the influence of passion and prejudice upon the actions and opinions of men, that it is next to impossible to influence any one for good whilst we treat him with distance and distrust.   To plead for union, and at the same time exclude the really pious from the communion of the body and blood of the Saviour, is, in the very nature of things, to destroy the practical power of our plea.[7]

This controversy ran for not less than two years, and at times became bitter.   Before it had run its course the whole question of the "pious unimmersed" received a thorough discussion.   Could a pious man, who had not been immersed, be saved eternally?   The question tended to renew another controversy of former years, raised in Campbell's famous Lunenburg letter of 1837, and on which many brethren then did not find themselves in agreement. But, before drawing conclusions from this controversy, it is best to see now the other side.

George W. Elley of Kentucky was the first to give a reply to Pendleton's answer.   There appeared to be real alarm in his heart as he viewed the replies in the *Harbinger*.   He asks, "Is not such a practice the breaking down of all the landmarks separating Christ's from human kingdoms?"[8]   Elley clings tenaciously to the

---

[5]Isaac Errett, "Letter from I. Errett," *Millennial Harbinger,* Fifth Series, Vol IV, No 12 (December, 1861), p. 711

[6]Robert Richardson, "Letter from Dr R Richardson," *Millennial Harbinger,* Fifth Series, Vol IV, No. 12 (December, 1861), p. 712

[7]W. K. Pendleton, "Remarks," *Millennial Harbinger,* Fifth Series, Vol IV, No 12 (December, 1861), p 713

[8]G W Elley, "Communion with the 'Sects,'" *Millennial Harbinger,* Fifth Series, Vol V, No 1 (January, 1862), p 39

principle that in New Testament time only those belonged to the church, only those were Christians who had been immersed What right, then, do we have to declare that men today can be Christians without immersion, as Errett and Pendleton were declaring. Can these men claim they are restoring the primitive order of things and at the same time set aside the primary necessity of the act of immersion?

Shortly after Elley's article appeared, Ben Franklin entered the controversy on the same side. Franklin merely wanted to know why, if it were admitted that no one but the immersed partook of the communion in primitive times, how can we claim to restore the ancient order, and today do it differently? And so he asks: "Where is the use of parleying over the question of communing with the unimmersed persons? Did the first Christians commune with unimmersed persons? It is admitted they did not. Shall we, then, deliberately do what we admit they did not do?"[9]

In the spring of 1863 Moses E. Lard wrote an article which he held in reserve for publication in the first issue of *Lard's Quarterly* in September, that year. Lard stood squarely beside Franklin and opposed W. K. Pendleton. The Lord's Supper, he argued, belonged properly to the kingdom, and those out of the kingdom had no right to it.

Basically there were two questions raised in the whole controversy The first one was, can a man be a Christian without being immersed? The second question was, does the church have a right to refuse the Lord's Supper to the unimmersed? The value in these questions is that they were revelatory of certain attitudes toward the Bible.

On the first question both Isaac Errett and W. K. Pendleton proved themselves to be true prophets of liberalism. While they agreed that no man was a Christian in New Testament times without immersion, yet we live in different times, times when we are compelled to admit that the good, pious men in all sects are Christians. It is not at all difficult to see why certain brethren thought of them as completely departing from apostolic grounds. They admitted that it took immersion in primitive time to make Christians. Why not now? If not now, what then was the value of restoring New Testament Christianity? On what ground could

[9]Ben Franklin, "The Limits of Religious Fellowship," *Millennial Harbinger*, Fifth Series, Vol V, No 2 (February, 1862), p 120

they defend themselves that they were even *trying* to restore it?
It was plain to men like Ben Franklin and Moses E. Lard that
Errett and Pendleton had exalted their human opinions above the
revealed word

Errett and Pendleton's attitude was truly symptomatic   In years
to come a large host of liberal brethren were to adopt the same
idea Lard and Franklin were to be looked upon as literalists and
extremists, and some, like W. C. Morro, in his book, "Brother
McGarvey," frankly say so.   All it took to be a Christian was to
have a pious character   Either immersion was essential to salvation
or it was not.   If pious character were all that was necessary, why
not abandon this thing of telling men to be baptized "for the remission of sins", especially when they could secure this remission
by having only good, pious characters?

For the most part the churches of Christ down through the
years have maintained that immersion is essential to being a Christian   They have refused to try to substitute opinions for this plain
declaration of scriptures.   Let this be called "exclusiveness,"
"phariseeism," "literalism," and an "extreme" or come what may,
still, it is loyalty to God's word, and shows a respect for the revealed will, and that's what counts

The second question was, does the church have a right to refuse
the Lord's Supper to the unimmersed?   From a practical point of
view Errett's conclusion on this point has been followed by the
churches of Christ down through the years, viz, they neither invite nor reject others from coming.   God has not made the church
a police force to guard the Lord's table from the unimmersed.   The
whole tenor of New Testament teaching is each man partaking of
the communion is to examine himself   Self-examination is the
prerequisite for participation   By the very nature of the case, the
church *could not if it tried* guarantee that only those partake of
the Lord's Supper who should.   Therefore, most gospel preachers
follow the practice of teaching the truth on the subject, showing the
Lord's Supper to be for Christians, those that have been immersed
for the remission of sins   If, after the truth is taught, a member of
a sect violates it, the responsibility is his, not the church's

By 1865, the year at which we bring this volume to a close, the
war between the states had ended.   The church had weathered the
issues created by the war without any serious disruption.   But
could she long continue without disruption with so many symptoms

present, indicating serious trouble? What were those clouds on the far-off horizon? Were they dark or were they white? Those whose hearts were heavy and anxious over Zion, strained their eyes to see, and then, with a look of consternation, declared they were indeed dark Then there were those who thought this was no time to look for dark clouds. The nation around lay bleeding and broken from four devastating years of submission to Mars. The Country's president lay dead, and every home, from the log cabin in the wilderness to the White House was draped in black, and thousands walked in mourning In such an hour of desolation there had to be something bright somewhere, and if not in the future, then where? And so some refused to look for fear of what they might see. But no matter There was but one thing to do · press on with renewed strength and zeal. The corresponding secretary of the Missionary Society on October 17, 1865, spoke truly:

As behind the cloud, the sun shines more brightly, or as through the rain drops only can we see the rainbow, so through the tears of the past we have at length beheld the gorgeous dawning of the rays of peace over our so lately war-scourged land Terrible indeed were the sacrifices; bitter the tears, deep the flow of human blood, made not to cease until reddened yet again, from the heart of a murdered President, and yet through all these times, hath God brought us safely to this happy anniversary hour A country saved, a race delivered and peace restored, may well fill us with a profoundest gratitude to God, and bow us humbly at His feet Amid these blessings, with such joys around us, with such hopes before us we can well afford to extend a new the right hand of fellowship to each other, without regard to dividing lines, from Main to the Gulf, and from ocean to ocean. With this Spirit, let us strive to forget the past and enter with a new life and strength upon the labors of the future.

O God, thou hast taught me from my youth;
  And hitherto have I declared thy wondrous works.
Yea, even when I am old and grayheaded,
O God, forsake me not,
  Until I have declared thy strength unto
  the next generation
                              —Psalms 71 17, 18

BIBLIOGRAPHY

PERIODICALS

Campbell, Alexander, *Christian Baptist*, (1823-1829)

Campbell, Alexander, *Millennial Harbinger*, (1830-1870)

Fanning, Tolbert, *Christian Review*, (1844-1847)

Fanning, Tolbert, Lipscomb, David, *Gospel Advocate*, (1855-1861, 1866-1948)

Ferguson, Jesse B., *Christian Magazine*, (1848-1853)

Franklin, Ben, *Western Reformer*, (1843-1849)

Franklin, Ben, *American Christian Review*, (1856-1948)

Lard, Moses E., *Lard's Quarterly*, (1863-1868)

Loos, C. L., *The Disciple*, (1851-1853)

Mathes, James M., *Christian Record*, (1844-1866)

Stone, Barton W., *Christian Messenger*, (1826-1845)

HISTORICAL BACKGROUND

Barrett, John Pressley, *The Centennial of Religious Journalism*, (2nd ed.), (Dayton Christian Publishing Co, 1908)

Baxter, William, *Pea Ridge and Prairie Grove*, (Cincinnati: Poe and Hitchcock, 1864)

Bennett, William W., *Memorials of Methodism in Virginia*, (Richmond Pub by the author, 1871)

Bond, John, *History of the Baptist Concord Association*, (Nashville Groves, Marks & Co, 1860)

Campbell, Alexander, *Debate on Christian Baptism*, (Campbell vs McCalla), (Buffalo· A Campbell, 1824)

Campbell, Alexander, *Debate on Christian Baptism*, (Campbell & Rice), (Lexington A T Skillman & Son, 1844)

Cauble, Commodore Wesley, *Disciples of Christ in Indiana*, (Indianapolis Meigs Publishing Co, 1930)

Fisher, George Park, *History of the Christian Church*, (New York Charles Scribners Sons, 1946)

Fortune, A W., *The Disciples in Kentucky*, (Lexington· ———, 1932)

Garrison, W E., *Religion Follows the Frontier*, (New York Harper & Brothers, 1931)

Gates, Errett, *The Disciples of Christ Story of the Churches*, (New York Baker & Taylor, 1905)

Gates, Errett, *The Early Relation and Separation of Baptists and Disciples*, (Chicago Christian Century Co, 1904)

Green, Francis Marion, *Christian Missions, and Historical Sketches*, (St Louis John Burns, 1884)

353

Haley, Thomas Preston, *Dawn of the Reformation in Missouri,* (St. Louis Christian Publishing Co, 1888)

Hayden, A S, *Early History of the Disciples in the Western Reserve,* Ohio, (Cincinnati Chase & Hall, 1875)

Hockett, Homer Carey, *Political and Social Growth of the American People, 1492-1865,* (New York MacMillan Co, 1940)

Lewis, John T, *The Voice of the Pioneers on Instrumental Music and Societies,* (Nashville Gospel Advocate Co, 1932)

Loos, Charles L, *First General Convention,* (Louisville· Apostolic Guide, 1891)

Moore, William Thomas, *A Comprehensive History of the Disciples of Christ,* (New York Fleming H Revell Co, 1909)

Morrill, Milo True, *A History of the Christian Denomination in America, 1794-1911,* (Dayton Christian Publishing Association, 1912)

Oats, Sargeant, *Prison Life in Dixie,* (Chicago Central Book Concern, 1880)

Qualben, Lars P, *A History of the Christian Church,* (New York Thomas Nelson & Sons, 1940)

Rogers, James Richard, *The Cane Ridge Meeting-House,* (Cincinnati: Standard Publishing Co, 1910)

Scobey, James E, *Franklin College and Its Influences,* (Nashville: McQuiddy Printing Co, 1906)

Srygley, Fletcher Douglas, *Seventy Years in Dixie,* (Nashville· Gospel Advocate Co, 1891)

Watters, A C, *History of the British Churches of Christ,* (Indianapolis: Butler School of Religion, 1948)

Wilcox, Alanson, *History of the Disciples of Christ in Ohio,* (Cincinnati: Standard Publishing Co, 1918)

Young, Charles A, *Historical Documents Advocating Christian Union,* (Chicago Christian Century, 1904)

BIOGRAPHICAL

Baxter, William, *Life of Elder Walter Scott,* (Cincinnati· Bosworth, Chase & Hall, 1874)

Boles, H Leo, *Biographical Sketches of Gospel Preachers,* (Nashville Gospel Advocate Co, 1932)

Campbell, Alexander, *Memoirs of Elder Thomas Campbell,* (Cincinnati: H S Bosworth, 1861)

Donan, P, *Memoirs of Jacob Creath, Jr,* (Cincinnati Chase & Hall, 1877)

Franklin, Joseph and Headington, J A, *The Life and Times of Benjamin Franklin,* (St Louis John Burns, 1879)

Grafton, Thomas W, *Life of Alexander Campbell,* (St. Louis: Christian Board of Publication, 1897)

Haley, J J, *Makers and Molders of the Reformation Movement,* (St Louis: Christian Board of Publication, 1914)

Hanna, William Herbert, *Thomas Campbell, Seceder and Christian Union Advocate,* (Cincinnati Standard Publishing Co, 1935)

Hopson, Ella Lord, *Memoirs of Dr Winthrop Hartly Hopson,* (Cincinnati · Standard Publishing Co, 1887)

Lamar, J S, *Memoirs of Isaac Errett,* (Cincinnati The Standard Publishing Co, 1893)

MacClenny, Wilbur E, *The Life of Rev James O'Kelly,* (Raleigh, N C Edwards & Broughton, 1910)

Moore, Allen R, *Alexander Campbell and the General Convention,* (St Louis · Christian Board of Publication, 1914)

Morro, W T, *Brother McGarvey,* (St Louis Bethany Press, 1940)

Power, Frederick D, *Life of William Kimbrough Pendleton, LL D,* (St Louis Christian Publishing Co, 1902)

Richardson, Robert, *Memoirs of Alexander Campbell, Vols I, II,* (Cincinnati : Standard Publishing Co, 1897)

Rogers, John, *The Biography of Elder J T Johnson,* (Cincinnati ———, 1861)

Rogers, John I, *Autobiography of Samuel Rogers,* (Cincinnati Standard Publishing Co, 1880)

Segar, Charles V, *Lectures on the Pentateuch,* (Cincinnati Bosworth, Chase & Hall, 1871)

Smith, Elias, *The Life, Conversion, Preaching, Travels, and Sufferings of Elias Smith,* (Portsmouth, N H Beck & Foster, 1816)

Srygley, F D, *Larimore and His Boys,* (Nashville: Gospel Advocate Co, 1898)

Stevenson, Dwight E, *Walter Scott Voice of the Golden Oracle,* (St Louis Christian Board of Publication, 1946)

Stone, Barton W, *Biography of Elder Barton Warren Stone,* (Cincinnati · J A & U. P James, 1847)

Tipple, Ezra Squier, *Francis Asbury, the Prophet of the Long Road,* (New York The Methodist Book Concern, 1916)

Ware, C. C, *Barton Warren Stone,* (St Louis Bethany Press, 1932)

Williams, John A, *Life of Elder John Smith,* (Cincinnati · Standard Publishing Co, 1870)

RECORDS

Spencer, Claude E, *Periodicals of the Disciples of Christ and Related Groups,* (Canton, Mo 1943)

Minutes of Concord Baptist Association.

Minutes of Mahoning Baptist Association.

Minutes of Meetings of American Christian Missionary Society (1849-1865)

INDEX

THE SEARCH FOR
THE ANCIENT ORDER

A History of The Restoration Movement
1849-1906

BY

EARL IRVIN WEST

Vol. 2
1866-1906

EARL WEST
RELIGIOUS BOOK SERVICE
722 N Payton Rd.
Indianapolis 19, Indiana

Remember the days of old,
Consider the years of many generations
  Ask thy father and he will show thee:
Thine elders and they will tell thee.
                    —Deut. 32: 7.

DEDICATION

To the Irvington Church of Christ, Indianapolis,
Indiana and to its elders—Charles Dean, John Smith,
Lewis Hurley, Gillespie Embry, and Loyd Gaines—without
whose patience and understanding this history could never
have been written, this volume is affectionately dedicated.

DAVID LIPSCOMB

CONTENTS

ACKNOWLEDGMENTS

The author acknowledges the assistance of a host of friends in making this volume possible He expresses his gratitude to Olan Hicks, editor of the *Christian Chronicle* and to Homer Hailey, teacher of Bible at Abilene Christian College for valuable suggestions on the manuscript, to E. C. Coffman of Houston, Texas and John T. Lewis of Birmingham, Ala. for help on the chapter of Austin McGary; to C. E. W. Dorris of Nashville, Tenn for the use of his library and suggestions on the manuscript; to Ben F. Taylor of Newcastle, Indiana for his assistance on the study of James A Harding, to Monroe Hawley of East St. Louis, Illinois for assistance on the chapter on Liberalism; to Enos Dowling of Indianapolis for the use of the Butler University collection of restoration material; to B C. Goodpasture, editor of the *Gospel Advocate* for valuable information on David Lipscomb; and to the countless other friends whose words of encouragement have helped vitally in producing this work.

PREFACE

All around the room my silent servants wait—
My friends in every season, bright and dim,
angels and seraphim.
Come down and murmur to me, sweet and low ,
And spirits of the skies all come and go
Early and late.

Thus sang Proctor the praises of his books. "A taste for books is the pleasure and glory of my life," wrote Gibbon "I would not exchange it for the riches of the Indies." Cicero thought that a room without books was like a body without a soul. Jeremy Collier said, "Books are a guide in youth and an entertainment in age. They support us under solitude, and keep us from being a burden to ourselves. They help us to forget the crossness of men and things, compose our cares and passions, and lay our disappointments asleep " "He that loveth a book," someone said, "will never want a faithful friend, a wholesome counselor, a cheerful companion, an effectual comforter."

A wise man wrote, "Of making many books there is no end; and much study is a weariness of the flesh." He who would undertake to add another publication to the endless parade of books marching before the attention of men should have something more than personal interest in doing so. The only excuse the author offers for the writing of this volume is that he feels there is a definite need for it. His method of writing has been colored by the consciousness of this need. Every attempt has been made to make the book easily readable and understandable. No one is more conscious than he of the lack of literary finesè the volumes could claim. The author is also conscious of departing from routine standards of historians in inserting many quotations that others might regard useless. Most historians it is true would have passed these controversies with much less attention. The author realized that many who read these volumes will not have this material accessible to them, that unless it was inserted here, many would remain ignorant of it. The volumes, therefore, have been written, not with the intention of meeting the high standards of literary criticisms, but to supply the need in the church of the present day.

It can hardly be denied that young preachers are filling the church today who have but scant knowledge of the historical background of the issues the church now faces and did face less than a century ago But there is nothing new in this When John F Rowe visited one of "our colleges" in 1883, he asked a professor if the students were taught the rise and progress of the "current reformation," and whether they were acquainted with the literature of "our distinctive plea." The professor replied: "they have not, and as for myself, I have not read up " Rowe then remarked:

And yet we establish colleges and ask the brethren to support them, with the avowed object of training young men to know the Bible, to know the plan of salvation, to know the difference between our distinctive plea, and the shibboleths of sectarian parties and to understand the ground reasons of our separation from all entangling alliances with the sect world If the country is to be flooded with a hungry horde of pastors who are unacquainted with the aims and objects of the fathers of the Reformation, we see no practical benefit in "Bible Colleges " The title is a misnomer and the pretension is a sham [1]

There is a timeliness in these words which has not diminished with the passing years

If any reader regards any of the pioneers of the restoration or any of the quotations given here from them as an authority today, he misses the point of the history. This attitude is disastrous to the search for the ancient order In the final analysis it is the New Testament that is the authority The pioneers would be the last to insist that their words be the present standard for the church

Too, there is something merciless in our ability to forget the heroes of the past, and their battles for the truth This is what Sir Thomas Browne calls, "the iniquity of oblivion " The author feels some satisfaction in lifting some of the outstanding pioneers from an engulfing darkness. Most historians have brushed aside men like David Lipscomb, Moses E Lard, Ben Franklin and Jacob Creath, as inconsiderate legalists who lacked true spiritual attainments On the contrary they were men who deeply loved the truth, and accepted the chastisement of others rather than

---

[1]John F Rowe, "Lift Up A Standard For The People," *American Christian Review*, (Oct 18, 1883) p 332.

renounce their convictions. They are men who need to be remembered, and it is hoped these volumes will help do this.

Therefore, in presenting this work to the public the author feels that if it fulfills the need, and inspires the church to greater work in channels of loyal adherence to great and true principles, all his time and effort will have been repaid. It is with that desire that these volumes are sent forth.

INTRODUCTION

There is no chapter in church history this side af apostolic days more thrilling to the lover of truth than that of "the restoration movement." At the beginning of the nineteenth century there burst forth throughout the country a general wave of spiritual and religious unrest. It began in England with such men as Glass and the Haldanes, and in this country with Mr. O'Kelly, Abner Jones, Barton W. Stone and others. Men were fighting their way out of the maze of sectarian and denominational errors and prejudices. The cry of their hearts was, "Back to the Bible and to the Christ of the Bible."

The list of these early pioneers of the spirit of religious liberty was swelled by names such as that of Thomas Campbell and his son Alexander, Walter Scott, John Smith, John Rogers, the Creaths and scores of others who came later. The heart thrills today as one reads of their struggles for truth, the. joy of their souls in finding it, and the urgency with which they proclaimed it everywhere. From rented halls and borrowed meeting-houses in the cities and towns to the school-houses and brush arbors of the back-woods, they heralded the newly discovered message of the ancient gospel of Christ and the apostles. Honest men and women of all sections gave a listening ear. The waters of rivers, creeks and man-made reservoirs were kept agitated by those sturdy pioneers as day by day they brought to be immersed the converts to the ancient faith. Like a great rolling tide, sweeping everything before it, the movement swept onward into the west, into the south, and across the ocean into England. Men began to wonder if the complete overthrow of sectarianism and the restoration of the true faith were not to be the "millennium" of the apocalypse.

But alas! the day came when men within the ranks of the church began to betray the faith by tendencies to compromise with those without, allowing the world and human errors of judgment to weaken and destroy the force of their plea. Their attitude toward the Scriptures changed. The temptation to be like the nations about them was more than some dared resist. Innovations entered and departures resulted—but not complete and entire! Noble men arose here and there with unsheathed sword to declare, "Hitherto thalt thou come, but no further, and here shall thy proud waves be stayed." A remnant was rescued from the tide of digression and the plea for the ancient order of things was saved The cause of Christ began again to invade the ranks of sectarianism and worldliness till once more the number of God's people in the States and abroad can be numbered in the hundreds of thousands. God still had his "seven thousand" who refused to bow the knee to Baal

In this second volume of his history, Mr. West has done a monumental work in gathering together facts and statements of the period long hid from the public's view He has spent months delving into the literature of the movement from its beginning to the turn of the present century With painstaking care he has sifted and sorted these materials, till he has given to the general public a clearer picture of the spirit and struggles of the men of that day than has any other historian.

In the past we have been treated to historical sketches and books written from the viewpoint of the liberal wing—men bereft of sympathy for the conservatives and their position, and oftentime by those lacking in sympathy for the Bible itself In this particular volume, the author deals with the underlying causes of the division that came within the ranks of Christians—a division which resulted in the two groups known as Christian Churches and Churches of Christ From contemporary writings and authenticated traditions Mr. West brings to light many facts hitherto lying silent and undiscovered in the periodicals of the times. He seeks to let such men as David Lipscomb, Ben Franklin, Tolbert Fanning and those laboring with him on the one hand, and Isaac Errett, W K Pendleton and their co-laborers on the other, present their own arguments and sentiments for the positions assumed For the first time the Gospel Advocate, the American Christian Review and other contemporary periodicals among the conservative wing are allowed to express fully the sentiments of those opposing the innovations.

In reading this book one is able to see more clearly than before what were the issues in the controversy, and to appreciate more deeply the convictions of men who stood against what they considered to be innovations leading to digression and apostasy. But besides this rich outlay of historical data, the reader will find such chapters as the one on the colorful life of Austin McGary and his contributions to the cause in Texas most entertaining and stimulating.

Second to the Bible, a study of this period with its great aims and oppositions, its faithful and its deserters, its trials and its victories, will do more to enlighten and strengthen, to warn and direct the Christian than any other literature known to the present writer. Enlightenment is one of the greatest bulwarks against error. As it continues to fire the hearts of men and women with enthusiasm and greater determination, and to arouse a deeper consciousness of the rich heritage of present-day Christians, this book will live long, ever contributing to a better understanding of the restoration of primitive Christianity in this present generation.

Mr. West is comparatively a young man, but an untiring and thorough student. It is a pleasure and an honor to be asked to write this introduction. Brother West was a student in classes conducted by me in Abilene Christian College in the thirties. I have followed with interest his persistent study of history and his diligence in seeking the truth on the issues discussed in both volumes of THE SEARCH FOR THE ANCIENT ORDER. And, although he writes from the viewpoint of the conservative body, he has sought to keep bias and prejudice completely out of the story. His aim has been to present truth as the historian should present truth. For him I predict a continued useful life in the service of God, and for his book that it shall be reckoned among the most valuable brought forth by members of the church of Christ in this generation

HOMER HAILEY

Abilene, Texas.
June, 1950

CHAPTER I

REBIRTH OF THE GOSPEL ADVOCATE

It was late in the year 1865. A horse and buggy moved slowly up a lonely pike south of Nashville, Tennessee. The lone occupant of the vehicle was a squat middle-aged man. There was nothing in his appearance to suggest that he was a preacher, nor was there anything in his disposition to admit the fact. He was a farmer, and his home was twelve miles south of Nashville on a small country road. "This thoroughfare," as J. M. Barnes later described it, "is what the Hillsboro Pike becomes after it ceases to be a Pike."

The horse and buggy crept into the city limits, and then moved toward the center of town. The streets were crowded with blue clad soldiers under orders to keep peace. Here and there loitering aimlessly, were young men still wearing the gray. Silent and sulking, they had returned from the war to houses that were burned to the ground, and farms that were gutted by war's havoc. They shrank reluctantly from plunging into the task of rebuilding the glory that had belonged to the South.

The horse and buggy pulled up before a dingy printing office and the occupant stepped down, tied the horse, and pushed through the doorway. An armload of papers was laid on a table—all written in longhand. The printer picked them up and scanned the copy of the first issue of the *Gospel Advocate* that would be published after the war between the states. The date on the top would read, January 1, 1866. Above the date would be the names of the editors, T. Fanning and D. Lipscomb. The front page would also say that this would be Vol. VIII and No. 1.

In a moment David Lipscomb returned through the door, untied his horse, stepped back into the buggy and directed his horse toward his farm.

The cessation of a war usually brings as many problems as it settles, and this was certainly the case of the war between the states. Probably the nation had not seen a period when she was more demoralized than in those first few years after this conflict. The South was beaten and suffering badly. Her fields were without crops, her cities for the most part lay in shambles; her youth lay dead on the battlefields, her uncultured slaves were now free, some arrogantly defying their former masters, and creating strong resentment against the black race   All in all it was a picture of desolation and ruin the like of which no section of the nation had ever previously known

E. G. Sewell lived south of Nashville and the impression of the war was vivid in his mind.   Speaking of his experiences, he wrote:

He has again and again stood in his yard or sat in his house and heard cannons booming like distant thunder, when he knew great battles were raging and human lives were every moment being rushed into eternity, while others were lying wounded and helpless, bleeding and agonizing, upon the cold ground.   He has listened to skirmishing with small arms, when cavalrymen could be seen dashing and retreating, while the fire of small arms was too rapid to count.   It takes a man of quiet nerve to remain unmoved while such things are going on so close by.

We were living about halfway between the two great battles, one close to Franklin, Tenn., the other near Nashville, Tenn., during General Hood's noted raid against the forces then encamped at these two places.   We could hear the cannonading almost equally well at both places.   After the battle at Franklin, when the Union forces fell back to Nashville, and the other side soon followed, the people living along the way had the stragglers from both armies to feed.   By the time the two armies had passed toward Nashville, homes were emptied of all they had on hand to eat, and our prospects looked gloomy as to feeding our own families, but while the armies were getting ready for the great battle near Nashville, we had time to hustle out, go to mill, get up some meal and flour, hunt up a little meat and such like, to live on again   By the time we did this the Nashville battle was fought. Hood and his forces fell back south, followed by the Union forces, then the stragglers from both armies had to be fed again   So we were again cleaned up of what we had to eat and were again ready to begin to stare hunger in the face; but before we got very hungry the armies passed on again, and again the people were fortunate enough to find supplies to keep hunger down a while longer   . [1]

The industrial North fared much better, but with the assassination of President Lincoln found it hard to control animosity against the South, even though few southerners welcomed the news of Lincoln's death   Inflation, hunger, hatred, rapacity—these swept over the country   The whole nation was enveloped in a

[1] E G Sewell, "Reminiscences of Civil War Times," *Gospel Advocate,* Vol XLIX, No 27 (July 4, 1907), p 424.

cloud of gloom. Just what the result would be nobody really knew.

Wise observers have pointed out that the condition of a nation politically reflects itself in the condition of the church. Certainly the condition of the country in those first years following the close of the Civil War was reflected in the Church. Probably the restoration movement knew no days of greater conflict than it was now to see. The controversies over instrumental music and the missionary society now began to rage, picking up momentum with the passing of years. Many brethren attempted to walk cautiously, fanning the flames as little as possible. W. K. Pendleton wrote in the *Millennial Harbinger*:

Upon the threshold of this new year of 1866, we desire to renew our vows, and to devote with increasing zeal our energies to the sacred cause of humanity, religion, and truth . . .

The world is suffering for the restoration of apostolic Christianity; the great heart of the times pants for something which it does not see in our present divided Christendom [2]

Ben Franklin, contemplating the general religious condition of the times, wrote:

The religious condition of the country is alarming, terribly alarming. The sectarian establishments in this country are tottering, crumbling and tumbling into one general chaos in all quarters.[3]

Franklin went on to point out that Episcopalian clergymen were fleeing into Roman Catholicism, the Methodist and Presbyterian churches were divided, and the courts were filled with disputes over their church property. Infidelity seemed to be having a grand jubilee. Meanwhile, Franklin held out that the only hope for the world was in the cause for which he and his brethren were pleading. They alone had the answer, and yet, their internal condition made them incapable of carrying on successfully. To accomplish the great work set before them, Franklin urged that they must (1) "set themselves in order in the house of the Lord," (2) "gather together in one harmonious and glorious union," and (3) go to work in earnest to convert the world.

---

[2] W K Pendleton, "Introduction," *Millennial Harbinger*, Vol XXXVII, No 1 (January, 1866), pp 3, 4

[3] Ben Franklin, "Introductory Address," *American Christian Review*, Vol X, No 1 (January 1, 1867), p 4

There were those like David Lipscomb who looked upon the war as divine punishment for evil in the nation. He wrote:

> In days that are past, God blessed us with all the bounties of life We grew rich, and in this world "had our good things." We hoarded our riches, and spent them upon our passions and vain desires. How little we consecrated to God and the good of our fellow man ! God in his providence sent a fatal besom of destruction over our land, and how fearful the desolation! Where once abounded wealth, and comfort and happiness, what deep poverty now much more abounds; what pressing want; what sorrow of heart that refuses comfort for those who are not Shall we, in beginning life anew, again pursue the same course that brought us to so disastrous an end? Shall we not, with the first dawn of returning peace, from our pinching necessities, consecrate the first fruit of our toil to the Lord, as the earnest of a more fruitful discharge of our duties for the future, as almoners of his manifold grace and stewards of his bounty?[4]

The moral in the words is as interesting as the general picture of the desolated condition of the land.

Yet, despite the demoralized condition of the brethren and the internal strife that prevailed, the church had enjoyed a substantial growth. In 1867 Ben Franklin wrote, comparing the condition of the church that year with that of twenty years previous. In 1847 the church had between one hundred and fifty thousand and two hundred thousand members, but twenty years later the number was conservatively estimated at a half-million Moreover, in 1847 the work was just beginning in Iowa and Michigan, but by the postwar period, it had penetrated into Kansas, Nebraska, California, Wisconsin, Minnesota, Jamaica, Australia, Wales and New Zealand. Twenty years before, gospel preachers were numbered in the hundreds, but in 1867, they could be numbered in the thousands. Twenty years before there were eight or nine monthly papers and one weekly, but in 1867 there were twenty-five regular publications in the brotherhood The brethren in 1847 were distributing no tracts at all, but twenty years later were spreading over one hundred thousand a year Finally, in 1847, Franklin pointed out that there were only two colleges among the brethren,

⁴David Lipscomb, "The Advocate," *Gospel Advocate,* Vol VIII, No. 1 (January 1, 1866), p 3

but twenty years later, there were ten colleges and not less than
forty or fifty high schools.[5]

The records of the American Christian Missionary Society for
those early post-war years show the strength of the church in
various localities. B. U. Watkins reports in 1866 that there were
sixteen churches in the state of Minnesota with a total of one
thousand members. Kansas boasted of sixty-nine churches with
three thousand, one hundred members. California had opened
up now and mission work was being done there. Robert Graham,
upon moving from Fayette, Arkansas, went to San Francisco,
arriving there on July 18, 1865, becoming the harbinger of gospel
truth to this section of the Pacific coast. On foreign fields the
Jerusalem mission was closed, but the Jamaica mission was still
open, although in 1866, it was being maintained only by native
preachers. The next year, J. O. Beardslee was back on the island,
but again stayed only one year, abandoning the work once again
to the natives. The corresponding secretary of the Society reported in 1868 that the missionary organization was doing work
in Jamaica, Nebraska, East Virginia and in the city of Troy, New
York. Barrow was in Nebraska where in the previous year, he
had baptized one hundred and forty-six persons. The state now
had twenty-two congregations with two thousand members.

In the South the church, although in destitute circumstances,
was recovering. P. S. Fall was still in Nashville. Justus M.
Barnes preached in Alabama. J. S. Lamar was in Georgia.
W. H. Hopson was in Virginia. The war had made contact between
the churches virtually impossible. Brethren in the South began
planning meetings where they could revive interest among themselves. The church in Murfreesboro, Tennessee, in their Lord's
Day meeting on April 8, 1866, decided to send an invitation to
the churches of the South, including Kentucky, Missouri, and
Maryland to come together in a general consultation meeting, to
discuss the needs of the church. W. H. Goodloe, evangelist at
Murfreesboro, sent out the invitation, and accordingly the meeting was conducted early that summer.

But of all the attempts to get back to normality in the South,
there is none more significant than the republication of the *Gospel
Advocate*. When the war began, it became impossible to con-

---

[5]Ben Franklin, "Now and Twenty Years Ago," *American Christian Review*,
Vol. X, No. 13 (March 26, 1867), p 100.

tinue publication of the *Advocate* All mail service was immediately stopped The *Advocate* could neither be distributed nor could material reach it. Added to this the high state of excitement in the South produced a corresponding slackening of interest in a religious publication like the *Advocate*.

When the *Gospel Advocate* made its reappearance on January 1, 1866, the most noticeable change was the replacement of William Lipscomb as a co-editor by his younger brother, David. For the next forty years the name of David Lipscomb was to be the most prominent one in the churches of the Southland. No man did more to stabilize the church during the critical years ahead. Certainly no study of the restoration movement from 1866 to 1906 could be complete without a knowledge of this great man.

Franklin County, Tennessee, in the year 1831—the year David Lipscomb was born—was hardly more than a wilderness. Mail service was unknown. Newspapers never reached back into the farm homes. A stagecoach line from New York to New Orleans ran through the county near the farm of Granville Lipscomb. A tavern was located not far away where the stages changed horses on the journey. News came in from the outside world in this manner. Roads were but winding snake-paths of mud. Life was rugged, simple, primitive and difficult. Clothes were of the home-spun variety, and meals consisted, not of the dainties of modern-day living, but primarily of that which was grown on the farm. Schooling was hard to secure, and the man who could read and write was looked upon as an educated individual.

Here into Franklin County moved Granville Lipscomb from Virginia in 1826. He was the oldest of ten children born to William and Ann Day Lipscomb There is much about the early life of Granville Lipscomb, David's father, that we would like to know, but apparently will never know. It seems probable that he was born in Louisa County, Virginia about the year, 1800 Granville Lipscomb might have married before leaving Virginia for Tennessee. Information on this is scant. In 1896 David Lipscomb met an elderly woman by the name of Betsy Broadaway who went to school with Granville Lipscomb's first wife in Spottsylvania County, Virginia Granville was the oldest of ten children, Dabney was the fifth child, and John was the youngest.

These three boys were very devoted to each other. Soon after arriving in Franklin County, their father was killed by a falling tree, the first major tragedy they experienced in their new home.

Following the Revolutionary War, North Carolina paid her soldiers by giving them land grants in the valley of the Cumberland. The Tennessee Historical Society has the journal of John Lipscomb who served as an Ensign in the company of Capt. William's Sixth North Carolina Regiment. He is described as a "happy-go-lucky, waggish fellow" who left his home state on April 25, 1784 to journey to Nashville. John Lipscomb's journal begins when Lipscomb left the Holston on June 11, 1784.[6]

It is not likely, however, that this John Lipscomb was the same individual who was an uncle to David Lipscomb but who had the same name. The latter John Lipscomb would have been too young to have been the same person.

All three of these boys—Granville, Dabney, and John—were members of the Primitive Baptist Church that met on Bean's Creek in Franklin County. Granville was a deacon, and a very devout man. The *Christian Baptist* was circulated in their neighborhood and all three read it. They determined that they would take the Bible as their only rule of faith and practice, and so stated their position to the Baptist Church. They were immediately tried for heresy and excluded from Baptist fellowship. At Winchester, not far from them, was a Newlight Church, a congregation established on the principles advocated by Barton W. Stone. The three brothers immediately became identified with this congregation. Later, however, Granville Lipscomb and his wife were united with the church near Owl Hollow in Franklin County.

After accepting the New Testament as their only rule of faith and practice, the boys thought it wise to give their time to a diligent study of the scriptures. Soon they concluded that slavery was against the will of God, and determined to do something about it. All three boys were now married, and had families. They owned farms and a few slaves, although the exact number is not known. Carrying out their convictions, they moved in 1835 to

---

[6] John P Brown, *Old Frontiers* (Kingsport, Tenn, Southern Publishers, Inc, 1938), pp 232-239

Sangamon County, Illinois, near Springfield Here the slaves were freed Among the first recollections of his life, David Lipscomb later recalled, was the year spent in Illinois Here, two sisters and a brother died 'In a short while his mother also died. Disheartened by these tragedies, all of which took place in such a short time, Granville decided to take the remainder of his family back to Franklin County. When he returned to Tennessee, David was the youngest of his three children All three were down with malaria fever and were "as much dead as alive." Mrs. F. C Van Zandt, a neighbor lady, warmly mothered David Lipscomb in those critical years. Parenthetically it might be noted that in a few years Mrs Van Zandt and her husband moved to Texas Isaac Van Zandt, her husband, was elected to the Texas Congress He was later sent from the Republic of Texas to the United States as a minister, and helped to negotiate the treaty of annexation for Texas

David Lipscomb attended a Sunday School class taught by his father at the Salem Church in Franklin County. No child ever had a more consecrated father. Each night before retiring the children listened to their father read a portion of Scripture and comment upon it

A Baptist preacher by the name of Elder "Billy Woods" was a near neighbor of the Lipscomb's, and although Granville Lipscomb highly regarded him, he had no patience with his doctrine Young David, then a lad of less than six, often heard his father speak of Woods' "false doctrine." but in his youthful mind could not distinguish between a "false doctrine" and a "falsehood." David promptly informed Woods one day that according to his father, Woods was "such a liar "

At the age of thirteen David and his brother, William, went to Virginia to spend a year with Lipscomb's grandfather, who was a deacon in the Baptist Church at Lower Good Mine in Louisa County There was an active Sunday School in which the pupils memorized scripture. Lipscomb during this time memorized the four gospel records in addition to the book of Acts He argued with his grandfather that baptism was for the remission of sins and refused to join the parade of young people to the mourner's bench.

In those early days it was unusual for a farmer to accumulate much wealth If he eked out a living, stayed out of debt, and reared a family with an average amount of food, he considered himself successful. But Granville Lipscomb, through industry and thrift, became a moderately wealthy man. He married again, bought a few slaves, and earned a livelihood above the average for that day. Still he was very religious. The slaves were assembled regularly for worship The Bible was read to them The slaves were given instructions in how to read and write by a member of the family. In later years Lipscomb was heard frequently to remark that some of his best religious impressions came from an old negro woman. Probably she was one of these slaves

The year, 1845, was an important one for David Lipscomb. He was now fourteen years old. Tolbert Fanning, who only recently had opened Franklin College, near Nashville, made a journey through Franklin County, preaching on the way Young David was just recovering from typhoid fever. He spoke to no one about it, but made up his own mind to send for Fanning. When Fanning tested David by asking him why he wanted to be baptized, David replied, "to obey God." With this statement, Fanning baptized him in a box.

In January, 1846 Lipscomb entered Franklin College, and three years later graduated from this institution, delivering the valedictory. Here, he was constantly under the influence of Tolbert Fanning, an influence from which Lipscomb never escaped Lipscomb was truly Fanning's protegè He adopted that fearless independence of mind so characteristic of Fanning, and consequently in later years showed no reluctance at standing alone upon his convictions. Lipscomb adopted Fanning's attitude toward many of the issues of the day Holding the same position as Fanning on such issues as missionary societies, christian participation in war, and in a measure, on church organization, it is not likely an exaggeration to say that Lipscomb portrayed the attitude of Fanning in his own life more than of any other living man

As a student, Lipscomb decidedly was above the average although not probably at the top of the class. Tolbert Fanning's class record has come down to us. A survey of Lipscomb's record **will** prove of interest The record is monthly and runs from **January** to July, 1846.

January		February		March	
English	8	English	8	English	8
Mathematics	8	Mathematics	8	Mathematics	9
Nat. Hist.	6	Nat Hist.	7	Nat Hist.	8
Music	5	Music	6	Music	6
Physics	8	Physics	9	Physics	10
Punctuality	9	Punctuality	9	Punctuality	10
Deportment	8	Deportment	9	Deportment	9
				Sacred Hist.	5

April		May		June	
English	8	English	8	English	9
Mathematics	9	Mathematics	9	Mathematics	8
Nat. Hist.	7	Nat Hist.	8	Nat. Hist	7
Music	6	Music	6	Music	6
Physics	10	Physics	9	Physics	7
Punctuality	10	Sacred Hist.	7	Punctuality	10
Deportment	10	Deportment	10	Deportment	10
Sacred Hist	8	Sacred Hist.	8	Manners	5

July	
Latin	5
Greek	6
Mathematics	8
Music	6
Physics	7
Punctuality	10
Deportment	10
Manners	5

It would seem as though Lipscomb's poorest grades came in "manners," a fact which is especially interesting. Years later Lipscomb recalled that the last "whipping" he ever remembered getting was for stealing a kiss from a "cherry-lipped Baptist lass" while a student at Franklin College

Upon graduation from College. Lipscomb moved to Georgia and became the manager of a large farm It is unlikely that his stay in Georgia was over two years. Shortly we find him back in Franklin County, working on a farm About this time the Nashville, Chattanooga, and St Louis railway, which was to pass through his father's farm, was being laid so Lipscomb worked on the project, cutting away some of the high ground,

In a short while he owned a farm of his own, and even had a few slaves. He was well on his way to becoming a highly successful farmer

David Lipscomb, like his father, had a tremendous interest in the Christian life, and, like his father, devoted a considerable portion of his time in studying the Scriptures. He had given very little of his time to thinking about being a preacher. To him, every man who was a Christian, should dedicate his life to the service of God in whatever way and manner he could. He did not regard preaching as a profession. At no time in his life did he like to be thought of as a preacher He had a natural timidity. In later years he could rarely stand before an audience without a feeling of embarrassment He was merely a Christian doing what he could to serve the Lord, who earned his living by farming. He once wrote:

I started out to preach believing preachers were appointed by laying on of hands. I failed to submit to it, because I did not care to be considered a preacher I began preaching because I thought I could do some work in that line that would be helpful. and all the help that could be given was needed then I have had no ambition for official places or honors in the church or out of it I desired to do what I did as a layman. I did not know how long I would continue in the work or when I would quit it I did not wish to continue a day longer than I could do good. I soon saw that Barnabas and Saul had preached ten or twelve years before they had hands laid on them, and those scattered abroad from Jerusalem, both men and women, "went everywhere preaching the word " I felt sure with these examples that I was on safe ground in preaching what I could. Then I did not care for anyone to feel any responsibility for supporting me So I preferred that kind of work.[7]

In 1875 Ben Franklin went to Franklin, Tennessee, to conduct a protracted meeting. Prior to this he had only a slight acquaintance with Lipscomb On this trip he became better acquainted with him. Franklin later wrote his impression of David Lipscomb in the following words:

Brother Lipscomb is a plain and unassuming man, with the simplicity of a child. He has good native sense, much power and influence, and is greatly devoted to the cause There is not the least danger of his ever turning *clergyman*. He has not an inkling

<hr>

[7]Quoted by E A Elam, "An Endorsement," *Gospel Advocate*, Vol XLVII, No 24 (June 15, 1905), p 369

in that way. He lives in utter disregard of the notions of the
world, puts on no airs, wears just such coat, hat and pants as suit
him. We were much pleased with him as far as our short acquaintance went.[8]

Simplicity in life, and thorough devotion to the cause of Christ—
these were David Lipscomb's two marked characteristics. By
1852 he had become a successful farmer. Having studied his Bible
considerably, he was eager to use his influence to promote the
cause of New Testament Christianity. As a young preacher, he
looked with great admiration upon Jesse B. Ferguson, then a
popular preacher for the church in Nashville. Very shortly there
came the rumblings of discontent, bursting into war between the
Christian Magazine and the *Millennial Harbinger*. The experience common to youth came now to him. Observing older brethren
in whom he had confidence fall into violent conflict, brought
disillusionment. But this dreadful experience was worth a
thousand sermons. Lipscomb had learned not to put too much
confidence in men. At first he seriously considered going back
to the church of his fathers, the Primitive Baptist. But a
closer study of the Bible revealed Ferguson's errors to him. He
became stabilized, and weathered the storm. He was now a wiser
man, having learned to trust man less and God's word more.

Lipscomb informs us that his first attempts at preaching the
gospel took place only three or four years before the opening of
the Civil War. Thus his first sermons were delivered about 1857
or 1858. However, before this time he had been actively serving
in the church. In the summer of 1855 one finds Lipscomb at
Salem, Tennessee, where he is serving as secretary of the executive
committee of the "Christian Churches in the Mountain District"
of Tennessee He announces a cooperation meeting to be held in
Woodbury, Cannon County, to start on the fourth Sunday in
September, 1855.[9]

George Stroud of Warren County, Tennessee, was the first to
suggest to Lipscomb that he should publicly proclaim the gospel.
Lipscomb went with him to a Lord's Day appointment. Previously he had studied carefully about ten verses of Scripture and
felt he was fully prepared to discuss them. When he stood up to

---

[8]Ben Franklin, "Visit in Tennessee," *American Christian Review*, Vol
XVIII, (1873), p 220
[9]David Lipscomb, "no title," *Gospel Advocate*, Vol I, No 3 (September,
1855), p 88

speak, however, he read the verses, but could not remember what he had planned to say. He finished reading the chapter, hoping the thoughts would come to him, but they did not. He was greatly embarrassed, and sat down in confusion. He asked Stroud to preach. Stroud was so taken back that he got confused, and could not preach, and the meeting closed, a great embarrassment to both.

After services both men took dinner at the home of a brother, neither mentioning the events of the occasion. After dinner, they mounted their horses, and rode off together. Finally Stroud spoke.

"Brother David," he said, "I hope you will not let this discourage you "

Lipscomb replied courageously: "Well, Brother Stroud, I will not be discouraged, if I can help it; but I confess that it is enough to discourage a young man to see a man who has been preaching fifty years make such a failure as you made today."

The war came in 1861. Lipscomb had fully made up his mind what he would do, having become thoroughly convicted that a Christian could have no part in it. He now lived on a farm at the edge of Nashville, and preached regularly. He publicly spoke out against the war, and took no part either in Southern or Northern politics. He was, however, denounced by men of both sides, but this did not deter him from preaching his convictions He wrote letters to public politicians, stating his position He lived apart from the war as much as possible, took care of his farming, and preached the gospel.

The disastrous effect of the war upon the South made Lipscomb decide, even before the war ended, to take more active steps to revive and reunite the scattered and discouraged brethren. He determined that when the war ended, the *Gospel Advocate* should be reborn to aid in this purpose. Then the question of editorship came before him. Fanning could not handle it alone, and Lipscomb himself did not feel competent. Furthermore, he was comparatively unknown as a preacher or writer. He had published only one article in any brotherhood paper, and it was not under his own name. We are never told just what this article was and when and where it appeared. In the hope of securing an editor for the *Advocate,* Lipscomb took a trip to Lexington, Kentucky,

in the fall of 1864 to attend a meeting of the Kentucky Christian
Missionary Society.   Upon the recommendation of J. W Mc-
Garvey, a brother was urged by Lipscomb to move to Nashville
and edit the *Advocate*.   Who this brother was we are never told
McGarvey himself promised to write for the *Advocate,* but never
did.   The reason undoubtedly is found in the *Advocate's* opposition to Missionary Societies of which McGarvey was an ardent
supporter.

The prospectus had been released sometime before January 1,
1866, when the *Gospel Advocate* appeared.   It well declared the
platform to be adopted by the *Advocate's* editors.

Our purpose is to maintain the right of Jesus Christ to rule the
world, the supremacy of the Sacred Scriptures in all matters spiritual, and to encourage an investigation of every subject connected
with the church of Christ, which we may consider of practical interest.   "The Kingdom of God" was a real, permanent institution,
"the pillar and support of the truth," upon a proper appreciation
of which the welfare of the world and the happiness of man depend,
her origin, organization, history, labor, and mission, her relation
to worldly powers, civil, military and religious, and her final
triumph, will occupy much of our attention.   The education of
the world for Christianity, and the training of Christians for
immortality, will constitute an important part of our labor.[10]

It will be of great interest to study in more detail the editorial
policy adopted by Lipscomb and Fanning, for in a large measure
it shows the character of the two men.   The war had left the
brethren South and North filled with hatred.   Neither Lipscomb
nor Fanning could escape the conviction that brethren who had
taken part in the conflict had abandoned God and the Bible.   But
the main suffering was now a thing of the past, and it was their
desire to build upon something better and to put the church on
a more substantial basis for the future.   Consequently, in the
"Salutatory," Fanning wrote:

After an anxious and painful silence of four dreary years, we
thank God most devoutly for the favorable auspices under which
we are permitted to address you.   No one has "set on us" to
injure us physically, or intellectually; and we trust to Heaven,
that it is our privilege to send our kind greetings to thousands
from whom we have long been separated.   While it is not our

[10]T. Fanning and D. Lipscomb, "Prospectus of Volume VIII of The
Gospel Advocate," *Gospel Advocate,* Vol VIII, No 2 (January 9, 1866),
p. 32.

purpose to make many promises, we feel that it is due to our brethren and the cause of our Master to say that it is our earnest wish to cooperate with all good men in setting forth the claims of the Messiah to the lost of earth. We have no local or peculiar institutions to defend, and nothing new to set forth. We will cheerfully labor with our fellow servants in the Kingdom of Christ in promoting every interest suggested in the word of life; and it shall be our constant study to oppose every cause antipodal to the reign of the Messiah. We earnestly desire to cultivate the most kindly feelings towards all men, and should we consider it incumbent upon us, to oppose the views and practices of any of our race, we hope to be able to do so in the spirit of love and meekness. Yet we desire to act independently, and when called by duty to oppose error and forewarn the deluded, we trust that we may be able to do so in the fear of God.[11]

The rebirth of the *Gospel Advocate,* then, in 1866, had a direct relationship to the general feelings among brethren North and South. Lipscomb wrote later:

The fact that we had not a single paper known to us that Southern people could read without having their feelings wounded by political insinuations and slurs, had more to do with calling the *Advocate* into existence than all other circumstances combined.[12]

With these facts generally stated, it is little wonder that the *Advocate* in the years immediately ahead was often accused of harboring a sectional spirit. It was not the purpose of either Lipscomb or Fanning to make the *Advocate* a paper exclusively for the South. In short, it was not to be sectional. Yet, neither of the men would deny that he felt a deep sympathy for Southern people. The bulk of the brethren North felt that the *Advocate* was championing the rights of Southern people, so they looked upon Lipscomb's strictures on civil government as "sour grape" psychology, since the South had been beaten in the war. This background considerably aided the *Advocate's* growth in the South, but hindered it in the North, where it had little or no influence. In years to come, this fact was to have more significance. The *Advocate* opposed bitterly the use of instrumental music and the missionary society. Consequently, churches in the South for the

---

[11]Tolbert Fanning, "Salutatory," *Gospel Advocate,* Vol VIII, No 1 (January 1. 1866), p 1

[12]David Lipscomb, "The Advocate and Sectionalism," *Gospel Advocate,* Vol VIII, No 18 (May 1, 1866), p 273.

most part stayed loyal to earlier restoration principles. In the North, where the *Advocate* was little read, and where the *Christian Standard* was more extensively read, the majority of the churches went with the general movement, accepting innovations Thus the innocent and proper motives of Fanning and Lipscomb became the occasion for further alienations.

The editors of the *Advocate* assumed a thoroughly independent position, fully resolved that they would submit themselves only to Christ Fanning remarked

We have received several letters from brethren assuring us that if we will defend certain peculiar interests and submit a satisfactory platform, we shall have a very large patronage indeed In reply, we respectfully suggest that in our early youth we repudiated all human creeds in religion, and we have never regretted it We now see no adequate cause for changing our position [13]

Upon the rebirth of the *Advocate*, the editors followed in a measure that attitude which they took in 1855 when the *Advocate* was first born They wanted the columns of their paper to be used as a means of having open and free discussions of all questions of interest to the church It was not the original purpose of the editors in reviving the *Advocate* to wage war on the missionary society, but of freely discussing the issue in the desire that unity might be achieved Consequently, Lipscomb wrote .

Any Christian Brother shall have the same freedom to our pages, on any subject that we may deem of interest, that the Editors themselves have In one word the *Gospel Advocate* shall not be partisan for or against Missionary Societies, nor for or against Christians engaging in war or politics, but shall be open to us free, full and candid investigation of the matters from those occupying positions on these and other practical questions as our space will admit [14]

To open a paper to full and candid discussions of all questions that effect the interest of Zion always presents the problem of personalities No matter what attitude the editors assumed, they opened themselves to criticism from the readers. While asking for full discussions of all issues, Lipscomb made no effort to steer away from personalities, realizing the futility of such an attempt.

[13]Tolbert Fanning, "Our Platform," *Gospel Advocate*, Vol VIII, No 1 (January 1, 1866), p 13

[14]David Lipscomb, "Errata—Our Future," *Gospel Advocate*, Vol. VIII, No 45 (November 5, 1866), p 717

Some years later, when F. D. Syrgley was criticized for inserting personalities into his articles, he tersely replied that whenever he saw a good-sized chunk of error lying around separate and apart from a personality, he would attack the error and let the personality alone. Lipscomb determined that he would watch closely the general spirit conveyed through these discussions, and would insist upon Christian charity and kindness being shown on every hand. Lipscomb had much to say on this subject at various times.

In announcing certain changes in the *Advocate* for 1868, Lipscomb restates the old policy in the following words:

Our purpose in the future, as in the past, shall be to encourage the free and full investigation of every subject having a practical bearing upon the spiritual welfare of the human family and the Kingdom of our Redeemer. We shall always demand that all investigations be conducted in a kind, Christian spirit. All vain theorizing on impractical questions and endless learned and unlearned theories and logomachies, and all personal strifes and contentions, shall be rigidly kept out of the *Advocate*.[15]

Men become identified with issues and thus cannot avoid being noticed. Lipscomb felt that carrying unrestrained personal quarrels desecrated the paper. He writes:

We intend hereafter, more rigidly than in the past, to exclude all personal quarrels and bickerings. The *Advocate* was not established to attack, nor to defend, the characters of individuals, either its Editors or others. It hereafter shall be desecrated to no such ends. It matters but little to the great interest of the cause of God in the world whether I or any other man be a hypocrite or not. Principles and institutions that effect the interest of humanity, not men, shall demand our attention. It is only as men become identified with such principles and institutions that we shall ever notice them.[16]

Nathan W. Smith of Jonesboro, Georgia, had been a faithful preacher during the war, and had undergone great suffering during the conflict. On one occasion he felt that he had been personally abused in the *Advocate*. While attempting to smooth over ruffled feelings, and, at the same time, to set forth the *Advocate's* policy, Lipscomb wrote:

The *Advocate* was never established to emblazon before the world the personal shortcomings of the brethren. The most pre-

---

[15]David Lipscomb, "Our Next Volume," *Gospel Advocate*, Vol IX, No 43 (October 24, 1867), p. 842

[16]David Lipscomb, "Errata—Our Future," *Gospel Advocate*, Vol. VIII, No 45 (November 5, 1866), p. 717.

cious earthly treasure the earth possesses is the character of her true and worthy children, and faults personal in their nature, of which we are all, to a greater or less extent, guilty, will never be lightly paraded to the public, to the detriment of the cause or the annoyance of any brother [17]

Like other editors, Lipscomb frequently received criticism from brethren who did not like to see discussions and personalities carried on in the press Such criticisms, he thought, generally indicated a lack of understanding of the role of a periodical. Papers possessed no authority They were but clearing-houses for ideas, avenues by which brethren came to a mutual understanding. That they were abused was readily admitted. On the whole point, Lipscomb once wrote:

Some of our brethren are very fearful of discussion of questions that continually arise among the brethren They seem to think the time will come when there will be no difference of sentiment, no discord or jars, no need for the investigation of subjects connected with the interests of our Master's Kingdom. They seem to think if there are differences of sentiment, they had better not be discussed. It makes a bad impression upon the world . . . Do you wish to make the impression that there are no differences, when differences do exist? That would be to perpetuate a deception upon the public, to act a falsehood. . And yet, there is a matter of conducting discussion, a proper spirit in which it must be done, in order that the greatest good may be, thereby, effected. Personalities, bitterness of feeling, and unkind inuendoes are unworthy of Christian men, and always harm the cause they are used to sustain Bitterness is not force, nor is personal denunciation argument We hope our scribes will remember these things, and like David of old, forget all personal insults and indignities in their holy indignation at insulted and injured truth, and in the name of Christ, with Christ's spirit, battle manfully for the truth as it is in Christ the Lord.[18]

After the first few issues of the *Advocate* appeared at the close of the war, Fanning gradually withdrew himself into the background Almost the entire editorial work was done by David Lipscomb When Fanning was asked why he did not write more, he replied:

The *Gospel Advocate* we consider ably edited without a line from us. We are not disposed to flatter, but we find Brother D

---

[17]David Lipscomb, "Letters from Nathan W Smith," *Gospel Advocate*, Vol X, No 4 (January 24, 1868), p 85
[18]David Lipscomb, "Discussion," *Gospel Advocate*, Vol VIII, No 6 (February 6, 1866), pp 83, 84

Lipscomb a strong and vigorous writer, an earnest man, and one who knows and loves the truth Of course, he is mortal—has faults, is not an angel, but we know not where to find a writer amongst the brethren better qualified to instruct in apostolic Christianity.[10]

In those early years following the war, the *Gospel Advocate* had great difficulty in getting on a sound financial basis. There were times when it looked as though it might be forced to cease publication. Were it not for the sacrifices of David Lipscomb, it unquestionably would have ceased During 1866 and most of 1867 he lived twelve miles from the office and had to ride this distance on horseback This took a great amount of time, and often the *Advocate* was sent out without any proofreading As an effort to avoid this, Lipscomb lived apart from his family for days, staying in unwarmed quarters, and munching cold lunches. Such personal sacrifices kept the *Advocate* going when otherwise it would have failed.

After the war, and for many years following, it was generally known that Lipscomb's health was very frail. He went to the consultation meeting at Murfreesboro in June, 1866, but had to return early because of illness By the spring of 1867 he was in "constant pain" It was evident something had to be done His condition he describes as "general biliary derangement, torpidity of liver, costiveness, alternated with a looseness of bowels" He complains that for several years he had known "severe paroxisms of pain" Upon hearing that a physician in Cleveland, Ohio, could cure such conditions by a "water cure," he determined to try it. He went to Cleveland via Cincinnati, visited congregations on the way, heard several preachers, met and talked with Isaac Errett The water cure, he thought, helped him temporarily For many years he suffered occasional hemorrhages that each time they occurred caused several days of suffering The last of December, 1879, he took a severe cold and coughed so often and so violently that he had grave doubts that he would ever recover Doctors declared his trouble to be "related to" asthma In later years his health greatly improved, but until he was fifty years of age he constantly knew frail health.

Lipscomb's ill health received considerable attention from many

[10]Tolbert Fanning, "Why Do We Not Write More·" *Gospel Advocate*, Vol VIII, No. 35 (August 28, 1866), p 560

brethren, especially from those who did not agree with his position. The *Advocate* has gained a reputation for speaking out
against things that were wrong, but the feeling existed that it
went to an extreme   L. B. Wilkes, one of the editors of the
Apostolic Times, probably expressed the popular attitude of brethren toward the *Advocate* when he wrote:

> The *Advocate* is sound in the faith; sometimes, I have thought,
> it is a little too sound—so straight that it leaned a little over.
> But its faults, and I think it not wholly free from them. generally
> lean toward the safe side.[20]

Now this being "too sound," as Wilkes put it, was at times laid
to the ill health of David Lipscomb. Isaac Errett put it in the
following words:

> We like Brother Lipscomb for one thing—his entire frankness.
> There is nothing of the assassin in his warfare—no sulking about
> the pathway of his opponent with cowardly insinuations, ready to
> hurl them murderously at the reputation of an unsuspecting and
> unarmed antagonist. He comes into the field armed *cap-a-pie*,
> publishes his cause of quarrel, throws down the gauntlet, and
> waits, in true knightly posture, for an honorable tilt. He may,
> perhaps, be charged with an excess of frankness. We are inclined
> to think that ill health and a somewhat atrabilarious temperament
> lead him sometimes to indudge in gloomy apprehensions wl ich
> give an undue soberness to many of his editorials. But we always
> know where to find him; and if we must have a controversy, we
> prefer to deal with an open and honorable disputant.

Lipscomb's reputation for having an "excess of frankness" was,
at times, made the butt of a joke. Before his father Ben Franklin,
died, Joseph Franklin was a loyal devotee of the truth, and was
one of the spiciest writers in the *Review*. He came to Nashville
in December, 1877, and visited many brethren, David Lipscomb
being among the number. In his characteristically pungent style,
he later remarked: "Brother 'Dave' has a mighty fine way about
him, but he don't mean it all." He was striking, of course, at
Lipscomb's "excess of frankness."

In the years immediately after the war, the *Advocate* had great
difficulty securing enough subscribers to continue   In 1866
the paper had no office, but was printed on contract by another

---

[20]L. B. Wilkes, "The Gospel Advocate," *Apostolic Times*, Vol I, (1869),
p. 12.

concern. Nashville was then occupied by a large Federal army Living conditions were bad, labor was high Postal facilities were very limited Only the larger thoroughfares had postal facilities at all, and these were inadequate. Lipscomb had not the funds to put into the paper to make it go In the spring of 1866 he announced that the *Advocate* did not have enough subscribers to carry it through the year without serious loss to the editor. By the fall of 1867 the condition was worse The October 17th issue was delayed, and Lipscomb explained that this was due to lack of funds. Five hundred dollars had been given to him to buy a press He loaned this money out with the understanding that he could get it back at any time Unfortunately, this promise fell through. During the fall of 1867, Lipscomb begged brethren to send him one thousand subscribers The *Advocate* reached a financial crisis that year, and closed out with the November 7th issue.

The paper appeared again in 1868, greatly enlarged, and changed in some details Even though Lipscomb was not financially able to make this improvement, he went ahead upon the theory that brethren would support it if it were a better periodical This year, Lipscomb assumed full responsibility for the editorship The year before P. S Fall had become a co-editor. Fanning also was a co-editor A new feature of the paper was an "Alien's Department" edited by Dr. T W Brents, consisting of essays on fundamental Bible teaching, intending to instruct the alien on how to become a Christian These essays were later collected together into a tract called "The Gospel Plan of Salvation," which later became the book by the same title.

The year 1868 saw the *Gospel Advocate* emerging from the financial storm. By June, Lipscomb announced that the *Advocate* was now on a self-sustaining basis By October, he suggested that it was past the crisis and in better condition than ever. Throughout the year 1869, Lipscomb carried the load alone Both Fanning and Fall had become too preoccupied with other matters to take an interest in the *Advocate* Elisha G Sewell was now invited to move to Nashville The invitation was readily accepted, and Sewell became co-editor of the *Gospel Advocate* January 1, 1870.

In later years David Lipscomb was to exert a tremendous

influence upon the course of the church in the South, an influence which cannot be exaggerated and must not be underestimated. The interest that lay closest to his heart was the welfare and purity of the church. He was a giant in Israel in those days. John F. Rowe spoke of him in the following words:

The *Gospel Advocate* is to hand, and, as usual, full of valuable thought and interesting reading. Brother David Lipscomb, with his efficient aids, is doing a large and good work, for which the Master alone can bestow a corresponding reward. I know Brother David well, and have always had the most undoubted assurance that the welfare of society and the purity of the church were the interests that fill his great heart.[21]

There were some, like V. M. Metcalfe, who believed that Lipscomb was providentially the man provided for those critical days of the restoration movement when men were abandoning the appointments of God for human opinions. It took a courageous, intelligent man, and withal a charitable one to sweep back the tide of innovations then engulfing the church. In view of this Metcalfe wrote:

He is getting old, and in the course of nature will not be here many more years to earnestly contend for the purity of the church and simplicity of the gospel I don't know of a brother who is more frequently misquoted and misunderstood than Brother Lipscomb. While everybody concedes that he is a man of ability, yet few know his real worth I have known him intimately for over twenty-five years, and I have never known a more godly or self-sacrificing man. Many suppose from his writings that he is a cross, ill-natured, sour old man, yet just the reverse is true. He is tenderhearted and loving as a child—can be led to do almost anything unless he thinks it wrong; then all the earth can't move him. He is loyal to the teachings of the Bible. I have never known a man just like him in all of his makeup. I believed that God in His providence has used him in the last twenty-five years as he has no other man to elevate the standard of the church of Christ and keep it pure from innovations. God has given him wisdom and power for accomplishing good. He has not been unfaithful.[22]

The Lipscomb story—his controversies, his activities, and his teachings—will largely fill the history into which we now launch

[21]John F Rowe, "Items," *Christian Leader*, Vol 1, No 2 (October 14, 1886), p 4

[22]V M Metcalfe, "Our Bible School," *Gospel Advocate*, Vol XXXV, No 22 (June 1, 1893), p 341

CHAPTER II

ISAAC ERRETT

Any estimate which one places upon the work and ultimate influence of Isaac Errett will be colored largely by the individual's viewpoint. Historians among the Disciples of Christ invariably look upon Errett as the one who saved the restoration movement from becoming "a fissiparous sect of jangling legalists." This group hails Errett as the prophet of spirituality and liberalism. His life stands, therefore, as the epitome of that type of thinking, which, after the Civil War swept over the church. A closer investigation may raise some doubts about the validity of this claim. But, whether we regard Errett as the champion of liberalism and "saviour" of the church from "jangling legalism," or as the prophet of digression, still, his influence in the restoration movement is so important that a chapter must be devoted to him.

Errett was the fifth child of Henry and Sophia Kemmish Errett, and was born in New York City on January 2, 1820. His parents were very devout and belonged to a very strict religious sect. His membership in this sect went back to November, 1810 at which time this group consisted mainly of emmigrants from Scotland. The "holy kiss" seems to have been regularly practiced along with other peculiar religious observances

Henry Errett, however, did not live long He died in 1825, when young Isaac was only five years old. Isaac scarcely remembered his father. In this respect, as in many others, the experience of Isaac Errett was the antithesis of David Lipscomb Lipscomb remembered his father, and hardly recalled his mother. Isaac Errett's mother, upon the death of her husband, was compelled to open a boarding house to earn a living for her family. Despite her difficulties her children were sent regularly to worship services where they listened to long speeches, endless prayers, and great theological discussions.

When Errett's mother married a Scotchman by the name of Sauter, the family moved to a farm in Somerset County, New Jersey. Here the boys in the Errett family learned to work long hours on the farm Their stepfather was a hard-working man,

23

a strong disciplinarian, and with his enthusiasm for money, sometimes forgot to take into consideration the full welfare of his family In 1832 he emigrated to Pittsburgh with his family where he set up a saw-mill, and put the boys to work. They worked from daylight until dark. They built up a resentment for their stepfather. Although he provided them with a home, he gave little love and tenderness. His life was occupied with making money. It was a mistake which he in later years realized.

The church in Pittsburgh borrowed freely from the Scottish background of its members. The "holy kiss" was practiced—at least for a while. Strict discipline was maintained. If a member of this church married an individual who was not, he could look for a public and personal chastisement from the leaders in the congregation. "Foot washing" was never practiced but was seriously considered.

The lives of the great pioneer preachers all display varied childhood backgrounds. Just how far the background of Isaac Errett influenced his thinking is difficult to say. Errett's youthful training made him thoroughly acquainted with the very strict interpretation of the letter of the law. This was his religious background and he rebelled stubbornly against it. His later outlook tended to react against what he considered a following of "the letter of the law." On the other hand, men like Jacob Creath, Jr., who knew in their youthful days the tyranny of human creeds and human opinions, became thoroughly obsessed with the conviction that any departure from the strict letter of the law would lead to apostasy. Consequently, Jacob Creath—and many like him—reacted violently against the projection of human opinions, and human innovations into the work and worship of the church. Certainly some significance is to be attached to these backgrounds

Isaac Errett, and his older brother, Russell, were very close. Being religiously inclined, they acted together. on nearly all important matters So, in the spring of 1833, when both boys heard Elder Robert McLaren preach, each was baptized by him in the Allegheny River They were now members of the church in Pittsburgh, and each was faithful in every way.

About this time Isaac Errett began thinking of his future. He secured a position in a bookstore where he worked here for nearly a year. In the meantime he decided that he would become a printer, and became an apprentice under a Mr. A. A. Anderson, editor of a paper called "The Intelligencer." Errett contributed several articles for this periodical, which friends observed, definitely indicated superior talent, a foreglance of his later greatness as a writer. In later years, after he began editing the *Christian Standard,* and his writings were before the brotherhood continually, Errett displayed an elegance of style, and a power of diction that few could equal. Perhaps this early experience contributed to this end. He stayed with the printing business under Mr. Anderson until 1839 when he resigned to accept a position as a teacher in a school in Roberson Township, Allegheny County, Pennsylvania.

It was during this time that he began to develop into a preacher. The church in Pittsburgh had various social meetings at which the young people were invited to speak. Errett spoke frequently The older people noted at once his sincerity, his interest in spiritual affairs, and gave him more and more encouragement. His first "regular discourse" was delivered on April 21, 1839. His subject was the promise which God made to David that his kingdom would not fail. As the custom of the church was to set apart its evangelists with a solemn ceremony, Errett was thus "set apart" on June 18, 1840.

The Pittsburgh church was singularly fortunate in the fact that some of the outstanding preachers frequently visited and delivered discourses there. It was Errett's good fortune to hear Alexander Campbell, Thomas Campbell and Walter Scott on various occasions. It can be safely assumed that he heard many of the other prominent evangelists such as Samuel Church.

For the four years following his being set apart as an evangelist, Errett's fortunes were cast in Pittsburgh. Sometime in 1840 a new congregation was established in this city on Smithfield Street. In October Errett resigned his teaching position to devote his full time to preaching for this congregation. Here he baptized his first convert, Mrs. Sarah Ann King. Here, too, Errett became acquainted with Miss Harriet Reeder, and on October 18, 1841, they were married. But the church at Pittsburgh, like most congregations in those days was indifferent toward the preacher's salary. Errett cast his eyes in the direction of a more fertile field where he could more capably support his family.

In 1844 Errett moved to New Lisbon, Ohio on the Western Reserve Here the eloquence of Walter Scott had blazed forth many years before, and through his proclamation of the plan of salvation the church had been planted. The congregation, at the time Errett went there, appears to have been in a bad condition but the nature of that condition is not explained Errett, however, rode the storm and managed to see a measure of peace and growth come to the work.

It was five years later, on March 28, 1849, that he moved to the church at North Bloomfield, Ohio. But again, Errett ran into some of the old trouble—poor support. The next spring, by mutual agreement with the congregations, he began preaching part-time for the church at Warren, Ohio For the next six years his labors were given mainly to the Warren congregation. He frequently went on evangelistic tours, and on one such tour, held a meeting at Bethany in 1854 While still at Warren, he debated Joel Tiffany, a Universalist. It was while Errett was preaching at Warren that his name came more frequently before the brotherhood until he assumed a more prominent role.

In political sentiment Errett was pronouncedly a man of the North. He looked upon slavery as a great evil. When the Fugitive Slave Law was passed requiring northern people to return run-away slaves, Errett remonstrated. He considered this to be against Christian principles. The sermon which he delivered at Warren in 1851 on the "Design of Civil Government And The Extent of Its Authority" clashed with the views of Alexander Campbell. Campbell printed it in the *Millennial Harbinger* as a very capable rebuttal, and replied. Errett's rejoinder was printed and Campbell answered it in footnotes.

In spring of 1856 Errett made plans for a move from Ohio Michigan was attracting him. He purchased a farm near Lyons, and on May 9, 1856 made his transfer from Ohio. For the next few years his work was to be done in this state. In 1857 he became the corresponding secretary for the American Christian Missionary Society and held this position until 1860. Meanwhile, he traveled extensively in evangelistic efforts. In Michigan his labors extended to Ionia and Muir. In 1861 he was made a co-editor on the *Millennial Harbinger*. The same year he was an agent for securing funds for Bethany College.

The war came, and Errett threw his influence solidly behind the North.   He made frequent political speeches, often going into camps to make rousing addresses to the boys in blue   He applied to the Governor for a commission as a colonel that he might raise corps to take to the field.   The Governor refused, saying he had given out all the commissions that he could.   Errett's brother, Russell, was a Major in the Union army.   His son, James, enlisted, but severe illness prevented any active participation J. W. McGarvey wrote Errett in an attempt to enlist his opposition to Christian participation in this carnal engagement.   Errett however, refused.   The cause of the Union was too close to his heart so he did all within his power to promote it.

Late in 1862 Errett considered casting his fortunes with the church in Detroit.   For a number of years there had been a small congregation in the city, and it now met in the City Hall   Late that year a group left this congregation to start another church on Jefferson and Beaubian.   The separation in the church appears to have been peaceable, although it seems evident that there were serious differences among the brethren.   Alexander Linn, brother-in-law to Colin Campbell, was with the old congregation   Linn was as loyal to the truth as a man could be, and was one of the future leaders in the battle against digression in Detroit.   Richard Hawley and Colin Campbell, on the other hand, were the chief men in the new congregation, and were liberal in spirit and outlook.   They employed Isaac Errett as their new preacher.   The building, which had been purchased from the Congregationalists, was dedicated by W. K Pendleton on January 11, 1863 [1]

During these Civil War years, and particularly while Errett was in Detroit, his liberal attitude appeared.   Errett had been laying the ground-work for the one-man pastor system in the *Millennial Harbinger*   He carefully, however, avoided dissension. The articles were conducted in the form of a dialogue, with "Eusebius" suggesting the ideas Errett wanted to put across.

But, soon after taking up the work with the church in Detroit, Errett published what he called "A Synopsis of The Faith And Practice of The Church of Christ."   The "Synopsis" consisted of ten articles setting forth the faith and practice of the church, in

---

[1] W K Pendleton, "The Cause in Detroit," *Millennial Harbinger,* Fifth Series, Vol VI, No 1 (January, 1863), pp 27-31

addition to a series of by-laws, emphasizing the regulations of the order and business of the church. Most brethren felt that the "Synopsis" amounted to a creed. Those interested in reading it may find it in full in *Lard's Quarterly*, September, 1863, pp. 95-100. There was strong objection to this "creed" Ben Franklin published it in the *American Christian Review*, and voiced his opposition. But the strongest objections came from Moses E. Lard:

There is not a sound man in our ranks who has seen the preceding "Synopsis" that has not felt scandalized by it. I wish we possessed even one decent apology for its appearance. It is a deep offense against the brotherhood—an offense tossed into the teeth of a people, who, for forty years, have been working against the divisive and evil tendency of creeds.[2]

Also while in Detroit, Errett secured a name-plate to put over the office-door. On it was engraved the words: "Rev. I. Errett." At this early stage in the restoration movement it was enough to shock the brotherhood. This was looked upon by many as a definite departure from apostolic principles. Neither Jesus nor his apostles, nor an evangelist in primitive times set himself aside by this "popish" designation, the brethren reasoned. The very fact that Errett selected such a designation as "Reverend" indicated to many that he had a closer affinity to Rome than to ancient Jerusalem. The fuller discussion of this issue is reserved to a later chapter, but it is enough to note here Errett's general viewpoint.

On April 7, 1866, the first issue of the *Christian Standard* came from the press. Isaac Errett was the editor. To relate the full story of the establishment of this paper involves many little known details. The chief source of information has been J. S. Lamar's, "Memoirs of Isaac Errett," which is such a biased production that the full facts are not revealed. To Lamar Errett was an idol. His two volumes on the life of Isaac Errett, which were first published in the *Christian Standard* in 1892 in serial form, show him to be utterly incapable of grasping the point of Errett's opponents. The volumes are wordy and extravagant, and seldom is Errett spoken of except with an adjective such as "sweet," "pious," "godly," "spiritual" The opponents of Errett were

---

[2]Moses E Lard, "Remarks on the Foregoing," *Lard's Quarterly*, Vol. 1, No. 1 (September, 1863), p 100.

invariably "earth-born spirits," "legalists," etc. Those who agreed
with Errett were the "leading minds in the brotherhood," those
who disagreed, were "disgruntled," "jealous," etc. When it came
to writing that phase of Errett's life that dealt with his controversies with other men, Lamar was incapable of doing justice
to Errett's opponents. That he relied much on his imagination is
evident, and the result, so far as it respects these controversies.
is as much fiction as history. When Lamar's articles appeared
in the *Christian Standard,* there were those who answered them,
presenting some of the fiction. David Lipscomb was one. L. F.
Bittle was another. Bittle appraised Lamar's treatment of the
establishment of the *Christian Standard* in the following words:

It is well that the people be informed of the facts in regard
to the origin of the Christian Standard Brother J. F. Rowe
knows a great deal about the matter. Will he not give an impartial statement of the case? J. S. Lamar, like the majority of
biographers, feels bound to eulogize his hero and to make the most
of the latter's deeds and motives. But the result is fiction not
history.[3]

But why was the *Christian Standard* established? Was there
a particular need for the paper? That certain brethren felt there
was need for such a paper is obvious else it never should have
been started. But as to what that *need* was is a different question.
Lamar pointed out the inadequacy of the currently published religious papers. He writes:

There were several weeklies, also, among them the "Review"
and "Gospel Advocate," but these were not satisfactory. They
were regarded as being narrow in their views in many respects,
hurtful rather than helpful to the great cause which they assumed
to represent I would say nothing here derogatory of the editors
of these papers. They represented and fostered that unfortunate
type of discipleship to which allusion was made in a previous
chapter—a type with which the leading minds among the brotherhood could have no sympathy. We may credit these writers with
sincerity and honesty, but we can not read many of their productions
without feeling that we are breathing an unwholesome religious
atmosphere They seem to infuse an unlovely and earth-born
spirit, which they clothe, nevertheless, in the garb of the divine
letter, and enforce with cold, legalistic and crushing power. The
great truth for whose defense the Disciples are set, demanded a

---

[3]L F Bittle, "The Truth in History, " *Octographic Review,* Vol XXXV,
No 32 (August 9, 1892), p 6.

wiser, sweeter, better advocacy—an advocacy that should exhibit
the apostolic *spirit* as well as the apostolic *letter.*[4]

Thus Lamar assures the reader that the *Christian Standard* was
needed because the *Gospel Advocate* and the *American Christian
Review* were edited by men of "unlovely and earth-born spirits"
who were cold, and legalistic.   Now the fiction in this is easily
discernible.   Plans for starting the *Standard* were under way by
1864.   The *Gospel Advocate* had appeared as a small, monthly
paper from 1855 to 1861, having ceased because of the war.   The
first issue of the *Advocate* as a weekly did not appear until
January, 1866.   In April that year Isaac Errett wrote to David
Lipscomb requesting back copies of the *Advocate* saying he had
not yet seen an issue of it.   Yet this paper which Errett had
not seen was the occasion for starting the *Standard.*   To state
that brethren were influenced to establish the *Standard* because of
the "earth-born spirit" of the *Advocate* but betrays the prejudice
Lamar felt and shows the undying contempt in which he held the
Advocate.   This is the element to which Bittle referred when he accused Lamar of resorting to his imagination—not to facts.

The *American Christian Review* was being printed as a weekly
before this time by Ben Franklin.   It was widely received: indeed, it was the most popular paper in the brotherhood, and it
was this fact that worried an element of prominent men in the
brotherhood. Franklin, on almost all issues before the church, stood
opposed to Errett, Pendleton, and preachers of kindred thought
The editor of the *Review,* they considered "narrow" and "bigoted."
Knowing Franklin's popularity with the majority of the brethren,
it was their constant fear that Franklin's "narrowness" would
fasten itself upon the brotherhood, and prevent the restoration
movement from following along more "liberal," "progressive" lines.
No person can go back to the study of this period and fail to see
that the chief reason for the establishment of the *Christian Standard*
was to kill the *Review,* and lead the brotherhood away from
Franklin's influence into these more liberal channels.

The fact that the Civil War was in progress only aggravated
the situation. Ben Franklin announced himself opposed to Christian
participation in the war, insisting that he would not kill those

---

[4] J S Lamar, *Memoirs of Isaac Errett.* Vol 1 (Cincinnati The Christian
Standard Publishing Co, 1893), pp 300, 301

people that he had for years been trying to convert to Christ. He
announced that the *Review* would not discuss war and politics.
When the American Christian Missionary Society passed its
resolutions backing the Union and denouncing the South, Franklin
remonstrated.   Indeed, this did more than anything else to turn
him against the Society.   He saw at once that it could be a
powerful weapon for evil.   Isaac Errett was connected with the
Society, and had endorsed the war resolutions. His close friend,
James A. Garfield, who was influential in starting the *Christian
Standard,* stood by his side   Garfield had forsaken the pulpit
for a name in politics, had fought in the Union army, from Shiloh
across to Chickamauga, and then resigned to be elected to Congress
from his home district.   Garfield, too, severely denounced the
South, even advocating the confiscation of all their lands and
property. Franklin strictly refused to allow the *American Christian
Review* to become the mouthpiece for agitating hatred among
brethren.   In 1867 while David Lipscomb was in Cleveland to
get a water cure for his sickness, he met Isaac Errett for the first
time.   Errett preached in Cleveland then and edited his paper
from there.   At this time Errett heaped abuse upon Franklin. He
informed Lipscomb that the *Standard* was started because Franklin
refused to allow them to publish their views on the duty of
Christians to support the government in time of war.[5]

Thus, that the *Christian Standard* was started in part to kill
the influence of Ben Franklin and the *American Christian Review*
is plainly evident.

There is another factor regarding the establishment of this
periodical which comes to us from John F. Rowe, and is completely ignored by Lamar.   In 1864 there lived at Corry, Virginia,
a wealthy brother by the name of G. W. N Yost.   Rowe was
then an agent for the Missionary Society, and the Society, upon
learning of Yost's wealth, sent Rowe over to get a part of it.
Yost was in the oil business and at that time was making about
one thousand dollars per day.   He had taken a particular liking
to Rowe, and donated to him five hundred dollars, requesting that
he secure a preacher and some singers, come to Corry and hold
a meeting.   Anything left over should go to the Society.   Rowe

[5]David Lipscomb, "The Truth of History," *Gospel Advocate,* Vol XXXIV,
No 28 (July 14, 1892), p 436

secured the services of A. W. Way, and the church was established at Corry. Yost paid for the erection of a meeting house.

Yost tried to prevail upon Rowe to settle in Corry. He volunteered to start and pay for a paper to be published from there. Rowe informed him that a first-class paper was needed, but should be published from a larger city, preferably New York. Yost requested Rowe to edit it, but Rowe refused, insisting however, that he would consent to be an associate-editor. When Yost asked him to recommend an editor, Rowe named Isaac Errett Errett then lived in Muir, Michigan. Rowe wrote him, and his letter was signed jointly by J. H. Jones, who was then engaged in a gospel meeting with him, who was also a close personal friend of Errett. We are not told what Errett's answer was at this time, but that a correspondence ensued which kept the idea alive.

To get the full Rowe story it will be necessary to anticipate some events. The result of Yost's proposal to Rowe of a paper was a gathering at Newcastle, Pennsylvania in the home of the Phillips brothers. Here, the *Christian Standard* was organized. Errett insisted upon publishing it from Cleveland; Rowe, from New York. Errett suggested to Rowe that the paper would have no associate-editor, but left it open for Rowe to write any department he chose. Rowe selected the department of "Book Reviewer," but in a few months received word from Errett that this department would be edited by B. A. Hinsdale. Errett then proposed that Rowe write one article a month for which he was to be paid one hundred dollars Rowe confesses that he wrote four articles and then broke all connection with the paper.[6] Thus, Rowe informs us that the *Christian Standard* was at first the result of Yost's suggestion to start a paper for Rowe, but that Errett saw fit slowly to push Rowe out of any place of responsibility.

Here, we have in its earliest stages two threads of action, each contributing to the establishment of the paper. The first was the desire to kill the influence of Ben Franklin and the *American Christian Review*. There melted into this stream of thought another which, happily for the Errett group, approached at the right time to furnish the occasion for carrying out the former

---

[6]John F Rowe, "Reminiscences of The Restoration," *American Christian Review*, Vol. XXIX, No 24 (June 10, 1886), p 188.

purpose—Yost's desire to establish a paper just for John F. Rowe.

Referring again to Lamar's theory on the establishment of the *Christian Standard,* there is yet another angle to investigate. Lamar indicates that there was a popular clamor for the *Standard.* He says, first, that this clamor came from the "leading minds" whom he suggests were "wiser, sweeter, better" than the "unlovely and earth-born spirits" that dominated other periodicals. On this point David Lipscomb wrote:

> In one word, Brother Lamar's theory as to the origin of the *Christian Standard* is, that the whole enterprise was projected by the "leading minds among the brotherhood" and that those "leading minds" were "wiser, sweeter, better" than the "unlovely and earth-born spirit" which dominated such papers as the *American Christian Review, Lard's Quarterly,* and the *Gospel Advocate,* and inspired such men as Benjamin Franklin, Tolbert Fanning, Moses E. Lard, David Lipscomb, E. G. Sewell, and Phillip S. Fall. Such is Brother Lamar's theory.[7]

But were these men "wiser, sweeter and better" than these other brethren? Certainly in no one's estimation but their own, and in this case they were not exactly altogether free of prejudice. It was not without point that Lipscomb called Lamar's attention to the contrast in character of these men. James A. Garfield was every inch a Union man   He led an army, made up greatly by members of the church, into the battles of Shiloh and later, Chickamauga. Returning from the war, he thundered wildly against the South. Errett himself preached war sermons, applied for a commission, and otherwise encouraged war. While this was going on, David Lipscomb preached openly in the South against Christians fighting either for South or North. Active opposition was raised against him. After preaching a sermon in middle Tennessee against Christians going to war, a man, standing in the doorway of a church building, said if he could get a dozen men to help him, they would hang David Lipscomb [8] Lipscomb found it difficult to believe that Errett's group were "sweeter, and better" than Franklin, Sewell, Fall, Lard, and Fanning

These facts abundantly show that Brother Lamar's talk about the brethren who started the *Christian Standard* being "wiser,

---

[7]David Lipscomb, "Concerning the Width and Sweetness of Things," *Gospel Advocate,* Vol XXXIV, No 24 (June 16, 1892), p 370

[8]David Lipscomb, "Correction," *Gospel Advocate,* Vol. XXXIV, No. 29 (July 21, 1892), p 453

sweeter, better" than the brethren who differed from them is the veriest twaddle. It is time to call a halt to such palaver. The plain truth is that "our brethren" differ among themselves on some points. The *Christian Standard* merely represents one party in those differences—simply that and nothing more The brethren in one party are neither wiser nor sweeter than those in the other, save in their own estimation.

All this is perhaps none of my business, but in justice to such men as Harding, Lipscomb, Elam, Smith, Sewell, Larimore, Taylor, Butler, Kurfees, Wilmeth, Burnet, Brents, Gowen, Creel, Bryant, Grant, Northcross, and hundreds of others, I protest against the complacent self-righteousness and brazen egotism which sneers at those who differ from Brother Lamar and *Christian Standard* as "being narrow in their views of scripture truth" and "unlovely and earth-born spirits" with whom "the leading minds among the brotherhood" can have no sympathy.[9]

Lamar's explanation that the *Christian Standard* was the result of a demand from the brotherhood indicates that he again relies more upon his imagination than upon facts. For a year and a half after starting, the *Standard* came near being a financial disaster. The stockholders washed their hands of the paper and gave it to Errett. This fact alone does not necessarily reflect against the merit of the paper. The *Gospel Advocate* during this time came near going under The truth is that those were hard times financially, and people with limited means did not subscribe freely to new papers. Lamar was not frank enough to face this fact. His hero-worship of the *Standard* would not permit it. He was dedicated to the task of showing that the whole brotherhood was up in arms against the *Review, Quarterly, Advocate*, etc , and were clamoring for the *Standard* In trying to sustain this position, it is a curious fact that Lamar was never able to see his own contradictory statements. Writing of the association which was formed to establish the paper, he says,

The association was not only to issue the paper, but to publish books, tracts, etc , and the paper itself was *wanted*, "everybody" had been calling for it, and its circulation would certainly be very large. . .

But in the same paragraph Lamar adds:

. . . The "Standard" with all its backing, had to establish a

---

[9]David Lipscomb, "Concerning the Width and Sweetness of Things," *Gospel Advocate*, Vol. XXXIV, No 24 (June 16, 1892), p 370

character for itself, and win its own way, little by little. to popular favor and support. . .

"Everybody," he insisted, wanted the *Standard,* and yet, by way of apologizing for the disappointingly small subscription list, he urged that the *Standard* had to win its way little by little Again, Lamar explains the low subscription:

Still, the brotherhood as a whole had not, at this time, been educated up to this high standard Their leading weekly, before the appearance of Mr. Errett's paper, was the "American Christian Review" edited by B. Franklin of Cincinnati—which, though in some respects strong and influencial, was run on a lower plane, and catered to a lower taste. *Its* readers, therefore, missed in the "Standard" the tone to which they had become accustomed, and that slugging sort of belligerency which had been weekly exhibited for their delectation and applause Many, consequently, who most needed the blessed influence of Mr Errett's gentler and sweeter spirit, had to be trained and schooled to appreciate it [10]

There is no way to harmonize such statements , they are plainly contradictory. To say that the whole brotherhood wanted the *Standard* and then apologize for its small circulation which nearly caused it to fail on the ground that the brotherhood as a whole was not yet educated *up* to such a standard, is a plain contradiction of facts. The plain truth of the matter is that Ben Franklin was the man of the people. There were a few men with both money and position who disliked Ben Franklin's close adherence to the scriptures, and who were determined to sell the church over to their liberal ideas. The fact that a hundred thousand dollar concern went broke in the attempt attests the fact that Franklin's influence was far more powerful than they imagined.

This lengthy discussion has been necessary because of the prevalent misunderstanding regarding the establishment of the *Christian Standard* We turn our attention now to the events which led to the birth of this periodical How far-reaching Rowe's letter to Errett in 1864 regarding the establishment of a paper may be hard to say. Nevertheless, in May, 1865, the idea of starting a paper gained momentum. During the month, the Ohio Christian Missionary Society met at Ashland, Ohio at which time a conference was held privately among some individuals to discuss the project. A committee was appointed further to investigate the possibilities.

---

[10] J. S. Lamar, *Memoirs of Isaac Errett,* Vol I, p 334

Of all procedures of preparation, the most significant was a meeting held at the home of the wealthy Phillips brothers—Thomas W., Charles M., I. N., and John T., who lived at Newcastle, Pennsylvania. The date was December 22, 1865. Those present included Isaac Errett, J. P. Robison, W. K. Pendleton, James A. Garfield, C. H. Gould, John F. Rowe, J. K. Pickett, J. B Milner, O. Higgins, E. J. Agnew, John T. Phillips, C. M Phillips, Thomas W. Phillips and W. J Ford. J. P. Robison was selected as chairman and W. J. Ford was requested to serve as secretary. T. W. Phillips then proposed the following resolutions.

RESOLVED, First that the present aspect of affairs, in connection with the religious interest of the "current Reformation," requires the aid of a new religious weekly newspaper.

RESOLVED, Second, that in order the more surely and successfully to effect the establishment and support of such a weekly, a joint stock company should be formed to raise the means necessary, and to direct the conduct of the same.[11]

The resolutions, being considered separately, were passed upon and accepted.

The next order of business was the selection of a site for the location of the new periodical. C. H. Gould recommended Cincinnati; Robison, with the encouragement of Errett, recommended Cleveland; Rowe advocated New York. Cleveland was finally agreed upon as the site. The committee on legal affairs relative to the obtaining of a charter and getting the necessary papers for organizing was then appointed with James A. Garfield, J. P. Robison and W. S. Streator selected. This meeting was adjourned with the understanding they should meet again four days later in Cleveland.

Accordingly, the meeting in Cleveland was held on December 26, 1865. The capital stock of the corporation was set at one hundred thousand dollars to be sold in shares of ten dollars each. The name of the company was selected as "The Christian Publishing Association." The price of the paper was fixed at two dollars and fifty cents a year, with the first issue scheduled to appear in April, the following year. J. H. Jones moved that Errett be made the editor-in-chief, and the motion was carried unanimously.

---

[11]J S Lamar, *Memoirs of Isaac Errett*, Vol I, p 302

From this time events moved more rapidly. The charter for the corporation was obtained January 2, 1866 A Board of Directors was appointed consisting of James A Garfield, W. S. Streator, J P. Robison, T. W Phillips, C M Phillips, G. W. N. Yost, and W. J. Ford. The first meeting of the Directors was held February 14, that year. Streator was appointed president, W. J. Ford, secretary, and J. P. Robison, treasurer These three men, according to the rules of the corporation, were to form the Executive Committee It was agreed that Isaac Errett, as editor-in-chief should manage all business of the paper and select his own associates, subject to the approval of the Executive Committee. At this meeting the title, *Christian Standard* was selected for the periodical.

Regarding the name of the paper, Errett wrote later:

We propose, therefore, to lift up the *Christian Standard,* as a rally point for the scattered hosts of spiritual Israel, to know only "Jesus Christ and Him crucified: His cross, His word, His church, His ordinances, His laws, and the interests of His kingdom "[14]

Prospects for the success of the *Standard* looked very hopeful. It had immense wealth behind it, in addition to the cooperation of certain men of influence. The subscription list of the *Christian Record,* then being published in Indianapolis with Elijah Goodwin as editor, was turned over to the *Standard.* Thus the new paper had about eight thousand subscribers immediately given over to it.

The direction a new periodical proposes to travel at once indicates the viewpoint of its backers. In those days it was customary for such a new-born enterprise to start with a "Prospectus," so the *Christian Standard* followed the custom. Their prospectus read.

A joint stock company, under the name of The Christian Publishing Association, proposes to publish, in the city of Cleveland, Ohio, a weekly religious newspaper, to be called "The Christian Standard." Isaac Errett, editor.

The "Standard" proposes—

1. A bold and vigorous advocacy of Christianity, as revealed in the New Testament, without respect to party, creed or an established theological system.

2. A plea for the union of all who acknowledge the supreme

[14]Isaac Errett, "Our Name," *Christian Standard,* Vol I, No 1 (April 7. 1866), p 4.

authority of the Lord Jesus, on the apostolic basis of "one Lord, one faith, one baptism."

3. Particular regard to practical religion in all the broad interests of piety and humanity. Missionary and educational enterprises, and every worthy form of active benevolence, will receive attention While the "Standard" is designed to be preeminently a religious paper, it will freely discuss the moral and religious aspects of the leading questions of the day, in literature, education, moral and political science, commerce—in short, all that bears seriously on duty and destiny.

4 A Christian literature, involving a review of books and such discussions of literature, science and art as may serve to excite inquiry and promote the intelligence and taste of its readers

5. A faithful record of important religious movements in the old world and the new. While it is intended to make the "Standard" an organ of the interests and movements of the brotherhood of Disciples, it will not fail to present such a view of the teachings and proceedings of all denominations and benevolent societies as will keep its readers posted in all the important affairs of the religious world

6. Such a summary of political, commercial and general intelligence as is suitable for a family and paper

Scriptural in aim, catholic in spirit, bold and uncompromising, but courteous in tone, the "Standard" will seek to rally the hosts of spiritual Israel around the Bible for the defense of truly Christian interests against the assumption of popery, the mischiefs of sectarianism, the sophistries of infidelity, and the pride and corruptions of the world.

The editor will be aided by an able corps of contributors

The "Standard" will be published in quarto form, suitable for preservation, and will be about the size of the Cincinnati "Commercial" The first number will be issued in March or April next

Terms, two dollars and fifty cents a year, invariably in advance No club rates. Address

ISAAC ERRETT
Cleveland, Ohio.

Nearly all of the papers published this prospectus   There was one notable exception—the *Gospel Advocate* Lipscomb had two reasons for refusing to encourage the *Standard's* circulation. The *Standard* was an advocate of the missionary society, to which Lipscomb objected. He wrote:

The Standard is edited with ability, and in a fair and liberal spirit. It is the only weekly now that is an advocate of the organizations of human societies in religion Whether from a retusal upon the part of the conductors or not, articles upon but one side of this question ever appear in the Standard.[13]

Another objection Lipscomb had was that the *Standard* was too favorable to Christians participating in politics and taking active part in wars. To encourage the circulation of the *Standard* would have, from his point of view, been to encourage Christians to kill their fellowman. But in his objection, Lipscomb is charitable. He says,

It (the Christian Standard) is ably edited by Elder Isaac Errett a man whose reputation for ability and polish as a writer and speaker, certainly is second to that of none among our brethren The Standard, in its matter and execution, bears all the marks of both pecuniary and mental ability, skillfully used [14]

When the first issue of the *Standard* appeared, Errett gave the promise that it would contain a variety of material to make it interesting He proposed to give a record of activities of the various denominations, a practical application of Christian principles, and special attention to the Christian ministry. He made it clear that he intended to be independent.

In regard to the general style, tone, and spirit of the paper, we can only say that we have an ideal which we shall strive to realize We shall seek to be gentle and courteous, but we are determined to be independent Deference to the counsels of age and experience, respectful attention to the suggestions of friend and foe, suitable regard to honest convictions and prejudices—these we can promise. but, after all, our own convictions must control us. We forewarn our readers that we set out, not to please them, but to please God; to strike sturdily at error and wrong, and to utter freely our convictions, on grave and weighty themes, which can only be made profitable by free and manly discussion [15]

In the spring of 1866 Isaac Errett moved from Michigan to Cleveland, Ohio where he set up his office in the rear of 99 Bank Street. The first issue was brought from the press of Fairbanks, Benedict & Co, on April 7, 1866. The motto was: "Set up a Standard, Publish and Conceal Not." The first number was destined to become a memorial edition, for just as it was in the process of being drawn up, the aged Alexander Campbell passed

[13] David Lipscomb, "Our Exchanges," *Gospel Advocate*, Vol IX, No 4 (January 24, 1867), pp 72, 73

[14] David Lipscomb, "An Explanation," *Gospel Advocate*, Vol VIII, No 26 (June 26, 1866), p 425

[15] Isaac Errett, "Salutatory," *Christian Standard*, Vol I, No 1 (April 7, 1866), p 4

away   Some of the front page of the first issue was devoted to
a memorial of Campbell

The first five years of publication were extremely difficult ones
The first year the paper did not pay expenses   Subscribers complained that the price was too high, so in October, 1867, Errett
dropped the subscription rate to two dollars   At a meeting of the
executive committee on April 15, 1867, a resolution was passed
to discontinue the paper after January 1, 1868 unless more subscribers were forthcoming.   By December that year, however,
despite the fact that the subscription list was in little better condition, the committee decided to continue its publication throughout the next year.   A month later the stockholders decided to
abandon the whole enterprise, and gave it to Errett to salvage
from it what he could

Prospects for the paper proved no better in 1868   Errett was
having hard financial difficulties   During the spring, he received
an invitation to move to Alliance, Ohio, to become president of
Alliance College   The invitation was accepted with the understanding that he could continue to edit the paper.   Errett announced :

We have made arrangements with the Christian Publishing
Association, by which the *Christian Standard* has become our own
property   This involves no change whatever in the character and
aims of the paper.   . We will not conceal from our readers that
we accept considerable risk in this arrangement , but we are encouraged from the past to hope for entire success

It has already become public, but not in our columns, that we
have accepted the Presidency of Alliance College   This will not,
for some time to come, necessitate any change of location, as we
shall not enter on our duties in the College until next August or
September   Nor will it make the slightest change in the character
of the paper   A few friends of other educational institutions have
expressed fears that the *Standard* will become a special organ of
Alliance College   These fears are all unfounded   The college has
nothing to do with the paper [16]

Instead of increasing, the subscription list slowly dwindled   Errett
himself began to entertain serious thoughts of abandoning it   Just
at this point Mr R. W. Carroll, president of the firm, R   W
Carroll & Co, which had printed so many books published by

---

[16]Isaac Errett, "A Change," *Christian Standard,* Vol III, No 8 (February
22, 1868), p 60

the brethren, heard of Errett's plight, and proposed to buy the *Christian Standard* and retain Errett as editor. Errett gladly accepted the offer and on July 31, 1869 the first issue of the *Christian Standard* from Cincinnati appeared

Being released from the College, the necessity no longer exists for its continuance here, and we therefore transfer it to Cincinnati as the most desirable center of operation.[17]

J. S. Lamar was now called to be associate-editor.

The arrangement with the R W Carroll Co. was that Carroll was to own the paper and use it as a business project. The new owner was not a member of the church, but a Quaker While there is little doubt that this move saved the *Standard* from complete collapse, there were those who criticized it One of the editors of the *Apostolic Times* wrote.

Brother Errett, were the editors of the *Apostolic Times* to sell out their paper to a company of infidels, and then engage themselves to said company to edit the paper, as in the interest of primitive Christianity, what would you think of the act? Would you defend it? If not, why?[18]

At any rate, the move was made; the *Standard* was saved, and the years ahead were much less difficult ones

It will be unnecessary at this point to follow in detail the life of Isaac Errett from this year, 1869 to his death in 1888, or to follow his thinking through the controversies ahead, as these matters shall come before us often in the next chapters. Needless to say the ensuing years were ones of labor mostly centered around the paper, the missionary society, and preaching efforts Errett's health gave way. By the year 1887 it was much worse His friends suggested a trip overseas, and raised $1,500 for this purpose. So there came a significant event in his life—his overseas trip to Europe.

Errett's traveling companion was Z. T. Sweeney of Columbus, Indiana, who is perhaps best remembered by the name, "Zach." On the night of January 13, 1887 a farewell party was given in the basement of the Richmond Street Church in Cincinnati. Four hundred were present, among the number being Archibald McLean,

---

[17] Isaac Errett, "Removal of the *Christian Standard* to Cincinnati," *Christian Standard,* Vol IV, No 30 (July 24, 1869), p 236

[18] Anonymous, "Card from R W Carroll & Co," *Apostolic Times,* Vol I, No. 22 (September 9, 1869), p 171

secretary of the Foreign Christian Missionary Society, and many
of the local preachers Farewell addresses were given and then
a round of refreshments made by the ladies. Six days later Errett
and Sweeney left Cincinnati, and on January 22, in the middle
of the afternoon, the steamer, "Umbria" eased its way out of New
York harbor with Sweeney and Errett aboard bound for Liverpool.

It was Sunday afternoon when the ship docked at Liverpool
The next morning they were off for London on a train. W. T.
Moore, then in London, met them He was pacing up and down
the platform when the train pulled in.   Two or three days of
sight-seeing followed

On Thursday evening, Moore, Errett and Sweeney went to the
famous Baptist Tabernacle to listen to C H. Spurgeon Spurgeon
was just back from his vacation, and this was his first sermon
upon returning Errett glanced over the tabernacle and sized it
up as capable of seating about six thousand people   There must
have been half that many present at this mid-week service, he
thought. He listened to the singing, and was struck with the fact
that no mechanical instrument was used So he says,

It proves that there can be edifying congregational singing without the organ, and that the organ is not absolutely essential to the
edifying performance of this part of public worship, even in large
assemblies [19]

Spurgeon's sermon, he noticed, was very ordinary How, then,
account for his reputation? Errett felt that the secret of Spurgeon's
power lay in his ability to adapt himself and his material to his
audience The crowds, he noticed, were made up entirely of
common working people Spurgeon's language was simple, his
illustrations homely and to the point

From London, Sweeney and Errett went to Paris, then to Italy,
then to Africa, and finally to the Holy Land Late in June, they
arrived back home Sweeney's arrival at Columbus, Indiana partook of the nature of a political convention. The big tabernacle
was ready for him Beautiful flowers were across the pulpit
The organ was also decorated and a large sign across it read, "Welcome Home" Chairs were draped in red, white and blue Flags
from every nation hung from the gallery When the train arrived,

[19]Isaac Errett, "Letters of Travel—No II," *Christian Standard*, Vol
XXII, No 9 (February 26, 1887), p 68

bearing "Zach" Sweeney, four great white horses, drawing an elegant landau, came down the street to meet it. Behind it came the Sunday School with a brass band. Following this came throngs of people, cheering his arrival.[20]

Upon returning home Errett settled down to his work, but his health was no better. The announcement which appeared in the *Standard* on December 22, 1888 came very much as a surprise to most readers:

Unexpectedly we are called upon to make the mournful announcement that Isaac Errett, our beloved chief, passed to his reward on the morning of Wednesday, December 19, at his home at Terrace Park, twelve miles from Cincinnati. . .

The funeral service will be held in Cincinnati, Saturday next, December 22, 10:30 A.M.[21]

The funeral service was held in the Central Church in Cincinnati at the appointed time. Robert Graham told the story of Errett's life; C. L. Loos described the elements of his character, and J. H. Garrison preached the funeral.

At the time of death men have a way of being charitable Errett had made many enemies, who looked upon him as the man most responsible for leading the church away from its apostolic moorings into digression. Yet, these men tried to be charitable. J. Perry Elliott wrote in the *Christian Leader*

Although I had known for sometime that Brother Errett's health was very feeble, I was not prepared to hear of his death so soon. One by one our old brethren are passing away, and now only a few remain of those who, fifty years ago, were so earnestly pleading for a return to the divinely-ordained order of worship. Brother Errett was greatly admired by a host of brethren, and will be sadly missed, and I question if any brother can be found who can satisfactorily fill his place as editor of the *Standard*.[22]

R. B. Neal of Louisville, Kentucky, wrote the news of Errett's passing to the readers of the *Gospel Advocate*·

Few if any have attained to the high eminence as a leader upon which he stood. I was reared and nurtured in some prejudices

[20]S. F Fowler, "Reception to Z T Sweeney," *Christian Standard*, Vol XXII, No 28 (July 9, 1887), p 222

[21]Anonymous, "Death of the Editor-in-Chief of the *Standard*," *Christian Standard*, Vol XXIII, No 51 (December 22, 1888), p 822

[22]J Perry Elliott, "Sundries," *Christian Leader*, Vol III, No 1 (January 1, 1889), p 4

against the *Standard* and stand today opposing some of the influences of that paper, but association in office and mission work with Brother Errett won my highest regards for him as a manly and Christian gentleman. He stood by me in the hour of greatest need. He was gentle, courteous, liberal, manly and yet, there was something of the slumbering lion in his nature—those who once aroused it cared not to repeat the experiment.[23]

In the *Octographic Review,* Daniel Sommer wrote the news. He perhaps was a little more frank than some of the others, but was kindly even so.

Elder Isaac Errett, founder and editor of the journal called "Christian Standard" is dead. He died of bronchial affection December 19 at his home near Cincinnati. He will be greatly missed. For years we hoped that he would live long enough to see the full development of the policies that he advocated But it was the Lord's will that he should not, and so we bow in submission [24]

---

[23]R B Neal, "Elder Isaac Errett," *Gospel Advocate,* Vol XXXI, No 1 (January 2, 1889), p. 1.

[24]Daniel Sommer, "Publisher's Paragraphs," *Octographic Review,* Vol XXXII, No 1 (January 3, 1889), p. 1

CHAPTER III

THE SOCIETY CONTROVERSY (1866-70)

The meeting of the American Christian Missionary Society in October, 1865 showed a discouraging outlook for the cause of organized missions. Funds were slow arriving. John F Rowe who was traveling in Ohio and Pennsylvania was the only agent for the Society in the field. The Jerusalem Mission had been closed and a committee favored keeping it closed J. O Beardslee had returned from the Jamaica mission, leaving it to native workers. The Society voted to reopen this mission when a man could be found to go.

By 1867 Beardslee had returned to Jamaica, but funds for the support of missionaries were but little better. W. K. Pendleton, in an effort to bolster morale delivered a forceful address in favor of the Society in 1866. At the 1867 meeting both J. W. McGarvey and Moses E. Lard delivered addresses in its behalf. By the next year Beardslee had returned from Jamaica, and the only missionaries the Society was keeping in the field were here in America. In Nebraska, in Virginia, and at Troy, New York the Society had men located. This year, Thomas Munnell took over as corresponding secretary, replacing John Schackleford. R M Bishop, former mayor of Cincinnati, was president, having been placed in this office upon the death of D S. Burnet.

To a few brethren there seemed to be abundant evidence that the Society movement in the church was now dead. In California early in the fall of 1866 an annual convention voted to adjourn *sine die* for a "want of scripture precedent" for such conventions. Joseph Franklin, son of Ben Franklin, wrote in the *Review* the next year:

That "Our Societies" are falling into disesteem is evident from the fact that Presidents, Boards and Secretaries everywhere, last fall, filled their annual addresses and Reports with defenses and excuses for failure. Let them go. The Gospel was preached before them, during their existence in spite of them, and will be preached after they are dead.[1]

---

[1]Joseph Franklin, "'Our Societies' and the Preaching of the Gospel," *American Christian Review*, Vol X, No. 2, (Jan 8, 1867) p 10

Perhaps the chief reason for the Society's decline in popularity was its "war resolutions." Many thought the Society had over-stepped its right in declaring itself favorable to the North At the close of hostilities, the Society passed the following resolution

Resolved, That we have great reason for thanksgiving to the Ruler of Nations, not only in return of peace to our suffering country, but also in the emancipation of the slave, and the triumphant vindication of our free and beneficial government.

The resolution doubtless looked innocent enough, yet in that day it could only mean one thing: The Society was passing measures of a political nature Tolbert Fanning and David Lipscomb were quick to see this implication, and to observe how it had stepped out of bounds. After pondering the above resolution, they wrote:

Is this resolution one of the objects of said meeting? Is it one of the means of disseminating the Gospel? This resolution has done that Society more injury than it will ever do it good Is this a political or religious resolution? or is it both religious and political? . . . Those brethren who can believe that this is the way to disseminate the Gospel can do so; and those brethren who believe that political resolutions are the Gospel can do so, and those who desire to contribute to such an object can do so *we cannot do it*[4]

Despite the fact, however, that these "war resolutions" seriously hindered the Society, that which hindered it even more was the change in Ben Franklin's attitude toward it In 1857 Franklin had served as corresponding secretary, and had often defended the Society. Too, Franklin had put himself in an enviable position. As editor of the *American Christian Review*, then the most popular paper in the brotherhood, he wielded an extensive influence. Even W K Pendleton admits. "It is the most popular paper amongst us, and wields an influence that should fill its editor with a profound sense of responsibility for its proper conduct, as regards all the great interests of the church."[5] As long as Franklin backed the Society, Society advocates could rest easy, but when he turned against it, these same advocates found themselves facing the most difficult struggle in the history of the organization

---

[4]Tolbert Fanning and David Lipscomb, "A Reply to the Call of W C Rogers, Corresponding Secretary of the A C M Society for Aid to Disseminate the Gospel," *Gospel Advocate*, Vol VIII, No 13. (March 27, 1866) p 206

[5]W K Pendleton, "Items." *Millennial Harbinger*, Vol XXXIX, No 12, (Dec 1868) p 712

Franklin had during the war looked with some misgivings upon the actions of the Society. He became profoundly impressed with the fact that such societies could be instruments of evil as well as good. Through the years that he had defended their right to exist, he had never done so with his conscience fully acquiescing in his utterances. With all of his large heart he wanted the brotherhood to be united; nothing pulled harder upon the threads of his soul than that the church might be divided. There were times when he stretched his conscience almost to the breaking point, trying to back the things the brotherhood apparently wanted, when he himself felt they could not be defended. Finally, he could do it no longer. By December, 1866, he announced his change in position, and came out fully ready to clash with society advocates.

Woe be to that man who changes his position on any issue in religion! He can be sure that the brethren will never allow him to forget it. J. S. Lamar went back to 1858, the year Ben Franklin carried on his controversy with Oliphant of Canada, mentioned in our previous volume, and dragged a few skeletons out of the closet. He printed Franklin's answers to Oliphant in defense of the Society to remind Franklin and the brotherhood of the change C. L. Loos, in commenting upon Lamar's item, wrote·

Now it is true that a man may change, and has a right to change his views. But when and how this could have taken place with the editor of the *Review* is very inexplicable to us It must date from the very shortest possible period,—less than a year; and what could possibly have occurred within six months to effect so sudden and radical a transformation, we are unable to see. . . .[4]

Loos then referred to a meeting held by the Ohio State Missionary Society at Akron in the spring of 1866 which Ben Franklin had attended, saying that Franklin at that time was very much in favor of the Societies. Thus he dated Franklin's change somewhere between the spring of 1866 and the·beginning of January, 1867. He wonders what could have happened in that period of time to cause this change and how Franklin would now meet the arguments for the Society that he himself had formerly made. Loos showed that, in spite of Franklin's opposition, he had no intention of laying aside the Missionary Society. He adds.

---

[4] C L Loos, "Bro Franklin's Argument for the Missionary Society," *Millennial Harbinger*, Vol XXXVIII, No 5, (May, 1867) p 243

If anyone asks why we thus call attention to the course of the editor of the *Review*,—our answer is that Brother F. is using his influence in his paper to the detriment of a work most near and dear to us, and thousands among us, and we are resolved to stand by this work, in true devotion while life lasts   . . Nothing that our opposing brethren have said has had the slightest influence in weakening our convictions in this respect, but has only made our attachment to the cause stronger.

Franklin, in answer to Loos, admitted that he had changed his views on the scripturalness of the Missionary Society. He furthermore admitted *trying* to defend the Society, but added that he was no longer willing to do so. With regard to his action at the Ohio State Missionary Society meeting in the spring of 1866, Franklin admitted being there and making a reply, but declares that Loos twisted it out of its context, for he was not upholding a Society, *as such,* but missionary work. Franklin adds that he went to that Society meeting with some misgivings already in his mind about their scripturalness. He had hoped to find something there to settle his mind on the subject, but came away disappointed, realizing there was no other course open to him but to oppose them.

W. K. Pendleton was another who remonstrated against Franklin for his change. He wrote:

Brother Franklin, we know, with many others, thinks that the Missionary Society at Cincinnati did some unconstitutional things during the war,—and we think so too;—but we think that far too much ado has been made about this already. Many *Churches* did impudent and unchristian things also—and are doing them every year;—but does this prove that churches are dangerous things and ought to be abolished? These are incidents of our human frailty and must be met with the wisdom and charity which are higher than passion and sweeter and more blessed than revenge.[5]

About this time J S. Sweeney wrote to Franklin about his change, as follows:

There seems to be at present considerable excitement among the brethren all over the country, growing out of the controversy about the Missionary Society, and it has been of late not a little intensified by the position you have—or are supposed to have—assumed in reference to the question.[6]

---

[5]W K Pendleton, "Missionary Movements," *Millennial Harbinger,* Vol. XXXVIII, No 3, (March, 1867) p 147
[6]J S Sweeney, "Sweeney to Franklin," *American Christian Review,* Vol X, No 20. (May 14, 1867) p 156

To this Franklin replied:

We did, under certain *limitations and restrictions,* to which we found finally the Society could never be held, defend the Society scheme against brethren Oliphant, Fanning, and others, but never saw our way exactly clear.

George W. Elley was yet another to remind Franklin of his change. Elley lived near Lexington, Kentucky, and was a Society devotee. He wrote to Franklin, suggesting that some were saying he was with the *Gospel Advocate,* as though this would make his action criminal. He wanted to know exactly what the attitude of Franklin was toward Missionary Societies. Franklin replied:

It is not *missionary work* to which we are opposed, but empty plans, schemes and organizations, after sectarian models, which have proved failures; expensive, cumbrous and lamentable failures in *doing missionary work,* filling our publications with speeches, reports and resolutions, as also unpleasant controversies and discouraging the brethren.[7]

Despite the risk involved, Franklin made this change. Some did not hesitate to remind him that his paper would be forced out of existence. But Franklin was undaunted. He wrote:

At all events, we have come to the time to rest the question whether *love and devotion* to the creation of a few individuals, in the form of an outside society, with laws and names unknown to the law of God, is sufficient to sink a man of more than thirty years' labor and devotion to the spread of the gospel, *solely because he will not go for the Society.*[8]

Thus Ben Franklin took his stand against the Society. His influence, together with the unpopular war resolutions, found the American Christian Missionary Society in 1866 badly in need of repairs and rapidly losing in popularity.

At this crisis, the Society invited its great apologist, W. K. Pendleton, to defend it. Pendleton's address before the convention of 1866 was intended to do just this. The importance of this address in a study of the society controversy cannot be overemphasized. It was published in the *Millennial Harbinger* for

---

[7]Ben Franklin, "Our Position Defined," *American Christian Review,* Vol X, No 11, (March 12, 1867) p 84

[8]Ben Franklin, "Prof C L Loos and the Harbinger," *American Christian Review,* Vol X, No 24 (June 11, 1867) p 188

1866, beginning on page 494. In our previous volume, some reference was made to it, but it is fitting that more attention should be given here. So far as the Society's defense went, it is the *summum bonum* in arguments for it. Almost all arguments draw their force from it. Pendleton's address, too, took on added significance by the interpretation which he set upon some of the basic principles of the restoration movement, and which set the pattern for future thinking by the more liberal element.

In an analysis of Pendleton's arguments, we note first his answer to the charge that the Society meant "we are departing from original ground." It was freely pointed out to the Society advocates that the organization was unknown to the early restoration movement. Some charged that Campbell in the *Christian Baptist* definitely opposed them Pendleton's answer to these charges showed his skill and displayed his eagerness to pin a charge on the Society's opponents which they had previously pinned on its advocates. To say the Missionary Society is wrong because it was unknown to the earlier restoration is but to follow human opinions, and this is contrary to the very genius of the restoration movement Obviously, this was a weak rebuttal, and Pendleton seemed to sense it, but where prejudice rules, weakness is strength. To the charge that Alexander Campbell had earlier opposed the Society, Pendleton simply asserted that this was a mistaken impression. The merit of this answer has already been discussed, but, at any rate, Campbell's words in the *Christian Baptist,* taken at their face value, are not as far-fetched as Pendleton suggested.

Pendleton's second argument was given in answer to the charge that the Missionary Society was not scriptural. He says:

You say, "Your Missionary Society is not scriptural"—and you mean by this, that there is no special express percept in the Scriptures commanding it. We concede this without a moment's hesitation. There is none, but what do you make of it? Is everything which is not scriptural therefore wrong ?[9]

That the scripture is silent about a missionary society. Pendleton readily admitted. He contended, however, that this did not make it wrong. Speaking again of the Society's opponents, he said:

---

[9] W K Pendleton, "Address, by W K Pendleton," *Millennial Harbinger,* Vol XXXVII, No 11, (Nov, 1866) p 501

Does he say that it is not *positively and expressly* commanded; then we demand by what canon of interpretation does he make mere *silence* prohibitory? You reply, the canon which forbids anything as a rule of Christian faith or duty, for which there cannot be expressly produced a "Thus saith the Lord," "either in express terms or by approved precedent." . . .

The annunciation of this principle needs much comment. Earlier in the restoration movement Thomas Campbell had spoken that great motto, "Where the Bible speaks, we speak, where the Bible is silent, we are silent." The bulk of the brotherhood had interpreted that motto to mean that whatever is unauthorized is forbidden. To most brethren the expression was simple, and meant that these people who advocated a return to the ancient order would practice in their religious beliefs only those things for which they found authority either by direct command, apostolic example or necessary inference. They had used the motto to sweep everything before them. They had challenged every sectarian, body of religious people the country over to show divine authority for their existence as a body. This was enough. Men, finding they were members of bodies unknown to Holy Writ, were freely abandoning them, and beginning to plead for others to follow them to safe, authorized ground. When, therefore, a group of brethren projected a Missionary Society, they naturally inquired of themselves, "Where is the authority?" Finding none, they said the Society had no right to exist.

Now Pendleton asserted that this view of that old motto is altogether wrong; that it was not at all what Thomas Campbell had in mind. With this he returned to study the early restoration. Campbell, and a few others, had formed the "Christian Association of Washington." It was before this group that this motto was first announced. Pendleton asserted that this association was not a church; that it took money for membership; that it had an Executive Board and a Secretary and Treasurer. In these respects the "Christian Association of Washington" was in itself nothing more than a Missionary Society. Pendleton was striking a telling blow. He pressed the point home:

Now it was this organization, which in the very act of forming itself, announced this canon! Did they mean to condemn themselves? Were they simpletons or hypocrites?

Obviously then, Thomas Campbell himself, the man who penned

the great motto, did not mean by it to exclude such organizations as the missionary society   This was Pendleton's point, and it had its effect

Unfortunately at the time of this address Robert Richardson had not yet written his monumental work, *Memoirs of Alexander Campbell.* The story of what had happened when the Declaration and Address was written had been handed down mostly by word of mouth.   True enough, articles of historical nature appeared once in a while in the *Millennial Harbinger,* but these were not exhaustive or critical.   It remains a fact that the knowledge the average man possessed in 1866 of happenings sixty years before was only hazy.   Pendleton was closely associated with Alexander Campbell, having married in succession two of his daughters, and had been vice-president under him at Bethany College.   His knowledge of the early restoration therefore went unchallenged   He was able to plant an interpretation of this vital principle of the restoration in the hearts of many leaders that opened the floodgates for all innovations the liberals may desire

But what are the facts in the case?   What did Thomas Campbell mean by the great motto, "Where the Bible speaks, we speak, where the Bible is silent, we are silent"?

Regarding the "Christian Association of Washington," it can be said that those who comprised it were neither simpletons nor hypocrites! Pendleton in this case was but a prejudiced juror and was, therefore, incapable of sensing every side of the issue The terms as "simpletons" and "hypocrites" were but appeals to prejudice.   The truth is that these people—Thomas Campbell included—were just coming out of sectarian practices and had yet a very imperfect grasp of what it meant to "speak where the Bible speaks and be silent where it is silent."   Of the minds of these people at the time the "Christian Association of Washington" was formed, Robert Richardson informs us:

It is true, indeed, that the individuals who had been for some time attending Mr Campbell's meeting were, by no means, all settled in their religious convictions, and that they differed from each other, especially in relation to a proper gospel ministry For, while all were disposed to confide in the Bible as the only true guide in religion, yet there were those who, conscious that they were imperfectly acquainted with its teaching, naturally experienced some misgivings as they felt themselves slowly drifting

away from the well-known shores and landmarks of their respective
religious systems into the wide ocean of Divine truth, which
seemed to them so boundless and as yet but imperfectly ex-
plored. . .[10]

Speaking of Thomas Campbell himself, Richardson says:

Neither Thomas Campbell himself, however, nor those associated
with him, had a full conception of all that was involved in these
principles. They only felt that the religious intolerance of the
time had itself become intolerable, and that a reformation was
imperiously demanded [11]

The above points W. K. Pendleton found it convenient to overlook. When Campbell announced his great motto and formed
the "Christian Association of Washington," neither he nor his
associates had yet a full conception of all that was involved That
it was right to take only those things that were authorized, they
could not doubt, but to see in advance where this would lead them,
they could not.

Campbell's attitude toward infant baptism may be taken as
typical of his attitude Soon after announcing his famous motto,
James Foster approached Thomas Campbell with the question,
"How could you, in the absence of any authority in the word of
God, baptize a child in the name of the Father, and of the Son,
and of the Holy Spirit?" Robert Richardson informs us that
Campbell's face changed color. He became irritated and offended,
and tersely replied, "Sir, you are the most intractable person I
ever saw."[12] A short time later Thomas Campbell did reject
infant baptism. On what ground? On the ground that there
was no authority for it in the word of God, the very principle his
motto had laid down. Why did Campbell not see, at the time he
announced his motto, that infant baptism was unscriptural? The
idea had never dawned on him then Was he a "simpleton" or a
"hypocrite"? Obviously not As Richardson explains, "He had
not yet a full conception of all that was involved in this motto."

Contrary to Pendleton's assertion, Campbell did mean to say
that whatever in religion is not authorized in the divine word
cannot be used. His application of this principle to the subject

[10]Robert Richardson. *Memoirs of Alexander Campbell*. Vol I, (Cincinnati Standard Publishing Co, 1897) p 234
[11]Robert Richardson, *Memoirs of Alexander Campbell*, Vol I, p 245
[12]Robert Richardson, *Memoirs of Alexander Campbell*, Vol I, p 240

of infant baptism shows him to be applying it in exactly this manner.

At any rate, Pendleton brushed aside this interpretation of the motto, and put a new one on it. He affirmed that it was meant to be applied to creeds and confessions of faith as terms of communion and fellowship. In short, all Campbell meant to say was that human creeds and human opinions cannot be forced upon us. If we want to practice a human opinion, this is our liberty, but if someone wants to force one upon us, we have the right to refuse, Pendleton argued.

The annunciation of this interpretation of Campbell's great motto is significant. It can be safely said that the bulk of the brotherhood had not so understood it. But now, Pendleton's interpretation began to be picked up by leading minds of the more liberal type and put into use to sanction every human opinion they wanted to urge upon the church. Upon this interpretation of the motto was based every innovation which was brought into the church. The door was now down, and human opinions, as they applied to the work and worship of the church, multiplied. To try to sweep back the avalanche by calling for divine authority was like trying to dry up the ocean with a sponge. Pendleton's interpretation was picked up by Isaac Errett and the *Christian Standard* and then by J. H Garrison and B W Johnson in the *Christian-Evangelist* to resound down through the years to the present. Nevertheless, an element remained to whom the call for divine authority still meant something. They believed that whatever in the practice of religion was not authorized by the word of God was wrong. The *Gospel Advocate* and the *American Christian Review* maintained this conviction down through the years.

These two types of thinking are responsible for even modern-day differences in religious practice. The use of instrumental music, missionary societies, and the many other practices, based on no divine authority, are but symptoms of the real trouble, which lies basically at this point.

To insist that nothing could be practiced in religion for which there is no divine authority was, to Pendleton, a horrifying thought. It was such a binding thing! It would make us too narrow and too strict. He said:

Let it not be said, then, that the disciples of Christ are to take the silence of Scripture on a given subject as a positive rule of prohibition against all freedom of action or obligation of duty. No rule could be more productive of evil than this

To ask for divine authority for everything in religion would mean that we couldn't have church buildings, blackboards, lights in the building, etc., they argued. Men became fearful of what it would mean to ask for divine authority. They soon shrugged off the idea as something utterly ridiculous.

Basically, this fear is to be accounted for by a failure to consider the fact that man is connected with two realms—the worldly and the religious. In what type of business shall a man earn his livelihood? Shall he be a doctor, lawyer, business man, farmer, etc.? Give book, chapter and verse What kind of car shall a man drive—Chevrolet, Pontiac, Ford? Give the scripture. These things belong to the world, and no scripture is needed or expected So with the meetinghouses, lights, blackboards, etc. These belong to the worldly realm, and have never presented much of a problem

Ancient Israel erected idols with her own hands and bowed down to worship them. Men tend to become infatuated with creatures which they make with their own hands, and become blind to their faults. W. K. Pendleton was an intelligent man and certainly thoroughly honest, yet, he was so infatuated with the society, the creature which his hands had formed, that he saw in everything the means to justify it.

The basic apology for the Society Pendleton based upon his conception of the church universal, and in this he followed closely the reasoning of Alexander Campbell. No man is prepared to see the Society as Pendleton saw it without beginning where Pendleton began. First, he filled his mind with the thought of the church in its universal aspect, ignoring for the time being the local church. God gave to the church—in its universal sense—the responsibility to convert the world But God did not give the *method* by which the church—in its universal sense—was to convert the world. Therefore, whatever method the church—in its universal sense—uses is acceptable The method is a matter of expediency The church universal is left free to decide for itself. This is briefly the defense he made for it

Some day somebody will do the cause of Christ a real service by taking the concept of the church universal, and giving it a thorough analysis based upon the scriptures and upon church history for the past two thousand years. The church is spoken of in the New Testament in a universal sense There is a body of people characterized by the fact that they follow Jesus that comprise the New Testament Church in its universal aspect.

There are some things about this truly significant. It is significant, for example, that the church universal has never known but one officer—Jesus Christ himself, who is Head over the body, King over his Kingdom The apostles were the ambassadors of this King to the church universal. They were not officers of the church, were never appointed by the church and existed before the church did The study of church history reveals the fact that every time men thought in terms of the church universal, they ended up by forming organizations which in their work substituted themselves in the place of Christ. Roman Catholicism is the highest embodiment of the church universal concept, and claims that its pope is the vicegerent of Christ on earth. So far as the church universal on earth is concerned, as viewed by a Romanist, the pope is virtually Christ.

Protestantism thought in terms of the church universal, and set up synods and conferences. These synods and conferences have written creeds, created confessions of faith—in short, have made laws for the church universal, a prerogative that belongs to Christ. In the final analysis these synods and conferences assume the position of Christ over the church universal Some, like the Baptist denomination, have tried to throw off the concept of the church universal for a time, and insist upon strict congregational polity. Yet they invariably thought in terms of the church universal and established associations which soon began to dictate to the local churches, a prerogative that again belonged to Christ. In the restoration movement, brethren thought in terms of the church universal, and with that concept formed a Missionary Society. Looking back on this history, as we can now, who can fail to see that this Society became the master, and soon dictated to the churches, a prerogative which belongs only to Christ.

That Christ intended for the world to be converted through individual congregations being established in every local community and thence, exercising a saving influence over that community seems too obvious for dispute. The plan the author of Acts lays down is that the gospel is to spread from Jerusalem, thence to Judea, then to Samaria and to the uttermost parts of the earth. The gospel radiated out, local congregations were planted, and exercised a saving influence upon the community. In one generation the gospel was sounded out to the whole earth, and that without a missionary society It is an indictment, not against our organization, but against our individual religious fervor that the same is not done today. The only church organization known to the New Testament is that of a local church, not the church universal. The only officers of the church are those of the local church, not the church universal. The individual congregation of Christ's disciples is the only missionary society then known to the Scriptures.

THE ISSUES

Up to this point a general view of the Society controversy has been given No analysis of the controversy as it respects the basic issues has been given. Broad, basic principles have been given, but now, in order to make the study of the controversy more complete, the issues must be considered

The first charge that was hurled against the Society which was that it was a *substitute for the church*. The Society had no divine authority for its existence, it owed its inception to human wisdom and human opinions Whereas God left the evangelizing of the world to local churches scattered throughout the world, the Missionary Society was, in effect, a substitute for God's plan It implied an imperfection in the divine plan and suggested that human wisdom could improve upon divine Therefore, as some men, particularly David Lipscomb, looked at the Society, man could only defend the Society by first defending his right to substitute human plans for the divine. This, in summary, was the most serious charge hurled its way.

In 1866 Tolbert Fanning and George W Elley carried on occasional discussions in the *Gospel Advocate* over the Society Fanning, as his custom was, placed this charge in the lap of Elley, feeling confident of his position Fanning wrote:

These missionary societies are not composed of churches, but of individuals, by paying a certain amount of money. In the work accomplished by them, the credit is mainly given to them and not to the church. Indeed, according to President Elley's statement, these associations plant churches, set them in order, and supervise them generally. . . .

Our view is that, such societies are employed as *substitutes* for the churches, that they stand on ground the churches are entitled to occupy, and that they do, to all intents and purposes, usurp the authority of the churches, and thwart the designs of Jehovah. They make void the churches of Jesus Christ and the law of God.[13]

After the war, Jacob Creath, Jr, was no less an opposer of missionary societies than before. On the whole study of the realm of the church, Creath had a clear insight. His language was generally supercharged with denunciations which only served to bring down upon his head the anathemas of those favoring the Societies. He gave an excellent view of the church and societies when he wrote:

If some of our own preachers will come among us and preach the gospel, and not politics, we will help to support such a man. But if any man comes among us sent out by one of these humbug societies, we shall let him pass. Ancient Christianity was spread by individuals, and not by societies or proxies, as is the modern gospels. And when a man becomes worthless, and his brethren have no confidence in him at once, he seeks an office in one of these falsely called missionary societies. The Jerusalem Church spread the gospel, or her members did *individually*, after the resurrection of Christ, before another church existed to assist her, through Judea, Samaria, Phoenicia, Cyprus, Antioch, and to the uttermost parts of the earth in the first century of the Christian era. (Acts, chapters 1, 2 and 11.) As this mother and model church spread the gospel, so did the other churches individually (not from societies), such as Antioch in Syria (Acts 13), and Thessalonia sounded out the gospel in Macedonia and Achaia (1 Thess. 1, 8). Let any church now do the same as these ancient churches did; let each member do all he can to spread the gospel. If a church or person is not able to do anything to spread the gospel, nothing is required of that person. Christ never gathered where he did not strew   It is required of us, according to what we have, and not according to what we have not. . . .[14]

Creath was striking at something fundamental just here which many congregations have found it convenient to overlook. God never requires of an individual Christian, or a congregation of Christians, any more than it is possible to do. The need for a

[13]Tolbert Fanning, "The Advocate and G W Elley," *Gospel Advocate*, Vol VIII, No 40, (Oct 2, 1866) pp 627-28

[14]Jacob Creath, "Missionary, and Other Organizations Besides the Church, for Carrying Forward the Work of God," *Gospel Advocate*, Vol VIII, No 3, (Jan 16, 1866) pp 41-42

Society arose from the fact that local churches felt themselves incapable of sending out the gospel, so they established societies to do the work which God ordained for the church.

David Lipscomb developed this point even further. After pointing out that the societies were founded on the assumption that the churches cannot or will not do the work of God as well as societies, he charged that the societies actually hinder and stifle church action. When the Society prospers, the congregations become inactive, allowing the work to be taken over by these human organizations. Instead of promoting church action, they check it.

The fact that many individuals and churches in sympathy with this Society encourage church action, does not at all militate against the fact that the society itself has a tendency to destroy church operation. For just to the extent that an individual gives of his means to the society, he withdraws it from the church.[15]

This business of the society's being a substitute for the church was to Lipscomb a serious matter.

To operate through an institution of man's devising in preference to the church of God is, in our esteem, to exalt man as of superior wisdom and power to God. To call in question the efficiency of God's appointments, as the best (we had like to say the *only*), that can be ordained for the accomplishment of God's designs, is to call in question the wisdom or power of God. As highly as we respect Brother McGarvey (and there is no man living, of his years, that we had formed a higher appreciation of for his work) and his associates, there are questions here involving too high, holy and sacred interests, both to God and man, for us to yield an iota.[16]

The Missionary Society had no more ardent supporter than Thomas Munnell, who, for a time served as corresponding secretary for the American Christian Missionary Society During much of the year 1867, he and David Lipscomb carried on a discussion over the Society through the pages of the *Gospel Advocate* While there shall be occasion to refer to this correspondence in the future, it is interesting at this point as it reveals Lipscomb's basic objection to the Society.

A chief objection we make to your societies is, that they ignore the overruling and guiding hand of God, and organize a human

---

[15]David Lipscomb, "Destroying Church Cooperation," *Gospel Advocate*, Vol IX, No 6, (Feb 7, 1867) p 114.

[16]David Lipscomb, "Destroying Church Cooperation," *Gospel Advocate*, Vol IX, No. 6, (Feb. 7, 1867) p 115

association to do that which God has reserved for himself   God says to man : you operate according to my directions in the various spheres, and with the instrumentalities I ordain for you.   I will overlook, I will guide, I will harmonize the various parts, and direct the vast complicated whole forward to the accomplishment of the designed mission without a jar or a discord.   All I require of you is to faithfully operate the parts I assign to you.   The action of the societies seem to say : No, Lord, we are not content to operate in the limited sphere assigned to us; we will take a general oversight, and take upon ourselves the responsibility of harmony, and controlling the vast whole   We will sit in the place of God, and do His work.   The great misfortune to the churches, Brother Munnell, is not a lack of cooperation—but a lack of *operation*   If man will only faithfully operate, then God will superintend the cooperation.[17]

Lipscomb saw the Society standing opposed to the very genius of Christianity when he wrote :

Human societies spread by organic force—the religion of the Saviour spreads as a leaven.   Human societies are based on the right of man to form organizations through which he will worship his Maker.   This is the fundamental error of Romanism.[18]

A year later, Lipscomb argued in the same vein in these words :

We feel just as sure that the missionary societies are corrupt and corrupting—the last one of them—as we do that human political organizations are corrupt   We feel just as sure that they are subversive of the Lord's institutions as we do that the societies and organizations of the Romish hierarchy are subversive of his appointments   They stand precisely upon the same footing—have the same living principles as these do [19]

John T. Walsh saw ample reason to object to the Society on the ground, viz., it was a substitute for the divine plan to do the work of the Lord.   Walsh wrote :

I think it is an undeniable truth, that men never departed from *primitive Christianity* until they lost faith in it   And no Christian ever yet adopted human systems and appliances until his faith becomes weak in the divine . . I repeat, therefore, that what we need is not a new plan of missionary work, but more faith in the old Jerusalem plan.

. . . We want *more faith and less machinery, more work and less talk*, more faith and less planning.   The Lord has given us

[17]David Lipscomb, "Discussion—Missionary Societies." *Gospel Advocate,* Vol IX, No 11, (Mar 14, 1867) p 208
[18]David Lipscomb, "Discussion—Missionary Societies," *Gospel Advocate,* Vol IX, No 23, (June 6, 1867) p 446
[19]David Lipscomb, "The Societies," *Gospel Advocate,* Vol X, No 33, (Aug 13, 1868) p 763

the plan, and bids us go work in his vineyard, but instead of going to work with the tools He has furnished, we spend all the day in making *new ones* which in our wisdom, we think will work better. Let us quit it, and go to work with a hearty good will.[20]

The only Missionary Society the Lord ever owned, Walsh contended, was the church.

The church of Christ is the Lord's missionary Society. He is its Head, and every member of it, male and female, young and old, rich and poor, learned and unlearned, black and white. *is* a LIFE-MEMBER AND DIRECTOR! The terms of admission are *faith* and *obedience*. The terms on which they continue members consist in the observance of "all things WHATSOEVER I have commanded you." and among the "all things" the injunction to "give as the Lord prospers" us stands out prominently and imperatively. *All must obey it'* and thus "show their faith by their works! In a word, let original Christianity be restored in faith and practice, and nothing else will be needed.[21]

No sooner had Ben Franklin changed his position on the Society than he announced his first conviction that Societies took the place of the churches, and were man-made substitutes for the church of Christ. He writes:

The circumstance that they had no missionary societies in the first age of the church, *of itself,* does not prove that we may not have them. But the fact that the Lord ordained the congregations, with their officers, and made it their work to convert the world with the additional fact that we have their example in sending our preachers, with the circumstance, that they had no missionary societies, but the churches, proves that it is wrong for individuals to create missionary societies, separate from the churches, as *substitutes* to do the work which the Lord appointed for the churches The congregations of the Lord, divinely appointed and constituted societies or bodies. for the worship of God, fitted for every good work—specially for the propagation of the gospel The simple question is, whether we shall honor the churches in working in them and making them effective as the Lord's appointed societies, in converting the world. or declare them *insufficient* to do the work which the Lord committed to them, and *substitute* a creation of our own hands, to do the work of the *churches ordained by the Lord.* Others may do this latter, but we *cannot*[22]

---

[20]John T Walsh, "Reply to G W Elley," *American Christian Review.* Vol X, No 25, (June 18, 1867) p 194

[21]John T Walsh, "Reply to G W Elley," *American Christian Review.* Vol X, No 25, (June 18, 1867) p 194

[22]Ben Franklin, "Explanation for Bro G W Elley," *American Christian Review.* Vol. X, No 19, (May 7, 1867) p. 148.

Quotations could be multiplied *ad infinitim,* but these are enough to indicate the viewpoint of the chief opposers of Missionary Societies. The organization of the Society merely indicated that man had lost faith in primitive Christianity; that he felt that he could by his own human wisdom devise a better plan to convert the world than the Lord furnished   The implication was that the church was insufficient to do the work God committed to it, and so human wisdom was at liberty to devise a better system of operation   We close this particular point with the words of Hiram Christopher, which probably go beneath the whole principle to the real one:

The Missionary Society had its origin in a false pride and shame, and a desire to be like the denominations around us   With all our condemnations of denominationalism, we have yet not the independence of mind to discard their machinery. We are afraid that they will get ahead of us, and this fear leads us to adopt some of their machinery. The first of these human instrumentalities was the Missionary Society.[23]

The second defense was that the Society was but an expedient. The church universal was charged with preaching to the world, but God did not provide its method; therefore, it was left to human-expediency to devise the best plan. This, of course, completely overlooked the fact that the church universal *was* given a method, the method being the work of the local congregation. The gospel radiated from Jerusalem to the "uttermost parts of the earth," local congregations being planted, and influencing a saving power upon their community. The local congregation, then, was the only missionary society that God ordained.

But advocates of the Society never tired of putting the Society on the plane of expediency, and then insisting that the whole controversy over missionary societies, was one of which plan to adopt   As a means of justifying themselves, charges of inconsistency were laid at the door of the Society's enemies who, it was said, were guilty themselves of working through human organizations. More shall be said of these charges

The use of expediency as a defense for the societies was suggested by W. K. Pendleton, as has been seen already. Pendleton, beginning with the concept of the church universal, emphasized that since God made no provision for the *method* the church

---

[23]H Christopher, "Dr Christopher vs Missionary Society," *American Christian Review,* Vol X, No 27, (July 2, 1867) p 211.

universal was free to adopt any of its own by which to convert the world. But Pendleton backed off carrying this line of reasoning on out to its logical conclusion, for his reasoning would lead to the conclusion, that since the local churches are incapable of spreading the gospel throughout the world, there must be a universal organization of the church with some sort of earthly controlling center that would overlook and direct the work of the local congregations.

In so far as the principle involved here is concerned, it is basically Romanism. To assert that the church universal, to do the work God gave it, must, by human wisdom, devise an earthly, central controlling station to direct the operations of the churches is to work on the same principle that led Romanism to the papacy. It would have been argued, of course, that this universal organization would have no power except as a *servant* of the church and not its *master*. The future of the restoration movement was to show that this reasoning was but idle dreaming. A society without some power or control would have been a helpless thing. If it could not, for a time, control the churches which were the *source* of its income, there were yet other controls it could have essential to its existence. It had to have the control of the *use* of its funds. It also had to have control over its missionaries. It is idle to say that a Society could exist without controlling *where* its funds would be spent, and *who* would be its employees, it missionaries The only one control the society lacked, and it did not lack this completely, was the power to control the source of its income. As time went on, these churches *where* the Society had spent its money, in turn, became the *source* for other revenue.

No one saw more clearly the logical end of Pendleton's reasoning than David Lipscomb who studied the address carefully. Lipscomb wrote:

The only defense that can be made of these institutions is, that there must be a universal organization of the church of God with an earthly, central head, that overlooks and directs the operations of all the numerous local organizations or congregations The premises that lead to this conclusion were laid down not very definitely by Brother Pendleton, in his last address at the last meeting of the Cincinnati society The logical result of these premises, we gladly note, he shrinks back from declaring. This, to our mind, is the most objectionable ground the societies could be placed upon. Brother Pendleton's use of the terms, universal church in connection with the society organization, we think can have no other meaning.[24]

With many, there was an inability to comprehend churches co-operating without forming some sort of a human organization. Consequently, some advocates of the society conceived that the whole controversy was very simple in that some advocated *organized* mission work and some *unorganized*. This retort was flung by Thomas Munnell to David Lipscomb in their discussions of 1867, but Lipscomb replied that if two distinct bodies (churches) blend themselves into one organization, their works become the operation of the third body, and not a cooperation of the other two It is this newly organized body that is working, and the churches, so far as this work is concerned, have lost their identity

But, as mentioned before, the Societies, in defending their right to exist on the ground of expediency, continually charged that their opponents were inconsistent. It was commonly asked, "If you insist upon a "thus saith the Lord" for everything, where is your scripture for a meeting-house?" The answer to this one came in an effective way from Jeremiah Smith, brother of B. K. Smith, who preached in Indianapolis. Jeremiah Smith replied:

The advocates of missionary societies uniformly and trium-phantly, as they seem to think, appeal to building meeting-houses in justification of having missionary societies to spread the gospel and build up Christian churches; and claim that Christians are left by the Lord free to plan and devise as to both, and that they are necessary expedients to forward the Lord's cause and kingdom

Is building a meeting-house any part of the Lord's kingdom, or of its institutions? Certainly it is not; for there is not a word said about it in the New Testament. It is not any more so than in building a dwelling-house, a barn, or opening and cultivating a farm is. Is the "sounding out of the word of the Lord." the conversion of sinners, the planting and building of Christian con-gregations, any part of the Lord's kingdom, or of its institutions? Certainly they are; for they are frequently named and enjoined in the New Testament. Then the argument is wholly fallacious: it is proving spiritual things by arguments pertaining to earthly things. .[25]

Again, advocates of the Society affirmed its opposers were in-consistent in that they printed papers while having no divine

[24]David Lipscomb. "Destroying Church Cooperation," *Gospel Advocate,* Vol IX. No 6, (Feb 7, 1867) p 115
[25]Jeremiah Smith. "Missionary Societies Human Expedients." *Gospel Advocate,* Vol VIII, No 49, (Dec. 4, 1866) p 780.

authority for such. Moses E. Lard was never too hearty a devotee
of the Societies, although he could never refrain from the belief
they did have a right to exist. To him, it was similar to a paper,
so he wrote:

I am printing a *Quarterly*, the avowed object of which is the
propagation and defense of the gospel. But this *Quarterly* is
unknown to the New Testament. Should I therefore abandon
it? Not an honest man in our ranks will affirm it. But this
Quarterly has precisely the same origin which the Society has—
human discretion, and not only proposes, but actually does, the
same work. If, now, my *Quarterly* is right in itself, that is, if it
has a just and legitimate existence, and may lawfully do the work
it proposes, then the man does not live who can show that a
missionary society *per se* wrong, and may not cause the gospel
to be preached With emphasis, I plant myself here, and maintain that the same argument which would rebate a missionary
society because it originates not in the New Testament, and would
deny to it the right to cause the gospel to be preached, must of
necessity rebate the *Quarterly*. And in candor I must go further,
and say I have no respect for the dullness which perceives not
the analogy nor the casuistry which denies to the resulting conclusion its just weight.[2b]

The article is strongly worded, as all of Lard's were, yet, it is
one of the ironies of the restoration movement that Lard could
never see the force of this argument as applied to instrumental
music in the worship. He opposed the instrument on the ground
the New Testament was silent on it, yet this argument meant
nothing to him when applied to the Society.

The same argument was put to Lipscomb by Thomas Munnell
in their discussions of 1867. Where is the authority for publishing the *Gospel Advocate?* To this Lipscomb answered:

So far as the publishing of a paper is concerned, it is nothing
more than teaching, exhorting, reproving by the written word,
instead of the spoken. The apostles set us the example of doing
this Printing is nothing more than the multiplication of the
copies of the *written* word. Who says we have not example for
this? It has no organization about it, but is the work of an individual in the church, and responsible to the church. There is
no more organization than there is in one individual writing a letter
to a brother Now the editors of the Advocate are each responsible

[2b]Moses E. Lard, "A Few Words on Missionary Societies," *Lard's
Quarterly*, Vol IV, No 2, (April, 1867) p. 151

to the church of which he is a member for what he writes and does.[27]

But by far, that which the advocates of the Society viewed as a more serious inconsistency on the part of the Society's opposers, was that men who objected to the Society on the ground it lacked divine authority, would also establish schools, and in them teach the Bible. Soon after the close of the Civil War, Tolbert Fanning led a movement to establish a large university in Middle Tennessee where Christians would teach. An "Educational Association" was organized to help raise the money. Fanning was never allowed to forget that such schools were human organizations exactly the same as the missionary society and without scriptural authority. Isaac Errett responded to Fanning in these words:

But he must allow us to say, that to us the absurdity is so glaring of opposing Missionary Societies on the ground of their lack of scriptural authority, and at the same time getting up human schemes of "Christian education," that it is hard for us to keep back the conviction that there is some other cause for this opposition to the Missionary Society than the mere lack of Bible authority.[28]

It is not likely that either Fanning or Lipscomb recognized this problem as being so great in the eyes of their opponents as it was. They gave what appears to be far too little space discussing this phase of the issue. To neither of them was there any real problem here, and it was difficult to admit the honesty of those who presented this argument. Lipscomb could but reply, "general education is not a work God has committed to the church."[29] Fanning would but say, "these matters are under the supervision of the worldly-wisdom side of our nature."[30]

The whole subject of the colleges teaching Bible will be more fully dealt with in a later chapter, so a brief word is all that is needed here. It is vital to see Fanning and Lipscomb's point of view. Man was a creature of a "worldly" side to them, and they particularly preferred this term. By it they did not mean evil, as we have sometimes come to associate the word, worldly.

[27]David Lipscomb, "Discussion—Missionary Societies—No 3," *Gospel Advocate*, Vol IX, No 13, (March 28, 1867) p 249
[28]Isaac Errett, "Missionary Societies," *Christian Standard*, Vol I, No 33, (Nov 17, 1866) p 260
[29]David Lipscomb, "Discussion—Missionary Societies—No. 3," *Gospel Advocate*, Vol IX, No 13, (March 28, 1867) p 248
[30]Tolbert Fanning, "Letter—No 2," *Gospel Advocate*, Vol IX, No 15, (April 11, 1867) p 281

Instead, man, living as he did in the world, had to use this wisdom of the world. The matter of earning a livelihood, securing an education, making business investments, and a thousand and one other such details which a man carries on in his life, have nothing to do with religion, and consequently, the Bible does not advise a man whether he must be a farmer, doctor, lawyer, teacher; or whether he must go to school or not go, or whether he must invest in business or not. Such things are completely outside the realm or scope of Bible teaching.

It dawned on neither Fanning nor Lipscomb that because a Christian school-teacher taught the Bible while giving a general education, that he was doing the work of the church. Neither man had anything good to say for "theological seminaries" or schools that existed to prepare preachers, for this was the work of the church.

The crucial discussion, then, of the missionary society's right to exist centered in the concept of expediency, its apologists all the while charging that the opposition was inconsistent in decrying the missionary society while maintaining their own right to have meeting-houses, publish papers, and teach in colleges. Lipscomb and Fanning maintained that these latter functions were beside the subject, and insisted that the missionary society was a substitute, devised by human wisdom, for the church which was established by divine wisdom. It was, therefore, to be thoroughly rejected as unscriptural and contrary to the will and desire of God.

While the crucial point upon which the whole issue turned has been seen, it would be wise to look at some of the lesser issues involved. It was charged that the missionary society was a cause of division in the brotherhood. The restoration movement had been conceived upon the ground of the need for unity. It maintained that its plea was the only catholic ground upon which the religious world could be united. Later an element of brethren brought in innovations which were unknown to the scriptures. Brethren could not agree upon these, and to promote them was to abandon the only catholic ground whereby the world could be united. Consequently, David Lipscomb wrote

We have long been satisfied that the only safe, scriptural, catholic ground upon which all Christians could stand, and work together in harmony as the people of God, was "The Word of God, the only rule of faith, the church of God, the only institution for the people of God."[31]

Perhaps, however, the most serious side issue to the whole controversy was the charge that the Society was a virtual dictator of the local congregations, it was the *master* instead of the *servant*. Admittedly, this fact was not as true in 1866 as it later came to be, but traces of this tendency were already abundantly evident. Especially did it show up in the experience of the *Gospel Advocate* upon its rebirth in 1866.

Prior to 1866 Tolbert Fanning had become thoroughly convinced that the Society was contrary to the will of God. As for David Lipscomb, this was not true. He informs us later that he had never seriously studied the question; certainly had no intentions of making it a cause of dissension with the brotherhood. In 1864, while contemplating the rebirth of the *Advocate* as soon as the war should end, he paid a visit upon a meeting of the Kentucky State Missionary Society, and tried to persuade a man, much in sympathy with the societies, to move to Nashville to edit the paper.

No sooner had the "Prospectus" been issued than Lipscomb got his first personal taste of the spirit of these Societies. On November 27, 1865 Thomas Munnell, soon after seeing a copy of the "Prospectus" wrote a letter to Lipscomb and Fanning

Dear Brethren Your Prospectus was handed to me today, with a request to use my influence for its circulation. Before I do so, I want to ask if it is to oppose our Missionary Societies? I have been laboring two years to build up our Kentucky Society, and could not favor the introduction of a paper to war against it all I am told that anti-mission is to be one feature of the "Advocate." If the "Advocate" will come out and help us in all our good work, I could wish for it a large circulation in our State, otherwise, my influence, much or little, will be against it I would be glad to see the Brethren cooperate in every good work, and hope we will be able to do so.

Two weeks later the following letter came from George W. Elley of Lexington, Kentucky:

Brethren Your Prospectus, or circular, for a renewal of the "Gospel Advocate" was received some days since. It would have been noticed earlier, but for other and various demands upon my time I am more than glad that Tennessee, and the

---

[31]David Lipscomb, "Convention Abolished," *Gospel Advocate*, Vol IX, No 4, (Jan 24, 1867) pp 70-71

South, is to have a paper in their midst   Here, the impression exists with some of our leading men, that its editors are unfriendly to Missionary Societies, and if so, I fear that but little can be done for its circulation in our midst   .[32]

It was evident from these two letters that these men, both officers in the Kentucky Society, would refuse to support any paper that would not support the society.   Fanning's reply to both of these letters but shows his independence of mind as well as his determination that no group of men could start a human organization and then dictate the policy of the *Gospel Advocate*

You will, doubtless, believe us brethren, when we assure you that we had not conferred together in reference to Missionary or other Societies unknown to Holy Writ; but we felt in our heart, that we should enjoy almost inexpressible happiness in once more cordially cooperating with our beloved Brethren, from whom we have long been separated, in every good work, without reference to differences of opinion.   But alas! we knew not what a day would bring forth, and when we hoped to find a hearty welcome, we met with a new creed to which we were to subscribe, or be thrust from your fellowship.   One which, neither we, nor our fathers knew, nor were able to bear, and we were plainly told that unless we could and would subscribe to doctrines which we had not studied, we must be regarded as enemies   Brethren, pardon us for very respectfully begging you to stop and think before you go too far.   What have you done already?   You have positively hurled us from your territory and Christian cooperation, unless we subscribe to, and promise to advocate something that you certainly could not pretend was authorized by Jesus Christ, or any of his apostles [33]

Some years before Fanning had learned the lesson for himself that the Society could be a friend of no man who was not first a friend of it.   To feel the indignation of the Society one needed only to let it be known that he was not one of its advocates   Ways and means would be found to limit his influence   Fanning found this to be true, when, in 1859, he attended the annual convention of the Society in Cincinnati   Isaac Errett was corresponding secretary, and carefully cut Fanning off.   Of this Fanning later wrote:

Years ago I attended the annual meeting of the American Christian Missionary Society in Cincinnati, with the disposition

---

[32]Thomas Munnell, George W Elley, "Missionary Societies," *Gospel Advocate*, Vol VIII, No 2, (Jan 8, 1866) pp 20-21

[33]Tolbert Fanning, "Missionary Societies," *Gospel Advocate*, Vol VIII, No 2, (Jan 9, 1866) pp 20, 21

to respectfully protest against the whole proceeding, but the managers hedged up my way—kept my mouth closed, except a little I was enabled to wedge in by telling some of my experience; but I went far enough to say to hundreds of preachers present, that most of the brethren in my section performed their labors through the church. This was said with the hope of provoking a discussion, but at the close of my experience—for nothing else could I get to tell—Brother Isaac Errett, the Grand Secretary, rose with a paper prepared, Resolved That there was no difference in fact, in doing our work through the church, as presented by Brother Fanning, and through other agencies. This was called by an editor years afterwards, "The courtesy and urbanity," of the society, through the influence of which Brother Fanning, "could not have much influence" In the first place, the Secretary and Society, were not willing for it to be seen that there is the least difference between God's plan and man's plan in doing religious work, and, secondly, by a flattering trick, the Secretary shut my mouth. This was worldly wisdom—shrewdness [34]

Still another side-issue in the whole Society controversy revolved around the charge that the Society was a poor business investment in getting the missionary work done. In the spring of 1866, J. W. McGarvey wrote a series of articles in the *American Christian Review* on how to settle the controversy. McGarvey proposed that every rich man who could, should support independently an evangelist in the field   Then, every congregation that could, should also support an evangelist. Then, those congregations which independently could not support a missionary, should collaborate "This agency," says McGarvey, "would be what a missionary society ought to be, and what they all must be, if they continue to be at all."

Lipscomb's answer was intended to show the carelessness of McGarvey's words. If McGarvey wanted every rich man to support a missionary, would this not leave the church out of it altogether? Actually McGarvey did not mean to say this, nor did Lipscomb mean to try to interpret him so, but the language of McGarvey was extremely weak. Relative to the third point in McGarvey's proposal, Lipscomb wrote:

We suppose Brother McGarvey means that a sufficient number of weak churches should combine to sustain one evangelist, not that all the weak churches in the world, or the United States, or one State, should unite in one unwieldy and complicated associa-

---

[34]Tolbert Fanning, "Letter—No 2," *Gospel Advocate*, Vol IX, No 15, (April 11, 1867) p 282

tion, that swallows up and destroys the integritism, identity and sense of responsibility of the individual congregations, and with a machinery so expensive in its operations as to absorb from one-fourth to one-half of the contributions before it can be got into operation.[35]

Lipscomb goes on to say that if this is what McGarvey means, and if the brethren will really do this, then those who are opposing them will not raise a voice or pen against them again. The discussion would cease at once, Lipscomb promised, if brethren will go to work through local churches, and not through extra, expensive machinery like the society He charged that at times from twenty-five to forty per cent of the total money received went to pay the expenses of employees of the Society.

It was only to be expected that in the heat of such a controversy passions should be aroused, and personalities should creep into the arguments. Apologists for the Society denounced in bitter terms the opposers. It was claimed that these opposers did not believe in "cooperation" or in "mission work." They were looked upon as bitter men, with no spirituality and little love for lost souls. C. L. Loos wrote:

The evidence from all quarters of our land, and from other lands, demonstrate that this great matter of missions—organized associations for cooperative efforts to send the gospel abroad—is really no longer a doubtful question among us, that it is decided and accepted. The whole matter has been thoroughly sifted in the past quarter of a century, and may now be regarded as settled . . . those few who have been of late days persistently and noisely denouncing missionary associations, have, by the unsanctified bitterness and rudeness of their attacks, given full evidence of the causes of their opposition—a lack of knowledge, of an enlightened piety and a true spiritual culture. To attempt to teach such men is well-nigh useless, as it is almost hopeless [36]

To charge men with lacking piety, having no knowledge of a true spiritual culture because they opposed the society was a grave and uncalled for charge The whole controversy, on the part of Ben Franklin, David Lipscomb and Tolbert Fanning, was not intended to be a personal attack despite the personal element which was often injected.

Even one so famous for spiritual culture as W. K. Pendleton

---

[35]David Lipscomb, "The Way to Settle the Society Question," *Gospel Advocate,* Vol VIII, No 19, (May 8, 1866) p 292

[36]C L Loos, "Ohio Missionary Meeting," *Millennial Harbinger,* Vol. XXXVII, No 6, (June, 1866) pp 274, 275

found it easy to thrust these abuses upon the Society's enemies
In his reply to Carrol Kendrick, he praises Kendrick by observing
that his article had none of the "trivial captiousness of ill-natured
opposition; no frivilous dogmatism, no irreverent treatment of
the great work of preaching the gospel. no scoffing at the pious
efforts of God's noblest men to extend the borders of Zion."
Speaking of Kendrick, he remarks that "he would not throw an
envious, or captious criticism across the path of the just, nor
hinder the preaching of the gospel, though done by a missionary."
Pendleton advised:

> Let men who have missionary work, . . take counsel together
> . . and let us not be disturbed. or distracted in our work. by
> outside railers, who seem to rejoice in nothing so much as their
> own success in preventing the preaching of the gospel [17]

Personal thrusts develop attitudes, and attitudes govern conduct. Franklin, Lipscomb and Fanning were quick to feel a
righteous indignation at these bitter remarks. To be represented
as men who were trying to prevent the preaching of the gospel
was something uncalled for considering the fact they had dedicated
their lives to the cause, and had consistently encouraged it from
the beginning They were opposed to that presumption on man's
part which allowed him to create an organization to do the work
which God gave to the church. It implied that God's plan was
imperfect, and that man could improve upon it. It implied that
human wisdom could improve upon the revelation of God's will
in the scriptures This assumption, along with all of its implications, these men totally rejected.

---

[17]W K Pendleton, "Divine Missionary Society," *Millennial Harbinger,*
Vol XXXVIII, No 5, (May, 1867) p 255

CHAPTER IV

THE INSTRUMENTAL MUSIC CONTROVERSY
(1866-70)

The issue which was to find little abatement, and which was more directly to effect a division among brethren was centered around the use of instrumental music in the worship. Actually, of course, the use or non-use of the instrument was symptomatic of an attitude toward the scriptures. Because many felt the use of the instrument was in direct violation of a basic principle which was necessary to maintain if the church was to return to the ancient order, they vigorously opposed it. Although it was frequently contended that the use of the instrument was a comparatively innocent practice, advocated even by some very spiritual-minded men; when viewed from the standpoint that it transgressed upon a very dear and essential principle, many were unwilling to compromise with it. It was this point that gave the controversy its vehemence. Certainly no study of the cross-currents of feelings giving rise to division in the ranks of the advocates of restoration principles could be complete without a detailed analysis of the instrumental music controversy.

It is right, however, to preface this material with a brief account of the beginning of another religious periodical among the brethren, viz., the *Apostolic Times*. The only apology needed for this apparent departure from the analysis of the controversy is the importance of this paper to the controversy. The editors of the *Times* were set for the defense of the church against the use of the instrument, making their paper fill a vital role in the controversy.

Lard's Quarterly had hardly died in the year, 1868, until plans were immediately begun to establish a new paper The greatest names in the brotherhood were enlisted in a splendid array of talent for an editorial corps. These editors were Moses E. Lard, John W. McGarvey, L. B Wilkes, W. H Hopson, and Robert Graham, and were leading men in the church. Wherever the plea for restoration was known, these names were household words   The last three mentioned are less known to the church today and perhaps stand in need of a brief introduction.

Lanceford Bramblet Wilkes gained his greatest fame with his series of debates with Jacob Ditzler, an ardent polemic of the Methodist variety.   One of these debates was published, and shows Wilkes' scholarship, thoroughness, and greatness.   Fame also came to him as an educator.   In 1856 he was president of Christian College in Missouri   Before that, he and W. H. Hopson had started and conducted Palmyra Female Academy in Palmyra, Missouri, the home of Jacob Creath, Jr.   Additional fame came to him because of his excellent ability as a proclaimer of the word of God   In 1853 he was the preacher for the church at Hannibal, Missouri, and he stayed here on and off until the close of the war   In the fall of 1865 he moved to Springfield, Illinois to preach   Later in life he moved west, and died in Stockton, California the first of May, 1901.

Wilkes was of sallow complexion, with light hair and blue eyes, weighing one hundred sixty pounds.   He was born in Maury County, Tennessee on March 27, 1824   When only five years old, his family moved to Miller County, Missouri and here Wilkes grew to manhood   He heard the gospel preached by J M. Wilkes and J. H. Haden, and was baptized in the James River near Springfield, Missouri on the second Lord's Day in August, 1848 by J. M. Wilkes   He entered Bethany College in the spring of 1849, but at the constant urging of J. H. Haden, came back that summer to Missouri and graduated from the State University under the presidency of James Shannon   He possessed a well-disciplined mind richly stored with great knowledge which probably made him a candidate for an editor's post on the *Apostolic Times* while the plans were yet in their formative stages.

Aside from Lard and McGarvey the most familiar name among the editors to present-day students of the restoration is undoubtedly that of Winthrop H. Hopson.   Hopson ranked foremost among the pulpiteers of his generation, seconded only by Moses E. Lard himself.   In personal appearance Hopson was meticulously neat, tall, erect and dignified The poorer, undignified class of people shrank at first from his presence, but soon Hopson would win them over by his humility and spirituality which made him "all things to all men."   Sometimes this portly dignity was used as the means of a joke on Hopson.   In 1859 he conducted an evangelistic meeting for the Eighth and Walnut Streets Church in Cincinnati. A writer of the *Western Christian Advocate,* a denominational periodical, went to hear and criticize Hopson. He timed Hopson's sermon—it was one hour and thirty-seven minutes to the tick. He says of him,

> He had on a good pair of whiskers as well as a fair representation of the article *mustache.* These he stroked with great complacency for a time, and then took out a penknife and began to whittle his nails.[1]

As a preacher, Hopson was a very gifted speaker. Many men of his generation bore testimony of this fact. In 1853 Alexander Campbell held a meeting in Hannibal, Missouri which Hopson attended. At this time, Hopson was conducting the school at Palmyra with L. B. Wilkes. Campbell writes of Hopson:

> Brother Hopson is one of our most gifted preachers, and when an evangelist, was so laborious as not to lose a day in the year. We cannot but regret that such a man as he should be confined to the sphere of a preceptor in any academy, male or female.[2]

Hopson's great reputation as a speaker grew out of his ability to make the truth plain to the common man. Ben Franklin enjoyed listening to him. Franklin writes:

> While Dr. Hopson is a fine scholar, and instructive to the highest order of society, he is also emphatically *the man for the people.* He possesses, pre-eminently, the happy art of presenting great truths in the plainest and easiest terms, and thus making them not only clear and appreciable to the whole people, but, at the same time, so interesting that all feel sorry to see him close.[3]

W. H. Hopson was a protegè of Samuel Rogers. Early in the decade of the 1840's, Rogers was preaching in the Gasconade Valley in Missouri when Hopson first came to him. Hopson was now tall, neat, graceful and slender. Hopson possessed letters from Abram Miller of Calloway County saying that Hopson wanted to be under Rogers' care as a preacher. Rogers put Hopson to delivering the discourses, and he himself would conclude with the exhortation. Hopson was now about eighteen years of age; yet he was clear, logical, and forcible, and child-like in

---

[1] Ben Franklin, "Doctor Hopson," *American Christian Review,* Vol. II, No 7 (February 15, 1859), p 26.

[2] Alexander Campbell, "Notes of Incidents in a Tour Through Illinois and Missouri," *Millennial Harbinger,* Fourth Series, Vol. III, No 2 (February 1853), p 66

[3] Ben Franklin, "No Title," *American Christian Review,* Vol II, No 3 (January 18, 1859), p. 10.

his simplicity, and always humble. Hopson's wife was Rebecca Parsons, daughter of Col. James Parsons, Samuel Rogers also baptized this young girl.

Hopson's son-in-law was R. Lin Cave, who for several years preached for the Vine Street church in Nashville. In his old age, Hopson lived with his son-in-law, and died in Nashville on Friday evening, April 20, 1888.

Robert Graham, the last of the five editors of the *Apostolic Times* to be noticed, was born in Liverpool, England on August 14, 1822. Because his parents were rigid Episcopalians, young Graham was reared as a member of the Established Church. Very early in life he moved from England to America, and settled in Allegheny City, Pennsylvania where Samuel Church was the distinguished preacher. Graham at first became a member of the Methodist Church, but later, when he discovered that there were many phases of Bible teaching which he could not harmonize with the practices of this denomination, he was baptized by Samuel Church.

Graham, by trade, was a carpenter, but gave a part of his time to devoted study. The first of January, 1843 he entered Bethany College, then only recently having been opened. He paid his way through by working as a carpenter on some of the buildings of the College which were under construction. After graduation, he traveled extensively in the interest of the college, settling finally in Fayetteville, Arkansas. Although he moved around considerably in later life, his most noticeable work was done in this city.

Thus briefly have we been introduced to the men who were behind the *Apostolic Times*. The first issue of the paper was scheduled to be published by the middle of April, 1869. During the fall and winter of 1868-69 preparations were rapidly made to launch the paper. The very fact that it had such an array of editorial talent, gave its friends high hopes of success. It was announced that subscriptions would cost $2 50, and anyone who secured ten subscriptions would receive one free. We have in our possession a letter, written by Moses E. Lard to W. C. Huffman, and preserved for us by Minnie Mae Corum on the subject and written at this time. The letter reads,

Lexington, Ky. Mar. 11, 1869

Dear Brother Huffman,

Yours of the 6th inst with names and P. O. order for $25 is

duly rec'd for which accept our cordial thanks. Our paper will be out early in next month We shall feel deeply obliged for a continuation of your efforts in its behalf. When out, the paper will be the largest and finest sheet ever issued in our ranks.

> Yours most fraternally,
> M E. Lard.

The "Prospectus" for the *Apostolic Times* appeared in the December, 1868 issue of the *Millennial Harbinger*. The "Prospectus" of the paper is important as it informs one of the direction the periodical proposed to go. The Prospectus for the *Times* said:

In compliance with the wishes of many brethren, expressed through a period of several years, the undersigned propose to issue from the city of Lexington, Kentucky, a weekly paper bearing the above title. It will be issued as soon as three thousand paid subscriptions have been received.

The absorbing object of the paper will be the propagation and defense of the Gospel as it came, pure from the lips of Christ and of the apostles. On this grand theme it will decline even the semblance of a compromise. Whatever aids this, it will aid, whatever opposes this, it will oppose. To the primitive faith and the primitive practice, without enlargement or diminution, without innovation or modification, the Editors here and now commit their paper and themselves with a will and purpose inflexible as the cause in whose interest they propose to write.

The paper will bear itself high over all political issues and geographical boundaries both in its matter and spirit. It will stand neither for the North nor the South as such, neither for the East nor the West as such, but in all places and at all times for the Truth alone and its friends.

The paper will aim to foster with tender solicitude and profound sympathy all our great educational enterprises. These, it is true, will be held as subordinate to the higher interests of Christianity, but as subordinate to these only, and hence, as entitled largely both to our space and aid.

Much room will be devoted to General Church News and Church Statistics. It is proposed to make this feature of the paper one of peculiar interest.

Important literary and scientific books, especially religious books, will be appropriately noticed. But endorsement where not merited may not be expected. We shall praise only where we think it is due.

The labor of the paper has been properly divided and distributed among its editors, but as editors, they are all equal, all alike pledged to its success, and are jointly responsible for its matter and manner

Each paper will contain eight pages, and each page five columns

The paper will be of the finest quality, the type new, and the work executed in the best style.

The price of the paper will be $2.50 per year. But to every person who will send us ten names with $25, we will send one copy gratis.

All preachers and other brethren who may feel willing to do so, are hereby requested and urged to act as Agents in procuring and forwarding both names and money Let names and money be sent in as soon as practicable. Large lists of names are solicited.

All communications of every kind to be addressed to "The Apostolic Times," Lexington, Kentucky.

If the paper is not issued, the money will be returned

> Moses E. Lard
> Robert Graham
> Winthrop H Hopson
> Lanceford B Wilkes
> John W. McGarvey [4]

The first number of the *Times* came off the press dated April 15, 1869. The Motto written across the top was, "The Bible Alone—Its faith in its purity, its practice without a change." The leading editorial was written by Moses E. Lard as a commentary upon that motto.

The Bible—first purge it of the corruptions of men, and then not a line does it contain which we decline to believe with a whole sound heart What it does not contain, as matter of faith or matter of duty, we value not at the price of a single mill For us it contains only the thoughts of God, and of Christ, and of those who spoke for them. Our love of these thoughts falls only a little below our love of him who paid the ransom of his life to save us ; nor could we more readily consent to see them corrupted than we could to see that bosom smuttered on which we yet hope to recline a weary head when the present troubled life is ended . .

There is in the Bible, especially in the New Testament, something called *the faith*. It is not of this exactly that our motto speaks It is of the matter of our faith or what we are to believe This matter must be kept pure, pure as when it dropped from the lips of him who is its source. . . But according to our motto, the Bible practice must remain unchanged In this we especially allude to the practice of the primitive Christians, as prescribed in the New Testament No changes must be wrung on this, neither must innovations be incorporated with it. But here a few distinctions seem called for By practice we do not mean *every thing*

---

[4] W K Pendleton, "Prospectus for the 'Apostolic Times,'" *Millennial Harbinger,* Vol XXXIX, No 12 (December, 1868), p 713

done by the first disciples. We mean strictly those acts which they performed *as* Christians in obedience to divine direction What they thus did we must do, what they thus did not, we must not do. In this respect their lives must be our model, their practice the law of our conduct.[5]

After the first issue of the *Times* appeared, considerable reaction was seen along different lines. Commenting upon the first appearance of the paper, W. K. Pendleton writes in the *Harbinger*.

We cannot be suspected of partiality or flattery when we say that, no paper among us has a more imposing Corps of Editors. They are brethren of high talent, large experience, approved "soundness," and deep devotion to the cause. . .

The first numbers bristle a little at the apprehension of hostile spirits somewhere in the regions of the air; evince a slight magnetic tremor, under the disturbing influence of some as yet not well determined antipolar forces, that call for watchfulness; and that give due notice that an eye is upon them.[6]

Neither Isaac Errett nor David Lipscomb appreciated very much seeing the *Times* begin Both the *Christian Standard* and the *Gospel Advocate* were having difficult times getting started. The *Standard* was in 1869 going through its most critical year when at any moment the paper could be a serious financial loss The *Advocate* had weathered the worst of its troubles, but even so the paper needed to be on a better basis Isaac Errett, upon seeing the first issues of the *Times,* then wrote the following.

We have received the first number of this journal, the prospectus of which we published sometime ago. It is about the size of the *Standard,* has the same form, and *of course* presents a commendable appearance. . . On its editorial staff are men of established reputation both as preachers and writers, and we expect from them a bold and vigorous advocacy of the truth as it is in Jesus. Among our best minds there is much doubt as to the expediency of starting a new weekly. On this there is much to be said on both sides. For ourselves, whatever our private judgment may be, we cheerfully recognize the right of these brethren to start a new paper, and bid them welcome to this field of toil.[7]

It was customary for David Lipscomb to be frank even if it came to his own discredit. At various times he had tried to get every single editor of the *Apostolic Times*, except one, to write

---

Moses E Lard, "Our Motto," *Apostolic Times*, Vol. I, No 1 (April 15, 1869), p 1

[6]W K Pendleton, "The Apostolic Times," *Millennial Harbinger*, Vol XL, No 5 (May, 1869), pp 294, 295

[7]Isaac Errett, "The Apostolic Times," *Christian Standard*, Vol IV, No 18 (May 1, 1869), p 141

for the *Advocate* They had all refused Now that they had started the *Times,* Lipscomb was frank enough to recognize that they would hurt the circulation of the *Advocate.* Consequently he was not glad to see the *Times* published, and he would not cover up this fact.

We will not say we are glad of the proposal of publication, for we are not. We regret that these brethren could not find some one of the papers, already in existence, worthy to publish their productions, inasmuch as quite a number of them are barely supported now. . .

We regret it, because we are conscious they will, to some extent, injure the circulation of the *Advocate,* when it is not in a condition to bear the loss of a few hundred subscribers.[8]

The *Apostolic Times* editorially occupied what was after the war the popular middle-of-the-road ground It, on the one hand, favored the missionary society, yet, on the other hand, it bitterly opposed instrumental music For a few years this was the popular position, but as time went by, many could not see the consistency of such a position and it gradually faded out of existence. To oppose instrumental music as being a human addition to a divine *worship* was the same *in principle* as opposing the missionary society as a human addition to a divine *work.* Moses E Lard and J. W. McGarvey could never see it this way The *Christian Standard* saw the position, and on the same ground that it accepted the society it was led to accept the instrument. The *American Christian Review* and the *Gospel Advocate* saw it this way, and on the same ground they were led *not* to accept the society, also rejected the instrument Clearly, the *Times* was not occupying a consistent position, but while the issue was yet in its definitive period, the *Times* represented a large bulk of the brotherhood.

THE CONTROVERSY

After the war, the practice of using the instrument in worship was gradually increasing, and in almost every case where it was brought into the worship a serious eruption was occasioned But as yet, the instrument was not being introduced at a very rapid pace In the spring of 1868 Ben Franklin hazarded the guess that there were ten thousand congregations in the brotherhood,

---

[8]David Lipscomb, "No Title," *Gospel Advocate,* Vol XI, No 4, (January 28, 1869), p 73

and not over fifty of them had used the instrument in worship. Even so, the practice was coming unless something could be done to stop it, and most enlightened brethren could see this. John Rogers, one of the great pioneers of Kentucky, died in 1867, and on his death-bed worried considerably over the ever-increasing introduction of the instrument.

In the larger city congregations the introduction of the instrument generally was accompanied with considerable anxiety in the brotherhood. In 1867 the church in St. Louis purchased a new building from the Episcopalians The building was located on the corner of Seventeenth and Olive Streets. In the deal was a three thousand dollar organ. The question of what to do with the organ immediately arose. A staunch group, led by Dr. Hiram Christopher, brother-in-law of J. W. McGarvey, opposed the instrument, and so, it was not immediately brought into the worship. For two years the agitation continued. At this time the church had one elder, A. Johnson, who favored the organ. A meeting was held the first of the year, 1869 to vote on the matter. Seventy-eight voted for it, and ten voted against it, but the elder recommended putting off using it until after the spring semi-annual meeting of the American Christian Missionary Society which was scheduled to be held in St. Louis in May, that year. A popular vote was later taken which showed that one hundred and four favored using the instrument and twenty-four opposed it. The opposition, although in the minority, was determined enough that for two years the instrument was rarely used. A gathering storm indicated division was on the way. Late in 1870, Robert Graham, Isaac Errett, Alexander Proctor, I. N. Rogers went to St. Louis to quiet the trouble. A compromise was reached whereby the instrument, for the sake of peace, was kept out. This lasted only a few years when the advocates of the organ took control, and those who opposed it were forced to leave and establish another congregation

In Akron, Ohio about this time a similar situation occurred. Ben Franklin was invited in April, 1868 to conduct an evangelistic meeting. The church had in the past on various occasions used the instrument, but in Franklin's presence had always refrained. But on this occasion, Franklin went into the building and took his seat, waiting for the singing to start, and then for his time to preach. But when the singing began, so did the instrument.

Franklin, opposed as he was to the instrument, was faced with a serious problem of what to do. He informs us of his thoughts during these few moments:

We have not been more tried in a long time. While this was going off, we reflected and turned the matter in every way possible. What was to be done? We never felt more unhappy. Are brethren determined, we involuntarily thought, to deteriorate the worship into music, and compel us to endorse it? If we refuse to preach, it may, we further thought, create a lasting trouble, and some may blame us for it. We decided to preach, and did so, but with a heavy heart, in view of the worship having been thus degenerated before our face.[9]

Nine-tenths of the congregation, Franklin was convinced, did not want the instrument, but the influential one-tenth promoted it. As to his own position, Franklin explained it as follows:

We have no prejudice against an organ, melodeon, piano, violin, or Jews' harp, but we do not intend to worship with any of these, or even tacitly to endorse the use of them, or any one of them in worship. . . We intend no man shall quote us, while we are living nor when we are gone, as endorsing or in any way giving countenance to the evil complained of. If brethren will introduce the instrument into worship, *they shall themselves be held responsible. We shall not be.* We therefore desire brethren not to invite us to hold a meeting for them, if they intend to play on an instrument in their worship. *We know positively that it is safe to keep it out.*[10]

In Chicago, Illinois still another similiar circumstance occurred. A new church building was purchased at the corner of Indiana Avenue and Twenty-fifth streets. This congregation was newly organized in June, 1868, and moved into its new building on January 17, 1869. D. P. Henderson was the preacher, and the organ was put in over his protest.

The organ is but a common melodeon, and even this is tolerated under protest by Brother D. P. Henderson, who is preaching for the congregation, and who is very much beloved for his work's sake by the whole membership.[11]

In the summer of 1870 the church in Memphis, Tennessee put in the instrument. David Walk, the preacher, chiefly instigated

[9]Ben Franklin, "Notes by the Way," *American Christian Review*, Vol. XI, No. 20 (May 19, 1868), p. 156.
[10]Ben Franklin, "Notes by the Way," *American Christian Review*, Vol XI, No 20 (May 19, 1868), p 156
[11]C W Sherwood, "The Cause in Chicago," *Christian Standard*, Vol. IV, No 8 (February 20, 1869), p 58

it, and put on a concerted drive to raise the necessary funds. At the same time the famous Christian Chapel in Cincinnati, corner of Walnut and Eighth streets underwent a change. A new building was secured costing one hundred and forty thousand dollars. Eight thousand dollars was spent for an organ. W. T. Moore was the preacher for this congregation. Upon the completion of the building, he preached a sermon on the subject, "It is Finished." Ben Franklin was ashamed, and severely condemned Moore for applying Christ's words on the cross to such a lavish expenditure of money in Cincinnati. Robert Richardson wrote Franklin adding his remorse to Moore's conduct and stating that Alexander Campbell would never have agreed to such an act. Franklin, a few years later, confided to a friend that he could have wept with joy at receiving such a letter.

With the gradual increase in the number of instruments being added to congregations, it was clear that the restoration movement was taking on a new color, one of which for the most part the earlier pioneers had never dreamed. J. W. McGarvey very accurately summarized the condition when he wrote:

We are moving; we are progressing; at least some among us are advancing. Whether you think the movement forward or backward depends very much upon the way you are going yourself. Once we had no men among us who were known to tolerate instrumental music in worship. After that there arose some who contended that whether we use it or not is a mere matter of expediency. More recently, a few churches have actually used it, and their preachers have approved, but have not often ventured publicly to defend it.[12]

The apology chiefly used for introducing the instrument was the rapidly changing world. The frontier had pushed on westward; larger cities were growing up in the mid-west. Science was making new discoveries. The train was increasing its speed and efficiency, tying the country closer together. New standards were arising, and consequently, society was raising its requirements. Some felt that a worship without an instrument was all right in a society that was accustomed only to the backwoods, but new standards of respectability were now set up, and the church to be progressive must meet these standards. So McGarvey wrote:

---

[12]J. W McGarvey, "A Little Farther Along," *Apostolic Times*, Vol I, No. 2 (April 22, 1869), p 13.

This question of instrumental music is becoming a serious one. There are many who favor it, and who will listen to no argument against it. By the cry of progress and conformity, it is making its way over the heads and hearts of many of our best brethren and sisters. . .[13]

One N. A. Walker found himself doing a profitable business. He was a preacher, but also sold mechanical instruments. He was busy most of the time holding evangelistic meetings, and usually managed to sell an organ to the church while he was there. For the year, 1869, he reported that he baptized three hundred people, and used an organ in every meeting he conducted except one. J. B Briney, who in these earlier years was much opposed to the organ, but who later turned to favor them, thought he detected in Walker's attitude a feeling that the organ helped to convert people to Christ. Briney replies very firmly:

I suppose he has an improved edition of the commission to this effect: "Go preach the gospel and play an instrument to every creature!" What a mistake the Saviour made in leaving the instrument out of the commission. When N. A. Walker can convert (?) three hundred persons per annum by the use of the instrument, while he might fail altogether with the simple gospel!

. . . With N A. Walker I am personally unacquainted, but how to reconcile a disposition to travel through the country sowing the seed of discord and strife among brethren with the spirit of the Master, I know not . .

He knows that its introduction has caused strife and contention in various places, and, in some degree, injured the influence of some congregations   He knows that some of his preaching brethren can not conscientiously preach for a congregation where an instrument is used.   He knows that leaving the instrument off can do no harm, while taking it on must work mischief.   He knows all this and much more, and yet he is going through the country introducing the instrument wherever he can, and organizing churches with it in. . .

Concerning him, I can only say to the brethren, "Ephraim is joined to his idols, *let him alone.*[14]

Many were not persuaded that the adoption of the instrument would mean progress at all, but instead a definite departure from apostolic principles.   The clash in views was evident.   In the quest for progress the instrument was being used over the protest

---

[13]J. W McGarvey, "Brother Hayden On Expediency and Progress," *Millennial Harbinger*, Vol XXXIX, No 4 (April, 1868), p 216
[14]J. B Briney, "The Organ or the Gospel—Which?" *American Christian Review*, Vol. XIII, No 7 (February 15, 1870), p 50

of men who were conscientiously opposed to it.   McGarvey propounded the following question to A. S Hayden:

There is a view of this question which I wish to present directly to Brother Hayden, and all conscientious men who stand with him for the use of organs.   It is this: You know that such are the convictions of a very large number of the best and most intelligent class of your brethren, that they will resist to the very last extremity the introduction of instrumental music in worship, and that they will never, while they live, permit it to rest anywhere in peace.   Such being the case, how can you, in the light of apostolic teaching, press the innovation in the manner that you do?[15]

The whole question of division growing out of instrumental music received only minor attention between the years, 1866-70 By its very nature it is such a thought that sincere men will put off considering as long as possible in the hope it will not be necessary to consider it.   Nevertheless, John I Rogers laid down a pattern which the minority by and large found it necessary to follow in the years ahead.

In cases of rebellion, defection or corruption, our duty is simple If the whole congregation, after all laudable means have been used, persist in the use of organs, or any other objectionable thing, we must withdraw from such disorderly congregations, and go where we can worship with a good conscience.[16]

Tests of fellowship over the organ were not frequently discussed during these years, although J. B. Briney speaks out forthright on it.

All of our brethren who favor the use of the organ, and some of those opposed to it, say that this must not be made a test of fellowship.   Did those brethren ever seriously ask themselves this question—who is it that makes the organ a test of fellowship? . . . The New Testament Scriptures know nothing of the organ — They are silent here.   Our consciences will not allow us to worship with the new element   The others say, we have the majority.   This is a question of expediency, and in all such questions the majority *rule*.   The minority reply, you can give neither precept nor example for the use of the instrument   We desire to live in fellowship with the congregation in which we have seen so many happy days, but we can not do it if you bring in the new item of worship.   We regard it as unauthorized and corrupting; as calculated to carnalize the worship   But, say the

[15]J W McGarvey, "Brother Hayden On Expediency and Progress," *Millennial Harbinger*, Vol XXXIX, No 4 (April, 1868), p 217
[16]John I. Rogers, "Objectional Language," *Apostolic Times*, Vol II, No. 26 (October 6, 1870), p 206.

majority, we have determined to use the instrument, and you can either accept that or withdraw from the congregation. Here, now, is a new test of fellowship. Who has made it?[17]

The question of division will be handled in another chapter; nevertheless at this point, some attention needs to be directed toward the subject if anything like a complete picture of the controversy is to be given.

It was stated at the outset of this chapter that the use or non-use of the instrument in worship was founded on basic concepts of the religion of the New Testament Opponents of the instrument considered the use of the instrument to be in violation of an important principle Moses E. Lard expressed this in the following words ·

The question of instrumental music in the churches of Christ involves a great and sacred principle. But for this the subject is not worthy of one thought at the hands of the child of God. That principle is the right of men to introduce innovations into the prescribed worship of God. This right we utterly deny. The advocates of instrumental music affirm it. This makes the issue.[18]

Ben Franklin strongly had the same feeling.

There is not an excuse in existence for forcing this new element into the worship and imposing it on those who cannot conscientiously worship with it   There is not a man anywhere who claims any authority for the new element, nor one whose conscience demands it. There is not a saint who cannot without any violation of conscience worship without it . We can remain on safe ground, the common ground and the ground on which we have stood in peace and war—on what is *written*. The worship in all its parts—all its elements—is a matter of *revelation—divinely prescribed*. Nothing is acceptable worship, only that which the Lord ordained.[19]

On the other side, friends of the organ planted their whole apology for its use squarely upon the matter of expediency as they had formerly done in the case of the missionary society. The champion of this view came to be Isaac Errett and the *Christian Standard*

Until the spring of 1870 Errett had remained silent upon the subject of the instrument. The columns of the *Standard* carried

[17] J B Briney, "Who Makes the Test?" *Apostolic Times*, Vol II, No. 22 (September 8, 1870), p 169
[18] Moses E Lard, *Lard's Quarterly*, Vol IV, No 4
[19] Ben Franklin, "Explanatory to Brother Franklin," *American Christian Review*, Vol XIII, No 21 (May 24, 1870), p 164,

articles pro and con, but little or nothing came from its editor. It was the spring of 1870 before Errett finally broke his editorial silence and stated his position. Afterwards, N. A. Walker humorously remarked that heretofore "we both claimed Brother Errett until I believe we are both willing that the other shall now have him." Actually, Errett was sincere enough. He was not straddling the fence, but held that the instrument was an expediency, although an *unnecessary* expedient and, therefore, should be counseled against. To Errett's credit it must be admitted that he was following a profound conviction which he had announced much earlier in the *Standard*.

. . In a matter of expediency, where we have no conscientious leanings toward or against a proposed scheme, we desire to shape our counsels so as to promote harmony, and this we can better do after watching the current of public sentiment.[20]

Believing, as he did, that the use of the instrument involved only a matter of expediency, he waited to see what the current of public sentiment was toward it   After sensing this current, Errett speaks out

Hitherto, while allowing a limited range to the discussion of the question in our columns, we have refrained from any expression of our own opinion   The discussion, generally speaking, has not been to our taste   We disliked the dogmatical spirit in which it commenced, and have not seen a time until now when we thought the public mind in readiness for a calm and dispassionate judgment, if, indeed, we have yet reached the most favorable mood for satisfactory investigation   Nearly all that we have published in the *Standard* has been in opposition to the use of instruments, and some of the articles—as those from the pen of Dr Richardson—have been strong, clear, and dignified. We have held back some able essays on the other side, hoping that the differences would be adjusted without much discussion, but we are satisfied, from numerous indications, that some suggestions are needed just now from those who have not hitherto shared in the controversy, and who have reserved their counsel for a time when both parties might be induced to listen.[21]

In the next week's issue of the *Standard* Errett wrote:

We may as well state now, that we intend to counsel against the use of instrumental music in our churches   Our object is to persuade brethren who favor such use to hold their preferences in

[20]Isaac Errett, "Missionary Societies," *Christian Standard*, Vol I, No 33 (November 17, 1866), p 260
[21]Isaac Errett, "Instrumental Music in Our Churches," *Christian Standard*, Vol V, No 18 (April 30, 1870), p 140

abeyance for the sake of *harmony;* for as the love of harmony is
that which leads them to see that the deeper and more precious
harmony of *soul* must not be sacrificed by the lovers of harmony
to the inferior harmonies of sound. . . . It is a difference of opinion.
It is wrong to make this difference a test of fellowship or an
occasion of stumbling.[22]

Thus Errett put instrumental music on the foundation of mere
opinion, at the same time counseling against its use. In still the next
week's issue of the *Standard* Errett elaborated upon his feeling
that the use of the instrument was a matter of opinion by saying:

Before proceeding to give our reasons against instrumental
music in public worship, we desire to elaborate more fully the
thought presented in our last article on this subject, namely, that
the real difference among us is a difference of opinion as to the
expediency of instrumental music in public worship, and therefore,
it is wrong to make this difference a test of fellowship, on one
hand, or an occasion of *stumbling,* on the other.[23]

No sooner had Errett expressed himself on the subject until the
Apostolic Times replied. W. H. Hopson expresses his satisfaction
at seeing the *Standard* speak out against the instrument, but declared a disappointment at the ground on which Errett counseled
against the instrument. L. B. Wilkes was glad Errett spoke out,
but declared that Errett gave an uncertain sound. Wilkes declared
that ". . . it will require some sharper thinking than I am capable
of to discern 'whether the snake that made the track is going
South or coming back.' "[24]

Two distinct attitudes toward the instrument now became
apparent. Errett championed that one which placed instrumental
music forth as an opinion, being neither right nor wrong in itself.
Over against Errett was Ben Franklin, who wrote strongly on
the other side in these words:

We put it on no ground of *opinion* or *expediency*. The acts of
worship are all prescribed in the law of God. If it is an act of
worship, or an element in worship, it may not be added to it. If
it is not an act of worship, or an element in the worship, it is
most wicked and sinful to impose it on the worshippers. It is
useless to tell us, *It is not to be made a test.* If you impose it on
the conscience of brethren and, by a majority vote, force it into

[22]Isaac Errett, "Instrumental Music in Our Churches," *Christian Standard,*
Vol V, No. 19 (May 7, 1870), p. 148
[23]Isaac Errett, "Instrumental Music In Our Churches," *Christian Standard,*
Vol. V, No 20 (May 14, 1870), p. 156
[24]L B. Wilkes, "Instrumental Music," *Apostolic Times,* Vol. II, No. 9
(June 9, 1870), p 68

the worship, are they bound to stifle their consciences? Have you a right to compel them to submit and worship with the instrument? They stand on the *old ground*, where the first Christians stood, as we all admit, and where we have all stood. If you press the instrument into the worship, we care not whether you call it an *element* in the worship or an *aid*, and drive them away, because they cannot conscientiously worship with the instrument, *you cause division—You* are the *aggressor—*the *innovator—*you do this, too, for the accompaniment of corruption and apostasy, admitting at the same time that you have no conscience in the matter.[25]

Clearly, then, to Franklin instrumental music was no matter of opinion. Man had no right to add an element of human origin to the divine worship, for such inescapably had to be an innovation. The two views, championed by Errett on one side and Franklin on the other, were poles apart. Down to the present day they have been the fundamental reason why fellowship between the churches of Christ, on one side, and the Disciples of Christ denomination, on the other, is inconceivable. If the use of the instrument is purely a matter of opinion, then, admittedly, any dispute about it borders on the ridiculous. If, however, the instrument is a human innovation, an addition to the divine worship, then it is sinful to use it. This latter view being accepted, there is no possible, consistent ground for compromise with the former.

The whole field of expediency received a thorough investigation during these years, 1866-70. What is meant by expediency? What is excluded and what included? Relative to the subject, Moses E. Lard sounded an ominous note when he wrote:

The subject of expediency, as interpreted by some of us, may yet prove the rock on which the reformation for which we are pleading goes to pieces. This is not said in the spirit of alarm; it is the utterance of a calm conviction. I do not deny that expediency is sometimes right, nor that the New Testament, in very special cases, sanctions it. Certainly not. . . . When we plead expediency to justify practices unknown to the apostolic age, we are not within the limits of the expedient. We are then violating the word of God. Expediency is no law for innovations, either in faith or practice; and he who pleads it to this extent has abandoned the only rule which can save us from ruin.[26]

---

[25] Ben Franklin, "Two Standards," *American Christian Review*, Vol XIII, No 24 (June 14, 1870), p. 188

[26] Moses E Lard, "Innovations in Divine Worship," *Apostolic Times*, Vol I, No. 3 (April 29, 1869), p. 20

A writer, signing his name "Alexis," writing in the *Christian Standard,* was equally pessimistic on the outcome of the plea of expediency. He wrote.

It was expediency that caused the Pope and Church of Rome to make the change from immersion to sprinkling and pouring in Christian baptism, and that caused the same "Church" to introduce the *organ* into the worship of God, or what was styled that worship. From the Roman Catholics the Episcopalians got it, and thus it has come on down to us of the present day. The chart of God's word is the only safe guide in religion. As long as we *adhere* to that, properly or correctly interpreted, there is no danger, but when we *leave* it, there is no telling where we will float to or land.[27]

Some of the clearest thinking done on the subject of instruments appears to have come from Robert Richardson, Campbell's biographer. In 1868 and 1869, he conducted a lengthy discussion in the columns of the *Christian Standard* with H. T. Anderson. Anderson's views of expediency is best summarized in these words which he wrote:

I am no advocate for instrumental music in churches But the Doctor with his legalism cannot legislate it out of the churches. I might easily say to him, where there is no law, there is no transgression. · There is no law against instrumental music in churches, therefore, those who use it are not transgressors [28]

Briefly, there was no law *against* the use of instrumental music; therefore, it is permitted by expediency. This was one view of expediency. Robert Richardson, an opponent of the instrument, set forth the other side. Expediency, Richardson pointed out, is not *without* the law, but *within* it. Before there can be expediency, there must be law. To illustrate his point, he uses the subject of Prayer. The Bible prescribes prayer, but expediency determines the place, the space of time, and' the posture of prayer. Then he writes:

As it regards the use of musical instruments in church worship, the case is wholly different. This can never be a question of expediency, for the simple reason that there is no law prescribing or authorizing it If it were anywhere said in the New Testament that Christians should use instruments, then it would become a

[27]Alexis, "Alexis on Instrumental Music in the Worshipping of God in Christian Congregations," *Christian Standard,* Vol IV, No. 19 (May 8, 1869), p 145
[28]H T Anderson, "Law and Expediency," *Christian Standard,* Vol IV, No 24 (June 12, 1869), p 186

question of expediency what kind of instruments was to be used, whether an organ or melodeon, the "loud-sounding cymbals," or the "light guitar"; whether it should cost $50 or $500 or $1,000, and what circumstances should regulate the performance.[29]

Richardson's words summarize his point. "The use of musical instruments in church worship can never be a question of expediency, for the simple reason that there is no law prescribing or authorizing it."

On still another occasion, Richardson writes plainly of the subject of expediency:

My position was simply that, as expediency has to do with the manner, time, means and circumstances connected with the doing of things, no question of expediency can rightfully arise until it is *first* proved that the things themselves are *lawful* and proper to be done I feared, and my fears have been fully confirmed by some who have since written on the subject, that expediency was supposed to occupy a wide sphere *beyond* the boundaries of law, and, in its jurisdiction, to be quite independent of law. My view is, that with us, it can have no place at all until law has first authorized something to be done, and that, therefore, its exercise must be restricted within the limits of some law, or rule of life and action.[30]

The one view of expediency was that whatever the word of God did not specifically disallow was permissable. Since the word of God did not condemn instrumental music, it was allowable. But, Richardson pointed out that nothing is expedient which is not first of all lawful. It is a command of God to pray, but it is left to expediency to decide the place, time, and circumstances. J B. Briney emphasizes this further by saying:

Expediency cannot be allowed to affect the character of a divine ordinance. Whatever adds to, subtracts from, or in any way modifies a divine ordinance, affects its character. Such are the principles that must regulate the work of expediency in the kingdom of God.[31]

It was evident during the years of 1866-70 that the restoration movement was undergoing a change. This is plainly so as to relates to the question of instrumental music. Earlier the pioneers had resisted the use of the instrument as an innovation, but advo-

---

[29]Robert Richardson, "Expediency," *Christian Standard*, Vol III, (1868), p 409.

[30]Robert Richardson, "Expediency Once More," *Christian Standard*, Vol IV, No 10 (March 6, 1869), p 73

[31]J B Briney, "The Doctrine of Expediency," *Apostolic Times*, Vol I, No 7 (May 27, 1869), p 55

cates favoring it were now creeping out here and there. Early in 1870 Enos Campbell wrote an article for the *Millennial Harbinger*, signing his name "E," in which he favored using the organ. Alexander Campbell had now been dead four years. But Campbell's widow wrote to Enos concerning his article, in a letter dated March 28, 1870. The letter but indicates the change that had come over the brethren. The part bearing on instrumental music is given here:

. . . You know full well, too, that as sure as the morning and evening sacrifice was attended to, that the songs of Zion resounded in this old mansion. But never was instrumental music tolerated or called in to aid the worship in the family. No, the revered patriarch [Alexander Campbell] advocated the "melody of the heart" in unison with the "human voice divine" in the worship of the family and in the church; and if he were upon earth now, he would do the same. He wrote about it and spoke about it. That you are well aware of, and he never yielded to the teachings of men in regard to the matter   He never approved nor recognized "expediency" as a doctrine to introduce it into the worship of the living God [32]

But yet, instrumental music was bound to come   Many would at first reject it, but once they were lulled into complacency by its soothing tones, they would be in the future unwilling to listen to any argument against it. Richardson observed:

The introduction of a musical instrument into a church is a triumph of the sensual over the spiritual. The innovation once affected, the sensual mind seeks to justify the act by plausibilities, as any error may be sustained, and to trust to Christian forbearance of those who are unconvinced, until the habit of hearing the instrument shall at length silence their scruples. There will be no joy, however, I fancy, at the great day, in a triumph thus gained over conscientious conviction, where the soothing strains of music are employed, not to "admonish" or enlighten, but to put to sleep, the guardian of the soul. [33]

[32] S H Campbell, "Letter From Sis Campbell," *Apostolic Times*, Vol II, No 13 (July 7, 1870), p 99
[33] Robert Richardson, "Expediency," *Christian Standard*, Vol. III, (1868), p. 409

Chapter V

THE LOUISVILLE PLAN

It has already been seen that the American Christian Missionary Society emerged from the Civil War with considerable doubt as to any successful operations for the future. The "war resolutions" caused many brethren to cock an eyebrow. It became evident that a perfectly innocent-appearing organization could soon become a legislative body for the whole church. Society leaders, however, met this opposition by admitting the mistake, but declaring that such mistakes did not militate against the right of a society to exist. Moreover, the cessation of hostilities immediately turned the attention of the people to thinking of rehabilitation, which drew some attention away from the Society .The Society now faced the worst crisis of its entire history. Whether it should live or die would depend upon the course of events in the next decade.

The original minutes of the Convention meetings from 1866 to 1869 indicate the impending crisis. W. K. Pendleton was called upon in 1866 to defend the Society. Being the successor of Alexander Campbell at Bethany, and the close ally of Campbell, his voice was tantamount to that of the sage of Bethany. It will not be necessary again to traverse the ground of Pendleton's defense. It is only necessary at this point to notice what he says of the state of the Society among the brethren:

It can not be denied, that we have not grown in power and means of good, as there was reason to expect. Instead of a steadily swelling treasury, our contributions have been less and less liberal. Instead of establishing new missions, we have allowed some that were started with enthusiastic zeal, to perish in our hands. . .

Pendleton's speech doubtlessly boosted many despairing spirits among Society advocates, but the crisis was by no means over. More defenses were needed, and the next year both Moses E. Lard and J. W. McGarvey were called upon to speak "in advocacy of the right of the brethren to have a society."

Considerable criticism had been incurred by the Society for its policy of making membership contingent upon the payment of money. To avoid this criticism the Society had abandoned this

93

method of raising money   The result had been a severe loss in
finances. By 1868 Thomas Munnell, Isaac Errett. W. K. Pendleton, G. W. Elley, and A R. Benton were ready to ask that the
following resolution be adopted :

Resolved, That in view of the abandonment of life-membership
and life-directorships, which have been the main and permanent
sources of income to the Society, we recommend to the Board
that they devise and carry out a plan of annual and life subscriptions, whereby a constant income may be secured, and a
reliable basis laid for permanent operations in the cause of missions.

As an attempt to improve the organization of the Society, the
number of vice-presidents was lowered from twenty-five to three.
But still enthusiasm was lacking

Enemies of the Society during these years were all but holding
a jubilee. Tolbert Fanning expressed himself frankly that the
Society was dead; David Lipscomb appeared to think that all
that remained was to gather up the broken fragments of a wasted
effort. Their joy was considerably heightened when Ben Franklin,
in 1866, threw the influence of the *American Christian Review*
against the Society   Franklin, influenced largely by the war
resolutions of the Society, began to see in it a potential danger
to the future of the church   Both Fanning and Lipscomb felt
that Franklin belonged on their side, and there is little doubt that
Society advocates viewed Franklin's friendship with considerable
uneasiness. No man could champion the principles that Franklin
held without sooner or later finding the missionary organization
in direct contradiction to them. When, therefore, Franklin turned
against the Society, considering his place and position in the
brotherhood, it threatened to be a blow from which the Society
could not recover.

Quite naturally if the Society was to recover, it would be much
to its advantage to win Ben Franklin back to its side. If Franklin
could never be made to be an *advocate* of the Society. something
should be done to draw a halt to his outspoken opposition. To
this end a movement began to win Franklin back, and to unite
the opposing forces of the brotherhood behind the Society.

Robert Milligan, president of the College of The Bible. in
Kentucky University, led the way for this move   In the October
16, 1866 issue of the *American Christian Review,* Milligan presented an essay in which he attempted to "place our Missionary

Society on a true and scriptural basis." It was intended to be a "golden mean" between extremes His plan was to leave off a constitution, by-laws, and other such objectionable features. and to organize the society into district, county, state, and national organizations.[1] Later, the idea was suggested through the *Millennial Harbinger* This plan received some semblance of support from Ben Franklin even if his endorsement is somewhat weak Franklin wrote:

We have all the time since our first efforts in the work of the Lord, felt some scruples about Missionary Societies, formed after sectarian models, but for years tried to be satisfied that if they were confined exclusively to missionary work, they might be employed without objection But, after writing more to reconcile the brethren to them and give them efficiency than any other man among us we were forced to the conclusion that there was no possibility of confining them *exclusively* to missionary work, that they opened the way for dangerous and mischievous elements to be thrown in, spreading contention in every direction; that such confederations were wrong in themselves; that their constitutions were nothing but annoyances, opening the way for amendments, modifications, or changes of some sort. distracting our meetings, and were not only useless but injurious Having been compelled to this conclusion some four years ago, we have been unable to make any defense of these Societies deserving the name, or to advocate them in any effective manner since.[2]

Nevertheless, Franklin did agree that Milligan's plan was far preferable to the Society as it had been known.

By the spring of 1869, criticism against the Society had abated very little In May that year, a semi-annual meeting was held in St. Louis at which the discussion ran high as to what could be done about all of the opposition. At a recess following one of the dinners, W. T. Moore proposed to W. K Pendleton that they take a walk As they walked. they discussed the Society, the opposition, and possible remedies At the next session of these St. Louis meetings, W T. Moore arose and suggested that a Committee of twenty persons be appointed to consider the whole question and present a report at the regular meeting in October that year in Louisville This proposal was accepted and twenty persons were selected to discuss this subject. Among the twenty

[1]Tolbert Fanning, "Religious Service Through Human Organizations," *Gospel Advocate,* Vol VIII, No 45 (November 6, 1866), pp 709-711
[2]Ben Franklin. "Brother Milligan On Missionary Societies," *Millennial Harbinger,* Vol XXXVIII, No 1 (January, 1867), p 14

were, W. T. Moore, Isaac Errett, Moses E. Lard, Ben Franklin, C. L. Loos and W. K Pendleton.

The annual convention of the American Christian Missionary Society was held October 19, 20, 21, 1869 in Louisville, Kentucky. The Committee of Twenty met together in Louisville prior to the meeting of the regular convention. Three days and nights were spent in the home of W. H. Hopson, who then preached for the church at Fourth and Walnut Streets in Louisville Finally, the committee was prepared to present its plan before the convention.

R. M. Bishop, president of the Missionary Society, prefaced the presentation of the famed "Louisville Plan" with these words:

But the present meeting, brethren, is likely to prove one of the most important we have ever had. It can not be denied that we have reached a crisis in our missionary operations. For the past fifteen or twenty years our missionary efforts can not be regarded more than experiments I do not mean by this to undervalue what we have done; for when we take into account all the circumstances, we have certainly done well. I mean simply that we have now reached a period in our history when we must do better, and that the experiences of the past ought to enable us to adopt such a plan of operations for the future as will be commensurate with the good work to be accomplished.

On Wednesday of the meeting the Committee of Twenty gave printed copies of the Louisville Plan to each person present, so that it could be carefully studied [3]

W. T. Moore, chairman of the Committee of Twenty, presented the proposed plan to the Convention. It was adopted with only two dissenting votes—both L. L. Pinkerton and John Schackleford considering it impractical. Later Isaac Errett wrote:

It was gratifying to notice that the same spirit which characterized the sessions of the committee, largely prevailed in the deliberations of the convention. And we think it would be difficult to find a body, made up of from five to six hundred delegates, coming together from all points of the country, representing so many varied interests and phases of a religious movement, who would discuss questions of vital interest with more deliberation than was done at the Louisville convention.[4]

The Louisville Plan, as it was adopted, proved to be everything

[3] J W. McGarvey, "The Great Missionary Convention," *Apostolic Times*, Vol I, No 29 (October 28, 1869), p 227
[4] Isaac Errett, "The A C Missionary Society," *Christian Standard*, Vol. IV, No. 45 (November 6, 1869), p 356.

but a simple one. Briefly, it consisted of national, state, and district organizations. The national organization consisted of a General Board and a Corresponding Secretary. The General Convention was to appoint nine men, who, with the corresponding secretaries of the states, and the presidents of the state boards constituted the General Board. Likewise, the smaller societies were modeled on the same order. Each state was to have a general board and a corresponding secretary. The numerous districts were to have boards together with a secretary. It was the responsibility of the district secretary to visit all the churches in his district. The district board was to retain one-half of the funds it received, and send the other half on to the state board. The state board was to retain one-half of its funds and send the other half to the national, General Board.

The reaction to this Plan was varied. Ben Franklin seemed to have satisfied his conscience that all was well. He wrote:

In our estimation, it is the most simple, natural, and wise arrangement ever made, and that it will commend itself to all who desire to do anything beyond their own immediate vicinities for the spread of the gospel. We have never seen anything proposed that came near meeting with the same approbation in a convention.[5]

Franklin, although a member of the Committee of Twenty, had said nothing in all the deliberations, nor did he speak a word in the convention that adopted the Plan. He makes it clear, however, that he regarded the Louisville Plan as entirely different from any other. It was not modeled after any sectarian scheme, he thought, and possessed no ecclesiastical authority—the two features of the former society that worried him most. As Franklin viewed the Louisville Plan, it was simply an agreement to work in certain ways; this was not, he insisted, a *society* but an *agreement*.[6] This point of view, it must be added, is one Franklin did not long retain. Only two years later, he was back, vigorously pressing a stern opposition to the Louisville Plan on the ground that it was a Society as the others had been.

For six years—from 1869 to 1875—the Louisville Plan occupied wide attention. The records of the annual conventions

[5]Ben Franklin, "The Annual Missionary Convention," *Millennial Harbinger*, Vol. XL, No 11 (November, 1869), p 606
[6]Ben Franklin, "Great Convocation," *American Christian Review*, Vol. XII, No 44 (November 2, 1869), p. 348.

during those years reveal that there was a lack of brotherhood support to the Plan. The Convention of 1870 met in Indianapolis in the new church building then located at the corner of Ohio and Delaware Streets The Plan was now one year old. R. M. Bishop, president of the Convention, reported that the Louisville Plan had been agreed upon by all State and District conventions since the previous year's meeting. There were no alterations in the constitution to suggest. A note of disappointment was sounded in that less funds were received than were expected, but Bishop reminds the brethren to keep in mind that the first year was in reality one of getting the machinery in motion. Then, too, some had openly predicted the Plan would be a failure and were withholding funds while waiting to see. The Corresponding Secretary, Thomas Munnell, reported that eleven states and thirty-six districts had been organized, but not enough funds had been received to do any foreign work So, all in all, the one hundred and two delegates and six hundred observers to the convention found little news to cheer them.

This first anniversary of the Louisville Plan found the convention searching earnestly for some remedy for the wide-spread indifference to the Society. John S. Sweeney, chairman of a Committee on Press, mildly criticized the various brotherhood papers for their half-hearted support, and pleaded for more enthusiastic publicity. As still another attempt to bolster sagging morale, Thomas Munnell made an appeal to the women to help. Munnell says,

Realizing that, as a people, we have never opened the way for the women of our churches to unite in any broad enterprise with us, we propose to invite their vast, though unemployed abilities to "labor with us in the gospel," both as solicitors among themselves and as missionaries in suitable fields.

Four years later Munnell's plea for the women to help was realized in the formation of the Christian Woman's Board of Missions.

The second anniversary of the Louisville Plan saw the annual convention back in Cincinnati. The date was October 19, 1871. The president, R. M. Bishop, again spoke. Men were needed, he stressed, who were more spiritual, more prayerful, and men who gave less time to discussion. The Corresponding Secretary's report showed that $48,123 33 had been given by the churches to the district organizations. However, only $2,600 had ever reached the General Convention. This was barely enough to pay the secretary's salary, and certainly allowed none for foreign missions.

Theoretically, one-fourth of the amount given by the churches to the district boards was to be sent to the General Board for foreign missions. J. W. McGarvey, however, had presented a suggestion that the churches who gave the money be allowed to say where they wanted it spent. It was a good diplomatic stroke, intended to avoid the criticism that the Society was dictating to the churches. However, it proved a blow to the Louisville Plan for the churches were asking their money be spent near home instead of being sent to the General Board. Ben Franklin saw some great significance to this.

Why did not about ten thousand dollars of the forty thousand raised come into the treasury in Cincinnati? Simply because, on some account, the churches that raised it, the districts, or the States, did not hold themselves bound to send their money, or one-fourth of it, there. The churches raised it, and claimed the right to expend it where they thought it would do the best service. This demonstrates that, in the judgment of the churches, the Board in Cincinnati is not needed, and they have not therefore, sent money enough to pay running expenses.[7]

Still, the Society searched anxiously for some way to get the churches more behind it. Perhaps if they showed the congregations they were doing something, that would help! Try to get their minds off of discussion and on the action! Get a man in the foreign fields! Attention now turned to this. The Franco-Prussian war had just ended in Europe and the two countries of France and Germany were before the people. War had plundered the countries, and people were destitute. German universities were filled with Rationalism, and the nation was largely godless. A mission to Germany, then, was recommended, and warmly received. Dr. W A. Belding personally offered two hundred and fifty dollars to the right man who would go. C. L. Loos delivered a warm speech on the subject. The scene of so much bitter contesting, Alsace-Lorraine, was the place of Loos' birth. He could speak German as well as English. It was suggested that Loos be the man to go, but Loos asked for time to think it over.

Action from the Society was also sought from another place,

---

[7]Ben Franklin, "General Convention," *American Christian Review*, Vol XIV, (1871), p 356

and one closer to home. The two hundred and fifty thousand inhabitants of Chicago had gone to bed on Sunday evening, October 8, 1871—less than two weeks before the convention met in Cincinnati—only to be awakened at one o'clock in the morning by one of the "most extensive and appalling conflagrations ever known in this country " At 9.45 that evening a small fire had been discovered at Halsted Street and Canal Port Avenue. A high wind blowing from the southwest blew the flames across the river at Twelfth Street. A general alarm had been sounded after midnight. Eighty-five thousand homes had been destroyed, eighteen thousand buildings burned down and eighteen hundred acres of land in the heart of the city lay waste. The fire had been checked when General Phil Sheridan ordered some buildings blown up at the corner of Wabash Avenue and Congress Streets.

O. A. Burgess, who had been preaching in Chicago, now brought the full story before the Convention. Two wealthy brothers in the church had lost a million and a half dollars. Isaac Errett had been visiting in the city that Sunday, and had stayed up until midnight, talking to these men about putting their money in spreading the gospel. Three hours later, these men were ruined financially.[8] At any rate, the Society was now given the opportunity to assist the cause in Chicago.

Still other action was demanded of the convention. Thomas Munnell continued to insist that the women ought to be given more active responsibilities to help the work. Then, too, the Society, undoubtedly feeling that they were not being given the publicity from the brotherhood they deserved, decided to publish a paper themselves. O. A. Burgess, still feeling the danger of too great-a centralization, asked that the publication be an individual enterprise. W C. Dawson, who, in only a few years after this, abandoned the church for the Episcopalians, asked that the Society run the paper, insisting that he feared no centralization of power. But, all of these steps pointing toward great activity, were not enough to bolster the sagging spirits of the Society advocates

The convention of 1872 met again at the Fourth and Walnut Streets church in Louisville By now the general outlook for the Society was even darker. Ben Franklin had again convinced him-

[8]Isaac Errett, "The Chicago Fire," *Christian Standard,* Vol VI, (October 14, 1871), p 324

self that the Louisville Plan was not a plan, but another Society, and the *Review* once again was turned against it. The nation was now in a dark economic depression. Little money was reaching the General Board. The brotherhood was filled with bickering and debate over the Louisville Plan. In the midst of such a crisis, R. M. Bishop urged the brethren to be settled and not waste time arguing. He declared that some had as their mission only finding fault. He ironically asks, "Must we continue to fritter away our resources and cramp our energies by attempting to settle the difference between *tweedle dee* and *tweedle dum* while the great world is begging us for the Bread of life?"

By the next year, the nation was in the middle of its financial panic. The Convention met back in Indianapolis, but conditions were still unimproved. Bishop was now in a fighting mood. He reviewed the history of the American Christian Missionary Society and the Louisville Plan. Then he turned his attention toward Franklin, criticizing the editor of the *American Christian Review* for changing his position He requests of the Society that it make up its mind that it cannot satisfy some critics. He cried out, "They mean to oppose us no matter what plan we adopt."

Still the Society was considering some changes that might help. $186,700.91 had been given to the boards in fourteen states of which $7,396.31 had come to the General Board. But the Convention feared going ahead with plans to open a foreign mission on such a small income. Some feared they would not get this if they did not go ahead. C. L. Loos had not yet agreed to go to Germany. How to get more money was the question. R. R. Sloan then suggested that the General Board be allowed to go directly to the churches with its appeal for funds. Heretofore, this was left up to the district boards. This resolution was passed, and the General Board made its plans to do this.

Once before when the Society was threatened with disaster, it had called upon its champion apologist, W. K Pendleton Up to the year, 1874, the outlook had steadily grown worse. W. K. Pendleton was again called. The Convention was held in October in Cincinnati, at the Richmond and Cutter Streets church. R. M. Bishop spoke cautiously and thoughtfully reminding the convention that "we as a religious people" have reached a crisis Success is nowhere in sight, so something drastic had to be done.

Churches were still not giving to the General Board, but instead were requesting that their funds be spent near home. As an attempt to answer charges against the Society, W. K. Pendleton then spoke. He reviewed the quarter-of-a-century history of the Society, recalling the names of the preachers who had been behind the Society, and of the glorious memories of associations with these preachers. When Pendleton had spoken in 1866, his speech served to steady the Society and prevent collapse. Now in 1874 his speech was like a shot in the arm. They convinced themselves more than ever that they were on scriptural ground, although some drastic changes were now in order. Considerable discussion was given to the subject of foreign missions and of changing the constitution. These changes were not to be brought about for another year. Perhaps, however, the most important event of that meeting had to do with the establishment of the Woman's Board of Missions.

Mrs. C. N. Pearre of Iowa City, Iowa on the morning of April 10, 1874 conceived the idea of a missionary society among the women. She, knowing Thomas Munnell's interest in the project, wrote to him about it. To this Munnell replied, "This is a flame of the Lord's kindling; and no man can extinguish it." Mrs. Pearre then contacted J. H. Garrison of St. Louis, then the editor of the *Christian* and got a favorable response from him Isaac Errett visited Iowa City about this time, and encouraged Mrs. Pearre. He followed this by writing several favorable articles in the *Standard*. He suggested also that the women plan a meeting in Cincinnati that October at the same time the General Convention would meet to talk over plans.

In accordance with this suggestion the women met in the basement of the Richmond Street church while the General Convention met upstairs. Mrs. R R Sloan presided while Mrs. Pearre outlined her ideas. These meetings resulted in the formation of the Christian Woman's Board of Missions on October 22, 1874.[9] A vote was taken and the women's decision was to reopen the Jamaica mission which had been grossly neglected.

The Foreign Christian Missionary Society, organized in Louisville, Kentucky, October 21, 1875, was the direct result of the

[9] Elmira J Dickinson, Helen E Moses, Anna R Atwater, *Historical Sketch of The Christian Woman's Board of Missions*, (Indianapolis Christian Woman's Board of Missions, 1911), p. 5-9

discontent over the Louisville Plan. The new society really had
its genesis the year before at the Convention in 1874. W. T.
Moore, noting the discussions on foreign missions and seeing
that nothing was to be done, called a group of men together in
the basement of the building. A committee was then appointed
to make definite plans to present at the next year's convention.
On this committee were W. T. Moore, Joseph King, A. I. Hobbs,
Thomas Munnell and B. B. Tyler. The next summer this committee met in Indianapolis and drew up a tentative constitution
for the proposed new Society. They wanted an American Board
to work in the home field, with a Foreign Christian Missionary
Society established to work in foreign fields. In October, 1875,
then, when the annual convention met in Louisville, this committee presented its plans to the assembly. Errett delivered a
speech, speaking tenderly of the dying love of Christ, until all
eyes were wet with tears. W. T. Moore presented the plans to
the convention which plans were readily adopted. The Foreign
Christian Missionary Society now was born. Isaac Errett was
elected its first president. The constitution called for life directors
by a payment of $500, life members by a payment of $100, and
annual members by a payment of $10.

The next issue of the *Christian Standard* carried the reports of
the Convention, and the plans for the new society. "The Foreign
Christian Missionary Society proposes not to be a rival of the
General Missionary Convention but a co-worker with it," wrote
Errett. The General Convention remained so that it consisted of
voluntary association of members and not delegates of the churches.
Writing of the need of such a society, Errett said,

A great many brethren have been anxiously waiting for years
to see foreign missions initiated by the General Convention and
stood ready to work with it. Nothing has been done. Nothing
is likely to be done. The foreign fields are entirely unoccupied
by us.[10]

Henry S. Earl was present at the 1875 convention that organized
the Foreign Society. He had formerly preached for three years
in England, and for ten years in Australia. He announced to
the Society that his intentions were to go back to England right
away. He was going whether the Society was organized or not,

[10]Isaac Errett, "Foreign Missions," *Christian Standard*, Vol X, (1875).
p 353

but proposed to go now under this Society. The Society could make little promise of financial aid, but did manage to send him five hundred dollars the first year and nine hundred the second.

No sooner however, had the Foreign society been inaugurated than Isaac Errett struck out defiantly at all who opposed the Societies·

We offer our sympathy to all those brethren who regarded our missionary convention as dead, and were eagerly and rejoicingly anticipating its funeral services. We have determined not to go on with our dying. This may be a severe affliction to them, but we hope they will bear it with becoming resignation. It will slaughter the reputation of a few false prophets, but it will carry joy and gladness to thousands and tens of thousands when they learn that the convention not only is not dead, but is developing a more vigorous life, and promises to increase and abound in effective labors for the spread of the gospel.[11]

OPPOSITION

Having now surveyed the history of the Louisville Plan from its origin in 1869 to its death in 1875 when the Foreign Christian Missionary Society was started, our attention now goes back to this history to be studied from the point of view of its enemies The minutes of the various convention meetings, from which the previous material was gleaned, show that the Louisville Plan was not widely received   Nor did all of the opposition appear in outspoken criticism of the Plan, for the very fact that most churches failed to support it indicated their opposition to it.

When the Plan first was announced, ironically enough most of the prominent preachers gave it their support. J W McGarvey· referred to the Plan as the "New Missionary Scheme," and declared that it virtually destroyed the American Christian Missionary Society. It has already been seen that Franklin hailed it as something new, not a society but a *plan* whereby the churches could cooperate for evangelizing the world   Isaac Errett did not agree with the judgment of those who proposed the Louisville Plan but promised his support   W. K Pendleton did not feel that it would answer all the criticism of the objectors, but agreed to support it.   Moses E Lard urged the brethren to get fully behind it.

---

[11]Isaac Errett, "The General Missionary Convention," *Christian Standard,* Vol X, (1875), p 348

Despite the backing of these prominent evangelists, the churches did not rally to the new Plan In Missouri it was strictly opposed, especially in Bates and Cass counties. D B Swink, writing in the *Christian Pioneer* cautioned that if the State Evangelist came to churches around this section of the state, advocating the Plan, he would be opposed "as a Sectarian under any other name." Swink referred to such men as a Brother Davenport, who lost little love on the Louisville Plan.

Those thoughtless brethren in the State Meeting, calling such men as Brother Davenport, croakers, has made them more determined than ever.—I tell you, brethren, the Louisville Plan we do not want, and will not have. Those that attempt to introduce it here will be responsible for the dissensions it causes.[12]

In Georgia the Louisville Plan caused resentment among the churches. Nathan W. Smith wrote from Jonesboro, Georgia on December 27, 1870 that not over three churches in the state would support the Plan if they knew what it was. It was their impression that it was a cooperation meeting to send out T M Harris Smith writes: "What will be the result of this movement time will show. It has brought division and sorrow with pain of heart to some of our best brethren already."[13] Likewise in Mississippi, the Louisville Plan received a severe knocking around before it was ever accepted. J. H. Curtis wrote in the *Apostolic Times*

May the Lord bless us and his cause in Mississippi. There is a puny, but would be "big injun—me," opposition to our great "Louisville Plan," and some pop-guns have squirted water on it, but they are impotent efforts, claiming rather our pity than contempt, for these assaults do not rise to the dignity of demanding grave reply after all that has been said In our own State there is no opposition [14]

David Lipscomb, however, found himself assuming no different attitude toward the Louisville Plan than he did toward the Missionary Society. True indeed, such Societies were always a potential threat to the liberty of the individual congregations, and Lipscomb opposed them on this ground Still, the Louisville Plan and the American Christian Missionary Society were alike unknown to

[12]D. B Swink, "The Louisville Plan," *Gospel Advocate*, Vol XII, No 42 (October 27, 1870), p 991
[13]N W Smith, "Church News," *Gospel Advocate*, Vol XIII, No. 2 (January 12, 1871), p 30
[14]J H. Curtis, "Louisville Plan," *Gospel Advocate*, Vol XII, No 36 (September 15, 1870), pp 843-844

the scriptures, and an attempt to substitute human wisdom for divine revelation. So, the announcement that the Plan had been adopted found Lipscomb just as opposed to it as he had ever been to the Society. Consequently, he wrote:

I am just as sure that the scheme is weak and impracticable as I am of anything undemonstrated. I am sure every congregation in the land will do ten times as much acting for itself and controlling its own means as it will to have its means sent up to Cincinnati and other places to have a board at Cincinnati and other points tithe and control it. This, the Plan contemplates. We feel sure that thousands of good brethren all over the country feel just as I do, that it is anti-scriptural in organization, subversive of the work and organization of the churches, inefficient in operation and corrupting in influence Believing this, our consciences demand we should protest earnestly against it.[15]

Of course, Jacob Creath, Jr., "the iron duke of the restoration," could be counted upon to oppose it To oppose all human institutions to do the work of the church was with him the magna charta of all principles of living.

When I am dead I should like for it to be engraved upon my tomb-stone—
"Here lies Jacob Creath, who opposed all Societies to spread the gospel except the individual churches of Jesus Christ, because he believed such Societies to be destructive of the liberty of the churches and of mankind.[16]

On The Louisville Plan Creath wrote:

These meetings are a violation and a departure from the form of sound words, from speaking of spiritual things in spiritual words —of being silent where the Bible is silent—which is the fundamental principle of our cause We had as well look for all the acts and deeds of Papists and sects, and all their councils, as to look for the names or doings of these two meetings. They are to be rejected by our people. This one reason is sufficient for their rejection, and until they can find the names of these meetings in the New Testament, they are bound to abandon them. They want apostolic precept and example. They have no "Thus saith the Lord."[17]

---
[15]David Lipscomb, "Mississippi and Louisville Plan," *Gospel Advocate*, Vol XIII, No 2 (January 12, 1871), p 38
[16]Jacob Creath, "Letter From Jacob Creath," *Gospel Advocate*, Vol XIII, No 2 (January 12, 1871), p 30
[17]Jacob Creath, "Some Thoughts On the Great Guns Placed on the Ramparts of the Missionary Fortifications in St Louis, Mo in May, 1869 and Louisville, Ky, October 20, 1869," *Gospel Advocate*, Vol XI, No 48 (December 16, 1869), p 1139,

The *sunnum bonum* of all arguments in defense of the Society by its advocates was to be found in the word, expediency. All discussions of the question eventually backed up to this word and settled here. Moses E. Lard, always an advocate of Societies, wished this point to be kept clear, and tried to use it to soothe down ruffled feelings. His article in the *Apostolic Times* was copied by David Lipscomb in the *Gospel Advocate* and considerably discussed. Lard wrote:

It should be remembered that' the "Louisville Plan" is wholly unknown to the New Testament. By that book, therefore, it is neither required nor sanctioned; consequently, if good brethren see fit to oppose it, they should neither be blamed, especially when their opposition is temperate and courteous, nor spoken of slightingly. . . On the other hand, if good brethren think the "Plan" right—that is, consistent with the Scriptures, and wish to see it, as a probable means of good, fully put to the test, their convictions should certainly be respected, and ungentle things should not be said against them. If, in the end, the plan does not promise well, it will be abandoned. This will be its death. But if great good shall result from it, it seems to me that it will be difficult to defend opposition to it.[18]

David Lipscomb replies:

It is seen there the ground upon which the Louisville Plan is placed by him. "It is wholly unknown to the New Testament." "It is neither required nor sanctioned." We confess our surprise to see Brother Lard accept an institution in the kingdom of God on such ground. He opposes instrumental music. It rests precisely on the same ground. It is neither required nor sanctioned by the New Testament.[19]

Lipscomb had for sometime been convinced that the Society was an organization gotten up by power-thirsty men wanting some means to control the churches. Such convictions as this were deeply settled in his mind. To express them would give an opponent the right to accuse him of uncharitableness in judging the motives of another. Lipscomb realized this, yet the conduct of the Society seemed to amply prove his contention. When the Society started, the advocates claimed it to be a mere expedient. They claimed that they were merely unselfishly interested in spreading the gospel. If brethren did not want to work through

[18]Moses E. Lard, "Louisville Plan," *Gospel Advocate*, Vol. XII, No. 36 (September 15, 1870), p. 848.
[19]David Lipscomb, "Louisville Plan," *Gospel Advocate*, Vol. XII, No. 36 (September 15, 1870), p 848.

the Society, they could refuse. It was, according to the society enthusiasts, one among a possible number of ways to preach, and men could use their own judgment as to whether they chose to work this way. Lipscomb always believed that this was so much propaganda designed to win favor. Actually, the Society proved to have little sympathy with any man who would not work through it, nor with any church which would not support it. Friends of the society admitted that since it was but an expedient, if the churches did not want it, it would be dispensed with. Certainly in that decade between 1865 and 1875 the Society had plenty of evidence that it was not wanted Churches refused to support, and not enough money was received to pay the salaries of the officers. The minute it was left to the churches, upon the suggestion of J. W. McGarvey, to decide where their money should be spent, funds to the General Board were less than ever. The Society over the country had alienated brethren, divided churches. Why did it not go out of existence?

With the passing of years this question more and more was raised in David Lipscomb's mind. In 1892 the Society's Convention was held in Nashville, Tennessee. Largely through the efforts of David Lipscomb and E. G. Sewell together with the *Gospel Advocate,* the churches in middle Tennessee opposed the Society. The cause had grown there rapidly without it, and churches were at peace among themselves, all working hard in spreading the truth. Not over three preachers in middle Tennessee favored the Society. Yet, it held its annual Convention there in the hope of swinging some of these churches in line with it. Was the Society *really* interested in peace among the churches? Was it *really* indifferent to the method of spreading the gospel? Lipscomb could never believe so.

The Society worked furiously to convince the bulk of the brethren to ignore the opposition. Thomas Munnell, its corresponding secretary, wrote:

It is a cheap, shoddy piety that spends itself in finding fault and breathing suspicions of the motives and conduct of others. But it wants brains and genuine piety to organize the forces of a people numbering half a million, and bring out their resources into healthful development We beg our brethren in all the states to turn a deaf ear to controversy and fault finding, and make a bold strike at their conventions for higher achievements the coming year. Strike a higher key, and raise a louder note, and sing a grander strain. . .[20]

W. C. Dawson, writing in the *Apostolic Times* of July 6, 1871, criticized harshly the opponents of the Louisville Plan and recommended brethren to stop subscribing to papers that opposed the plan. John T. Poe of Huntsville, Texas replied to Dawson very vigorously:

We are not surprised at this. We *are a little* surprised, however, to find this advocated so early in the race for clerical power. We expected to see it but not yet. We expect to see the time, too, if the Plan succeeds well, when all preachers will be required to subscribe to the Louisville Plan, or support themselves entirely in the work. Why? Because the Plan is to be made *popular,* like circuit-riding in the M. E. Church. If you want a support in the ministry, you must join the circuit. Send your name up to Conference (Convention) and have the preachers elect you. The Pope, or Bishop there, will assign you your field of duty.

It will take but a few years of the present state of things to require another great Reformation, to relieve the church from its thraldom. . .[21]

Ben Franklin, finally convinced that the Society was unscriptural did not swerve from a steady opposition to it. The Conventions themselves were the source of brotherhood troubles. Therefore, Franklin wrote:

The conventions themselves are the wrongs, and we cannot cure the evil by attending and trying to mend them. There is but one cure for them and that is to abolish them. The way to do that is not to attend them.[22]

Franklin now insisted that the differences have not been about evangelizing nor cooperation, but about forming ecclesiasticisms which grasp power, usurp authority to tax the people, and which also usurps authority to negotiate union with "other denominations." This ecclesiasticism also wants to employ "pastors" for churches and have the right to try heretics.[23] Franklin sensed this trend, and set himself for the remainder of his life, against it.

It may be at once seen that the controversy over the Society

---

[20]Thomas Munnell, "Missionary Work," *Christian Standard,* Vol VII, No 1, (August 17, 1872), p 260

[21]John T Poe, "The Plan Again," *Gospel Advocate,* Vol XIII, No 33 (August 24, 1871), p 783

[22]Ben Franklin, "Anti-Missionary," *American Christian Review,* Vol. XVIII, (1875), p. 52

[23]Ben Franklin, "Evangelizing," *American Christian Review,* Vol XVIII, (1875), p. 28

was moving out to a different sphere of argument. In its earlier years the controversy settled on expediency, and while this remained the core of the argument; brethren now sensed a different type of danger: that of a power-grasping ecclesiasticism to control the churches. On the other hand, the opposition found itself gradually moving into a more closely definitive period in its argument. If the Society were wrong because it was a human institution doing the work of the church, then where was the line to be drawn between the society and printing establishments, church buildings, etc. This effort to sharply define the principle of differences was to occupy some attention in coming years.

The Society appeared to its advocates as a comparatively innocent looking organization. Perhaps Robert Richardson best summarized the feeling of the friends of the Society on the question when he wrote:

In the discussion about Missionary Societies, it is, I believe, agreed upon by all parties, that to the church is committed the duty of propagating the Gospel. Those who approve of missionary societies, do not, however, regard the Societies at all apart or distinct from the Church. On the contrary, they consider the Missionary Society as a proper organization, through which the church can accomplish the work They do not conceive the Society at all to be independent of the Church, but to be merely a convenient arrangement, through which the church may best carry on the work committed to her.[24]

What could be wrong with it when viewed in this light? Thoughtful people often raised this question in their own minds.

One such individual was L. C. Wells of Burksville, Kentucky. In 1873 Wells wrote to the editor of the *Gospel Advocate* presenting a defense of the Society, but earnestly desiring more light. Wells suggested that the word, society, if particularly odious be dropped. Like Richardson, he presented the Society as not separate and apart from the church, but the church systematically at work. He then presented an illustration. Suppose a congregation wanted to erect a meeting house. It would select two or three men to buy a site, purchase the material, employ workmen, etc. The church is at work, but working systematically through the men especially appointed for certain responsibilities. No one in this case would complain that they were not authorized by the

[24]Robert Richardson, "Missionary Work," *Christian Standard*, Vol II, (1867), p. 201.

New Testament   Then to draw the parallel, he said the church
is really God's missionary society.   Suppose the church were to
select a few men to oversee the missionary work, it would not
be unscriptural.   Suppose a few congregations went together and
appointed a committee to look after missionary work, nothing
could be wrong with this, he contended.   Certainly this is not a
society, but the congregations at work.

David Lipscomb replied that the building committee in the
illustration is the church at work if it furnishes the means, and
builds according to the wishes of the church and then ceases its
function when it is done.   But the Society maintains an organic
existence distinct and separate from the church   It elects its own
officers, and acts independently of one and all churches.   If this
institution really is the church, then it must follow that its officers
also must be officers of the church, but certainly they were not [25]
Wells had been bothered by the whole problem, but when he received Lipscomb's answer, saw the distinction and changed his
mind.

W. D. Jourdan wrote to the *Apostolic Times* early in 1872
drawing a line of distinction on the whole question   Jourdan
wrote:

It is true, God has left out of law many things that, in the
course of time, fall within the direction of the church, such as
building houses of worship, of what material they shall be, at
what place, or how large they shall be   But not so in relation to
matters upon which he has expressed his will, here we must not
add one word, much less make, and enforce any plan whatever.
The Louisville Plan, to my mind, assumes the ground that God
has given no plan for raising money to maintain his cause on
earth, or if he has, that his plan has failed . . If he has given no
law or plan for this purpose, what necessity caused us to originate
one? . . .
But if the Louisville Plan claims for itself an existence on the
ground that the plan of God has failed, it shows, at least some
friendship in the attempt to resuscitate or aid the failure of its
maker; but what confidence could we have in its success, more
than we could have in the plan of God?[26]

The opposition to the Louisville Plan was effective   The

---

[25]David Lipscomb, "Thoughts on Missionary Cooperation," *Gospel Advocate,* Vol XV, (1873), pp 721-726
[26]W. D Jourdan, "The Louisville Plan," *Apostolic Times,* Vol III, No 51 (March 28, 1872), p 401

churches refusing to support it, left the Society destitute of funds. The decision to abandon the Louisville Plan in 1875 and establish the Foreign Christian Missionary Society was significant in that it was also a decision to abandon all attempts to please the element opposing societies in the brotherhood   Henceforth all efforts to promote the society were to be exerted among its friends, and no attempt would be made to even notice the opposition.   It was virtually an admission that there was division in the brotherhood, and an abandonment of any attempt to reconcile the opposing forces.   Indeed, by the year 1875, the brotherhood was already divided so far as the fundamental issues were concerned.   The next quarter of a century was merely an era when congregations, members, preachers were lining themselves up on one side or the other

Chapter VI

KENTUCKY UNIVERSITY

As events were now developing, the entire brotherhood was to find itself seriously effected by troubles at Kentucky University at Lexington in that decade between 1865 and 1875. These unfortunate happenings helped create a certain type of thinking respecting the whole issue of human institutions, their place and work, which has continued to be a major problem.

The history of Bacon College has already been briefly recounted Starting in 1839 at Georgetown, Kentucky, Bacon College later moved to Harrodsburg, where it found the attempt to be a first-class school filled with so many problems that it finally closed At the instigation of John B Bowman, new hopes were suddenly revived for the school in 1857 Bowman had the vision of making it into Kentucky University. Very quickly he raised sufficient funds to make this seem possible Then came the Civil War. Despite the handicap of the war, the College remained open, but in 1865 a serious fire blasted its hopes At this moment an invitation was extended for it to join forces with Transylvania University in Lexington, and so from that date, Kentucky University became a name closely allied with Lexington.

In 1862 John W. McGarvey moved from Dover, Missouri to preach for the Main Street Church vacated by the resignation of Dr. Winthrop H. Hopson. Three years later, when Kentucky University moved to Lexington, McGarvey was invited to join the faculty of the College of the Bible which was then under the presidency of Robert Milligan McGarvey's name had by now become a household word among members of the church His commentary on Acts of The Apostles was already before the public and widely acclaimed. His enthusiastic defense of the pioneer's older practice of not using the instrument of music had often found his name in the *Millennial Harbinger* and the *American Christian Review*. McGarvey, sensing the opportunity to extend his influence, readily accepted the position as teacher of Bible in the College of The Bible when it was offered to him in 1865

The center of activities in the brotherhood was already passing from Bethany to Lexington, Kentucky. Alexander Campbell, old and feeble in 1865, had substantially yielded the sceptre to his younger contemporaries It was Campbell who had made Bethany, and his passing meant in a measure the passing of Bethany as the Jerusalem of the restoration But natural causes were also at work The frontier had pushed westward. Lexington was no longer a city on the far reaches of the west, but a cultural center of the western United States The moving of Kentucky University together with the College of The Bible to Lexington was of great interest to the brotherhood

That trouble was eventually due to arise in this University was but natural, and probably few informed brethren saw any method of avoiding it Basically, there was a clash in ideologies for the school This clash sooner or later had to be forced into the open

Kentucky University opened at Lexington for its first session on October 2, 1865. The College of The Bible opened with thirty-seven students As it was now organized the University was divided into five separate colleges, the College of Arts, Agriculture and Mechanical College, College of Law, Commercial College and the College of The Bible John B Bowman, who had raised all of the money, was the supervisor of the university officially known as the regent Each College had its president, Robert Milligan was the president of the College of The Bible.

The Agriculture and Mechanical College was a more recent addition to the University. Congress had previously granted thirty-thousand acres of land to each state for each representative and senator that it had in congress for an Agriculture and Mechanical College. Three years had been allowed for each state to accept the offer. Two years went by and nothing was done in Kentucky to accept it Finally, Transylvania had applied to have the A. & M College annexed to it But, about this time, Kentucky University was joined to Transylvania Bowman, in the meantime, had raised one hundred thousand dollars and had purchased Henry Clay's home of four hundred and thirty-three acres at Ashland At any rate, Kentucky University by 1866 found itself in possession of an A. & M. College together with a four hundred thirty-three acre experimental farm in nearby Ashland.

By now, however, some had already begun to wonder just where Kentucky University stood in relation to the brotherhood.

It had been their understanding that the University belonged to them. The largest percentage of funds donated to the school had been given by members of the church in the belief that the school would be run on thoroughly Christian principles. The charter was intended to make this clear. Regent Bowman was to have gathered around him a Board of Curators, and he, together with the Curators, was to supervise the school. The charter stated that at least two-thirds of these Curators should be members of the church. Section No. 8 of the Charter read as follows:

For the ownership and control of said university, at least two-thirds of the Board of Curators shall always be members of the Christian Church in Kentucky At no time shall any member of the faculty be a member of the Board [1]

Members of the church in Kentucky, therefore, gave freely to the university. They expected the faculty to be members of the church, and thought they were to see a university where they could send their children to secure an education that would heighten their respect for the church When the faculty more and more became made up of individuals not in sympathy with the church and when the University began to annex the A. & M. College, which meant it had formed an alliance with the state, a rumble of discontent began to sweep over the brotherhood Particularly was this true in Kentucky.

Bowman had gathered around him a Board of Curators largely imbibed with his own educational ideas. Both for their day were filled with "liberal" ideas for the school, but their language, clothed as it was with the verbiage long familiar to the brotherhood, caused considerable misunderstanding. Both Bowman and the Curators claimed they were running a university on "non-sectarian" principles. The brotherhood breathed a sigh of relief. But they were soon to learn that the connotation of "non-sectarian" was not necessarily fixed. Bowman conceived of the churches of Christ as another sect. Instead of making Kentucky University be sympathetic toward their cause, he would conceive of a school that would serve equally as well the denominations. For the first time many brethren realized that they were looked upon as a sect.

There was a certain ambiguity in the terms that made the real truth difficult to see. To announce to the brotherhood that the

---

[1] Moses E Lard, "Who Owns Kentucky University?" *Apostolic Times,* Vol III, (1871), p 244.

school was "non-sectarian" satisfied them for they believed the
school was sympathetic to them   But the denominations understood by "non-sectarian," that it advocated the principles of no
one religious group   Such ambiguity those close to the school
could sense   McGarvey sensed that the brotherhood was being
deceived by Bowman and the Curators.   Moses E. Lard, who
had moved back to Lexington at the close of the war where he
edited both *Lard's Quarterly* and later, the *Apostolic Times*, agreed
with McGarvey.   The feeling became more widespread.   The
church in Lexington soon became convinced that all was not well,
and gradually, this idea went out of the brotherhood

By the time the fall term of 1871 was ready to open, the undercurrent of feeling had picked up sufficient momentum that it was
at the bursting point   Only a matter of days before the term
opened, Ben Franklin addressed an article through the *American
Christian Review* to Regent Bowman and the University.

True, we grant, it is not to be *sectarian*, but it is to be *Christian*.
It must be under the control of *Christians*   The church of God
is no *sect*, and the gospel of Christ is not *sectarianism*   .

True, the Institution has the funds and can exist without
regard to the *will* of the donors, or the chief men among us   But
it can not get the patronage of *Christians* unless it is true to the
cause in the interest of which it has been raised up. . . We are
perfectly aware how pleased it is to talk about *liberal principles*
and an *unsectarian* Institution   But the religion of Christ is *liberal*,
and those who submit to it are *free*, in the highest sense, and
charitable too, but not, however, liberal, charitable and free enough
to be unequally yoked together with *unbeliever* and *sectarians*

We must have some assurance that the Institution will be
run with a more strict regard to the wishes of the donors and the
chief men in the State before our embarrassment will be removed
We desire to know that the University is not only *nominally* turned
over to the brotherhood, but run in accordance with their desires [2]

Kentucky University felt financially capable of running her
own affairs without the brotherhood's sympathy and proposed to do
so   It was the realization of this danger that had led Tolbert
Fanning and David Lipscomb to advocate that schools have no
endowment and that they might die upon the death of their
founders   Men would give money to richly endow a school

---

[2]Ben Franklin, "Kentucky University," *American Christian Review*, Vol.
XIV, No 39 (September 26, 1871), p 308.

and after they died, the money would be used to destroy the very thing they had tried to erect. Ben Franklin, hoping to get Bowman to put the school on a more acceptable foundation, thought it wise to call his attention to the need of getting back to the old foundation.

The leaven of discontent had now worked the situation up to the bursting point. Bowman and several of his faculty attended the Main Street Church in Lexington where McGarvey preached Bowman felt the pressure gradually pushing in on him He, with thirteen members of his faculty, suddenly decided to leave the Main Street Church and go "around the corner" to establish the Second Christian Church Moses E. Lard now jumped into the trouble, declaring that Bowman was violating the teachings of Matthew, chapter XVIII, and therefore, was guilty of disorder and schism. A vote was taken whether or not the church should withdraw from Bowman, and was sustained fifty to ten [3]

The story of the "church war at Lexington" now blazed forth before the whole country. A brother of one of the men who withdrew was connected with the secular press in Lexington. Soon, the *Lexington Press* and the *Louisville Ledger* were filled with news stories of the trouble. Quite naturally, their sympathy lay with Bowman and the Curators They declared that Kentucky University belonged, not to any one "sect" or "denomination" but to the people of Kentucky. They praised Bowman for his liberal stand, and denounced McGarvey and Lard as narrow-minded bigots who were jealous of Bowman's popularity and who were without a sufficient breadth of understanding and charity

The *Apostolic Times* charged head-long into the fracas. It met the attack of the secular press by frequent references to the charter and to the history of the school, declaring that the school was owned by the brotherhood of Kentucky who had been the largest contributors to it. It declared that Bowman and his curators were not thoroughly honest with the brethren, and that the secular press was a partisan witness in the whole affair.

The *Cincinnati Commercial* picked up the story and ran its side.

Three prominent members and leaders in the Christian denomination, Moses E Lard, J W McGarvey, L B Wilkes, who form-

[3] Ben Franklin, "A Church War at Lexington," *American Christian Review*, Vol (IV No. 46 (November 14, 1871), p 364

erly were residents of Missouri and came to Lexington since the
University expanded into its present broad proportions, with a
few others of less note, have been manipulating to get Regent
Bowman out of the university and have it conducted according to
their ideas of the fitness of things, which ideas happen to be of
a rather sectarian and illiberal character

News of the trouble spread into the brotherhood papers   J M.
Long of Chillicothe, Missouri, Bowman's ardent supporter, picked
out the above article from the *Commercial,* and printed it in the
Christian Standard, over the name, "Alumnus," along with comments of his own. Long had a standing grievance against Lard
and McGarvey of two years previously when both men had
severely criticized an article he had written for the *Christian
Pioneer.* Long had written some articles for the *Apostolic Times,*
but Lard and McGarvey had regarded them as unsuitable for
publication. Now, however, Long took advantage of an opportunity to criticize them   After quoting the article from the *Commercial,* he concluded by saying,

The whole difficulty lies in the fact that the large hearted founder
of Kentucky University is too broad and catholic for them   They
want a college that shall be run on a narrow and strictly sectarian
gauge. In view of this we would say that Kentucky University
is not the college for them, it is not suited to their dimensions [4]

Both Lard and McGarvey expressed their disappointment that
Isaac Errett had allowed such an article to be run, especially since
it was unsigned   Errett, however, explained that his only purpose
in printing it was to elicit some denials of it

Regent Bowman was thoroughly convinced that Lard and Mc-
Garvey had been planning a campaign to oust him from his
position   McGarvey and Lard felt greatly embarrassed when
Bowman presented a statement from Thomas D Butler of Louis-
ville, Kentucky, affirming this point   Butler was a member of
the Fourth and Walnut Streets congregation in Louisville where
W. H Hopson preached   According to Butler, shortly after the
Apostolic Times was started in the spring of 1869, Hopson re-
ceived a letter from Lard and McGarvey   The letter requested
Hopson to get a brother to write a question and send it to the
Times, which letter was to ask the *Times* questions about the
handling of Kentucky University by Regent Bowman   One

[4]Alumnus, "Regent Bowman and Kentucky University," *Christian Standard,* Vol VII, No 2 (January 13, 1872), p 11

question that was to be asked was, "Why is it that the Regent has employed only nineteen professors from the Christian Church whilst eleven of the professors in the university are from elsewhere?" Another question to be asked was, "Is John B. Bowman, who is only a Kentucky farmer, the fittest man for the Regency of Kentucky University while we have so many college-bred preachers in the State?"

Furthermore, according to T. D. Butler, Lard and McGarvey suggested that they were ready to start a war against the Regent but they knew it would not do for them to start it themselves. T. D. Butler charged that soon after W. H. Hopson received this letter, he confided the matter to him asking him to write these questions for the *Times*. Butler had refused and had stopped his subscription as a result. Now, Butler wrote these facts out, signed them, had them notarized, and gave them to J. P. Torbitt of Louisville, Kentucky, one of the curators of the school. Torbitt, in turn, gave the statement to Regent Bowman, who now used it against Lard and McGarvey.[5]

No sooner, however, had Bowman published such a letter than a strict denial came from W H. Hopson that he had ever had such a conversation with T. D. Butler. Lard and McGarvey, moreover, emphatically denied that they had ever written such a letter. The matter was presented vigorously to the Fourth and Walnut Streets church, but neither Butler nor Hopson backed down from their previous statement. The result was this argument entered a stalemate. A committee in the Louisville church was appointed to go into the matter, but nothing could be proved. The result was a re-affirmation of confidence in both men, but a severe upbraiding of Butler for ever publishing such a thing even if it were true.

Ben Franklin now began to view the Kentucky University troubles with great alarm He lashed out against Bowman, claiming the church in Kentucky had lost complete confidence in him Bowman is charged with trying to turn a Bible institution into a secular institution.[6] R. M. Bishop, president of the American Christian Missionary Society, was one of the leading members of

---

[5] Anonymous, "The Lexington Difficulties," *Christian Standard*, Vol VII, (April 6, 1872), p 106

[6] Ben Franklin, "Kentucky University," *American Christian Review*, Vol XV, (September 24, 1872), p. 316

the Board of Curators of Kentucky University. Franklin turned
against Bishop   The speeches which Bishop delivered before the
Conventions of 1872 and 1873 were presented while Bishop was
still nursing the wounds of this conflict with Franklin over
Kentucky University.

David Lipscomb had been watching the trouble with keen interest. It was characteristic of Lipscomb to view so many troubles
as largely political in origin, and that was the way he viewed this,
although Franklin denied politics had anything to do with it.
Lipscomb charged that Bowman was a radical in politics and
in sympathy with the "progressive" party in the church. He
claimed the Regent had filled the Board of Curators with his
radical political friends, and of filling the faculty with the same.[7]
That Lipscomb probably had some ground for making such charges
seems evident, but if so, they nowhere appear in the controversy
itself.

In spite of the controversy that was raging the matter rocked
on in that vein until the summer of 1873. An Executive Committee was now appointed to go into the matter and bring forth
a decision   Bowman was chairman of the committee, which gave
assurance that an impartial decision was out of the question
McGarvey, at any rate, was asked to hand in his resignation. At
the instigation of many of his close friends, McGarvey refused.
The Executive Committee, however went before the Board of
Curators with its decision, and the Board officially dismissed Mc-
Garvey as a teacher   Shortly afterward, McGarvey wrote:

The purpose long cherished in the heart of John B Bowman
has at last been accomplished. Mordecai no longer sits at the
king's gate refusing to bow down when the great Haman goes
in and out.[8]

McGarvey had for sometime been considering the matter of ceasing
to teach and to preach and write. Now that he was out of
Kentucky University he determined to give his time to preaching,
and to writing a new commentary on Matthew and Mark

The churches of Kentucky took the dismissal of McGarvey as
in effect an attempt to pull the university away from the brotherhood altogether. They had confidence in McGarvey, and knew

---

[7]David Lipscomb, "Kentucky University," *Gospel Advocate*, Vol XV,
(1873), p 882
[8]J W McGarvey, "My Removal," *Apostolic Times*, Vol V, No
(October 2, 1873), p 4

him to be loyal to their principles. Many decided not to surrender without a fight. A petition, signed by many members of the church in Kentucky was handed to R. M Bishop, chairman of the Board of Curators, but to no avail By the next spring the brethren were determined to try again

Meeting in Louisville, Kentucky on May 28, 1874 a group of brethren agreed to appeal the matter to the State Legislature to change the management of the University. Their proposal was that a Board of managers would be selected by the church in Kentucky to manage the school. These would be elected for five years. Each manager was to be a member of the church. When fifty congregations should propose it, a change in the management of the institution could at any time be brought about. A committee of twenty-one brethren was appointed to try to secure this legislation When the State Legislature met, the vote in the House of Representatives was forty-eight for the change, and forty-seven against. In the Senate, the vote was sixteen for, and twenty against. Since a majority vote in both chambers was necessary, the measure automatically ended.

During the summer of 1874, matters at the college looked dreary so far as the brethren were concerned. Many students were leaving the school, not to return. It was evident that something drastic had to be done. Brethren now began to reconsider the subject. Kentucky University, with its alliance with the State, its A. & M. College, was not the Bacon College of 1847. The pet cub had grown to be a roaring lion and who knew what to do with it? Theoretically, Kentucky University was owned by the churches of Kentucky, but the State also had some claim to the school now. For the churches to try to maintain an ownership of such a University seemed to many ridiculous. How could the church in Kentucky, by its very nature, own such a school? James Challen thought along this line very clearly Speaking of the University said, "Now this is a pretty business for the churches in any State to be burdened with." He pointed out that the churches could not look after Kentucky University. "Brethren." he declared, "stop this thing. There is evil and mischief in it that will outlive the movers of it."[9]

---

[9]James Challen, "Old and New," *Christian Standard*, Vol IX, (January 17, 1874), p 17

As many brethren now thought about it, they began to see that the college could be an instrument of evil as well as of good. Ben Franklin now started out to write a series of articles entitled, "Educational," but which he did not finish. At any rate, he states a new conception that he had concerning the schools. It had never before occurred to him that a school might be a source of evil as well as of good. He stated an opinion that colleges ought to stay with secular work and leave the teaching of the Bible to the churches. He resolved to give this whole subject some careful consideration The question he asked was, "Ought the *church* to build a college of arts and sciences and make it denominational?" He was determined to think this through and come to some more definite conviction about it.

David Lipscomb himself now cocks an eyebrow toward such schools as Kentucky University. His idea of schools, patterned mostly after those of Tolbert Fanning before him, had never been too closely related to that of many in the brotherhood. Fanning had never favored building up Franklin College with a large endowment that it might last through the years. On this point Fanning and Alexander Campbell had formerly differed. Fanning saw that good men might give to a college for an endowment, but years after they were dead, their money might be used to tear down the thing they were trying to build. Lipscomb had the same conviction. He wrote:

We think the most fatal mistake of Alexander Campbell's life, and one that has done much and we fear will do much more to undo his life's work, was the establishment of a school to train and educate young preachers . .

We think the idea of taking young men and withdrawing them in a preacher's school to make preachers of them, results in evil in many ways, without one particle of good attached Christ did not take his teachers from that class. . .

All schools conducted by Christians ought to teach the Bible thoroughly to all who attend no matter what their anticipations for life may be.[10]

During the early part of the decade of the 1870's, Joseph Franklin wielded a powerful pen for the ancient landmarks He followed his father with the greatest of enthusiasm. Unfortunately in years to come a sadder chapter appeared in his life. Less than

---

[10]David Lipscomb, "Schools for Preachers," *Gospel Advocate*, Vol XVII, No 15 (April 8, 1875), p 346

five years after his father died, he began showing signs of yielding his position, and yet later, threw all of his influence behind the very cause he had once fought so vigorously. As Joseph Franklin viewed the situation at Kentucky University, he was led to some extreme points of view. "The arguments in favor of Bible Colleges," he wrote, "are fallacious and the results do not justify expectations. He lays a very serious abuse down at the door of these colleges.

We have been promised trained men who could fairly represent us in the world of letters and science. What have we got? Occasionally there is one such (who would have had an education had there never been a Bible college), but for one such *scores* of pedantic striplings who prate about the illiteracy of our ablest men snivel because people prefer common sense instead of their dry speeches, and make indecent haste to sell out the reformation for the fellowship of sectarians.

Young Franklin goes on to conclude:

I believe, therefore, that the "Bible College" is just the same old sectarian *pod auger* we used to know as the "theological seminary." The current scandal of Kentucky University illustrates and enforces my argument.

During these years also, when Kentucky University was having its troubles, a series of articles made its appearance in the form of letters written to Jacob Creath, Jr by B F. Leonard who lived in New England. Leonard wrote under the name of L. E. Bittle. He never became widely known as a preacher, being more or less secluded in New England. Yet for a score of years beginning at this time, Leonard's writings carried great weight. His letters to Jacob Creath pretended to be written by an outsider, criticizing the brotherhood. The articles are at times rather severe, and were a vital factor in helping to mold a certain attitude toward the Bible Colleges. To Creath, Bittle wrote:

You have abandoned the old and more appropriate name of "Theological Seminary" for that of "Bible College": but because you have thus exchanged names it does not follow that you have in hand an institution differing in any wise from that possessed by the "sects."[11]

Bittle lays the accusation before Creath that the brethren will not listen or pause to consider that such colleges may be wrong. "They take for granted that "whatever is, is right" and are seldom willing

---

[11]B F. Leonard, "Letters to Jacob Creath," *Gospel Advocate*, Vol XVI, (July 2, 1874), pp. 631-635.

to listen candidly to a person who demands of them a valid reason, or rather, who shows them that they have no such reason, for things which they hold or practice   Men like horses, love to travel in a beaten path with the wheels in the ruts "

Bittle's articles frequently cause one to wince a little, but they are good in that there is more truth here than one sometimes likes to admit   Against Bible Colleges he lays some pretty severe charges   "One charge that I have to bring against them is that just intimated—they are worldly.   Like all other colleges, they are founded on money, not on the Bible "   He points out that they have to have an endowment, talent and patronage.   Their success depends upon courting the favor of the world   He charges that whenever a crisis occurs, they can be counted on to take the most popular side in opposition to all principles of right, if need be   He has a word of warning:

I may be misinformed, but I believe your Bible Colleges are no exception to the general rule   Their abuses may not yet be plainly manifested, but they will surely show themselves in all their deformity.

To prove his charges he asks Creath what the colleges had done to check the avalanche of innovations.   He charged that they were all either silent or advocating the wrong side

The troubles at Kentucky University between the years, 1871-75, largely planted the seeds for the controversy to arise in later years against the right of Christians to operate schools in which they could teach the Bible   So far as its lasting effect in the brotherhood is concerned, the controversy at Kentucky University did both good and evil   For some men it served the purpose of helping them to clarify their thinking that schools might later be started which would avoid the errors of the College of The Bible   Evil was done in that men used the controversy at Kentucky University to set them off on the road of wholesale denunciation of schools, no matter how organized, and no matter the principles beneath them.   The churches of Christ have not yet outgrown the full effect of the troubles at Kentucky University nor are they likely to do so in this generation

Going back now to the historical sequence of the University conflict, the future, from the summer of 1874, indeed looked dark   Nothing of great consequence happened to clear the trouble through the following winter   But by the next summer the Board of

Curators had become convinced that something needed to be done to regain the favor of the brotherhood It was decided to give the College of The Bible over to the control of the "brotherhood of Disciples," with an understanding that a vigorous campaign for endowing the college would be pressed. In effect, the College of The Bible was now being separated from Kentucky University. so that the churches of Kentucky would now only look after this college rather than the entire University. The peace was likely the only sensible one that could be brought about under the circumstances, but it was probably little comfort to members of the church to see thousands of dollars formerly given to endow a university slip from them.

The Board of Curators now began taking more steps to get the College of The Bible on a more thoroughly acceptable basis. In June, 1875 the Board appealed to the Kentucky Christian Educational Society to appoint two professors for the College The Educational Society immediately laid this matter before the Committee of Twenty-One, who theoretically represented the will of the churches. Meeting on June 24, 1875 in Louisville, the committee suggested Robert Graham as president of the College of The Bible (Robert Milligan, former president had died a few weeks before.) John W McGarvey was suggested as professor of Sacred History. So, with Graham and McGarvey constituting the faculty, the College of The Bible reopened in the fall of 1875

Two years later it was evident to all that the brotherhood of Kentucky had not rallied to support Graham and McGarvey. The College of the Bible while virtually separate from Kentucky University was not organically separate. The brethren, despite their confidence in both Graham and McGarvey, could not wholly bring themselves to support the College. On July 10. 1877 the Kentucky Christian Education Society met again to discuss what plan to pursue. Meanwhile, the Board of Curators, who still controlled the College of The Bible, decided to dismiss Graham completely and put McGarvey on a part-time basis This step was necessary due to the lack of funds. The action of the Board had virtually disbanded the College of The Bible. The Education Society for the time being could do nothing

The churches in Kentucky immediately became alarmed At a mass meeting of the brethren on July 27, 1877, it was decided that an independent College of The Bible should be formed in Lexing-

ton   At this meeting, they elected Robert Graham, president, and
J W McGarvey, a teacher.   I B Grubbs was also added as a
teacher   For the next quarter of a century the College of The
Bible was associated with these names

As the curtain was being drawn on the drama of the troubles
of Kentucky University, an unfortunate act seemed necessary to
be played   The chief role was to be played by Moses E. Lard.
The decision on the part of the brethren to establish an independent
College of The Bible struck forcibly at the pride of both John
B Bowman and the Board of Curators   The decision virtually
was an admission that the brethren had no confidence in them
Consequently they met the decision for an independent college
with a bitter, non-cooperative spirit   They were strictly forbidden
to meet in the class rooms of Kentucky University, so for a year
the new independent college was forced to meet in the church
building.

Bowman was thoroughly determined to continue the College of
The Bible in connection with the University as a rival institution
of the new independent school   Bowman now looked over the
field for a president   What Bowman now needed more than
anything else to accomplish his purpose of defeating the other
college was a president for the College of The Bible that would
be thoroughly acceptable to the brotherhood.   To get one that
was not was to be defeated before he started.   A few years before
he cared little for this, but now it was absolutely imperative.   He
turned his attention, therefore, to Moses E Lard, who accepted
the offer and became president of the College of The Bible at
Kentucky University.

This was a strange sight indeed.   To the brotherhood generally
Moses E. Lard now seemed to be backing Bowman against his
old friend, McGarvey and against the brotherhood at large in
whose interest he had formerly worked   Such conduct from Lard
seemed unexplainable to them   When they turned to Lard for
an explanation, none was forthcoming.   Brethren shook their
heads and wondered   The periodicals of the brethren ignored
the strange contradiction of Moses E. Lard.   Scarcely did it appear to be discussed except in private conversations of brethren.
Lard himself felt keenly his ostracism.   He moved around silently.
He wrote little, preached little.   Despondency clouded his life;
his disposition became somewhat saturnine.   His wife became ill,

and financial troubles piled in upon him. Life was miserable, so he turned to studying the Scriptures about the life to come, and had some strange misgivings. Then he developed cancer of the stomach. Lard went down to his grave in June, 1880 a sad, broken-hearted man, a much misunderstood man. But the brotherhood threw a mantle of charity over the last three years of his life, and chose to remember him for what he had been.

Actually, however, Lard had not forsaken the brethren at all in becoming president of the rival College of The Bible. Bowman, while consulting Lard about taking the presidency, had privately and confidentially promised that he would step down from the Regency after one year if Lard would take the position. Lard now saw an opportunity of saving Kentucky University for the brethren. When therefore, he became president it was with the hope that Bowman would step down and Kentucky University would be given back to the brethren. But this fact Lard could not tell the brotherhood as yet. Not having any way of explaining his position, he had but to take the criticism as working against their interests.

Under these circumstances the College of The Bible under Lard naturally failed It was only a year in doing so On June 11, 1878 Kentucky University offered the independent College of The Bible the use of its classrooms Here the college met until 1895 when it built its new building which still is in use at Lexington.

Chapter VII

POST-BELLUM DAYS (1865-75)

"These are times that try men's souls," wrote Thomas Paine of those pre-revolutionary war days in colonial America. No less was that decade after the close of the war between the states a time to try men's souls—for the world, for the nation, and most of all for that half-a-million people in America pleading for a return to the ancient order of things. Internal problems were mounting, division and discord were threatening. The restoration plea was being put to its most severe test. The entire future course of the restoration was to depend upon the events of this decade.

These indeed were trying times for the world. The Franco-Prussian War found Europe once more in a baptism of blood. Russia, nursing the wounds of her Crimean War, was watching defiantly for another chance for a struggle in the Balkans which later came by a series of revolts starting in 1875. In England Prime Minister Benjamin Disraeli was slowly pushing English imperialism to the far stretches of the world. America meanwhile, was trying to recover from her Civil War. A grateful nation put General U S Grant in the presidency. Unfortunately however, he met with a financial collapse scarcely equalled by any in the history of the nation. In one year, five thousand business concerns failed. Three million wage earners were out of work. Republican Senator George F Hoar declared that never had corruption gotten so firm a hold on a government as it did during Grant's administration. Postmaster-General Creswell swindled the government out of over three hundred thousand dollars.

Yet these were memorable days. The eloquence of Henry Ward Beecher thundered from Brooklyn. These were the days of Dwight Moody, Ira D Sankey and Charles H Spurgeon days when David Livingstone was doing his final work in Africa, when the doctrine of papal infallibility was being shaped into dogma by the Vatican. These were times when the word, crisis, is written high over the passing of all events.

The restoration movement now launched into an era of intense controversy, both internally and externally. Debating became the custom of the day. Almost every issue of the brotherhood periodicals carried a news item of at least one debate. The following list may be suggestive of the times: In 1871 David Lipscomb met Jacob Ditzler at Gallatin, Tennessee; the same year Clark Braden debated Sam Binnus, a Universalist, at Reynoldsburg, Ohio J Carroll Stark met W. M. Rush, a Methodist, in Gallatin, Missouri F. G. Allen debated Robert Hiner at Mt. Byrd, Kentucky on infant baptism. Braden met A. J. Fishback, a Spiritualist at Sturgis, Michigan. D. R. Lucas met D. B. Ray ("Battle Flag" Ray), a Baptist, at Clayton, Illinois. Jesse L. Sewell met John R Strange, a Methodist, in Hart County, Kentucky. It was common for T. W. Brents and Jacob Ditzler to be debating during these years. Ditzler also found a frequent opponent in L. B. Wilkes. A. J. Lemons met N. Ramsay, a Baptist, in Arkansas. H. T. Wilson debated R. T. Hanks, another Baptist, at Pickensville, Alabama. J. S. Sweeney traveled to Sherman, Texas to meet Jacob Ditzler in 1875, etc.

That the restoration movement was deepening itself, may be indicated in the publishing of so many books. The appearance of McGarvey's commentary on Acts in 1862 set off a wave of interest in commentaries. Lard encouraged McGarvey to put his work through a revision and make it the crowning work of his life. By 1865 Lard was prepared to announce his intention to write a commentary on Romans, which, however, he did not complete for ten years. After Lard's announcement of this intention, W. H. Hopson wrote to W. K. Pendleton suggesting that Pendleton write one on Hebrews and C. L. Loos, one on John. As matters proved it was left to Robert Milligan to write the commentary on Hebrews and B. W. Johnson to publish one on John.

Other great books were in the making. In 1868 the saintly Dr. Robert Richardson presented to the brotherhood his first volume of "Memoirs of A. Campbell," but it was another year before his second volume appeared. "From beginning to end." writes W. K Pendleton, "it shows evidence of an earnest and conscientious worker."[1] After the appearance of the second volume, James T. Barclay wrote:

---

[1] W K Pendleton, "Memoirs of A Campbell—by Dr R Richardson," *Millennial Harbinger*, Vol XXXVII, No 1 (January, 1866), p 43

The ardently cherished expectations of the brotherhood are at
last gratified in the happy completion of this great work—and
truly a complete work it is!

To mention that it is executed in the happiest style of the
gifted biographer, printed on the finest toned paper, and bears
the finished imprint of Lippincott's great establishment, is to
declare it worthy of a most conspicuous place in any library.   .
Nothing is hazarded by the assertion that no Christian preacher
can afford to dispense with this invaluable Thesaurus of our
ecclesiastical history   And the library of any Christian family
that is minus this lucid evolution of primeval Christianity from the
chaos of sectarianism is minus a great blessing [2]

Late in 1867 there came from the press of R. W. Carroll &
Company of Cincinnati, the book *Reason and Revelation* by Robert
Milligan, a book which never proved as popular as his later one,
"Scheme of Redemption," published in 1869   In 1870 Clark
Braden's debate with G. W. Hughey, president of the Cairo
district of the Methodist Church, was published.   J. C. Clymore,
a wealthy member of the church, spent four thousand dollars
producing it.   It was widely acclaimed as one of the great debates
of the restoration, John R. Howard declaring that it sustained the
same relation "to the present state of the controversy" as the
Campbell-Rice debate did in its day.

T. W. Brent's famous work, "The Gospel Plan of Salvation"
made its appearance during these years.   In 1867, Brents edited
an "Alien's Department" in the *Advocate*   Late in 1868 he prepared a series of tracts on the gospel plan of salvation and printed
them in the *Advocate*.   Later these tracts became the basis for
his book

As the church expanded her borders she came more and more
in contact with the denominational world, setting off strenuous
conflicts   The deepening of the church found her leaders undertaking more exhaustive research resulting in the production of
literature calculated to strengthen the church   Yet, another movement, synchronous with these, not quite so favorable to the church
was also developing in that decade between 1865-75.   With the
word, progress, as its key, the church internally was attempting
to expand into many forbidden areas   The missionary society
and the instrumental music, discussed in previous chapters, were

---

[2] J T. B., "Dr Richardson's Memoirs of Alexander Campbell," *Gospel
Advocate*, Vol. XII, No. 1 (January 1, 1870), pp 1-3

but two expressions of the attempt at progress. Back of these and underlying them were dangerous trends of thought The history of the restoration cannot be recounted without some attention to these trends.

TRENDS

Moses E. Lard, writing in the spring of 1865, sounded an ominous note for the future of the church. Lard then wrote:

The prudent man, who has the care of a family, watches well the first symptoms of disease. He does not wait till his wife is helpless, and his children prostrated He has learned that early cures are easy cures, while late ones often fail. On this experience he resolutely acts, and the world applauds his wisdom. Why should not the same judicious policy be acted upon in the weighty matters of religion? . . .

Our churches and people now stretch over a tract reaching from Maine to the farthest coasts of the Pacific, and almost from the Lake of the woods to Panama. Within this wide area exists one of the noblest brotherhood, *and within their hands only,* is kept the cause which is the last hope of earth. . .

But Lard goes on to express more vividly his picture of the future.

He is a poor observer of men and things who does not see slowly growing up among us a class of men who can no longer be satisfied with the ancient gospel and the ancient order of things These men must have changes, and silently they are preparing the mind of the brotherhood to receive changes.[3]

While Moses E. Lard, writing in 1865, declared he saw a group of men growing up in the brotherhood, not content with ancient gospel, but wanting something different; observers writing in later years looked back and declared a great change had come over the church. L. F. Bittle wrote to Ben Franklin at the close of the decade under discussion, saying,

For the last few years your people have had a great deal of unpleasant controversy, and some harsh wrangling, over matters entirely unknown to the past generation of Disciples. They, too, had their troubles, no doubt, and some of them may have said bitter words in consequence of personal disagreements. But they never had anything like the alienation that now exists in certain places in regard to matters which should not be so much as named among a people who claim to stand before the world as the repre-

[3]Moses E Lard, "The Work of the Past—The Symptoms of the Future," *Lard's Quarterly,* Vol. II, No 3 (April, 1865), pp 251-262

sentative champions of the Bible, and the Bible alone, as the rule of faith and practice [4]

Henry Hathaway was an old elder in the church at Covington, Kentucky where Ben Franklin had preached for many years Late in 1868 Hathaway wrote to Franklin:

When I embraced Christianity the church was a city sitting upon a hill, all beautiful and joyous, a green spot in this world of sin Now the pride of life, the lust of the eye and the lust of the flesh are crowding into Zion, the beautiful city of God.[5]

Indicative of the line of thought was the feeling at a meeting of brethren held in Louisville, Kentucky during the summer of 1868 David Lipscomb attended, found many pleasant things, but heard some unfavorable comments:

Some were saying it was useless to try to get back to primitive Christianity, could not be done, and if done, wouldn't be desirable in this present age. We heard the assertion made that without more organization than God gave the churches in the beginning, the world could not be evangelized .

Robert Graham who was ordinarily a man of milder moods, saw there was a radical change underway in the church during these years Graham wrote:

. . there is among ourselves a falling off from the simplicity of the gospel, a conforming to the mode of the *other* denominations, the loss of zeal for the spread of the gospel for fear people will think us solicitous only to build up a party, the decrease of Bible reading and study among us of late, the growing disposition to recognize the distinction of clergy and laity in our churches, and among much more that might be named, our conforming to the unscriptural phraseology of sects, to say nothing of our adopting many of their anti-scriptural customs With the uniform experience of past ages before us, the tendency of men to-make the gospel popular under the plea of extending its influence, and that, too, even at the cost of its purity and power to save, should make us keen to detect and fearless in our condemnation of all departures from the faith [7]

A catacysmic event has upset all the routine of living for society after the war and it sensed that its foundation had been

[4] B F Leonard, "Who Are Responsible?" *American Christian Review*, Vol XVIII, No 4 (January 26, 1875), p 29
[5] Henry Hathaway, "Covington Church," *American Christian Review*, Vol XII, No 1 (January 5, 1869), p 2
[6] David Lipscomb, "The Louisville Meeting," *Gospel Advocate*, Vol X, No 31 (July 30, 1868), p 723
[7] Robert Graham, "The Signs of the Times," *Apostolic Times*, Vol I, No 1 (April 15, 1869), p 4

shaken and started a search for a new one. Some believed that this change in society demanded a change in the church to fit the times.

The frontier had pushed to the west, and the mid-west found itself no longer a sparsely-settled wilderness but a deepening, rapidly-increasing settlement. Crude log cabins, the huts of frontier life, were being replaced by larger, more permanent homes Railroad lines tied the towns together, and gradually industries grew in larger cities. As the cities grew, men lived on fixed incomes The backwoodsman became an oddity. Culture, education, money—these came more and more to mark society.

When, therefore, the Civil War closed, thoughtful brethren contemplating the future, recognized that in certain areas changes must come. Preachers would change their styles of delivery, churches would build better meeting houses. There was little conflict over these points. Brethren were ready to admit the influence of environment in these realms, they were hardly prepared, however, to see the church undergo a complete change in those realms of scripture teaching where the authority of God's word was at stake. Conflict, fierce and unrelenting, was at this point inevitable.

The demand for progress among some took on various characteristics In some cases it threatened the basic conception of what constituted a New Testament Church There was a definite trend to make the church another sect among sectarians; another denomination in denominationalism. There was also abundant evidence of a definite revolt against the past Men who symbolized the previous generation were set for a stormy session. Progress also courted a more fashionable appeal to the rich by what many considered an extravagant expenditure for church buildings The cry for progress also demanded a new position for the preacher and a different content to his message Many were convicted that if they had to surrender the fundamental teachings of the Bible, teachings the earlier pioneers held, they would refuse "progress" at all costs. It was this method of looking at the question that gave the controversy additional fierceness.

Ben Franklin stood as a living symbol of the past Against all departures from the word of God, he steeled himself for a vigorous fight He became, therefore, a target for the friends of "progress" in the church In the spring of 1872 Franklin wrote

It is now an undisguised fact that there is a party in the ranks that have been troubled for years about *our influence,* or *the influence of the* REVIEW.   The party in question have and do now consider our influence in the way of what they desire to accomplish.   We have known this for years and understood it through and through, and had not at any time, and have not now, a doubt about the cause of it.   We have watched this opposition closely, and thought about it, and the grounds of it, as well as how the difficulty could be relieved . .

Franklin stated that for years he had tried to be kind, ignore the bad feeling against him, but now it could no longer be done

Who are they that are against us?   They are the men who think that much of the work by A Campbell will have to be *undone*. the friends of the organ in worship, of extravagant, fine and houses of worship, festivals, fairs, organ concerts in churches, etc [8]

Because Franklin refused to go along with the popular trend of progress, he was spoken of as being a "millstone around the neck of the reformation "   It is interesting to ask the reason for this

Wherein are we a "millstone around the neck of the reformation?"   In our decided and determined opposition to the departures being made from the primitive gospel   In our opposition to church fairs, festivals, church concerts, organ concerts, useless outlay in gorgeous and fashionable temples of folly and pride, called "churches," instruments of music in worship, etc   We have sinned against *Dr. Progress, Mrs Fashion, Sirs Custom*. and offended the taste of their friends and the *spirit of the world in* general, and have thus become a millstone around the neck of pride, folly, arrogance and self-importance in general, the lusts of the flesh, the lusts of the eye, and the pride of life in general
We have failed to appreciate church fairs, festivals and entertainments, as a means of raising money for the Lord
We have no scheme to defend, no hobbies to ride, nor enemies to pursue   We have our Lord and His cause squarely before us. To please Him and maintain his cause is all we have to do   .
We are opposed to *no man,* but opposed to all *departures from the faith.*   We stand not in opposition to men but error   .[9]

Trouble between Ben Franklin and Isaac Errett had been

[8]Ben Franklin, "The Editor of the Review," *American Christian Review*. Vol XV, No 19 (May 7, 1872), p 148
[9]Ben Franklin, "Prophecy Revived," *American Christian Review*, Vol XV, No 27 (July 2, 1872), p 212

smouldering for some time. The two men were not standing on the same foundation During the years, 1871 and 1872, the two clashed bitterly on several issues. Errett began to refer to Franklin as an "alarmist" G. W. Rice, in answer to Errett, wrote:

But, after all, he appears to us to be more alarmed than any of those he would hold up to ridicule and to be laughed at. He is no alarmist himself. He never warns the people against danger either from within or without No, no, in his view of things there is no danger Henry Ward Beecher is no alarmist, either. Anything that has the semblance of religion is acceptable with him Baptism, or no baptism, immersion, sprinkling, pouring, or no water at all All, or either, or none Who ever heard from him a note of warning against departures from the simplicity of the Apostolic Practice and worship? Did he reach his present position at a single leap? Was it not by small beginnings under the specious plea of *expediency?* a word that, with some among the Disciples, has become a screen and a vail to pull over the eyes of the confiding and unsuspecting, and behind which some of our wise ones and learned scribes, not excepting our humorous brother of the *Standard,* fly, when hard pressed for something to justify their departure from Apostolic practice [10]

It was obvious that the abuse heaped upon Ben Franklin by the *Christian Standard* came not because Franklin was departing from the faith and introducing innovations Franklin had undergone no change. The *Standard,* however, conceived its role to be that of "moving forward," adapting the church to changing environmental factors. Franklin resisted these changes, clinging to the older practices Very correctly, then, did Franklin write:

We learn that a few men among us are now expressing regret that we are taking *such a course in our old days*—that we are *spoiling all we did in former years,* etc In this they are like the man standing on the landing boat, who thinks the shore is coming to him, they think that change is in us, but are unconscious of the *change in themselves* They point to nothing in which we have changed, nothing new in us. Their trouble with us is about the new things they are introducing, the new departure they are making, their *progression,* which is really retrograding We have put a vast amount of hard work into this cause—the great reformatory movement in which we are engaged, and men whose voices are now still in death, and whose faces are no more seen among us, have put forth their best energies and most faithful efforts, till

---

[10]G W Rice, "Alarmists," *American Christian Review,* Vol XV, No 43 (October 22, 1872), p 340.

they breathed their last breath, and we do not intend now to give up the work, nor the glorious principles for which we have so long battled, but intend to stand by these principles firmly till the last, and to the men true to them, and that intend to stand by them

What *course* are we pursuing that they regret? What principle or truth are we departing from? Can they tell? Not a man of them. What good work have we not stood to firmly from first to last? We defy them to point to one. What has happened false in principle or practice that we have not opposed squarely all the time?[11]

Franklin and men of a similar school of thought were looked upon as being "perverse" and "stubborn." A correspondent, signing his name "Carl Crab," wrote an article, entitled "Franklinian Stupidity," as a satire against these men.

The term at the head of this article is not used in any offensive sense, but simply as a brief descriptive phrase by which we recognize a large class of the brotherhood, of whom the editor of the *Review* is almost a perfect specimen.

It is the common conclusion among the more liberal and progressive brethren that the above-minded class have, for years past, been exhibiting a stubborn and perverse stupidity in reference to the progress of the age.

Long since they became a real pest upon the body ecclesiastic, by standing directly in the way of those grand conceptions being realized which the more literary, refined, and charitable brethren have presented from time to time for the adoption of the Christian brotherhood.

It is really provoking to think that so many propositions for the adoption of means and practices intended to popularize our religious movement, and break down these distinctions between us and the other denominations which have to some degree united them in opposition to us, should be so stupidly and perversely opposed.[12]

Twenty years earlier Franklin was regarded as a champion for the truth. Although he had not changed his position, and was still fighting for the same principles, Franklin was regarded as a "pest upon the body ecclesiastic" and a "millstone around the neck of the reformation." What strange bewilderment must have clouded the mind of Ben Franklin!

The trend toward denominationalism. The demand for progress was also characterized by the fact there seemed to be clear indi-

[11]Ben Franklin, "A New Phase," *American Christian Review*, Vol XV, No 47 (November 19, 1872), p 372

[12]Carl Crab, "Franklinian Stupidity," *American Christian Review*, Vol XV, No 14 (April 2, 1872), p 105

cations that the church was drifting to the status of another sect among the sectarians. Reference to the above correspondence by Carl Crab will show that the "progressive party" considered it provoking that anyone would resist their attempt to break down the barriers with the denominations and resist the attempt to popularize the church with these denominations.

L. F. Bittle, in another of his famous letters to Jacob Creath, struck at this general disposition:

The greatest danger that threatens you, as a religious brother-erhood, is the rapidly growing disposition, manifested by your so-called educated men, to elevate your people into the dignity of a sect, a denomination, with a name, policy and organization in harmony with those employed by the various parties into which Christendom is so unhappily divided [13]

Moreover, the addition of a new periodical, the *Christian Quarterly,* in 1869 aroused considerable fears for a time that it might be influential in leading the church into this conception of things The editor was W. T. Moore. In 1859, a decade earlier, Moses E. Lard had announced his intention of publishing a periodical to be called *The Christian Quarterly* The intention of calling it this title appears to have stayed with Lard almost to the time of the first issue, when he switched to the name *Lard's Quarterly* The history of *Lard's Quarterly* has already been told. That it failed in the middle of 1868 because of the lack of subscribers is known Now, at the beginning of 1869, W. T. Moore started a *Quarterly,* using the title that Lard had previously intended to use. As men, W. T. Moore and Moses E. Lard were the antithesis; either would have been glad to have reflected upon the other. Did W. T Moore establish the *Christian Quarterly* almost as soon as *Lard's Quarterly* failed as a taunt to Lard? One can but wonder.

Moore was popularly regarded as a man of extreme liberal ideas Sometime previous, he had been responsible for publishing Campbell's famous *Lectures on The Pentateuch.* In the introduction, he had written of the church as a denomination which had been founded by Thomas and Alexander Campbell and that it was a branch of the Baptist denomination. Then, more recently Moore had preached that the church of the New Testament was in a

[13]B F Leonard, "Letters to Jacob Creath—No II," *American Christian Review,* Vol XVI, (July 22, 1873), p 225.

state of infancy, but that it needed to grow into manhood [14]
Moore, himself, said of the *Quarterly*, that ". . . its main contention was for a liberal interpretation of the Disciple movement and
a support of all worthy enterprises in the interests of the movement "[15]

The appearance of the *Christian Quarterly* was hailed as a great
step forward by most brotherhood periodicals   David Lipscomb,
however, saw it to be an omen of evil things to come, and so he
wrote

Almost every paper among the brotherhood, to some extent,
save the *Advocate* and *Apostolic Times*, has given an unqualified
commendation ot the first number of the *Quarterly*   Yet if some
things and matters that are there given prominence be true or
right, the present effort at return to Apostolic Christianity is a
senseless and criminal movement   I refer to the article on "Indifference to Things Indifferent "   Saying nothing in reference to
the bitter, unchristian spirit that pervades it, the tendency of its
matter is to destroy entirely the plea for conformity to the word and
institutions of God   We must express, too, candidly our fears
of the influence of the *Quarterly* under its present management
A *Quarterly* should be eminently sound and discriminating in its
teachings—a display of superficial learning is nothing

Lipscomb proceeded to speak of W. T Moore as one who had
courted the "association and fellowship of the sects in their clerical
association," and then added

Now, brethren, without prejudice or querulousness we protest
that such things are unpardonable in a *Quarterly*, that the tendency
of these things is to destroy the moral power and spirit of the
children of God   The tendency is to lower their claims as the
churches of Christ and degrade them to a position of a mere sect
among sects [16]

The trend toward fashionable church buildings   There was
perhaps no event that stirred up more bitter feelings than the
opening of the wealthy Central Christian Church of Cincinnati,
where W T Moore was the preacher   R M Bishop, president
of the American Christian Missionary Society, former mayor of
Cincinnati, and later, governor of Ohio, was one of its elders   At
the opening of its new church building early in 1872, Ben Franklin

[14]David Lipscomb, "Indications of Progress," *Gospel Advocate,* Vol XV,
No 22 (May 29, 1873), pp 515-521
[15]W T Moore, *Comprehensive History of the Disciples of Christ* (New
York Fleming H Revell Company, 1909), p 558
[16]David Lipscomb, "Christian Quarterly," *Gospel Advocate,* Vol XI, No
17 (April 29, 1869), p 395

apparently felt that the time of the Antichrist was here, and he was less sure than ever that W. T. Moore might not be he. Instrumental music, missionary societies, and other similar steps had caused heated controversy, but nothing excelled the intensity and bitterness that arose when the Central Christian Church moved into its new building.

The Central Christian Church spent one hundred and forty thousand dollars for a new meeting house and eight thousand dollars for a new organ, the organ not having previously been used in this congregation Ben Franklin attacked this as an appeal to the worldly, the carnal, and pride in human hearts. It was a positive indication that the church had surrendered the spirit of Christ for the spirit of the world, thought Ben Franklin.

That Franklin was both right and wrong in various phases of this controversy seems to us evident. That Franklin was right in opposing the introduction of the organ is readily admitted, but the principle would have been the same had the organ been given to the church. The spending of eight thousand dollars for an organ merely made it worse. That this congregation had apparently forsaken the spirit of Christ for the spirit of the world will appear more evident in the further remarks. The only question is, did the expenditure of one hundred forty thousand dollars indicate this worldly spirit?

Ben Franklin would have been the first to agree that the building of a church building was a matter left purely to human discretion. While God commands meeting for worship, the place of meeting is left to human wisdom. The cost, size, looks, and structure of that place of meeting is left to the discretion of man, for God does not legislate upon these matters. All of this Franklin recognized. But, was there a place where a line could be drawn between extravagance and necessity? It was right that these brethren should have a building to meet their needs. Was it human pride that caused brethren to want to erect a structure extravagant enough to attract the worldly great, and compare with the finest cathedrals of sectarianism? Franklin thought so, and truly the lesson of history appears much in his favor. It is a historical fact that churches spending extravagantly on buildings seldom remain satisfied with the simple gospel more than one generation.

The Central Christian Church was, in the days when Alexander Campbell published the *Christian Baptist,* known as the Sycamore

Street Baptist Church It was a branch of the Enon Baptist Church located on Walnut and Baker Streets just above Third Street The Enon Church had become so large that a new congregation had been proposed Letters of dismissal were granted to one hundred and fifty members who formed the nucleus of the Sycamore Street Baptist Church Jeremiah Vardeman, who was converted through reading the *Christian Baptist*, was the preacher for the Enon Baptist Church

At first, the Sycamore Street Congregation had met in the Council Chamber on Fourth Street, then in Talbott's schoolhouse on Fifth Street, then in an upper room in an old copper shop on the corner of Vine and Columbia After this, it built its own meeting house on Sycamore Street above Fifth. This was in the fall of 1828 James Challen was the first preacher for this new congregation, although he at times alternated with D. S. Burnet. Walter Scott preached here for a short time in 1829. In 1837 Campbell debated Purcell in this building

Through hearing Alexander Campbell and through reading the *Christian Baptist*, the Sycamore Street Baptist Church had dropped its practices and begun working for a restoration. Since most members lived in the west part of town, its building was sold to the Methodists, and the church started meeting at Walnut and Eighth Streets It was in this building that the first convention of the American Christian Missionary Society was held Here, the church continued to meet until 1872

In 1870 the congregation started the construction of a new building on Ninth Street near Central Avenue The estimated cost was one hundred thousand dollars which reached to one hundred and forty before it was finished In January, 1871, a lecture room was completed, and dedicated A year later, the whole building was finished For style, architectural beauty, it surpassed anything known to the brotherhood

The dedication of the new building was held on February 11, 1872 The house was packed and the aisles were filled with chairs to seat the overflow audience For the first time in the history of the congregation the sound of the organ came from behind the pulpit. W T. Moore spoke on the words of Christ on the cross, "It Is Finished " He remarked that when Christ spoke those words it was both an occasion of sorrow and gladness —sorrow because Christ was dying, but gladness because his death meant the work of Christ in human redemption was finished He applied these words to the building in which they were meeting

Franklin's ire knew no limitations He charged that the organ had been introduced over the protest of the majority

Many pretty things have been said by those determined to make the church a fashionable place of resort and entertainment They would not introduce the organ if it would create the least disturbance! if it would wound the conscience of any member of the church! etc, etc. But the "Central Christian Church" have put it in, knowing that an overwhelming majority of their brethren cannot worship with it, and flourish it before our faces in the public prints in their description of their extravagant building, in which they have expended more money than has been given to the General Missionary Society during the past ten years from all sources.[17]

Franklin, to make it clear that he was not an extremist, wrote in the next week's issue of the *Review*

We are not unreasonable, nor an extremist, nor would any allusion we made, nor logic used by us, lead to having no house in which to live or in which to meet and worship; but there is a vast difference between a comfortable and plain house in which to live, or in which to meet and worship, and extravagant temples rivaling the worldly temples around us. We may and ought to have the former, but ought not to have the latter.[18]

Forty years earlier Franklin had come to Cincinnati to preach for the congregation on Sixth Street. On the way to worship that morning an old man advised him to remember that he was preaching to *people,* so preach the same in the city that he did in the country. A few years after that, when the Episcopalians erected a building costing one hundred thousand dollars, "we talked of it as an example of extravagance beyond all endurance." Then he recalled that Alexander Campbell had told the Baptists that the only thing that kept them from being as vain and pompous as the Episcopalians was the lack of means. "But," Franklin went on,

little did he think then that those professing to be Christians, Disciples of Christ, and standing with him pleading for the "ancient order of things" and the "gospel restored" would ever have opened the way for such a document as the one we reproduce in another column to be flourished before the world This is the "gospel restored"—the "ancient order of things"—with a ven-

---

[17]Ben Franklin, "Central Christian Church," *American Christian Review*, Vol XV, No 8 (February 20, 1872), p 60
[18]Ben Franklin, "Central Christian Church," *American Christian Review*, Vol XV, No 10 (March 5, 1872), p 76

geance! This worldly and carnal display will send grief home to many hearts of the old saints. Many thousands now living will grieve [19]

Reaction among the brethren was divided   Isaac Errett came to the rescue of the Central Church, declaring that such a price naturally sounded high to a country man.   E. P Belshe, however, backed Franklin ardently.

If the Pope should happen to visit Cincinnati and lose his way to the Cathedral, he might sit pretty comfortably in *Central* and take notes of the advancement of his religious institutions [20] Robert Richardson, biographer of Alexander Campbell, wrote Franklin, saying that Campbell would never have agreed to such an expenditure of funds. Going further, he writes.

  . While I have no disposition to denounce or harshly to criticize the erring, I cannot but express my sincere regret at the course which the Central Church in your city has thought proper to adopt in relation to the matters above mentioned [21]

Indicative of the drift in this congregation was the following advertisement which appeared in one of the secular papers:

GRAND ORGAN CONCERT
At Central Christian Church, Thursday Evening, February 29, 1872, for the Benefit of the Ladies' Furnishing Committee

PROGRAMME
PART I
1. Overture to Masniello—Auber; M Dell
2 Offertoire, op 23 in Ab.—Batiste; C. M. Currier
3. Solo and Chorus (organ arrangement)—Handel. Wilbur F. Gole.
4. Offertoire—Wely; Henry G. Andre
5. Organ Solo—Batiste; Henry J. Smith

PART II
1. Offertoire in G—Wely; M. Dell
2 Serenade—Schubert, Wilbur F. Gole
3 Selections—Henry J. Smith
4. Improvisation on Home Melodies; C. M. Currier

[19]Ben Franklin, "Central Christian Church," *American Christian Review*, Vol XV, No 8 (February 20, 1872), p 60
[20]E P Belshe, "Dim Religious Tone," *American Christian Review*, Vol XV, (May 7, 1872), p 149
[21]Robert Richardson, "Brother Moore Again," *American Christian Review*, Vol XV, No 16 (April 16, 1872), p 124

5 Fantasie—Andre, Henry G Andre
Admission,,one dollar
The Church will be opened at seven o'clock. Concert will
begin at eight

After the above advertisement appeared, Ben Franklin copied it
and then added:

Reader, what say you of this? Primitive Christianity! Ancient
order of things!²²

The objection to the course of the Central Christian Church
lasted only a few months and was intensely bitter. As a controversy it was contemporary with that at Kentucky University, instrumental music and the Louisville Plan. Moreover, the same
parties were arrayed against each other in each case. The conduct
of the Central Church probably did more than anything else to
convince Ben Franklin and his associates of like-mind that the
opposition had completely forsaken the spirit of Christ in favor
of the world. The breach in the brotherhood was to grow wider

The trend in preaching The cry for progress also expressed
itself in new trends for preaching Indeed, this was the point
where the drift now centered. Some brethren were·becoming
extremely intolerant toward the preaching of the "first principles."
Preachers stressing these were less popular than before. The cry
for higher spirituality was everywhere heard. J B Briney, realizing a change had come over the content of the sermons, wrote
the following:

There are some among us who seem to have imbibed quite an
antipathy to first principles They love to talk about a "higher
spiritual," a "deeper piety," a "broader love," etc Were it not
that these men make such lofty pretensions to a "higher spirituality," you would be led to think that this is the very article they
most need. . . .

The man that is tired of the first principles of the doctrine of
Christ is tired of the only thing that can convert men to God, and
lift their souls in holy aspirations toward heaven. But when a
man says he is tired of first principles, what does he mean? Does
he mean he is tired of faith? No He has much to say about
faith It is his theme on all occasions Does he mean that he is
tired of repentance? Certainly not He is for repentance, *theoretically*, at least What, then, is the substance of all this opposition to first principles and to the men who are devoted to them?
Simply this· "I am tired of baptism for the remission of sins"

²²Ben Franklin, "Central Christian Church," *American Christian Review*,
Vol XV, No 13 (March 26, 1872), p 100

This is what you get when you summer all this talk about a "higher spirituality." etc, down [23]

Men were heard to speak frequently of "legalism" and "the spirit of the New Testament " Preachers were now preaching, not the "letter" of the New Testament, but the "spirit" of it, an attitude that Errett championed J S Lamar, his biographer, defined the point of view as follows

The conditions by which we are confronted, being wholly unknown to the apostles, their practice *cannot be* applicable to these conditions in letter, and must be pleaded only in its spirit [24]

A class of men yet remained, however, who preached the first principles, who insisted upon a "Thus saith the Lord" in their preaching Against this class of men, the ugly title of "legalist" was continually hurled Ben Franklin, Moses E Lard John W McGarvey, David Lipscomb, and Tolbert Fanning were now classed as "legalists " Some who laid claim to have progressed a little more had reached the point of denying completely that there was a law under Christ This spirit, David Lipscomb saw arising, and wrote

We have been pained for some time to see reproach cast upon those who insist upon faithful obedience to the law of God, as the condition of his blessing, as *legalists,* and the principle that required the submission as *legalism* Some of our progressive brethren have even gone so far as to deny there is any law in the New Testament as there was in the Old

The tendency of our brethren's speculative distinctions on these subjects is to weaken the scene of obligation to comply with the full requirements of God's will, and to give people license to follow some impulse, passion or prejudice which they may conceive to be the suggestion of faith within, that becomes law to itself [25]

Moses E Lard, however, looked with some pathetic humor upon these more progressive men He wrote·

They are partial to the "pious" in other sects; yet they pounce unmercifully upon the faults of their own brethren They appear doubtful that their brethren are right in anything They claim to have made greater progress in spirituality, in the inner life, and in the secret walks with God

Are they less tyrannical than others? or more lowly in their look, in their walk, or in their talk? Eat they less than their

[23] J B Briney, "What We Need," *Apostolic Times,* Vol III, No 21 (August 31, 1871), p 161

[24] J S Lamar, *Memoirs of Isaac Errett,* Vol II, p 253

[25] David Lipscomb, "Legalism and Obedience," *Gospel Advocate,* Vol XIII, No 17 (April 27, 1871), pp 389, 390

brethren of the vulgar rout; pray they more, or just less coarsely? Give they more than others to the cause of God, work they more assiduously, or grumble less? In what do they excel? I clamor, in what? . . . No one emotion of piety ever trembled in their souls to which their brethren of the baser sort are strangers. Closely as they have gone to the presence of God, so closely have gone we; deeply as they have drunk at the fount of spiritual life, so deeply have drunk we. Not a flower blooms on the tallest peak their feet have ever pressed whose fragrance we have not inhaled These men lack the gift to see themselves as others see them [26]

These "progressive" men, Lard went on to say, were sweet and pious as long as a sectarian was their mark, but they were "ferocious as a hungry hippopotamus" when a brother was to be dispatched. In the pulpit their greatest delight appeared to be to preach so that no one knew what they believed. Their greatest desire was to let the world know they were out of sympathy with their brethren These men, in their pursuit of a "higher spirituality," had abandoned preaching on the gospel plan of salvation

Ben Franklin admits that "progress" is a good word, but he expressed a fear that brethren misunderstood it. These who cried for "progress" showed an extreme dislike for a "Thus saith the Lord" and for a "It is written," said Franklin. He agreed that men needed progress in knowledge, but he called upon these men to distinguish between progress and apostasy. He also pointed out that those who advocated progress would do well to improve upon their tempers "We never allude to any of their progressive ideas," writes Franklin, "when we do not expect most harsh treatment." "These men who know more," he adds, "ought to show a little more patience until we learn better or die off."[27]

The place of the preacher. Not only had the demand for progress caused the type of preaching to be changed, but it brought also a change in the place and position of the preacher. Moses E Lard, writing in 1865, declared this to be one of the symptoms of future apostasy Whereas God ordained a group of elders to rule the local congregations, Lard declared that a new class of officers, unknown to the Bible, had now arisen. These were the "pastors," men who took the oversight away from the elders. Lard writes:

---

[26] Moses E Lard, "The Progressive vs The Sound," *Apostolic Times,* Vol I, No 1 (April 15, 1869), p 1

[27] Ben Franklin, "Progress," *American Christian Review,* Vol XIV, (August 22, 1871), p 268

There is no such function or position in the church as that of
pastorate to be filled by a special class of men different from the
elders   . Now, in view of the truth as here stated, we cannot
but feel alarmed at the disposition on the part of many of our
churches—a disposition which is clearly on the increase, to create
a new office in the church, and to fill it with a class of men wholly
unknown to the Bible.[28]

In another chapter considerable attention will be given to the
study of the pastor as he arose in the restoration movement. Consequently, only a word need be mentioned here. Before human
innovations could get far in the church, a human organization over
the local church had to be devised. The "pastors" of the church
possessed greater authority than they deserved. Most of them
were young men, born and bred of a more modern spirit. Their
consent was readily given to the modern innovations. Those who
did little consenting often did less opposing. Joseph Franklin
wrote

I steadfastly believe that the current innovations might have
been kept out, or might be put out, if preachers were not afraid to
attack them. The Jews cried, "Give us a king." God gave them
Saul   The people now cry: "Give us pastors! give us music;
give us fairs, festivals and lotteries! give us conventions and societies! Allow us innocent amusements! And God is giving them
over to ungodliness and worldly lusts. Presently the profoundly
respectable denomination, "The Disciples' Church," will receive
the right hand of fellowship as an "evangelical church." And then
God will raise up another people who will defend the honor of His
name [29]

It is not without some justification that later in the restoration
many looked at the "pastor" as a potent cause of the departures.

Already in the restoration movement discussion was arising over
the adoption of titles by the preachers which were then peculiar to
the Protestant or Roman Catholic clergymen. Alexander Campbell had been averse to adopting such titles for himself. He wrote·

My name is Alexander Campbell, and by this *alone* I choose to
be known among men   Neither *Mr* nor *Rev* nor *Bishop* accord
with my feelings, calling nor the cause which I plead. . . .

Some of our acquaintance would, methinks, look very much
abashed to be saluted *in the great day* with the title *Reverend*,

[28]Moses E Lard, "The Work of the Past—The Symptoms of the Future,"
Lard's Quarterly, Vol II, No 3 (April, 1865), pp 251-262
[29]Joseph Franklin, "Preachers," *Gospel Advocate,* Vol XV, No 10
(March 6, 1873), pp 234, 235

Elder, Bishop, or *Deacon,* by him who will render to every man according to his works! And how the *Doctors of Divinity* will hang their heads in the presence of that *Paul* whom they have so often misquoted, and of that Saviour whose command. *"Be not called Rabbi,"* they have so often condemned, imagination cannot point, nor ink and paper describe [30]

During the summer of 1853, the following question was sent to the *Millennial Harbinger* "Is it in accordance with the teaching of the Head of the church for her Elders and Evangelists to assume the honorary title of Reverend?" A W. Campbell answered it by saying:

The Christian Church has no honorary titles to confer upon any of her members Her titles are all official, and refer to a work, or class of duties to be performed

The titles of Reverend, Right Reverend, Most Reverend, Reverend Father in God, Reverend and Holy Father, Most Reverend and Holy Father, Lord God the Pope, are all titles of the same category, and we have placed them in the ascending series, from the positive of spiritual pride to the superlative of blasphemy.

These are all contraband wares in the city of our God, but very saleable and desirable in Babylon the Great, where the articles are manufactured. . . [31]

Tolbert Fanning in no uncertain terms blazed away in condemnation of preachers who assumed the title of "Reverend" He wrote:

When Cornelius met Peter, he fell at his feet to REVERENCE him, but Peter took him up and said, "I am a man—worship God." It is idolatry, rank and vulgar, to worship any being in Heaven or upon the earth, save the Father, whom we approach through the Son Rome taught her slaves to reverence the priests, Protestants have adopted the custom, and, worse still, modern infidels, and profane Unitarians, Universalists, and flesh-serving Spiritualists, most wickedly apply the term "Reverend" to their scoffing priests. God will not suffer this insolence forever. Let no good man assume titles which are alone applicable to Deity We assert not too much when we state that all such Popish designations are of the enemy, and become not an humble follower of Jesus of Nazareth.[32]

While, then, preachers of the gospel had a strong aversion to wearing the title, Reverend, earlier in the restoration, by the close

[30]Alexander Campbell, "Bishops," *Millennial Harbinger,* Vol I, No 9 (September, 1830), p 428

[31]A W Campbell, "Queries," *Millennial Harbinger,* Fourth Series, Vol III, No 8 (August, 1853), p 473

[32]Tolbert Fanning, "The Term Reverend Applied to Man," *Gospel Advocate,* Vol II, No 6 (June, 1856), p 192.

of the Civil War the name was beginning to find more frequent use   The church obviously was drifting into the full status of another denomination   The first person of any great significance to apply the title to himself was Isaac Errett.   When he moved into the new church building at Detroit, accepting the position as its minister, he nailed up a beautiful silver doorplate inscribed with "Rev. I. Errett" on it.   At the time considerable objection was raised against it, but to Errett it was an innocent enough title to assume.   J. S. Lamar explains it thus:

. . . It is coming to be more and more widely understood that the Saviour's words do not prohibit the use of any designation which simply makes known *the fact* that the man to whom it is applied is a *preacher*.   It is distinctions *among* preachers—the acceptance of high-sounding titles which elevate the parties *above* their brother ministers—that the divine word seems to forbid   The word *Reverend* before a man's name is universally understood to indicate simply that he is a minister of the gospel   It bears no significance of personal superiority or official eminence [33]

The term admittedly found some struggle before it became acceptable to most preachers.   Thomas Munnell, one of the leading liberal-minded men of this decade, wrote an article with reference to William Pinkerton, son of L. L. Pinkerton   Through no fault of Munnell's, the printer allowed the title "Rev." to be placed before his name.   Brethren arose up in arms.   Munnell correctly explained the error, but then added:

If I had called a minister of the gospel "Rev," I have no idea that it would be a sin against the Holy Ghost   Brother Walk states about the truth when he says it simply means that a man is a preacher, and is certainly a very brief statement of that fact   The term to me is not a desirable one on account of the abuse of it by others, but in itself it is as harmless as any other.[34]

Thus it is seen that in the decade between 1865-1875 the restoration movement had entered a period of transition.   Old principles were being restored; old mottoes were being given new applications.   When the full effect of this transition was to be later felt, the church resulting was to be vastly different than that proposed by the earlier pioneers.

Against these departures, the preachers tabbed "legalists" rebelled, and the restoration movement headed toward an era of

[33]J. S Lamar, *Memoirs of Isaac Errett,* Vol II, p 278
[34]Thomas Munnell, "My 'Rev,'" *American Christian Review,* Vol X, No. 27 (July 2, 1867), p 209.

division. But, who was to be responsible for this division? L. F. Bittle wrote:

Elijah was not to blame for the drought and famine that for three years or more cursed the land of Samaria. He was not the troubler of Israel as Ahab said. It was the wicked king himself that by departing from the way of the Lord, and bringing in the religious devices of his idolatrous neighbors, had incurred the displeasure of the Almighty, and the prophet was but the instrument of divine vengeance.

So it is now. The folks that built costly meeting-houses to please the eye, and introduced organs to gratify the ear, and have since apologized for these things, against the protestations of a great brotherhood, are responsible for all the alienation that has in consequence occurred. The men who left the New Testament plan of evangelizing, and organized sectarian societies to usurp the authority of Christ by creating offices and delegating powers unknown to the apostles, thus rightful independence, and who still in spite of brotherly admonition and scriptural argument, persist in their wild schemes, are responsible for all the strife that their plans have enkindled.[35]

[35]B. F. Leonard, "Who Are Responsible?" *American Christian Review,* Vol XVIII, No 4 (January 26, 1875), p 29

CHAPTER VIII

THE RISE OF NEW LEADERS

Elisha G Sewell and John F Rowe were not closely related in work nor did they agree on some major points of controversy Each, however, had great influence during the last quarter of the nineteenth century. Although each man was born about the same time—only three years apart—death, however, came to Sewell in 1924 and to Rowe, in 1897 Thus, Sewell's work extended a quarter of a century longer The former was a prominent leader of the church in the south, whereas, the latter was equally prominent in the North Each made his contribution and is deserving of a place in the history of the church of the nineteenth century.

E. G SEWELL

"Old-timers" of today who remember the church in the South have the names, "Lipscomb and Sewell" stamped upon their memory Seldom was one man mentioned without the other The two first met at a gospel meeting held near McMinnville. Tennessee around 1858 E. G. Sewell was a student at Franklin College under William Lipscomb, David Lipscomb's older brother This connection afforded Lipscomb and Sewell opportunities to renew their friendships frequently Later, in 1870, when David Lipscomb found himself in need of help in editing the *Gospel Advocate*, he was sagacious enough to see in Sewell an ideal co-worker From January 1, 1870 until Lipscomb's death in the fall of 1917, "Lipscomb and Sewell" formed a team in shaping the cause in the Southland.

The *Gospel Advocate* was conceived to spread the word and encourage the church to better work Neither of its editors, therefore, wrote much about himself This admirable modesty is unfortunate for the historian whose information is necessarily limited

E. G. Sewell was born in the mountainous plateau region of Overton County, Tennessee near Wolf River on October 25, 1830 His birthplace was within one mile of the Kentucky State Line and about twenty-one miles from Livingstone, the county

150

E G SEWELL

seat   Prior to his birth, twelve children had already been born
into the log cabin home of Stephen and Annie Sewell   When the
thirteenth child was born, he was a boy—the eighth—and, like
the other children, had to have a Bible name   Accordingly, he
was christened, Elisha   All but one of the eight boys bore Bible
names   The pair of twin boys was called Caleb and Joshua.
Joshua had died in infancy   Four of the seven boys became gospel
preachers—Isaac, Caleb, Jesse and Elisha

Stephen and Annie Sewell, parents of Elisha G, were of
English descent   Stephen had formerly lived on Clear River in
North Carolina but had moved into East Tennessee where he

married. He and his wife lived in a cabin of hewed logs. It was a double house of the type that was very popular in those early days. There were two rooms down separated by an open hall, and a half-story upstairs. There was a chimney at each end of the house. The upstairs was used for bedrooms. Glass windows were unknown to them.

Living conditions, compared to modern standards, were very poor. It is not likely, however, that they considered them so. In their own way they had comforts. They worked hard and sacrificed much. Their clothing was home-spun. Each boy was given a plot of ground to plant for himself. The crop he raised was sold and the money often used to buy clothing. On Christmas morning each child was given a suit of jeans, and a pair of shoes of undressed red leather This, together with what they bought for themselves, lasted until the next Christmas.

The Sewells were all Baptists. Methodists were scarce in Overton County, the Baptists being most prevalent religious sect. Meetings were great occasions back in these rural churches, and were largely social assemblies. Newspapers were almost non-existent, and the preacher, who went from one community to another, was the chief source of news His importance was thus magnified, despite the fact his ability as a preacher might be negligible.

Country meetings were generally conducted upon Saturdays and Sundays, and people from ten to twenty miles away attended. Saturday's social gathering was largely an exchange of news. People came with no intention of listening to any preaching. Frequently there were several preachers present for the Sunday services, and Baptist custom authorized each to speak. Since each was thought to be guided by the Spirit, the messages were impromptu, and pronounced for their longevity. Often a service which began on Sunday morning lasted on until three or four o'clock in the afternoon. Customs regulating the conduct of listeners were loose, so no one apparently minded how long the service lasted. People were continually getting up and walking out. Sometimes they would go to the spring a half-a-mile away, chat for half-an-hour and then get up and go back for another "hearing." The young people, of course, utilized the time in getting their "courting" brought up to date.

The Sewell family became interested in the restoration plea

through the conversion of an elder son of Stephen Sewell, William B. Sewell to the Church of Christ. In 1840 W. B. Sewell, E. G. Sewell's older brother, married a woman, who was a member of the Church of Christ. W. B. in deference to his wife's wishes, occasionally attended services with her, and learned to appreciate them. Very shortly, he was partaking of the Lord's Supper with these people. So far as the Baptists were concerned he had crossed the rubicon—straight into the darkest heresy.

The Wolf River Baptist Church was a member to the Stockton's Valley Association of United Baptists, a strict group in protecting its orthodoxy. The charge against William B. Sewell came immediately before the Wolf River Baptist Church. As the trial continued, it was evident that this was a matter of house being divided against house; it was Sewell against Sewell William D. Sewell, an uncle of E. G and William B, acted as the moderator. At the trial, William B. raised his New Testament in one hand and the article of faith of the Baptist Church in the other, and asked to know by which he would be tried. People were divided, and William B. Sewell was voted out of the Baptist Church without a trial.

The Sewell boys—Jesse L., Isaac, Caleb and Elisha particularly —regretted deeply the course their brother had taken Jesse L., the oldest of the boys, decided to convert him. William B. expressed a willingness to be converted if it could be shown from the scriptures that he was wrong. To this end Jesse searched the scriptures, but in the process was himself converted. Soon, Isaac and Caleb and the whole Sewell family, except E. G., had abandoned the Baptist Church for the return to apostolic ground. E. G. was younger than the other boys, consequently less versed in the scriptures. He refused to be moved by his family's decision, insisting instead upon studying the Bible for himself. Sewell, in the spring of 1849, started reading his New Testament. On the fourth Lord's Day of October that same year, he was immersed by Jesse L. Sewell, an elder brother. Thus, William B. Sewell, although himself never a gospel preacher, influenced his family, and through them preached the "unsearchable riches."

Family worship was a regular activity with the Sewells. Until Isaac and Caleb left home to teach, it was customary for them to conduct the worship. After this, it was suggested that E. G. conduct it. This became his first attempt at anything related to a public service for the Lord. In the fall of 1851, at the private house of a neighbor, E. G. preached his first sermon.

Education for E. G. Sewell came with great difficulty. As a youth he picked up what learning he could around the rural community, but this was inadequate. The acquiring of a wife, and soon a family, only increased the difficulty. On November 22, 1853 he married Miss Lucy Kuykendall near Cookeville, Tennessee, and for convenience and economy moved in with his father-in-law. Matthew Kuykendall, his wife's father, encouraged him to continue his education in spite of being married. Two years passed, and late in 1855 Professor G. A. Kuykendall took Sewell to Spencer, Tennessee to investigate Burritt College where W. D. Carnes was president. Carnes was sympathetic and encouraging so Sewell rented a house and began preparations to enter school in February, 1856.

Burritt College held Sewell only two years. He studied Latin, Greek and mathematics. A congregation of New Testament Christians met in the town. However, a doom fell over the school when W. D. Carnes left as president. One night Carnes' residence was burned. He could not escape the conviction that he had many enemies who were seeking to ruin him. He could not, therefore, be persuaded to remain longer at Spencer, so moved to East Tennessee University. Carnes' successors at Burritt disappointed Sewell, and before long, he was back to the home of his wife's parents, five miles north of Cookeville.

The same year Sewell moved to Franklin College to study under Tolbert Fanning and William Lipscomb. His return to the Kuykendall home found him in despondency so far as his educational possibilities were concerned. His wife and children demanded his time and money, and this responsibility left scarcely any probability of further education. Nevertheless, when he heard that Fanning and Lipscomb proposed to educate twenty young men at Franklin College with board and tuition free, he decided to look into it. He found he could make arrangements to go, but what was he to do about his family? Providentially, the way was revealed. An unmarried brother of his wife's proposed to open up a boarding house and school at Bloomington Springs but had no one to superintend it. Room and board were offered to Sewell's wife and three children if his wife would take the position. She accepted and on September 1, 1858 E. G.

Sewell entered Franklin College. By studying arduously Sewell completed his course here in one year, graduating in June, 1859

After leaving Franklin College, he gathered up his family and went to the home of James C. Owen in Williamson County. Through the Civil War and for the next five years after, he spent his time preaching in Middle Tennessee. With the exception of a part of 1866 when he was in Mississippi, most of Sewell's preaching was confined to Wilson, Williamson, and Rutherford Counties.

Nothing enlarged the border of Sewell's influence more than his work on the *Gospel Advocate*. Beginning on January 1, 1870 and extended forward over fifty years, the name of E G Sewell became familiar to *Advocate* readers. Upon receiving the invitation from David Lipscomb to assist in the publication of the *Advocate,* Sewell accepted the opportunity with little reluctance. His family had continued to grow, and, as Sewell was absent so much from home, the task of caring for the family was getting to be too great for his wife. Too, his observation was that the *Advocate* was growing, and that he was being extended an opportunity to do a larger and possibly more influential work. Besides, Nashville was growing. Although the church in 1870 was weak in the city, possibilities existed for a large extension of the work. It was not therefore a difficult decision to make.

Edgefield, Tennessee lay east of Nashville across the Cumberland River Long since it has become a part of Nashville proper 801 Boscobel Street in Edgefield became the address of E. G Sewell on January 1, 1870 and remained his address as long as he lived. This street was then in the outskirts of town. A large pasture across the street offered a good opportunity for the Sewell's to keep a cow. With the passing of time, however, the city grew, and Sewell's living changed with differing environmental circumstances.

Were one writing a biography of a military general, there would be much of the wild, the turbulent, the picturesque to recount to make the pages gleam with activity. But to recall the history of one of God's servants, a man who lived a quiet, peaceful life, there is little of the colorful and the romantic The remainder of Sewell's life was occupied in preaching and writing The first fifteen years in Nashville found him working earnestly to build

up a congregation in East Nashville.   Probably the greatest disappointment of his life came when this church adopted the innovations flooding the church.   To recall the meetings Sewell
held would be to little advantage.

Moderation in everything was one of his prominent characteristics.   The impression he left upon all was that he wanted to
please God and go to heaven.   He made no effort to please men
nor did he make any pretense to be great despite the fact that
his was true greatness.   He loved to read the Bible, and even
upon the most unusual occasions would be found with the Bible
upon his lap, almost completely oblivious to his surroundings.   He
was gentle, earnest, and persuasive in his appeals to sinners.   His
heart was filled with loving-kindness toward all men.   In personal
appearance he was always neat.   Some remarked that E. G.
Sewell was the "cleanest-looking" man they ever saw.   He never
appeared to be anxious about anything.

The Sewell home became known for its hospitality.   As the
church grew in Nashville, and the *Gospel Advocate* became more
widely read and known, the city became a radiating point for
the gospel in the South.   Traveling preachers found themselves
welcome at Sewell's home.   He not only *extended* invitations to
Christians, but in sincerity and earnestness, *urged* them to be his
guests.

E. G. Sewell was methodical.   F. B. Srygley stayed in the
Sewell home while he conducted a tent meeting at Tenth and
Fatherland Streets in 1891.   At precisely the same time every
morning Sewell would rap on the door and call out, "Well,
preacher, are you ready for breakfast?"   Syrgley was then a
young man, and had always heard that a preacher should eat
little "supper" if he were going to preach that night.   Syrgley
enjoyed eating too well to want to follow that counsel, and therefore, was glad of the advice Sewell gave him, "I always eat about
the same amount whether I preach or whether I listen to some
one else preach."

Death came to E. G. Sewell on Sunday, March 2, 1924 at 1:45
A. M.   He died at his old residence, 801 Boscobel Street where
he had lived fifty-four years   His funeral was conducted the
next day at the Russell Street Church in Nashville with S. H.
Hall and J. C McQuiddy preaching.

JOHN F. ROWE

The *American Christian Review* was unquestionably the most influential paper in the brotherhood for over a quarter of a century after 1856. The editor, Ben Franklin, was, doubtlessly, the most popular preacher in the church after Alexander Campbell. For eleven years John Franklin Rowe served as an associate-editor under Franklin later to become his successor as editor of the

Review. Rowe, too, founded the *Christian Leader* in 1886, and served as its editor until his death in 1897. Thus, through a period of intense crisis the name of John F. Rowe was often before the church. Whether his lasting influence be regarded as important or not, it is a historical fact that he played a major part in the later years of restoration movement

Martin Rowe and his wife Martha Magdalena Alshouse Rowe

were a young couple living on a farm near Greensburg, Pennsylvania in 1827.   Both were of German descent; poor but industrious, and devoutly Lutheran   To them was born on March 23, that year an infant son whom they named John Franklin. In accordance to their religious beliefs the infant son was taken to the Lutheran Church nearby and "conscripted in infancy" by sprinkling.

Migration was characteristic of the times.   It was a common sight to see wagon trains pushing westward, and to hear friends and neighbors discuss moving.   When, therefore, John Franklin was only twelve years old, his family migrated into Ohio and settled near Wooster   Here, John F. Rowe spent his childhood

Being a farmer did not militate against his following some other occupation as well   Martin Rowe followed the trade of a bricklayer, and quickly taught this trade to John F   However, Rowe informs us that when he was twenty years old, he took up the trade of a shoemaker.   This gave him a work he could perform in the winter time when the weather made bricklaying impossible. He worked every day from seven o'clock in the morning until nine o'clock at night, and saved small amounts of money.   During these early years, he attended "Parrott's Academy."   Educational opportunities were limited, so Rowe read extensively and became well informed on many subjects, especially history.

The winter of 1827-28, when Rowe was twenty years old, he first came in contact with the restoration plea.   His associates were heard to speak contemptuously of the "Campbellites," who were then conducting a meeting at Bentley's School House.   Meetings were commonly conducted with two preachers on the ground —one to do the preaching and the other the "exhorting."   Almon B. Green, a logical and argumentative man, was the preacher, and J. Harrison Jones was the exhorter.   A man of strong emotions, also tender and somewhat eloquent, Jones had strong persuasive ability with the sinner   Known affectionately to his many friends as "Uncle Harry," Jones became a close friend and adviser to John F Rowe in later years   It was out of curiosity that Rowe went to the meeting at first, but soon he became interested and obeyed the gospel.

The event changed the whole course of his life   Jones was his constant companion, and by traveling with him, Rowe soon heard the greatest preachers of the restoration   Rowe gradually built up an attitude of hero-worship toward Alexander Campbell, the "sage of Bethany " Meanwhile, his sincerity and earnestness caused him to make friends easily Sensing an ability in Rowe for great service in the church, the money was raised to send him to Bethany College.

It was September, 1850 when Rowe arrived at Bethany, carrying a letter of introduction from J. H Jones. Rowe somewhat presumptiously took the letter to Campbell's study where he obtained his first glimpse of the famous preacher. Because there were no other chairs in the study, Campbell piled up some books for a seat and said jokingly to Rowe, "Please, Sir, take a literary seat " Jones had said to Rowe, "Tell Brother Campbell that we want him to make a man of you," and Rowe now passed on the message. Campbell replied, "That, my dear Sir, depends on the kind of material they have sent me." Rowe wilted momentarily but Campbell's simple manners soon put him at ease.[1]

John F. Rowe came to Bethany College with the intention of remaining only one year, but when Campbell urged J H. Jones to arrange for another year, it was done. During this second year at school, Rowe started preaching. On one of these attempts he rode an old gray horse twelve miles, taking four hours on the journey, to preach a sermon he had gathered from some of Alexander Campbell's notes. After he started preaching, he stopped only after an hour and twenty minutes and then from pure exhaustion. When he returned home, he weighed and found he had lost four pounds in the last twenty-four hours

Rowe's stay at Bethany later furnished many happy memories Here he had heard Thomas Campbell deliver his last address, and was later in the funeral procession that took the elder Campbell's body up to the cemetery on the hill At Bethany Rowe enjoyed the companionship of great men. Among these were T. M. Henley, O. A. Burgess, J. S Lamar, J A Meng, and J. M Barnes. While a college student, Rowe served as one of the editors of the *Stylus,* the college paper. He was also still a student when he married Mary Editha Pardee, daughter of Judge Allen Pardee of Wadsworth, Ohio, the marriage occurring in September, 1852 It is not unlikely that J H. Jones figured in this for Mary Pardee was Jones' sister-in-law Graduation from college came

[1]John F Rowe, "Reminiscences of the Restoration, No 2," *American Christian Review,* Vol XXIX, No. 18 (April 29, 1886), p 141.

in July, 1854. John Schackleford was called "the beloved disciple"; O. A. Burgess was the "son of thunder"; J. S. Lamar was the "son of consolation and good hope," and J. F. Rowe held the "pen of a ready writer."

Upon departing from Bethany, Rowe went to spend the summer at his wife's home in Wadsworth, Ohio. That fall he became an agent for the Ohio State Missionary Society. He spent about five weeks, in the company of John Reed, traveling over the western part of the state. In the spring of 1855 he moved to Springfield, Illinois at the invitation of W. A. Mallory, editor of the *Christian Sentinel,* to be co-editor. Most of his work was traveling in Illinois, getting subscriptions to the periodical. A part of the time he had as his traveling companion C. D. Roberts. Roberts was the financial agent for Alexander Campbell, who was in Illinois buying up land for Campbell. This land later contributed considerably to Campbell's wealth. These trips through Illinois provided Rowe with a romantic life. He and Roberts rode horseback constantly, and while hurrying across the fields often scared up prairie chickens which looked like a thick cloud floating away on the horizon.

During the time Rowe lived at Springfield he became acquainted with Abe Lincoln, who was then a young lawyer in the same town. Rowe once engaged Lincoln to try a suit for him, which for some reason was stopped. He stayed at Springfield for two years, and during the time encouraged the church to have Isaac Errett conduct a meeting. Here their first child, Eugene Pardee, was born. The *Sentinel,* however, was so much in debt that Rowe could not be paid his salary, so he sold his furniture to pay his landlord, left town, owing a note for $15.00. It was ten years before he could pay it, and was following from state to state with a threatening suit.

Financial difficulties followed Rowe most of his life. In 1857 he moved to Oskaloosa, Iowa, upon the invitation of A. Chatterton, assistant editor of the *Evangelist,* to help raise funds to establish Oskaloosa College. The agreement was that after the school was financially secure, Rowe would be made a professor. The financial depression that year crushed many men, Rowe being among the number. He was forced to return to his work of bricklaying for two dollars a day.

The times were hard. Northwest of Oskaloosa, lived an old

preacher named Anderson, who had lost everything the winter before except a cow and two pigs   Rowe lived here for three days on a diet of prairie chicken and corn bread   The tame prairie chickens lolled on a fence while Rowe picked them off with a shotgun.   Often he walked ten miles without pay to preach the gospel.   Once he was forty miles from home without a cent and walked the whole distance.   Before leaving Oskaloosa in the spring of 1859 to return to Wadsworth, Ohio, Rowe was forced to sell everything except his bed-clothing to pay his debts.   Only because his father sent him $50 00 could he make a return trip.

Rowe's activity during the Civil War centered in Ohio.   The summer of 1859 he worked as a bricklayer for $5.00 a day, at the same time preaching at Manchester.   At the opening of the war, he preached in Holmesville, Ohio.   It was Rowe's practice to take no part in the war or in politics, however, he once delivered an address to the Soldier's Aid Society   For two years he worked as a member of the Board of the Ohio Christian Missionary Society, but considering himself a "nonentity," he resigned.   Because he secured five thousand dollars for the Society from the Phillips Brothers of Newcastle, Pennsylvania, the Society raised his salary two hundred dollars a year.

G. W. N. Yost of Corry, Virginia, a wealthy man, cleared a thousand dollars a day in the oil business.   He and Rowe became fast friends.   Yost's interest in establishing a paper, and Rowe's part in this, has already been recounted   The result of this series of incidents was the creation of the *Christian Standard*. Rowe never felt that he could understand Isaac Errett. so consequently, he gave little enthusiasm to his support for the *Standard*. Yost agreed to pay Rowe one hundred dollars a month as salary for Rowe to write on any brotherhood publication.   When Rowe stated the facts to Ben Franklin, Franklin placed him on the *Review*, giving him a one hundred dollar bonus to begin.   After that, Ben Franklin became John F. Rowe's idol.

It was 1867 that Rowe became connected with the *American Christian Review*, a connection he retained until the close of 1886. It is as a writer that J. F. Rowe is best remembered today. The brotherhood had few men that could wield a pen with Rowe's pungency and clarity.   Ben Franklin certainly held this opinion for in 1872 he wrote him :

Brother Rowe has stood side by side with us in the columns

of the *Review* for years, as our readers can testify. We have but few men who can write as he can; certainly not a half a dozen.[2]

When the *Review* of February 12, 1878 appeared, Rowe was listed as the assistant editor. Franklin then said of him:

Long has he worked at our side, and well do we know how to count on him. His pen scarcely ever slips, nor is it ever still. Nor does he stop with *writing,* but he is an *incessant* preacher. He is fully out now as the successful preacher and writer. We trust the way is now open for him to be more abundantly useful than ever before. He is ready for the work and in it. The Lord strengthen his hands and encourage his heart.[3]

After the death of Ben Franklin, Rowe took over the editorship of the *Review,* Daniel Sommer wrote of him,

Critics, sharpen your pens; he is a good subject to work on He will neither coax nor drive into either good or bad; but convince him, and he will go himself into whatever is right.[4]

The reader may have guessed already that John F. Rowe was never a prominent preacher. The harsh truth is that Rowe bordered upon a failure as a preacher. He declared that when he came from Bethany College, he possessed a great knowledge of the Bible which he had learned from Campbell, but lacked the ability to organize and present it. This was true. He had deep convictions, and a great knowledge of the Scriptures. He was a good student, never reaching the point that he felt he had enough sermons to retire from further study. W. O. Tomson said of him, "As a preacher, Brother Rowe is not what many call a pulpit orator. . . He is clear and forcible and convincing and never fails to send conviction to every honest heart."[5]

Shortly after the Civil War, Rowe moved to Akron, Ohio where he lived the remainder of his life. In the fall of 1886 he became the editor of the *Christian Leader,* a paper which he founded. His break with the *American Christian Review* that year will be studied in another chapter.

The last decade or more Rowe lost much prominence. It is not too difficult to understand Rowe's thinking, and to some extent

[2]Ben Franklin, "John F Rowe," *American Christian Review,* Vol. XV, No 48 (November 26, 1872), p 380

[3]Ben Franklin, "John F Rowe on the Warpath," *American Christian Review,* Vol XXI, (February 12, 1878), p 53

[4]Daniel Sommer, "The Present Editor," *American Christian Review,* Vol XXI, No 48 (November 26, 1878), p 377

[5]W O Tomson, "John F Rowe," *American Christian Review,* Vol. XXIII, (June 15, 1880), p. 186.

throw a mantle of charity over these years. The church passed
a period of intense trial. By 1880 the issues in the brotherhood
had, for the most part, been thoroughly discussed. Men arrayed
themselves up on the various issues, but the question that now
forced its way to the front demanding serious attention was that
of fellowship. Many had taken the position that the use of the
instrument and the missionary society were wrong, unscriptural
and sinful. But, it became evident by 1880 that many churches
were going to use the instrument and support the society anyway.
The influence of the *Christian Standard,* particularly throughout
the North, had been great enough to become a rallying point for
those advocating the instrument, and using the society. Whereas
one group insisted the instrument was wrong, the other insisted
it could be used. Could fellowship remain?

This question forced its way upon the church. There were
some who had formerly strictly opposed instrumental music whose
opposition subsided   J. B. Briney had stood vigorously behind
the opposition to the instrument, but now wavered   So did
Joseph Franklin, son of Ben Franklin. What happened with
these more prominent leaders happened to many less known.
Others remained loyal to old convictions. If instrumental music
were sinful, there could be no fellowship with it, and ten million
churches using it would not make it any more right than it had
ever been. A serious division was threatening and Rowe shrank
from it. He firmly believed instrumental music was wrong, but
how to continue to fellowship advocates of it was a problem the
full force of which he never met. Uncertain sounds came from
him   A small organ, he declared was permissible, just so it
was not a large one. Brethren naturally rebelled against him on the
one hand. On the other, while some congratulated him for his
liberal spirit, he was never ardently received because of his pronounced belief against the use of the instrument. His influence,
therefore, in his last years was localized

Rowe's death came at four o'clock in the afternoon of Wednesday, December 29, 1897. Ill health prevented his being at the
Leader office since May of that year   As far back as two years
previous, he had a heavy mental strain that affected his health.
In May, 1897, he suffered a nervous breakdown   His friends
advised him to take a vacation   That August, he and his wife
went to West Virginia for a vacation and in October returned to

Cincinnati. By this time he was partially paralyzed. It was evident that he could not recover. So he returned to Akron, to spend his last days.

Still later he partially lost his power of speech. His last articles which appeared in the *Leader* through November and December in 1897 were written under the most adverse circumstances. He was in bed when he dictated the articles to members of his family, who, at times, asked him several times to repeat his statements. His last words were directed to his son, Fred L., who still resided in Cincinnati, and who managed the *Leader* in the absence of his father. Rowe said to members of his family, "Tell Fred not to waver—keep the *Leader* pure and clean." These were his last words.

The funeral was conducted at the home of his second son at one o'clock on Friday afternoon, December 31, 1897. F. M. Green, then residing at Kent, Ohio, and a close friend of the family, preached the funeral. He read the words of one of Rowe's favorite songs, "On Jordan's Stormy Banks I Stand," before preaching the sermon.

CHAPTER IX

THE PASSING YEARS (1865-1885)

The passing of a score of years following the Civil War witnessed a rapid transition in every phase of American life. The nation in 1876 celebrated its centennial, and many awakened for the first time to the realization that this was a growing country. After the peace treaty of 1783 the colonies had a combined area of 820,680 square miles, but a century later, 3,603,884 square miles. The population increased from 2,803,000 in 1783 to 44,-000,000 by 1876 The centennial celebration on July 4th in which thirty-eight states participated, indicated the growth of a century.

The cessation of hostilities following the war however, little abated the nation's political problems Days of reconstruction were ahead for the South, but the passing of twenty years saw most of these problems settled. Poverty had followed in the path of the war. The ripest manhood in the South were dead or badly crippled. In the transition the South paid a heavy price. Money was scarce, and the panic which hit the nation in 1873 and which lasted for several years, further burdened the nation. This environmental circumstance, of course, reflected itself upon a point of emphasis among preachers The man who was paid a thousand dollars a year was mercenary The emphasis in the South was on preaching to the poor, David Lipscomb in the *Gospel Advocate* ever being their champion. Preachers farmed for a living, and gave what time they could to preach. While they should receive much praise for this, the fact is that most could not have done otherwise had they desired

"Man's extremity is God's opportunity" says a very truthful maxim Since the rich and powerful seldom have time to think of God, years of hard struggle against depression prove splendid time for the growth of the cause of Christ. Environmental factors all favored the growth of the church The war had taught the more thoughtful people the need of searching for God, and the years of poverty made it more compelling Too, the predominately rural population contributed to the growth. The automobile had not yet been invented so few people traveled far from home   A gospel meeting was a big occasion in the average rural community, when nearly everybody generally attended   The occasion was quite frequently as big a social event as a religious   This, too, was a suitable environment for great debates   Behind the seriousness of a religious discussion there was for the average person in a rural community an occasion for sport.   Aside from the seriousness of the event, people came to enjoy themselves with this unusual event.   Preachers seemed to sense this and injected personal thrusts and humorous stories at the expense of their opponents   In later years, however, people were to find their enjoyment and sport in other events, and, on the whole have insisted that debating be what it should be—a serious search for truth.

Society as a whole, then, was prepared for the gospel.   When a preacher showed the willingness to make the sacrifice to preach to a rural community, he could be sure of a good audience.   The physical equipment was hardly essential since any school house, brush arbor, or large shade tree would suffice   Given an average preacher one could be assured of baptizing thirty to sixty people.   A preacher, who in the course of five years baptized less than five thousand people, apologized often for it.

The national census for 1870 ranked the churches of Christ fifth in size in the nation, having 2,822 local congregations.   It was widely rumored that the church numbered some half-a-million.   The feeling generally was that this report was inadequate, and that a more accurate report was needed.   When the General Convention of the Missionary Society met in Cincinnati in October, 1879 a committee was formed to gather the statistics.   F. M. Green, J. B. Briney, R. Moffett, Elias Sias and L. D. Carpenter were on this committee.

Census reports among the churches of Christ through the years have every reason to be inaccurate.   Because the churches are locally independent, with no central headquarters, no power of compulsion can be made to the local churches to make them report.   Some reluctance had been felt to be placed in the same category with denominational churches as census reports imply   When, therefore, F. M. Green wrote to David Lipscomb, urging him to assist in getting up the census, Lipscomb declined.

God had not made any specific law to King David against

numbering the children of Israel, but God condemned him when he did it, reasoned Lipscomb. David, upon discovering the number of his people, would have been inclined to place his confidence, not upon God, but upon the strength of numbers, thought Lipscomb. So he reasoned that the same inclination would be felt in the church. Moreover, he regarded the Missionary Society as a representative of only a small minority of the churches To come before the world with a claim to be the representative of the churches in America would be false.[1]

The Society, however, gathered its statistics A large majority of the churches, not having any sympathy for the Society, failed to report to it, so it was far from being accurate The report, however, presents some idea of the general growth of the church up to the year, 1880.

States	Congregations	Preachers	Members
Alabama	35	28	3,250
Arkansas	56	45	5,928
California	49	38	5,775
Colorado	16	12	1,750
Connecticut	6	4	775
Dakota	7	5	675
District of Columbia	1	2	425
Florida	14	11	900
Georgia	72	48	9,850
Illinois	795	650	85,250
Indiana	675	580	78,950
Iowa	200	98	15,500
Kansas	125	78	16,860
Kentucky	595	485	79,525
Louisiana	12	7	1,500
Maine	7	5	725
Maryland	5	4	1,695
Massachusetts	7	5	1,200
Michigan	75	49	6,000
Minnesota	7	5	725
Mississippi	15	12	2,370
Missouri	565	395	60,900
Montana	6	4	675
Nebraska	75	41	13,580
New York	49	39	5,950
North Carolina	95	79	14,700
Ohio	425	217	45,500
Oregon	45	24	4,750
Pennsylvania	95	88	13,400
South Carolina	25	18	2,825
Tennessee	275	195	38,890
Texas	165	138	16,500
Vermont	3	2	425

[1]David Lipscomb, "Statistics Wanted," *Gospel Advocate*, Vol XXI, No. 32 (August 7, 1879). p 503.

Virginia	150	115	16,500
Washington Territory	1	1	75
West Virginia	65	48	7,750
Wisconsin	21	12	2,575
Wyoming Territory	1	1	95
Totals	4,768	3,488	563,928[2]

The centers of numerical strength may be readily grasped from the report. Illinois, Kentucky, Indiana, Missouri and Ohio were the numerically strong states. In Illinois, where there were over 85,000 members, the church was largely in rural areas. In 1871 Chicago had but two congregations. Twenty years later there were seven.[3] John S. Sweeney preached at this time for the church at Sixteenth and Wabash Avenues.[4]

Kentucky had eighty thousand members in 1880, but her strong centers were at Lexington and Louisville. The church at Lexington had been established on Main Street in 1834 by James Challen. Here, the Campbell-Rice debate was held in 1843. The church had always known good preaching. W. H. Hopson labored here from 1859 to 1862. The war caused Hopson to leave, and J. W. McGarvey followed him. During the battle at Richmond, Kentucky the building was used for a hospital, but aside from this, the war did not greatly disturb the growth of the church. By 1871, it was evident that the church had outgrown its old building. It was found that the First Presbyterian Church, corner of Broadway and Second Streets, had its building for sale at $15,000. The money was quickly raised and the house purchased. The first meeting in the new building was held on May 1, 1870 at which J. W. McGarvey spoke, relating the history of the church in that city.

In Louisville, the history of the church dated back to 1825 when P. S. Fall established a Baptist Church in this city. Fall became converted through reading the *Christian Baptist,* and began preaching apostolic principles. The Baptist Church divided, and the first congregation worshiping purely upon primitive grounds, was organized. In the next few years the location of the building shifted.

[2]David Lipscomb, "Those Statistics," *Gospel Advocate,* Vol. XXIII, No. 8 (February 24, 1881), p 114

[3]A J. White, "Two Years in Chicago," *Christian-Evangelist,* Vol XXXI, No 4 (January 25, 1894), p. 57.

[4]C W Sherwood, "The Cause in Chicago," *Christian Standard,* Vol. IV, No. 8 (February 20, 1869), p 58

The church met first at Green and Sixth Street. Then it bought another house on Second Street between Jefferson and Market. A few years later it built on Fifth Street between Chestnut and Walnut. By 1860, it was ready to build again. On May 18th, that year, the cornerstone was laid for a new building at Fourth and Walnut. A basement was finished here by March 17, 1861. Then came the war, and the building could not be completed. For nine years they continued to meet in the basement-building. W. H. Hopson moved to Louisville to preach for this church in 1868. At that time the church numbered nearly six hundred members. Work was being pushed on the upper part of the structure. The first meeting was held in it on April 23, 1870. The building had been completed at a cost of one hundred thousand dollars. At this first service in the new building the aging Samuel Rogers was present as a visitor and led the first prayer. Hopson used as his text Jeremiah 6: 16.

The Fourth and Walnut Streets Church was the original church in the city. After the war, other congregations arose. By 1870 there was a congregation of over four hundred members on Chestnut Street. The year before a smaller congregation had been established on Jefferson Street.[5] In the spring of 1876 forty members began meeting in Robinson Hall. R. B. Neal, an energetic and capable preacher, was the leading spirit in its establishment. In September that year this group purchased a lot on Campbell Street between Main and Market, and the following March completed their building. On the 18th of the month, J. W. McGarvey preached the dedicatory sermon for the Campbell Street Church, using Jeremiah 6: 16 as his text. Moses E. Lard, who was then engaged in a meeting at the Chestnut Street Church, was present and spoke a few words.[6] The Campbell Street congregation later became the Haldeman Avenue Church.

At this time the Fourth and Walnut Streets Church claimed to be the largest congregation worshiping after apostolic principles in the nation. When J. S. Lamar left here in 1876, it had eight hundred members. That spring B. B. Tylor came to preach to be followed in 1882 by A. I. Hobbs. With this array of more

[5] W H Hopson, "The Walnut Street Christian Church, Louisville, Ky.," *Apostolic Times*, Vol II, No 6 (May 19, 1870), p 45
[6] J. W McGarvey, "My Visit to Louisville," *Apostolic Times*, Vol. IX (April 12, 1877), p 225.

liberal spirited preachers, the church finally adopted instrumental music, and went with the general "progressive" movement. In the western part of the city about this time a few disciples left the Fourth and Walnut Streets Church when the instrument went in. By 1884 their number had increased to one hundred and twenty members Their meeting house was first a livery stable which was bought by the Methodists. The brethren purchased the building from the Methodists, remodeled it to suit their purposes. This congregation was known as the Portland Avenue Church. It was here F. G. Allen preached in 1879-80 while editing the *Old Path Guide* "Weeping Jo" Harding and R. B. Neal had been his predecessors

The report of the Convention for 1880 showed Indiana to be third in point of membership with seventy-eight thousand Prominent congregations were found at Indianapolis, Bloomington and Bedford. John O'Kane preached the first sermon in Indianapolis in 1833 at the log cabin house of Ben Roberts, who lived at the corner of Market and Illinois Streets. After the war, this congregation, with around five hundred members, met at Delaware and Ohio Streets. In 1869 the church dropped the name, church of Christ, and called itself the "Central Christian Church." Northwest Christian University was founded in 1855, and was located at Fourteenth and College. This was in those days out in the country. It was hard for students to go to Ohio and Delaware Streets to the Central Church, so classes were started at the University early on Sunday mornings, which led to the establishment of a church across from the campus in 1868. Eventually this became the Third Christian Church. The Second Christian Church was a colored congregation at Fourteenth and Illinois Streets, established in 1866.

These early churches, like many others in the brotherhood, put in the instrument and generally went with the "progressive" movement. The Third Christian Church in Indianapolis put in the instrument sometime late in the 1870's. The exact date is not known Twelve brethren who could not conscientiously worship with the organ began in 1878 to worship on South New Jersey Street in a Danish Chapel Dr Joshua Webb, one of the members, went from house to house preaching Alfred Ellmore began a meeting here on May 2, 1880, which lasted for twenty-nine days and ended with forty-one baptisms [7]   Four years later while the church was meeting on Mulberry Street. John F. Rowe conducted a meeting for the same congregation   Rowe enjoyed a renewal of friendship with the editor of the *Indianapolis Journal,* John C. New *(later, Indianapolis Star),* who had been Rowe's classmate at Bethany College in 1854, and previously the assistant United States Treasurer.[8]

At both Bloomington and Bedford strong congregations were established. The church at Bloomington started in 1828   In 1879 it had one hundred and seventy-five members. W. B. F. Treat and I. N. Porch made Bloomington their home and preached constantly in the surrounding territory. J. M. Mathes, one of Indiana's stalwart pioneers, editor of the *Christian Record,* lived at Bedford. By 1880 he was getting old, but he knew well the history of the work in Indiana. In the earlier days when Indians were plentiful in Indiana, Mathes was offered the position as chief in one of their tribes because of his tall, stalwart physical frame. Although he refused, they gave him the title of "Big Fire." Mathes lived in a little country home near Bedford, was an elder in the congregation which exercised great influence in the southern part of the state.

The state of Missouri boasted sixty thousand members in 1880 Some forty-five years before this time T. M. Allen, Thomas McBride and Samuel Rogers were among the earliest preachers of the ancient order in the state. They had traveled from one settlement to another, each with a sleeping bag and a few provisions. Thomas McBride died years before, but in 1877 the ninety-year-old Samuel Rogers was living with his son, John I. Rogers, in Danville, Kentucky. However, death cut off his earthly life two years later. T. M. Allen had died in 1871.

There were three schools run by the brethren in the state during these years. Christian University, at Canton, was in 1876 divided into four colleges—College of Arts, College of Literature and Science, College of the Bible, and Commercial College. The brethren also supported Christian College at Columbia and a female school, which at this time had J. K. Rogers as president. There

---

[7]A. Ellmore, "Indianapolis Meeting," *American Christian Review,* Vol XXIII, (June 29, 1880), p 205

[8]John F Rowe, "Mission Work in Indianapolis," *American Christian Review,* Vol XXVII, No 17 (April 24, 1884), p 133

was also a female orphan school at Camden Point in Platte County.[9]

Ohio, fifth largest in the nation as it respected the numerical strength of the brotherhood, had been a rallying ground for the plea of the ancient order since Walter Scott had preached on the Western Reserve fifty years before. Cincinnati, the "Queen City of the West," had six congregations in the year 1880. The largest was the Central Church, where at this time David Walk preached, but where sometime earlier W. T. Moore gained fame. In one sense, this was the Central Church of the brotherhood. In 1868, B. A. Hinsdale wrote of this congregation: "It contains many elements of power—wealth, character, social position, and if it does not exert a very considerable influence in the city, it it not because the Lord has withheld His blessings."[10]   R. M. Bishop, one of its elders, was mayor of Cincinnati during the Civil War, and in 1874 he was elected governor of Ohio. The meeting house cost over one hundred thousand dollars—a large sum for those days. The Central Church, however, became the seat for innovations—instrumental music and missionary societies.

Richmond Street, Eastern Avenue, and Fergus Street were the other three white congregations in the city. Ben Franklin had preached for the Richmond Street Church shortly after the war, but A. I. Hobbs was the preacher in 1880. Two colored congregations—one on Harrison Street and at College Hill were also found here.

Aside from these "strong hold" states for the church, the cause was realizing rapid growth in all regions north of the Ohio River and east of the Mississippi. In Minnesota and Wisconsin the cause yet remained weak, as it did in most of the New England states. B. U. Watkins reports from St. Paul at the close of 1875 that a small congregation is found in this city. And in New England the plea was hardly as well planted as in the states to their west. By 1876 Baltimore, Maryland, had but two churches. The original congregation here was the North Street Church. In 1840 the Paca Street Church was formed from it through a division. Through the years the little fellowship existed. In 1876

[9]Messrs Davis and Durrie, "Christian Church at Fulton, Missouri," *Apostolic Times*, Vol. IX (April 5, 1877), p 213.

[10]B. A Hinsdale, "A Week in Cincinnati and Covington," *Christian Standard*, Vol III, No 2 (January 11, 1868), pp. 12, 13.

the North Street Church reorganized under the name Dolphin Street Church and a more active fellowship was realized.

The larger cities in Michigan soon had congregations. Grand Rapids, the second city of Michigan, had about twenty members to begin meeting in 1874. S. E. Pearre moved here in February, 1875, to become the first preacher. But Detroit still remained the stronghold. On August 3, 1842, Alexander Linn came to Detroit from Glasgow, Scotland. He found Thomas Hawley and his family conducting worship in Hawley's house, so Linn joined in with them, and thus began the church in Detroit. Linn was then in the mercantile business, but after 1870 he devoted his full time to preaching the gospel.[11] About 1869 the Plum Street Church was organized at Fourth and Plum Streets with thirty members. The older congregation was meeting on Washington Street and using the instrument. By 1882 Plum Street had three hundred members and was renowned for carrying on its work with the leadership of its elders and not employing a preacher.[12] In 1883 the Plum Street Church established a congregation at Fourteenth and Ash, erecting a building that cost $2,600.

The church was spreading west of the Mississippi. A steady stream of migration poured across the Mississippi following the war, swelling the population on the vast prairies and to the Pacific. In the fall of 1877 Pardee Butler asserted before the state meeting of the Kansas Christian Missionary Society that fifty thousand members of the church had left their homes in the east and moved into those territories lying between the Missouri River and the Pacific Ocean.[13] The first congregation in Kansas, however, antedated the war. Butler went to this state in the spring of 1855, and in June gathered a large crowd on the banks of Stranger Creek, Atchison County, on a land claim belonging to Caleb May. A month later the first congregation was established at near-by Mount Pleasant, and became known as the Round Prairie Church. The Topeka Church was slow in beginning. D. H. Johnston went here in 1865. Five years later he published a call for all members of the church to meet in the courthouse. Thirty members organized

[11]J M L Campbell, "Alexander Linn," *American Christian Review*, Vol XXV, No 18 (April 27, 1882), p 141
[12]James A Harding, "The Plum Street Church of Detroit, Michigan," *Gospel Advocate*, Vol XXIV, No 19 (May 11, 1882), p 298
[13]Pardee Butler, "Address to the Brethren in Kansas." *The Christian*, Vol. XV, No 38 (September 20, 1877), p 5

themselves, renting a hall for three hundred dollars a year. Three years later they had two hundred members, when the financial depression hit the nation. Money could not be raised to pay rent, so the church disbanded.[14] At Wichita the first congregation was established on July 4, 1880, by T. J. Shelton and J H. Rosecrans, who held a thirty days' meeting and added forty-three persons to the church.[15] Considerable activity, then, took place in Kansas. Pardee Butler asserted that in that part of the state lying north of the Kansas River fifty congregations had been established since the war. All but twenty died out by 1877, and these were in poor condition. Beneath the pessimism is the symbol of struggling life.

In Arkansas and Louisiana the plea for the ancient order was felt. The church at Little Rock felt the impact of the war. Though not dividing openly, the war engendered an undercurrent of hard feelings. When J. H. Garrison conducted a meeting for the congregation in 1877, he found it greatly discouraged. David Lipscomb visited here eight years later, and remarked that the congregation was about holding its own—nothing more. Small, struggling churches were springing up over Arkansas. On June 25, 1875, Joe Waldrop came to Fort Smith and found a small congregation three or four years old. At Alma, Russellville and Dardanelle little churches were existing. Over the entire section the influence of Robert Graham, who had lived at Fayetteville before the war, was still felt. At Hope and Prescott, congregations were organized in 1882. At Texarkana, J. C. Mason preached almost steadily in 1884 and 1885.

In New Orleans, as late as 1883, the church had a poor foundation. When a correspondent named "Zenas" visited here that year, he wrote:

. . . The church in New Orleans was planted by Alexander Campbell many long years ago. Many malign influences have dwarfed its growth. The baleful glare of Jesse B. Ferguson's "post mortem" gospel; the soul-chilling doctrine of Dr. Thomas' Elpis Israel; the "word alone" theory, and perhaps worldly conformity, have all contributed to its present depressed, uninfluential and lifeless condition.

The writer of this notice had supposed that the labors of such men as James Shannon, J. A. Dearborn, R. B Roberts, Drs. John

---

[14]D. H. Johnston, "Topeka Church," *The Christian*, Vol. XV, No 29 (July 19, 1877), p 2.
[15]A A Glenn, "Christian Church, Wichita, Kansas," *American Christian Review*, Vol XXIII, (August 3, 1880), p 242.

R. McCall and A. A Jones, William Edwin Hall and his potential "Iron Preacher," etc, had built up a large and influential church in this Southern city He therefore expected to see crowded aisles and pews, of brethren residing in the city, and throngs of members of the church from Texas then in New Orleans, who were supposed to be anxious to hear a preacher of so much renown as David Walker Imagine the writer's astonishment when, entering the auditorium, he saw a small assemblage of not more than forty, embracing in the number Sunday school scholars, teachers and visitors A very intelligent looking brother engaged in teaching a class, consisting of one old colored sister, pointed toward the rostrum, and then, for the first time, I saw Dr Walk (the word doctor is used in its proper sense, teacher) When Geranius found his father, "Marius, a destitute wanderer, a hunted outcast weeping amid the ruins of Carthage," he saw not a sadder countenance than that of Dr Walk, at that time The diminutive Sunday school was a sufficient explanation of the gloomy face A brother named Allen, in a very sprightly and fluent way, expounded II. Tim 1 to the Bible class of five or six men He seemed to be anxious to teach, and, in his explanations, went doubtless was in earnest, and, perhaps, realized that expansion was as good as thoroughness . .[16]

As the tide of immigration swept westward, members established small churches in the communities where they settled At Denver, Colorado a small congregation was organized in May, 1873. Six years later another was established in the city, and A I Hobbs visited here in 1880 to attempt a union between them

The tide of immigration swept across the prairies, scaled the mountains and rolled on to the coast of California. Brethren were plentiful enough in the state that already they were thinking about establishing their own schools. Pierce Christian College was located at College City in Colusa County, six miles west of the Sacramento River It had an endowment of forty-five thousand dollars given to it by a Brother Pierce W. J Carpenter was president here in 1876 Hesperian College was located in Woodland, Yolo County, having a thirty-five thousand dollar endowment. B H Smith, formerly of Christian College, Missouri, was at this time the president At Santa Rosa there was a Christian College built in 1872 by J M Martin Florence College was located at Hollister Alexander Johnson was president [17]

[16]Zenas, "The Church of Christ in New Orleans," *Gospel Advocate*, Vol XVII, No 23 (June 10, 1885), p 358

[17]G O Burnett, "Our Colleges in California," *Apostolic Times*, Vol VIII, (August 24, 1876), pp 530, 531

David Lipscomb declared that the 1880 census report of some thirty-eight thousand members was grossly an understatement. In middle Tennessee, where the influence of the *Gospel Advocate* was strongly felt, the church had a rapid growth In West Tennessee the large growth was due largely to preachers like John R. Howard who had preached there much earlier. East Tennessee remained almost destitute of churches By 1878 no effort had been made to establish the church in Chattanooga on a sound footing. Twenty members lived in that city of twelve thousand people, but there was no meeting house. The brethren of middle Tennessee neglected Chattanooga, and the General Missionary Society grasped the opportunity to plant itself in Tennessee by sending a preacher to the city. It gave the Society an inroad into the state and paved the way in a few more years for the establishment of a state missionary society.

Joseph Franklin visited Tennessee in the fall of 1877. At Gallatin he found a congregation but writes of it: "The congregation in Gallatin has been built up by a series of very successful protracted meetings under Brethren Hopson, Gano, and others, but seems to have been deficient in systematic and regular instruction of the Disciples."[18] At Hendersonville a congregation had been established that spring. W B. Wilson, a member of the Fourth and Walnut Streets church in Louisville, had moved to Hendersonville in the fall of 1876, where he went to work to build up a congregation. By the spring of 1877 it had only eight or ten members.

In Alabama, by 1885, the cause was still in its infant stages. There were no congregations in Athens, and Decatur, although a group of brethren were meeting in Huntsville. James A. Harding had held one or two very successful meetings here. At Tuscaloosa, a small church was established in 1881 by a Brother Beasley At Falkville, there was a small church. Hartselle, thirteen miles south of Decatur had a congregation which was established in 1884. When V. M. Metcalfe visited Birmingham in 1882, he referred to it as a "magic city of ten thousand inhabitants" which had grown up in only ten years. There were more saloons in the city he thought, than any city he had ever

---

[18]Joseph Franklin, "Incidents of Travel in Tennessee," *American Christian Review,* Vol XXI, No 2 (January 8, 1878), p 9

seen, but no church after the New Testament order. Twelve members lived here in 1876 when J. M Barnes arrived, but because they refused to hold regular meetings, Barnes would not return.

The cause in Alabama was hindered by the death of J M Pickens on February 3, 1881 Pickens lived in the northern part of the State and operated a small school near Mountain Home. T. B. Larimore, after leaving Franklin College, went to Pickens' home and taught school with him several months. This gave Larimore the idea for Mars Hill College. Pickens, however, was an excellent preacher, and did much to establish the cause in northern Alabama. But, on February 3, 1881, Pickens, with a young man by the name of William Davidson, walked down a road toward a neighbor's farm. Another youth jumped out of the bushes, shot at the Davidson man and killed him. Pickens knocked the gun from the killer's hand and ran. The assassin picked up the gun and shot Pickens three times, killing him instantly Pickens was only forty-five years old, and ready to do his greatest work [19]

A volume would be required to write the history of the church in each of the various states. These sketches can only convey a general impression of the growth of the cause.

STATUS QUO

In imparting a general view of the passing years something must be said about the state of the church.

A marked difference in the state of the brotherhood may be seen twenty years after the war. In the North the *Christian Standard* and the *American Christian Review* were locked in combat. Each paper represented a different type of thinking. Society as a whole was changing. The increase in population, the advancement of science, greater educational opportunities— these were inherent causes. The *Christian Standard,* keenly aware of this fact, assumed its greatest task to be that of redefining the earlier restoration principles in terms of the growing demand for progress. The *American Christian Review*, while not opposed to progress, clearly assailed the redefining process The Bible truths were static, the Bible teaching the same thing in 1885 that it had taught in 1845, and any attempt to change the church to alter

---

[19]Sarah E Williams, "Particulars of the Death of J M Pickens," *Gospel Advocate,* Vol XXIII, (February 17, 1881), p 102

the laws of God to conform with the changing environmental factors in society, the *Review* considered objectionable.

A point of contention was the familiar motto coined by Thomas Campbell in 1809 "Where The Bible Speaks, We Speak, Where The Bible is silent, We Are Silent" Isaac Errett saw that a redefining of this motto had to be made if the church was to conform to an age of progress. Errett therefore, wrote that Campbell meant *"that nothing should be urged as a term of Christian fellowship* for which there could not be a *thus saith the Lord"*[20] Errett declared that Campbell was too intelligent to teach that everything should be avoided in our religious belief and practice except those things for which there could not be found a "thus saith the Lord" W K Pendleton's address before the Society convention in 1866 had declared substantially the same thing It is evident Errett's thunder was only that of Pendleton pitched in a higher key.

In January, 1884 John F. Rowe began a series of editorials in the *Review* on the explanation of the motto and directly attacked Errett's viewpoint If Campbell meant that "nothing should be made a test of fellowship except that for which there could be found a thus saith the Lord," what an unusual principle this was on which to start a movement of restoration, wrote Rowe. What denomination ever wanted to make its peculiar beliefs and practices a test of fellowship anyway? If this be what Campbell meant, why not join the ranks of the denominations and give up this plea for restoration? Rowe saw in Errett's interpretation a trend toward making the church another denomination for every denomination wanted to be allowed to hold its basic peculiarities while fraternizing with others with different peculiarities. So Rowe wrote:

The serious trouble now with some of our people is, not that they wish to make *their* "human opinions and human inventions a term of communion," which, as a question of divine law and authority, does not seem to enter into their calculations; but the trouble is that there is a large party opposed, upon the authority of God's word, to the introduction of "human opinions," and especially "human inventions," "into the constitution, faith or worship of the church" If there is "no harm" in these innovations upon the prescribed order of heaven, why talk about "reforma-

---

[20]Isaac Errett, "The Basis of Christian Fellowship," *Christian Standard*, Vol XIX, (January 12, 1884), p 12

tion" at all? Why talk of the restoration of the apostolic church? Why should we prate of Christian union upon the basis of the Bible? If we may infringe upon the order of heaven in one place, we may in every other place Grant this assumption of power and "our providential mission" is at an end. we have already degenerated into a sect [21]

The *Review,* therefore was prone to look upon the cause of restoration with great alarm It seemed to them as though the *Christian Standard* would guide the church in complete departures from apostolic grounds Innovations came into the church, with the encouragement of the *Standard* The *Review* cried aloud of dangers, but the *Standard* was perfectly complacent William Baxter, author of the biographies of Knowles Shaw and Walter Scott, a year before his death wrote to the *Review* in defense of the *Standard* His articles were signed "BW," his initials reversed He declared he could detect no dangers. To this Alfred Ellmore responded with a strongly worded article.

. . . Please read in the same paper an article from Brother G. W. Rice, in which he is straightening the crookedness of the *Standard* on mission work. He certainly knows that the *Standard is* and *has been,* for years, apologizing and excusing, which amounts to defending, the following list of departures, viz : The *organ and choir in worship, the employing of a* pastor *to take charge,* of the church, missionary societies, with their *salaried secretaries, ministerial associations,* etc all of which are unknown to the New Testament [22]

E C. Weekly summarized the "status quo" in 1881 in the following words:

"Behold how good and how pleasant it is for brethren to dwell together in unity." The church of Christ, when first organized, was a unit. continued a unit until a human creed was made We were once, as a religious people, a unit in our faith and worship. But how things have changed in some churches called Christian churches, within the last few years! Some of our editors and preachers are now contending for human institutions—organs, festivals, societies, etc , while other editors and preachers are reviewing and exposing all such institutions and things as unscriptural and hurtful Yet both parties say, "Where the Bible speaks, we speak, and where the Bible is silent we are silent."

[21] John F Rowe, "The Silence of the Scriptures," *American Christian Review,* Vol XXVII, (January 17, 1884), p 20
[22] Alfred Ellmore, "A Very Dull Scholar," *American Christian Review,* Vol XXII, No 7 (February 11, 1879), p 53

Yet they continue to controvert questions not found in the Bible. . .

Dear Brethren, do come back, and be satisfied with the purity and all-sufficiency of the holy Scriptures Let us all unite once more in contending for the unity of the faith. "Let all envy and strife be put away from you and be kind one to another, forgiving one another as God for Christ's sake hath forgiven you [23]

In summarizing the work for the year, 1877, J. A. Headington found sufficient cause for optimism.

Our own people, the chosen of God, during the past year have not been idle Vast numbers have been added to the fold of Christ during the past year Matters of doubt and uncertainty have been put to the test, weighed in the balances and found wanting. Great conventions, salaried secretaries and mammoth missionary schemes are below par at the closing out of the year 1877 [24]

PUBLICATIONS

Periodicals and books, spreading the plea for a return to the ancient order, were rushing from press telling effectively the story of the restoration.

On January 1, 1879 there was published at Louisville, Kentucky the first issue of the *Old Path Guide* by its editor Frank G. Allen, minister of the Portland Avenue Church Its prospectus announced that it would be called *Apostolic Age,* but Allen, considering that it might be confused with the *Apostolic Times,* changed the name to *Old Path Guide.* Financially, the paper was a success. The first year netted the editor six hundred dollars, a tidy profit for those days The *Guide* proved also to be a popular paper Dealing less with the prominent issues than other periodicals, its pages contained solid material on the fundamental principles of Christianity. In stating the purpose of the *Old Path Guide,* F. G. Allen wrote:

In the providence of God the Old Path Guide is now started on its mission of love and loyalty to Christ Its object will ever be to guide the world into the old paths in which men walked with God in the golden days of uncorrupted Christianity. Than this, it has no higher aspiration That it may ever be true to this end, the divine aid is especially invoked.

[23]E. C Weekly, "Condition of Things," *American Christian Review,* Vol XXIV, No 38 (September 20, 1881). p 297
[24]J A Headington, "The Passing Years," *American Christian Review,* Vol XXI, No 1 (January 1, 1878), p 5

F G. ALLEN

The Old Path Guide has no sympathy with that form of liberalism which regards divine appointments necessary only for the weak—that divine legislation is not for strong men, but only for babes in Christ.[25]

Through sheer determination F G Allen had become a preacher of considerable influence in the brotherhood His early childhood

[25]F G Allen, "Introduction," *Old Path Guide,* Vol I, No. 1 (January, 1879), p 1

was not different from that of other pioneer boys in Kentucky
There were the same hardships—endless hard labor on the farm
plus little or no opportunity for education   It was on March 7,
1836 that Sarah A Allen gave birth to Frank G , her fifth child.
But she was to be the mother of eight more of Francis Allen's
children, and the thirteen were to present no easy task at rearing

Both parents were Methodists, but not "fussy about it "   His
mother was not a "shouting" Methodist   His father though
religiously inclined could never "get religion" at the Methodist
altar   Despite this fact he believed Methodist doctrines, and lived
and died a member of that church   Allen at the age of ten, joined
the Methodists during a revival near his home at LeGrange,
Kentucky   Even as a boy, he enjoyed church services   Years
later Allen could remember the texts and the sermons the Methodist preachers delivered in his early youth   He wrote "I had
high regard for preachers, and from early life was fond of their
company, and since I have become one myself, the society of
good, faithful men of God brings me as near heaven as I shall
ever be in the flesh [20]

Occasionally Allen showed indications of a great character   He
was an average boy in that he liked to hunt, and enjoyed too,
being slightly mischievous   Many honestly believed that he would
some day be a criminal and be hanged   Even his own father held
this conviction   There were, however, glimpses of greatness in
him   From the coon skins he sold he would purchase books
to study by the fireplace   By sheer determination he overcame
physical handicaps and frail health   He had the markings of an
outstanding person, once the spark could be ignited in him that
would cause him to put his full powers to work toward one, worth-
while goal

Allen met Jennie Maddox in the summer of 1855 while he was
working as a harvest hand for her uncle, and it appeared to be
a case of "love at first sight."   September 11, 1856 they were
married   His wife's father, G. W. Maddox was an elder at
Pleasant Hill Church in Oldham County, Kentucky   He was
one of the most enlightened men on the Scriptures in the brotherhood   Allen became attached to his father-in-law, and learned
the gospel from him   He was slow to accept the truth, since he

---

[20]Robert Graham, *Autobiography of Frank G Allen* (Cincinnati Guide
Printing and Publishing Company, 1887), p 13

had looked upon "Campbellism" as the worst of all heresies He discussed religious subjects at great length with his father-in-law, and in May, 1861 was baptized by William Tharp during a meeting at Pleasant Hill.

In August, 1862 Allen entered Eminence College. It was not easy for a married man with a family and no money to attend school But he rented a house and three acres of ground at the edge of town so he could raise hogs His wife raised chickens Knowing he was short of funds, Allen decided to work more strenuously and crowd four years of school work into two He was the only married man in the classes—that is, until J B Briney came along a year later to join him However, by working too hard, Allen ruined his health, and was never again well At Eminence, Allen formed a close friendship with I. B Grubbs that remained through life.

Leaving school in 1864, Allen went first to Campbell County, Kentucky where he opened a school of his own He preached some in the neighborhood, too For the next ten years Allen preached, taught school, and conducted religious debates In 1876 he became an editor on the *Apostolic Times* with I B Grubbs and Samuel A Kelley In 1879, while living in Louisville and preaching for the Portland Avenue church he began publication of the *Old Path Guide*

The major publications of the brotherhood from the close of the war to 1885 remained the *Christian Standard, American Christian Review, Gospel Advocate,* and the *Apostolic Times* The *Old Path Guide,* new in the field of religious journalism in 1879, realized great prominence through its short life In 1885 it united with the *Apostolic Times* to form the *Apostolic Guide* The *Times* and *Guide* each represented that type of thinking characteristic of the brethren in middle Kentucky for thirty years after the war McGarvey, Grubbs, Allen, Lard, and S A Kelley each believed in organized societies and defended them vigorously upon the ground of expediency They were, on the other hand, bitter enemies of the instrument in worship Men of their mind in middle Kentucky were slow to agree that both the society and the instrument stood on the same principle As the fact slowly dawned on many, the "middle ground" faded away It was evident, therefore, to many of those central Kentucky preachers that some adjustment had to be made in their positions F G

Allen showed signs of seeing the error of societies when death came to him in 1885. J B Briney, a devotee of the "middle ground" made his adjustment by adhering to the instrument. although in his earlier years he was staunchly against it. McGarvey himself was the last of the die-hards of the position. In his later years he moved from one congregation to another as the instrument was introduced, refusing to worship with one.

Various smaller periodicals exercised an almost entirely local influence   They were effective, however, as far as their influence went   In Missouri, the *Christian Pioneer* began republication in 1872. D. T. Wright and John R. Howard had issued the first number in 1861   Wright continued the publication until November, 1870. The first of 1872 he began to republish the paper, now having W C Rogers as co-editor, and putting it forth weekly from Chillicothe, Missouri [27]   *The Christian,* another Missouri publication, which later joined with *The Evangelist* to form the *Christian-Evangelist,* will be noticed in another chapter.

Early in 1876 W E Hall of New Orleans sent forth the first issue of the *Iron Preacher*   This paper was a successor of the *Southern Christian Weekly.* The same year the *Texas Christian* took the place of the *Texas Christian Monthly*   The Wilmeth brothers, J R. and C M , published it from McKinney

Aside from periodicals, brethren were now giving considerable attention to writing books   In the spring of 1863, during the darkest days of the Civil War, McGarvey had sent forth his commentary on Acts.   McGarvey was a young man—a little beyond thirty years of age—and to the present day his commentary has proved to be among the most popular books in the brotherhood. In presenting his commentary McGarvey wrote.

I have now ready for the press a commentary on Acts of Apostles, to the preparation of which, I have devoted all the time which I could spare from my ministerial labors, for three and a half years. The peculiarities of the work are chiefly these
1st   It presents the real meaning of the text, as developed in the writings and teaching of our brotherhood, the only people of modern times who have understood and appreciated this book.
2nd   On every passage which presents any of the great issues of the day, the question is argued in full   In this way nearly all

---

[27] D T Wright, "Prospectus of the Christian Pioneer for 1872—Vol 11," *Apostolic Times,* Vol III, No 45 (February 15, 1872), p 354

the issues which we have formed with the sectarian world come
up for discussion in the course of the work

3rd   It is adapted to circulation among sectarians and the un-
converted, and contains much matter designed for the edification
of the brethren.

4th.   It contains a complete biography of Paul, the blanks in
his history left by Luke being filled up with facts derived from
the epistles

5th   It contains a revision of the text, in which the common
version is modernized and corrected

6th.   The text and comments are so confined that the latter
will not read like a dictionary, as in most commentaries, but the
whole will be continuous and connected, like any other book.   It
is a book to be read, and not merely a book of reference [28]

The appearance of McGarvey's commentary on Acts in 1863 set
off a wave of interest in commentaries on the New Testament
Brethren dreamed of the day in the near future when an entire
set, written by the more scholarly men connected with the restoration would be before the world.   Bosworth, Chase and Hall,
prominent publishers of brotherhood books, announced in 1871
that eleven volumes of New Testament commentaries to be called
"The New Testament Commentary" were in preparation   The
writers were J W McGarvey, W. K Pendleton, J S Lamar,
Isaac Errett, C L Loos, Robert Richardson, W. T. Moore and
Robert Milligan   A meeting was held in Cincinnati that year
with the publisher and the writers to make all arrangements [29]
As it worked out only McGarvey, Lamar, and Milligan completed their assignments.

McGarvey's commentary on Acts has never been surpassed by
any writer connected with the restoration   It was eagerly awaited
by the brotherhood at large   Ben Franklin wrote :

The work he now proposes to bring before the people is one of
much importance and merit, and we are assured it will have a
widely extended and profitable circulation   It is a commentary on
the part of the New Testament most needed and one of the kind
demanded.   We are satisfied this work will meet the expectation
of the brotherhood as fully as any book that has appeared for
many years [30]

---

[28] J W McGarvey, "A New Commentary on Acts," *Millennial Harbinger*,
Fifth Series, Vol VI, No 5 (May, 1863), p 211

[29] Bosworth, Chase and Hall, "A New Commentary," *Gospel Advocate*,
Vol XIII, No 12 (February 23, 1871), pp 279, 280

[30] Ben Franklin, "The New Commentary on Acts," *American Christian
Review*, Vol VI, No 19 (May 12, 1863), p 74

W K Pendleton received his copy soon after its publication, and wrote of McGarvey's book

The good sense and sound judgment of its laborious and ingenious author are more and more revealed at every reading.   One feels safe in following Brother McGarvey, for it is evident that he is conscientiously particular as to where he leads us   He loves the truth, and would go very far out of his way to correct even his own errors   Such men are not apt to recklessly impose upon others as accurate and certain, that of which they are themselves in doubt [31]

David Lipscomb, who had a reputation for considerable reservation in giving praise, was jubilant with McGarvey's work:

Whatever may be the minor faults of his production, we think it one of the best volumes that has been issued from the press for a number of years   As a commentary upon this most important portion of Sacred Scripture, and upon the plan of introduction into the Kingdom of Heaven, therein developed, for clearness and justness of conception, and as an aid in understanding the varied instructions and allusions of the divine teachers, by a thorough inquiry into the different circumstances and stand points from which they spoke, it is superior to any work known to us.   We heartily commend it to all of our readers who feel an interest in the understanding of this most interesting and important part of Holy Writ [32]

W. H Hopson not only commended the book, but issued with a valuable suggestion   He wrote of the book, "I regard it as a felicitous performance, decidedly creditable to the author and to Bethany College, his Alma Mater, and eminently useful to the cause of truth"   Hopson then suggested that Moses E Lard undertake a writing of a commentary on Romans; that W K Pendleton undertake to write on Hebrews, and C L Loos on John   He then suggested that others undertake writing until the whole New Testament is completed [33]

Not all, however, hailed McGarvey's work as being so praiseworthy   John Shackleford, writing in the *Independent Monthly* in 1869 complained that it was published too soon; that five or six more years should have been given to it   Those knowing the bitterness with which Schackleford and his co-editor, L D

[31] W K Pendleton, "Commentary on Acts of Apostles," *Millennial Harbinger*, Fifth Series, Vol VII, No 1 (January, 1864), p 38
[32] David Lipscomb, "New Publications," *Gospel Advocate*, Vol VIII, No 1 (January 1, 1866), p 10
[33] W H Hopson, "A Suggestion," *Millennial Harbinger*, Vol XXXVII, No 1 (January, 1866), p 43

Pinkerton, were assailing the brotherhood on many points, will be likely to take his criticism with the proverbial grain of salt. He complained that McGarvey goes at the law of pardon much as a lawyer goes at a contract McGarvey was, however, coldly logical and almost destitute of sentimentality

Completion of the writings on the New Testament were not made altogether according to plans. Moses E Lard announced in 1865 his intention to write a commentary on Romans Eight years passed and the work was still not finished, Lard scarcely finding the time to proceed. In 1873 he went into almost complete oblivion, brethren frequently inquiring what became of him. An occasional reply came back that he was busy, writing his commentary. Finally, at the close of 1875 Lard announced that his commentary had been turned over to the printer.

McGarvey on Matthew and Mark, Lamar on Luke and Milligan on Hebrews were all forthcoming about the same time.

Aside from writing commentaries, increased interest was shown in other fields of writing Attention to biographical material was manifest. After the death of Alexander Campbell in 1866. Robert Richardson produced the classic history of the restoration, his biography of Campbell. Thirty years earlier when Richardson had approached Campbell, revealing his ambition Campbell was receptive Campbell was only dead a short time when his widow asked Richardson to start the biography Richardson's eyes were bad, so his daughter, Emma, was conscripted for amanuensis. It was his intention to complete the work in one volume, but it became evident that two would be necessary—possibly three. After completing the first volume in the summer of 1868, Richardson sent a copy to his friend, John R. Howard, accompanied with the following letter:

When I last wrote to you, I hoped to be able to comprise the whole in one volume, but afterwards found it best to make two vols, and publish them consecutively Indeed to carry out my plan fully would require at least *three* vols, such as I send you I must however endeavor to embrace what remains in another of equal size [34]

The book required three years to be written, and was a financial loss for Richardson He paid all publication costs himself. but the sale of the book was so limited that he lost money

---

[34] John R Howard, "Memoirs of Alexander Campbell," *Christian Standard,* Vol III, No 33 (August 15, 1868), p 258

Since Richardson's death falls within the score of years now being surveyed, a brief sketch of his life will not be out of order A E. Meyers visited the Richardson home early in the spring of 1876 and found him recovering from a stroke of paralysis which had come to him on February 18. His general health appeared good Meyers commented that he "can not articulate any words distinctly," and was only with great difficulty that he could write at all

On the morning of October 22 Richardson arose before six o'clock, apparently quite well It was the Lord's Day The morning was spent in reading the Scriptures, and afterward, Richardson ate a hearty lunch That afternoon he took a little walk, then he retired earlier than usual Suddenly the family heard unusually heavy breathing from his room, and dashed to see about him. It was evident that Richardson had another stroke. Without uttering another word, he slipped quietly into death Three days later his body was laid to rest in the cemetery at Bethany.

Born in Pittsburgh, Pennsylvania on September 27, 1806, Richardson was the son of a wealthy Irish merchant, Nathanael Richardson Although Episcopalian in religious background, the Richardson home became the stopping-off-place for Thomas and Alexander Campbell and more frequently, of Walter Scott. Scott early became Richardson's idol, for Richardson attended his school at Pittsburgh and later rode horseback many miles to get Scott to immerse him. He attended a medical school at Philadelphia and became a doctor

Richardson, however, did not limit his interests to the medical profession, for he was first a Christian He was a preacher, teacher and writer as well. As a preacher, he was somewhat diffident. His thoughts were excellent, but his flow of words was very uneven, making his sermons boresome to an audience. In any of the great gatherings of the brotherhood Richardson was never a featured speaker In 1830 he began writing for the *Millennial Harbinger* under the title, "Discipulus" He was an elder in the Bethany church and a teacher in the college for twenty years

The popular reputation Richardson has gained depicts him as a mild-tempered. soft spoken individual This was not always the case I. B. Grubbs says of him, "When earnestly opposing what he deemed seriously erroneous, he was somewhat caustic, and was sarcastic to a degree that made him formidable to an opponent."[35] Isaac Errett wrote

Pure in life, studious in habit, retiring in his disposition, unostentatious in his labors, supremely devoted to truth for truth's sake, his service to the cause of Christ were great and valuable, and his genuine merit was greater than his fame. His real worth was known only to the few that were intimately acquainted with him [36]

The publication of the *Life of Elder John Smith* caused a minor upheaval of animosity between the *Christian Standard* and the *Apostolic Times* Petty jealousies were frequent. The *Christian Standard* in 1869 was near bankruptcy The *Times,* on the other hand, was just beginning, its outstanding corps of ambitious editors probably a little ashamed that the subscription was no higher than it was. When on August 21, 1869 it was announced that the *Standard* would begin carrying in serial form John A. William's biography of Smith, which later would be put in book form, The *Times* vigorously protested Obviously they had been outmaneuvered. Nevertheless, William's biography did increase the *Standard's* circulation and helped to put it over the crisis

Two years before Robert Milligan announced to the world his publication *Reason and Revelation* the object of which was to set forth the province of reason in "matters pertaining to divine revelation," and to "vindicate the paramount authority of the Sacred Scriptures" The book was widely acclaimed as a leader in its field, but *Time,* the true evaluator of all books, was not so generous David Lipscomb wrote of "Reason and Revelation":

Our author has done this work well His reasoning is sometimes faulty; his conclusions on minor and secondary matters is not always correct, and his exegesis of scripture, in one or two instances, is not the proper one from our stand point. Yet the work as a whole is good, and far surpasses any work on these subjects known to us [37]

One other major publication work occuring during these years needs some attention. In 1880 McGarvey's *Lands of The Bible*

[35]I B Grubbs, "Dr Robert Richardson," *Apostolic Times,* Vol VIII (November 9, 1876), p 712
[36]Isaac Errett, "Death of Dr R Richardson," *Christian Standard,* Vol XI, (November 4, 1876), p 349
[37]David Lipscomb, "A New Work," *Gospel Advocate,* Vol IX, No 45 (November 7, 1867), p 895

was published   This book related to McGarvey's studies a year earlier in Palestine

On Saturday, March 1, 1879 McGarvey celebrated his fiftieth birthday   The next day he preached at a joint meeting of the congregations in Lexington, a farewell sermon.   The following day at three o'clock he left for Palestine   Monday morning McGarvey walked upstairs to his library, and looking for a moment over his books, he spoke aloud   "Good by, my dear old friends, and if I never see you again, God bless you for the good you have done me, and the happy hours we have spent together"   Downstairs, he went to the kitchen to tell the servants good by   The old colored servant, Jim, was morose   He wanted to go to Palestine, too   But McGarvey joked that a whale might swallow him up to which Jim replied, "If he do, I can't he'p it   I want to go anyhow   I ain't never seen nuthin' and I want to see somethin' before I die"   The work at the Broadway Church was turned over to H Turner   Robert Graham and I B Grubbs agreed to keep the College of the Bible going   So that afternoon, McGarvey took the train for Philadelphia

On March 5, 1879 on board the steamer, "Pennsylvania" McGarvey sailed for England.   With him were his cousins, Frank Thomson, a farmer who lived near Lexington and W. B Taylor of Elizabethtown, Kentucky, a former student of the Bible College [18]   McGarvey sent regular dispatches to the *Christian Standard* while W B Taylor wrote regular articles for the *Gospel Advocate*   It was on this trip that McGarvey drowned.   The claim was his heart had stopped, but he was brought back in a matter of moments to life   Upon his return to Lexington, McGarvey wrote his book based upon his travels in the holy land

THE PASSING PREACHERS

The years which now occupy our attention witness the passing of H T Anderson, a preacher known chiefly for his translation of the New Testament from Greek into English.   His death occurred September 19, 1872 in Washington D C   His last years were decidedly unfortunate ones   In his old age he could preach little   His business management had been very poor, and for

---

[38] J W McGarvey, "Letters of Travel," *Christian Standard*, Vol XIV, No 11 (March 15, 1879), p 81.

his financial maintainence he was at the mercy of the brotherhood His association was mostly among the Baptists He evidenced decided leanings in their direction Baptists were quick to take advantage of it, and from that day to this Anderson has been quoted frequently, much to the embarrassment of many gospel preachers

Around 1870 a movement was started, repeated every few years since, of a reunion with the Baptists. T. J Melish, once a member of the church, went to the Baptists Later he left them and went to the Episcopalians. At this time, he was editing a Baptist periodical, *Journal And Messenger* Early in 1871 Anderson wrote for the *Journal And Messenger* articles favoring the Baptists He wrote.

I must be permitted to say for myself that I have been with the Disciples for nearly forty years, and I know them . . I now have to say, after studying the Scriptures for forty years, and after having made a second translation of the New Testament, that the dispensation of the Gospel is a dispensation of grace, as such it must be received into the heart by faith and love, not by work or works [19]

The implication the Baptists saw was, of course, that baptism was not necessary to salvation.

It was one of Anderson's conviction that the "form" of expressions used by the brotherhood were standing in the way of a union with the Baptists These "forms" he deprecated So he says,

I am in favor of a union with the Baptists, and I believe in it My purpose in writing was to state, sharply, what I understood to be obstacles in the way of union, and to remove those obstacles. I think I have already affected some good in that direction I know my brethren I know that they have certain *forms of words* current among them, that are hindrances to their own progress "Baptism for the remission of sins," is one of those forms, "law of pardon" is another I know that for more than forty years they have been explaining themselves, and are yet unexplained. The form of words, "baptism for the remission of sins," is unexplainable, and should be thrown out of use No one believes it, and yet it is constantly used

. You teach, "Baptism for the remission of sins " I teach,

---

[19]Isaac Errett, "H T Anderson on the Disciples," *Christian Standard*, Vol VI, No. 8 (February 25, 1871)

"Christ crucified for the remission of sins." Which of us is most likely to reach the Baptists?[40]

In Anderson's case it is little wonder the brotherhood did not understand him, and so refused to support him.

These passing years also bring to our attention the death of James T. Barclay, whose last years were spent in northern Alabama. From the day he became ill—October 20, 1874—until his death, his son, J. J. Barclay was constantly by his side. At noon on Wednesday, October 28, at the age of 68 years, he died. The next 'day J. M. Pickens preached the funeral.[41]

The passing of Dr L. L. Pinkerton should be briefly noted. In the more recent years Pinkerton's prominence in the brotherhood declined so that he was seldom used as a preacher. An unknown writer pens in the *Apostolic Times* a pathetically candid article:

It is well known to our readers that for some years past he has been to a great extent alienated from the Christian Church, having adopted some views in religious matters which were in direct antagonism with cherished convictions of the Disciples, and having become involved in much personal animosity toward conspicuous brethren. During this period he has not held membership in any congregation, and his services as a preacher ceased to be in demand, so that he sought secular employment and was, at the time of his death, employed by the Federal Government as a detective in the mail service.[42]

President Robert Milligan of the College of The Bible in Lexington went to his death on March 22, 1875. His life has been sketched in our first volume J. W. McGarvey preached his funeral, and in it related an incident instructive of the value of guarding one's Christian influence. During the days of Milligan's illness, the doctor recommended a drink of whiskey for its medicinal value, but Milligan refused. He pointed out to the doctor that he was the president of the College of 'The Bible and that he would rather die sooner than allow some action of his cause one of the young men in the school to stumble Richardson, then, very appropriately wrote of Milligan:

---

[40]H T Anderson, "H T Anderson's Reply," *Christian Standard,* Vol VI, No 12 (March 25, 1871), p 90
[41]Robert Richardson, "Dr J T Barclay," *Christian Standard,* Vol IX, (1874), p 364
[42]Anonymous, "Dr L L Pinkerton," *Apostolic Times,* Vol VII (1875), p 32

To the church here, however, the loss of Brother Milligan is no common calamity   High in position, great in influence, eminent in example, abundant in labors, his relations to the brotherhood at large were coextensive with the reformatory movement in which we are engaged, and to which he has been in many respects a valuable auxiliary.   So amiable was he in spirit, so gentle and unobtrusive, so free from self-assertion and pretension, that his departure and the cessation of his labors may alone enable the brotherhood to realize their value and to appreciate properly the power of that beneficent influence which he constantly exerted while quietly and faithfully fulfilling the various public duties in which he was engaged [13]

On October 10, 1871 at Columbia, Missouri died one of the great in Missouri preachers   Thomas Miller Allen stood beside Samuel Rogers as foremost in establishing churches early in Missouri.   T. M. Allen was born in the Shenandoah Valley in Virginia on October 21, 1797.   Both of his parents died when he was but a child.   At the age of seventeen he enlisted as a volunteer in Captain Peter Hay's Company and served six months in a regiment of the Virginia Militia in the war with Great Britain.

The familiar figure of T. M Allen around Missouri always was of a stout man with a crippled arm at his side   On May 10, 1816 he was returning to Virginia from a visit to Kentucky when six miles west of Washington, Pennsylvania a violent storm struck.   A tree suddenly fell across his path, killing his horse and a young lady companion riding beside him.   Allen received the crippled arm.

On March 24, 1818 he was married to Rebecca W. Russell, Barton W. Stone performing the ceremony.   He settled on a farm near Lexington and studied law at Transylvania University.   Allen was a Mason, being master of the lodge of which Henry Clay was a member.   In 1822 he moved to Bloomington, Indiana where he practiced law   His law partner was James Whitcomb, who was later elected Governor of Indiana and then still later a United States Senator from Indiana.

Allen moved back to Kentucky early in 1823.   In May of that year he was immersed by Barton W. Stone   He had heard Stone and E. R. Palmer preach at the residence of General Robert S.

[13]Robert Richardson, "Robert Milligan," *Christian Standard,* Vol X (April 10, 1875), p 116

Russell who resided on North Elkhorn in Fayette County, Kentucky Thereafter, Allen went to work for the Lord He was a member of the "Old Union" congregation in Fayette County which Stone established with six members In the spring of 1825 Allen began preaching.[44]

In the fall of 1836 he purchased a farm on Two Mile prairie in Boone County, Missouri. After settling here, he was influential in establishing congregations throughout the state. He proved to be moderately wealthy due to exceptionally good business judgment and successful farming. Before the war, he had been able to purchase several slaves. Their attachment became so great that when they were freed following the war, they refused to leave the Allen home.

Early in February, 1880 William Baxter went from his home in New Lisbon, Ohio to Newcastle, Pennsylvania for a meeting. Suddenly he became ill with typhoid fever On February 11th he, too, passed away. Three days later Alanson Wilcox preached the funeral at New Lisbon.

Baxter was born in Leeds, Yorkshire, England on July 16, 1820, and came to America when he was eight years old. Although his parents belonged to the Church of England, young Baxter was baptized by Samuel Church into the Methodist Church at Allegheny City. Church later became one of the foremost proclaimers of the return to the ancient order, although in these early days he was in the Methodist. In 1841, after becoming converted to the restoration, Baxter entered Bethany College Upon graduation, he preached a year in Pittsburgh, and then three years at Port Gibson, Mississippi. Later he preached at Baton Rouge, Louisiana. The war years he spent at Fayetteville, Arkansas with Robert Graham. After the war, he preached for the Sixth Street church in Cincinnati for two years before finally moving to New Lisbon.

Baxter was outstanding for his writings. He contributed several poems to the *Millennial Harbinger* His book, *"Pea Ridge and Prairie Grove"* is one of the best stories of the activities of the brethren during the Civil War to be found Later, he wrote

---

[44]Anonymous, "Death of Elder T M Allen," *Apostolic Times*, Vol III, No 30 (November 2, 1871), p 235

biographies of Walter Scott and Knowles Shaw. In these writings he gained fame, but was never an outstanding preacher.

The death of James Challen should be noted Challen, born at Hackensack, New Jersey on January 29, 1802, died in Cincinnati on December 9, 1878 Challen's early life was spent near Lexington, his parents moving here when he was only seven. In earlier life he was skeptical of all religion, but under James Fishback, one of Kentucky's foremost Baptist preachers, was led into the Baptist denomination After graduating from old Transylvania University, Challen preached for the Enon Baptist Church in Cincinnati Through reading the *Christian Baptist* he was converted to the restoration, and led most of the Baptist Church to apostolic principles

In 1834, after the death of his father and younger brother, Challen went to Lexington again, and established the Main Street congregation In 1850 he moved to Philadelphia where he preached eight years He moved, then, to Davenport, Iowa for ten years, and finally back to Cincinnati where he preached until he died [45]

John O'Kane, pioneer preacher of Indiana, died on January 5, 1881. He had established the first congregation in Indianapolis in 1833. Out of the fifty-six years he had preached the gospel, twenty-seven had been spent in Indiana.

O'Kane was born in Rockbridge County, Virginia on September 22, 1802 His father, Henry O'Kane, was a scholarly schoolteacher, and left an imprint on his son which never left him John O'Kane became an unusually good Bible scholar, being very proficient in Greek, and having an excellent knowledge of Biblical criticism. Joseph Thomas, the "white pilgrim" baptized young O'Kane in 1825, and almost immediately O'Kane began to preach.

Around 1830 O'Kane read an article in the *Christian Messenger* on baptism written by James Matthews. It caused O'Kane to completely change his views on baptism. Two years after this, O'Kane moved to Milton, Indiana and thus began his long life of work in this state.

He had the personal appearance of a good preacher. His slender six feet, two inch body stood erect, making O'Kane the embodiment of dignity in the pulpit. His voice was deep and solemn. He

---

[45]Isaac Errett, "Death of Elder James Challen," *Christian Standard*, Vol XIII (December 14, 1878), p 400

stood nearly perfectly still all the time he preached.   He was not eloquent, but his earnestness was impressive to an audience

He was laid to rest in Bellefontaine cemetery in St Louis [46]

These events, then, present the reader some idea of what was transpiring between the close of the war and the year, 1885

---

[46]L H. Jameson, "John O'Kane," *American Christian Review*, Vol XXIV, (March 15, 1881), p 81

CHAPTER X

A CHRISTIAN PRESIDENT

The attention of the brethren turned in June, 1880 toward the nation's capitol. There was a very definite reason One of its members, a prominent gospel preacher was nominated by the Republican convention that year as its presidential nominee The following November the public elected him to the nation's highest office—the presidency of the United States James Abram Garfield had traveled that difficult road from the log cabin in the wilderness of Cuyahoga County, Ohio to the White House. It was a long, rough and toilsome way, but Garfield by sheer determination accomplished the fete.

There was nothing new in a leading member of the church seeking a political office. R. M. Bishop, an elder in the church in Cincinnati, was mayor of the city during the Civil War, and was elected Governor of Ohio in 1874. The father of D S Burnet, Jacob Burnet, was mayor of Cincinnati in earlier days. In 1880 preachers of the church apparently became very much interested in politics. D. R. Dungan, that year, was a candidate for Governor of Iowa but was defeated. J. M. Pickens ran for Governor of Alabama the same year and also was defeated. The citizens of Indiana got out a petition urging O. A. Burgess to run for Governor on the Republican ticket, but the urge was not strong enough to get him the candidacy. R. M. Gano of Dallas, Texas, one of the brotherhood's prominent Texas preachers, was urged by the Greenbackers of Texas to run for Governor, but Gano refused. The *Christian Preacher* wrote, "Brother Gano could do more good preaching the gospel than ten Congressmen could making laws, even if they always made good ones. The Gospel of Christ is superior to the Greenback gospel." Still later, Ira J. Chase was governor of Indiana in 1892. Chase was one of Indiana's gospel preachers before running for Lieutenant-Governor. J. A. Brooks was vice-presidential nominee on the Prohibition ticket in 1888.

The Populist State Convention of Texas nominated Addison Clark for Superintendent of Public Instruction in 1894 David

197

JAMES A GARFIELD

Lipscomb complained that gospel preachers were forsaking the pulpit and seeking honors in governmental positions From the small village to the nation, church members were filling offices ranging from constables now to the presidency This tendency touches a study of the restoration on its periphery, and a consideration of it is of value to this total study to see the different points of view aroused in James A Garfield's election to the presidency

In 1831 the Western Reserve, in northeastern Ohio, was a dense wilderness, the scattered population being predominately New Englanders James A Garfield's parents were typical of the inhabitants   Abram, Garfield's father, was born in December, 1799.   His mother, Eliza Ballou, was born in Richmond, New Hampshire on September 21, 1801   Both had immigrated from New England to the promising lands to their west   Settling in Cuyahoga County, they built a log cabin thirty by twenty feet long consisting of one door and three windows, and a puncheon floor.   The roof was made of oak clapboards held down by long weight poles.   The family slept on straw in the attic.

James Abram Garfield was born in this log cabin on November 19, 1831   The hardy pioneer parents worked hard to have a home for the children   In May, 1833 the beginning of a tragedy occurred   A forest fire broke out.   The neighbors pitted their efforts against this demon of nature, finally conquering it, but Abram exhausted himself, caught cold and died   James A. was now only eighteen months old   The rearing of the family was left up to Garfield's mother who patiently labored to provide for it, and guide the children.   Consequently, Garfield had a respect for his mother in later years that caught the admiration of the nation.

Garfield's brother, Tom, was eight years older   At night they slept together in the attic.   Garfield would often kick the covers off, and half awake, would cry, "Thomas, cover me up "   After a battle during the Civil War, Garfield lay on the ground beside a distinguished Union officer   The covers came off, and Garfield murmured in his sleep, "Thomas, cover me up "   The words awakened him   Memories of the childhood days drifted before his eyes . He covered his face and wept softly

At the age of sixteen, Garfield agreed to cut wood at twenty-five cents a cord and his board for his uncle who lived near Newburgh   All the while he entertained the dream of being a sailor. The idea was a disappointment to his mother who desired for her son something greater. But she patiently acquiesced temporarily in his planning, thinking the dream might be exploded.   In July, 1847 Garfield went to Cleveland to a cousin, Amos Letcher, and secured a position running a boat on the Ohio and Pennsylvania Canal   At the end of the summer, he returned to his home, still determined to become a sailor. and thoroughly satisfied with himself for the summer's work

Wise guidance was now needed   The mother suggested that he go to school so that he could teach school in the winter and work at the canal in the summer. Her hope was that an education would make him forget the canal work. The plan worked perfectly. Through the influence of Samuel D. Bates, a gospel preacher who lived at Marion, Ohio, Garfield decided to enter Geauga Seminary at Chester. So, on March 6, 1849 he presented himself to this school. The next winter he taught school, and the following spring returned to Geauga During the summer of 1850 he worked as a carpenter near Chester, and that winter, returned to the seminary once more.

That same fall, Western Reserve Eclectic Institute was born at Hiram, Portage County, Ohio with A S. Hayden as president. Garfield continued to finish his term at Geauga, and the following year transferred to the Eclectic Institute He remained here until the fall of 1854 when he transferred to Williams College to study under the famous educator, Mark Hopkins He graduated from this school in 1856 taking the highest honors in the class, and then, returned to Hiram to become president of the Eclectic Institute, a position he held until he entered the Ohio State legislature.

GARFIELD'S RELIGION

Elder A A. Lillie went to a school house at Organge in March, 1850 to conduct a meeting The school was located about forty rods from where Garfield was reared. During the meeting, Garfield came to him privately, frankly admitting that he had some skepticism, and asking for reassurance that the Bible was the word of God Lillie, instead of censuring the boy for his doubt, admired his frankness and absolute honesty in seeking after truth. The next night, he preached a sermon on "What Is Truth?" that thoroughly satisfied Garfield's inquiring mind. At the close of the sermon, Garfield and seven others stepped forward The next day all were baptized. The date was March 4, 1849.[1]

From his mother Garfield had learned the practical walks of the Christian life. Upon his leaving home, she asked him to remember that every evening at sunset she would be reading the Bible It became Garfield's practice through life to pause at sunset and read the Bible, for he had the consciousness that he was now reading with his mother. Likewise did she teach him to

---

[1]F M Green, *A Royal Life* (Chicago Central Book Concern, 1882), p 153

pray. While in the army, Garfield never forgot this, and was
often referred to as the "praying colonel." Moreover, he was
always faithful to meet with the church for worship. He met
with the church in Washington D. C. for the first time in the
fall of 1861 while he was yet in the army. Later, when president,
Garfield attended every service, even to the regular social gatherings He mixed and mingled with the people, shook hands with
them, and inquired of their personal health. It was his constant
conviction that "there is nothing that can make youth so shapeful,
manhood so strong, and old age so beautiful, as the religion of
Jesus Christ."

The first sermon Garfield preached was at Hiram in the winter
of 1853-54. After that, he was a popular speaker in the town.
Garfield and Alexander Campbell met in August, 1860. Campbell
was then seventy-two and Garfield was only twenty-nine. The
meeting was at Alliance, Ohio. Campbell preached in the morning,
and Garfield spoke in the afternoon In a letter dated June 19,
1855 Garfield wrote to a friend.

Your favor of the 4th inst was received about ten days ago,
but I have been entirely unable to answer until this time. A day
or two after it came I left for Pittstown, New York, to attend a
yearly meeting of Disciples, where I spent some four days, and
last Saturday I left again for Poestenkill, and spoke to the people
Saturday evening, and three discourses on Lord's Day. . We had
good meetings in each place, and much interest I cannot resist
the appeals of our brethren for aid while I have the strength to
speak to them.   I tell you, my dear brother, the cause in which
we are engaged must take the world It fills my soul when I
reflect upon the light, joy and love of the ancient gospel, and
its adaptation to the wants of the human race I long to be
in the thickest of the fight, and see the army of truth charge
home upon the battalions of hoary-headed error. . [2]

Garfield's regard for the religious conception he espoused may
be easily seen. While in later years, his political career far overshadowed his religious, he remained faithful to Christ until his
death His preaching was often criticized, it is said, by the older
pioneers in that it dealt more in the ethical realm than upon the
"first principles" Still members of the church never doubted his
allegiance to these principles.

In the halls of Congress he later gained much fame as a debater

---

[2] F M Green, *A Royal Life*, p 121

on political issues   Earlier he was winning considerable fame as a religious debater   At Chagrin Falls in Cuyahoga County, Ohio he debated an infidel by the name of William Denton.   Brethren were highly pleased with his success

The family of Garfield needs special mention.   At the time of his death, Garfield's family consisted of eight persons—himself, his wife, Lucretia Rudolph Garfield, his aged mother, and five children.   His children were Harry, James, Mollie, Irwin and Abram.   Two of his children had died in infancy.

During the winter of 1850, 51, Garfield taught school at Warrensville, Ohio.   One of his pupils was a girl by the name of Mary L. Hubbell.   Later she went with him to school at the Eclectic Institute.   It was generally assumed around the school that they were engaged, although many felt that she was not suited for Garfield   Garfield himself soon came to realize this, but the affair had gone so far that to break it off without offending the girl became with him a major problem.   Often he talked to his close friend, C. E. Fuller, about the matter, and Fuller's advice was to go ahead and break it.   But considerable criticism came to Garfield over it.

Garfield first met Lucretia Rudolph, the girl he married, at Geauga Seminary in Chester.   Her father, Zeb Rudolph, shortly afterwards moved to Hiram to open up a boarding house for boys attending the Eclectic Institute   Rudolph had four children— Lucretia, John, Joseph, and Ellen.   At this time. 1851, Lucretia was about nineteen, the oldest child of Zeb Rudolph.   She taught a school two and a half miles north of Hiram, and·was only home on the week ends.   By disposition, she was a little reserved although attractive.   She and Garfield were married on November 11, 1858 by the president of Western Reserve College at Hudson.

Through their thirty-two years of married life, Garfield displayed a devotion to his wife that was the contributing factor to their marriage success.   In those months previous to his assassination his wife was severely sick.   The newspapers carried daily stories of her condition, and the country watched anxiously for her recovery.   Garfield was deeply concerned. and often said he would resign his position as president if it would help his wife to recover.   But just as news came forth that she was better, he was himself shot down.

The first years of their married life were spent at Hiram.   Garfield purchased a small farm, adjoining the college campus. When he went to Washington as a congressman, he at first rented the property. There is no indication that Garfield was ever materially wealthy. After his third election to Congress, he borrowed money from an old army friend, and bought him a lot and built a house on it.

Garfield's national fame came first as a soldier before he gained popularity in politics. Shortly after the outbreak of the war, he applied to Governor Dennison of Ohio for a commission with the right to raise a regiment. On August 14, 1861 he was commissioned a Lieutenant-Colonel of the Forty-Second Regiment of Ohio Volunteers. Two days later he was mustered into service at Camp Chase, Columbus, Ohio. Many of the soldiers in Garfield's regiment came from students in Hiram College. (Western Reserve Eclectic Institute) Three months were spent in drilling the soldiers, and by the first of December, they were ready to march Southward toward the conflict.

On December 15, 1861 Garfield reported to General D. C. Buell at Louisville, Kentucky. General Buell was a stern soldier, and was somewhat skeptical of Garfield's ability. Nevertheless, an assignment was forthcoming General Zollicoffer was advancing from Cumberland Gap through Kentucky to Mill Spring Confederate General Humphrey Marshall was threatening to over-run the whole of eastern Kentucky. General Buell's plans called for a main drive on Bowling Green southward, but the attack could not be risked until the pressure from the east could be relieved General George H. Thomas, then a rising colonel, was assigned the task of stopping Zollicoffer, and Garfield was assigned the one of halting Marshall

Marshall was known to be encamped at Paintsville up the Sandy Valley with five thousand men. Garfield gathered four regiments of infantry and eight companies of calvary and drove on Marshall. The confederate general was forced to retreat from Paintsville to Prestonburg, but Garfield pressed the battle winning decisive victory. For this triumph, President Lincoln made him a Brigadier-General The commission came on January 10, 1862, giving Garfield the distinction of being the youngest general in the army.

He was now summoned to return to Louisville, but upon his arrival found that General Buell was at Nashville, and was ordered to follow him there. When he got to Nashville, the battle at Shiloh was shaping up, and Buell had already gone to join Grant. Garfield was ordered to Shiloh, and on April 5 was reassigned to the Twelfth Brigade of the Sixth Division of the Army of Ohio. The Sixth Division was one of Ohio's most active early in the war. It fought in upper Virginia until late in November, 1861 when it was ordered to Louisville to join General Buell The Sixth was on the way to join Grant at Donelson when it heard of the fort's surrender. It turned up the Cumberland to Nashville. It was the first of the Union armies to march through the city, and was the first to hoist the national flag over the Tennessee state capitol building.[3] Garfield joined the division in time to take part in the last day's fighting at Shiloh.

After the Shiloh battle, he pursued the enemy southward to Corinth, then eastward through northern Mississippi and Alabama. Later he made headquarters at Huntsville. In August that year he became ill with ague and was sent home. Early in the fall he reported to Secretary of War Edwin M. Stanton in Washington where he was detailed as a member of a court of inquiry to investigate the case of General McDowell. On November 25, he was detailed to try the case of General Fitz-John Porter in a trial which lasted forty-five days This trial demonstrated Garfield's ability as a lawyer.

In January, 1863 he was ordered to report to Major-General Rosecrans at Murfreesboro, Tennessee He was made Rosecrans' chief of staff to reorganize the Army of Cumberland into a more efficient fighting unit During this time, General Grant was sweeping down the Mississippi basin, threatening to cut the confederacy in two But Rosecrans was immobile. People inquired why. The President and the war department were pushing Rosecrans to advance against the enemy, but Rosecrans refused. He addressed letters to each of the seventeen generals under him, asking their opinions and all agreed that an advance was impossible.

Garfield had by now come to an independent decision but the same one that the President, the war department and General Grant had already reached. Unlike European wars, this war was not to be won by occupying strategic cities, for the South

[3]T J Lindsey, *Ohio at Shiloh* (Cincinnati C J Krehbiel & Company, 1903), pp 58, 59

had no strategic points. Victory lay only in meeting the enemy and destroying her army and the sooner this could be done, the sooner the war would be over. Garfield, therefore, studied the matter thoroughly, and recommended to Rosecrans a march east-ward against General Bragg. He figured that discounting the number of soldiers needed to remain in Murfreesboro and hold the city, Rosecrans would still have over sixty-five thousand with which to face the enemy. Rosecrans and his army generals dis-agreed, and let it be known that Garfield alone would be personally responsible for what happened. Garfield assumed the responsibility, and the army moved eastward fighting a series of battles climaxing in the battle at Chickamauga.

Chickamauga was Garfield's last battle, and here he won national fame. The prize at Chickamauga was the Rossville Road, and General George H. Thomas was told to hold it at all costs. The enemy got reinforcements, and beseiged relentlessly Thomas' right flank. General Thomas was swept back in retreat. Longstreet paused to reorganize the attack, thinking victory now certain Enemy forces three times as strong as Thomas were surrounding him, and the general could not know it. Garfield made a daring run on a horse fully exposed to enemy fire to convey the news to Thomas. Thomas immediately retreated further saving the Army of Cumberland from complete destruction. The War De-partment now made Garfield a Major-General.

But Garfield's army career was now at an end. With no effort at all on his part, his friends had placed his name before the public, and had elected him as a representative of the nineteenth district of Ohio in the national Congress. Reluctantly, Garfield gave up an army career, and on December 5, 1863 took his seat in the House of Representatives at Washington

His interest in politics went back only to about 1856. In the fall of 1855, while he was yet a student in Williams College, John Z. Goodrich, a Congressman from Massachusetts, delivered an address on the Kansas-Nebraska bill that held Garfield speechless. Afterward he confided in a friend that he was ignorant of this subject and would familiarize himself completely with it. Much later Garfield became one of the best informed men in the nation on slavery question. Up to this time he had been a Whig. He was disinterested in the Know-Nothing Party, but afterward became an ardent Republican. His first political vote was cast for John C. Fremont.

His first political speeches were delivered at Hiram in 1856. Three years later he began to speak at County Mass Meetings That year he was elected to the Ohio state legislature. During the winter of 1861 he was admitted to the bar. In January, 1860 he took his seat in the Ohio legislature, becoming its youngest member.

For seventeen years he was a member of the House of Representatives. He delivered forty speeches before Congress, addresses that were classics in rhetoric and logic.

On the night of the assassination of President Abraham Lincoln, Garfield was in New York City. In the early morning it was learned that Lincoln was shot. The streets were immediately filled with silent crowds. There was no business transacted. People milled around—no laughter, no mirth, but each anxiously awaiting news of the President's well being. The morning papers blazed the story more fully. The president had died; Secretary Seward's throat had been cut, and attempts were made upon the lives of other cabinet members. It looked as though the government itself was being overthrown, and people feared for what news might yet be forthcoming. Posters asking the crowd to meet around the Wall Street Exchange were placed up, and fifty thousand came. They were angry. The South, they felt had caused this. Two men were heard to say, "Lincoln ought to have been shot long ago !" In a matter of moments their bloody bodies lay still on the ground—one dead and the other dying A frenzy swept the crowd ; silence changed to hateful words, and the swearing of vengeance. Suddenly, Garfield stepped out on a balcony before them all and spoke:

Fellow-citizens!

Clouds and darkness are round about Him. His pavilion is dark waters and thick clouds of the skies! Justice and judgment are the establishment of His throne! Mercy and truth shall go before His face! Fellow-citizens! God reigns and the Government at Washington still lives.[4]

The effective of this speech was to cool the rising temperature of the crowd, and put some semblance of reason back on the throne

Garfield's reputation in politics was on the whole excellent. His

---

[4] F M Green, *A Royal Life,* p 299

enemies in the presidential campaign laid three charges against him which the nation never seriously accepted. It was charged with corruptly purchasing ten shares of stock in the Credit Mobilier Corporation. He was accused, also of fathering a bill in Congress to raise the salaries of the congressmen, and of a corrupt practice in the DeGalyer contract for the pavement of the streets in Washington D. C. The South had a strong dislike for Garfield due to his part in the war, and his strong Northern political bias. Once Garfield favored the confiscation of all southern property, a thing for which David Lipscomb found it hard to grant forgiveness.

Early in life Garfield had formed a resolution against seeking for a position, but to allow the position seek him. He went to the Republican Convention in Chicago on June 2, 1880 with no thought at all of receiving the nomination for a candidacy. Grant, Sherman and Blaine were the three most likely prospects to get the honor to carry the Republican banner in the coming presidential campaign. Garfield ardently backed John Sherman of Ohio. Thirty-three ballots were taken, and on none of them was the name of either man enough in the majority to receive the nomination. Garfield's name appeared on the thirty-fourth ballot. On the thirty-sixth he was swept into the position as the Republican party's candidate for the presidency. Three weeks later the Democrats nominated General Winifield Scott Hancock as his opponent.

As a matter of repeating a historical fact, Garfield was elected in November, and the following March 4th, was duly inaugurated into office.

That which proved the cause of so much trouble at the outset of Garfield's term of office proved to be the cause of his death in only a few months. Civil service examinations to fill governmental positions were as yet unknown. Close to one hundred thousand positions were to be filled either directly or indirectly by the President. Members of the church were quick to take advantage of Garfield's presidency. They flocked into Washington from as far away as Texas with letters from churches, thinking they would now have an easy picking of political jobs. But Garfield refused. He would not be guilty of appointing his own brethren for positions for fear of the charge of biasness. He said to his Chaplain Mullins: "Keep my brethren away from me; it annoys and wounds me for them to come asking for office because of our religious relations." Brethren would meet him in public places, rush up to him, shake hands with him, and say, "How are you, Brother Garfield?" Mullins stated that John B Bowman would have been made Secretary of Interior and B. A. Hinsdale, ambassador to England except for the fact they were members of the church.[5]

Charles J. Guiteau, a French Canadian by birth, and a "vagabond and dead-beat" by profession came to Washington D. C. on Sunday evening March 6, 1881—two days after the inauguration ceremonies He stopped at the Ebbitt House for one day, and then moved around in Washington from place to place On Wednesday, May 18th, he determined to kill the President The last of May he went into O'Mara's store, corner of Fifteenth and F Streets and looked at the pistols. He came back on Wednesday, June 10th and purchased a gun for $10.00 The next day he spent practicing

On Sunday morning, June 12th, Guiteau sat in the park across from the White House He watched the President and his family come out, get in their carriage, and drive off to church He hurried to his room, got his pistol, and started to church. Garfield entered the building at five minutes past eleven, during the reading of the Scriptures Dr Bayton and wife, friends of the Garfields, from Cleveland were his companions F. D Power, regular preacher for the congregation, was out of town, and S D. Moore of Hagerstown, Maryland, was the visiting speaker. Guiteau took a seat several rows behind Garfield His intention was to shoot the President then, but he feared hitting someone else He noted, however, that the President sat near an open window, and determined upon another plan. Guiteau was outside the window the next Sunday morning, but Garfield was out of Washington on official business, thus thwarting the vile purpose

On Saturday, July 2nd, Garfield arose early at the White House, and spent the early hours attending to considerable executive business He was preparing to leave for a two weeks trip into New England First on the itinerary was a scheduled stop at Williams College to address a graduating class Other members of the party went ahead to the Baltimore and Potomac Railroad Depot to take their seats in the President's car Secretary of State,

---

[5]Chaplain Mullins, "Garfield's Religion," *Gospel Advocate*, Vol. XXV, (March 8, 1883), p. 156

Blaine and Garfield drove up in a carriage as the time was nearing 9:30 A. M. The carriage stopped at the B Street entrance, and both men stepped out to walk arm in arm into the station. They passed through the outer "Ladies' Room," on into the main corridor. Just as they did Guiteau darted from behind a door directly in back of Garfield, lifted his gun and shot twice. The last shot was fired only four feet from Garfield's back. The President staggered and fell. Mrs. S. V. White, the woman in charge of the Ladies' Room was standing only six feet from the President and watched the deed. She was the first to reach him. She lifted his head and found he was deathly pale but still conscious. One of Garfield's sons rushed up, bent over his father, and began sobbing frantically. A Dr. Sunderland, a former Chaplain in the Senate, was near. He rushed to Garfield and said: "Mr. President, you are in the hands of the God you have long trusted, and I say to you that the heart of this whole people will go out to God in prayer that you may be spared." The President calmly replied: "I know it, Doctor. I believe in God and trust myself in his hands."[6]

In ten minutes a thousand people were at the depot. The President was placed upon a mattress, and vomited violently. He was carried to an office. The ambulance drove up, and surrounded by twelve mounted police, it moved the President to the White House. Meanwhile, the ticket agent grabbed Guiteau, and he was quickly placed under arrest.

The nation watched anxiously through the months of July and August and up to the middle of September. At times, there seemed to be indications that the President would recover. Finally, on September 19, the eighteenth anniversary of his famous ride at Chickamauga, Garfield passed quietly away. Some years earlier an agreement had been made between Garfield, Isaac Errett, Dr. J. P. Robinson and J. Harrison Jones that the survivors would attend and take part in the funeral services of the other. Each of these men, therefore, spoke at Garfield's funeral.

The election of a member of the church, and a former gospel preacher at that, to the presidency of the United States reflected itself in different ways upon the church. It is for this reason that Garfield's life needs to be told, and that a chapter on him needs

[6]John F. Rowe, "Universal Sympathy for Our Beloved President," *American Christian Review*, Vol. XXIV, No 29 (May 19, 1881), p. 228.

to find a place in restoration history.   The first reaction was one largely localized in the South.

During the Civil War, David Lipscomb became seriously impressed with the idea that the whole study of the relation of the Christian to civil government needed to be gone over completely. It became his conviction that the general conception held by most church members was wrong.   Consequently, in reviving the *Gospel Advocate* in 1866 Lipscomb announced at the beginning that the subject of the Christian's relation to civil government would be thoroughly examined in succeeding issues.   Point by point he proceeded to investigate the subject.

Lipscomb declared that there were currently three ideas of the relation of the church to world powers   The first was that the church should form alliances with world powers and use these powers to advance her own cause   This was the Roman Catholic idea.   The second idea current was that the political governments are of divine origin and should be thus sustained for this reason. This is the Protestant idea   The third idea is that the two institutions—the church and civil governments—are two separate and distinct systems.   Each was necessary in its own sphere.   The church was perfect and needed no human help; that God allowed those who refused to submit to the divine governments—the church —to form governments of their own and in them to accomplish their own desired ends   While the Christian is to have no part in this government, he will quietly and meekly submit to it where its laws do not conflict with that of the church.[7]   Of course, further elaboration was demanded

Tolbert Fanning 'left the imprint of his own character profoundly upon Lipscomb.   There is, however, no indication that Lipscomb borrowed his conception of the Christian's relation to civil government from Fanning, but that he was influenced in the direction he went by Fanning hardly admits of any doubt   When. after the war, several brethren urged Fanning to run for a political office, he refused.   Undoubtedly with his turn of mind he could have been an outstanding success in politics.   But in refusing political offices, Fanning explained his reasons ·

To be sure, we do not affirm that no Christian man or woman ever ascended a throne, but we are quite sure that no Christian

---

[7]David Lipscomb, "The Church of Christ and World Powers," *Gospel Advocate*, Vol. VIII, No 2 (January 9, 1866), pp 28-30

ever ruled a nation by the principles of Christianity The fact is, that the laws of Christ are not suited for the government of any of Satan's subjects. We, moreover, give it as our candid conviction, drawn from scores of examples, that no Christian man can engage in human legislation, or give, even a part of his time to the affairs of human government without being greatly injured spiritually. We do not pretend to give a reason for it; but we simply state the fact of corruption attached to all that busy themselves in politics, and the ordinary excitements incident to human governments. Ambition and false pride, have led many of our brethren into legislative halls, state and national, but in every instance, they are swallowed up and lost in vice, or greatly injured by their associations and labors [8]

Beginning therefore in 1866 at a time when the South lay prostrate from the war, Lipscomb started setting forth the Christian's relation to civil government as he conceived it The idea was somewhat novel to the brotherhood and that it took more hold in the South than in the North can be explained on two grounds Lipscomb was a citizen of the South, and hence the prejudice then so current against Northerners was not an obstacle to the spread of the idea. Then, too, the South was pyschologically prepared for such teaching. A deep sense of the futility of earthly things and of the instability of human governments filled the South, making a fertile field in which to plant the seeds of Lipscomb's theory. An analysis of this theory will prepare the mind of the reader to understand how the impact of Garfield's election was received in the South.

Civil government denoted to David Lipscomb governments founded by men in contrast to that founded by God, the divine. He writes,

We shall use the adjectives, civil and political, when connected with the institutions of earth, as indicating those of human origin, in contradistinction to those of divine origin. Civil government then, is a government founded by man for the well-being of the human family, in contradistinction from a government founded by God for man's well-being.[9]

Definitions now out of the way, Lipscomb goes on to inquire (1) as to the origin of each government. (2) the relation of each to the other at the beginning. (3) and the changes in each with

[8]Tolbert Fanning, "Shall the *Gospel Advocate* Take Any Part in State Matters?" *Gospel Advocate*, Vol VIII, No 3 (January 16, 1866), pp 33, 34
[9]David Lipscomb, "The Church of Christ and World Powers," *Gospel Advocate*, Vol. VIII, No 4 (January 23, 1866), p 56.

reference to the other through the years and how these changes were regarded by God.

Starting then, with the creation of the world, Lipscomb pointed out that God possessed all authority and assigned to each created object its functions and positions and powers. God empowered man to "subdue the earth," etc. (Gen. 1: 28) No man, it is suggested, can occupy any position, or possess any authority, apart from the appointment of God. Man is empowered with the right to subdue and control lower creation. But who governs man? Shall he govern himself? No! God reserves the sole right to govern and control the man. Man's assumption to rule himself is an interference of the divine prerogative. God has always made provision for exercising His right by keeping a government of his own before man. In the garden of Eden, He controlled man by direct commands. When Adam refused this government by yielding to the Satanic suggestion to control himself, he was driven from the garden During the patriarchal dispensation, God governed man—those who would submit—through the fathers. When the family grew, God changed the government from a family to a nation. When the Jewish nation refused the government of God, that form of government was abrogated and the church was inaugurated. All the people of God who submitted to the government of God belonged to the church.

Turning from this brief history, Lipscomb now raised the question of the origin of human governments. His answer was that human governments owe their origin to that portion of the human family that refused to submit to the government of God, and who, in rebellion, set up their own government. The first reference to a human government, says Lipscomb, is in Gen. 10: 10. Here it is seen that this government originated in man's rebellion against the government of God. He writes, "In its beginning it was the embodiment of man's effort to throw off the rule of His maker "

Down through the history of the Old Testament what was the relation of the human government to the divine? Genesis, chapter fourteen, says Lipscomb, shows five kings, rulers in the earthly governments, at war with Abraham, a servant of God, one who submitted to the government of God. The history of the Jews shows that God forbade His people from forming alliances with human governments   (cf. Ex 23: 31, 2; 34: 12, 16; 1 Kgs. 11: 2)

Every time an alliance was formed between the divine government, the Jewish nation, and the human government, the kingdoms of the world, the Jews became weak and disobedient. This nation is a type of the church. For members of the church to form alliances with human governments weakens them and makes them disobedient to God.

It was, therefore, a profound conviction of David Lipscomb's that for Christians to enter into politics was not only wrong in principle but sinful against God. He refused to vote and urged others to refuse. Likewise, of course, did he refuse to participate in carnal wars which were but strifes between political governments brought on by jealousy and greed Human governments, owing their origin to man's rebellion against God, would be overthrown when men the world over would all submit themselves to the government of God.

With David Lipscomb no-man believed anything who was not willing to suffer for what he believed. Suffer, Lipscomb surely did. On November 13, 1862 he induced the elders and evangelists of ten or fifteen congregations in Middle Tennessee to send letters to both the President of the Confederacy and the President of the United States at Washington D. C. declaring their intentions to have nothing to do with war on either side. At the beginning of the war, then, Lipscomb was accused by the South of being disloyal to the Confederacy. He was often threatened and one or two vowed to hang him, but he persisted in his belief When the Federal troops took over Nashville, Lipscomb showed the same indifference as he had toward the South, and was accused by them of being a Southern sympathizer The truth is, he would have nothing to do with either government, he would be a Christian and meekly submit no matter the government under which he lived.

Jacob Creath, Jr., who at the beginning of the war showed some bias in favor of Christians' participation, found himself gradually changing as the war progressed Before long, he quite independently, had reached conclusions similar to those of David Lipscomb After commending Lipscomb for his articles, Creath wrote:

In August, 1863 or 4, I was in the state of Illinois, preaching the Gospel, and one Saturday evening I was sitting in the shade reading the Bible, near a railroad, and a man walking on the

road turned in at the gate and came to me and addressed me thus ·
"What," said he, "are you reading the good book?" "Yes" said
I, "it is a good book, provided people will obey it." He immediately
introduced the subject of the war which was then raging, and
justified the war from God's commanding Moses to kill the
Canaanites and Saul the Amalekites. I asked him if God had
given a command to men, under the Gospel, to kill each other
as he did to Moses and Saul to kill? He said if I called killing
men in war, murder, I did not understand the language. I told
him when you took a man's life, you had killed him, whether
privately or in war, and that I knew the distinction, when done,
between homicide, manslaughter, and murder in self-defense, or
a self-murdering defense, and returned him his compliment of
ignorance, and closed by saying to him, "Now, Sir, you are a
stranger to me, and I to you. I never saw you before, but I
presume you are some sort of a religionist, or sectarian, full of
war up to your chin. I will state a few facts to you for your
future reflection Our Saviour whom you profess to follow, never
killed a man while on earth—he never commanded a man to be
killed—he never shed a drop of human blood, and the only time
when violence was used by one of his followers, he ordered him
to put up his sword, and wrought a miracle to heal the maimed,
and more than that he was murdered outright and downright by
God's elect nation Now, sir, compare your pleading for wholesale murder with the life of him whom you profess to follow,
and slander by calling yourself one of his people" He was off
quickly. I learned afterwards he was a Presbyterian priest.[10]

Lipscomb had to defend his doctrine. It was charged that his
theory violated 1 Pet. 2. 13-14, and Romans 13: 1-5 Inspiration charges every soul to "be in subjection to the higher
powers for there is no power but of God; and the powers that be
are ordained of God." To this Lipscomb pointed out that every
person possesses some power but yet there is always a higher
power. Every soul must be, according to Lipscomb, in subjection to that power which is over it. A servant must be in
subjection to the "higher power" of the master; a child to that
of its parent, a citizen to the "higher power" of the magistrate,
and a magistrate to the higher power of God. "The powers that
be"—all of them are subordinate in the present dispensation to
Christ, he wrote.[11]

---

[10]Jacob Creath, "War and Peace," *Gospel Advocate*, Vol VIII, No 41
(October 9, 1866), pp 650, 651

[11]David Lipscomb, "Romans 13 1," *Gospel Advocate*, Vol VIII, No 4
(January 23, 1866), pp 59, 60

Lipscomb pointed out that during the Civil War, both sides used Romans 13: 1-5 to justify killing in the war. The citizens of the Confederacy used it to prove that they had a right to slay the citizens of the North, and the citizens of the Union used it to justify their killing the citizens of the Confederacy. The Christian under the Confederacy thought Romans 13: 1-5 taught him to submit to the Confederacy, but at the same time, that verse was teaching him to rebel against another government, the Union. Was not the Union a "power that be" the same as the Confederacy? By submitting to either government the Christian was rebelling against another "power that be."[12] This dilemma led Lipscomb to believe that something was wrong with men's interpretation of this scripture. What was it?

In March, 1867 Lipscomb raised the question without answering it. Is it absolutely sure that Paul is speaking of the "powers that be" refers to civil governments? Possibly there was some doubt at this writing in Lipscomb's mind. Fanning had believed that "higher powers" referred to church authorities, those whom the Holy Spirit had made overseers of the flock. The overseers are to see that the law is obeyed. "They bear now the sword in vain" refers figuratively to the fact that he bears not the authority in vain, said Fanning, and the paying of tribute referred to paying contributions.

Lipscomb toyed with this idea a month or two and then rejected it. The "higher powers" did mean civil governments, but to understand Paul, chapters twelve and thirteen of Romans must be studied together. Chapter twelve closed by declaring that vengeance belonged to God. The next chapter shows that God takes this vengeance through His agents. Christians are not God's agents for this vengeance, but the civil government is. The wickedness of the world compels a work to be done which a good man cannot do. Christians are ministers of mercy; civil government, a minister of wrath. The civil government is ordained of God as a minister of God's wrath.[13] Hell is ordained of God as a place of the punishment of the wicked, but this does not justify a Christian in helping Satan. Nor does it justify him in assisting

---

[12]David Lipscomb, "Defense of the Government," *Gospel Advocate,* Vol IX, No 11 (March 14, 1867), pp 215, 216

[13]David Lipscomb, "The Higher Powers," *Gospel Advocate,* Vol IX, No 27 (July 4, 1867), pp 521-525

civil governments in being ministers of God's wrath.   So reasoned
Lipscomb.

The statement of Lipscomb's theory presented problems to be
answered one of which was that of withdrawal of fellowship.
Lipscomb, teaching as he did, that it was wrong for Christians to
vote, hold political office, etc, had the question brought before
him: Should congregations withdraw fellowship from those who
voted, held office, and fought in carnal warfares.   R. C. Horn
of McKinney, Texas wrote Lipscomb in 1875 inquiring what to
do about such people—disfellowship them or not.   Lipscomb
answers by saying,

While saying this much, we are yet unwilling to say that we
think a church ought as yet, to withdraw themselves from one for
voting. (The brethren will excuse us for not using the word,
exclude. It is not a scriptural word, nor does it convey a scriptural
idea.) The reason for this is, the brethren have not been sufficiently
taught upon the subject. The Scriptural means for correcting an
evil has not been sufficiently used to resort to this extreme measure
We have spoken upon the subject, written upon the subject, talked
publicly and privately upon the subject, having come as near
making a hobby of the subject as any one, (expect to do it more
in the future and have no dread of being called a hobbyist), yet
we have never to a single individual taken the pains to present
the subject in such fullness and with such earnestness, as to be
ready to give him over to Satan for rejecting it [14]

Lipscomb goes further and wrote:

Now if others have made such efforts to patiently instruct and
persuade their brethren the truth on this subject, have exhausted
all patience, forbearance and long suffering in teaching them the
way of the Lord, publicly and from house to house, and they
wickedly refuse to hear that law, then it may be right to withdraw
yourselves from such. But no Christian, observant of the laws
of the Lord, can properly withdraw from a brother, aiming to do
right, but ignorant of the truth of God.

For fifteen years, then, Lipscomb's position on the Christian's
relation to the civil government had been permeating the South,
and had picked up many adherents   When, therefore, in June,
1880 Garfield was nominated for the presidency, Lipscomb wrote:

After days of wrangling and strife the better elements of the
party seemed to triumph and they nominated Gen. James A.
Garfield as the candidate for President   General Garfield is a

[14]David Lipscomb, "Queries on Civil Government," *Gospel Advocate,* Vol
XVII, No 17 (April 22, 1875), p 399

member of the church of Christ, was once a preacher, or as he prefers to style it, a lecturer among the disciples of Christ, went into politics, was a member of the Ohio State Senate at the breaking out of the war, went into the army, was a general for a time, became General Rosecrans' chief of staff, and in this position at the time of Rosecrans' march through Middle Tennessee to Chattanooga. Since the war he has been a member of Congress. We presume he has maintained his personal and religious integrity as well as any man with his surroundings and his position could. There have been some ugly charges made against him, but we think, not sustained. . .

But now, dear brethren of the South who wish and argue for good, pious, religious rulers, what are you going to do about Brother Garfield? Are you going to vote for him, or will you take up an ungodly Democrat, if they should nominate such a one? . . .[15]

In the predominately Democratic South, this was a bitter pill for members of the church to swallow. Whether to vote for a member of the church when his politics was Republican or vote for a Democrat who was not a member. Lipscomb wrote:

Many Christians justify themselves in voting and taking part in politics on the ground that Christian men are needed in politics and in official positions. If Christians are needed in politics, the purer the form of Christianity, the better We have been sure that they were mistaken in this reason. I do not mean that they were conscious of insincerity, but that they deceived themselves. We intend to make this deception evident to all who are willing to be undeceived. Gen. Garfield is a member of the church of Christ. He is a man in good standing in that church. He is intimate with a great number of well-known and leading disciples of Christ. They all regard him as a man of honor and integrity. . .

His neighbors esteem him. They have repeatedly elected him to represent them in the highest positions of trust and honor in Congress, with constantly increasing majorities His party in the Legislature of his State unanimously elected him to the United States Senate. They knew him In Congress he is personally esteemed by both political friends and opponents No man in Congress, we have been assured by his most determined political opponents, is more highly esteemed personally than he. He is popular and respected personally by all in Congress Under these circumstances, no Christian can believe or report or take up the public evil reports against Garfield, without violating all the obligations of Christian brotherhood.

[15]David Lipscomb, "Words of Caution," *Gospel Advocate,* Vol XXII, No 26 (June 24, 1880), p 401

We say this much about him while having no sympathy whatever with his course   We have watched his course for years ; we knew his character and position before the war, as a man of culture and refinement, with strong religious sentiment   We watched him to see the effect of the soldier's profession and work on his character   We were to him an unknown but interested observer of his course while in military power here in our State   We have watched his course with interest from the day he took his seat in Congress till now, to see what effect politics and political associations would have upon his earnest religious nature and strong resolute will   We have been strengthened by this observation of his course, in our conviction that no Christian can go into politics and maintain a Christian character ; at the same time that politics are not aided by the intrusion of religion into its domain   But we are satisfied that we know of no man who has gone into politics, who has become so thoroughly identified with the affairs of government, and yet so well retained his Christian character and religious interest as has General Garfield.

We hold that wherein Gen. Garfield has not failed in religious integrity in the political arena, ninety-nine out of every hundred Christians would fail.   Moreover, I do not believe in a hundred years past, so much of earnest, intelligent religious character, in one person, has come so near the Presidency as does now in the person of General Garfield   The chances are, that so much will not again for a hundred years to come.[16]

Lipscomb declared that if he did not believe that Christians had no business in politics, he would vote for Garfield himself.

But Lipscomb was a Southerner, writing to Southern readers who bore no good will toward Republicans.   To get his point across he was charitable in the extreme.   His readers mistook this charitableness for weakness, thinking that now since a Christian was running for President, he was surrendering his former point of view   Lipscomb, however, was intending to show he bore no bias against Garfield while yet declaring that a Christian had no business in holding political offices.   From Hallville, Texas an old brother, John H. Cain, wrote in anger : "Brother Lipscomb : I am very old and feeble and do not wish to be insulted with your black Republican politics.   You will please discontinue my paper."

The *Gospel Advocate* felt the reaction of Lipscomb's theory. Joseph Franklin, early in 1880, was announced as a new associate-editor.   Joseph Franklin, son of Ben Franklin, was then going

---

[16]David Lipscomb, "Christians and Politics," *Gospel Advocate*, Vol XXII, No 29 (July 15, 1880), p 449

through a period of confusion and readjustment. Ten years earlier he had stood squarely behind his father, and steadfastly fought all human innovations. Upon his father's death and the assumption of the editorial chair by John F. Rowe, young Franklin changed. Turning from the *Review,* he went to the *Gospel Advocate,* but the election of Garfield and its repercussions in the *Advocate* caused him to suddenly announce his resignation. Meanwhile, Lipscomb found himself on the opposite side of the issue from John F. Rowe, so both men discussed the issue, which was carried in both the *American Christian Review* and the *Gospel Advocate* in the summer of 1880 while the candidates were lectioneering.

Garfield's election to the presidency turned the attention of the brotherhood—and the world—to the church in Washington, D. C. Garfield began regularly attending the church upon his first election to Congress in 1863. In the spring of 1869 the congregation purchased a small, frame building from the Methodists. Reporters sneeringly referred to this as the "Campbellite shanty." After Garfield's nomination, the church felt its own inadequacy, and cries went up for funds to build a new house of worship. V. M. Metcalfe visited this congregation late in 1880, and reported that the church had begun to use a small organ in its worship. He noted that Garfield seldom missed a single service, even to attending the social meetings.

Garfield Memorial Church was badly needed, thought many brethren. The task of raising funds was turned over to the Missionary Society. David Lipscomb was critical of the move— not that a meeting house was not needed but to build one because of Garfield, to refer to it as the "Garfield Memorial Church," was totally contrary to the principle of returning to the ancient order. G. W. Rice, publisher of the Review, however, thought such a building was not needed. He wrote:

A week ago I expressed my opinion about the proposed meeting-house in Washington City. I now repeat, such a house is not needed. The one now there is sufficiently large for all the purposes of the church at that place It has been said as a good and sufficient reason for building a fifty thousand dollar house in Washington—we want and need a court church in Washington City, it being the seat of government of the United States—That we need and must have a large and elegeant house where the President and his family can attend and be seen. . .[17]

Both Lipscomb and Rice were objecting fundamentally on the same ground, although Rice couched his objections in strongly-worded terms. That Washington needed a new meeting house was evident. To build one in honor of President Garfield, to build one as a means of show, to parade the church before the government in Washington was a fundamentally carnal and worldly spirit. This is the seat of the objections

Plans for the erection of the building went on even after Garfield died. By the spring of 1882 the congregation was ready to let out the contract. The cornerstone was laid July 2, 1882, the first anniversary of the shooting of the President Five thousand people attended that simple service, among them President Arthur himself. B A. Hinsdale delivered the major address. The new building, to be known as the Garfield Memorial Church was to be completed at a cost of $33,700, a rather costly project considering the times.

This hero worship, and calling a church, the "Garfield Memorial Church" was too much for Lipscomb. He wrote of Garfield:

His course was one of dishonor to the church; with ability and assured success as a servant of that church, he surrendered it for service in the worldly kingdom. If Garfield's career was acceptable, why not all young men of popular talents turn from the ministry to law, war and politics? Did I believe his course was acceptable to God, I would yet turn from the service of the church to that of the world Is it strange when the church counts him who turned from service in her offices and works, to the work of the world, worthy of so much more honor than those who serve faithfully in her sanctuaries. . .[18]

Garfield more than any other man had proved to be the exception to the rule. Politics corrupted him less than it did any other person. For strength of moral character and of devotion to God the presidency has never known Garfield's equal.

---

[17]G W Rice, "Washington City Mosque," *American Christian Review,* Vol XXIV, No 11 (March 15, 1881), p 85

[18]David Lipscomb, "Hero Worship," *Gospel Advocate,* Vol. XXIV, No. 30 (July 27, 1882), p 467.

CHAPTER XI

DARKENING HORIZONS

In 1865 Moses E Lard argued that division was virtually impossible, for in the first place, the teaching of the church virtually condemned it, and furthermore, the churches had no ecclesiastical tribunal to declare it. Added to this, thought Lard, was the fact that the local autonomy of the congregations was a decided barrier to division. Three years later, Ben Franklin voiced his approval of Lard's sentiments Reviewing the history of the restoration, he found in such cases as the Jesse B. Ferguson trouble, the war, slavery and the society controversy that the church had weathered these threats of division with no serious breach in its ranks. These facts were encouraging to the belief that division was out of the question

The passing of another decade, however, made many less confident of continual unity. Some were now speaking of "organic union and disunion" among the brethren, inquiring fearfully if "organic disunion" will ever come. But David Lipscomb alleged that he had not the least fear of "organic disunion" for the reason there was no "organic union" among the churches to be broken. In the next place, he contended, any union which existed among the churches was not dependent upon any action of will or resolution of the members themselves Lipscomb's explanation was there was no such thing as "organic union" among the churches in New Testament times. The New Testament never speaks of union of churches, but only of unity among all the people of God Christ prayed that individually, all of His disciples might be one— not one in organic union, but one like the Father and the Son are one—in purpose, in love, in desire That which made all disciples one in New Testament times was a common belief in the same person, Jesus, and a "walking in the light as he is in the light."[1]

W. B. F. Treat concluded that division was no longer out of the question. He preached for the church at Bloomington, Indiana and saw the congregation divided over the introduction of the

---

[1]David Lipscomb, "Union, True or False," *Gospel Advocate*, Vol XXII, (June 10, 1880), p 374

221

organ   After reviewing Lard's reasons why the church could not divide, Treat added:

But the last few years have been eventful ones in our history and by experience we have received lessons which some of us had hoped never to learn   It is strictly true that we can never divide while, as individuals and as congregations, we have the grand watchword with which this movement began: "Where the Bible speaks, we speak; where the Bible is silent, we are silent."

But it begins to occur to the minds of many that there is a possibility of division over things not in the Bible!   That any great number of men among us would insist on organizations, customs and practices not mentioned in the Bible, and force these into the Church, does not appear to have been included among the possibilities by the scribes who decided that we could never divide.[2]

Treat added:

If the worldly, unauthorized customs and practices that are popular with innovationists and sectarians are forced into the Church, over the protests of godly men, division is not only imminent, but it may become a necessity and a virtue!   The law of Christian unity is based upon the recognition of the supreme authority of Christ, and nothing in the gospel of Christ requires a believer to submit to unauthorized practice in religion

R B Trimble of Mayfield, Kentucky also contended that it *was* impossible for the people of God to divide.   The very fact that a few people were dissatisfied with apostolic principles and abandoned these for "human innovations" did not imply that God's people had divided   "They went out from among us because they were not of us."   So Trimble wrote:

There is now, ever has been, and ever will be division of sects   But that there is now, or ever will be, a serious division of the true children of God, is that which I do not believe   That good and bad are caught in the gospel net, no one who is a discerner of events, or at all acquainted with Bible history, will, for a moment deny   There are great fears expressed by some of the brethren that the church will be divided.   I have no fears of division among the true friends of Jesus.[3]

Trimble pointed out that those who would make the church another denomination, who would put in the organ, and champion the missionary societies were never really converted to the truth anyway.

[2]W B F Treat, "Can We Ever Divide?" *American Christian Review,* Vol XXII, No 19 (June 6, 1879), p 145
[3]R B Trimble, "Are the Children of God Divided?" *American Christian Review,* Vol XXII, (1879), p. 43.

If division must come, Lipscomb refused to regard it as the worst calamity possible. He wrote:

We have not doubted, for years, that if the course of adding innovation to innovation, pursued by many, is persisted in, that division and separation will come Nay, it ought to come. God will cause it to come . . If a separation will, and ought to come, it may be asked, how will it be brought about? All the true disciple has to do, is to firmly stand for the truth, and to be true to it. God in His providence will then bring it.[4]

Likewise, J. W McGarvey, sensing that division was threatening, did not fear it as the worst of calamities. His article, first printed in the *Old Path Guide* in 1885 was copied into the *Gospel Advocate*.

. . . I have but little sympathy with those brethren who seem to dread disunion among ourselves as the direst of all evils. If we would inspire sensible men around us with a desire for union with us, we must be careful to show them that we do not and will not maintain unity with anything unscriptural, whether it shows itself within our ranks or outside of them. Truth first, union afterwards, and union only in the truth. This is our motto.[5]

With the passing of time the war drums beat a steadily increasing tempo The danger of division was increasing hourly. The horizon was dark By 1883 some declared that division was present The editorials of John F Rowe in the *American Christian Review*, which began in the fall of that year are among the best Rowe ever penned. The fever was now at its height, and Rowe's strongly-worded articles were intended to check the trend. To dip back into the past and breathe the atmosphere of these editorials is to give one a sense of the anxiety of the hour, and an appreciation of this crisis in the restoration.

Rowe compared the plight of the church in 1883 with the condition of ancient Israel

As a people, we have not yet passed into actual captivity; but we see premonitions of such a captivity all around us. Of these premonitions, or prognostication, we shall speak hereafter. That there have been gross departures from the principles of radical reform, with which we started, that the original simplicity of the gospel has been shamefully marred by perversions of the truth, that the hearts of the righteous have been made sad by a secularized worship; that false rules of Bible interpretation have

[4]David Lipscomb, "Union and Schism," *Gospel Advocate*, Vol XXV, (December 26, 1883), p 822
[5]J W McGarvey, "no title," *Gospel Advocate*, Vol XXVII, (January 7, 1885), p 7.

made powerless our distinctive plea; that efforts have been made
to destroy the independence and individuality of the congregations
of Christ; that efforts have been made to subordinate the congregations to the will and dictation of organized conventions—a concern
distinct and separate from the church of Christ, and *under whose
protecting wing every folly and innovation hides itself,* that many
mock at the proposition, "Where the Bible speaks, we speak,
where the Bible is silent, we are silent"; that all who stand upon
the original platform of principles, as enunciated by the Campbells,
and resist all innovations upon the apostolic order, are proscribed,
persecuted, and socially ostracized—are questions of the most
serious nature, and patent to all observing eyes [6]

Rowe reported that letters were pouring into the *Review* office,
asking if this "reformation" were to go forward, or "to degenerate
into a sect." While it appeared that a division was inevitable,
Rowe affirmed there was no present danger of it.

As long as the evil which God pronounces against does not
take an organic form, and as long as a yoke of bondage is not
actually fastened on the necks of the people, an actual separation
need not take place. Until such a condition of things actually
confronts us, and before we are bound hand and foot by a system
of ecclesiasticism, we are morally bound by our pledges to the
great Head of the church, in our places to beat back the tide of
innovations, and by invincible courage and resistless pluck, hold the
fort, secure every possible advantage and repel the enemy.

Here was a call to resist all innovations. But, suppose in spite
of all struggles, the innovations sweep over the church anyway,
what then? In the same editorial Rowe added:

If, however, in their struggles at the post of duty and as faithful members in the one body, the true Israel of God are over-
powered and the church of Christ loses its apostolic identity by
the presence of organized ecclesiasticism and priestly domination,
in that it will become necessary, according to the mandates of
God quoted above, to actually separate and make a new rally
upon the original ground.[7]

About the same time Rowe declared that two distinct parties
were growing up in the church One, he calls the "ancient order
of things," and the other, "the new order of things." Each stands
antagonistic to the other.

That there is rapidly growing up among us a new order of

---

[6]John F Rowe, "Lift Up a Standard for the People," *American Christian Review,* Vol XXVI, (September 13, 1883), p 282
[7]John F Rowe, "Lift Up a Standard for the People," *American Christian Review,* Vol XXVI, (September 13, 1883), p 292

things in contrast with the old order of things, as advocated by Alexander Campbell and his associates, is a fact that is becoming more apparent and pronounced every day. Anyone who will take the pains to read the *Christian Baptist,* edited fifty years ago by Alexander Campbell, and continuing seven years, will discover in reading his series of articles on *"The Ancient Order of Things,"* that, when placed in contrast with much of our church literature of the present day, and in contrast with much of our pulpit teaching there is growing up and taking form "The Modern Order of Things." It pains us to make this statement, but the fact is so patent and palpable that it is in vain to try longer to conceal it We might as well prepare to meet the issue first as last. We are grieved to say that the line of separation is becoming more distinct every day. There are two classes among us—those who represent "The Ancient Order of Things" and those who represent "The New Order of Things." It is manifest that these two parties are not only not acting in sympathy, but that the men of the New Order of Things are determined to crush down, if possible, the Ancient Order of Things.[8]

In the intensity of a controversy like this one now raging. one finds at least the partial answer for the future course of the restoration. Why did so many churches in the North adopt the innovations? The answer is partially explained in the fact that the *Christian Standard* "outmaneuvered" the *American Christian Review* at almost every turn. John F. Rowe was of a positive conviction that the rise of innovations would divide the church. But while opposing innovations, Rowe did not act consistently in what he believed. There is, on the one hand, a leader of the forces opposing innovations who was not consistent; on the other there was a leader shrewd enough to capitalize upon these inconsistencies, and the reason is found for many churches and brethren who were "on the fence" favoring innovations

Rowe, in opposing Isaac Errett published ten items on which the scriptures were silent, and charged that the *Standard* was promoting these, and therefore, causing division Included were such items as the instrument of music, missionary societies, etc. But as a last item, Rowe accused the *Standard* of promoting "lesson leaves," Bible School Quarterlies, of which the Bible was silent Errett was shrewd enough to single out the "lesson leaves" and ride it mercilessly. He had, of course, very little difficulty in

---

[8] John F Rowe, "The Old and the New Order," *American Christian Review,* Vol XXIII, No 13 (March 30, 1880), p 100.

making Rowe's position appear ludicrous, and since Rowe had declared "lesson leaves" to be in the same category with instrumental music and missionary societies, the answer to "lesson leaves" was the answer to all—so concluded the readers of the *Christian Standard*. What drove Rowe to such an extreme?

Moreover, Rowe in opposing the missionary society, charged their conventions with causing division. Yet, late in 1883 he recommended a mass meeting of the brethren who opposed innovations to get together in a conference and republish the principles on which they stood. So he proposed fighting conventions by forming an opposing convention. James A. Harding was quick to point out Rowe's inconsistency:

It is clear that if division comes in the ranks of this reformation, it will come through the conventions. Were the anti-organ, antimissionary society men to do what their opponents have already done, that is, were they to meet in such mass meetings, an organic division would inevitably result. Such a division could not take place without the conventions. There would be nothing larger than a church to divide; for there would be among Christians no other organization than the local congregations.[9]

Why could not Rowe see his inconsistency? The answer is difficult to find; we only state it as an inescapable fact.

THE CAUSES OF DIVISION

Underlying the fearful fact of division were certain causes. As an attempt to understand the threat of division, it will be necessary to understand some of these causes.

The growing use of instrumental music. Despite the fact that during the war, the instrument was fought severely as an innovation, its use grew at first slowly and then more rapidly. Ben Franklin declared in 1867 that not ten congregations in the brotherhood were using the instrument, but by 1885 that number had greatly multiplied.

The story of its introduction in most cases is a story of division, law suits, and bitterness. In the summer of 1872 the instrument came into the church at Frankfort, Kentucky. This congregation for years had been accustomed to strife, and the introduction of the organ only fanned the flames more. About 1870 the church house burned and the necessity for a new building was pressed.

---

[9]James A Harding, "Will We Divide?" *Gospel Advocate*, Vol. XXVI, No. 1 (January 2, 1884), p 10.

T. N. Arnold, the preacher, raised the money. Mrs. E. H. Tubman of Augusta, Georgia, a wealthy widow who had proved a benefactor for the erection of many church buildings, came to the rescue The building was finished the summer of 1872 and by August, the church was ready for the dedication ceremony.

Isaac Errett and W. T. Moore, neither of whom opposed the organ, came to Frankfort. Errett was to preach the dedicatory sermon and Moore continue with a protracted meeting. A minority in the church planned the program, and all the details were unknown to Arnold and the elders. On Saturday before the scheduled service it was learned that an instrument was to be used. A petition was gotten up objecting to the move, but in spite of their objection the organ was used. Great division followed for years to come.[10]

Late in 1880 the church in Bedford, Indiana, put in the instrument. Uncle "Stever" Younger, who had given one thousand dollars on a new building, had worked hard in building up the congregation. When the organ was injected into the worship, he and fifty others were excluded.[11] A short time earlier the church at Bloomington, Indiana, had a similar experience. W. B. F. Treat came to Bloomington in 1870 and preached for the church four years. Afterwards, he turned his attention to evangelistic work, although still making Bloomington his home Weak preaching produced weak members in the years that followed. The sermons were mere lectures or moralizing, "such as would be popular in any sectarian church." The organ was introduced. Treat and some others left and began meeting in the courthouse The introduction of the organ took place in November, 1877. In the following spring Ben Franklin came to Bloomington and conducted a meeting in the courthouse. Treat began preaching monthly here.[12]

On Sunday, June 26, 1881, the church at East Cleveland, where Jabez Hall preached, dedicated a new organ costing two thousand dollars. The church had tried to secure the services of Isaac Errett for the dedication, but another appointment kept Errett

---

[10]W H Hopson, "The Frankfort, Kentucky, Christian Church," *American Christian Review*, Vol XV, (September 24, 1872), p 317

[11]W. H. Krutsinger, "Bedford (Indiana) Church Split," *American Christian Review*, Vol XXIV, No 3 (January 18, 1881), p 21

[12]Ben Franklin, "Bloomington, Indiana," *American Christian Review*, Vol XXI, No 23 (June 4, 1878), p 180

from being present. The pastors of several denominational churches were invited, and a professional organist, from the First Methodist Church, was hired   A. S Hayden, who worshipped there, wrote the following to John F. Rowe:

Can you imagine how all this idolatrous affair looks to me, for it is naught else, it being the instrument first, middle, and last The prophet Amos, in speaking of the manner in which Israel worshiped, uttered this language. "Woe to them that chant to the sound of the viol, or invent to themselves instruments of music like unto David " If it was woe unto them then, what will it be to those who live in this day of the printed word and gospel light?

To this John F. Rowe remarked:

So far as our distinctive plea is concerned, that "Disciple Church" is gone. Indeed, it was carried away into Babylon years ago, and this is one of our "missionary churches" too! *Two thousand dollars* for an organ is what they call "missionary work." We have our doubts that this church has contributed one thousand dollars in the last ten years for missionary work. . . As Jabez Hall "the pastor," and "three of the wealthy brethren," have thrown down the fences, of course the members can go in and out and find pasture—which ministers to the flesh—in any of the "sister churches " Of course the communion table is open to all streaked, ring-necked and speckled sectarians. Jabez Hall was educated at Bethany College   Shades of Alexander Campbell! How have the mighty fallen! Yes, it is *"money* that makes the mare go "[13]

The church in Anderson, Indiana, which had long been divided, introduced the organ during April, 1882   On March 15 that year, George P. Slade came for a meeting. Four years earlier Slade had astonished the brotherhood by carrying on a one-sided discussion with McGarvey in the *Review* alleging that the Greek word *Psallo* included an instrument. Possessing a natural bias 'for the instrument, Slade came to Anderson and used his influence to promote the organ [14]

At Augusta, Georgia, still earlier Mrs Emily H. Tubman gave a hundred thousand dollars for a new building   The lot cost $35,000; the parsonage cost $10,000, and the meetinghouse $55,000. The persons planning the building left place for an instrument, but Mrs. Tubman refused to allow it. She tore down a picture of John baptizing the Saviour and put in its place the words, "Repent

---

[13]John F Rowe, "Organ Dedication at East Cleveland," *American Christian Review,* Vol XXIV, No 31 (August 2, 1881), p 242
[14]Charles R Cravens, *History of the Central Christian Church* (n p , 1925), p 52

and be baptized every one of you in the name of Jesus Christ for the remission of your sins," etc. (Acts 2·38)[15]

The Central Church in Cincinnati, one of the most prominent in the brotherhood, put in the instrument in February, 1871. A short time before, while the church still met in its old house, a vote had been taken on the instrument. T. M Allen of Missouri happened to be visiting that day, and threw his weight against the movement, cutting off the use of the instrument temporarily

Still the use of the organ increased. At Wellington, Kansas, the organ was introduced in 1884. At Bowling Green, Kentucky, there was trouble in the church in 1879. M. J Ferguson, a graduate of Bethany College and Harvard University, aided in putting in the mechanical instrument John T Poe wrote from Texas: "The old church at Huntsville has put the organ *in,* and some of its best members *out.*" Carroll Kendrick, who had only recently moved from Texas to California, wrote in March that, year that the new church in Santa Ana had just included the organ in its worship

By 1885 other congregations were taking steps preparatory to introducing the instrument. When Mrs. Alexander Campbell returned to Bethany in June, 1884, she found the organ in the vestibule, it already having been used in the Sunday School and on two different occasions at church services during her absence' She wrote:

I have attended the worship of the church the last two days since I came, and am happy to say the sound of instrumental music grated not upon *my ear,* but most excellent, solemn, congregational singing, in which I heartily enjoyed uniting I have worshiped in the church, but with a protest elsewhere to the organ I must say, however, I could not endure to worship in the church at Bethany if the instrument which had introduced so many discordant notes amongst dear brethren and sisters was made part of the worship instead the music rising from the heart of God's children . . [16]

Mrs Campbell was an ardent opposer of the use of the instrument all her life, borrowing her conviction undoubtedly from her husband.

With the cases of the introduction of the organ growing, op-

[15]Anonymous, "Items, Personals, Etc," *Gospel Advocate,* Vol XVIII, No 3 (January 20, 1876), p 72

[16]Mrs Alexander Campbell, "Letter from Mrs Alex Campbell," *American Christian Review,* Vol XXVII, No 29 (July 17, 1884), p 227

posers found themselves wondering what they should do. Should they cease their opposition and acquiesce to the majority rule? On the other hand, could one who believed its use sinful adopt its use? The problem was serious, nor was it likely that their solution would at first be uniform.

J. M. Mathes, one of Indiana's pioneer preachers, had always opposed the use of the instrument just as he had the missionary society When the society was accepted by a majority of brethren in 1849, he surrendered his opposition in deference to their wishes. His last years were spent near Bedford, Indiana. He watched Indiana churches adding the instrument. He never relinquished his opposition, and yet wrote:

I am opposed to the organ in the worship, but make no *factious* opposition to it. I suffer no organ to drive me from my place in the church of Christ, nor from my duty as a disciple of Christ.[17]

Isaac Errett put the use of the instrument entirely on the plain of expediency. Consequently, when a brother wrote him, asking for advice on what to do when the instrument was introduced, Errett responded:

Unquestionably, in such a case the wishes and convictions of aged and wise brethren should be respected   The law of love requires us to waive our own preferences, even when such preferences are right, rather than destroy the peace of the church or wound the feelings of our brethren. God cannot bless rude and unfeeling attempts to overrule the judgment and scruples of good brethren by the force of numbers, even when such judgment and scruples may be forced in error. . . . But where a majority thus acts, the minority should firmly protest against the action, and rid themselves of responsibility, and then patiently endure until a change comes. Sooner or later, unless the fear of God is entirely lost, time works out a remedy for such evils.

When the question of what the minority should do when the majority voted in the organ was sent to the *Apostolic Times*, one of the editors replied:

If they make the organ a matter of opinion or expedient, as the organ party professes to do, then according to their own professions, they ought not to bring the organ in. They cannot do this without giving offense. But we put it on no such grounds as this. The worship of God is divinely prescribed in the law of God. The acts of worship are clearly set forth. These acts we can perform. This is the true worship when performed in spirit and in truth.

---

[17]J. M Mathes, "The Organ Once More," *The Evangelist*, Vol XVI, No 13 (March 31, 1881), p 197

Majorities have no right to vote a new element into worship No majority can compel a man to submit to something for worship that is not found in the divinely prescribed acts in the Scriptures We will worship according to the Scriptures in every item, small and great; but we will not have anything imposed on us not found in the prescribed worship. We can, we trust, find some who will worship according to the Scriptures, with whom we can worship, and with these by the blessing of the Lord, we will meet and worship the Lord—the Jehovah.[18]

Shortly afterwards, a man wrote, objecting to the *Times'* attitude toward the introduction of the instrument, declaring, "This makes every man's conscience, and every man's notion of divine teaching in regard to worship, the basis of union" To this the *Times* replied that this is wholly incorrect, but that it makes the word of God the basis of union, and requires each man to adhere to the word of God The *Times* asked, "The only question is, how long shall the minority hold membership in a congregation that has abandoned the word of God?"[19]

Ben Franklin, seeing the magnitude of the problem, simply wrote:

A new question is being started, it is this: "Do you intend to make the organ a bar of fellowship?" We do not propose to *make it anything*. We want simply to have nothing to do with it . . The question is not about bars of fellowship, but about *worshiping with the organ* Can you compel brethren to *worship with the organ?* You certainly cannot If you introduce the organ and drive persons from the worship with it, and who cannot do it in good conscience, you are the cause of the disturbance and will find yourself held responsible. We are certain the Lord does not require us to worship with the organ, and *we will not do it.* If any man brings into the worship a new and foreign element, and thus places pious people in such a position as to compel them to worship with the organ or not worship with him, he introduces the disturbing element and is to be held responsible for the trouble. In reference to such the commandment is, "Mark them who cause divisions," etc "[20]

But as the years passed, there seemed to be no means in sight to settle the question. Franklin inquired: "But what is to be

---

[18] Anonymous, "Two Questions and Four Answers," *Apostolic Times*, Vol V, (April 24, 1873), p 4

[19] Anonymous, "The Organ and Conscience," *Apostolic Times*, Vol V, (May 15, 1873), p 4

[20] Ben Franklin, "The Frankfort, Kentucky, Christian Church," *American Christian Review*, Vol XV, No 39 (September 24, 1872), p. 316

done? How can we avoid strife? Let the organ come in and say
nothing against it?" He admitted that there was much bitterness
over the organ, but insisted that this bitterness was all on the
other side, a statement not altogether too accurate. But he was
firm, "We are in the right, and intend by the grace of God to
maintain it."[21]

Some questions of differences among brethren might be settled
by putting the question on the plain of expediency, but it was
becoming increasingly obvious that this subject of the use of the
instrument could not be settled on any such grounds If a man
honestly believed the use of the instrument to be a sin, who could
expect him to participate with it? E. M. Schrock wrote to Ben
Franklin saying: "If you prefer to worship without an organ, it
is none of my business; and if I wish to use an organ. it is none
of your business " This rather rude and harsh way of putting
it was precisely the position of those defending the instrument on
the grounds of expediency. But Franklin replied ·

But now, "If you prefer to worship without an organ, it is
none of my business; and if I wish to use an organ it is none of
your concern " But suppose we both meet in the same congregation, how can this rule be carried out? Can you worship *with*
it and we *without it?* No, sir; if you worship *with it,* we must
worship *with it.* If we worship *without it,* you must worship
without it

It is not my course that "creates strife." The course of the
organ folks in bringing the organ, which "is outside of the Bible"
into the worship prescribed in *the Bible,* creates the strife, and
frequently divides the church. They are the responsible party,
the cause of strife and division.[22]

It was not possible for brethren who thought the instrument sinful
to worship along side of those who thought it expedient Opposers
of the instrument were failing to see why, if the use of the instrument was outside the Bible, it was expedient to put it into the
worship and divide the church. Unfortunately, Franklin's death in
1878 came in the middle of the conflict Had he lived longer, it
is but a matter of conjecture what course the restoration would
have taken. One cannot escape the conclusion that some breathed

---

[21]Ben Franklin, "Question of Fellowship," *American Christian Review*.
Vol XVIII, (1875), p 316

[22]Ben Franklin, "no title," *American Christian Review,* Vol XXI, No 1
(January 1, 1878), p. 4

easier now that Franklin was gone. J. M. Barnes sensed this and wrote:

No doubt there are men who claim to be brethren, that rejoice that he [Ben Franklin] is dead. But they should remember that, like Abel, "though dead, he yet speaketh." His great works will live far into the periods of the future, and the unborn will call him blessed. He was truly a great commander, one that could see far into the future, and as such often has he lifted his warning voice to the host, among whom he so nobly battled, and sought to lead to higher scenes and purer joys. Often has he pointed out to the brotherhood a Judas, with his innovations, and time has proven him correct. Men hated him then, and now they hate his name and influence. But, Brother Rice, there will grow out of the church of Christ, in the United States, a sectarian party They will be composed of the progressive and organ element. Let them go; the sooner, the better. They are a curse to the cause we plead. I like Brother Lard's position, as expressed in his *Quarterly,* in regard to the organ, not to preach for a congregation that uses an organ. . . . We will fight for the truth against innovations.[23]

J W. McGarvey, in 1881, wrote a series of articles on instrumental music in the *Apostolic Times* strictly insisting that its use was a positive sin. A year later, however, the rumor was spread abroad that McGarvey had changed his position To make his position perfectly clear, McGarvey wrote in a letter dated May 10, 1883, the following:

I have not withdrawn my opposition to the organ I would not hold membership with, nor contract to preach for a church using one. Its introduction against the conscientious protest of a minority is high-handed wickedness, and can be prompted by no spirit but that of the world and the flesh [24]

Along with McGarvey was J A. Meng of Moberly, Missouri. Writing in 1879, Meng declared that in the state of Missouri only six congregations were using the instrument He was opposed to it. but what should he do about worshiping with these that used the organ?

Were I to go there, I would have either to worship with the organ at the expense of my conscience: or, if I got them to let it remain silent while I was there, I would have the satisfaction of knowing and seeing that some of the members were staying away.

[23] J M Barnes, "Correspondence," *American Christian Review,* Vol XXII, No 7 (February 11, 1879), p 51

[24] J W McGarvey, "Beliefs Here and There," *American Christian Review,* Vol XXVIII, (March 12, 1885), p. 82.

Why staying away? Anything wrong about the things commanded? No, not that They could not "hear the organ's peal" in the
worship of their lowly Redeemer. Why this trouble, this unpleasantness, this non-fellowship? Any precept, precedent or necessary
inference, in the way of that union sweet and dear esteem that
should be manifest in all our actions toward one another? No.
Nothing of the sort. But, instead of that, human devices have
crept in, the leaders have turned the people away from the simplicity of the worship to serving idols; those idols are dearer than
their brethren for whom Christ died, and those strongly resemble
those people of whom the Lord said, by the mouth of the prophet,
Hosea. "Ephraim is joined to her idols, let him alone."[25]

Thus there were two attitudes toward the organ. One insisted
that its use was a matter of expediency; the other insisted that it
was a human innovation into a divine worship and, therefore,
sinful Between these two positions it was evident that there was
no compromising or midway point, a fact that has always permanently stood in the way of a reunion between the churches of
Christ and the Christian Church. Here, then, was the point of
departure, the parting of the ways, the instrument giving the
impetus to a division which neither the war, slavery, the Ferguson
fiasco, or even the missionary society had done.

The issue and the corresponding decision were brought squarely
before the minds of the brethren. Most who opposed the instrument stood their ground, refusing all fellowship with it. Some,
like Joseph Franklin or J. B. Briney, however, were backing off
from the logical consequence of their own reasoning They concluded that if other brethren could not be convinced the instrument was sinful, they should surrender and go along with them.
Franklin soon abandoned the major principles of his father. His
old friends were disappointed. W. S Harper of Greenville, Ohio,
expressed a great disappointment, and wrote an article imagining
the delight the denominations were feeling in Joe Franklin's change.
He pictures the denominations saying:

What a different man Brother Joseph is from his father! Old
Ben was as unyielding as a pharisee, had the New Testament at
his tongue's end, and his manner of presenting arguments was so
overpowering that it was not safe to be in hearing distance of his
harangues. He has robbed us of many of our most valued members We had to build our fences high and strong against him.
But, thanks be to God, the scales are changed Old Ben was called

---

[25] J A Meng, "New Tests of Fellowship," *Gospel Advocate*, Vol XXI,
No 11 (March 13, 1879), pp 169, 170.

a Commoner; we will dub his son a Leveler. We must welcome Brother Franklin into our pulpits and to our homes [26]

J W McGarvey found himself shut out in coming years He never ceased declaring the use of the instrument to be sinful. When the churches in Lexington, Kentucky, were introducing it, McGarvey moved from one congregation to the other, refusing to stay where the instrument was used. Nevertheless, his major influence went with the side of the advocates of the instrument, but it is doubtlessly true he never felt fully at ease with his company.

In the South, David Lipscomb used the columns of the *Gospel Advocate* very little in discussing this issue. The question was raging furiously in the *Review* and the *Apostolic Times,* but Lipscomb seemed to be unconscious of any need for the discussion in the *Advocate,* feeling that these two papers were sufficiently discussing it. Too, he was waging war against what he considered the greatest of the evils facing the church—the missionary society. With Lipscomb one missionary society was far more dangerous to apostolic Christianity than "a whole orchestra of instruments." This did not mean that he entertained the slightest inclination toward the instrument. In the Southland closely following the Civil War, churches were poverty stricken and could not buy instruments. By the time they could financially afford to own them, they had been indoctrinated sufficiently against them Meanwhile, as the controversy raged in the North, Lipscomb for the most part watched as an interested observer

At first, Lipscomb shrank from drawing lines of fellowship against the proponents of the instrument. In 1871 he wrote:

. . . The *Times* and *Review,* if we have not misunderstood their teaching, have advised brethren to withdraw from and refuse to worship with a church that adopts the organ While we condemn the organ certainly as wrong, unauthorized and corrupting, we have never decided that it is a Christian's duty to go to this extremity. Churches became corrupt in primitive times, and yet no such advice is given in the Scriptures. So we hesitate, while we heartily and earnestly condemn the innovation as at once the outgrowth and promoter of evil. . . .[27]

At the time of writing the above, Lipscomb felt a keen sense of the inconsistency of both the *Times* and the *Review.* Both papers

[26]W S Harper, "Spirit of Sectism," *American Christian Review,* Vol XXVII, (February 28, 1884), p 69

[27]David Lipscomb, "Piece of News," *Gospel Advocate,* Vol XIII, No 12 (March 23, 1871), p 277

recommended withdrawing from churches using the instrument; yet, both papers favored at this time the missionary society. The war was now raging against the Central Church in Cincinnati for its new extravagant building and the adoption of the instrument. Lipscomb failed to see just why the *Times* and *Review* could back the Louisville Plan and yet condemn this church as worldly when money for the plan went to the very men behind this congregation. So he asked:

For ourselves, could we open the door of expediency sufficiently wide to take in the plan, we could certainly take the organ, too, without an extra effort, and we think it is not principle but prejudice that causes a person who accepts the one to reject the other.

It is evident that Lipscomb saw earlier than most men that the instrument and the society stood or fell on the same ground.

Lipscomb's first thrust against the use of the instrument came in 1878. "Although," he wrote, "not speaking much concerning it, we have not regarded it with indifference." While admitting that the instrument was used in Old Testament times, he argued that it is incompatible with the worship of the church.

Instrumental music passed away with the other appeals to the merely sensuous and imaginative in men. Instrumental music as a part of divine worship was associated with bleeding beasts as sacrifices and the incense offering. There is just as much reason and authority for the revival of either of these as for the revival of instrumental music in worship. They are both more directly the commands of God, and neither of them have been more clearly or definitely excluded from his worship than instrumental music. Those who adopt one cannot reject the other.

Those who introduce instrumental music give up heart worship of Christ for the formalism of Judaism. It is another indication of that which was the trouble in apostolic times and has been since, the tendency to go back to the forms, the ritualism, sensuousness of Judaism It shows how difficult, even now, it is to appreciate and cling to that which is purely spiritual in nature.

It was not accidental, or incidental, or unintention, or an oversight that Christ and the apostles ignored and left out of their worship instrumental music. They did it advisedly, because the nature of the religion was contrary to such worship. When Christ and the apostles left it out, who dare replace it in their worship? The incense, as a sweet smelling savor, affects the imagination of some persons just as powerfully as does instrumental music others [28]

---

[28]David Lipscomb, "Instrumental Music in the Worship," *Gospel Advocate*, Vol. XX, No 35 (September 5, 1878), p 551.

The flame of division leaped high in Louisville, Kentucky, and helped undoubtedly in setting a precedent for opposers of the instrument. Around 1881 the Fourth and Walnut Streets Church put in the instrument, causing several conscientious people to depart. A. I Hobbs shortly afterwards came to this congregation as its preacher. While he had no part in the division, his actions seemed to sustain the introduction of the instrument F G. Allen, then editing the *Old Path Guide* in Louisville, said to Hobbs, "I have as little fellowship for a church that forces an organ in, and thereby drives good brethren out, as I have for one that practices infant sprinkling." However, Allen had made Hobbs associate editor of his paper, an action which appeared to be inconsistent. Meanwhile, from Hobbs there came constant taunts thrown at the brethren asking what they were going to do about the instrument; it was in and they could do nothing about it. To this James A. Harding worded a strong reply, and wrote:

I think it is high time to give them an answer based upon the word of God What does the Bible say we should do with regard to schismatics? Let the Sacred Writings answer Rom 16: 17, "——"; 2 Thess 3: 6, "——"; 2 Thess 3. 14, "——", Titus 3· 10, "——."

Now it appears clear to me that brethren Yancey, Cline, Hume, and others, were as inconsistent in going to those union meetings at Fourth Street Church, as were brethren Marshall and Stanley in fraternizing with those sectarians at Cynthiana And it appears, furthermore, that brethren McGarvey and Allen are equally inconsistent in hobnobbing with these same and other factious people in missionary conventions, etc . Let us follow the Scriptures and avoid these people The innovators are rapidly gaining ground in Kentucky in the face of an overwhelming majority who are opposed to them, and who favor standing by apostolic teaching and practice in the worship, simply because those who are for the old paths do not stand firmly and consistently by what they believe to be right.[29]

Two years later A. I. Hobbs wrote in the *Apostolic Guide* on division, charging that there were "those who seem to be doing what they can to bring on a conflict which may result in division " Deeply deploring this condition, he strongly condemned those opposed to the instrument as causes of this division To this Harding replied:

---

[29]James A Harding, "Another Inconsistency," *Gospel Advocate,* Vol. XXV, No 21 (May 23, 1883), p 323

The First Church at Louisville determined to use an organ in worship. A number of the members, some of them among their oldest and best, could not agree to this. The Holy Spirit had left the instruments of music out of the worship, upon the institution of the church of Christ, and they thought it would be sinful to put back into the worship of God that which his Holy Spirit had deliberately taken out. They could not use the organ in the worship without doing that which they believe to be presumptuously wicked. In this they agree with many of the most pious and learned among all religious people who claim to be guided by the New Testament. But the majority of this church deliberately kicked these excellent people out of their number by bringing in the organ anyhow. The majority does not claim that the organ is necessary to the worship; it does not claim that the organ was used in apostolic times; it merely claims that it will make the music sound better; for the sake of having their ears tickled with a pleasant sound, they drove out the most excellent members; for the sake of a "box of whistles" they cut themselves off from a number of God's faithful children. This wicked work was done with the full sympathy and concurrence of A. I. Hobbs; since it was done, he has defended the church in its action. As F. G. Allen once said, so say I now, I have no more fellowship for a church claiming to be a church of Christ that will introduce an organ and thereby drive out good brethren than I have for a Methodist society. And what more, I intend to do what F. G Allen has not done, I intend to stand by the statement, to carry it into practice as a preacher and an editor. I would as soon edit a paper conjointly with an infidel as with a man who has thus stabbed a church of God. Such a man does more harm to the cause than any infidel. The majority in this First Church of Louisville caused division contrary to the doctrine of Christ, and we are to mark them and avoid them, if we are to obey the Saviour.[30]

A year earlier Harding drove forcefully at the seat of the trouble:

There are many whom we are told to "mark" and "avoid"; men from whom we are to "withdraw" ourselves; men who trouble the churches of God by forcing upon them untaught questions; who gratify their own tastes by forcing organs and other such things into the worship, thereby driving numbers of the oldest and best members out. From such let us turn away.

It is worthy to remark that the things that are troubling the churches are the inventions of men; the organ, the human missionary society, the suppers and festivals for raising money, etc..

[30]James A Harding, "Christ Came to Us to Divide Us," *Gospel Advocate,* Vol. XXVII, No 32 (August 12, 1885), p 498

are the bones of contention . . . Did not the apostles get along without the organ? Yes! Are not these things divisive? Yes! They have rent more churches, alienated more brethren, and caused more heartaches among the children of God than any other things that have troubled the Zion of our King in this century [31]

Harding's articles were fast helping to mold an attitude among the readers of the *Gospel Advocate,* and undoubtedly set a precedent when circumstances similar to those in Louisville would occur other places. The use of the instrument, being sinful, would not be tolerated, and brethren who thus considered them sinful were now quickly ready to draw lines of fellowship against the innovators.

The trend toward denominationalism. Turning now from the study of instrumental music as a cause of division, our attention now centers upon a trend—a trend toward making the church another denomination On this trend more attention shall be given in another chapter At this point it is enough to see it as a cause of alienation among brethren

Sensing a danger that the church was drifting unconsciously into becoming just another sect, John F. Rowe wrote:

That which gives us the greatest apprehension is the tendency to drift unconsciously and imperceptibly into a miserable sect, a condition of things which is overtaking us because of the supreme indifference of our people on the question of a restored Christianity.[32]

The plea for a return to the ancient order as advocated by earlier pioneers embodied among other things the restoration of the New Testament Church. No one denomination laid claim to being identical with the New Testament Church, but claimed to be a "section" of it. Thus denominations were constantly referred to as "sectarian bodies." The restoration movement proposed the destruction of all denominations by replacing the identical church of the New Testament—an event to be accomplished by close adherency to the word of God, without addition, subtraction or substitution A conviction that this principle of action was at once practical and scriptural was the driving force for many of the church members The denominations refused to see the charitableness in the plea, but pressed the charge that brethren had started

---

[31]James A Harding, "Will We Divide?" *Gospel Advocate,* Vol XXVI, No 1 (January 2, 1884), p 10

[32]John F Rowe, "The Old and the New Order," *American Christian Review,* Vol XXIII, (March 30, 1880), p 100

a denomination of their own—the last thing brethren were interested in doing. But, because they insisted upon not being a denomination, but rather identical with the church of the New Testament, their enemies called them narrow and legalistic.

After the Civil War, a trend set in among many brethren to reduce the church to the status of another denomination. Some openly defended using the word denomination with reference to the churches of Christ. That there were Christians in all denominations now began to be openly advocated. The term, Disciples of Christ, was now elevated to the dignity of a denominational appellation, and the Disciples of Christ denomination, with its "reverends" and "pastors," a royal sect among sects, was now a reality. Some openly declared that a return to the New Testament Church was not desirable if it were practical, as did W. T. Moore, when he spoke before an Indiana Convention in Rushville. W. B. F. Treat openly laid the charge at the door of Isaac Errett of having as his supreme desire the making of the churches of Christ another denomination among denominations.[33]

Symptomatic of this trend was the attitude toward the "pious unimmersed," and the growing practice of union meetings with the denominations. But this analysis of the trend will be further treated in another chapter.

The silence of the Scriptures. A third factor underlying the division was the attitude of the brethren toward the silence of the Scriptures. Thomas Campbell's reason for rejecting infant baptism was that the Scriptures were silent on this point. Lacking apostolic authority, the brethren refused to practice it. After the Civil War, this way of measuring religious practices was entirely abandoned by many of the more progressive fringe. Some, however, looked upon this abandonment as dangerous in the extreme. If man were allowed of his own free will to add anything he desired to the work, worship, and organization of the church, there was no end to what could be introduced. Man's desire being the limitation, caused brethren to see no ending of the innovations that could now be introduced. Jacob Creath wrote:

When a man leaps the falls of Niagara, can he stop before he touches the bottom over the falls? When a man leaves the *Bible alone*, there is no rest for him this side of Rome. The most that

[33]W. B F Treat, "President, Scribe, Affairs, Etc ," *American Christian Review*, Vol. XXIII, (June 15, 1880), p 185

can be said for all those persons who have ceased to the *silence* of the Bible is that they are only partly in the reformation [14]
Creath proceeded to charge that they are standing a straddle of the line, having one foot in the reformation and the other in sectarianism. "They are neither on one side or the other," he wrote

But the principle of remaining "silent where the Bible is silent" was, with David Lipscomb, a vital one. When John H West of Murray, Kentucky, wrote Lipscomb in 1873 inquiring for light on the subject of instrumental music, Lipscomb replied:

We do not think anyone has ever claimed authority from the Scriptures to use the organ in worship. They only claim it is not condemned. It is used as an assister of the worship. Its service is part of the worship and very frequently a substitute for a portion of the worship. Our worship to God is regulated by the laws of God. We have no knowledge of what is well-pleasing to God, in worship, save as God has revealed it to us. The New Testament is at once the rule and limit of our faith and worship to God.

This is the distinctive difference between us and other religious bodies. Others accept the New Testament as their rule of faith, but do not make it the limit of their faith. They add other things as articles of faith and acts of worship than those contained in the Bible. We seek for things authorized, they for things not prohibited. Our rule is safe—theirs is loose and latitudinarian. Ours confines us to God's appointments. Theirs opens the worship and service of God to whatever will please men. Our rule limits man's worship to the exercises approved of in the Bible [15]

On the same point Lipscomb wrote later:

The arguments in favor of the use of instrumental music in the worship have been chiefly a ridicule of the idea that we are limited by the New Testament in our worship. That that principle has been sometimes abused, misapplied, and by ignorant persons perverted, we are well aware. But the principle properly applied, is a good one, is the only safe one to guide Christians. The true work to be done is not to ridicule the principle, but to show its proper application and wherein it is or may be abused. [16]

Those prone to look upon the silence of the Scriptures as a measure of acceptable religious practice insisted that Campbell meant no such thing by his motto, "Where the Bible speaks, we

[14] Jacob Creath, "Our Reformation," *Gospel Advocate*, Vol XXII, (1875), p 1123
[15] David Lipscomb, "The Organ in Worship," *Gospel Advocate*, Vol XV, No 36 (September 11, 1873), pp 854, 855
[16] David Lipscomb, "Instrumental Music in the Worship," *Gospel Advocate*, Vol XX, (1878), p 566

speak; where the Bible is silent, we are silent." Nathan J. Mitchell, author of "A Pioneer Preacher of the Ancient Gospel," and the founder of many congregations in the Bald Eagle Valley of Pennsylvania, recalled that he frequently traveled with Thomas Campbell and heard him preach many times. He insisted that he knew what Thomas Campbell meant by his motto, and quotes Campbell as frequently saying:

The order of the primitive churches, as to worship of God, under the immediate personal teaching and supervision of the inspired apostles, was equivalent to a command to us moderns; and that the silence of the inspired apostles, on any theme, was to be sacredly and unscrupulously regarded as much as the positive teaching.[37]

As a side line of this point, the word liberty now came into popular vogue. Some insisted that the cause of restoration was intended to unshackle men from the bondage of "legalism," and insisted that the additions to the church which had been introduced were allowable on the ground of the liberty. But yet, in this David Lipscomb thought he saw a definite swing away from the understanding of the earlier pioneers. Liberty of opinion they did not conceive to give them free license to push something into the worship for which there was no apostolic authority and compel men to either accept it or get out. Times had indeed changed! So Lipscomb wrote:

This principle of holding of opinions is one that has greatly changed in its use since it was first laid down by the Campbells. With them opinions might be held as private property, but must not be taught or imposed upon others. A noted example of this was the case of Aylett Raines, who was a Universalist or Restorationist. He could hold this as an opinion, but he could neither teach it or create strife, or force it on others as a condition of union or fellowship. He, without surrendering the opinion as untrue, agreed he would hold it as private property and preach the gospel. He did this, and, it is said, in holding the opinion as private property, not preaching it, he lost sight of the position altogether. According to the present interpretation of the principle, Aylett Raines would have been at liberty to preach Universalism on every occasion he saw fit, and none could have said nay.

For a man to make an opinion a principle of action, where others must act with him, is to force them to conform to his opinion, or to withdraw from his association. When a man has an opinion

---

[37]N. J. Mitchell, "no title," *American Christian Review*, Vol. XXII, (February 18, 1879), p. 57.

that an organ is admissible in the church service, and forces it in, he compels every man to accede to his opinion, or to withdraw from the church. When a man holds the opinion that sprinkling is baptism, and insists on acting on that opinion, he forces everyone in the church to accede to his opinion, or to withdraw from the church. This is making an opinion the test of fellowship; making others accept and act on our opinion, or withdraw from the fellowship of the church.[38]

But one other question now seemed pertinent, viz, who was to be charged with the responsibility for this division?

THE RESPONSIBILITY

Late in the summer and early in the fall of 1883 John F. Rowe undertook to write a series of editorials in the *American Christian Review* entitled, "Lift Up a Standard for the People," the very title suggesting that this threatened to be a blow to the *Christian Standard*. Rowe's editorials were charged with implications of the unsoundness of the *Standard*, and of the fact it was largely instrumental in leading the restoration away from its earlier points of emphasis. Finally, Rowe climaxed his editorials with one entitled, "The Duty of the Hour," which David Lipscomb pronounced the finest Rowe had ever written. Rowe called for "frequent consultation" among the men of faith to "republish to the world our platform of gospel principles." It was a strongly-worded fighting challenge to stand firm against the mighty inroads of innovations then engulfing the brotherhood.

Isaac Errett at once accepted the challenge for a struggle. In the *Christian Standard* of November 24, 1883, Errett replied to Rowe, doing so by charging that there was a coalition of brethren who were set to create disunion, and capture as many preachers and congregations as possible. Errett, while admitting that this charge was based only upon rumor, even named the persons involved. They were supposed to be John F. Rowe, J. C. Holloway, Alfred Ellmore and D. L. Kincaid. Errett responded to Rowe by insisting:

This looks very much like a feeler, and is in harmony with much more that has appeared in that paper, only a little bolder. It may help our querists and our readers generally to interpret the foregoing utterances in their real import, if we state that there are rumors in the air to the following effect: That there is already a

---

[38]David Lipscomb, "Strange Developments," *Gospel Advocate*, Vol. XXVI, No. 11 (March 12, 1884), p 166.

combination of men engaged in an organized effort to capture as many of our preachers and churches as possible, with a view to such a separation as is implied in the foregoing extracts; that the movement—which has been carefully concealed from public notice, except as it gleams forth in obscure intimations in that paper, and is practically a secret combination—is under the leadership of John F. Rowe, assisted by such men as D. L. Kincaid, J. C. Holloway, and A. Ellmore; that those whom they wish to gain, but are not quite certain of, are pledged to profound secrecy before they are informed of their plans; that their purpose is to spot both churches and preachers who are not in favor of their movement, and by importing men of their own stripe, to hold every inch they can; that every man who favors the *Standard,* or missionary societies, or will tolerate an organ, is unsound and marked as one who causes division and they are pledged to each other to do all they can to lay every preacher of this kind on the shelf, and assist their own men of finding fields of labor where they can be sustained; that the question of division is a fixture, unless the Missionary Society as an organization is abandoned. At present it is reported to be to all intents and purposes a secret combination—a conspiracy against the unity and peace of our churches.[39]

This editorial was as if a bombshell had been dropped upon the church. John F. Rowe replied vigorously. denying totally the charges Errett specified:

So far as I am personally concerned, I deny emphatically that I know of "a combination of men engaged in an organized effort to capture as many of our preachers and churches as possible, with a view of such a separation." We demand the proof or a retraction. Errett's charges continued to burn deeper. Rowe charged that Errett was but creating a sensation with which to increase the subscription of the *Standard* Moreover, the journalistic ethics involved were not too flattering to Errett, Rowe thought. Serious charges were made based only on rumor to the effect that a secret combination had contrived to cause a major division in the church. Rowe wrote:

Are not panics started on "rumors," especially if they originate with responsible parties? If rumors of the insolvency of a reliable banking house are floated among the people, do not such "rumors" shake the confidence of the people and create a panic among the depositors? And are they not greatly injured by the wanton circulation of such base "rumors"? And yet, the writer has the

---

[39]Isaac Errett, "Is There a Combination to Create Division Among Us?" *American Christian Review,* Vol. XXVI, No 48 (November 29, 1883), p 380.

effrontery to say. "We regret that our *benevolent motive* is not understood or appreciated." Yes, it is the benevolence that a wolf has for a lamb! And yet the writer has the temerity to say that "their present air of injured innocence is uncalled for." A wolf might, with propriety, smack his lips and impudently vociferate the same language of insult.[40]

Errett was called upon to prove his statements or retract them, neither of which was forthcoming. Alfred Ellmore wrote to Errett:

But you have arrested four men, and virtually charged them with treason against this divine union: and though you had the nerve enough to make the arrest. yet when it came to the trial in court, your knees smote together, your courage failed you, and you withered like a fresh-mown flower.[41]

But Errett refused to believe that this "secret combination" did not exist. and refused to retract his statements, while at the same time he refused to prove them. Rowe was now furious. He closes off with Errett by writing the following terse statement:

I hold the editor personally responsible as my wilful defamer and detractor, in an implied charge of leading in a secret combination to produce divisions, until he either sustains his implied charge by documented testimony or makes an honorable detraction.[42]

But on what was this rumor based?. The whole affair owed its origin to a private conversation between D. L. Kincaid of Perry, Illinois, and H. T. Buff. Kincaid confided in Buff that he thought there was a division coming in the ranks of the brotherhood, an observation requiring no profundity to be sure. Kincaid remarked that he was saddened over it but nevertheless feared it was coming. He remarked to Buff that he had talked over this matter with Brother Holloway and Brother Wolfe, and both felt the same way. He said he judged from the recent editorials of John F. Rowe that he, too, must feel the same way. Buff then remarked that he would like to write about this matter. Kincaid replied that he did not want to get into the controversy and requested his name be withheld. but authorized Buff to use anything he had spoken to him. From this basis, Buff told Isaac

[40]John F. Rowe, "Adding Insult to Injury," *American Christian Review* Vol XXVII, No 1 (January 3, 1884), p 4
[41]A. Ellmore, "A Call for Proof," *American Christian Review*, Vol XXVII, No 3 (January 17, 1884), p 21
[42]John F. Rowe, "The *Standard's* Desperation," *American Christian Review*, Vol. XXVII, (January 31, 1884), p. 36.

Errett, and from him through the *Christian Standard* that a "secret combination" was being formed to cause division. Naturally, the four brethren charged felt great indignation, for there was no real basis for the charge.

Yet, once more, Errett proved to be the better of the two strategists, and Rowe lost considerable prestige among the opposers of the innovations. Coming as it did in that critical time when many were on the fence respecting the innovations, Errett won a singular victory.

Once before, in 1880, John F. Rowe had used severe language in condemning instrumental music, and announced that division was coming. Once before, Errett accused Rowe of construing to cause division in the church. Rowe had to give a defense, for he would not be construed as the cause of division. So he wrote: "We have never said that we would declare 'nonfellowship' because of the presence of the organ." He further stipulated that every congregation must act independently. If a congregation puts in the organ, and does it in the fear of God, "have I a right to interfere with the independent act of said church, and does the constitution of the kingdom of Christ allow me to break the peace of that church and throw it into confusion?" Rowe proceeded to point out that while he is opposed to the instrument, he would not cause division.

Why does not our critic discriminate between the fact of *opposing* an injurious practice and *compulsory toleration and endurance* of such a practice? We have never said that we would declare "non-fellowship" with any church because of the presence of the organ . . The organ is not the only thing we oppose, while we are compelled to tolerate and endure it. We have always been opposed to select choirs, but have endured and tolerated them. . . . Paul was opposed to paganism, but he preached in pagan temples. . . . God himself is opposed to polygamy and slavery, yet he tolerates and endures these evils. That is exactly our position on the organ question. We have *never* said that we intend to make the use of the organ "a test of fellowship" in the churches.[43]

Rowe was placed in a dilemma. On the one hand, he held that the use of the instrument was sinful; yet, on the other hand, he would fellowship preachers and congregations introducing the organ. This is precisely the position that Errett wanted Rowe to

[43]John F. Rowe, "Self-Contradiction," *American Christian Review*, Vol XXIII, No 17 (April 27, 1880), p 132.

take   Despite the fact that Rowe could never see he was inconsistent, he lost considerable prestige in the brotherhood generally
Because he believed the instrument to be sinful, Errett's party
connected with the *Standard* could not welcome him with open
arms   But because he would not stand behind the logical consequence of his own declarations on the subject, brethren who agreed
with him in opposing the instrument gradually placed less confidence in him as a leader in the church.   On the diplomatic checker
board Rowe had played his man once more against Errett and
lost.

Standing beside Rowe in opposing the instrument were his two
stalwart generals, J. A Meng and W. B F Treat.   Both men
were powerful writers, and influential men, but both looked with
alarm at Rowe's inconsistency   J. A Meng wrote to Rowe that
his attitude "is the very thing to make the advocates of every
possible innovation laugh and almost dance for joy."   Meng
declares that none of the apostles knew of any such church independent as Rowe imagines   Each congregation, says Meng, is
independent so far as its own worship and work is concerned.
But all congregations are under the same King, and under the same
laws   Meng affirmed that if a thing like the organ is not prescribed, it is not lawful, and then cannot be introduced except in
violation of the constitution of the kingdom

. . The organ is *not* commanded, is *not* prescribed, is not lawful, consequently can't be expedient, and no one has any right
to contend for it in the worship who is willing to "Speak where
the Bible speaks, and be silent where the Bible is silent "[44]

W B F Treat also spoke out against Rowe, concluding his
attack by saying,

But we shall pursue this subject no further.   Brother Rowe is
wrong and no amount of bluster can make him right   While we
feel no disposition to "crack the whip of censorship over him,"
yet we must remember that his mistakes are of more consequence
than formerly because of the highly responsible position he occupies

All of this had occurred in 1880 to conclude one of Rowe's attacks against the *Christian Standard*   That battle had ended with
Rowe losing considerable prestige   When therefore, in 1883 Rowe
pressed home the declaration that division was coming. Errett
managed once more to boil the issue down to a charge that Rowe

---

[44] J A Meng, "When Shall the Controversy End?" *American Christian
Review*, Vol XXI, (March 19, 1878), p 89

was the cause of division, and Rowe once more backed into his corner, still declaring he would fellowship a church using the instrument, although he believed its use to be a sin. In 1867 Rowe had declared that an organ was permissible provided it was under the elders. Now, in 1884 he admitted that an organ was permissible provided it was a "little organ." The effect, of course, was disastrous. Errett had succeeded in maneuvering so as to drive a wedge between Rowe and men of his mind. Alienation now set in between Rowe and his own brethren. A coolness developed between W. B. F. Treat and Rowe, and the *Review,* with its own editorial corps badly divided, was in no condition to press a successful attack against the innovations being promoted by the *Christian Standard.*

Meanwhile, neither Isaac Errett nor John F. Rowe was prepared to accept the responsibility for the imminent division. Errett wrote in the *Standard* for October 19, 1872:

The greatest danger that we see is that of making *tests of fellowship* of opinions or expedients concerning which we have no right to judge one another. Let us be careful at this point and we are safe.[45]

Once more Errett wrote:

It is becoming growingly evident that the way is being thus prepared for an attempted division in our ranks, to the extreme dishonor and injury of the effort so prosperously for the last half century for the union of all Christians on a scriptural basis. . .

Let our brethren be on their guard against every attempt, secret or open, to create division among us. There is nothing to justify it. It can only be done by the introduction of false tests of fellowship. Generally our people are too well schooled in the principles of New Testament Christianity to be captured by factionists, and are too thoroughly devoted to these principles to tolerate. even for an hour, any proposal to be false to them, come under what guise it may.[46]

This reasoning was logical, provided of course, one agreed that the use or non-use of the organ was an *expedient* and not an *innovation.* Errett's warning, therefore, could not have any effect on thwarting division.

Others believed that the instrument was unauthorized in the

---

[45]Isaac Errett, "Alarmists," *American Christian Review,* Vol XV, No 45 (November 5, 1872), p 357

[46]Isaac Errett, "The Responsibility of Division," *American Christian Review,* Vol XXVI, No 51 (December 20, 1883), p 404

scriptures. It was the act of bringing in unauthorized practices that was causing division, not the opposition to these things Errett wrote in the *Standard*, "We trust our brethren everywhere will frown on every attempt to produce alienation and division." G. W. Rice, publisher of the *Review*, replied:

So do we. This is sound doctrine. We do most sincerely echo it. But, are there now no elements of discord. alienation and division existing among us? Is the organ such? I think the *Standard's* editor will not deny that it has created much alienation and discord. Who is responsible for its introduction? Not us. We trust, therefore, the editor of the *Standard* and all other good brethren will frown on every attempt to introduce this element of discord and alienation.[47]

By 1885 division was upon the church The issue was now clear, and for the next twenty years churches were to be placing themselves behind one principle of action or the other. Congregations were yet to know division.

The *American Christian Review* entered the new era badly divided internally. John F. Rowe had not proved to be a man with the foresight of his predecessor, Ben Franklin. Underlying this divided state, too, was the fact that men felt themselves fully as qualified, if not more so, to wear Ben Franklin's shoes as John F. Rowe had been. A roaring current of suspicion and jealousy flowed freely through the columns of the *Review*. In these critical years the cause of the ancient order could ill afford this, and it cost heavily.

---

[47]G W Rice, "Alarmists," *American Christian Review*, Vol XV, No 43 (October 22, 1872), p 340

CHAPTER XII

"PROPHETS OF LIBERALISM"

Whether in the halcyon days of the restoration there could be found the seeds for the later liberalism that swept the brotherhood, may be doubted. Certainly, however, it can never be questioned that these seeds are discovered buried deep in human nature. There are always those who believe they sense something in the "spirit" of a thing contrary to what may be found in its "letter"; or, who, reacting against what they consider a radical extreme of isolationism devote their energies to popularizing a movement. The restoration period came to know these individuals following the war between the states. The church appeared to them to be too narrow and restricted, and their ambition therefore was to lift the brotherhood to a "dignified church" in a world of denominationalism, commanding at least some respect from these religious bodies. With the passing of years the number of men to take the lead in this type of thought became legion. To mention a few they were B. B. Tyler, A. B Jones, Alexander Proctor, George W. Longan, J. H. Garrison and W. T. Moore. In lasting influence the latter two are far more significant than the others. Before considering the liberal movement that arose in the church it is well to consider its two greatest promotors—J. H. Garrison and W T. Moore.

Garrison's influence came chiefly from the paper that he edited, *The Christian-Evangelist,* and not so much from his pulpit work There is little indication that Garrison was a superior preacher, although he was far from an inferior orator As an editor, however, he reached masses where as a preacher he reached the few The modern *Christian-Evangelist* is largely a product of Garrison's viewpoint, and its following stems from Garrison's liberalism.

Born in what was then Green County in the state of Missouri, Garrison was the twelfth child in a family of thirteen. The exact place was near Ozark, fourteen miles southwest of Springfield, and the date was February 2, 1842 Ten years before, Garrison's parents, James and Diana Kyle Garrison, had moved here from Hawkins County, in East Tennessee These were the years of migration when wagon trains moved from North Carolina and Virginia into Tennessee and Kentucky and thence, on to Missouri where rich land and plentiful game attracted the pioneer. Isaac Garrison, grandfather of J. H., had fought in the Revolutionary War, and following the conflict, had moved from North Carolina into East Tennessee. He came on westward with his youngest son, James, who was the father of J. H., and died in Missouri in 1836 at the old age of one hundred and four. Ten years after James and Diana Garrison settled near Ozark, Missouri, J. H. Garrison was born.

Garrison's childhood was similar to any other frontier boy. Educational opportunities were difficult to receive, most youths managing to eke out a few months of each year under some local pedagogue. The winter of 1860-61 Garrison acquired his most impressive bit of education at the feet of a "yankee" school teacher, Professor Charles P Hall who had opened an academy at Ozark. With the outbreak of the war, Hall closed the school, went back to New England, and later joined the Union Army

Religion played an important part in frontier life. Garrison's father belonged to the Missionary Baptist Church. Garrison himself was immersed into this church at the age of fourteen by a cousin, Ephraim Way, and became a member of the Prospect Baptist Church As yet, that body of people calling for a restoration of primitive Christianity was completely unknown to him.

Garrison's childhood was routine—endless work on the farm, interrupted occasionally by a few months in a country school, seasoned some by a sprinkling of religious emphasis But the spring of 1861 saw this routine changing for a more definite course ahead Rumblings filled Missouri of a Civil War that threatened to burst over the nation

Missouri was more largely populated by immigrants from Kentucky and Tennessee, who filled the state with pro-southern sentiment Still, Missouri's close proximity to Union territory gave it a substantial dotting of Union sympathizers The direction Missouri would tend in those critical days was hard to determine

In the spring of 1861, while political excitement filled the country over Lincoln's election, a business firm had recently completed construction of a court house in Springfield, and announced that on a given Saturday, a Confederate flag would be unfurled on top of it. In this area the country people were predominantly loyal to the Union and the city people, to the Confederacy. A large gathering was on hand. A man appeared on top of the building to unfurl the Confederate flag A Union man raised a rifle and took aim, but before he could fire, Garrison pulled his arm down. He gave an address, arguing with the people to put up a Union flag since war had not yet been declared, and then defend it if someone tried to take it down. Garrison's speech postponed any immediate bloodshed.

A short time later news that a Confederate Army was moving on Springfield reached the countryside. When Garrison learned of it, he packed his belongings and rushed to join the Home Guards. He came to realize that there was no immediate danger, so returned to help in the wheat harvest It was July 4, 1861 and Garrison was in the wheat field when he heard the distant roar of the cannon. Dropping his work, he ran to defend Springfield, a defense that proved futile. General Lyon led the small band of Home Guards in a battle ten miles south of Springfield on Wilson's Creek. Lyon was killed and the band of men was driven back.

Garrison entered more determinedly into the Union cause by abandoning the Home Guards and joining Company F of the Twenty-Fourth Missouri Infantry under Colonel S H. Boyd. Garrison, on March 6, 1862 was shot in the left leg while taking part in the battle at Pea Ridge near Fayetteville, Arkansas. He lay on the battlefield all night with no one to dress his wound. After attention finally was given to him, he was sent home. However, when he was well enough, he was made a Captain in his company and finally a major, a rating which he had when the war closed.

Near the close of the conflict, Garrison was acting as chief clerk in the Provost-Marshal's office where he became acquainted with A. N. Harris of the Tenth Illinois Calvary It was this acquaintance that changed the whole future course of his life. Desiring to send his two sisters northward to safety and at the same time, to locate them in a place where they could go to school, Harris recommended Abingdon College, a school operated by the brethren Garrison followed through with the suggestion, but sometime later was surprised when the sisters wrote to him that they had united with the "Christian Church " Later, at the insistence of his sisters, he enrolled in the same school.

This event proved the changing point in his career. Up to

now he had dreams of a future in politics. But when he heard
J. W. Butler, president of the college, lecture on the Bible, it
changed his interests greatly. The Bible now became a living
book. It was only a matter of time until Garrison, too, was
abandoning the Baptist Church.

A series of quick events set the pattern for Garrison's life in
1868 and the year following. One was his selection of a wife.
While a student in school, Garrison met Judith Elizabeth Garrett
of Camp Point, Illinois and became fond of her. Meanwhile,
J. H. Smart had met an older sister of Miss Garrett. In a double
ceremony held at Camp Point on July 2, 1868, Garrison and
Smart were married to sisters. Another event happening about
this time to set the pattern for his life was his connection with
J. C. Reynolds which led to Garrison's future work. Through
Reynolds' encouragement, he preached his first sermon at Macomb,
Illinois in 1868. About this same time, Reynolds was editing a
paper called the *Gospel Echo*. He insisted that Garrison become
an associate-editor. On January 1, 1869 the first issue of this
periodical under their partnership was sent forth. Thus, in a
short period of time Garrison had become a member of the church,
settled down in married life, begun to preach and started a career
in religious journalism.

It was not long before he realized that the *Gospel Echo* needed
to be a weekly and not a monthly publication, and that, furthermore, it needed to be in a larger center of operation. In casting
around for a future likely home for the home, he settled upon
the city of Chicago. To this end, the September, 1871 edition
of the *Gospel Echo* announced the prospectus for a new publication
to be issued from Chicago and known as the *Christian Missionary*.
The new publication was to begin in October that same year.
Then came the great Chicago fire that destroyed a large part of
the city. Garrison went to Chicago to determine what this fire
had done to his plans, and found that the men who were interested
in the paper financially were now unable to help. So, the plans
were abandoned. Garrison wanted to move to St. Louis as the
most central location in the country for a large publishing interest,
but abandoned this due to the lack of funds. He moved to Quincy,
Illinois and immediately laid plans to start publishing a paper

Meanwhile, an approach was made from several leading brethren
George W. Longan being the spokesman, to join the *Gospel Echo*

with *The Christian,* then being published in western Missouri.
The merger of these two papers marked an interesting develop-
ment in both papers   The *Gospel Echo* was first published in
Carrollton, Illinois in January, 1863 by E L Craig J. C. Reynolds
bought the paper in 1868 and moved it to Macomb, Illinois, J H.
Garrison joining him the first of the following year as an editor.

The Christian traced its history back much earlier.   D. Pat
Henderson was co-editor with Barton W Stone of the *Christian
Messenger,* Henderson going on with it after Stone's death   In
January, 1847 the *Christian Messenger* emerged with the *Bible
Advocate* and was published at St. Louis by John R Howard
The first issue of this paper had been published in August, 1842
by John R Howard and S B Aden from Paris, Tennessee   In
June, 1861 John R Howard and D T Wright started the *Christian
Pioneer* at Lindley, Missouri   On January 11, 1864 the office
burned and Wright moved the paper to Chillicothe, Missouri   On
November 3, 1870 the *Christian Pioneer* merged with *The Christian*
of Kansas City.[1]

T. P Haley, George W. Longan, Alexander Proctor, A B
Jones and George Plattenburg were editing *The Christian* in the
fall of 1871   They proposed to publish it on what they styled
more "progressive" style, but because the brotherhood was not
yet educated up to this, it was a losing proposition financially   In
the fall of 1871 *The Gospel Echo And Christian* began publication from Quincy, Illinois. The next January, a part of the name
was dropped so that it became *The Christian*

A year later, *The Christian* moved to St Louis   Garrison now
began the organization of a stock company called the Christian
Publishing Company with fifty thousand capital stock   The paper
began operations from its new headquarters January 1, 1874

Garrison in the meantime settled in St Louis and continued
his publication of the paper   There were, to be sure, financial
reverses which at times threatened the paper's existence   In
January, 1881, at the insistence of the Foreign Christian Missionary
Society Garrison took leave to go to England to join forces with
W T Moore   After a stay of less than two years, he was back
at St Louis

---

[1] J Edward Moseley, "The Story of the *Christian-Evangelist,*" *Christian-
Evangelist,* Vol LXXVI, No 1 (January 6, 1938), pp 24, 25   Cf Jesse H
Berry, "Elder D T Wright," *American Christian Review,* Vol XIV, No
33 (August 15, 1871), p 261

In 1882 another merger was negotiated which led directly to the establishment of the *Christian-Evangelist* B. W. Johnson was at this time editing *The Evangelist* at Oskaloosa, Iowa when negotiations began for the merger.

Barton W. Johnson, editor of *The Evangelist,* had by 1882 made a name for himself in the brotherhood This he did in spite of his frail health and diffident disposition Johnson never pushed himself and in brotherhood gatherings was never prominent He was, therefore, an ideal co-partner for a man as ambitious as J. H. Garrison But, from the log cabin in Tazewell County, Illinois where he was born in 1833, Johnson had taken advantage of every opportunity to distinguish himself as a brilliant student of the Bible Upon his graduation from Bethany College in 1856 he ranked among the foremost in his class. Soon after leaving Bethany, he was called to teach at Eureka College and very shortly became president. Beginning in the fall of 1863 he acted as an agent for the American Christian Missionary Society in Illinois The following spring he became corresponding secretary upon the resignation of D S Burnet.[2] In 1864 he took the chair of mathematics at Bethany College where he stayed until after the death of Alexander Campbell. Then he preached at Lincoln, Illinois before finally moving to Iowa to become president of Oskaloosa College It was while he was in this position that he accepted the position as editor of *The Evangelist* [3]

Meanwhile, *The Evangelist* had grown steadily It had bought out the *Christian Record* that J M Mathes had edited so successfully from Bedford, Indiana. Still later, it purchased the publishing firm of Bosworth, Chase and Hall which had printed so many brotherhood publications from Cincinnati *The Evangelist* changed its name to the "Central Book Concern" and took up headquarters in Chicago to have a larger area in which to work

Late in the summer of 1882 both *The Christian* and *The Evangelist* announced their intention of consolidating It was not by now a financial necessity on the part of either, but only that both had come to recognize that they covered the same general geographical area, and that the merger would result in a substantial

[2]W K Pendleton, "American Christian Missionary Society," *Millennial Harbinger,* Fifth Series, Vol VII, No 9 (September, 1864), pp 418, 419

[3]J H Garrison, "Departure of a Christian Hero," *Christian-Evangelist,* Vol XXXI, No 24 (June 14, 1894), pp 369-371

saving in effort, time and finances. "The Christian Publishing Company" would result from the merger. Accordingly, the first issue of the new *Christian-Evangelist* came from the press dated October 5, 1882.

In 1885 J. H. Garrison went to Boston at the insistence of the American Christian Missionary Society. He had been assured that he could continue his publication of the *Christian-Evangelist* although separated by many miles from St. Louis. By October 15, 1886 Garrison was back in St. Louis satisfied that the experiment could not be successful.

Until his death in 1926 Garrison gave his entire ability to promoting liberalism among the pioneer preachers. While at first he met with continued opposition, in the course of time he won many to his position From 1894-99 the stockholders behind the *Christian-Evangelist* showed increasing dissatisfaction with his policy and threatened a revolt. The trouble was finally settled when Garrison managed to buy out their interests. The story of this liberalism and Garrison's particular connection with it shall be related in another chapter.

WILLIAM THOMAS MOORE

It is not likely that the lasting influence of W. T. Moore is as great as that of J. H. Garrison. With the exception of the *Christian Quarterly* and the *Christian Commonwealth*, Moore published no paper that molded the mind of the brotherhood as did Garrison in the *Christian-Evangelist*. The *Quarterly* ran roughly only a decade. The *Commonwealth* was published in England, and therefore, very little touched the American brotherhood Nevertheless, Moore was a man of influence He played a vital part in the various organizations, especially in the Missionary Society, and in no small measure controlled its policy which in turn controlled the thinking of a large mass of brethren.

W. T. Moore was the son of Richard and Nancy M. Moore, and was a Kentuckian by birth Moore was born in Henry County, August 27, 1832. He was a mixture of Scotch-Irish, his father being Irish, and his mother, Scotch His parents had moved into Henry County from Virginia Moore was only nine years old when his father died, leaving behind him a widow with six children The burden of rearing the family fell largely on him.

so he had little time for an education. By the time he was eighteen, he could only read and write, but at that, had read the Bible through extensively. In 1850 he entered an academy at Newcastle, Kentucky. In the fall of 1855 he entered Bethany College and graduated in July, 1858 as valedictorian of his class.

In October after graduating from Bethany, Moore succeeded P S Fall as minister for the church in Frankfort, Kentucky He preached here until 1864. In June of this year he married Mary A. Bishop, second daughter of R. M. Bishop. Thus, Moore by marriage made close social ties with the leading men of his generation.

On January 1, 1865 he accepted the position as the preacher for the Central Church in Detroit, Michigan. When Kentucky University sent him an invitation a year later to become a professor, he resigned his work in Detroit and moved to Lexington. Hardly had he settled here until the Central Church in Cincinnati invited him to preach there. He accepted hoping to preach at this congregation and deliver lectures during the week at Kentucky University since the distance between cities was not so great. He found this too difficult so resigned at Lexington to devote his full time preaching in Cincinnati.

For twelve years, from 1866-78, Moore stayed in Cincinnati, then the "Jerusalem of the brotherhood." Here was headquarters for the American Christian Missionary Society Here the *Christian Standard* started and prospered, and Moore saw it through those crucial years when it battled financial depression. Here too, was a city in close proximity to Lexington, the locality of the College of The Bible If one were to take a map and draw oblong around Cincinnati and Lexington with each city as a focal point, he would have marked out the heart of the brotherhood geographically in 1866-78. In this "heart," W. T. Moore carried no small influence

During those twelve years, the Central Church underwent many changes. The erection of a building costing $140,000 was but one of them But possessing the finest building in the brotherhood was a high point of pride with the congregation.

In membership, in influence and in building, Central, Cincinnati became the cathedral church of the brotherhood One of the notable architectural features of the edifice is a great rose window high in its front. The most influencial church paper of that day denounced Mr. Moore for this "aping of Rome" and a number of prominent preachers took up the outcry against his supposed departure from the faith.[4]

In 1878 Timothy Coop, a prominent wealthy business man of Southport, England visited Cincinnati and convinced Moore that he should move to England to help advance the cause there. Under the sponsorship of the Foreign Christian Missionary Society Moore went to England   He spent eighteen years preaching in Southport, Liverpool, and London, most of the time preaching in the West London Tabernacle and editing the *Christian Commonwealth*. While he was here in England, Moore's liberalism caused considerable criticism in the brotherhood, but since that, too, will be given later, it will not be dwelt upon here.

It was 1896 when W. T. Moore returned to America.   He immediately became the first dean of the Bible College of Missouri which was affiliated with the State University at Columbia Moore and J. H. Garrison had a summer resort, with a cottage by the lake, at Pentwater, Michigan, and the two men spent much of their summers together.   In 1909 Moore moved to Indianapolis but when his wife's health failed, moved to Eustis, Florida, purchasing the old home of W K. Pendleton   Just before leaving England, Moore's first wife died, and he married Miss Emma S Frederick of Carthage, New York.   After spending ten years at Eustis, Florida, Moore moved to Clearwater, in the same state   His death occurred in the fall of 1926 and his burial was at the Spring Grove cemetery in Cincinnati

Moore distinguished himself in the pulpit   L L. Pinkerton said of him,

> His manner in the pulpit, whether of action or utterance, indicates deep earnestness   His style sometimes borders on the vehement, but never on the declamatory   The points in his discourses are generally well chosen, forcibly argued, and clearly illustrated, and, when practical, powerfully enforced   But his success as a minister is owing much less to his logic than to the warm and wide sympathy which pervades and vivifies it [5]

It is enough here to sketch this brief biography of Moore. His place in the controversy over liberalism shall be noticed again

---

[4]Anonymous, "Distinguished in Three Generations," *World Call*, Vol VIII, No 11 (November, 1926), p 37

[5]W. T. Moore, *Living Pulpit of the Christian Church* (Cincinnati R W Carroll & Company, 1868), pp 537, 538

CHAPTER XIII

THE RISE OF LIBERALISM

A cataclysmic occurrence stirred the brotherhood violently late in 1889 when R. C. Cave delivered a sermon filled with rationalism to the Central Church in St. Louis. The sermon with its repercussions was reported in the *St. Louis Republic* for December 9, 1889. Cave asserted that Abraham and Moses were grossly ignorant of the true character of God, and denied both the virgin birth of Jesus and the bodily resurrection of Christ. He described the Bible as an evolution, not a revelation, and declared that there was no such thing as a divinely-given "plan of salvation." Added to this was his affirmation that water baptism was not found in the great commission. Cave declared:

He who brings himself, according to his measure of knowledge and ability, into obedience to the will of Christ and into oneness of life and character with Christ, is a Christian and entitled to all Christian privileges, among which is membership in the church. To this basis I invite men.[1]

On the Wednesday night following this sermon on Sunday Cave embodied these beliefs in a series of resolutions which were presented to the church. The first resolution read, "The Christian Church makes nothing a test of fellowship but that which a man's own conscience tells him is right or true. . . Strict loyalty to self is the real loyalty to God."[2] The other resolutions were built around this one. The upsurge of the matter was that Cave insisted these resolutions must be accepted by the church or he would resign, adding a touch of dogmatism to the assertions. Liberalists are never dogmatic!!!

Both R. C. Cave and the Central Christian Church of St. Louis were long known for liberal tendencies This congregation resulted from the minority who in 1869 had attempted to introduce the instrument into the worship By 1871 the church had a separate existence, and for the next decade fraternized often

---

[1] A T Degroot, W E Garrison, *The Disciples of Christ A History* (St Louis Christian Board of Publication, 1948), p 388

[2] C. L Loos, "A Protest," *Christian-Evangelist*, Vol XXVII, No 1 (January 2, 1890), p 9

with the denominations   Later, Joseph H. Foy was its preacher. In 1884 Foy left the church to join the Episcopalians where he might receive "larger latitude of opinion " Later, however, Foy returned   J. H. Garrison preached for this congregation with some regularity for fifteen years   When R. C. Cave came from Richmond, Virginia on December 9, 1888 to serve as minister, he found fertile soil in which to plant his liberalism. Cave is described as "highly educated" and a "masterly orator " In character he was irreproachable. He possessed a magnetic personality.

On December 1, 1889 Cave preached a sermon dealing with God's revelation to the Old Testament characters in which he affirmed that an understanding of God was native to the soul, and questioned the understanding of God held by these Old Testament characters.

David, Elijah and Isaiah—all the worthies, whose names adorn the pages of the Old Testament story, while they were eagerly reaching out after God, were groping in darkness and grossly ignorant of his true character   These old Jews had a conception of Jehovah far higher than that of the heathen world round them, but still sadly imperfect and frightfully false.
She (the church) is not called upon to defend the Abrahamic and Mosaic conceptions of God , on the contrary, she cannot defend them without being disloyal to Him who came to displace them and give the world a different and higher and truer conception
We ask men to come to him (God) by Christ   And when we invite them to come to Him by Christ, *we do not mean that they shall come by virtue of any sacrifice that Christ has made to appease his wrath and render him willing to receive them,* but we mean that they shall come to him by Christ as their guide, their teacher, their exemplar, leading them to him [3]

The first reactions were violent. One denominational preacher accused Cave of leading the church to the devil, a prominent Baptist clergyman said Cave was "verging on Ingersollism." O. A. Bartholomew, minister of the First Church, reported :

Against Dr. Cave personally I have nothing to say—I must say that Dr. Cave is not in accord with the church on any one point, and his teachings are entirely at variance with the doctrine accepted by the Christian Church. . . Dr. Cave, in assailing the Old Testament, assails the inspired word of God, which is the foundation of the church. The church does not agree with Dr. Cave in any such belief, as he sets forth, which are his own views

St Louis Republic, December 8, 1889, p 26

and not those of the Disciples. Why he remains in the church while holding and preaching these views I do not know [4]

The next Sunday, December 8. Cave preached another sermon along the same line of thought as the first. Most of the congregation, captivated no doubt by his unimpeachable character. glowing personality and scholarly appearance, congratulated him. That evening he spoke on "The Beginning of Christ's Society" and invited men to come to Christ as they understood him, despite the fact they might not believe in miracles, or even in the Bible.

On the third Sunday, December 15, Cave preached to an overflow audience, again presenting his liberal views. At the conclusion of this sermon, a committee of brethren headed by Dr. R. M. King presented a series of resolution. No doubt these resolutions were the result of a gathering storm of opposition swelling up from the entire brotherhood. The resolutions in the main objected to a creed in any form and opposed any attempt to "fetter thought." They read,

Whereas a fellow minister, O. A. Bartholomew had said R. C. Cave was not in accord with the Christian Church

Whereas the Christian Church makes nothing a test of fellowship but that which a man's own conscience tells him is right or true, and that the very biggest exemplification of one's faith is shown in strict loyalty to self as the true essence of loyalty to God

Whereas, the Christian Church has no established written creed—

Whereas, the church recognizes no canon by which to judge man's orthodoxy

Whereas, the Central Christian Church acknowledges no ecclesiastical court

Whereas our only rule of faith and practice is loyal and faithful obedience to self

Resolved that the church unanimously support Cave

Resolved that disciples at Central Christian Church in no way approve any attempt of man to fetter liberty of thought. conscience or speech

Resolved that a copy of the above be placed on records of the church and sent to the papers.[5]

J. H. Garrison at first allowed the Cave matter pass with but little controversy. He was out of town when the resolutions were adopted but upon reading them the next day in the newspaper, called upon Cave. The next Wednesday night at Prayer

[4] *St Louis Republic,* December 8, 1889, p 26
[5] *St Louis Republic,* December 16, 1889, p 8

Meeting the service was turned over to a business meeting to discuss the resolutions   Garrison asked that another date be set to consider these resolutions, but he was refused   Cave insisted that a vote against them was a vote against him   Garrison promptly asked for a letter of dismissal for himself and his wife, and was followed by the same request from J H Smart and his wife. Later Garrison wrote out his objections to the resolutions insisting that they nullified the Bible as a guide

Very shortly Garrison drew up a letter of protest signed by sixty members of the church, and on Friday, December 27 presented this at a special meeting   F. E Udell acted as chairman of the meeting calling upon Cave to repeat his views, which Cave did This meeting adopted Garrison's protest and Cave promptly resigned. On Sunday January 5, J H Garrison spoke to the church on "Earnestly Contending For The Faith Once Delivered to The Saints." Twenty-nine of Cave's followers asked for letters of dismissal Dr R M King announced that a meeting would be held the next day to form a new congregation organized on "the oldline Campbellite basis " The congregation was organized under the name, "West End Christian Church" and Cave was invited to be the minister.

Garrison, editor of the *Christian-Evangelist,* admitted that he was pained deeply at Cave's bold declarations. When he and Cave met together privately to talk the matter over, Cave assured Garrison of his deep convictions on these matters totally at variance with the views of most of the brotherhood He admitted also that these views might cause a division in the Central Church, and asked Garrison's advice   Garrison advised him to go to another locality as soon as it was deemed wise, and establish another church upon his own views. Cave appeared to accept the suggestion, but Wednesday night, in the meeting that lasted until eleven o'clock, Cave appeared to be pressing his views, which led Garrison to ask letters of dismissal from the congregation for himself and his wife

Most of the brotherhood reacted violently against Cave. The *Church Register,* edited by J C Creel of Plattsburg, Missouri, published the following article which we copy from the *Christian Leader*

The course of Dr. Cave was not a surprise to some among us He has been known to hold views at variance with the disciples for several years; and yet he has filled some of the best pulpits of the Church. His foibles have been withheld from public gaze and criticism by means not necessary to mention until the crash came, which follows such a course as regularly as conclusion follows premises, and one of our churches has half its membership buried beneath the debris of his rationalistic air-castle. But was he alone to blame? I tell you No. The disaster was invited rather than avoided. There is a false idea of liberality among us that is ruinous in its tendency. Utterances that discredit all that is held as sacred among us, and even the express language of the inspired writers, are excused as mere differences of opinion. The more rash a man's statements in regard to the Bible the better his chances for a hearing at the annual meetings of our conventions, lectureships, etc. The remark is not without foundation that, "We used to preach the gospel at our conventions, but we've quit it"

Speculative subjects are discussed to the almost entire exclusion of the gospel of Christ. Men are known to hold views not only not believed among us, but views which, if practiced, would render nugatory the very commands of the gospel, still the most sacred interests of the Church are committed into their hands by men who know they hold such views This is plain language, but "the time for great plainness of speech has come. We speak that we do know and testify that we have seen." Do we wonder that such a result as the "Cave matter" should follow such a course as we have persued? The only wonder is that it was delayed so long.

Whenever men abandon the Bible as a standard of truth, and exalt their conceptions of truth to the dignity of a tribunal at whose bar the Bible itself is to be tried, there is not much uncertainty in respect to results.[6]

David Lipscomb saw in Cave's remarks something striking at the very foundation of the inspiration of the Bible So he wrote

The defection of R C. Cave, of St. Louis, pains us more, though does not surprise us as we heard intimations of it heretofore He is a man of irreproachable moral character, fine powers of mind, and extraordinary force and attractiveness as a public speaker. We have heard for some time, that he doubted the inspiration of the scriptures and called in question the miraculous conception of Jesus, and other truths vital to the Christian faith.

Recently he preached a sermon in St Louis an approved report of which has been published in the St. Louis *Republic*. In it, he clearly repudiates the inspiration of the Old Testament. He says "Those old Jews had a conception of Jehovah far higher than that of the heathen world around them, but sadly imperfect and frightfully false" "All the presentations of him were imperfect

---

[6]William Cobb, "Some Things Developing," *Christian Leader*, Vol. IV, No 7 (February 18, 1890), p 5

and more or less false " "Abraham and Jeptha were no more commanded by God to sacrifice their children, than the Hindoo mother is commanded to cast her child into the Ganges "

He says to the infidel, "There is and can be no conflict between you and us, as long as your attacks are directed against the Judaistic conception of Jehovah, whether you find it in the Old Testament story book, or nineteenth century creeds. Wherever found, it is false and dishonoring to the true God, and we invoke the Divine blessing upon your efforts to drive it from the world," and much of the same kind. While making no direct attack upon the New Testament, it is clear he rejects its teachings which conflict with his ideal of what God should be. He repudiates the idea that Christ suffered to satisfy the demands of God or law— or to ransom man or as a propriation for man—he is his example

To talk of denying the inspiration of the Old Testament yet maintain the inspiration of the New, is too absurd to talk of for a moment. Robert Cave has a logical, investigating mind. He attacks the inspiration and truthfulness of the statements of the Old—but he cannot believe the New inspired If the Old Testament is not inspired, the New cannot be. Jesus Christ and the apostles have unequivocally affirmed the inspiration of the Old Testament They have staked their claims to inspiration on the inspiration and truthfulness of the Old If the Old is not inspired of God and true, they were deceived or deceivers. Either of which is fatal to their claims. Christ refers to Moses as the law-giver sent of God, to Abraham as the friend of God, as seeing the day of Christ and rejoicing in it And makes Abraham's bosom the type of heaven Declares all true children of Abraham the children of God The apostles from the beginning of their career quote the law and the prophets as the word of God—given by inspiration "All scripture is given by inspiration and is profitable for doctrine, for reproof, for correction, for instruction in righteousness that the man of God may be perfect, thoroughly furnished unto all good works." This refers to the Old Testament scriptures. Again to Timothy "thou hast known the holy scriptures, which are able to make thee wise unto salvation, through faith which is in Christ Jesus." These scriptures pronounced holy and able to make man wise unto salvation, are none other than the Old Testament scriptures For none other were in existence in the childhood of Timothy Why holy? Why able to make wise unto salvation, if not from God?

Then to object to the Old Testament, because of the cruelty manifest in the commands given to Abraham and Jeptha, as abhorrent, and to accept the New with the crucifixion and death of Christ in it, is to strain at gnats and swallow camels If Jesus suffered and died as the scriptures declare, by the will of God, unless the Bible reason for that suffering be accepted, it surpassed in abhorrent cruelty a thousand fold all the cruelties recorded in the Old Testament combined. The scripture reason for the suffering of Christ, explains and justifies the lesser sufferings inflicted by the will of God on others. . .[7]

By 1890 the brethren were more conscious of the inroads of rationalism into the reformation than they had ever previously been. Garrison, in reacting against it, enlisted the assistance of some leading brethren to write on the fundamental principles. These articles, printed first in the *Christian-Evangelist* were later printed in the book, *Old Faith Restated,* a symbol of the doctrinal reaction. The *Gospel Advocate,* likewise sensing the danger in this type of modernism to the restoration, enlisted the support of a number of leading brethren to write articles against rationalism and in defense of the inspiration of the Bible. These articles were printed in the *Gospel Advocate* for 1890, and were never collected together in book form as were those in the *Christian-Evangelist.*

Garrison's opposition to R. C. Cave probably elevated him in the estimation of many brethren. Still, it is a matter of simple fact, that many failed to be impressed. Brethren frequently agreed that Garrison was as bad as R C. Cave in his beliefs, but his dwindling prestige demanded some retraction to boost the brotherhood's confidence in him. H. R. Tanner of Missouri tersely put it this way,

There is not a sensible man in Missouri or out of it who thinks that either Garrison or the congregation to which he belongs objected to Cave's doctrine. It was only an indignant brotherhood which made them turn on their brother pastor and hound him out of their pulpit.[8]

Though the criticism appears harsh, there is undoubtedly much truth to it.

David Lipscomb shared Tanner's conviction about Garrison. Cave, he felt, had been made the scape-goat when in reality Garrison had much more harmed the brotherhood by his friendly overtures to liberal-minded preachers than had R. C Cave. So Lipscomb wrote:

[7]David Lipscomb, "Sad Apostasies," *Gospel Advocate,* Vol XXXII, No 1 (January 1, 1890), p 6

[8]H R. Tanner, "Western Splinters," *Octographic Review,* Vol. XXXIII, No. 24 (June 12, 1890), p. 2

Whenever a man begins to draw the distinction between believing in Christ, and believing in the Bible, which reveals Christ, he does not believe in the Christ of the Bible or of God   And he who rejects the Bible, rejects the Christ of the Bible. And he is the only Christ that can save.   All other Christs are the creations of their own minds, deifications of their own conceptions There is a school of rationalism in the church of Christ, especially in Missouri. We have spoken of it heretofore. They use terms out of their ordinary meaning   They mean by inspiration, as Longan calls it, "inspired genius " The revelations of God are merely "the creations of genius," as Shakespeare and Milton's works are   They do not mean that the Spirit of God enters into, reveals the mind of God to man, and speaks through him

The Bible is the "creation of genius," not the revelation of God to man, by the Holy Spirit. Hence it is not the complete and perfect standard of religious truth   It is all to be subjected to the judgment of man, or to the spirit of holiness in man, as what of the Bible is true and what is not. "Inspired genius" may yet develop new revelations, and higher manifestations of truth   All this is sheer and unmasked infidelity to God, and to his Son Jesus Christ, and is a rejection of the Bible   It makes every man a law unto himself   Because of the disingenuous and equivocal use of the terms, the evil has been insideous in its workings, and difficult to define and expose. For one, we felt a sense of relief, when Cave declared his convictions in unmistakable terms. This was fair and honest in him, to let the world know in unambiguous terms exactly where he stood   The disciples owe to him a vote of thanks for his candor, and so far as we are concerned, he has it.

I object to those who have been teachers in this school of infidelity making Cave a scape-goat, while those denying the Bible to be of God, equally hurtful in their teaching, but less courageous and candid, are petted as "esteemed brothers."

Let us go to the bottom and make clean work in purifying the church of this corrupting infidelity. Longan and Proctor have been the leaders in this school. Others follow after them   They do not believe the Scriptures are given by inspiration of God, hence that they are not the final and perfect revelation of God to man, and the standard of truth

But anything now, short of thorough denunciation and exposure of the whole system of destructive of all true faith in God, as destructive as the claims of the Bible to be worthy the attention of humanity, as dishonoring to God and degrading to Christ, and a rejection of the Holy Spirit, and as destructive of all good to man in time and eternity, is treason to both God and man. Let us be true to the occasion and faithful to God, and great good will come to the church through this development   If we compromise in this matter, and fail to stand firmly for God's word and

God's honor, we betray the Son of God afresh and deserve shame and everlasting confusion.[9]

F. D. Srygley, who in 1890 began as front-page editor for the *Gospel Advocate,* watched the whole procedure with his characteristic note of humor. He thought of Mark 16: 16, "He that believeth and is baptized shall be saved." The *Christian-Evangelist* had been very lavish in declaring that the pious unbaptized should be saved. Srygley wondered what would become of the pious unbeliever, and so wrote:

The *Christian-Evangelist* and the *Apostolic Guide,* and the *Christian Leader* and the *Christian Standard* and, in fact, about every body else of much consequence have been pitching into R. C. Cave for the sermon he recently preached in St. Louis. So far as I have noticed, every body has been trying to prove that he is not in harmony with the current reformation. Well, suppose he isn't, what of it? I don't know any body that is in harmony with the current reformation, for that matter. I mean to say, the current reformation concedes to any man the right to differ from it, and about every body of any consequence exercises that right now and then To differ from "us, as a people" is not a very great thing after all. If R. C. Cave has done nothing worse than this, we are doing entirely too much cackling for the size of the egg. The Bible says, "He that believeth not shall be damned." That is the point I am watching. So far, I have not yet seen that point made. And yet, that is the very pitch and substance of the case. What must a man believe, to keep from being damned, and will R. C. Cave be damned some too for what he does not believe? That is the question It is needless to talk about what "we as a people" do or do not believe. For my own part, I stand by the Book—"He that believeth not shall be damned." And this I understand to be just such *believing not* as is set forth in those few whereases recently passed so flippantly by our erring brethren of the Central Church in St Louis. This thing must be fought to the end on that issue, and the *Christian Evangelist* may as well come down to the work at once. We have been lavish of our sympathy for the pious unimmersed What, now shall we do with the pious unbeliever? Is any body going to be damned? If not, I am disposed to say, in the language of the inimitable T. W. Caskey, "You may as well convert hell into a calf pasture and be done with it."[10]

Meanwhile, Garrison found it extremely difficult to countenance

---

[9]David Lipscomb, "Those Sad Apostasies," *Gospel Advocate,* Vol XXXII, No 6 (February 5, 1890), p 87.

[10]F. D Srygley, "From the Papers," *Gospel Advocate,* Vol XXXII, No 3 (January 15, 1890), p. 33.

Cave's "clear conscience" where the peace and welfare of the church was at stake. Garrison wrote to Cave, "If you, my brother, can look at the wreck of the Central Church, which a year of your ministry has wrought, with its divided homes and its saddened and alienated hearts, and with the fearful burden it imposes upon those who propose to stand by their colors, with a 'clear conscience,' as you say, that is the severest possible condemnation of the sufficiency of conscience as a guide in matters of religion."[11]

Srygley, on the other hand, failed to be touched by Garrison's display of conscientious opposition. After all, Garrison's editorial policy had not wrecked one congregation but scores the nation over, who objected to the policies advocated by the *Christian-Evangelist*. Srygley, after copying Garrison's note to Cave, replies:

That is a touching paragraph, and now I am expecting some one to "take up the thread" of the brother's exhortation and say to J H. Garrison: "If you, my brother, can look at the wreck of the whole brotherhood all over this broad land and in Texas too, which your editorial policy has wrought by way of pushing things many good brethren conscientiously believe to be corruptions of the worship—a wrangling brotherhood with its divided homes and saddened and alienated hearts, and with the fearful burden it imposes upon such men as McGarvey and Lipscomb who propose to stand by their colors on this society and organ question— if you can look on all this with 'a clear conscience,' that is the best possible evidence that you are a pretty bad sort of fellow too!" Verily it does make a difference whose ox is gored. In the language of the lamented Allen, "The case being altered, alters the case." When J. H. Garrison wants to push something which the brethren conscientiously believe to be a corruption of the worship, their conscientious convictions are small considerations, and he can not understand at all why they have such consciences anyhow. When R. C. Cave wants to push something which J. H. Garrison conscientiously believes to be a corruption of the worship, this matter of divided homes and saddened and alienated hearts, at once looms up as one of the biggest things in the whole business. As between R. C Cave and J. H Garrison in this matter of divided homes and such like things, there is precious little difference. My own opinion is that one of them is about as bad as the other if not worse . . .[12]

Within less than a decade following the Civil War it was

---

[11] J H Garrison, "The Difficulty in the Central Church," *Christian-Evangelist*, Vol XXVII, No 2 (January 9, 1890), p 23

[12] F D Srygley, "From the Papers," *Gospel Advocate*, Vol. XXXII, No 5 (January 29, 1890), p 63

thought by some that there was a strong inclination toward what is abstractly called "modernism" in Missouri. Then it was referred to as "rationalism," a term borrowed from German theological circles. Alexander Proctor and George W. Longan were especially singled out as accepting the usual theory of Biblical interpretation used by German and French Rationalists. Proctor and Longan rolled out the anathema of "legalism," especially directing it toward the editorial policy held by the *Apostolic Times* with Moses E. Lard and J. W. McGarvey the specific targets. Some of the strongest articles against this drift are to be found in the *Apostolic Times* between the years 1869-72. The term, legalism, however, although popularized by the *Christian-Evangelist* and re-echoed on down to the present day by men imbibed with the Garrisonian type of thinking, is one that those who use it most are least willing to attempt to define. What is legalism? Moses E. Lard wrote in 1871 in answer to Proctor which we copy from a later issue of the *Gospel Advocate*. Lard says,

Not to insist on obedience to these commandments is legalism. Against it, of late, not a little has been said, and nothing wisely. The term legalism I do not like. It is an offensive term, with a bad sense, as popularly used, and should, therefore, not be employed. *Obedience to the commandments of Christ is its exact equivalent, and should always be used in its stead.* But few men, however, could be found bold enough to speak against obeying the commandments of Christ. The result here would be too glaring. None could fail to see it, and few would hesitate to pronounce it infidelity. A more insidious method is adopted. Legalism is the thing inveighed against. But the act amounts to the same. Legalism and obedience to Christ's commands are the same Hence to speak against that is to speak against this. Nor have I any respect for the man who masks the law of Christ, and then speaks against it, than I have for him who insults it indirectly [13]

Thus Lard accused Proctor of making the idea of obedience to Christ under the guise of legalism, and fighting it under this name.

By the year 1890, David Lipscomb thought back over the last twenty years of his life and recalled many statements coming from Missouri preachers, all of which were closely allied to rationalism. He recalled that E. B. Cake, president of the Missouri Sunday School Convention and a frequent contributor to the *Christian-Evangelist,* had time and again declared that God and man were

---

[13]David Lipscomb, "Is Rationalism Rife in Missouri?" *Gospel Advocate,* Vol XXXII, No 12 (March 19, 1890), pp 182, 183

one. God talks to himself when he talks to man. Man hears and obeys the voice of God when he does what his intuition directs him to do.

In the April 16, 1886, issue of the *Apostolic Guide,* J. W. McGarvey began openly criticizing the tendency of Missouri preachers to accept liberalism in their thinking. For the next decade or more, McGarvey became increasingly conscious of the evil of this type of thinking to the restoration movement. His famous works on "Biblical Criticism," reprints from articles he wrote for the *Christian Standard,* are indicative of his strong reaction. At any rate, by 1886 McGarvey opened a campaign of criticism against the "advanced thinking" promoted by the Missouri Christian Lectures. He charged that Hedric's sermon in the 1885 lectureship on "The Philosophy of Remission of Sins" philosophized the atonement into nothing but a moral influence on the sinner and made the remission of sins into a mere turning of the sinner away from sin. It made pardon a figment of the imagination, according to McGarvey, and went so far as to deny possibility of pardon in the government of God. At the same lectureship McGarvey charged that Proctor had said that the Jewish idea of angels and demons were superstitions borrowed from Babylonia. McGarvey immediately thought it to be a shame that Jesus and his apostles did not have more scientific eyes and more rationalistic study so that they might have detected this. The same year, Longan had said it was a "piece of foolishness" for man to regard it as real history that the sun and moon had stood still, as the Biblical account affirms. The book of Job, Longan regarded, as not inspired.

Simpson Ely, president of Christian College at Canton, Missouri, wrote in the *Christian Register:*

The New Theology has been spreading with alarming rapidity during the last ten years. A mutual admiration society has been formed in Missouri, and when one member of the society would make a bold rationalistic statement, the other members would applaud.

Their very pompous actions would seem to say, "We are the only advanced thinkers." This society cannot brook opposition. Woe to the man that has the hardihood to question their position. Those who attended our lectureship will doubtless remember how the writer was throttled when he entered his solemn protest against charging the inspired apostle Paul with fallacious reasoning. Now the same man who charged Paul with fallacies, does, in the last *Christian-Evangelist*, deny that Mary and Elizabeth sang the beautiful psalms attributed to them by the sacred writers.[11]

Ely's last charges were directed toward Longan. But, according to Lipscomb, Longan had gone further, insisting that Matthew and Mark were confused upon the second coming of Christ, and therefore he denied their credibility. He also questioned the reasoning of Paul. Lipscomb charged that when the Scriptures say Jesus cast out demons, Longan understood that Jesus was a victim of heathen superstition.

Lipscomb now charged that this type of thinking and preaching had been going on in Missouri for ten years. Yet, the favorite writers for the *Christian-Evangelist* had been these very men promoting such "advanced thinking." When, therefore, Garrison appeared to be taken by shock at R. C. Cave's bold rationalistic assertions, Lipscomb joined with many others in questioning Garrison's sincerity. This type of thing had been going on under his nose for years, and he had constantly winked at it. What made him suddenly change? Too, Cave's attitude was a little strange. He had formerly preached for the Vine Street Church in Nashville, but had never proclaimed his beliefs on rationalism there. Why had he done it immediately upon coming to St Louis where Garrison attended church? Was it not likely that he felt that here he was among friends, and could afford to do it? At least no one had appeared more shocked at Garrison's rebuff than Cave himself. Actually, by 1890, there was a mounting antagonism to this new Missouri rationalism from all quarters. Although the charge is hard in its bluntness, many believed Garrison's action to be a political move to reinstate himself in the eyes of many who were losing confidence in him. Garrison admitted as much when he wrote:

. . . Some have, in their earnest zeal, even questioned my own soundness in the faith. I have no censure for them, but urge them to be patient and see whether or not the *Christian-Evangelist* shall prove worthy of confidence the brethren have reposed in it in this trying ordeal.[15]

The charge is not altogether groundless when all the facts are

[11]David Lipscomb, "Is Rationalism Rife in Missouri?" *Gospel Advocate* Vol XXXII, No 12 (March 19, 1890), pp 182, 183

[15]J H Garrison, "The Difficulty in the Central Church," *Christian Evangelist,* Vol XXVI, No 52 (December 26, 1889), p 820

considered   At least Lipscomb had no less confidence in R. C.
Cave than he did Garrison and let the fact be known.

This whole system is rationalism and skepticism of the most
bare-faced type   It destroys the credibility of the Bible, all ground
of respect for it as the word of God, and man's faith in Jesus as
the Christ, the Son of God   The man who defends these men or
their teachings, whether he intends it or not, aids and abets
the spread of rationalism and infidelity in the land   The man
who can see no apostasy in this widespread adoption and advocacy
of these destructive theories proclaims himself more than half an
apostate and infidel   For a man to denounce R. C Cave, who has
honestly declared his unbelief, and carried it and himself out of
the churches of God, and to overlook or close his eyes to these
ruinous teachings in the church, and to defend and cherish the
men who advocate them, as brethren, shows sectarian spirit, or a
moral cowardice that unfits for membership in a church of God,
and proclaims him unworthy to be accounted a disciple of the Lord
Jesus   I would prefer membership in any sect of Christendom
that holds to the Bible as the inspired and infallible word of God,
however it might pervert its ordinances, than to be in fellowship
with those who tolerate, cover up and cherish teachings denying
the inspiration of the Scriptures, rejecting the Bible as the infallible
word of God, destroying man's faith in it and in Jesus the Christ
as the Saviour of sinners, or who affiliate with and sustain the
men in this work of ruin to the best hopes of humanity   If the
Bible is the word of God, let us hold to it   If not, let it go to
the dogs. If it is not the inspired word of God, it is a book of
fables and falsehoods

Others besides Lipscomb and McGarvey sensed the leanings in
Missouri   In December, 1878, Proctor delivered an address on
"Rights and Ceremonies in Religion" before a Preachers' Meeting
in Kansas City   In this discourse he took the position "that in
the usual and scriptural sense of the words, there were no rites
and ceremonies in the New Testament."   One senses that somehow the ambiguity in the statement worried F. G. Allen as much
as the facts, for Allen replied:

Somehow in the last few years, a number of our preachers in
Missouri and some other states, have fallen into the habit of delivering addresses at these "Preachers' Meetings" and conventions
that require a great deal of explanation   Sometimes they are
months trying to get the people to understand what they meant
and what they didn't mean   There is no necessity for this. What
the Bible clearly teaches on any subject may be so presented that
the people will understand it—cannot help but understand it. We

are constitutionally shy of a speech that requires so much explanation.

We know nothing of the nature of Brother Proctor's explanation of his position, "that in the usual and Scripture sense of the words, there were no rites and ceremonies in the New Testament," but we are profoundly certain that it would require *a good deal of it* to enable us to "endorse the position."[16]

Indicative of the trend in the brotherhood was the revival of the controversy over the "pious unimmersed." From the earliest days of the restoration movement the question has constantly been asked, what shall become of the pious members of the denominations who die without being immersed? Preachers had proclaimed that the Bible taught baptism (immersion) to be necessary to salvation, but does this imply the unimmersed will be lost. Those who frankly faced this implication were considered uncharitable and legalistic. Those who managed to squeeze in room in heaven for the unbaptized somehow considered they had caught more the true spirit of the restoration and breathed a more spiritual atmosphere.

In a large measure this controversy revived itself around W. T. Moore while he was preaching in England. Timothy Coop, a wealthy English member of the church, felt that a trip to America to discover the reasons for success in the United States would probably help the English cause. He visited America and Cincinnati in 1878 and managed to persuade W. T. Moore to move to England. The Foreign Christian Missionary Society promptly made arrangements, and sponsored Moore in that foreign country

Moore left for England in the fall of 1878, locating first at Southport. There was a small congregation of disciples here, but Moore ignored this church and rented Cambridge Hall, a large auditorium. He selected fifty persons for a choir, none of whom were members of the church, and proposed to set forth "undenominational Christianity." David Lipscomb complained that Moore was deceiving the people, and so wrote:

The movement is announced in language which all persons, not acquainted with Mr Moore's position and mission, must understand to mean that, like Mr. Moody, he labors for no denominational object and does not seek to promote the increase of any special church, or party, but will leave his converts, uninfluenced, as to the sects they may please to join; than which nothing can

[16]F G Allen, "Editorial Notes," *Old Path Guide,* Vol I, No 2 (February, 1879), pp 77, 78

be further from the truth. In the only sense in which the people understand the term, Mr. Moore is intensely denominational, his mission is denominational—so much so that no one of the churches connected with the Missionary Society, whose agent he declares himself, would receive into its membership anyone of the most pious of Southport's believing people, who had not been immersed, and he is sent here for the purpose of planting or enlarging such churches [17]

In 1881 Moore began publication of his paper called *Christian Commonwealth*. During the spring of 1885 he made a recommendation through his paper calculated for union among all the denominations when he advocated that the church accept into her fellowship all members of denominations who were sprinkled for baptism, and who sincerely believed this was right, but that they should understand the church itself would only practice immersion

While both the *Christian Standard* and the *Christian-Evangelist* defended Moore, his proposal excited the ire of a considerable number of brethren   F. G. Allen led the way in attacking Moore He charged him with being the pastor of a church four hundred strong in membership, which was really a mixed Baptist Church. Allen charged that if Moore would preach the whole truth of God, that church would not keep him for twenty-four hours. Although Allen had a strong tendency to defend the society, and did , he found ample reason to turn his anger toward it   He declared that up to this time he had "kept his finger in his mouth" and would do so no longer. John F Rowe joined Allen's crusade against Moore, both charging that the *Christian Commonwealth* gave news reports of denominational activities in England while ignoring the brotherhood there   The *Commonwealth* had much to say about "Reverend Alexander McClaren, D D ," but nothing about an advocacy of a return to the ancient order of things

Alfred Ellmore reviews the work of Moore in the past and expresses no surprise at his conduct. He wrote.

And while we have nothing personal against Brother Moore and certainly wish him well, in well-doing, we say that when the brethren are through with his labors over there, we wish them to send him on to some other heathen (?) nation, for, while we would regard him as a citizen, we have no use for him as a preacher of

[17]David Lipscomb, "'Rev' W T Moore, M A , at Southport," *Gospel Advocate*, Vol XX, No 45 (November 14, 1878), p 715

the *ancient order* over here. We are perfectly satisfied he is not reliable as a leader and, therefore, speak out plainly.[18]

But David Lipscomb laughed up his sleeve in the typical "I-told-you-so" attitude. He believed the Society was fundamentally wrong, and anything it would do would be wrong. Moreover, he never doubted that the basic philosophy underlying the establishment of the Society was the conviction on the part of its friends that human plans could improve upon the divine. The Society itself represented a basic implication that God's way, the church, was unsatisfactory, and that man could improve upon it. The Society, to Lipscomb, represented man's attempt to change the divine plan He regarded F. G. Allen as being inconsistent in "keeping his finger in his mouth," but apologizes for Allen on the ground that Allen had been reared in central Kentucky among the friends of the Society Lipscomb never doubted that if Allen lived long enough he would stand with him in opposing the Missionary Society. For W. T. Moore, however, to allow people into the church upon sprinkling was, to Lipscomb, equivalent to Moore's assuming the authority to change the law of God. But so what? Wasn't this the basic philosophy that underlay the whole program of the Society? Lipscomb wrote· ". . . The same authority that changed the order of God in reference to the work of the church can change the faith. You have sown to the wind; you must reap the whirlwind."[19]

On October 29, 1885, the fourth anniversary of the publication of the *Christian Commonwealth*, a dinner was held in honor of the paper. W. J. Hocking delivered the toast of the evening Hocking was a high dignitary in the Church of England. He told the story of a man driving a wagon in Texas with four bullocks drawing it One was named Baptist, another Methodist, another Presbyterian, and another Episcopalian A man passing by inquired of the driver why these animals had been given such a peculiar name The answer was that the bullock by the name of Baptist was so called because he always headed for the water. the one named Presbyterian would do nothing except by rule, the one named Methodist was always kicking over the traces, and the

<hr>

[18]Alfred Ellmore, "Our Foreign Missionary," *American Christian Review*, Vol XXVIII, (August 6, 1885), p 253

[19]David Lipscomb, "How It Was Treated," *Gospel Advocate*, Vol XXVII, No 30 (July 29, 1885), p 470.

one named Episcopalian was so called for he always held his head high. Hocking applied the story   W. T. Moore was the driver, and the various men at the dinner—Methodist, Baptist, Presbyterians, and Episcopalians—were the animals.   Hocking then pronounced the *Christian Commonwealth* a "scriptural," "unsectarian" paper.   The paper was declared to be evangelical but not sectarian, scriptural but not uncharitable, progressive but loyal to Christian principles.

F. G. Allen printed this material in the *Guide,* but only brought down the wrath of the *Christian-Evangelist* and the *Christian Standard* against him.   Both insisted that if he were a gentleman he would apologize.[20]

W. T Moore's sincerity in his action is hardly to be questioned no matter how much one may disagree with his action of taking into the church those that were unimmersed.   Actually, Moore, Errett, and Garrison looked upon the situation in England as being analogous with that of Thomas Campbell when the latter in 1809 inaugurated the "Christian Association of Washington" when baptism was hardly a controversial question.   "The case being altered, should have altered the case"—to use a pet phrase of F. G. Allen—but Moore could hardly see it.   Neither Moore, Errett or Garrison were in precisely the same point with regard to advancement in knowledge in 1885 that Thomas Campbell was in 1809.   Campbell acted consistently with his beliefs.   If sprinkling or immersion had not yet entered a discussion of the Association, it was only because Campbell had not yet surveyed the field of thought on the subject.   He was acting in perfect accord with the convictions he had at that time.   With the passing years, he added considerably to his knowledge, altering his ideas radically as to the purpose and method of baptism.   In point of knowledge, the Thomas Campbell of 1845 was not the Thomas Campbell of 1809, and whether with his advanced learning of scriptural principles, he would have acted the same way in 1845 that he did in 1809 is highly questionable.   W. T Moore ostensibly believed that immersion was the only baptism, and that it was in order to salvation.   To waive this in the interest of Christian union as Moore did is not wholly analogous to Thomas Campbell, who in 1809 had not yet reached these convictions.   It is understandable

[20]A Recluse, "Jottings at Home," *American Christian Review,* Vol XXIX, No. 1 (January 1, 1886), p 2.

that Moore's act should be interpreted by David Lipscomb, F. G. Allen and John R. Rowe as a presumptious act on his part aimed at displacing the law of God with his own human wisdom.

The whole question of where the "pious unimmersed" stood with regard to their own salvation and the fellowship of members of the church displayed two attitudes The *Christian-Evangelist,* on the one hand, advocated the liberal spirit, displaying no reticence to shut its eyes on immersion when it deemed it wise, declaring at the same time that "the church of Christ believes that it is wiser to keep the spirit of a commandment than the letter." Of course, just how an individual kept the "spirit of a commandment," without doing what the commandment enjoined, the *Christian-Evangelist* never proposed to explain To this attitude, F. D. Srygley replied ·

This talk about the spirit and letter of commandments usually comes from men who want to *feel* goodish, but do as they please, in religion . . . To put the whole thing in its simplest form, the theory is that any man who is right in *spirit or motive* will be accepted of God no matter what the outward form of his conduct may be. It puts man's salvation wholly upon the ground of his own honesty, and taboos the idea that anyone will be damned who has the *spirit of obedience,* no matter how grave may be his mistakes as to the *letter* of God's commandments Much has been said against rationalists, but in my judgment they have done no more than follow this spirit-and-letter buncombe to its legitimate, logical consequences The point is, does God require man to conform his life to an external standard, or does he leave him to determine his own course by an internal light? Is man guided in religion by revelation from without, or by a spiritual light and nature *within* himself? Did religion originate in miracle, and is it perpetuated by teaching, or is it innate with man in principle, and developed by evolution? This is the only issue, and there are but two sides to the question Those who talk flippantly about keeping the *spirit* of a command while sneering at the *letter* of the law, or the exact thing commanded, are but the logical premises of which rationalists are the necessary conclusion, whether they so understand and intend or not. . . .[21]

As to the other attitude, F. D. Srygley in his own inimitable style, expressed the feeling of most members of the churches of Christ when he wrote:

Brethren, it is a waste of time to try to drag me into a discus-

[21]F D Srygley, "From the Papers," *Gospel Advocate,* Vol XXXII, No 33 (August 13, 1890), p 513

sion of this "pious unimmersed" question. As I understand the
New Testament, the "pious unimmersed" ought to be immersed
And in case they are not immersed, I know of no promise in the
New Testament that they will be saved   But, as to whether God
will make allowance for honest mistakes, and save those who think
they are obeying him when in reality they are doing something he
has not commanded in lieu of what he has commanded is a question for God to settle, and I decline to take any part in it [22]

To this same attitude, Isaac Errett came in the last years before
he died   In 1888 Errett was scheduled to speak on the Missouri
Christian Lectureship on the subject, "The Grounds of Christian
Fellowship " This was only a few months before he died   Because
of Errett's sickness, someone else read the paper on that subject
Errett had prepared   For several years Errett had given every
indication of backing the receiving of the "pious unimmersed" into
the fellowship of the brotherhood   His strong supporting of W T
Moore on that issue is but one indication of Errett's tendency
Still, in the address, Errett says

My own conviction, not hastily reached, is that we cannot consistently receive into fellowship, in our churches, the unimmersed
I say this with a full recognition of the Christian character and
eminent spiritual worth of multitudes of Pedobaptists, and agreeing
with Mr Campbell fully in acknowledging them as Christians in
the sense in which he employs that designation in the quotations
I have made.[23]

The very fact that J H. Garrison at the close of the address gave
it his hearty endorsement presents the enigma that was Garrison

The student of the restoration is not likely to be long in recognizing that such questions as that of the "pious unimmersed" are
but symptomatic· the basic question relates to the conception of
the church   On the one side men of a more conservative turn of
mind conceived of the church as *the* New Testament Church.   By
following the scriptures—without addition subtraction or substitution—they believed they would have *the* apostolic church, it
would not be a *sect* of the church as the Protestant denominations
claimed they were, but *the* church   But the liberal ranks in the
brotherhood frowned disgustedly upon this conception   Men who
had it were "narrow and legalistic and had not yet caught the

[22]F D Srygley, "From the Papers," *Gospel Advocate*, Vol XXXII, No
13 (March 26, 1890) p 193
[23]Isaac Errett. *The Missouri Christian Lectures, 1886-88* (Cincinnati
Standard Publishing Co, 1888), p 53

spirit of the restoration" was a typical Garrisonian statement, later to be applied with sophisticated airs against the *Christian Standard* But the development of a score of years between 1870 and 1890 was to show how far apart brethren were drifting in their thinking at this point.

In some circles the practice was constantly growing of fraternizing with the Protestant denominations W. T. Moore, as we have seen, practiced it regularly in England. At Madisonville, Kentucky, J. W. Higbee held a union meeting with the "other denominations." At Rushville, Indiana, D. R. Vanbuskirk waits on the communion table, assisted by a Presbyterian and Methodist clergyman [24] This disposition many could hardly countenance The aim of the restoration they conceived to be the exalting of the New Testament Church by the destruction of all sectarian bodies. Protestantism was the enemy to be destroyed that the apostolic church might alone remain. John F. Rowe, therefore, wrote:

We ask with all the seriousness of the judgment day before our eyes, and in view of our final accountability, can the Disciples of Christ affiliate with men who have produced such a mongrel of the holy and blessed religion of Christ? Can we in any sense identify ourselves with such sectarian bodies? Can we, in the fear of God, and as the conservators of the ancient order of things, religiously mingle with them and sit down at their communion tables? To do so is to return willfully into Babylonian Captivity Religiously, we must remain a distinct people, or else give the lie to all our pretensions of restoring the apostolic church, in doctrine, in faith and obedience, in worship and in discipline [25]

To avoid sounding too narrow and exclusive, some were willing to relegate the church into another sect in Christendom. In 1889 an editorial appeared in the *Christian Standard* saying:

We claim to be part of the church of Christ; we claim that the faithful in our fellowship are members of the church of Christ, and that our churches are churches of Christ, and that one of our churches is *a* church of Christ, but that churches as a whole constitute a church of Christ or *the* church of Christ we most positively reject [26]

---

[24] J. A Meng, "Let Us Have the Documents," *American Christian Review*, Vol XXV, No 8 (February 23, 1882), p 65

[25] John F Rowe, "The Duty of the Hour," *American Christian Review*, Vol. XXVI (November 1, 1883), p 348

[26] John F Rowe, "The *Standard's* Surrender," *Christian Leader*, Vol III, No 38 (September 17, 1889), p 4

Nine years earlier J. H. Garrison wrote in *The Christian*

If it be inquired, "What, then, is the name of our church?" we
reply, if by the term *our* is meant those of us engaged in this
reformatory work, *we have no church,* separate and distinct from
that to which all other Christians belong. The idea that we have
is the *sect idea.* It is an idea that has given birth to such names
as "the Methodist Church," "the Presbyterian Church," "the Baptist Church," etc   To speak of ourselves as "the Christian Church"
is to adopt this sect-idea and to put ourselves on the same basis
with all other sects   It is not necessary for us to say to our readers
that the church of God or the church of Christ, in New Testament
usage, includes all the saved—all obedient believers in Christ. This
is a well-known fact   What right have we to use these names in
any narrower or more restricted sense? To do so is to use them
in a sectarian sense

If it be replied to this that these sectarian bodies, by adopting
party names, have virtually repudiated the scriptural names, and
are, therefore, not entitled to them, we answer that, as separate
parties or bodies, they are not entitled to them; but that, unless
the act of consenting to be designated by a party name, on the
part of the individual Christians in these various sects, has served
their bond of allegiance to Christ, so that they have ceased to be
members of his body, they are a part of the church of Christ, which
he purchased with his own blood, and should, therefore, be included
in our use of the word church   But if the fact of their being members of a sect *has* dismembered them from the body of Christ, then
are they not Christians, and our plea for *Christian union is* without meaning. The plea for the union of Christians is based on the
idea that there is one family of God, one church of Jesus Christ,
and that the members of this one family are one church, by reason
of human weakness, ignorance and folly, in the past, are now
scattered, and divided into parties and sects, wearing party names,
rallying around party leaders and dogmas, and building up partition
walls between those who have a common Saviour and a common
destiny, and who should, therefore, love each other as brethren,
and help each other along the pilgrim way to the "better country."
To plead for the union of this divided family and to point out the
way to its realization is a work of such grandeur and dignity as
to commend it to the approbation of all conscientious, thoughtful
and unbiased minds, and to the gracious favor of Heaven

Again, in the July 15, 1880, issue, Garrison wrote:

In our last we were speaking of the impropriety of alluding to
our effort at reformation or restoration as "the Christian Church,"
or "the church of Christ"—thus employing Catholic terms in a
denominational sense   It is easy to see how this has come about.
All denominational movements in Christendom are styled *churches,*
with a prefix setting forth some leading doctrine or principle of

such denomination. Adopting this style of thought, and conceiving of our movement as a separate church, with a proper aversion to unauthorized and unscriptural names, it was natural that the name Christian should be selected in preference to any other adjective, as best descriptive of *our* church But the error lies either in conceiving of our religious movement as an ecclesiastical organization, answering to the name of church of God, and including all that the name includes in its scriptural usage, or else in regarding it as a denominational church, like the other churches about us

Sometime ago there was a controversy between some of our papers on the question, "Are we a denomination?" It occurs to us there is another question lying behind that that will help to answer it It is this · are we a *church?* If so, we are certainly a denominational church like the rest.[27]

Thus, germane to the spirit of liberalism arising in the brotherhood was the basic conception of the church To Garrison there were Christians in all churches, and the purpose of the restoration was to unite all of these Christians. Baptism, far from being essential to church membership, could be cast aside, thus opening the doors of heaven to the pious regardless of their immersion or lack of it The church in the final analysis was another sect and thus as denominational as the rest

Nor can anyone doubt that this viewpoint was growing rapidly in popularity. B. B. Tyler, another of its champions, preached in New York, and became involved in a controversy with John F. Rowe The New York preacher made it clear that baptism could be placed aside with him easily enough.

Let me as far as possible narrow the point of difference. I did not hold that immersion was the "dead fly." In this my brethren have misunderstood me The dead fly, in my estimation, *was the insisting on immersion as the sine qua non of church membership* I hold that as a large portion of the church of Christ (those considered by disciples as true members of Christ) are opposed to immersion, disciples ought to recognize their convictions [28]

Later, Tyler proceeded to teach that all men are the sons of God, and in this sense only is Jesus the Son of God [29] At Canton, Ohio,

[27]Joseph Franklin, "Sectarianism in the Reformation," *Gospel Advocate,* Vol. XXII, No 35 (August 26, 1880), p 545

[28]B B Tyler, "A Word to Rev Dr Tyler," *Christian Leader,* Vol IV, No 23 (June 10, 1890), p 1

[29]B B Tyler, "In What Sense Is Jesus the Son of God?" *Christian Leader,* Vol. IV, No. 43 (October 28, 1890), p 4

in August, 1889, Tyler, speaking before a large gathering of brethren, taught that all men would be saved who did the best they knew how, and in private conversation declared that unimmersed people would be saved. When it came to the subject of a union with the denominations, Rowe found reason to give Tyler's strictures a vigorous examination. Tyler had written:

The union of Christians is a subject very near to the hearts of a great multitude of the children of God. The interest increases. Prayers in behalf of unity multiply. Conferences to aid the cause are becoming common. Union is in the air. Everybody feels it. It is the watchword of the day. . Little by little we are finding a common platform in that word which lives and will abide forever. Coming out of the confusion of the Babylon of the great apostasy, modern denominationalism seems to have been unavoidable; but it was not so in the beginning. The believers then were one heart and one soul. This was and is the will of our common Lord. But our denominationalism must not be confounded with the sectarianism so severely condemned by the Holy Ghost in the New Testament. The sects condemned in the world of the Lord were companies of professed believers in the Son of God, turning away from Jesus, from his truth and from his Church. The denominations of our time represent the efforts of godly men to return in faith and in life to the religion of Jesus as he gave it to the world in the beginning. The various Protestant denominations represent stages in the journey from Babylon to Jerusalem.

Rowe responded by saying, "Let us analyze this piece of sectarian soft solder."

a. B. B. Tyler says, "The union of Christians is a subject very near to the hearts of a great multitude of the children of God." Well, sir, if a "great multitude are already the "children of God," why discuss Christian union at all? The idea is superfluous and preposterous . . .

l. "Little by little we are finding a common platform." "Are finding" is in the present tense. Paul says the "word of faith which we preach is nigh thee, even in thy mouth and in thy heart." If it is that near, it shouldn't take the honest, sectarian, theological doctors long to find the jewel. Again, does Brother Tyler pretend to affirm that the Disciples of Christ are "little by little *finding* a common platform"? He found it some years ago, but it now seems he lost it in the wide West, and that he is again "finding" it in New York City! Like the man who "got religion"—now he has it, and now he hasn't. . .

m. "But the good Lord will show us in his own good time the way out of the present difficulty." Please tell us by what means, outside of his revealed will, God will "show us the way out"? Are we to have new revelations? You had better spend your precious time, my brother, in showing the denominations the way in, provided you regard yourself as being in, and not simply occupying a "stage" in the "movement from Babylon to Jerusalem." If the Lord in his own good time intends to show us the way out in the remote future, then, in that case, the Bible has actually ceased to be an infallible guide!

So much sophistry in so small a space we have not, in a long time, seen in a sectarian sheet of the deepest dye. Alas, alas, the "Grand Restoration" is only a "movement," and another denomination has been added to a troop of phatasmagoria.[30]

It was inevitable that with the rise of this liberal spirit it should eventually affect the schools operated by the brethren. Butler University in Indianapolis was in for more than one session of constant anxiety over the encroachment of this spirit. In 1879 the university found itself in the midst of a war with the brethren over the question of whether or not only members of the church should compose the faculty. Love H. Jameson, president of the Board of Trustees, upheld using sectarians on the faculty, insisting that "our plea" was indefinite, and our principles broad and catholic. Jameson asked:

One of the most distinctive tents of Disciples, if I do not misunderstand them, is that sectarianism is wrong, and all Christians should be united. Holding such opinions, ought we to exclude a Christian man or woman from our faculty because they differ with us? . . .

F. G. Allen looked aghast at such a statement and replied:

With what singular uniformity do those who lend themselves to sectarian interests speak disparagingly and even contemptuously of the Restoration. . . . When men begin to champion sectarianism they have at once a strange idea of undenominational institutions, with them that institution which is composed and conducted in the interests of a number of denominations is undenominational, while that conducted by and in the interests of *no* denomination is *sectarian*.

With such men our plea for the restoration of primitive Christianity and the union of God's people on the Bible becomes at once a myth as unsubstantial and shadowy as the shade of Plato's ghost; or else a human creed to be condemned by an institution founded on the Bible alone, to the rejection of human creeds.[11]

---

[30] John F Rowe, "An Apology for Sectarianism," *Christian Leader*, Vol II, No 8 (February 21, 1888), p 4

[11] F G Allen, "Butler University," *Old Path Guide*, Vol. I. No. 7 (July, 1879), pp 269, 279.

But there were those who yet stood in opposition to this general trend toward making a sect out of the church. In this respect there are oddities in the restoration. F. M. Green was connected in sympathy with the *Standard*. He was secretary for the Society, and in 1886 was a member of the Ohio State Legislature, and thinking seriously about running for a United States Congressman. F M. Green's father was Philander Green of Kent, Ohio. No greater contrast in men could be found than in Philander Green and his son The father was as unyielding and determined as Jacob Creath He opposed everything that looked like progression, but his son was the opposite, working hard toward it. As the elderly Green thought back over the restoration movement, he wrote

I remember well when we had no meetinghouses to dedicate by professional dedicators or successful beggars for money We had no organs to entertain the congregations, but the natural one the Lord had given to his children We had no hired boys just out of college to play the clergyman and usurp the authority given to the heaven-ordained elders of the church of God I have lived to see nearly all things we once preached and practiced changed to the modern, fashionable, sectarian practices, where all expedients are used to entertain the people and gain thereby the recognition of the conflicting sects about us, to become popular, and be considered orthodox and really, one of the branches of the church. . . .

When I became a member of the church almost fifty years ago, I never expected or dreamed that I would live to see the change in doing the Lord's work, as it is called, that I have seen [32]

But Green comes to the battle fully ready to do his part in his declining years. Manby J. Breaker writes · "Christians are asked to unite on the basis of the primitive church in Jerusalem, but in reality no one wants to return to the condition of that church." Breaker goes on to say that the Jerusalem church had no Sunday School, lacked discipline and was badly organized But Green went to work on Breaker. "The farther some people get from Jerusalem and primitive Christianity," he writes, "the better they feel." Breaker had said there was in the Jerusalem church no definitely stated terms of membership Green says that of course the Missionary Society has membership on a money basis, and in this case every man knows when he has complied, but the Lord

---

[32] P Green, "The Testimony of One of the Pioneers," *Gospel Advocate,* Vol XXX, No 7 (February 15, 1888), p 12

didn't have as much sense as men have, and so didn't give any terms of membership.[33]

In addition to the liberalism expressed in the general conception of the church, there was yet another tendency which must be noticed. This relates to the drift toward a centralized ecclesiasticism which would serve as the "voice of the brotherhood" to exercise a control over the preachers and the churches. The Missionary Society in most cases became identified as this centralized ecclesiasticism, and so the debate over the Society now entered a second phase.

In 1882 the Missouri State Convention adopted a constitution which assumed the oversight of all the schools operated by the brethren in the state. The State Convention insisted that "all schools demanding recognition allow the nomination of their trustees by the State Convention." Three years later only two schools had complied with the request—Christian University at Canton and the orphan school at Camden Point F. G. Allen again took his finger out of his mouth and wrote:

The fact is, our conventions are making rapid strides in the footsteps of the post-apostolic church, which eventually led the great apostasy. If they do not soon become *legislative* in their action, it will be because their progress in that direction is arrested.

David Lipscomb said:

It seems to me that all hope that a society whose existence is itself an unauthorized usurpation, should refrain from unauthorized usurpation of power, is wholly against scripture and common sense. Like begets like.[34]

Rowe charged that the Convention was trying to control the school, and through the schools, to control the church

B. Bowen read a paper before the Kansas City Alliance of Christian Preachers on September 1, 1888, deploring the "present distracted condition of the churches" He said·

The Christian Church has no protection against an incompetent and vicious ministry If a man can deceive one congregation, he may wear, without contradiction, the name of Christian preacher. Our preachers are located with no reference to their peculiar abilities . . .

---

[33]P Green, "The Conclusion of the Whole Matter," *American Christian Review,*" Vol XXIX, No 40 (September 30, 1886), p 316

[34]David Lipscomb, "Societies," *Gospel Advocate,* Vol XXIV, No. (October 5, 1882), p 625

. . . The brotherhood, then, ought to have authority over individual congregations.[15]

The *Christian-Evangelist* now took the lead in advocating some centralized control over the brotherhood, fearing centralization less than excessive individual liberty   Depicting the general tendency on this point is the following from Samuel Magee

The *Christian-Evangelist* now advocates a conference, or some such institution with authority, to pass upon the ministerial qualifications of all preachers, that is, as to their moral fitness and doctrinal soundness, etc   Verily, this is progression with a quick movement.   But who gave the *Christian-Evangelist,* managed by poor, fallible, sinful, uninspired men, the prerogative to legislate and to dictate for the great Head of the Church?   Just as Christ commanded in the words of his commission, all disciples have authority to go out into all the world and preach the gospel, and who has authority to command otherwise?   The creed of the Christian is personal, not doctrinal nor dogmatical   Paul's statement is, "I know whom I have believed," not "what I have believed."   Paul was never alarmed concerning "the danger among us has always been in the direction of an extreme individualism rather than a tyrannical ecclesiasticism "   This is the danger our progressive movement fears! . .

. .   The state societies are everywhere taking advantage of every opportunity to foist an ecclesiasticism upon the churches of Christ   In Mississippi the State Society is making a desperate effort to secure and hold the title of all the church property in that state; in Kansas the Society has recommended that no preacher be employed unless indorsed by the Corresponding Secretary, in North Carolina the State Convention has, by a committee, "passed, ordained and placed on the roll of ministers" certain evangelists, and by the same committee "one candidate was rejected."   How does this strike you?   In Missouri the Society has taken control of all the educational institutions.   I want to know from whence this authority is derived!   Is not this whole thing a bold assumption?   How long will the disciples of Christ submit to this assumption?   How can we stand fast in the liberty wherewith Christ has made us free so long as we wear the collar of this man-made institution?   [36]

In October, 1882, James A   Harding attended the convention of the Society in Lexington, Kentucky, as an observer   Isaac Errett was the spokesman to raise money by selling life membership

[35]B   Bowen, "Centralized Organization of the Christian Church," *Christian-Evangelist,* Vol XXV, No 37 (September 20, 1888), p 581

[36]Samuel Magee, "Missouri Letter" *Christian Leader,* Vol IV, No 47 November 25, 1890), p 1

When a man asked Errett if he could purchase a life membership for his eight-year-old son, Errett replied: "Yes, or for one eight days old. We have infant membership here, though not in the church." Although Errett made his statement in jest. events proved that the Society had accepted money for infant membership. Harding took the Society severely to task only to be taken to task himself by F. M. Green.

A few months later The Northeastern Iowa Christian Convention modeled itself after the Methodist conference. The Convention proposed to put the churches and preachers under its oversight; to select preachers for the churches, to form circuits of the weak churches, and to send preachers to those circuits, and in addition, to establish new churches which would belong to and be under the care of the convention. Harding now wrote:

Well, things are progressing! The General Convention has begun to admit babies and outsiders to its membership and directorship; the Missouri Society proposes, I am informed, to take an oversight over the colleges and schools of the brethren of the state; the Northeastern Iowa Convention proposes to control and direct the churches and preachers in its district. . . . Truly, the world moves! Thank the Lord, we of the *Advocate* haven't any State Convention down here to run us and to manage things generally.[37]

Now that the State Conventions and the Missionary Society had grasped more and more power, brethren of the *Advocate* frame of mind saw that it was dangerous to oppose these organizations. The Conventions and the Society would work against any preacher or any congregation or paper that would not dance to their tune In Missouri, Dr. E. W. Herndon edited from 1882-89 the *Christian Quarterly*, aimed at the presentation of conservative principles where liberalism was running wild. When, however, Herndon printed an article on Christian Unity. insisting that to maintain this unity it was necessary to observe all God's appointments and institutions. Garrison saw in this an objection to the Missionary Society and promptly asked the brotherhood to cease subscribing to the *Quarterly*.

When J W. McGarvey wrote the *Gospel Advocate*, inquiring, "Please tell your readers how much error a man must preach in

---

[37] James A Harding, "The World Moves," *Gospel Advocate*, Vol. XXV, No 17 (April 25, 1883), p 266

order to deny the faith and forfeit fellowship," F D. Srygley was ready to answer.

As to how much error a man must preach in order to deny the faith and forfeit fellowship, if I may venture an opinion upon a rather limited observation along this line, backed by more than thirty years' experience of the *Gospel Advocate,* I would be frank to say the surest way to "forfeit fellowship" would be to modestly criticize the action of a General Convention or lovingly question the scripturalness of instrumental music in the worship. I have never done anything as heterodox as this, and hence my orthodoxy has never been questioned, nor has my fellowship yet been jeopardized. But I have made some edifying observations on this subject. While enjoying the loving fellowship of warm and confiding hearts, I have seen and felt that such men as the lamented Allen, the beloved McGarvey, and the fearless Lipscomb had indiscreetly forfeited their fellowship with us by their narrow policies of criticizing conventions and opposing organs in worship A man may repudiate all of the Old Testament and a good part of the New, deny the miraculous conception of Jesus, boldly assert that God inspires men today the same as in apostolic times, presumptuously point out the mistakes of Paul and knowingly pronounce the whole story of Eden a myth—all this and much more he may do, without forfeiting his fellowship. But if he should go so far as to intimate that a General Convention can make a mistake or that an organ cannot be scripturally used in the worship, his orthodox scalp would be dangling at the belt of some bold defender of the faith before he had time to offer an explanation or apology. We draw the line *here.*[38]

Despite all opposition the liberal tendencies multiplied greatly, and with the passing of a few years grew so rapidly that the *Christian Standard* sensed a stopping point must be found somewhere and began to draw back somewhat. The relation between the *Standard* and the *Evangelist* was for the most part cordial although a coolness developed.

At first it arose over the Hymn Book In a letter written April 3, 1885, by Isaac Errett to J. H. Garrison, who was then in Boston, Errett gave some hint as to the development of this "misunderstanding." Garrison had invited Errett to visit him in Boston, and Errett sent the following reply:

---

[38]F D Srygley, "From the Papers," *Gospel Advocate,* Vol. XXXII, No 1 (January 1, 1890), p 1.

STANDARD PUBLISHING CO.
No. 180 Elm Street
Cincinnati

April 3, 1885

Dear Brother Garrison:

Your favor of 1st inst. received. I had made up my mind to spend June in the East, especially that by personal observation I might be able to speak with emphasis as to the openings and the prospects there. At the same time, I fully appreciated the kindness of Brother Tyler in proposing to make a visit as pleasurable as possible. But the removal of Brother Mathews from the city necessitated new arrangements about the Bible Lessons—and the only solution of the difficulty was my consent to take back the work into my own hands. The third quarter's lessons must be prepared for issue in quarterly form before July 1, and this, in addition to my other work and the promises already made abroad, put it out of my power to go anywhere in June   I may be able, after a time, to transfer part of my other work to other hands. I would like to make the eastern trip sometime, and thank you for your kind invitation   I fear the hot season would not be a time when I could be of much service to you, as it is the season for vacation in religious matters; but I will keep the matter in mind and see what can be done in the future. It would please me to be able to make a statement as the result of my own observation that might call attention more definitely to the Boston enterprise, which I am very anxious should succeed

I had a letter recently from the Chn Publishing Co. I presume that, before long, we shall be able to come to some under; standing about a matter in regard to which there ought to have been no misunderstanding.

Wishing you all prosperity in the arduous work you have undertaken,

Ever truly yours,

ISAAC ERRETT

Alexander Campbell had in 1864 turned the *Christian Hymnal* over to the American Christian Missionary Society   The *Standard* published the Hymnal until 1882, when the *Christian-Evangelist* took over its publication. The *Standard* promptly put out a rival hymnal, and a controversy that grew extremely hot before abating developed between the *Standard* and the *Evangelist*

David Lipscomb in 1868 had written to Ben Franklin informing him that the American Christian Missionary Society was being used to build up the *Standard*. Although at the time Franklin doubted it, later he agreed. Commenting later, Lipscomb said:

It has been managed to build up the *Standard* until it has become rich, and so independent, that the Standard Publishing Company served a very practical and significant notice on the Society and the public, that if the Society refused to be subservient to its interest, it would destroy the Society.

As an illustration, Lipscomb referred to the Hymn Book question. Errett had an active part in securing the Hymn Book from Campbell for the Society. When the Hymn Book was revised, the Christian Standard Publishing Company put in a bid for its publication but was underbid. The Standard then published a rival book, and by this means sought to destroy the sale of the other book. Lipscomb interpreted it to mean that if any person dared to act contrary to the financial interest of the Standard, he could count on opposition. Lipscomb wrote:

It is a great lack of common sense, and an indication of ignorance of human nature, to think such institutions will not be run in the interests of designing and ambitious men.

They not only afford facilities for ambitious and selfish men controlling the affairs of the church, but they present temptations to lead men into selfish and corrupting courses; just as the opportunity to steal is a temptation to steal. The opportunity to acquire power tempts to do it, and the possession of it is a constant temptation to it for selfish ends. No man can endure constant temptation. We are not intending to say that we, or others, tempted as the *Standard* has been by its opportunities, would have done better. We are saying the temptation ought not to be offered any one[19]

In the controversy with Errett over the Hymn Book in 1883, Lipscomb revealed his feelings toward the editor of the *Standard*. He charged that a host of brethren, including Ben Franklin and Tolbert Fanning, had regarded Errett as a "trickster," that Franklin had no confidence in him, nor did the elders of the church in Detroit where Errett's ambition or financial interests were at stake. James W. Goss had said of Errett, "He is full of treachery—he won't do." L. L. Pinkerton had charged Errett to be a person who would back down on principle for the sake of popularity and gain. Lipscomb directly charged that Errett's character was not good for firmness and principle where these contradicted his own interests.

It was not, however, until after the turn of the century that any remarkable difference appeared between the *Christian-Evangelist*

---

[19]David Lipscomb, "Its Practical Working," *Gospel Advocate*, Vol. XXV, No 21 (May 23, 1883), p 326.

and the *Standard,* and the difference then largely settled on the matter of centralization and too hearty cooperation with denominational bodies. An organization was formed in February, 1901, by the Protestant churches of America called the "Federation of Churches and Church Workers." The membership was made up of a few local churches, not whole denominations. The next year at their Convention in Omaha, the Disciples of Christ took up the issue of whether they should join a proposed federation of Protestant Churches in America. Upon the suggestion of J H. Garrison. E. B. Sanford presented the plan. Garrison presented a resolution to this effect at the Convention. J. A. Lord, editor of the *Christian Standard,* cocked an eyebrow and raised the question whether this would be "recognizing the denominations " W. E. Garrison, son of J. H. Garrison, replied that it would only be recognizing that the denominations exist, not that they ought to exist. Another mass meeting was held at Norfolk in October. 1907, at which time it was agreed that the Disciples of Christ should join the proposed Federal Council soon to be organized. There was only one dissenting vote—that of J. B. Briney.

Garrison, of course, backed heartily the decision to join the Federal Council. Of those opposed, he wrote:

Those voting in the negative no doubt believed they were more loyal to the principles of our movement than those who favored it. But as a matter of fact they had never caught a true vision of its real spirit, intent and scope, as it is understood and presented by our representative men.[40]

Such a statement is typically Garrisonian

---

[40] J H. Garrison, *Memories and Experiences,* p 116

CHAPTER XIV

DANIEL SOMMER

"Of late years I have said the time will come that we will go so far from Bible Christianity we can well say, 'We had a prophet among us, but did not know it.'" So wrote J. D. Tant to Daniel Sommer twelve years ago.[1] The truculent Daniel Sommer was particularly adapt at making close friends and fierce enemies—only he preferred to call them "friendly friends" and "unfriendly friends," never enemies. He found a martyr's satisfaction in thinking of himself as the "most hated" and "most loved" man in the "disciple brotherhood" Despite, however, the obloquy of his "unfriendly friends," Daniel Sommer was unmoved in championing points of view which the brotherhood charitably at times called his "extremes" No matter how one may view the full effect of Sommer's work, it cannot be denied that before the year 1906, the enigmatic Daniel Sommer was a force with which to reckon. He has left his mark—whether for weal or woe will remain for the future to reveal.

The story of Sommer's life is an inspiring one. Although reared in almost absolute poverty, by sheer determination he became the protege of Elder Ben Franklin and one of the most popular preachers in the brotherhood He was "strong in the faith and robust mentally and physically" as W. B. F Treat once described him The appraisal is not overdrawn Sommer had complete confidence in the word of God, and a child-like trust in God's leadings It can hardly be denied that he was spiritually a giant He loved the Bible and studied vigorously He prayed constantly, and devoted himself earnestly to the work of God. Like Tolbert Fanning he was of an extreme independent term of mind, and took no man as an authority in religion. He freely challenged the great men His series of twenty-five articles entitled " 'Disciples of Christ' Challenged" which were run in the *Apostolic Review* in 1935 and 1936 show a refreshingly independent approach to the writings of Alexander Campbell.

---

[1] J D Tant, "An Open Letter," *Apostolic Review*, Vol LXXXI, Nos 49, 50 (December 7, 1937), p 5

Physically, Sommer was a giant. His excellent bodily condition enabled him to stretch his earthly life from the normal "three score and ten" to "four score and ten." His worn out frame yielded to death on February 14, 1940, and was laid to rest in Crown Hill Cemetery at Indianapolis

A little over ninety years before, Daniel Sommer was born in St Mary's County, in the state of Maryland The exact date was January 11, 1850.

Sommer's parents were both German His father, John Sommer, was a Hessian, and his mother, Magdalena Wyman was a Bavarian Both had emmigrated to America in 1835 They were married "at or near" Washington D. C in 1840 John Sommer died a comparatively young man, at the age of forty-one. Daniel Sommer was only a child at the time, and consequently remembered little of his father By trade, his father was a blacksmith He worked hard, but unlike most Germans, saved little Although not a drunkard, he did drink considerably, and consequently, too much of his money was lost in this way. When he died, he left his widow with no money and a large family. The future for the family looked dark

Sommer learned that tribulation is a difficult but necessary school in which to learn patience and perserverance When John Sommer moved his family near the village of Queen Ann in Prince George's County, Maryland around 1855, he contacted a severe cold in the process The cold developed into pneumonia, causing his death His penniless widow, burdened with a large family, went unselfishly to work. To earn money she sewed suits for the negro slaves owned by the rich plantation owners in that vicinity Usually a slave was allowed two suits a year by his master, so naturally, they sought for the best seamstress to make the clothing to last the longest

Queen Ann was a small village on the west bank of the Patuxent River, about thirty miles east of Washington D. C There were no churches of any kind here, and scarcely anything else to give it the reputation of being a village. Here, Daniel Sommer spent some of his early years The family lived in a log cabin, and each did some kind of work. Young Daniel set his traps, and in the winter brought in the game from his traps. The family lived for many days at a time on wild rabbit and corn bread.

In the spring of 1859 Daniel was hired out to do his first work
He was only nine years old, and the law said a boy could not do
public work under the age of ten   But his employer was a friend
and conveniently lied about his age   Roswell Marguder, his employer, was building roads through that section of Maryland, and
hired Daniel for a very small salary to help in the construction
Young Daniel arose before daylight, put his breakfast and lunch
in a sack, and walked several miles to be at the place of work on
time   He would walk back again at night, and fall exhausted
upon the floor of the log cabin, only to have the process repeated
the next day. Oft and on he worked at this job through the fall
of 1861. When the war came, workers were scarce and work
plentiful, so the boys below army age secured their full share
Although the war raged about him, Sommer lived in almost complete oblivion of it.

He entered school first at the age of seven   At first, he was
slow to learn and received considerable "teasing" about it. Nevertheless, he managed to take full advantage of his opportunities
and advanced very well. His school days lasted only a few months
each year for five years   He dropped out in the spring of 1862
to return to work   Until he entered Bethany College seven years
later, he was never again inside of a school   Through the winter
of 1862-63 he worked as a farm hand for four dollars a month
and his board

Up to the spring of 1863 Sommer had given very little thought
to religion   His parents were nominally Lutherans and had their
children sprinkled by Lutheran ministers   But they gave no
devoted time to practicing their religion   Along through young
life, Sommer had picked up a few bad habits, common to boys
of the world   He could curse a little, and in case of necessity
found it easy to lie occasionally   Old fashioned thievery was out,
but woe be to the person who left a penknife lying around without
a guard   These habits, then as now, were hardly considered too
bad for an irreligious boy who had never given serious thought
about his responsibility to God

In the spring of 1863 Miss Louisa V Harwood, an adopted
daughter of the store keeper in the village, decided to open a
Sunday School in a private house and invite the children of the
neighborhood. Sommer at first was but little interested but
later changed his mind   The young teacher presented her lessons

in an appealing manner so Sommer became interested. She encouraged the children to think about their soul's welfare and asked them to "repent and pray" to God. Sommer for one, took her seriously, and began for the first time to pray. It was not long until he was living an entirely different life.

At the close of 1863 Sommer left the plantation of William Fielder Howell where he had been employed, to work for Oden Bowie Here, Sommer had some unpleasant experiences, due in the main to the fact that Bowie expected too much out of the farm hands He left this farm on January 1, 1865 and the next day hired out to a farmer by the name of Mullikin Sommer's mother, meanwhile, lived in a tenant house on the farm.

Before the close of 1864 Sommer had grown careless about his religion, lapsing into indifference. About this time a revival meeting was conducted among the Methodists in McKendry Chapel Sommer was solicited as a likely candidate to come forward, "get religion" and "join the church." He convinced them that he had religion already, and so was promptly admitted into the church. He began now to be regular in attending Bible classes at the Methodist Church.

During the winter of 1866, Sommer chopped wood for a living It was during this time that he heard of a group of people called the disciples of Christ. He heard it rumored that these people had no knowledge of "heart-felt" religion, and had no experience in conversion They simply took the attitude, he heard, that if they did certain things, God was obligated to save them. The whole affair was rumored to be a cold, legalistic type of religion, and of course, was arduously condemned So, when Sommer had a day off from work, he went down to a creek to observe a baptism being conducted by D. S. Burnet, whom Sommer understood to be the preacher for the church in Baltimore, but who was now here in the country conducting an evangelistic meeting

In the winter of 1866 Sommer moved into Hartford County, Maryland Here he had his first real contact with the restoration At the "Mountain Meeting House," also called the "Jerusalem Church," there was a preacher by the name of Calderwood, commonly described as a man "too lazy to work between meals." Talk of him—evidently not too praiseworthy—and of his teaching often became the topic of conversation in the community When Sommer went to work for a man by the name of John Dallas

Everitt, a member of the church, young Daniel was now placed directly in the line for some wholesome teaching. When he reminded Everitt that he had been baptized—sprinkled when he was a baby—young Sommer was promptly told he had not been baptized at all. Step by step, through discussion and research of the Scripture, Sommer was led. For a year the discussions continued and Sommer found his convictions slowly changing. Finally, in August of 1869 he was baptized by Elder T A. Crenshaw of Middletown, Pennsylvania.

The question of selecting a life's work now renewed itself in Sommer's mind. His father had selected him to be a blacksmith because of his hardy physical makeup. Later, one or another possible vocation suggested itself. Now that Sommer was converted, and was intensively interested in the Bible, he began to toss about in his mind the possibility of preaching the gospel. When he spoke to some of the elderly men in the congregation about it, they encouraged him, but suggested that he first needed more education. Bethany College was the closest of the schools connected with the brotherhood Besides, it was the most illustrous. Alexander Campbell's memory hovered spirit-like around it. His son-in-law, W. K. Pendleton, was now its president. C. L. Loos, a highly-respected educator, was connected with the school. Robert Richardson, although growing old, was still there. Sommer, therefore, prepared to enter Bethany College.

He came to Bethany in the same state of poverty that had characterized his entire life. Consequently he worked hard to pay his way, and went greatly in debt besides His educational background· was very limited—not having put in over five years, and those were disconnected and under inadequate circumstances in country school houses Sommer entered Bethany far below other students both in educational background and financial security, but no student ever entered with more determination. At first, he took Latin, Greek, and algebra, but dropped the algebra to take rhetoric.

The first disappointment that Sommer felt with the brotherhood came during his student days at Bethany. He noticed that there were two classes of disciples in the church. One class believed that the Bible was a revelation to the saint and sinner. The other believed it was only a revelation to the sinner. The rule with the latter class was that God gave a revelation to tell the sinner how to become a Christian, but beyond that, the rule was "love God and do as you please." There were no laws governing the church, and in the final analysis, sincerity alone was sufficient. President W. K. Pendleton was a champion of this point of view.

"The smooth and compromising manner of President Pendleton," wrote W. B. F. Treat, "had no charms for him" (Daniel Sommer). He reacted violently against this. Although C. L. Loos was less addicted to this type of thinking, he was still the friend of human societies outside the church to do the work of the church, and in this connection Sommer had his first serious trouble.

The lady members of the church in Bethany decided to raise some money to buy new curtains, a new carpet and to paint the building. C. L. Loos, an elder in the congregation, gave a talk before the congregation one evening favoring the plan. A Ladies' Mite Society was organized and the announcement made that the hat would be passed that each person might give his mite to this work. The Mite Society held frequent meetings, which in Sommer's opinion degenerated into something very worldly. It was the custom of the church to invite different preachers among the students to speak at the Sunday evening services at the church. When Sommer received his invitation, he chose the first Psalm as a text, and closed the discourse with a severe blast at the Mite Society. This blow staggered the Society and in a matter of few days it died peacefully, but the blast shook Sommer's popularity considerably around the school.

The Mite Society was the first deviation from apostolic principles that Sommer found in the church after becoming a Christian. He was proud of the fact that he had publicly attacked it, and that his flagellations against all unscriptural practices were never known to stop as long as he lived. Sommer wrote:

I denounced publicly the first deviation from apostolic simplicity that I found among "disciples," and I have been acting on the same principle ever since. For a brief period I thought that "mutual teaching and exhortation" should be the order at the time of worship without what is called a "sermon." But I soon learned that when any one imitating the apostle Paul as a preacher was present at such a meeting then that one should be used as Paul was at Troas. Then for a brief period I thought that we should not offend the objector to classifying children and others in order to teach them in the meeting house. But I soon learned the evil results of doing nothing special for children on Lord's Day, and thus I turned from my mistake on that question . .[2]

Sommer's self-appointed role as a critic of brotherhood activities cost him dearly in friends, and gave him a reputation not altogether too envious   It is seldom that an individual can voluntarily select the role of a critic but what he can become overbalanced in this department of his work, and go to an extreme.   One can repose, however, in some felicity with the thought that it is better to have a watch dog that barks too much than one that barks not at all.

In the spring of 1871 Ben Franklin, editor of the *American Christian Review,* came to Wellsburgh, West Virginia to conduct an evangelistic meeting   Quite naturally, Sommer had heard of Franklin, as had nearly every member of the church   From what he had heard about Franklin, he rather liked him, but he wanted to go see him and be sure   He asked and secured permission to miss classes one day at the College and went to Wellsburg to be with Ben Franklin   It was a case of love at first sight, and the love was fully returned   The aging Ben Franklin took a liking to young Sommer, and Sommer in turn idolized Ben Franklin   To the day of his death, Sommer never ceased regarding Franklin as the quintessence of gospel preachers. Sommer could well recall that at this meeting he found Franklin brokenhearted   Franklin now lived in Cincinnati where the Central Christian Church was erecting its $140,000 meeting house and putting in it an $8,000 organ   This case of extravagance was unparalleled in restoration history   So thought Franklin   His spirit was low when he met Sommer and he poured out his heart to his young protegè, and Sommer drank it in at the same time— consciously or unconsciously—firmly resolving to duplicate this man's life in his own

Sommer's stay at Bethany College covered less than three years   During the Christmas holidays of 1872. he went to a place called Dutch Fork in Maryland and conducted a meeting   He did not return to take the final examinations that year, and dropped out of school   On his occasional excursions into Maryland, Sommer. too, had had other interests in mind the nature of which was

[2]Daniel Sommer, "'Disciples of Christ' Challenged—No 18," *Apostolic Review,* Vol. LXXXI, Nos. 5, 6 (February 2, 1937), p 8.

clearly revealed when on this return trip he married Miss Kate Way.

For a short time immediately following his marriage, Sommer preached for one of the churches in Baltimore. There were two congregations here. The Paca Street Church where D. S. Burnet had preached until his death, and the congregation for which Sommer now preached had long been divided. The Paca Street congregation now had a preacher, who, in Sommer's opinion, was somewhat less than a Christian as it respected his morals Sommer's stay was somewhat shortened and occasioned by considerable inter-congregational animosity.

During the time he lived in Baltimore, however, Sommer made a fast friend of George Austen, one of the elders. Austen had succeeded in establishing congregations in the bordering territory, and was one of the leading men in the church in that day He was a harsh critic of Sommer's at a time perhaps when Sommer needed this After hearing Sommer twice on one Lord's Day, he wrote his young friend the following letter ·

Your forenoon's discourse was only tolerable At night I knew you had made a failure as soon as I heard your text. Your gesticulations were stiff and awkward, your intonations of voice were forced and unnatural; your outlines were only ordinary, and the filing-up was miserable [*]

Such harshness was far from pleasant, but Sommer profited by it

After a brief stay in Baltimore, Sommer moved to Kelton, Pennsylvania where he preached for the next five or six years. This congregation was one that George Austen had established. In the absence of any documentary evidence, it is not unlikely that Austen played some part in the changing of the locations.

At Kelton, Sommer took the opportunity for constant growth. Little of any significance came from him before the brotherhood. In 1872 he wrote his first article for Ben Franklin which was published in the *American Christian Review*. Three years later a few short articles appeared. Then there is silence until the fall of 1878 when Sommer wrote for the *Review*. Aside from these occasional flings at writing, Sommer kept busy in evangelistic meetings, his unusual ability becoming more widely known. From November 8 to December 14, 1878, he was in a meeting at

---

[*]Daniel Sommer, " 'Disciples of Christ' Challenged—No 22," Vol. LXXXI, Nos 13, 14 (March 30, 1937), p 8.

Reynoldsburg, Ohio. A. E. Sprague who heard him through the entire meeting wrote of him:

He is a young man not yet in the prime of life; his voice strong and clear; his enunciations exceedingly good; his knowledge of scripture rarely excelled; his energy untiring; his manner and address pleasing; all these, together with his exemplary walk, and great reverence for the word of God, makes him a man of no ordinary ability.[4]

In the spring of 1879 while still living at Kelton, Sommer was bitten by a mad dog, which gave him hydrophobia. Two physicians attended him, dosing him heavily with lobelia.

He felt heavily the blow of Ben Franklin's death in the fall of 1878, for he and Franklin had corresponded frequently, and already Sommer had sent in a series of articles entitled, "Educating Preachers" which were aimed at the culpableness of Bethany College. When John F. Rowe took over the editorship of the *Review,* Sommer continued his writing for several months, but eventually dropped from the contributors.

While preaching in Kelton, in Chester County, Pennsylvania, Sommer had occasion to receive a high compliment from Ben Franklin. In April, 1878 Franklin wrote Sommer of a congregation needing a preacher. The particular place offered twice the salary Sommer was then receiving, and from every point of view was attractive. But Sommer declined, writing to Ben Franklin that he was needed at Kelton more than at the other congregation. Although Franklin regretted that Sommer would not make the move, he admired the spirit, and so wrote:

We like this letter, though it does not agree to what we had in view. It is in the spirit of the pioneers in our great work, and of the primitive men in the church. The question with Brother Sommer is not *how much money* he can make out of his fine gifts and the gospel, but *how much he can do* in the great work of saving men.[5]

In 1880 Sommer moved from Kelton, Pennsylvania to Reynoldsburg, Ohio, stopping by Columbus for a short time on the move. In 1883 he began editorial work on his own. Together with L. F. Bittle he started a small monthly paper called the *Octograph.* The name was coined by Bittle to denote the "writings of eight,"

[4]A E Sprague, "Daniel Sommer at Reynoldsburg, Ohio," *American Christian Review,* Vol XXII, No 4 (January 27, 1880), p 30
[5]Ben Franklin, "The Right Idea," *American Christian Review,* Vol XXI, No 20 (May 14, 1878), p. 156.

referring to the eight writers of the New Testament. The paper was thus to be thoroughly apostolic. Bittle is one of those little-known heroes of the restoration. For a few years, while the *Review* was published by Franklin, he flamed into brilliance before the brotherhood in his opposition to the "digressive" tendencies. Among *Review* readers, he was extremely popular.

In the fall of 1884 Sommer moved to Martel, Ohio, and the following spring, on to Richwood. At this latter place the church had only seventy-five members and was unable to support a preacher. Besides they were deeply in debt. Sommer agreed to preach for them temporarily for nothing. The congregation was, when Sommer came, using an organ, supporting the missionary societies, and selling pies at church festivals to raise money. Sommer, of course, pitched heavily into these. J. J. Moss, one of the liberal preachers, came by, conducted a meeting, and the result was an open division in the congregation.

As a preacher, however, Sommer was continuing to gain a great prominence. George W. Rice, after hearing him preach, said, "As an earnest and clear-headed gospel preacher he falls behind no one in the rank. For zeal, devotion and earnestness in preaching the gospel I place him next to Brother Franklin."[6] On another occasion Rice said of Sommer's preaching:

It forcibly reminded me of the preaching of the pioneer days, when men were ready to spend and be spent in the restoration of the apostolic gospel and order of things . .

He is so full of the gospel that he has thrown everything else overboard—knowing nothing else but Jesus Christ and him crucified. By doing this, he fills every person so full of the gospel that all innovations are given up and forgotten where he preaches.[7]

Ben Franklin, too, had always high regard for young Sommer as a promising gospel preacher. Shortly before he died, Franklin conducted a meeting in Detroit Speaking confidentially to O. M. Benedict of Sommer, Franklin said:

I consider Brother Sommer as one of the most promising young men in my whole acquaintance. God has given him a grand physique, a strong, grasping mind, a sharp pen, a fairly-ready

---

[6]George W Rice, "Why I Am Now on the Review," *Octographic Review*, Vol XXX, No 24 (June 30, 1887), p 1

[7]George W Rice, "Daniel Sommer as a Preacher," *Octographic Review*, Vol XXX, No 43 (November 10, 1887), p 8.

tongue, and his heart is attuned to the grand principles of this great *Restoration movement* [*]

When Edwin Alden, owner of the *American Christian Review,* presented the paper for sale in the summer of 1886, Sommer was quick to take advantage of the opportunity to purchase it   The following spring the name was changed to *Octographic Review*   For the next seven years the paper was published first from Cincinnati, then from Richwood.   All of the while, Sommer was casting about for a better location.   Indianapolis immediately appealed to him due to its central location in the heart of the great brotherhood.   But he was not adverse to moving it somewhere else.   For a short time brethren in Missouri made a bid for it, but this did not materialize.   Gradually Sommer became more and more in demand as a preacher in the state of Indiana, a fact which made Indianapolis seem more than ever like the best location from which to publish the *Review*.   Early in 1894 then Sommer moved to this city.   His office was at first at 66½ North Pennsylvania Street, but in two or three months was moved to West Udell Street in north Indianapolis.   The first issue of the *Octographic Review* to come from Indianapolis was dated March 20, 1894

The church in Indianapolis had grown considerably since John O'Kane had conducted the first evangelistic meeting there in 1833   Out of O'Kane's effort had gradually developed what became known as the Central Christian Church.   With the establishment of Northwestern Christian College in 1855 in the city, members of the church were attracted to the city   When, following the Civil War, the instruments of music began filling all the churches, brethren who opposed these found themselves forced to start their work all over again.

Taking the lead in this new birth was Dr. Joshua Webb   Born on August 13, 1809 in Columbiana County, Ohio, Webb was baptized by Elder William Schooley when he was only fifteen   At the age of twenty-one he began to preach   He spent his entire time preaching for the next seven years, and usually with marked success.   At Beaver Creek in Maryland the whole Lutheran Church dissolved its denominational status and adopted the name, Christian.   At this time the Lutherans, becoming alarmed, sent their favorite, S. K. Hoshour of Hagerstown, Maryland to confound Webb, but

---

[*]O M. Benedict, "To the Readers of the Review." *American Christian Review,* Vol. XXX, No. 1 (January 6, 1887), p 5.

Webb succeeded in leading Hoshour to restoration principles. Webb's health broke and he ceased preaching. He studied medicine for three years, and practiced in Maryland and Ohio before coming to Indianapolis in 1865. He promptly became a member of the Central Church.

In 1878 after the Central Church had introduced the organ, Webb withdrew and began meeting with a few in what was called the Danish Church on South New Jersey Street. Shortly afterwards, Webb purchased a frame house from the Sixth Presbyterian Church, and had the building on the back of his lot behind his home on Mulberry Street. This congregation met three times every Sunday. The forenoon service consisted of short talks from the members—never any preaching. In the afternoon, they had Bible study, and of course, these were conducted without lesson leaves. At night, there was an evangelistic service.

When John F. Rowe visited Indianapolis in the fall of 1887 he found seven congregations, consisting of fifteen hundred members. The number included those using the organ. A new congregation had recently been established in West Indianapolis by Abram Plunkett. Wesley Davidson was one of the elders. The congregation had over a hundred members. It had not added any "innovation." On Home Avenue the "Third Church" had recently been established. D. R. Vanbuskirk was a leading member here. The congregation had three hundred and fifty members. The next year, 1888, Z. T. Sweeney, who was then riding a high crest of popularity, spoke at the dedication of a new church building.

Rowe had made frequent excursions into Indianapolis. When he visited the city again in 1890, he found a new congregation meeting on Madison Avenue. Two years later he came back to the city and went with J. W. Perkins, J. Perry Elliott, H. I. Shick and B. N. Davis to the newly founded North Indianapolis congregation. Rowe preached in the forenoon and Perkins in the evening The congregation had only twenty members, nearly all of whom were young married people.

When, therefore, Daniel Sommer moved to Indianapolis in 1894, he identified himself with this church in North Indianapolis, and until his death preached off and on for this congregation. Sommer's first major activity in Indianapolis was to announce a ten week's Bible Reading to begin in May, 1894 and close the last of July. The cost was to be about fifty dollars. A dozen young men or so came to the Bible Reading. In later years, he lost some of his ardor for these readings insisting that it gave young men the idea they were preachers long before they were ready to preach.

Sommer never distinguished himself as a religious debater although he did engage in several during his life. His first debate was held with a German Baptist in Ray County, Missouri. Before the discussion, Sommer wrote, "Debating will be new business to me and I have no idea that it will be enjoyable." It did prove enjoyable, however, and Sommer found considerable satisfaction in this type of teaching.

It will not be needful to trace the life of Daniel Sommer through the years to his death in 1940. Much of this would be relatively modern history with which the average reader would already be acquainted. These facts of his life are given that cover the years of his life that relate especially to those covered in this volume. On some points of study with which this volume deals Daniel Sommer plays a prominent role.

Any estimate that one may place upon the life's work on Daniel Sommer will understandably be colored by the background of the biographer. We could wish in this matter as in all others to be true, honest, and charitably objective. That Daniel Sommer was a great preacher, possessing a great mind and heart, no person at all acquainted with his life can for a moment doubt. He was fearless, independent, and ambitious. Deploring as violently as he did the "digression" that swept the churches, it was hardly possible for him to look with any charity or much understanding upon anything, whatever it was, that played any part in causing this "departure."

Sommer's experiences at Bethany College found him departing from school with absolute disgust at the idea that a preacher needed a college education. The trouble at the College of The Bible in Kentucky University found the two men Sommer admired most—Ben Franklin and Jacob Creath, Jr.—turning against Bible Colleges Sommer was a young preacher; they were older preachers Their turning against these colleges at a time when Sommer's heart was already chafing at the bitter memory of Bethany, helped form a conviction in Sommer's heart. Too, Sommer could never think of himself in any role except the successor of Elder Ben Franklin, whom he regarded as the greatest gospel preacher since apostolic times. Franklin in his latter years opposed colleges, and the man who wore his mantle would be likely to do the same

That Sommer went to extremes at times, even he himself admitted. In championing for a short time the view that preaching had no place at the morning worship, he saw soon was an extreme and abandoned this course. For our part we are not willing that his extremes should blind us in seeing the real greatness in the man, nor shall our willingness to see his greatness stand as an obstacle to our seeing his extremes.

Sommer's point of view on issues that developed before 1906 will be discussed in other chapters.

Chapter XV

THE REVIEW'S TROUBLES

In the August 26, 1886 issue of the *American Christian Review* there appeared a very startling report in the form of an editorial, making public the fact that the *Review* was having critical financial times. More than this, the editorial announced the resignation of John F. Rowe and George W. Rice—the former as editor and the latter as publisher. Brethren had little knowledge of any trouble, and so sat tensely waiting to see what would happen. Soon the facts came forth, but before they had finished doing so, the *Review* was injured seriously.

In 1873 the nation had experienced a severe financial panic. During this time, the *Review* was threatened. Edwin Alden, a business man who made his money acting as an advertising agent, came to the paper's financial aid by paying its debts as well as those of George Rice, the *Review* publisher. These totaled about fifteen thousand dollars. From that day, it was agreed that Alden should use the *Review* for his advertising, but the editorial policy would be directed by Ben Franklin. Alden was to have no say about how the *Review* should be run editorially, nor was he to do any advertising out of harmony with Christian principles. This arrangement had proved very satisfactory. In spite of the fact he was not a member of the church, his relations to Ben Franklin and Rice during those years was very cordial.

But, early in 1886, Alden faced the fact that his business was losing money. Before long he was fifteen thousand dollars in debt Nothing remained for him but to sell the *Review* to save himself from complete bankruptcy. He immediately, therefore, began negotiations with two men—A. E. Childs and Geroge F. Hussey, neither of whom was a member of the church, and to them the *Review* was turned over.

Alden in conducting the whole transaction had failed to consult with either Rowe or Rice. Actually he was under no obligation to do so since he was the paper's owner. Rowe and Rice, true to human nature, felt left out. The new owners of the *Review* were strangers to them, and it is not unnatural that they should feel some misgivings as to the future. Moreover, the fact that Rowe would have liked to purchase the *Review* for something around nine thousand dollars doubtlessly influenced his revolt against Alden, so Rowe threw a gigantic bluff in the hope of getting the paper himself. It was a big chance, but if it succeeded, he would be able to purchase the *Review* at almost half its real value. Rowe took the chance and lost. Unfortunately he injured not only himself but the cause of which he was a symbol.

The editorial of August 26 was written by a Presbyterian preacher in Cincinnati and published over the names of Rowe and Rice. Why they induced this preacher to write the editorial for them is hard to explain. The editorial accused Alden of taking money that did not belong to him and of manipulating the business to his own selfish ends. Alden remained silent in the face of their accusations for some time. At first, brethren as a whole sympathized with Rowe. The idea of trying to edit a paper owned by a member who was not even a member of the church was enough to arouse their sympathy. In later years, however, Alden seems to have completely vindicated himself in their good graces by establishing a reputation for honesty despite the blow he received.

Three weeks after his first editorial appeared, the September 16, 1886 issue of the *Review* came out with the brief announcement from George W. Rice that John F. Rowe had been forced out as the editor of the paper. Rice proposed to carry on until further developments. The next issue of the paper appeared with W. B. F. Treat as the editor.

Fifty-one year old Treat was a short man with grey eyes, auburn hair and a heavy beard. He had been connected with the *Review* while Franklin edited it, but had found himself very often in disagreement with Rowe. He was a native of Morgan County, Indiana, and had been preaching for thirty years, although at one time he had served four years in the State Legislature of Indiana as a Senator. For a short time he had been associate-editor of the old *Christian Record* which had been edited by J. M. Mathes at Bedford, Indiana.[1]

The affair aroused Rowe's suspicion. Several months before the sale of the *Review*, Treat had resigned his work on the paper.

---

[1] J. W. Perkins, "Briefs Here and There," *American Christian Review*, Vol. XXX, No. 1 (January 6, 1887), p. 5.

After the trouble between Alden and Rowe, Alden had taken a trip and talked privately with Treat about becoming editor. Rowe, not knowing this, wrote to Treat, asking his advice about starting another paper. Treat advised both Rowe and Rice to do this, but afterwards explained that Rowe had asked him between two courses, one of which was starting another paper, which in his opinion would be more desirable. Treat said he did not think much of either action, but of the two, starting another paper seemed more desirable, and had so advised Rowe. At any date, when Treat, after advising Rowe to start another paper, was announced as editor of the *Review,* Rowe immediately concluded that a conspiracy to kill his work and influence had been under way.[2]

No sooner had Rowe left the *Review* until he made immediate plans to start another paper. His new paper he would call the *Christian Missionary* but later changed his mind and called it the *Christian Leader.* The first issue appeared dated, October 7, 1886, and its make-up and appearance was the *Review's* twin. Across the top was written: "One Faith, One Lord, and One Immersion." J. Logan Richardson, brother of Robert Richardson, Campbell's biographer, was the publisher of the *Leader.* John F. Rowe was editor and Alfred Ellmore, corresponding editor. In the first issue Rowe stated the purpose of his periodical:

It will be the constant aim of this journal to bring men and women in spiritual contact with Christ and His apostles. . . We shall aim to glorify the church of Jesus Christ, and not waste our time on the glorification of human missionary societies. . . We shall strive to build up in every congregation an intelligent and competent eldership, and, if possible, we shall by the grace of God, avoid all angry controversies with our brethren.[3]

In the next issue of the *Leader,* the editor laid down an eight-point program designed to be a guiding policy for the periodical. The *Leader* should be, (1) "thoroughly apostolic, yet abreast of the times." (2) It should not shun to declare the whole council of God. (3) While courteous to all men, the *Leader* should uncompromisingly present only God's standard of righteousness (4) It must avoid all untaught questions that gender strife. (5) It must do nothing through strife or vainglory. (6) Bible thoughts

[2]John F Rowe, "Overture for Reconciliation," *Christian Leader,* Vol I, No 8 (February 22, 1887), p 4
[3]John F Rowe, "The Christian Leader," *Christian Leader,* Vol. I, No 1 (October 7, 1886), p 4.

should be expressed in Bible language. (7) It should avoid all personal wranglings. (8) It should make an agressive battle for the truth.[4]

The immediate effect of establishing the new paper was a dividing of the forces of the old *Review*. Alfred Ellmore, who had been connected with the *Review* for many years, left it to join Rowe on the *Leader*. W. H. Krutsinger of Ellettsville, Indiana who had written Indiana items frequently for the *Review* transferred his editorial labor to the *Gospel Advocate* Afterwards, Krutsinger writes:

There is no more *American Christian Review*. The paper that Franklin founded and ran until his death is a thing of the past The best thing you can now do is to take and read the *Gospel Advocate*.[5]

The *Christian Messenger*, published at Bonham, Texas carried an article directing the old readers of the *American Christian Review* to subscribe to the *Leader*, a statement that solicited strong resentment from Treat. These petty differences, however, were indicative of things to come.

Meanwhile, the months of October and November, 1886 passed, and Edwin Alden felt that he must sell the paper, the deal with Childs and Hussey having failed. The issue of December 9, 1886 announced that business negotiations were under way for the paper to be purchased by a "prominent evangelist," who would act as owner, editor and publisher.[6] Two weeks later the *Review* announced that Daniel Sommer had purchased it. On the front page of this issue was a large picture of Elder Ben Franklin, indicating not only Sommer's admiration of the deceased gospel preacher, but the determination to return to the editorial policy of the great Hoosier preacher.

The fact of Deniel Sommer's purchasing the *Review* came as a blow to Rowe and his editorial corps on the *Leader* There is every reason to believe that Rowe still had considerable hopes of securing its ownership J. L. Richardson dangled the bait before Alden, offering through the *Leader* to buy the *Review* but

[4]John F Rowe, "The Kind of Paper Wanted," *Christian Leader*, Vol I, No 2 (October 14, 1886), p 4
[5]Daniel Sommer "Peculiarly Unfortunate," *Octographic Review*, Vol XXX, No 19 (May 26, 1887), p 1
[6]W B F Treat, "Important Notice," *American Christian Review*, Vol XXIX, No 50 (December 9, 1886), p 398

"not at a price double its value." It is not likely that anything would have pleased Rowe more than to purchase it at his own price, not at Alden's. When, therefore, Daniel Sommer entered the discussion, Alden went the second mile in making a financial arrangement whereby the "prominent evangelist" could make the purchase

David Lipscomb had watched the negotiations with some interest. When Alden first attempted to sell the *Review* to Childs and Hussey, Lipscomb wrote, "We presume this will not in any way seriously modify the *Review*. The work of the *Review* is needed especially in Ohio, and we would dislike to see anything occur that would cripple its influence in the least." Shortly after Sommer bought the paper, Lipscomb wrote:

Brother Daniel Sommer, a man of most excellent repute, as a true and faithful Christian and a teacher of the Bible, has bought the *Review* This removes the objectionable feature of the ownership, and we think the publishers of the *Review* and *Leader* ought to make an earnest effort to combine the two papers Their circulation must be within the same section and among brethren who ought to work together in harmony. We know, under these circumstances, there must be clashing interest and partisan spirit excited We know the subscriptions of the two combined will not be more than sufficient to sustain one paper so as to enable it to do effective service. We have only the kindliest feeling toward all persons concerned, and, while we think it not well for men not Christians to have the power to appoint and dismiss teachers for Christians, we wish to say that we have had dealings with Mr Edwin Alden as advertising agent for fifteen years past, and although we lost by his failure, nothing ever occurred to induce the belief that he was not an honest, fair-dealing man.[7]

The December 23, 1886 issue of the *American Christian Review* was the first to carry the name of Daniel Sommer as "proprietor and publisher." W. B. F. Treat was listed as editor; Dr. J. C. Holloway, George T. Smith, and J. W. Perkins were corresponding editors. The paper was now published at the northwest corner of Fifth and Vine Streets in Cincinnati.

Daniel Sommer's assumption of control of the *Review* was the signal for the beginning hostilities. John F. Rowe opened the cannonading with vociferous barrage in the January 18, 1887 issue of the *Christian Leader*. Rowe charges that Sommer is

---

[7]David Lipscomb, "A Friendly Suggestion," *Gospel Advocate,* Vol. XXIX. No 4 (January 26, 1887), p 54.

deceived and that an "outsider" still owns the *Review*. Sommer rejoins with the accusation that Rowe had deliberately plotted the overthrow of the *Review* and had trumpted up some false charges against Alden. Moreover—and this hurt Sommer worse —Rowe, says Sommer, stole the subscription list of the *Review* in order to start the *Leader*. Readers of the two papers for some time were let in on the flagellations Rowe and Sommer each gave the other. Meanwhile, readers of the *Christian Standard* and *Christian-Evangelist* found additional reason to believe that the opposers of the society and instrumental music lacked Christianity, and the *Leader-Review* warfare increased the popularity of their point of view considerably.

The history of the *Review* for the past decade was now brought out for an inspection. Who was the person Ben Franklin had in mind to be his successor as editor of the *Review?* There could be little question that Franklin, well-meaning though he was, had unconsciously encouraged a jealous spirit among his admirers. As a means of encouraging young men, Franklin held out to them the possibility that they might succeed him as the editor of his paper. Several young men, each one thinking of himself as fit to wear Franklin's mantle, found themselves jealous of each other, and that jealousy split the forces of those who opposed innovations in the North.

W. B. F. Treat declared that a few months before Franklin's death he spent two weeks with him, and they had discussed his successor. According to Treat, Franklin had mentioned James A. Meng, L. F. Bittle, Daniel Sommer, Joel A Headington, but John F. Rowe was definitely placed "at the foot of the list." Treat testifies that Franklin stated his confidence in Rowe was completely gone Franklin had charged that Rowe was "the same color as the bush he was in." In Ohio, where the Society was strong, Rowe favored the Society, but in Pennsylvania where it was opposed, Rowe had opposed it [8] There can be little doubt that L. F. Bittle was Franklin's first choice except for the fact that Bittle's health would probably have prevented his attending to the rigors of the editorship.

It will be recalled that Franklin's death occured unexpectedly. It was therefore left to George W. Rice, the publisher of the

[8] W. B. F. Treat, "The Conspiracy," *American Christian Review*, Vol XXX, No 8 (February 24, 1887), p 60

Review, to name the successor. The decision was by no means simple. Joel A. Headington was opposed to Rowe and threatened to quit the paper if Rowe were named as editor. Rowe, on the other hand, would do the same if Headington were chosen. Rice, after taking all things into consideration, decided in favor of Rowe. At the time of making his choice, he wrote:

I know that his [Ben Franklin] mind settled on Brother John F. Rowe as his successor. Believing that to be his wish and will, I have placed Brother Rowe in that position. This I have done without any hostility to anyone else. Brother Rowe has been connected with the *Review* as contributor and assistant editor longer than anyone else, and has had more of Brother Franklin's correspondence than any other brother that has ever contributed to the columns of the paper. . . .[9]

Daniel Sommer, on the other hand, seemed to question very little in his own mind that he himself was Ben Franklin's choice of a successor. In the spring of 1878, six months before Franklin's death, the editor received a letter from Sommer. The letter was never published, so one can only judge what was in it by the answer it received. In a letter to Sommer, dated May 30, 1878, Franklin replied that Sommer's letter to him had caused him to think much of the qualifications of a successor. The man, Franklin confessed, that he liked most was Bittle, but he feared Bittle's health would not permit him to edit a paper. Therefore, Franklin wrote that the only thing he could do was to open the way for some man in the brotherhood to make himself a record, "to write himself into the confidence of the brethren." Franklin stated to Sommer that he had recently thought of Sommer as a likely successor for the following reasons: (1) Sommer was a young man —then only twenty-eight   (2) He had good bodily health.   (3) He had industry, endurance, perseverance and determination.   (4) He had sufficient education.   (5) He had had severe experiences for a young man.   (6) "I believe you intend to keep the faith," wrote Franklin.

The *Review* editor then proposed that Sommer begin writing himself into the confidence of the brethren. Franklin advised Sommer to write under some name, like LUTHER, and advised Sommer to write about some "live issues."[10] Acting upon this

[9] G W. Rice, "Brother Franklin's Successor," *American Christian Review*, Vol. XXI, No 46 (November 12, 1878), p 364
[10] Daniel Sommer, "History," *American Christian Review*, Vol XXX, No 9 (March 3, 1887), p 65

advice, Sommer prepared a series of articles on "Educating Preachers," signing them "Evangelist." The articles began to appear in October, 1878, the same month Franklin died. Sommer, therefore, lacked the time to "write himself into the confidence of the brethren" that he might be Franklin's successor Nevertheless, enough had been said to him by Franklin to lead him to believe that he was the veteran editor's real choice of one to succeed him

When, therefore, Rice announced John F. Rowe to be the new editor of the paper in the fall of 1878, Sommer disagreed. He immediately wrote to Rice announcing his intention to stay with the *Review*, but no one can fail to see his disagreement of the choice. Sommer's letter to Rice said in part:

I am not an aspirant, and I hold myself above narrow and ungenerous thoughts. From the time of Brother Franklin's death my constant prayer was *that* one might be chosen editor who was best fitted for the position. *I acquiesce in what you have done as the best for the present,* and in this time of its need I intend to stand by the *Review* with whatsoever power I may have. No petty considerations shall turn me from it. I am thinking about the interests of our brotherhood, and not about individual and personal aggrandizement. While your columns are open to me I intend to write for the *Review*, pay or no pay."

It would be a "dull scholar" indeed who could not see that Sommer's concern over an editor for the *Review* did not involve some personal interest of his own in the position

For two years events proceeded with Sommer continuing his sporadic writing for the paper. Rowe, sensing in Daniel Sommer a competitor to his editorial position, found it hard to keep his ruffled emotions quiet. Rowe hardly greeted Sommer's attempt to "write himself into the confidence of the brethren" cheerfully. When, in the spring of 1880, Sommer negotiated arrangements to move from Kelton, Pennsylvania, to Reynoldsburg, Ohio, he arrived at the latter city on May 1st, only to plunge into conflict with Rowe. Two or three days later Mrs M R. Lemert approached him with a letter she had received from Rowe. Mrs. Lemert was a very forward woman, having gained some degree of prominence in her discussions in the *Review* with leading preachers The letter from Rowe to Mrs. Lemert was not made public. Nevertheless, Sommer assured his readers that it came as a terrible

---

"Daniel Sommer, "History," *American Christian Review*, Vol. XXX, No 9 (March 3, 1887), p. 65.

shock to him.   One can but surmise that it must have been a personal thrust.

Sommer immediately discontinued writing for the *Review*. Three years later he and L F. Bittle began publication of the *Octograph*, perhaps in an attempt to "write himself into the confidence of the brotherhood."   In purchasing the *Review*, Sommer states his reasons as being:

One of our purposes was to save the enterprise of Benjamin Franklin's grand life from ruin, another was to occupy a position in which we could do the greatest possible good, and in order to do this our purpose was to lift the *Review* out from its entanglements.[12]

The vituperations between Rowe and Sommer continued for several months, but eventually each grew weary of the struggle and swore off putting such personal thrusts before the public. The armistice undoubtedly helped both periodicals.   Actually the whole warfare did little except to gratify the personal pride of each.

With the passing of time the feelings mellowed, and notable changes came in both papers.   In the spring of 1887 both George W. Rice and J. L. Richardson abandoned the *Leader*.   "Time has mellowed the whole matter," Rice wrote, "and then added that he could now see that Alden's sale was not a "sham," and so offered his apology to Mr. Alden.   Richardson confessed he was in error in advising Rowe to publish another paper, and made public his confession through the *Review*. Alfred Ellmore, one of the popular writers and preachers of the time, went with the *Leader*. There was nothing personal in his action.   He had made the promise to Rowe and Rice when the trouble first occurred, and he went with the *Leader* to keep his word.   Ellmore wrote:

The all-important question with me is, "what is my duty?"   I am anxious that the right prevail.   I seek not caste, fame or wealth, but duty.   An humble seat just inside the door is all I ask.   Life is too brief and too precious to be thrown away.   But I would rather fail sustaining the right than triumph in wrong   I would rather die with the few, being right, than to live and prosper with the many in the wrong.[13]

However, Ellmore's stay with the *Leader* was not calculated to be

[12]Daniel Sommer, "The *Review's* Farewell," *American Christian Review*, Vol XXX, No 11 (March 17, 1887), p 81
[13]Alfred Ellmore, "Wheat and Chaff," *Christian Leader*, Vol I, No 11 (March 15, 1887), p 4

of long duration. In the fall of 1893 the *Leader* changed its form, doubtlessly copying the *Christian-Evangelist*. About the same time Alfred Ellmore is noticeably dropped from among the contributors. The reason, he explains later, is that John F. Rowe had gone over to the "digressive element," alluding, of course, to Rowe's willingness to worship with a "small organ," but not, "O ye gods," said Rowe, a large one.

Meanwhile, Sommer's editorial work began in earnest. He made definite changes that he thought would contribute to the success of the paper, the first major change being the dropping of all secular advertising. It was the custom generally to advertise frequently in the papers everything from Royal Baking Powder to Hood's Sarsparilla. Most papers could not have eked out an existence through the lean years without this advertising. Sommer thought the practice so deplorable that he dropped it immediately, and began frequent criticisms of other papers who did advertise. The *Gospel Advocate* had by advertising sustained itself and was at the time in no financial position to drop them. Sommer made a lengthy attack on the *Advocate* for its practice, and David Lipscomb watched, but like F. G. Allen, had "kept his finger in his mouth." He considered Sommer "a good man and in many respects a most excellent teacher," yet Lipscomb felt Sommer "looks at things from a narrow and selfish standpoint."

On the whole the *Advocate's* relation to Daniel Sommer during the first part of Sommer's editorial labors was very cordial. James A. Harding, then riding the crest of popularity with his work in the *Advocate*, often found the enigmatic Sommer hard to understand. In an editorial printed in the *Review*, February 3, 1887, Sommer wrote on "Which Is the More Excellent Way?" Sommer attacked those preachers who preached where the organ was used, but in doing so insisted that it be silent. For this Harding found strenuous objections, although David Lipscomb advocated the same. If a congregation, reasoned Lipscomb, will not keep the organ silent out of respect for God, why should it do so out of respect for *me?* But on this point a considerable number of preachers who were all united in their disagreement of the use of the organ found room for contention. W. B. F. Treat, while preaching for the church at Martinsville, Indiana, which used the instrument, was content to work along with the church in he

hope of leading them back. But Harding looked with dismay on
the practice, and wrote:

. . He [Daniel Sommer] is the present owner and publisher
of the *American Christian Review,* and is also one of the chief
writers for that paper. He has been regarded as one of the most
earnest, faithful and powerful of the younger class of writers and
speakers among the disciples (he is, I presume, yet under forty),
and also as one of the most apostolic in his teachings. He was a
great favorite with Brother Benjamin Franklin, the founder of the
Review For a number of years Brother Sommer has edited and
published a small periodical called the *Octograph,* but of late he
has obtained possession of the *Review,* a paper that has always
taken a leading rank among us of those that oppose the missionary
societies, fairs, festivals, organs, etc.

But within the last few months there has been a change all
around in the management of the paper, and it appears that this
is to be followed by a very decided change in its tone. . . . It has
a new owner, a new editor-in-chief, and a new staff of editorial
contributors, and (if I am not mistaken) it is beginning to show
a very different spirit from that manifested by its bold, aggressive
and devoted founder A truer, nobler, grander man than Benjamin Franklin I think I never met. I read his writings for nearly
a quarter of a century; that is, from the time I was about ten years
of age till he died He was often in my father's house (they were
intimate friends), and I knew him well. He often spent months
in our region conducting protracted meetings, and, when he did,
it afforded me great pleasure to hear him preach, and to go with
him from house to house, for I realized that there was in our
midst indeed "a prince and a great man," a notable leader of the
hosts of God. No other man was holding back so mightily the
tide of innovation that was sweeping in upon us; no other was
so vigorous in the endeavor to eradicate the seeds of division and
the causes of stumbling

Since his death I have watched the course of the *Review* with
great interest, and I have seen much in it that was good, very
good, and much that was evidently written in bad spirit and poor
taste.

When Brother W. B. F. Treat became editor of it, I was glad,
for I said, "Whatever may be the merits of the Rowe-Rice-Alden
embroglio, a strong, true man is at the helm." But, much to my
disappointment and sorrow, it was but a little while till I learned
that Brother Treat was even then preaching regularly as the hired
minister of a church that uses an organ with every song they sing,
notwithstanding his supposed opposition to the pastor and the
organ

When Brother Sommer appeared as the owner and publisher of
the paper, my hopes revived, for I had known of him, through

some of the Detroit brethren, as a sturdy, faithful, resolute, apostolic man; but when this article which we are about to review appeared, my confidence in the *Review's* remaining true to the Divine teaching was sadly shaken. However, such has been my confidence in Brother Treat and my hope for Brother Sommer that, I think, there is not a man who would be happier than I were my fears to prove groundless. . . .[14]

Nothing very serious, however, developed from Harding's objections. For some reason the truculent Harding found Sommer slightly objectionable it seems, and the two men hurled their criticisms back and forth for years.

The last copy of the *American Christian Review* came before the public March 17, 1887. Sommer announces that the *Review* will henceforth be united with the semimonthly *Octograph*, and its new name would be *Octographic Review*. The name coined by L. F. Bittle was intended to be suggestive of the fact that the *Review* was to be thoroughly apostolic. The term "American" to Sommer was too local, and the term "Christian" was too sacred to be used in connection with a human enterprise. However, the term "Octograph" proved to be too burdensome, and in 1914 the name was changed to *Apostolic Review,* a name the paper held until Daniel Sommer's death.

The patrons of the *Review* found it difficult to familiarize themselves with the new name. It was odd, clumsy, and conveyed no real meaning to the average reader. The name *American Christian Review,* on the other hand, was alive with tradition, and had come to symbolize everything bold, vigorous and truthful in the restoration. *The Christian Standard* tersely commented on the new title. "It is to be hoped that none will claim that this name is the outcome of seeking Bible names for Bible things."[15]

Meanwhile, Sommer had bright visions for the future welfare of his paper. Cincinnati was hardly the place to publish the *Review,* and in the spring of 1887, Sommer thought of Indianapolis as the logical place. He wrote:

At this juncture we venture to say that Cincinnati is not the most central place. For years we have thought of Indianapolis as the city above all others from which the publication that would

---

[14]James A. Harding, "The More Excellent Way—A Reply to Brother Sommer," *Gospel Advocate,* Vol XXIX, No 11 (March 16, 1887), p 173
[15]H. McDiarmid, "Editorial Items," *Christian Standard,* Vol. XXII. No. 17 (April 23, 1887), p. 133.

work a revolution should be issued.   On this subject we have not changed our mind   Indiana was the home of the *Review's* founder, and doubtless is the state in which his influence was largely felt   Indianapolis is the city in which about fifteen lines of railroad center   Besides, it is perhaps more nearly than any other city in the center of our great brotherhood.   In due time the *Review* expects to recover from her wounds and recuperate wasted forces and move westward.   But for the present it is here in a beautiful town in a beautiful country which probably has as little iniquity to the square inch. as good health, as good and upright citizens as any other place that can be found eastward of westward, northward or southward.

Four months later Sommer wrote again after visiting in Indiana:

Something over four weeks ago we left home for this state (Indiana). and we must confess that the more we see of it the better we like it   The utter absence of aristocracy is delightful to a plain man   People seem to estimate each other at the point of character and regardless of wealth or grammar.   They do not affect to despise either, but character seems to be the highest criterion   Brethren of Indiana, we still think favorably of Indianapolis as the future home of the *Review*   It is a central place with excellent facilities   The Lord willing we shall get there. and we hope all the people will say, "amen."

According to a dream, therefore, that Sommer had entertained for some years, he moved the *Review* to Indianapolis in 1894.

Thus the *American Christian Review* had passed through an intensely interesting, if stormy, history.   The *Review* of Ben Franklin's day died when Franklin died in 1878.   The *Review* of John F. Rowe lived from 1878 to 1886.   The newborn *Octographic Review* with its successor, *Apostolic Review*, ran from 1887.

Chapter XVI

SONS OF THUNDER

In the course of time, if one remains loyal to principles of truth, he is likely to see victory shine out from the darkness of despair. At the close of the Civil War, David Lipscomb and E. G. Sewell went patiently to work in a war-trodden South to build apostolic Christianity. Their paper, the *Gospel Advocate,* was an unostentatious periodical hardly promising of any great influence. The few disciples were scattered, the mails were just opening, and srong, influential preachers almost nonexistent in their latitude. They remained true to their convictions. Occasionally they were laughed at, but in the process of time, the preaching which they had done in schoolhouses and in brush arbors counted where they could see it. The teaching of the *Advocate* took root. Congregations grew stronger, and younger men began dedicating their lives to preaching the gospel. By 1890 Lipscomb and Sewell were beginning to catch a glimpse of the sunset, but around them had arisen a young corps of preachers whose adventures portray the romance of the era.

James A. Harding, F. D. Srygley, F. B. Srygley, E. A. Elam, J. D. Tant, M. C. Kurfees, T. B. Larimore and T. R. Burnett were now entering their prime. The stories of each of these men, in addition to others, would make, if completely told, thrilling reading. Their sacrifices would cheer the hearts of more modern gospel preachers, and furnish inspiration for the church at large. The stories of two—Fletcher Douglas Srygley and James A. Harding —are told here for the reason that they influenced in a major way the movement that is being studied. In some respects both were similar Each was an intrepid soul. The logic of James A. Harding, and the fierceness with which he went at an opponent, added nothing to the felicity of his enemies. While Srygley used less of the real arts of a logician, he was, however, of a fiery temperament that shrank in fear of nothing He had a masterful and humorous method of meeting every attack. To Harding and Srygley for at least a decade the restoration in the South can give credit for some of its coloring.

F. D. SRYGLEY

T. R. Burnett once declared that in Texas, F. D. Srygley was called "the Mark Twain of the Reformation." If so, it is little question but that he deserved the sobriquet. After becoming front-page editor of the *Gospel Advocate* in November, 1889, he gave to the paper a punch and wit that undoubtedly widely increased its influence. The *Advocate* during these years had a well-balanced editorial force. David Lipscomb's articles were deep and thought-provoking. E. G. Sewell's thoughts elegantly flowed through his words. J. C. McQuiddy kept abreast of the happenings of the brotherhood, and both T. R. Burnett and F. D. Srygley gave the paper humor enough to brighten up every crisis. Burnett was no doubt right in viewing the *Gospel Advocate* of those years in the following light:

Srygley's brilliant periods, Sewell's smoothly flowing leaders, McQuiddy's newsy items, old David's heavy artillery, this scribe's pointed paragraphs—here is a bill of fare that will edify a man who loves good eating, and will give a digressive saint the dyspepsia.[1]

For a time there was some talk going via grapevine that F. D. Srygley was being specially groomed to take Lipscomb's place as editor of the *Gospel Advocate* The rumor seemed altogether ill-founded as Srygley well recognized, but even so, the application of a little humor to the case seemed appropriate:

A private letter from Texas, as well as hints from other quarters, would indicate that a few brethren are troubled to decide whether I am a proper person "to wear David Lipscomb's mantle after he dies" Seeing I have been in feeble health for several years, and that eminent physicians long ago decided I was beyond the aid of medical science and doomed to a premature grave, while D. L. is in vigorous health with every prospect of living to a green old age, I feel but little interest in the question. I think I can "rustle" around and keep a mantle of my own as long as I live, and the way D. L. is tearing around among rationalists just now, I am inclined to think his mantle will be pretty well ripped up by the time he is done with it.[2]

Rock Creek, Alabama, where Srygley was born, was a country post office "twelve miles from the nearest point on any railroad" in the rough, mountain country of Colbert County. It was six

---

[1] T R Burnett, "Burnett's Budget," *Gospel Advocate*, Vol XXXVI, No 23 (June 7, 1894), p 9

[2] F D. Srygley. "From the Papers," *Gospel Advocate*, Vol XXXII, No 12 (March 19, 1890), p. 177.

F D SRYGLEY

miles to the nearest country village It was here "in the hill country of north Alabama" that F. D. Srygley was born on December 22, 1856. His parents were James H. and Sarah Jane Srygley—poor, hard-working, devoted country people

Sarah Jane Coats Srygley, his mother, was thoroughly devoted in her religious life and left the imprint of her convictions upon her sons. She was born into a Presbyterian family on November 7, 1831, and her father, Benjamin Coats, was a Cumberland Presbyterian preacher. She was baptized by J. M. Pickens, one of North Alabama's prominent preachers, soon after the close of the war. Immediately after she was immersed in August, 1866, she and her husband established a congregation at Rock Creek. Although for years the number of disciples was only about eight or ten, they were faithful in their religious duties.

Srygley's father, James H., a poor laborer, settled in the mountains of North Alabama, west of Huntsville soon after the Indians were removed. At the time he settled in North Alabama, the richer plantation owners were beginning to purchase the rich land along the Tennessee River, so from one of them Srygley's father secured a job splitting rails. His pay was fifty cents a hundred plus his board.

It was twelve miles from his home to the place where he worked. He would walk the distance through the trails in the woods about sunup on Monday mornings. From Monday morning until Saturday night he could split fifteen hundred rails, and on Saturday night he would walk the twelve miles back home again. He spent Sundays chopping wood for his wife and looking after her provisions so she could be taken care of until he arrived home again the next Saturday. It was a hard life, scarcely promising of a future.

The Srygleys had five boys—F. G , F. W., F. D., F. B., and F. L. F. D. and F. B. were the only two that were preachers. One may naturally wonder why all the boys were named with their names beginning with an "F." There is hardly a way to find out. To the inquisitive F. D. Srygley wrote in the summer of 1880, "Those who are curious to know why all of our names commence with an F may write to our dear mother who lives at Rock Creek, Alabama, inclosing stamp to pay return postage." If anyone wrote, the answer was never published.

The little Rock Creek congregation shared in common with the other churches the hardships of life in the South after the close of the war. People had no money and could only give to the Lord's work what little they could raise on their farms. As late as 1876 members of the church in Lauderdale, Alabama, lacking money, were contributing wheat, corn, flour, meal, cloth, etc , to the church. At a time when the church needed ready cash, it merely sold some of its stored-up produce About this time when "Weeping Joe" Harding was trying to build a meetinghouse at South Tunnell in Sumner County, he took gifts of chickens, hauled them to Nashville and sold them to raise the money to build the house. People had no money, and the small band at Rock Creek shared alike in this.

T. B. Larimore was called from Tennessee to Rock Creek to preach for the small congregation. It was about 1868 or 1869. It was Larimore's first time to meet F. D. Srygley, then a poor country boy in his early "teens." Thirty years later, Larimore vividly recalled the scene:

More than thirty years ago, I went from Nashville, Tennessee— my native state—to Alabama, to Rock Creek, to the new historic Rock Creek meetinghouse My mission was to preach the word. The church there then numbered seven souls. As, the first time, I approached the door of that old log cabin "meetinghouse"—a penniless stranger in a strange land—I saw, standing about thirty feet away, to the right and in front of me, twenty feet from the path that I was traveling and thirty feet from the door I was approaching, a bright, little, black-eyed bareheaded, barefooted boy; a picure of health, happiness, and peace, and contentment; perfectly beautiful—to me—then as, on memory's page, r.ow. His cheeks were rosy; his eyes were black. Faultless in form and feature, he stood, silent, motionless and erect.

He was standing there to see the "preacher" as he passed, probably not caring to ever be nearer him than then Instinctively I turned toward him, went to him, took his little right hand into mine, put my left arm around him, and led him into the house. From that day to the day when, in the delirium of death, he, suddenly recognizing me, enthusiastically grasped me by both hands and thrilled my soul with an expression I can never forget, he was my devoted friend.[1]

No man ever had a closer friend than Larimore did in F. D. Srygley. It was exactly so—from that moment that Srygley first saw Larimore until the day when Srygley died, he was a firm admirer of T. B. Larimore. Srygley would often say in later years, "I'll criticize him [Larimore] when he needs it, if I want to; but no other man shall do it." Throughout their lives, they corresponded frequently, and when Larimore would come in the vicinity where Srygley lived, they were constantly together.

The first book Srygley wrote was entitled, "Larimore and His Boys." It recounted, besides the life of Larimore, the lives of some of the boys who studied under Larimore at Mars Hill College near Florence, Alabama. But there was one book that Srygley wanted to write to make the crowning work of his life. It would

---

[1]T. B Larimore, "F. D Srygley," *Gospel Advocate,* Vol. XLII, No 35 (August 30, 1900), p. 54.

be a complete compilation of the life and letters of Larimore.
Srygley was younger by thirteen years than his friend, and he
entertained some hope of living beyond the time of his former
teacher His ambition was to wait until after Larimore died, and
then compile the story of his life, believing he could die in peace
if he could but accomplish his

But as the century was nearing its close, Srygley became pain-
fully aware that his end was drawing nigh. Larimore had been
invited to hold a lengthy meeting at Nashville, the meeting beginning in December, 1899, and lasting for over two months Srygley
felt that he had better strike then. Reluctantly did Larimore agree
to the undertaking Miss Emma Page, a teacher of the Fanning
Orphan School, and later Larimore's second wife, was employed
to take down Larimore's sermons Srygley worked against time
to gather letters and information, but early in the summer or late
in the spring the material was turned over to the printer.

Srygley was already sick when the first copy of the book came
from the press. He was in bed when he examined it. Naturally
he found many mistakes; some errors to be corrected, but on the
whole he was well pleased. At the time, Larimore was near Nashville in a meeting, and came to pay a visit on his dying friend.
Srygley, from his bed, asked Larimore to get him the book After
pointing out an error or two in it that he wanted corrected, he said
to Larimore: "I would love to live to read it and all that may be
said about it in the press, revise it and perfect it; then I suppose
my work would be about done. I now think of nothing else that
I want to do." Later he added, "I may be mistaken, of course,
but I honestly believe, the Bible excepted, it is the best book I have
ever seen " He loved the book because he loved its subject.

In the month of August, before becoming eighteen years of age,
F. D. Srygley was baptized by T. B Larimore. For a long time
Srygley had been wanting to be immersed, but had been taught
that children need not hurry, so had waited until after he was
seventeen. Larimore's school near Florence had been opened only
three years before, so Srygley made plans to become one of its
students. His plan was to go to school in the winter and preach
in the summer.

The summer of 1876 Srygley left home "with a pair of saddle-
bags on my shoulder" to join John Taylor in a preaching tour
through northern Alabama. John Taylor was an old preacher,

then over seventy, and Srygley was only nineteen Srygley loved this old preacher for the sacrifices he had made Nearly twenty-five years later Srygley took what profit he had made from "Larimore and His Boys" and remembered Taylor A part of the profit from the sale of the book went in paying expenses for a little girl to attend the Fanning Orphan School. About two hundred and fifty dollars was spent in paying salaries for preachers who were in destitute fields. Eight dollars was spent to buy a gravestone for John Taylor. Srygley had known poverty. His heart was with the poor, and with any preacher, who would sacrifice to preach to the poor.

But, as he and Taylor went out in the summer of 1876 to preach, they planned for hardships Taylor had a good horse; Srygley had none. It was decided that both of them should ride together when the roads were bad, and take turns riding when the road was good. However, a good brother offered Srygley a colt "whereon yet never man sat," but he had to walk five miles to get it. During this summer's preaching, they preached often in private houses, under brush arbors, and in school houses

That winter, Srygley was back in school, but the next summer was out preaching again. This time he and Henry F. Williams of Maury County, Tennessee went forth together. Of the occasion, Larimore wrote·

Our two worthy young brethren, Henry F. Williams, of Maury County, Tennessee and Fletcher D. Srygley of Colbert County, Alabama left Mars Hill a few days ago, to begin their summer campaigns. They are noble young soldiers. They are entirely worthy of all the confidence that brethren and friends may repose in them. They love the ADVOCATE and will wield a strong influence in its favor.[4]

Young preachers are not likely to spend *all* their time in preaching. Most will find sometime for the more amorous affairs of life, and Srygley was no exception to the rule He "wooed and won" Miss Ella Parkhill of Mars Hill, Alabama, and on December 15; 1878 found himself with a sixteen-year-old bride. Of course, Larimore performed the ceremony.

Two little girls—Mamie and Jeffie—were soon born, but Mamie, the first, died in infancy The child's funeral was held and the baby was tearfully borne to the cemetery near Rock Creek After

[4]T B Larimore, "Correspondence," *Gospel Advocate*, Vol XIX, No 27 (July 5, 1877), p 423

the funeral, Ella wept bitterly for a tiny curl she had forgotten to clip from the child's head. Friends tried to console her, but she refused their tenderness. Late one night, Srygley went out to the cemetery, reopened the grave, clipped a curl, and took it back to his sorrowing wife. But in a matter of a few months, she followed her little girl to the grave.

It was December, 1880, being only a few months out of school, that F. D. Srygley moved to Paris, Texas. His stay in Texas was short-lived. Having made the acquaintance of John T. Poe, then living at Longview, Srygley one day walked with Poe out into the woods. The two sat down and Srygley spoke thoughtfully saying, "Brother Poe, I am going into the larger cities; I feel I have a work to do I cannot accomplish in Texas." Something discouraged him, and he turned his footsteps back toward Tennessee.

There is little question but that Srygley felt he could do considerable good through his writing. He had natural writing ability, worked hard at it, and the ability to treat a subject with that kind of concern it demanded. However, before that time came when he and David Lipscomb found mutual acquiescence on major issues, Srygley's editorial career was somewhat stormy.

Very early in this career did Srygley and Lipscomb find themselves in disagreement. Srygley was a mere youth, only twenty-two years old, whereas Lipscomb was nearing fifty when they had their first disagreement. It is possible, if not probable, that Srygley shared a common sentiment, felt in those earlier days that David Lipscomb was a "sour old man," and this seemed to have lead to a natural aversion to agreeing with Lipscomb. At any rate, Lipscomb wrote in 1879, advising the participation in sports. He commented that man needed more rest and relaxation, that he himself had had poor health the past several years, a thing he attributed to his lack of sufficient diversion. Srygley took exception. It was better for a Christian to spend an afternoon in visiting the sick than in some sporting event. Srygley succeeded in calling on himself a mild castigation.

Two years later, however, Lipscomb and Srygley sparred off on more serious matters—this time the subject of the Missionary Society. It was customary for T. B. Larimore to stear clear of controversial subjects within the brotherhood which left room for some of his younger admirers to doubt the importance of op-position to them. Later, some of Larimore's "boys" caused con-siderable anxiety in the brotherhood in the South over these issues that Larimore refused to oppose. It might have been a different story had Larimore indoctrinated these youths earlier against them. This is one of the few just criticisms to be made of Larimore's work.

Apparently lacking in any trepidation whatever, young Srygley marched against the senior editor of the *Gospel Advocate* late in 1881 on the subject of the Society. Srygley made no contribution in the way of new arguments for the Missionary Society. The fact that a host of noble pioneers disagreed with Lipscomb weighed heavily with Srygley. While not a forceful advocate of the Society, it was difficult for Srygley to see that it could not be excused on the ground of expediency. Lipscomb was kind but positive in his disagreement. He confessed his belief that Srygley was un-duly prejudiced and therefore, had not come fully to understand the real issue involved. Srygley took personal offense, thinking Lipscomb had been too hard on him, and withdrew his support from the *Advocate*.

F. G Allen had within recent years begun publishing the *Old Path Guide* from Louisville, Kentucky and toward this paper Srygley now turned. Allen, an extremely forceful writer, com-manded the respect of the more conservative bulk of the brother-hood, who occupied the "middle ground," viz, they favored the missionary society but opposed the use of instrumental music. The College of The Bible at Lexington was an educational center of this type of thinking, and a host of preachers flowed from its halls to melt here and there into the brotherhood activities. The passing of a decade made it increasingly certain that this middle-ground would pass out of existence. Some who saw it viewed the inevitable with bitterness. Such did Moses E. Lard. The majority, however, jumped from their sinking isle across the roaring currents of the controversies to the *Christian Standard*. They reluctantly accepted the use of the instrument. but their number gave a decidedly conservative coloring to the *Christian Standard* which it has in its own way retained through the years. J. W. McGarvey, who had furnished the music to inspire the vanguard of that hapless army of preachers, was oddly enough doomed to be its rearguard, being the last of that school of thought to pass. In the last five years of F. G. Allen's life he showed signs of leaning more and more to David Lipscomb's point of view. His life was cut down in 1886, but Lipscomb never doubted that had Allen lived longer, he would have stood solidly behind the *Advocate*.

When, therefore, Srygley left the *Advocate*, he became an ardent supporter of the *Old Path Guide,* and backed its editorial policy. Suffering severely from Bright's disease in 1884, he retired from the editorial staff of the *Old Path Guide.* For the next five years Srygley sat on the side-lines watching as best he could the current of events glide past On December 26, 1888 he married again— this time Miss Jennie Scobey, daughter of James E Scobey of Hopkinsville, Kentucky. His health was still poor, and Miss Jennie knew it. Later, F. B. Srygley declared that she had added ten years to his brother's life.

Upon the death of F. G. Allen, Russell Errett, owner of the *Christian Standard* took over the *Old Path Guide.* Srygley saw its editorial policy change, and watched the paper as it apologized for the use of the instrument of music in worship, and Srygley's ardor for the *Guide* cooled. The old wounded feeling against David Lipscomb healed some with the passing of time, and, although Srygley could not yet see entirely the way Lipscomb did, he decided that Lipscomb's "extremes" were on the side of safety. Having prepared his manuscript for "Larimore And His Boys," he and his wife made a trip to Nashville late in 1889 to see about getting it published. He met Lipscomb again. We are left to surmise the conversation they must have had. Judging from the fact that with the November issue that year, Srygley began his editorial work as "Front Page Editor" of the *Advocate,* old feelings were forgotten, and a basis of understanding reached.

No sooner had Srygley begun writing for the *Advocate,* than many waved the hand of despair. Was not Srygley known to favor the Society? Had he not been on the editorial staff of the *Guide,* a "progressive" paper? What then was wrong with David Lipscomb?

It is doubtful if many men have fully grasped the greatness of David Lipscomb, but in the attempt to do so one must not over- look the fact that it was his constant aim to be firm for the truth, oppose the wrong, and yet forbear with human weaknesses. Stating the principle on which he had worked all of his life, Lipscomb once wrote:

We have noticed those most extreme on one side are liable to run to the other extreme. Let your moderation be known to all men. Be firm for truth, steadfast in the maintainence of right, yet forbearing to the weaknesses of our fellowmen, knowing we also are liable to be drawn aside, and as we judge others, God will judge us. We have often borne with men that were wrong, tried to get them right, often failed, but have never regretted the forbearance Be true to the truth, oppose the error, but forbear with humanity.[5]

On this principle David Lipscomb acted. But he learned that it is difficult for an individual to love truth, stand by principle, and yet not bear personal animosity. He who tries it may often find that his own brethren will most doubt his altruism

Lipscomb felt that Srygley was still wrong, but that he was coming in the right direction; therefore, as a Christian he must forbear. Srygley had not reached that point of view that Lipscomb had, but he was going that direction To forbear in such case might incur the wrath of some brethren, but it would win the individual Srygley, aware of the criticism Lipscomb was getting, wrote on the serious subject in a vein of levity.

Speaking of boycotting, it might be well to say I am boycotted by extreme partisans on both sides of the progressive ditch and not on very good terms with myself just now I have been giving attention for some weeks to certain extreme parties in Alabama, and Missouri, and now I find myself besieged and completely cut off from my base of supplies by extremists on the other side of the question in Arkansas and Texas. The *Firm Foundation* puts it this way· "If the *Advocate's* policy is to shelter, defend and praise every "progressive" that will work for it, we think it may safely calculate on getting "thirty thousand subscribers" soon But if the paper is to be a faithful exponent of the views of Lipscomb, Srygley, Aten, *et al*, it will have to cut a broad swath— "weed a wide row"—so wide that we need not expect it to uproot every plant not planted by our heavenly Father. Those new men will slight their work when they come to some of the human plants, and I) I may look out for criticism frequently " This is bad news from Texas, with several townships yet to hear from, and the latest news from Arkansas, as reported in the *Christian Preacher*, adds despair to defeat The *Preacher* puts it thus

"The *Gospel Advocate* has recently added to its editorial

---

[5]David Lipscomb, "Thirty Years' Work," *Gospel Advocate*, Vol XXXVIII No 2 (January 9, 1896), p 20,

force, F. D. Srygley and A. P. Aten—the former a racy writer;
and the latter a very elegant one. Both have been on the editorial staff of the *Guide,* and are known to be progressive.
How they can consistently work with the *Advocate* we do not
understand We sometimes fear the "Old reliable" may be
made to capitulate by a modern Trojan horse scheme."
Speaking of horses, I wish I had a Trojan horse, or any other
kind of a horse, that I might ride him out of this mess. If I
only had a "Texas plug," a "Mexican broncho," or even a hobby-
horse, I might yet be saved. As to how I work with the *Advocate,*
I understood it on Paul's theory, "If meat make my brother to
offend, I will eat no flesh while the world standeth," and considering that I have to tussel with all intolerant extremists on
all sides of all questions, I find it pretty hard work on decidedly
light diet [6]

Srygley's interest in brotherhood periodicals was not limited to
his writing, for he owned a half-interest in the *Old Path Guide.*
When the Courier Publishing Company was organized in Dallas
to publish the *Christian Courier,* Srygley purchased two hundred
and fifty dollars worth of stock in that paper. In view of the
fact that the *Christian Courier* was intended to be the *Christian
Standard* of the west, Srygley was placed in an inconsistent light
as owning stock in a company while editing for another paper
directly opposed to it.

The Srygley family migrated from Alabama to Coal Hill,
Arkansas about this time. F. D. Srygley moved here in October,
1885. Two years later, his mother followed. Soon a colony of
three hundred or more had located here, most of them being
Srygley's relatives from Alabama. A few disciples met and built
a respectable meeting house. Srygley lived here about four years,
until he moved to Nashville to work on the *Gospel Advocate.*
While at Coal Hill, he worked as a real estate agent, preaching
some on the side as he was able.

Early in the year, 1900, Srygley went back to Coal Hill for a
visit. His mother had died the previous August. He tried to
preach at Marianna, Arkansas but the doctor sent him home,
knowing he was in a dying condition. From May until August,
1900, Srygley spent most of the time in bed, waiting for the end.
He refused to allow any public announcement to be made of his

---

[6]F. D Srygley, "From the Papers," *Gospel Advocate,* Vol. XXXII, No
12 (March 19, 1890) p 177

condition. Consequently, the announcement of his death came as a surprise to many readers of the *Gospel Advocate.*

J. C. McQuiddy broke the news through the *Advocate* with the following announcement:

On the morning of August 2 our dear brother, associate, and friend, F. D. Srygley, breathed his last. He was sick for about two months; but as it was his request and desire, no mention was made of his sickness. His affliction was heart disease, which produced dropsy.

We feel very deeply the loss, and know that this announcement will bring sadness to many hearts. He has been one of the editors of the Gospel Advocate since November, 1889. During all these years he has been a vigorous, clear, and forceful writer. He loved his work, wrote with great ease and rapidity, and has often said to me that he expected to spend his life in writing books and in the defense of the gospel of Christ. He was true to this purpose, for he wrote to the very last, and before the paper containing his last editorial work had reached our readers he was dead. But his work is not dead, and will continue to live to bless thousands. While his life was a short one, being hardly forty-four years old, yet he lived much and did much that will live on to ennoble and purify. In the later years of his life he spent much of his time evangelizing in destitute fields. In these years he did far more of this work than any preacher known to me. Often have I heard him say that the wealthy churches could easily secure the best preachers to preach for them, while the poor could not, adding that the Saviour went among the poor while he was on earth. The many truths he has taught and impressed so forcibly cannot die. His work in showing that what constitutes one a Christian makes him a member of the one body cannot be in vain. God will raise up others to carry forward this teaching.[7]

JAMES A. HARDING

The outbreak of the Civil War in the spring of 1861 nearly paralyzed the work of the church for a time. Nevertheless, Moses E. Lard in the fall of that year ventured over to Winchester, Kentucky to assist J. W. Harding in a gospel meeting. In the course of the meeting J. W. Harding's thirteen-year-old son, James A., was baptized. He was the oldest child of J. W. and Mary E. McDonald Harding, and the parents took great delight in the fact that he became a Christian.

---

[7]J. C. McQuiddy, "F. D Srygley," *Gospel Advocate*, Vol. XLII, No. 32 (August 9, 1900), p 505.

J A. HARDING

J. W. Harding was at home in Kentucky. For ninety-seven
years he lived around Winchester, traveling but little from there.
His father, Amos Harding, had moved into Kentucky from Boston

around 1820. Having become a tailor, he followed that trade for
a number of years. In 1839 he obeyed the gospel, and after that
he preached on Sundays, and worked either as a tailor or a
merchant through the week. He married Mary E. McDonald in
1844, and to them fourteen children were born. J. W. Harding
was throughly devoted to the work of God. He was an elder in
the Court Street Church in Winchester, Kentucky until the instrument of music was forced in in 1887. Thereafter, he and
fifteen others left and became the nucleus for the Fairfax congregation. Harding was active here until he died in 1919.

But the name of James A. Harding was destined to become much
more familiar than that of his father. Although from very early
in his life Harding intended to be a preacher, his first work was
teaching school. Harding later recalled that the first pay he ever
received was for teaching. When he was seven years old, his
mother had employed a colored girl about fourteen who wanted to
learn to read. Harding had just completed the "first reader," so
he passed his knowledge on to her, forcing her all the while to
get her lessons up well. If she were slothful, he flogged her, the
same as his teacher did him He took the colored girl through
the second and third readers. One day her father gave him a sack
of watermelons for teaching "his gal" to read.

Harding very largely paid his own way through school by teaching. At the age of sixteen he entered an academy taught by J.
O. Fox, an eminent Kentucky educator, to prepare for entrance
to College. He paid his board and tuition by teaching It was
the fall of 1866 that Harding entered the renowned school.
Alexander Campbell had died the previous March, but the memory
of Campbell permeated every phase of the school. Harding finished
at Bethany in the spring of 1869, and then prepared to go back
to Kentucky.

Harding intended to make the preaching of the gospel a life-
time career at this time. About the time James A. Harding was
born, his father began preaching. It was nothing unusual for
him to lead fifty to a hundred to Christ in the course of a gospel
meeting. This impressed young Harding.

As far back as I can remember I had it in mind to preach when
I became a man, so when I was about 19 I began to seek for op-

portunities to speak in the school houses away back 8 or 10 miles from town.[8]

Upon leaving Bethany College, Harding went to Hopkinsville, Kentucky and taught school. He stayed with the school five years, and attended faithfully the congregation in the town. Here, he met the daughter of Judge John B. Knight, a prominent member of the church, and married her. Three children were born to them, two of whom died almost immediately. In five years, his wife also died. Harding's second wife was Miss Pattie Cobb of Estill County, Kentucky.

While teaching school at Hopkinsville, Harding made the acquaintance of V. M. Metcalfe, a popular Kentucky preacher. They first met in 1870. Metcalfe was one who pushed Harding to preach. Often on the way to an appointment, he would stop by Hopkinsville, and take young Harding with him in his buggy. Before long, he had Harding preaching.

When Harding left Hopkinsville in 1874, he fainted because of malaria fever and was taken in a carriage to Winchester to recover. Just as he was recuperating, an old brother, John Adams came to get him to go back into the country and hold a protracted meeting. Harding protested vigorously that he had never held a meeting and had no meeting sermons. Adams talked roughly to him, and reminded Harding that he had been brought up in church and Sunday School and besides had been to Bethany College, and that he ought to be killed if he could not preach, and for him to "shut his mouth," get his horse and go hold that meeting. Harding went and held his first protracted meeting

Usually every great man has one outstanding quality that he epitomizes. Hardings's most outstanding quality was his faith in God. It was with him a settled conviction that if he did the work God wanted him to do, God would look after him, even to the performing of a miracle if necessary. He could have no doubt that if he ceased his school work and devoted all his time to the work of the Lord, God would care for him. It was not unusual for Harding to be found hundreds of miles from home, getting ready to depart for the depot without a cent in his pocket. If someone inquired how he expected to ride a train with no money,

[8]James A. Harding, "Why I Became a Preacher," *Christian Leader and the Way*, Vol. XX, No. 11 (March 13, 1906), pp. 8, 9.

he could expect the answer that God would look after him If
Harding had an appointment to preach at a certain place on Sunday, and if a storm arose Saturday night, washing out a bridge so
the train could not travel, it was a matter of certainty with Harding
that God had caused that, and for some reason God did not want
him to make that appointment.

Harding's absolute trust in God excites the admiration of all
who study his life. However, in his own day, as now, the men
were legion who believed Harding went to an extreme in his
views on divine providence. In 1883 Harding and J. C. McQuiddy
carried on a lengthy discussion in the *Gospel Advocate* on divine
providence. Neither moved the other from his views.

James A. Harding very quickly became a prominent preacher.
In 1882 Lipscomb made Harding a corresponding editor for the
Gospel Advocate. For the next five years Harding's weighty
thrusts in the *Advocate* helped establish the cause in Tennessee
where the *Advocate* was especially circulated. He was fearless in
his exposures of what he considered wrong. In 1882 he visited
as an observer the annual convention of the Society which met
at Lexington, Kentucky. Isaac Errett presided Harding heard
infant membership in the Society encouraged. He came home
more thoroughly convinced than ever that the Society was an instrument of harm to the church, and set to work denouncing the
organization. He was beset by anathemas and denials from F. M.
Green and Isaac Errett, but undaunted, Harding stayed with it
until he established his point. In 1899 Harding made a visit
to Dallas, Texas. Here he met T. R. Burnett, who gives perhaps
what is the best description of Harding in print·

Physically, he is a fine specimen of the genus homo, weighing
perhaps over two hundred pounds, and has a large blue eye and a
big red head. His fat, flush cheeks and thick, red neck indicate
that he is of thoroughbred stock or has been fed well at the pie
counter. He has doubtless made "full proof of his ministry" among
the yellow legged chickens of the blue grass regions of Tennessee.
I take it that he wears a No. 17 collar, sleeps well at night, has
a conscience void of offense toward God and man, and is full of
a laudable ambition to do a great work for the Master's cause
In personal appearance and manner of address, he is very much
like Brother C. M. Wilmeth, only he is larger in size. Like
Brother Wilmeth he fills his sermons with illustrations It is no
uncommon thing for his eyes to fill with tears while he is speaking,
but this is rather a help, and not a hindrance to his speech. . .

He is in all respects the soundest gospel preacher that I have heard preach in Texas. He believes the Bible from "lid to lid."[9]

His quick mind made him particularly adept in controversy. G. G. Taylor was giving an accurate appraisal when he wrote,

His mind is quick and his speaking ability extraordinary. His memory is excellent and he possesses the rare gift of calling to his service momentarily whatever is available for, and advantageous to, his cause He is always prepared for any emergency, and his zeal and honesty make for him friends on both sides of the controversy Take him altogether he has few equals in the controversial field [10]

But Harding's controversy was not limited to the columns of the Advocate. One of his first public discussions was with a Dr. Hayes, presiding elder in the Methodist Church, South. This occurred at Middletown, Kentucky, May 19-27, 1880. Perhaps his most famous discussion was held in Nashville with J N. Moody, a Baptist preacher. Harding followed this debate with a lengthy meeting on Foster Street with over a hundred additions to the church.

It was true that Harding was no less adept in evangelistic work as in debating. V. M. Metcalfe watched his young protege with considerable interest. Upon learning in the spring of 1882 that Harding was to preach for the small mission at Huntsville, Alabama, Metcalfe wrote:

Brother Harding is an old-style, solid gospel preacher, and the church that gets him to hold a meeting for them and expects him to go home as soon as he gets up an interest, will be disappointed I learned he expects soon to commence a meeting at Huntsville, Ala. They could not have made a better selection in a preacher I would urge the brethren in the surrounding country to attend the meeting and get acquainted with Brother H. He will do you good. Men of his strength, faith and earnest piety are seldom found. May the Lord bless him and all his faithful, struggling children.[11]

After closing a meeting with the famous Plum Street Church in Detroit in 1887, a correspondent wrote of him,

[9]T. R Burnett, "Brother Harding in Texas," *Gospel Advocate,* Vol XLI, No 32 (August 10, 1899), p 510

[10]G G Taylor, "The Sulphur Debate," *Gospel Advocate,* Vol XXVI, No. 25 (June 18, 1884), p 394

[11]V M Metcalfe, "Notes of Travel," *Gospel Advocate,* Vol XXIV, No 24 (June 14, 1882), p 367

A man of sterling character and wonderful memory. In my estimation as well as that of others he is a born orator, worthy of mention, with the same daring spirit which characterized the apostle Paul. . . From his well-stored mind a stream of seeming inexhaustible information flows forth, containing instruction for young and old, the rich and poor in every work of life [12]

Fortunately Harding was strong physically, making it possible for him to do strenuous work. J. W. Higbee wrote of him,

Brother Harding is about thirty-four years of age, and very stoutly built This enables him to endure a large amount of work without showing any signs of weariness He is a faithful and earnest student of the Scriptures for he has reached the healthful conclusion that there is but one absolutely good book in the world and that book is the Bible Not that he underestimates the value of other books or fails to study them, for he does not, but in his carefulness he has imbibed the spirit of the German proverb which truly affirms that the better is always a great enemy of the best; that is, the richest devotional books and newspapers are enemies if they keep one from reading the Bible [13]

In 1891 James A. Harding and David Lipscomb established the Nashville Bible School. For nearly a decade Harding was one of the leading spirits in this school In April, 1899 Harding edited a paper called *The Way*, which later united with the *Christian Leader* to become the *Christian Leader And The Way*.

After ten years with the Nashville Bible School, James A. Harding was providentially permitted to open the Potter Bible School at Bowling Green, Kentucky. The Nashville Bible School, at the close of its tenth session, could hardly see how it could lodge the number of pupils wanting admission the next session. C. C. Potter and his wife proposed to Harding to devote one of their farms to a Bible school and erect the proper buildings if he would secure the necessary faculty. The Potters had a one hundred and forty acre farm two miles from Bowling Green, the proceeds of which they wanted to use to support the school. Harding agreed to the proposal, and plans were immediately begun to erect the buildings for the new school. Potter's idea was that each college should be self-supporting When in later years the Potter Bible School failed to support itself, he paid all outstanding bills and locked the doors

[12]Vivian, "Plum Street Church of Christ," *Christian Leader*, Vol. I, No 17 (April 26, 1887), p 3
[13]J W Higbee, "The Madisonville Meeting," *Gospel Advocate*, Vol XXIV, No 24 (June 15, 1882), p 373

Albert T. Potter and Mary J. Dunn were married February 15, 1866 and to this union was born two children: a daughter who died in infancy and a son, Eldon S Potter. Albert Potter died September 28, 1873. Six years later, his younger brother, Clinton C Potter, married his widow. No children were born to them. Both cared tenderly for Eldon S Potter. Eldon never married. His death occurred October 9, 1899. This sadness over his death was a hard blow to C. C. Potter and his wife. When the opportunity of starting a Bible School came to them, they grasped it and named it in honor of Eldon S. Potter and as a memorial to him.

Upon the decision to start a Bible School at Bowling Green, C C. Potter felt concerned over David Lipscomb's reaction, and so determined to take a trip to Nashville to find what Lipscomb's attitude would be. He was overjoyed to hear Lipscomb say, "I wish there was a college in every county." About this time Lipscomb, in announcing plans for the eleventh session of the Nashville Bible School, wrote:

... There will be some changes for the future. Brother Harding and Brother Armstrong go to Bowling Green, Ky., to begin a similar school near that place. This comes of no disagreement or trouble in the faculty here; but means were offered to start a similar school there, and Brother Harding thought it would be best to accept and use this means, and the rest of us acceded to his ideas It has never been our idea to build up a school to monopolize the teaching of the Bible, but one of our aims has been to excite others to do likewise. We would be glad to see a school in which the Bible is taught to every pupil in every church in the land; indeed, we do not think children can be reared in the nurture and admonition of the Lord at home or at school without daily instruction in the word of God. . .[14]

His death occurred on May 28, 1922, and he was buried at Bowling Green.

---

[14]David Lipscomb, "Nashville Bible School," *Gospel Advocate*, Vol XLII, No 23 (June 6, 1901), p 361

Chapter XVII

REARGUARD ACTION

By 1890 the issues dividing the church were largely before the public. Little new in the way of arguments was being offered. Many had already weighed the thought and cast their lot with different sides. So serious a matter as an open breaking of fellowship comes with spiritual men only as a last resort. One of the most determining factors in this break is occasioned by the last-ditch fighting of the rearguard. Here, the battle is often the most intense. The straggling remnants of an undecided host found neutrality no longer possible, and now must plunge into the issues. As the break in fellowship now became more obvious, attempts to place the blame occupied men's attention. Fealty to principles of truth transcended personal interest. Fierce flagellation, dynamic onslaught of the enemies' ramparts, the last bitter cries of wounded pride—these naturally preceded zero hour. Finally came the silent, almost unnoticed, separation of ways, and in the distance was heard the mournful requiem of Israel, sobbing over a broken and battered Zion.

Rearguard action was not peculiar to any one front—North, South, East or West—between the years, 1890 and 1906, but this chapter concerns itself with the last-ditch struggle in Tennessee. Through these years the life's work of David Lipscomb was put to the test. By the dawn of the twentieth century Lipscomb could see remarkable differences in the status of the church in Tennessee. Gold, silver, wood, hay or stubble? What had he built? The slow, burning fires of opposition were now to test it.

GOSPEL ADVOCATE

The *Gospel Advocate* had literally grown beside with the church in Tennessee. David Lipscomb liked to say this was the oldest publication in the brotherhood, beginning, as he avowed, with the *Christian Review* in 1844 and coming down through its successor, the *Christian Magazine.* So much had Ben Franklin liked the *Christian Review* as edited by Tolbert Fanning, that he called his paper the *American Christian Review* after Fanning's paper.

If David Lipscomb's point be granted, that the *Gospel Advocate* began with the *Christian Review,* certainly some justification could be found for the claim that this was the oldest periodical in the brotherhood   Reviewing a fifteen year history of his connection with the paper, Lipscomb, writing at the beginning of 1881, could well recall the trials he had met   Never, he declared, had it been his intention to make money from the *Advocate.* In fifteen years he had never made over five hundred dollars, and most of that had been made during the year, 1880.   For the first four or five years of the paper's existence, he had given most of his time—and money—to keeping it going.

Lipscomb's bitter experiences had taught him to appreciate T. R. Burnett's "Texas proverb" which said,

There is more joy in a printing-office over one sinner who pays in advance, and abuses the editor on every occasion, than over ninety and nine church members who take the paper and sing its praises and puff the editor, but never contribute one cent to keep him out of the poor-house [1]

The policies Lipscomb used were hardly the best guarantee of a growing subscription list.   But still it grew   At the close of 1880, there were 3,200 subscribers; five years later the list had more than doubled.   This happened despite the fact Lipscomb was especially proud that he had never asked anyone to subscribe to the *Advocate*   Frequently, he had given the paper to individuals, and asked them to examine it, and if they felt it worthy, to act accordingly; but he never pushed subscriptions.[2]

Moreover, Lipscomb used the *Advocate* to oppose whatever tendencies he thought wrong.   It is safe to say that this is hardly an appeasement policy for the masses   When, therefore, a correspondent wrote to Lipscomb asserting that he was ashamed of the *Gospel Advocate* because of its "wrangling," Lipscomb replied:

I have no doubt Brother Harding, Brother Allen, and every honest lover of the truth, regrets the necessity of controversy with brethren, or anyone else.   The necessity of the controversy arises from the disposition in man to sin and to go into error.   So long as that disposition continues, so long the necessity of controversy will continue.   That disposition is constant, is unceasing

---

[1] T R Burnett, "Burnett's Budget," *Gospel Advocate,* Vol. XXXVII, No 9 (February 28, 1895), p 131
[2] David Lipscomb, "The *Gospel Advocate,*" *Gospel Advocate,* Vol XXIII, No 2 (January 13, 1881), p. 15.

in seeking to work. It must be met with remonstrance, with arguments, with exposure. These must be constant as that No movement for the better, even when originated by God himself has ever lasted one generation without the introduction of evil and wrong. That wrong must be met and exposed, or the error triumphs Our movement is not different from others The truth must be maintained by watchfulness, fidelity to the truth; by conflict from without and within Whenever a church is not engaged in active conflict with error within itself, it is floating down a broad stream to an open hell Those who introduce error are responsible for the controversies A man who will not oppose error when it presents itself is a traitor to God, to Christ who died to root out error and establish truth. . .

Brethren complaining indiscriminately at all when engaged in controversies, those who oppose as well as those who introduce error throw their influence for the error. It says, let error be introduced without opposition—error with quiet is preferable to truth with controversy. . .[3]

But the *Gospel Advocate* gradually grew into a large concern. Early in 1871 its office was moved to 36 Cherry Street between Union and Church. J. T. S Fall, the "best Job Printer in the City" published it, so in connection with the printing of the paper, a "first class Book and job printing office" went with it Twenty years later, the *Advocate's* business increased thirty percent in one year. That was in 1889-90. The same year the office moved to 232 North Market Street. A "first-class" office had been equipped, and presses were now being run by electricity.

In a large measure the *Advocate's* growth may be contributed to the bettering of economic conditions throughout the South. The close of the Civil War left the South in desolation, but as this condition improved, the *Advocate's* financial condition did the same. But that is only a part of the story. The paper never lost touch with the common man, and managed to carry items somewhat "off the beaten track" that appealed to its readers. If Louisiana strawberries were selling for twelve cents a quart in Memphis the previous week, the *Advocate* announced it. Nor did the paper become so serious about weighty problems to forget the lighter side. When a boy wrote Lipscomb and Sewell in 1876 saying, "I have a pet Raccoon, if you want it you can have it," Lipscomb could reply, "We don't wish the animal for our

---

[3]David Lipscomb, "Queries," *Gospel Advocate*, Vol XXVII, No 45 (November 11, 1885), p. 711.

use and fear it would be a disastrous speculation to go into the
'coon business.' " When, in the summer of 1879, Russell Errett
married Mary Glass, a Catholic, of Cincinnati, the *Advocate*
jibbed: "May the snows of many winters whiten the head of this
young editor Er-rett should come to pass that his fondness of his
glass should cease." With the addition of a younger corps of
writers later, levity became more the order of the day and
Lipscomb's "heavy artillery" thundered less frequently. J. C.
McQuiddy, the "office editor," compiled a column of "Miscellany"
each week in which most anything might be found. But, once in
a while, something like the following would fill it:

William Lipscomb, Jr is sick this week. J C McQuiddy is
at the World's Fair, E G Sewell is off holding protracted meetings.
David Lipscomb is greatly crowded with outside duties connected
with the closing of the Bible School, the Fanning Orphan School
and other matters, and the first page man is writing an extemporaneous speech which he has been notified he will be unexpectedly called on to make at a commencement occasion in a
few days. This explanation will account for nearly anything [4]

Each year David Lipscomb's editorials not only set forth the
perfect felicity he found in abiding solely by the word of God, but
the growth of the paper so dear to his heart. At the beginning
of 1886, he wrote:

This number begins the twenty-eighth volume of the *Advocate*
and the twenty-first year of our connection with it   Over one
thousand weekly visits have been made by the *Advocate* to its
readers during the last twenty years, very few of which failed to
have something from our pen. During this time we have doubtless said many things in a style that was not the best and some
things that had better never been said. But we have a clear
conscience that what we have said has been at all times with a
view to honor God and promote His cause on earth. We begun
our course with a firm conviction that the path of safety to man
and honor to God can be found in a faithful adherence to His
revealed will and to the examples approved by God in faith, in
worship and in work. We believed then that efforts to substitute
human inventions for the ways approved by inspired men, would
be a cause of division and strife among the disciples, and would,
also, by accustoming men to look to their own wisdom for help,
lead to a reliance upon the wisdom of men rather than upon the
wisdom of God, for guidance. It weans away from God, from His

---

[4] C. McQuiddy, "Miscellany," *Gospel Advocate*, XXXV, No 2 (June 1,
1893), p 344

word, from His appointments. It leads to reliance upon human wisdom, human inventions, human strength. It breaks down faith and trust in God, it leads to rationalism, to the exaltation of human wisdom, and human expedients, and to infidelity.

A number of persons prominent among those pleading for the return to the primitive order, has gone out from among us. They all traveled the same road. Beginning with the adoption of human experiences, they all have followed the pathway until they set aside all divine appointments that fail to accord with their judgment.

As a man has faith in God, he will implicitly follow God in His approved worship and manner of work. As he lacks faith in God, and trusts human wisdom, he will forsake, set aside God's approved acts of worship and modes of work, and follow the suggestions of human wisdom instead. "Blessed are the poor in spirit,"—those without spiritual wisdom or resource, without confidence in their own spiritual strength or wisdom, is the first condition of possessing the Kingdom of God, because in the consciousness of their own lack of wisdom they are willing to rely upon God, trust His wisdom, and be led by Him in and through His own appointments, and leave the results in His hands. To return to the primitive heaven-approved ways of the Church of God requires a stronger faith in God,—less faith in man Whomsoever we trust, we will follow. If we trust human wisdom, our own or another's, that we will follow. These things, then are tests of our faith in God

Twenty years' experience and observation in the workings of the Church, have confirmed me more strongly in the conviction that the stronger our faith in God, the more closely we will seek to follow His approved order in faith, in work, in worship. And the more closely we follow God's approved examples, the stronger our faith in Him will grow "A closer walk with God" we will seek. On the other hand, observation teaches clearly that the adoption of human inventions and devices in faith, in work, in worship, gradually lead further and further from God, and one innovation but prepares for a dozen others to follow. This has been the pathway in which every denomination in Christendom has traveled away from God. We are not better than others, if we travel the same pathway, we will like them wander from God. The besetting sin of the Jews, of all nations, of every tribe and kindred of earth, is to forget that God will be worshipped only in His own ways, and that the wisdom of man is foolishness with God.

We trust and pray as we grow older that we may more and more learn to trust God, and strive to walk continually more and more closely in His approved ways, that we may more and more distrust human wisdom and human inventions in religion Our future course in the *Advocate* will be in accord with this

prayer. Will all who believe that man's good will be promoted
by an unshaken trust in God, and a faithful walk in His ways,
work with us in promoting this end? As we have labored the
past twenty years of our life to this end, with increased confidence
in the wisdom of the course, we consecrate the remainder of it,
be it long or short, with the help of our Father, to a more complete devotion of all our powers to this work.[5]

Four years later Lipscomb wrote again:

This is the fifty second and last number of the 32d volume of
Gospel Advocate. This closes the 25th year of my editorial labor
on the *Advocate.* Over twelve hundred and fifty numbers have
been issued within this time. Very few of these numbers have
gone out that did not carry some word of teaching and instruction,
exhortation and warning from my pen. During this time, I have
tried to be true to the word of God and faithful to his teachings.
To maintain his teaching has been the leading and supreme aim
of my labor. I have wished to succeed in the publication of the
Advocate, and have not been indifferent to the esteem and approval of my fellowmen. But the controlling desire of my heart
and the leading effort of my life have been to understand and teach
the word of God, and to be faithful to him in all of his requirements, loyal to him in maintaining his church and all his services
as he gave them   This has been the key note of my labor from
the beginning. I now anticipate it will be to the end. . .[6]

The years stepped by quickly. Six more soon passed, and the
senior editor wrote:

Thirty years is an average lifetime   A comparatively small
proportion of the human family devote thirty years after they
grow to the affairs of life. The last number of the Advocate
closed thirty years of work for me in editing and publishing the
Gospel Advocate. I began with the first week of January, 1886.
The last number closed the year, 1895. I lacked a few days of
being 35 years old when I published the first number   I now
lack a few days of being 65 years old [7]

When the last *Advocate* of the nineteenth century was being
prepared, Lipscomb gave himself to some fond reminiscences. He
was knocking at the door of three-score and ten, and was all but
laying aside his life's labors. His faltering pen scratched out
these words:

---

[5]David Lipscomb, "Our Work," *Gospel Advocate,* Vol XXVIII, No. 1
(January 6, 1886), p. 6
[6]David Lipscomb, "Twenty-Five Years' Labor," *Gospel Advocate,* Vol
XXII, No 52 (December 24, 1890), p 829
[7]David Lipscomb, "Thirty Years' Work," *Gospel Advocate,* Vol XXXVIII,
No 1 (January 2, 1896), p. 4.

This number of the Gospel Advocate is the last one for the century, and closes thirty-five years of work I have given to the Advocate   This is considered an average lifetime, and usually spans the period of one man's active labors.   I had earnestly desired by this time to have closed up my business relations with the *Advocate* and the publishing company, that the business might rest on younger shoulders and that I might write only as I had something to say.   I have not been able to do so.   The difficulty has been to find a suitable person willing to do the work and meet the responsibilities for the pay there is in it   This, too, in the face of the impression made by many that it has been a source of profit to those who manage it.

There are not many names on our list now that were there thirty-five years ago. The generation then living has passed away, and a new one has arisen. A few that then were with us still linger on the shores of mortality, while the great number are gone. The rest must soon follow.

While my general health is now much better than it was when I began this work, I feel very sensibly the infirmities of age creeping over me, and the incurable disease, old age, will soon finish its work   I do not now believe I will dread or shrink from the change when it comes   I have tried through three score years and ten to keep a conscience void of offense toward God and man.   I remember when yet a youth my desire was to go through the world without any one's being able to say he was worse off by my having lived in it   I have tried to keep that before me through life   This falls far short of the ideal placed before man by God. This, if it were successfully lived up to, is only a negative life. The ideal God puts before man is, while injuring and harming none, to help all whom we can help   To do no evil is well; to do all the good in our power is the work to which God invites every human soul. I have tried to do that which would help my fellow-men. I have not always succeeded   I have not tried to do what would please them   I have tried to please them for their good to edification   I have tried to get them to be pleased with that which would build them up, do them good, and fit them for the service of God forever   Only in seeking the good of others can man find his own true good, only in seeking to live up and save others can he save himself   If all men could realize this, how it would change this world of woe into a heaven of bliss . .[8]

The passing years made not only David Lipscomb conscious of his coming demise, but many others as well. Some were reflecting upon the loss to the cause in the Southland. When "Uncle

[8]David Lipscomb, "The Closing Year and Century," *Gospel Advocate*, Vol XLII, No 52 (December 27, 1900), p 824

Minor," V. M. Metcalfe, paid a visit to the Nashville Bible School in 1893, he came away and penned his reflections about Lipscomb, saying:

> He is getting old, and in the course of nature will not be here many more years to earnestly contend for the purity of the church and simplicity of the gospel. I don't know of a brother who is more frequently misquoted and misunderstood than Brother Lipscomb. While everybody concedes that he is a man of ability, yet few know his real worth. I have known him intimately for over twenty-five years, and I have never known a more godly or self-sacrificing man. Many suppose from his writings that he is a cross, ill-natured, sour old man, yet just the reverse is true. He is tender-hearted and loving as a child—can be led to do almost anything unless he thinks it wrong; then all the earth can't move him. He is loyal to the teachings of the Bible. I have never known a man just like him in all of his makeup I believe that God in His providence has used him in the last twenty-five years as he has no other man to elevate the standard of the church of Christ and keep it pure from innovations. God has given him wisdom and power for accomplishing good. He has not been unfaithful.[9]

On May 23, 1906 a reunion was held in Nashville of the former students and teachers of the Nashville Bible School. Both E. G Sewell and David Lipscomb spoke While David Lipscomb did not possess the eloquence of E. A. Elam or T. B. Larimore, nor the wit of F. D. Srygley, nor the logic of T. W. Brents, there was something about him—his sincerity, his devotion to God—that made him a remarkable speaker. At this particular reunion James A. Harding came, and, having listened to the two sermons by Lipscomb and Sewell reflected:

> . . . They are seventy-five years of age, Brother Sewell being a few weeks the older. They have done far more for the cause of Christ in Tennessee than any other two men, I believe. I have been more intimately associated with Brother Lipscomb. In my judgment, since Campbell died, no man among us has been so powerful with the pen. At seventy-five he is still an intellectual giant. He is not an orator; but no orator has ever moved me as he does. Had I not clinched my teeth and pressed my lips together, I would have sobbed aloud; and in spite of me the tear would flow. It is said that when Pitt spoke at his best, a torrent of logic, red-hot with passion, flowed like a rushing river. But when David Lipscomb speaks of truth that enlightens the

---

[9] V. M. Metcalfe, "Our Bible School," *Gospel Advocate,* Vol XXXV, No 22 (June 1, 1893), p 341

mind, warms the heart and mightily moves the will, fills me. He is the Nestor of the brotherhood, the sage of Nashville, one of the greatest of the great men of the ages. He is not as great as Brother Sewell in some things, each would have been incomplete without the other. A fortunate union has been their long association as editors of the *Gospel Advocate*. May God greatly bless them both.[10]

Nor was an appreciation for David Lipscomb's work lacking in more extended areas. J. T. Showalter, then field editor of the *Octographic Review*, wrote of the *Advocate's* influence in these words:

Through that paper Brother Lipscomb has done a grand work for the church of the living God. Those that follow innovations fear and hate the logical and scriptural pen of Brother David Lipscomb. From what I can find out he has held the churches in Tennessee, and other places as well, nearer the apostolic simplicity, than can be found almost anywhere While it might be impossible to find, not inspired, who w uld not get upon the wrong side of some of the many questions now agitating the religious (?) world, yet in Brother David Lipscomb is found a man, to say the least, who is nearly always right when viewed from, and in the light of the New Testament. . .[11]

NASHVILLE CHURCHES

On the whole there was perhaps no city in the nation where the plea for the ancient order of things had been more successfully advocated than Nashville. In 1891 Lipscomb boasted that Tennessee had fifty thousand disciples, four hundred and fifty congregations and three hundred and fifty preachers, the bulk of which was located in middle Tennessee, in the environs of Nashville.[12] Seven years later the *Christian Guide* asserted there were five hundred and thirty congregations in Tennessee. When the editor of the *Christian Standard* visited Nashville in the spring of 1901, he reported there were eighteen congregations of New Testament Christians in the city—sixteen white and two colored. The whole population of Nashville was then a hundred thousand, and there were four thousand, five hundred members of the church.

[10] J A Harding, "The Nashville Bible School," *Gospel Advocate*, Vol XLVIII, No 24 (June 14, 1906), p 369

[11] J T Showalter, "Jottings from Virginia," *Octographic Review*, Vol XXXV, No 12 (March 22, 1892), p 5

[12] David Lipscomb, "The Convention," *Gospel Advocate*, Vol XXXIII, No 43 (October 29, 1891), p 677

The first congregation to plead for original Christianity in the city had its origin in 1820   The account of that earlier history has already been given. That year—1820—Nathan Ewing donated a lot on Spring Street (now Church) between Sixth (High) and Seventh (Vine). This was the lot where Loew's theatre now stands. Here, a six thousand dollar building was erected. On January 1, 1826 P. S. Fall moved from Kentucky to Nashville to preach for the church there.

The congregation very early belonged to the Baptist denomination, but the restoration principles, as advocated by Alexander Campbell, became thoroughly implanted in the church. In the summer of 1827 the congregation withdrew from the Concord Baptist Association. A year later the church voted to reorganize in full sympathy with the restoration plea. Out of one hundred and fifty members only six dissented.

In 1831 P. S. Fall returned to Kentucky. The church now had over three hundred members. Tolbert Fanning and A. Adams now preached here. After 1841 W. H. Wharton, a physician, preached for the congregation, but in 1847, after the church had succumbed to the eloquent charms of Jesse B Ferguson, there was a change of preachers and Ferguson located here. The next decade was one of "advance through storm." In 1849 the congregation decided to erect a new building on Cherry Street (Fourth Avenue) below Spring (Church Street). The new building, completed by 1852, was the most pretentious thing in the city. At a cost of $30,000 the congregation had built a meeting house that would seat twelve hundred.

Then came the Ferguson fiasco. The congregation divided and a new congregation was established near the present site of the Sam Davis Hotel. Meanwhile, it filed suit to get possession of the new building on Cherry Street. A year later, Campbell came to Nashville to try to save the church. It was December, 1856 before the group finally got possession of the new building. Early the next spring, a remnant of fifty-seven members recalled P. S Fall to come and rebuild the church   But that year, on April 8, the new thirty-thousand dollar building burned. The original building on Spring Street had been sold to the Shiloh Presbyterians, so now the congregation negotiated to purchase the old property.

The church weathered the storm of the Civil War, and gradually grew back to surpass its former numerical strength. The quiet, unassuming P. S. Fall had the respect of the towns-people as well as the congregation, and throughout the city, the congregation was spoken of as "Brother Fall's Church." The increasing infirmities brought on by age made it necessary for Fall to think of departing. In 1876 Samuel A. Kelley, one of the editors of the *Apostolic Times,* came to hold a meeting. He was urged to locate with the church, and on January 1, 1877 did so.

Kelley came with expectations of doing great things. "Consultation Meetings," as they were popularly called, had been widely accepted in Tennessee before and shortly after the war. Kelley called one to meet on November 20, 1877, and invited the brotherhood at large. Some illustrious men came. David Walk came from Memphis. Ordinarily, preachers in the church were and are plain men, dressing like common men. But. Walk had a dignity and dress that made him look more like a professional clergyman than any preacher in the church. When Joe Franklin saw him, Franklin avows that he didn't know whether to call him, "Brother Walk," or address him as an Irish Catholic would his priest.

At any rate, Kelley had not properly appraised himself of the thought among brethren in the Tennessee churches. Although "Consultation Meetings" were popular earlier, the brethren grew more and more suspicious of what they might become. William Lipscomb debated with Kelley the advisability of this meeting The result was that its total effect was killed, and Tennessee churches henceforth allowed all "Consultation Meetings" to die

Kelley's untimely death the next summer, paved the way for the coming of R. C. Cave to the congregation. Cave was the son-in-law of Winthrop H. Hopson Hopson, now old and feeble, followed Cave to Nashville, where Hopson died. R C. Cave's health was bad. He left Nashville in a year, and his brother, R. Lin Cave then settled down to preach for the church. R. Lin, like his brother, was brilliant and eloquent, and had everything to make him popular in the city. He had fought under Robert E. Lee in Virginia, and was one of those haggard, tired Confederate troops standing by at Appomatox when Lee surrendered. Consequently, at the annual Confederate reunions in Nashville, R. Lin Cave was usually the favorite speaker.

On the issues facing the church, Cave remained silent, but it was clear that his sympathies were with that larger body of northern brethren who favored innovations into the work and worship of the church. Through the years the older members of the original congregation passed. In the fall of 1876 Orville Ewing, Sr. and James Foster, Sr. died. leaving only one member of the original congregation left—Jesse March By 1885 the congregation had eight hundred members. but the bulk of its growth was from members moving into the city from other localities. They brought their affinity to innovations with them, and the congregation became fertile soil for the use of these additions to the work of the church. Yet, the church had had great preaching T. W. Brents had conducted a meeting here in November, 1877, which was followed by another one with Moses E. Lard, who was now sick, broken-hearted and unpopular. R. Lin Cave preached for this congregation from 1881 until 1897 when he resigned to become president of Kentucky University. His drifting with the popular current on the issues confronting the church was a pledge of things to come.

On March 27, 1887 the last service of the church was held in the old Spring Street property. P. S. Fall, now yielding rapidly to the inexorable pull of death. came back to preach the last sermon in the meetinghouse. For the next two years the church met in Watkins' Hall, awaiting the completion of its new building. In 1889 it was finished at a cost of $21,000, and henceforth became known as the Vine Street Christian Church. The introduction of the instrument came a short time later to nobody's surprise and with but little fanfare

Brethren in Nashville who had deep convictions against the more modern additions to the church were prone to mark off the Vine Street church as no longer an effective instrument to advocate pure apostolic Christianity. They found it necessary at the same time to hold a similar view toward the Woodland Street Church in East Nashville, or Edgefield In view of the early teaching that it had received. the reasons for Woodland Street's departure seemed less natural E G Sewell moved to Nashville in January, 1870 to become co-editor of the *Gospel Advocate* That year he baptized a number of persons as a result of some preaching done on White's Creek Pike in North Edgefield This group moved into an Odd-Fellow's Hall on Woodland Street.

The congregation continued to meet here until July, 1878 when it completed its new building

For twelve years E. G. Sewell preached here once a month. Except for the time he was away in meetings he was usually present to teach at a mid-week service. In 1875 the little church cooperated with the Owen's Station congregation in Williamson County to sustain an evangelist full time in the field. A good work in a small, unpretentious way was being done. But changes came in the membership. Members of the church moved in from other states. The congregations where they had formerly worshipped were in favor of Societies, and the Woodland Street church soon found itself with an element favoring these "modern fads" in the church. Sewell, by patient teaching, resisted the encroachment of the society element An undercurrent of feeling swam through the church.

E. G. Sewell, never one to stay where he was not wanted, yielded to the desire of the church for a new preacher. The selection was a young man, W. J. Loos, son of C L. Loos. The son was like his father. C L Loos had heartily sympathized with societies, and for a time was president of the General Missionary Society, and the son was strongly behind his father. Young Loos came to Nashville the first of 1883. In October, that year, he attended the national convention, and returned with the fire of Societism burning brightly in his soul He spoke to the Woodland Street congregation in laudable terms of the work the Society was doing, and insisted that he was ashamed to admit at the Convention that he was from Tennessee. The next Wednesday night, after Loos returned, Sewell kindly upbraided the young preacher, and Loos said no more about the Society publicly as long as he was there.

The first of 1887 R. M Giddens came to the Woodland Street Church The Society sentiment grew. Some women organized an auxiliary society despite the fact Sewell spoke against it. Soon the Ladies' Auxiliary Society had sent letters to the churches in Tennessee, asking for money so that it—the Ladies' Society—could employ a State Evangelist. Sewell objected to the elders, but the ladies were upheld In the summer of 1890 J. C McQuiddy and E G Sewell, along with forty other members, sent a petition to the elders of the Woodland Street Church—D. C. Hall, W. A.

Corbin, and B. J. Farrar—asking them to lay aside their society for the sake of peace, but the elders refused [13]

Yet, despite the fact that both the Vine Street Church and the Woodland Street Church adopted these innovations, other congregations planted on a more solid foundation grew up in the city. Most of these owed their origin to the sacrifices of godly men. In 1857 David Lipscomb went one bright Sunday afternoon to Fireman's Hall on Cherry Street in South Nashville Only three women attended. Lipscomb told them that if each would come back the next Sunday afternoon and each bring one other person, he would be back to preach. From this effort the College Street congregation had its origin. The work was slow and arduous. In the spring of 1877 the church appointed a committee consisting of R Averitt, Humphrey Hardison and Frank Anderson to receive funds to buy a lot for a building. They refused to build until they had all the funds. Later, the College Street Church began some mission work on Green Street, and the Green Street congregation resulted. In 1887 the College Street Church had a membership of one hundred thirty-six Many of these were former members of the Church Street or Vine Street congregation who were dissatisfied with the adoption of innovations.

The church in North Nashville was started with as little pomp and show. In 1867 David Lipscomb went out to the old army barracks and started preaching. The North Spruce Street congregation resulted Five years later Lipscomb went out to Watkins Chapel in the northwestern part of the city and preached. He conducted a protracted meeting here without a song ever being sung. [David Lipscomb could not sing.] The Line Street church grew out of this. In 1876 Lipscomb went west of the city and held a meeting in a schoolhouse. There was no town there then, but this effort resulted in the establishment of the church in West Nashville.

Meanwhile, in East Nashville, the church was likewise growing. The original members who formed the Woodland Street church were pushed out by the society element, and established the Foster Street church. Later, more people left the Woodland Street church because of its acceptance of innovations and started the church at

[13]David Lipscomb, "The Work of Strife," *Gospel Advocate*, Vol. XXXII, No. 36 (September 3, 1890), pp 566, 567.

Tenth and Russell Streets. By 1895 David Lipscomb could announce that there were ten white congregations in the city. There
were more members of the church in Nashville, in proportion to
its size, than in any city in the world. Yet, all of this was done
without the aid of a single society separate and apart from the
church. This work was accomplished by the zeal of individual
members, and stood as the strongest proof that the establishment
of Missionary Societies is not the sign of strong missionary zeal,
but rather the sign of the *lack* of it. Men never feel the need of
human organizations to do the work of the church until the church
loses its zeal.

Perhaps in no one year did the church in Nashville see greater
success than in 1889. A large part of this was due to the preaching
of James A. Harding. In the spring Harding conducted a meeting
for the church in South Nashville. In May of that same year, he
held a much-publicized debate with J. N. Moody, a Baptist preacher,
that was well attended. Following the debate, he went to the
northeast part of the city and preached for eight weeks with one
hundred and fourteen additions. This was done with the Foster
Street Church. Later, this congregation put up a building on
Grace Avenue and became known as the Grace Avenue Church of
Christ. That same spring F. B. Srygley and Granville Lipscomb,
preaching under the supervision of the College Street Church,
conducted a tent meeting in West Nashville. While the churches
were being established, new additions were mounting, the *Gospel
Advocate* announced that persons looking for money need not come
to Nashville, for they were spending right in their own city, establishing churches. Whether that be a selfish attitude is open to
question. Nevertheless, it is a stern fact that a part of the present-
day success of the church in the city is owing to that earlier attitude.

Still the work proceeded. P. W. Harsh reported in the spring
of 1895 the following:

We have arranged to have regular services at two places—one
at a little house on Carroll Street, near Wharf Avenue, where
services will be held as follows: Sunday School, 9.30 A.M., preaching Sunday, 11 A.M. and 7.30 P.M., prayer meeting Thursday,
7.30 P.M.—another in a hall, corner South Market and Molloy
(two blocks from Broad), Sunday at 3 P.M. and 7.30 P.M.;
prayer meeting Friday, 7:30 P.M. We have secured Jackson's

hall, on South Cherry, just beyond Decatur Railroad crossing, and expect to have regular services there in a short time. . . .[14]

It was a strong point with David Lipscomb that many congregations be established in the city instead of pouring money lavishly into one large one. David Lipscomb was in Philadelphia, Warren County, Tennessee, preaching, in 1857, when word reached him that the thirty thousand dollar building that the Church Street congregation had erected burned. He arose before the church and publicly expressed his joy. Writing about it nearly forty years later, Lipscomb said: "I still think it was a blessing from God."[15] Modest houses of worship with a people strong in missionary zeal was the combination Lipscomb liked, and which the churches had in these years

SOCIETY INVADES TENNESSEE

Late in 1889 R. M Giddens, the preacher for the Woodland Street church, went privately to David Lipscomb informing him that the ladies in the church had raised enough money to support an evangelist in the state He insisted that this mission work be done in Tennessee through the church, under the supervision of the elders, and he asked Lipscomb to run a notice of it in the *Advocate* E. G. Sewell prepared an article The *Advocate* was just ready to publish it when word came from Louisville that A. I. Myhr was on his way to Tennessee to organize a Tennessee State Missionary Society. For the next fifteen years Myhr was to be heading the conflict over the Societies in that state.

Myhr came to Tennessee from Missouri where his spiritual edification had mostly come through the liberalism of the *Christian-Evangelist*. His beliefs were very closely akin to those of R. C. Cave He came to Tennessee advocating that the preaching had to keep abreast of the times; that the preaching of twenty years ago would no longer do any more than the preaching of John the Baptist would do after Jesus came.[16]

The first meeting of the Tennessee Christian Missionary Society was held in Chattanooga in October, 1890 Present at the meeting

---

[14]P W Harsh, "Nashville Notes," *Gospel Advocate*, Vol XXXVII, No. 15 (April 11, 1895), p 235
[15]David Lipscomb, "Fine Houses for Worship," *Gospel Advocate,* Vol XXIV, No 4 (January 28, 1892), p 52
[16]David Lipscomb, "Further Comments on Brother Harsh's Queries," *Gospel Advocate,* Vol XXXIII, No. 2 (January 14, 1891), p 23

were nine preachers from Tennessee and three from without the state. R. M. Giddens and R. Lin Cave were present from Nashville. R. P. Meeks and a student came from Henderson, Tennessee. David Lipscomb went as an observer. The convention appointed a committee of seven to contact Lipscomb and see if harmony could be reached. Lipscomb wrote out his views, presented them to the convention, but they availed nothing. Nor did Lipscomb expect they would. Later he wrote:

We went to this meeting with no anticipation of changing the current of affairs. We had seen enough of the spirit of disregard of the rights and feelings of Brother Sewell and others, and the perversion of the property in East Nashville, to know the course had been determined upon. We were satisfied they would not stop to study the will of God or consider the feelings of their brethren. But we have spent over thirty years, during which the leading purpose and end of every day's work was to build up the churches of God after the model given by him in the Scriptures. The highest and only real ambition of my life is to see .the churches in good active working order in just that condition that the Holy Spirit sought to leave them. I have no confidence in human wisdom, common sense, sanctified or unsanctified, improving upon the model of organization, worship or work given by the Holy Spirit And if we cut loose from these, there can be no restraint to the fancies and follies of humanity. The departures may not be very marked or flagrant at first, but once under headway they will grow with accelerating force. We are certain this movement will affect the churches in Tennessee. Many have come into the churches that have but little confidence in God's provisions, and are dissatisfied with the simplicity of his order. It does not afford scope for display or gratify opportunity for the ambitious. The ways that human wisdom have invented seem more effective and more attractive to many. . . [17]

The exact cause of the establishment of the Tennessee Christian Missionary Society may never be known. Ostensibly, its devotees claimed that it was established to inaugurate, systematize and organize cooperative work in Tennessee. But Lipscomb himself could not be shaken from the conviction that the whole thing was started by the *Christian Standard* in the selfish matter of looking after its own financial interests.

This whole society movement in Tennessee has been whooped up by the *Christian Standard*. It has been well known to all

---

[17]David Lipscomb, "Convention Notes," *Gospel Advocate,* Vol XXXII, No 43 (October 22, 1890), p 678

familiar with the publishing interests that the Standard Publishing Company has steadily sought to obtain a monopoly of the publishing business among the disciples   It obtained its success by being recognized as the organ of the societies, general, foreign and state   When it failed to control the sale of the society hymn book, it published a rival one—Hymn and Tune book.   It now owns the *Guide,* and it, or Russell Errett, owns a large interest in the *Courier,* of Dallas, Texas, and directs its policy   Some years ago, through a third person, R Errett bought the *Christian Evangelist,* with all its publications   The owners learned, before the delivery of the property, that R Errett was the purchaser, and refused to deliver the property on the ground that they had been deceived in the transaction   To injure the *Evangelist* it has established an agency for the *Standard* and its publications in Kansas City, and encouraged other publications in Missouri calculated to injure the *Evangelist*

Russell Errett has, through several years past, made repeated efforts to buy the *Gospel Advocate*   When we would refuse to sell, he would raise the price of Popular Hymns upon us   Our readers all used it, and we were compelled to handle it, even if we had to do it without pay   But this determined us to publish a book of our own.

Five or six years ago, we made a contract to have a book prepared   When the matter was greatly prepared, Errett learned of it, and bought the book up , he has never brought it out   This was done, no doubt, to hold us at his mercy   We then got out Christian Hymns   The *Standard* has never extended it the usual courtesy of a notice, so we are told   But it is reported that it paid it the highest possible compliment by sending a messenger to its editor to induce him to get out one as good for the Standard Company.

A few months ago Errett proposed to transfer the *Guide* to the *Advocate* for an interest in the Advocate Publishing Company. While we would be glad to combine the two, we did not see how the *Guide* editors could work in harmony with the *Advocate,* nor did we believe the present readers of the *Guide* would remain with the *Advocate.* So we did not see that we would get anything in the trade

In every proposition to purchase the *Advocate,* or an interest in it, it was stipulated that Brother Sewell and I were to continue to edit it, and that it should be held to its present position   The idea was that it was to be held to its present position as suiting the southern brethren, and as their organ, just as the *Standard* is for the northern brethren   With these propositions has come to me the assurance that R Errett was half opposed to the societies, anyhow, and one reason given for wishing to transfer the *Guide* to the *Advocate* was his conscience hurt him because it was not being run in harmony with the wishes and purposes of F. G Allen, who founded it, while the *Advocate* is being run more nearly in harmony with his wishes than any other of our papers.

I am just as sure as I could be of anything human, that if we had sold R. Errett an interest in the *Advocate,* the present effort at organizing a society in Tennessee would not have been made Some favored it, but without the encouragement given by the *Standard,* no effort would have been made, and it would never have encouraged it, if Errett had owned an interest in the *Advocate.* These brethren are allowing themselves, consciously or unconsciously, to be used by R. Errett to break down all home enterprise among Christians in the different sections of the country, and to build up one great central monopoly in the hands of those who have no social, local or other sympathy with them, further than to use them in building up their own interests. . [18]

An undocumented statement has passed down from year to year for the past half century to the effect that David Lipscomb spent an entire night in prayer to God. One cannot refrain from thinking that if this event occurred, which is very likely, it must have taken place on the night of October 17, 1892. The next morning at nine o'clock the General Christian Missionary Society was to open its annual convention in the building of the Vine Street Christian Church. For several weeks the convention had been given considerable publicity. Both the *Christian Standard* and the *Christian-Evangelist* had been trying to encourage considerable enthusiasm. They pointed out that the churches of Nashville had a very great "prejudice" against the Society, and that a national convention in that city would show those people the greatness of the organization. Lipscomb was practical enough to recognize that his life's work might be undone. With the strong arm thrusts the Society was making at Tennessee, there was serious danger that the work of a life might be overthrown.

Actually, of course, it strengthened most opposers to the Society in their convictions. Society advocates had from the beginning contended their agency was but an expedient. They suggested that it made no difference to them *how* mission work was done, just so it was done. They contended that the minority who opposed the Society should submit to the majority who wanted it. Lipscomb always believed that this was so much propaganda, calculated for effect, but it was difficult to disprove it. The action of the Society in coming to Nashville was the most effective force

---

[18]David Lipscomb, "Convention Notes," *Gospel Advocate,* Vol. XXXII, No 45 (November 5, 1890), p 708.

to disprove it   Only two congregations in the city wanted it there
—Vine Street and Woodland Street—and even these were not
united in that desire   The bulk of the brethren did not want the
Society, and felt that its coming might promote division   The
Society ignored the majority when that majority was against it
In their efforts to try to convert the people to the Society method
of working they most effectively proved the contention that the
Society was much more interested in making converts to Society-
ism than it was in making converts to Christ.

But Lipscomb could not be sure of this before the Society came
to his city. Most brethren stayed away from the convention while
the visitors who did attend were those from Vine Street and Woodland Street   C. M. Wilmeth suggested a meeting of those who
opposed the Society with its advocates at the convention to see if
harmony could be reached   The advocates declined the invitation
because of the lack of time   A paper signed by David Lipscomb,
E G. Sewell, C M. Wilmeth, M C. Kurfees and a host of others
was prepared to be read at the convention   The following was the
paper drawn up:

To the General Christian Missionary Convention, Assembled in
Nashville, Tennessee —Dear Brethren in Christ: Inasmuch as your
body now in session in this city purports to represent the churches
of Christ, untrammeled by creeds, and there is a conspicuous absence of many myriads of brethren whose sentiments are voiced in
such periodicals as the *Gospel Advocate, Christian Leader, Octographic Review, Firm Foundation, Christian Messenger, Christian
Preacher, Primitive Christian* and *Gospel Echo*, and, inasmuch
as you have assembled in the State of Tennessee, which contains
about 40,000 Christians who profess to practice the primitive order
of things, and perhaps not more than 1,000 of these thoroughly
sympathize with your organization, and, inasmuch as arguments
and appeals have been made on the floor of your convention to win
these brethren over to your ways, we respectfully submit to your
august body this memorial

1. That we, believing as we do, that all should be one in Christ,
of the same mind and the same judgment, speaking the same things
and endeavoring to keep the unity of the spirit in the bonds of
peace, cannot countenance the corruption of the pure speech of
the Bible, and do deeply deplore the grievously divided state of
the church, whereby brethren are embittered against each other,
congregations are torn asunder and sections are arrayed one
against another

2 That, believing as we do, that whatever is not of faith is sin,

we cannot conscientiously cooperate in the organization or workings of any missionary society, home or foreign, with officers unknown to the New Testament and terms of membership at variance with the spirit and genius of the gospel, it being our firm and abiding conviction that in building up such societies we are pulling down that which our fathers labored to build up and are sapping the strength of the church for which Christ died.

3. That, believing as we do, that the Scriptures furnish us unto all good works, and that preaching the gospel stands preeminent as a good work, we boldly affirm and earnestly contend that the Bible contains a divine system of evangelism, powerful enough to shake the Roman Empire in its day and perfect enough to carry the gospel to the ends of the earth; and we modestly submit that, putting this faith into practice, we have demonstrated that in our day this divine plan is effectual, in that without other organization the primitive gospel has been planted in this region, a mission among the Indians has been sustained for many years, a mission in Turkey has been established and the Volunteer Band in Japan supported.

4 That we, in consideration of the aforesaid truths and facts and with no desire to destroy or cripple the work of any one engaged in preaching the gospel and teaching the way of salvation in either the home or foreign field, but believing that all now engaged can be sustained and more work be done in harmony with the examples of the apostles and inspired men, come before you with brotherly love and beseech you in the name of our Lord Jesus Christ that you abandon these organizations that found no necessity or recognition in apostolic times, and that you concentrate your zeal and energies in the churches of God, under the direction of their heaven-appointed officers, which we all admit to be common and scriptural ground, thereby removing a cause of widespread division and bringing about that union and cooperation in which there is strength and which will enable us to make more rapid conquest of the earth for Christ, and to this end we present this memorial, and for this consummation devoutly to be wished for shall we ever pray.

> C. M. WILMETH,
> DAVID LIPSCOMB,
> E. G. SEWELL,
> J A HARDING.
> M. C KURFEES.
> AND OTHERS.

At one point in the convention C. M. Wilmeth arose and read the paper. J W. McGarvey was chairman that day. A few brethren smiled while the paper was being read. McGarvey suggested referring the paper to a committee made up of himself, J. H. Garrison, C L Loos, B. B Tyler and F. D. Power. Garrison himself made a great joke of the whole affair [19]

Lipscomb attended the convention to observe its proceedings. The Women's Board of Christian Missions was there and Lipscomb heard women preach He observed that the Bible was about as popular as "last year's almanac " Not a verse of scripture was quoted Later he wrote:

A mere girl was put up to make a rambling talk on missions to Loos, McGarvey, Tyler, Darsie, and other wise men present It could not profit them It injured her and lowered the standard of womanly modesty

Candidly, if I believed the law of God iterated in precept and example all through the Bible, written from the beginning in the being and natural functions of woman, could be set aside and trampled under foot, as was done in this Convention, without sin, I would think that sprinkling could be substituted for baptism, or baptism be rejected altogether I would think the statement that Jesus was begotten of God could be rejected with impunity, or the whole Bible set aside without harm to man in time or eternity. I cannot see, if this is allowable, why we cannot substitute a creed, a confession of faith, a discipline like the Methodists, as containing the parts of scripture we think essential or like to follow, together with such additions by human wisdom as seem to us good Indeed, I prefer a fixed human standard to one unstable, dependent only on the passing humor of the men, women and children who come together

If that Convention was not an open, defiant rejection of God and his holy word, I would not know how to reject God or set aside the authority of his word I do not think delicious speeches or animal enthusiasm manifested by constant cheering and handclapping applause compensate in any way for the violated law of God. Nor do I think its being done for a worthy cause helps the cause or palliates the sin

If the Bible is of God, let us obey it If we are not willing to be governed by it, let us make no present, let us kick the book out of our homes and be a law unto ourselves.

Jesus Christ calls in Matt 15 7, those who profess to honor him, yet follow the teachings of men, hypocrites "In vain do ye worship me teaching for doctrines the commandments of men." Man's only duty is to obey God and leave results with him.[20]

---

[19] J H Garrison, "The Nashville Convention," *Christian-Evangelist*, Vol. XXIX, No 43 (October 27, 1892), p 677

[20] David Lipscomb, "Convention Thoughts," *Gospel Advocate*, Vol. XXXIV, No 45 (November 10, 1892), p 709.

The meeting of the Society did very little to convert the churches of Tennessee Most became thoroughly satisfied that they were wrong. As to the results Lipscomb wrote

We did not see or hear of a single preacher or brother among our Tennessee preachers that was not strengthened in his conviction that these things are all wrong and lead to division and strife, and gradually school men to neglect the Bible Quite a number even of those who had looked favorably on the societies went away disgusted. . . . I believe the effect of the convention here has been good, that the atmosphere will be purer, that the brethren and sisters who are in earnest will be more united, more content to stand upon the Bible, and be satisfied with its provisions; because they have seen in this convention to what extent good, God-fearing, strong-minded men like McGarvey, Loos and others can be carried by those organizations, unknown to the apostles, not mentioned in the New Testament.[21]

HENDERSON TROUBLES

Viewed from the standpoint of its later influence upon the cause through the next few years, the rearguard action which occurred at Henderson, Tennessee, in 1903-04 was at a particularly strategic point. Here, since 1874, had been meeting what was known as the Henderson Masonic Institute. Through the influence of J B. Inman the school came under the influence of the brotherhood and its name was changed to West Tennessee Christian College. Inman, reared a Presbyterian, moved into McNairy County, Tennessee, in 1856 He was preparing to be a Presbyterian minister when he heard Knowles Shaw, "the singing evangelist," and was converted. Immediately afterwards he began preaching for the congregation in Henderson. Meanwhile, through his influence the Henderson Masonic Institute became West Tennessee Christian College, and Inman was accordingly its first president.

Inman died in 1889 and G A Lewellan became the next president of the college. Three years later the faculty of the school is found to consist of G. A. Lewellan, president, H. G Thomas, vice-president, and R. P Meeks, head of the Bible Department.[22] The school was rapidly attaining a high literary distinction among Tennessee schools. In the spring of 1893, Lewellan, Thomas and Meeks suddenly resigned from the faculty, and shortly afterward

[21]David Lipscomb, "Convention Items," *Gospel Advocate,* Vol XXXIV, No. 43 (October 27, 1892), p 676

[22]J. C McQuiddy, "Miscellany," *Gospel Advocate,* Vol XXV, No. 19 (May 11, 1893), p 396

A G Freed, who had opened a school at Essary Springs, Tennessee. moved to Henderson to become president of the school   Enrollment grew and soon it was seen that a new building needed to be erected   In 1896, J F Robertson of Crockett Mills, Tennessee, promised to make a donation of five thousand dollars toward this end. with the understanding that the name of the college would be changed to honor his daughter, "Miss Georgia."   Consequently West Tennessee Christian College became Georgia Robertson Christian College in 1897

Freed made every attempt to improve the school.   One of his methods in doing so was to build up a better faculty.   N. B. Hardeman joined the faculty in 1897 as a teacher of Bible   Five years later E C McDougle became co-president with A G. Freed. and about the same time L L Brigance became connected with the school

It was inevitable that a struggle over innovations should occur. From the days of Inman the school as well as the church in the town had shown a decided partisan attitude favoring the more modern additions to the work and worship of the church.   On his way to Chattanooga in 1890 to establish the Tennessee Christian Missionary Society A. I. Myhr had stopped at Henderson and had received assurance of the backing of the church before going on to the meeting   Henderson was undoubtedly the most influencial point from the standpoint of the plea for a return to the ancient order that could be found in West Tennessee.   Developments there would doubtlessly influence the whole church in that part of the state—and as events have proved, very widely in the whole country.

By the turn of the century most Christians in Tennessee were making their viewpoint clear on these issues.   Gradually, eyes turned in the direction of Henderson.   R. P. Meeks, head of the Bible Department at the college, had a wide reputation for favoring the use of the instrument and the society.   C. A. McDougle, co-president, had the same reputation.   But A. G. Freed. N B Hardeman and L L Brigance did not have this reputation.   When A. G. Freed debated J. N. Hall of Fulton, Kentucky in April, 1902, some of the brethren signed a petition that they were against the organ and "human societies"   Among those to sign were J W Grant, G. Dallas Smith, L. L. Brigance and A. O. Colley.[23]

[23]John R Williams, "Notes from West Tennessee," *Gospel Advocate*, Vol. XLIV, No 18 (May 1, 1902), p. 283.

It was widely known what attitude the church at Henderson took. The attitude of McDougle and Meeks was also known. But, with Freed, Hardeman and Brigance on the other side of the issues, it as hard to tell about the total influence of the college at Henderson. John R. Williams, one of West Tennessee's prominent preachers, undertook to defend the school.

. . . As to Brother Freed, one of the presidents of the college, and Brother N B. Hardeman, one of the teachers, I am personally acquainted with both of them, have heard them express themselves publicly and privately, and know they are opposed to these things, notwithstanding the fact that, they have not removed them from the congregation at Henderson nor withdrawn from it. Brother Freed had laid his plans before me and convinced me of the course he would follow; and right here I will state that in a very short time it may be seen what that course was to be. . .[24]

But questions about Freed continued to arise. The Henderson church continued its course of favoring innovations, and Freed took some criticisms. G. Dallas Smith, knowing the man, came to his defense, and wrote.

During the past few years there has been a good deal of complaint against Brother A. G. Freed by well-meaning brethren who did not understand the man or the circumstances under which he labored. Many knew that the organ was in the church at Henderson, Tenn , and, without knowing Brother Freed's attitude toward, condemned him as being unsound in the faith. . . I have often doubted the propriety of Brother Freed's course and have so expressed myself to him and others, but I have never for a moment doubted his soundness in the faith. Brother Freed's idea was to educate them out of it, and his influence in that direction has been wonderful, as is shown in the number who have taken their stand with him recently. . . "By their fruits ye shall know them." When Brother Freed went to Henderson, if I am not mistaken, Brother N. B. Hardeman, who is now one of the very best preachers in West Tennessee, was working and worshiping in full fellowship with the progressives, for he had never known anything else. Now he is a great power in contending for the "old Book," without addition or subtraction. Why did he change? Brother Freed simply taught him out of it. Brother L. L. Brigance, another one of our splendid preachers, told me that he was not opposed to the organ in the worship when he entered the Georgia Robertson Christian College, about eighteen months ago Now

[24]John R Williams, "Notes from West Tennessee," *Gospel Advocate*, Vol XLV, No 5 (January 29, 1903), p. 77.

he is earnestly contending for the faith unmixed with any sort of human inventions . .[25]

The whole affair came to a head in a comparatively innocent gesture at the beginning of 1903. In November of the previous year A. M. St. John, one of the elders of the Henderson church, wrote E. A. Elam requesting him to come and conduct a meeting for the church. Elam had, upon the death of F. D. Srygley, become front-page editor of the *Gospel Advocate* and was regarded as one of the outstanding preachers of the state. St. John in his letter pointed out that the church was using the instrument and supporting the society, and that some day these things might be discussed "dispassionately," but for the present he was to preach only on Christian living. Elam agreed to come provided St. John would get all of the elders together and they should agree upon it. If agreeable to all, he would come the second Sunday in December, 1902.

A letter came from A. G. Freed, requesting the meeting be postponed until after the Christmas holidays. The elders however had decided not to use the church house for any such meeting because they feared Elam might speak against their practices. Freed, however, assured Elam that at a meeting of many of the brethren it was urged that Elam come ahead. Moreover, the young preachers in the school wanted to hear the issues discussed. The meeting was set for the second Sunday in January, and Elam prepared to go.

Meanwhile, the brethren had made arrangements for Elam to do his preaching in the Baptist meeting house, since the building of the brethren had been refused. Elam arrived on the Saturday before the second Sunday. On the way into town he was met by a committee of five from the church led by R. P. Meeks. They asked Elam not to hold the meeting, since the roads were muddy and people could not attend. Elam knew, of course, that the real reason was they did not want their practices opposed. Meeks admitted that opposition would stir up strife and that he did not want this condition there.

The meeting was held anyway in the Baptist meetinghouse. About seventy-five people dissatisfied with the innovations that had been brought into the church in the town, decided to hold

[25]G. Dallas Smith, "A Statement Concerning Brother A. G. Freed," *Gospel Advocate*, Vol. XLV, No. 11 (March 12, 1903), p. 171

separate services and worship according to apostolic precedent.
A. G. Freed and N. B Hardeman and "every young preacher in
the school" were included in this number. The church for the
present began meeting in the courthouse with Freed and Hardeman preaching.[26]

Very shortly the original congregation thought of checking this
opposition. A. I. Myhr was sent for, and came to Henderson to
hold a "Bible Institute" from February 23-25. W. J. Shelburne
of Union City, Tennessee spoke on "Ground And Authority For
The Organization of Missionary Enterprises" as the first address.
R. M. Giddens also spoke in defense of these innovations. Hardeman and several of the students attended, and challenged Shelburne
for a debate, but were only ridiculed.[27]

To bring things even more to a head was the debate held in
Henderson between J. Carroll Stark and Joe Warlick F. W.
Smith, recently returned from a trip to Texas where he had met
and learned to admire Joe Warlick, was in McMinnville preaching. Stark was also in the town, and became boastful of his
opposition to those against innovations. A challenge for a debate
was issued. Smith accepted, agreeing to get a suitable opponent
for Stark. When Joe Warlick was contacted, he was ready to
come. The debate began on November 4, 1903 and lasted for
four days.

The congregation of seventy-five had now grown to one hundred
and thirty and was meeting in a building of its own. Good attendance was seen at the discussion although not a single preacher,
favoring innovations, came except Stark himself R. P. Meeks
was out of town. A. I. Mhyr, although in the neighborhood, refused to come. F B. Srygley, N. B. Hardeman, L. L. Brigance,
A. G. Freed, F. W. Smith, Jesse P. Sewell and John E. Dunn
were among the preachers who did attend.

Debating on these issues now came prominently into vogue.
The only reason they were never more popular was because advocates of innovations could not be induced to publicly discuss
them. Constant sparring went on with J. B. Briney, but little
success followed it. In 1903 Briney challenged the *Gospel Review*

[26]E. A Elam, "A Meeting at Henderson, Tenn ," *Gospel Advocate,* Vol
XLV, No 6 (February 5, 1903), pp 81, 82
[27]E A Elam, "no title," *Gospel Advocate,* Vol XLV, No 16 (April 9,
1903), p. 225.

of Dallas, Texas for a debate   Briney was editor of the *Christian Companion* at this time.   Noting the challenge the *Advocate* casually announced that other papers had given Briney the same provocation the *Review* had for a discussion, and if, for any reason, the *Review* did not accept the challenge, Briney should rest assured he would not go without an opponent.   Briney retaliated with a suggestion for a debate in Nashville   The *Advocate* agreed providing the debate would be repeated in Cincinnati or Louisville.   Briney refused this stipulation.   It was agreed to have both a written discussion and an oral one.   Briney would conduct the written debate with M. C. Kurfees and the oral one with Joe Warlick.   It was agreed that the written discussion should be carried in both the *Gospel Advocate* and the *Christian Companion*.   Briney backed out of putting it in the *Companion* because instrumental music was no issue with his readers.   Finally it was agreed to have the oral discussion in Nashville, and the discussion was to be put in tract form, but the sale of the tract, Briney's promoters insisted was not to be pushed by either the *Advocate* or the *Companion*.   It was increasingly clear to the brethren, that Briney would discuss the issues only before an audience where the people were against these innovations; he would never stand to see them discussed before his own people.   Consequently the debate was dropped.

Before the discussions ended, Briney quibbled that he had wanted to debate with David Lipscomb, the champion of the opposition, all along   Why had he never challenged Lipscomb? Naturally, Lipscomb had to decline the challenge.   He was now getting old.   His sight was almost gone and his hearing extremely poor.   He rarely ever was outside the house at night.   Lipscomb had advised Elam and Kurfees all along that Briney was an unfair man, and had no intention of allowing those who believed like he did to hear the other side.   Elam and Kurfees had tried every way to discuss issues with Briney, but as Lipscomb predicted it was of no avail.   His opinion of Briney he summarized as follows:

I am told Brother Briney frequently gives me notices not very complimentary.   Over twenty years ago he convinced me he was not a fair or just man.   It was in a small thing, but the Master said: "He that is unjust in the least is unjust also in much."   F G. Allen about the same time published that he had never had to deal with a more unfair man than Briney, and the Old Path Guide published a cartoon of him astride a planked fence

Knowing these things, I discouraged the brethren giving him notice and insisted all correspondence with him looking to a discussion of questions was a waste of ink and paper   I never believed he had the most remote intention of a fair discussion with any one   His reason for not publishing a discussion was, his readers did not need it , yet proposed to discuss them himself in his paper   So he proves what I say . .[28]

By 1906 the rearguard action was nearly fought. The events preceding the break of fellowship had for the most part transpired. The overtures of the Society, the last ditch struggle of advocates of innovations had been resisted. A few congregations here and there, especially in East Tennessee, adopted these modern appendages. But the vast majority stayed with their earlier principles and were unshaken by the fiery trials   J H Garrison in 1890 prophesied that David Lipscomb and the *Gospel Advocate* were on their way out , that the brethren had tolerated them long enough, and was ready *en masse* to join the "progression" ranks. Garrison wrote:

Let me make a little prophecy, and you can file it away for future reference. Unless there is a radical change in the policy and spirit of the *Gospel Advocate,* its subscription list five years hence will be much smaller than now   More alliance has been made for Brother Lipscomb than would have been made for any one else, but there is a considerable element and a growing one in Tennessee that is tired of just such things as D L is getting off weekly. Mark my words. The majority of the live members of our churches in Tennessee will in less than five years be contributing to our foreign and home missionary societies. The *Advocate* need not support these societies in order to live. It could oppose them if it were done in a fair way, and keep up for a while at least. .   Every time the *Advocate* denounces those who contribute through these societies in effect as apostates, it makes life-long enemies to the *Advocate* and life-long friends of the societies. The response to an appeal to take Tennessee for organized mission work you will find is going to be prompt and liberal, and those who are working to that end are to my knowledge counting largely on the unreasoning opposition of Brother Lipscomb to help the movement.[29]

As events proved, Garrison was a failure as a prophet.

[28]David Lipscomb, "Criticisms," *Gospel Advocate,* Vol XLVII, No 9 (March 2, 1905), p 137
[29]F D Srygley, "From the Papers," *Gospel Advocate,* Vol XXXII, No 17 (April 23, 1890), p 257

Chapter XVIII

THE NASHVILLE BIBLE SCHOOL

Many years before the Nashville Bible School was established, David Lipscomb had settled his mind upon the value of such schools.

> We have always believed in Bible schools, Bible academies, and Bible colleges We have believed it the duty of every Christian who teaches to teach the Bible, to teach it as thoroughly and systematically as it can be taught to the pupils
> Our objection to Bible college has been that they were especially to make preachers The evil of the churches, the corrupting influence is found, we are sure, in the position of the preachers and the tendency to subject everything in the churches to the work of the preacher .
> If the brethren will just teach the Bible to all who will attend whether they intend to be preachers or follow any other call ng in life, they will do a good work and none will more heartily rejoice in that labor that I will [1]

Indeed, the real question with Lipscomb was, how a Christian could support a school where the Bible was not taught

> There has never been a question with me as to whether a Bible school is right or not The question that has troubled me is: Can a Christian teach or support a school that is not a Bible school? "Whatsoever ye do in word or deed, do all in the name of the Lord Jesus." (Col. 3: 17) To do it in his name is to do as he would do were he in our places. Does any one believe, if Jesus were here as we are, he would teach a school in which he was not permitted to teach the Bible as the most important consideration of life? If he would not, his servants should not Does any one believe he would send children to a school in which the Bible was not the chiefest text-book? . . .[2]

Nothing could be of more paramount interest to a Christian parent, in Lipscomb's estimation, than to see that his children were taught in a school where the Bible was studied daily.

> We have long insisted that Christians ought to have Christian schools for their children, and children ought to study the New

---

[1]David Lipscomb, "Bible College," *Gospel Advocate*, Vol XIX, No 32 (August 16, 1877), p 505
[2]David Lipscomb, "Teaching the Bible," *Gospel Advocate*, Vol XLVI, No 32 (August 11, 1904), p 505

Testament, especially, daily, as they study the spelling book or the reader. The lessons of the New Testament ought to be stamped indelibly upon the impressible minds of the children, before they are filled with other things. . .

. . . If Christians were half as determined that their children should be taught the Bible at school, as the opponents of religion are that theirs should not be, there would be schools all over our land teaching the Bible But as matters now exist in our relations with the world, the Bible will not be taught in the common schools.[3]

Shortly after the Civil War Lipscomb caught the "education fever," had the desire to establish a school, but in a few years that fever subsided. It was not that he had lost interest in schools but only that his other work overshadowed it. In the fall of 1877 he wrote:

We are glad to know of the prosperity of all our schools. We wish them much success We wish them to stand on a solid platform of true worth, that will raise them above all jealousy and sensitiveness. We once had a very fervid educational fever It has wholly subsided, so far as any disposition to work in that direction ourself. But we wish those who engage in it, usefulness and success. We find some who when giving our time and means to it, were lukewarm, are now quite fervid in their zeal. That is all right, we think. We find, too, that every brother who becomes identified with a location or school, thinks that the best location and school in the world. We have found they frequently change their opinions with a change of location.[4]

Members of the church around Nashville had been interested in schools since 1842 when Tolbert Fanning had organized what became Franklin College. This school flourished until the Civil War when it was forced to close. During the war, its buildings were used by the armies as barracks, but as soon as the conflict ended, plans were made to reopen it. On October 2, 1865 the school reopened. On October 28, a little boy, in the act of "burning out his chimney" accidentally caught the main building on fire. There was no insurance and the cost of the fire was estimated at forty-thousand dollars. For a short time George A. Kinnie and A. J ("Jack") Fanning tried to continue the school but with little success.

---

[3]David Lipscomb, "Schools," *Gospel Advocate,* Vol XXV, No 31 (August 1, 1883), p 482
[4]David Lipscomb, "Schools," *Gospel Advocate,* Vol XIX, No 37 (September 13, 1877), p 567.

For several years brethren were undecided as to what next to do. At a meeting of the Board of Trustees following the burning of the main building, it was decided to build a large college in Middle Tennessee. It was proposed that between two hundred and three hundred thousand dollars should be raised. There was a strong emphasis, of course, on the fact that these new buildings must be fire-proof. The school, it was hoped, would be sufficiently endowed that all worthy students could attend gratis. The people of Tennessee, however, were in hard financial circumstances. The money could not be raised, and the dream for a large school in Middle Tennessee was lost.

Tolbert Fanning's interest in educational advantages for the poor was not to be defeated so easily. He announced in June, 1867 that "Peace College" would be erected upon the ruins of Franklin College. A charter was granted and a Board of Trustees was provided. On the board were P. S. Fall, James Metcalfe, James C. Owen, O. T. Craig, David Hamilton, David Lipscomb, John W. Richardson, Tolbert Fanning and John Hill. But, one hears nothing more of "Peace College," so it likewise proved to be but a vision.

One dream, however, was realized   On December 10, 1866 the Tennessee State Legislature granted a charter for the founding of Hope Institute. On the board of trustees were E. G Sewell, P. S. Fall, V. M. Metcalfe, W. H. Goodloe, T. W. Brents and A. J. Fanning. This school was for the education of girls. Hope Institute continued to function until 1884 when the property was given over to the establishment of Fanning Orphan School. Fanning, before his death in 1874, had expressed a special interest in educating orphan girls. His wife, Charlotte Fanning, who had constantly guided Hope Institute kept this thought in her mind. Finally in 1883 she deeded one hundred and sixty acres of land, including Hope Institute, to the new Fanning Orphan School. In 1867 Fanning had spent $17,500 for sixty acres of ground plus the buildings for Hope Institute. The buildings, however, had suffered considerable decay. A Board of Trustees consisting of John G. Houston, J. C. Wharton, C. W. McLester, John H. Ewing, J. R. Handley, Dr. E. Charleton, A. J. Fanning, S. S. Wharton, P. S. Fall, J. P. McFarland, W. H. Timmons, O. T. Craig, and David Lipscomb, was appointed. The Board spent

Christmas week of 1883 looking over the grounds and making estimates of the amount of expenditure needed to put the buildings back up in first class condition. The outlay of money needed was negligible, the work was done, and in the fall of 1884 Fanning Orphan School opened to "train white girls for virtuous Christian lives."

But such a school by its very nature obviously could not meet all the needs. Nashville, educationally, had come to be looked upon as the "Athens of the South." There was a gradual realization that so far as the plea for the ancient order was concerned it was also the "Jerusalem of the South." David Lipscomb's frequent assertion that in proportion to population the church was better established in Nashville than in any city in the world was no doubt correct. The eyes of the church in the South were turned toward the capitol of Tennessee. Mars Hill College at Florence, Alabama, which T. B Larimore had run for seventeen years, closed its doors in 1887. Here, some of the South's influential preachers had been educated. This small school, like so many others, was constantly harassed by financial worries. When the doors closed, the youth of the South looked for other places to be educated. Bethany College, they felt, had been swallowed up by advocates of innovations which made it undesirable. The College of The Bible at Lexington had its attractions not only for its proximity to the South, but the name of scholarly J. W. McGarvey held some magic power But one major objection attached itself to the College of The Bible: its adherence to Society plans to do the work of the Church. McGarvey, while being a strong opponent of the use of the instrument, was a devotee of Society plans. C L. Loos, president of the College, was also president of the Foreign Christian Missionary Society, and there is ample evidence to show that he was an extremely partisan president So, both the College of The Bible and Bethany College were strongly objectionable to many of the members in the South It is not unlikely that many around 1890 expressed their wish to see a school established nearer home and free from these objectionable features

However, David Lipscomb was not the type of an individual to project an institution to hurt another. No matter how correctly this might at times be said of others it cannot be correctly said of Lipscomb that he would establish a school in Nashville for the express purpose of hurting the College of The Bible. McGarvey, however, was strongly suspicious, and as soon as the Nashville Bible School was established, accused Lipscomb of jealousy toward the College of The Bible, and of having a desire to hurt it. No one knew better than McGarvey, Lipscomb's opposition to Societies and of McGarvey's inconsistent position regarding them. But still, at this time, Lipscomb would practice patience with his errors in the hope of leading him—and the school—back on more apostolic ground.

In March, 1889 James .A. Harding came to Nashville to conduct a meeting. Before he left the city, he had been there seven months, and besides conducting meetings, held his great debate with J. N. Moody, the Baptist preacher. During the debate, Harding stayed in Lipscomb's home, and the two discussed the possibility of starting a Bible School in Nashville. Lipscomb asked Harding to join him in the project. Harding agreed that he would do so as soon as he had caught up on all his obligations to hold meetings, which would take him about two years. Of this talk with Lipscomb Harding later wrote,

Sixteen years ago I began a meeting in Nashville, Tenn., in March. The meetings were continued for nearly seven months. Brother David Lipscomb and I talked of the many fields that were white for the harvest for which laborers could not be found. Daily we were receiving pressing calls for evangelistic work for which we could not find workers. We did not have suitable schools in which to educate our children, and so they were being sent to sectarian or digressive institutions. The influence of these schools, so far as religion is concerned, is more or less baleful. And so we talked about starting a school in which we should teach the Bible daily to every student. I had been thinking about such a work, hoping and praying that I might have an opportunity opened to me to enter upon it, for about sixteen years. Brethren W. H. Timmons and W. H. Dodd joined us in the work. And so two years and six months after Brother Lipscomb and I began to talk about it the Nashville School was opened in a large, comfortable old brick building in Nashville, which had once been one of the fine homes in the city Six young men were enrolled the first day. We enrolled in all thirty-two that session. Our average daily attendance, I suppose, was about twenty-five. Our students led about 250 souls to Christ during the summer vacation During the session they had been great helpers to Brethren Allen and Mead in planting the Green Street Church, which is now one of the most earnest and faithful of the churches of the city, a congregation that has already developed from its membership several efficient preachers, including brethren Allen, Mead, McPherson, our young correspondent, James A. Allen, and others   Brother Dan Gunn at the time he began to preach, was a member of this congregation, I believe.   The Bible School did a great work in that first year. . .[5]

From that first private conversation between Lipscomb and Harding the discussion of the possibility of such a school was passed around. J C. McQuiddy gently broke the news that something was in the wind when he wrote in his column on "Miscellany" in the *Advocate:*

Nashville is justly considered the "Athens of The South " With many fine institutions of learning located here, this city certainly has a right to the title   We learn from the *Baptist Reflector* that the Baptists have completed arrangements for establishing a Female College in South Edgefield   The thought occurs to us, why have not the disciples a good institution of learning in this city?   We are sure it is not because the location is not a good one, not because there is no desire for a good school here among the disciples   We have known of the subject being discussed and agitated by some and all concurred in the opinion that by all means we should have a first class school here.   The Methodists are represented here by the Vanderbilt and the Nashville College for young ladies, the Catholics by St Cecilia, and then there is the Wards Seminary, claiming to be non-sectarian, the State Norman, Woolwine's High School, Montgomery Bell Academy, The Fisk and Roger Williams Universities, colored schools.   Besides these, the public schools, many small and select schools, and yet out of all these there is not one under the control of the disciples   It occurs to us that the right man could build up a first class school here among the disciples.   This is only suggestive. . .[6]

Gradually, interest in establishing such a school increased and by the following spring, McQuiddy could write,

That it is desirable to have a good Christian college in Nashville will certainly be conceded by all.   Nashville deservedly has the title, the Athens of The South.   While others have the finest educational facilities here, our people have not a single school in the city under their control.   If we wish to educate our boys and girls we must send them away from home   Those who desire

[5]James A. Harding, "Bible Schools and Colleges," *Christian Leader and the Way,* Vol XXIX, No 15 (April 11, 1905), p 8
[6]J. C. McQuiddy, "Miscellaneous," *Gospel Advocate,* Vol XXIX, No 33 (August 14, 1889), p. 522.

to educate their sons for the ministry have usually sent them to another state Is it possible that a great people in a great state and country cannot establish a good school for the education of their sons and daughters?

One brother is certainly in earnest about this matter He proposes to give ten acres of beautiful ground out about three miles from the city He says the ground is as beautiful as the Vanderbilt campus He has thirty-five acres and, at his death will deed all the land to the trustees of the college The street railway management now say, that the electric cars will be running there inside of twenty-four months We would be glad to hear from all who are interested in establishing a good college here and who will work to accomplish this end [7]

By the next January, the "rumor" that Nashville was to have a Bible School went far and wide. *The Apostolic Guide* of Louisville, Kentucky commented tersely,

It is rumored that a Bible College is to be started soon at Nashville, Tenn. in the interest of sound theology Rumor also intimates that T B Larimore is to be the presiding genius

When McQuiddy read the above in the *Guide,* he playfully rejoined,

Come now brethren, you are too old in the business to go publishing things on *rumor* Wonder if a *woman* is editing the News Department on the *Guide* [8]

It was not, however, until June that the public in general was allowed in on the news that the Bible School was to be a reality David Lipscomb wrote,

It is proposed to open a school in Nashville, in September next, under safe and competent teachers, in which the Bible, excluding all human opinions and philosophy, as the only rule of faith and practice, and the appointments of God, as ordained in the Scriptures, excluding all innovations and organizations of men, as the fullness of divine wisdom, for converting sinners and perfecting saints, will be earnestly taught The aim is to teach the Christian religion as presented in the Bible in its purity and fullness, and in teaching this to prepare Christians for usefulness, in whatever sphere they are called upon to labor Such additional branches of learning will be taught as are needful and helpful in understanding and obeying the Bible and in teaching it to others [9]

[7] J C McQuiddy, "Miscellaneous," *Gospel Advocate*, Vol XXXII, No 22 (May 28, 1890), p 346
[8] J C McQuiddy, "Miscellany," *Gospel Advocate*, Vol XXXIII, No 6 (February 11, 1891), p 90
[9] David Lipscomb, "Bible School," *Gospel Advocate*, Vol XXXIII, No 24 (June 17, 1891), p 377

As plans to establish the Bible School took on concrete form, the thought of a "superintendent" naturally arose. David Lipscomb pushed aside the thought that he might head the school. As a trustee at the Fanning Orphan School, editor of the *Gospel Advocate,* a gospel preacher and a farmer, he found his time mostly taken. He would consent to teach one Bible Class but that is all. As to a superintendent, attention turned first toward T. B. Larimore. Larimore had gained wide popularity as an eloquent preacher and a devoted Christian. Moreover, his experience at Mars Hill made it appear that he was the right man for the position. Larimore, therefore, was invited to accept the superintendency. His answer, however, was held up while he weighed the offer. By August, 1891, it was still thought Larimore would come, but no definite answer had been reached. It was planned to open the school in September, but the opening date was pushed forward to October. Early in September came Larimore's formal decline of the offer, and in his place, went William Lipscomb as a teacher. James A. Harding was made the superintendent.

What lay behind Larimore's rejection? Maybe nothing. Or again, maybe Larimore realized that his attitude toward Missionary Societies and instrumental music was not the same as David Lipscomb's and that sooner or later it may be the occasion of conflict. A few years after this, Hall L. Calhoun expressed to James A. Harding *privately* that he was against the society and the use of the instrument, but because he refused to state his position *publicly,* Harding refused to allow him on the faculty of the Nashville Bible School. When Harding spoke to Larimore about these issues, Larimore replied that he did not know what the Bible taught on them. Harding had already planned to use Larimore in a series of lectures at the Bible School, but now refused to allow Larimore to deliver them. Whether underneath, this may have had anything to do with Larimore's refusal cannot be for certain said. but it is interesting to notice the possibilities

During the summer, Lipscomb wrote·

The responses from those desiring to attend such a Bible school as we have spoken of, has been encouraging. There are from twenty-five to fifty young men anxious to enjoy the help at once of this school. The responses from those willing to aid with their means, in such a school. have not been so encouraging. Shall we

not brethren put such a school in operation and aid those who
wish to devote their lives to the service of God?[10]

David Lipscomb was undoubtedly correct in asserting a few
years later that the Nashville Bible School was started quietly
and without much publicity in response to a widespread demand.
School opened on Monday, October 5, 1891 in a dwelling house
at 104 Fillmore Street   There were six students to enroll the
first day.   Students came from Kentucky, Tennessee. Alabama,
Arkansas, California and Texas.   Thirty-two regularly enrolled
students entered the school that first year, twenty-four of these
were preparing to be preachers.   Besides these, there were twenty-
one others who attended a Bible class.   Nothing is said about
young women being enrolled although two or three years later
we are assured that from the very beginning a few girls attended
"though not many."   A boarding-house keeper who wanted to
dispose of his belongings was bought out, and the boys moved
into the house where they paid their board at the rate of two
dollars a week.   Tuition was three dollars a month to the boys
who could pay.   Those who could not, went free; no worthy
young man was turned away for lack of funds.   "No one," wrote
Lipscomb, "is trying to make money out of the school."

Courses taught included English, Latin, Greek, Mathematics,
Logic, Metaphysics, and Natural Science.   In addition, the Bible
was taught "above everything else."   There were three daily re-
citations from the Bible.   The first class was in a study of the
Old Testament, which by the close of the first session at Christmas,
was expected to complete the Pentateuch.   The second class was
on the New Testament, and the third studied the Bible in a
topical form.   Lipscomb taught the class in New Testament while
the other Bible classes were taught by Harding.   Every student
was required to have at least one Bible class a day.   He was
expected to memorize the contents of each chapter of the Bible.
The class in New Testament was expected to memorize all the
sermons of Christ and the apostles which are recorded in the
four gospels and in Acts.

The first year closed on Thursday night, May 26, 1892 Reci-
tations, essays and addresses were made by the young men.

The school now looked forward to its second year. J. W.

---

[10]David Lipscomb, "That Bible School," *Gospel Advocate*, Vol. XXXIII,
No 28 (July 15, 1891), p 445

Grant, a graduate of Kentucky University, was employed to teach. Thirty-four students enrolled that fall, "all save two or three, preparing to spend their lives in teaching the lost the way of life" During the school year these young men preached constantly in the city and country around Nashville. By March, 1893 the *Advocate* reported that forty-two persons had obeyed the gospel "under their ministry."

The second year of school had closed May 31, 1893. Forty-two young men had been enrolled. J. W. Grant and James A. Harding had taught full time, and David Lipscomb, one hour a day. Expenses had been increased the second year over the first. Tuition was now five dollars a month; board, two dollars and a quarter a week, and matriculation fees were three dollars It was estimated that total cost for the year would not run over one hundred and fifty dollars. Young men who wanted to preach, but who could not pay, were admitted free But this worked a hardship on the school, and Harding urged others to help out.

. . . It is a fact that many young men who want to attend the school cannot pay tuition and board. In some cases congregations send and sustain them; in others, individuals have done it; some have worked their way through. In no case has a young man, properly commended to us, been turned away because he lacked means. Next sessions we will need much more help in this line We would like to hear from individuals and churches who will take part in this good work The man who wishes to invest means for Christ, we think, cannot find a better field for investment. Any one, male or female, wishing to study the Bible will be received in the school.[11]

Very early in 1893 plans were begun for opening the school for its third session that fall. Lipscomb was impressed with the fact the school's present buildings were very unsatisfactory. Could a new location with more suitable quarters be found he felt confident of an enrollment of one hundred students. Consequently, in the September 7, 1893 issue of the *Gospel Advocate* Lipscomb announced that a tract of land consisting of two acres or more on which was a large brick building had been purchased This old building was made into a boarding house. Two large classrooms were erected and a home for the superintendent W H Dodd and wife volunteered to manage the boarding house free of charge. In

---

[11]James A Harding, "The Nashville Bible School," *Gospel Advocate*, Vol XXXIV, No. 31 (August 4, 1892), p 485

this new location on Spruce Street the Bible School opened its third
session. This term opened with Dr J S. Ward, a graduate of the
medical school at the University of Tennessee, added to the faculty.
Harding was now teaching Latin, Greek and Bible, Grant, mathematics and "the English branches"; and Dr. Ward, classes in
chemistry and physiology.

Gradually the influence of the school broadened. The young
preachers were encouraged to spend their summers preaching the
gospel in destitute fields. Grabbing their Bibles at the close of
a session, these youths would head for the country school houses
and brush arbors from Mississippi to Kentucky. During the
summer of 1893 all the "boys" together baptized over five hundred
people and established six congregations. The next summer the
number of baptisms was over one thousand, two hundred. During
the summer of 1896 it was estimated that in the five years the
school had been established its young preachers had 'led three
thousand and four hundred into the church, and had established
twenty-eight congregations.

The fourth session opened with the school becoming gradually
a more pretentious affair. During the summer of 1894 new buildings were erected on the South Spruce Street property that added
twenty-eight more rooms for the school's use   There were eighty-
nine students in all during this session, eighteen of whom were
girls. Forty-eight of the number were preachers. This was a
great enrollment, offering bright prospects for a school with as
lowly a beginning as this one. The next spring—the spring of
1895—Dr. T. W. Brents delivered a series of lectures for the
Bible School. As he walked across the lawn one day, he spoke
prophetically, "This is a big thing, a much bigger thing than I
expected to find here; there is no telling whereunto this will
grow."[12] At this time there were four buildings on the two and
a quarter acres on South Spruce Street—the "Recitation Rooms,"
boarding department for young men, and the homes of J. W.
Grant and James A. Harding.

From 1896 through the spring of 1902 the school had a yearly
average enrollment of one hundred and twenty-five students. That
same spring the grounds, buildings and equipment of the school
were valued at twenty-five thousand dollars. In that brief span

---

[12]David Lipscomb, "Bible School Notes," *Gospel Advocate*, Vol XXXVII,
No 26 (June 27, 1895), p. 407.

of time the school had grown considerably. At the turn of the century James A. Harding had resigned at the Bible School to go to Bowling Green, Kentucky to start the Potter Bible School W. Anderson, of Maury County, Tennessee, was chosen superintendent in his place. In 1901 the first sizable bequest of money was given to the school by Fannie Pond, who stipulated in her will that twelve thousand dollars should go to it, the interest of which was to pay the way of worthy young men to get an education.

In some respects the Nashville Bible School was undergoing some changes, whether for the good or not may be a mooted question. Coming shortly after Harding left to go to Bowling Green, the Nashville Bible School was incorporated The exact date of this was February 2, 1901 A Board of Trustees made up of seven men was appointed So far as the records go the separation was peaceful, and was occasioned by only one factor—Harding's desire to establish a similar school in Bowling Green However, it hardly takes more than a neophyte to know that the full truth, especially as it respects motives, is rarely put out for the public to read. It is not at all unlikely that the separation of Harding and Lipscomb at this time had occurred when Lipscomb announced his intention of incorporating the school to enable it to become a larger one.

In the attention given to degrees the Nashville Bible School also underwent some change with the turning of the century. In the summer of 1894 Harding wrote,

We confer no degrees. It is vain to use empty titles, and the degrees D D., A.B., A M , B S , Ph D , etc , in this country are just that, they are so common and so easily obtained But when a student has finished our four-years' course, maintaining a standing of seventy and above, we present to him as a diploma book. beautifully and substantially bound, stamped as a gift from the school to him. containing a statement of the length of time he has been with us, of the branches he has studied, and giving his monthly standing in each study for the entire time If he remains longer than four years this will be certified to in the book, and his monthly standing given The presentation will be publicly made, and will be, we think, more valuable than any degrees we could confer [13]

But, in the spring of 1901 Lipscomb announced,

The Nashville Bible School has been incorporated, and will

---

[13]J A Harding, "The Nashville Bible School Extracts from Catalogue," *Gospel Advocate,* Vol XXXVI, No 26 (June 28, 1894), p 405.

hereafter more rigidly encourage a regular curriculum of study, and will confer the literary and scientific degrees common in the college and higher institutions of learning.[14]

Now that the school was incorporated, and intended to give degrees and look toward more extended work, it was time to think about expansion On Granny White Pike, two miles below the corporate city limits, David Lipscomb had his farm. He gave this to the school, which necessitated immediate preparation on the buildings. So Lipscomb wrote,

. . . To continue the school, we must have more buildings. A good tract of land outside of the city limits, near the street car line, has been secured. Stone foundations of two buildings have been built and are ready for the brickwork. One of the buildings is forty-four feet wide and seventy-five feet long. It is to be two stories high, for a chapel and eight recitation and library rooms. The other building is in the form of a T, one hundred and sixteen feet by one hundred and twenty-five feet, and is to be three stories high. This is to be for lodging rooms for the boys, and also contains a kitchen and a dining room. There is a residence on the place that, with some additions, will furnish rooms for the girls From present prospects, we will need room for at least from one hundred to one hundred and twenty boys and at least fifty girls. These buildings will cost not less than sixteen or seventeen thousand dollars. If we could sell our present buildings for cash, we could realize twelve thousand dollars on them; but we do not think it possible to do this in time to help in the new buildings. We believe that with about five thousand dollars from friends abroad, we can place the buildings without debt. We have begun the building with the confidence that this amount would be cheerfully given for the work. We are compelled to begin now and press the work vigorously to be ready for use next September It will not do to have the school in debt, because the income of the school will not pay debts It really does not run the school as it should. Those conducting the school have made greater sacrifices to run it than they should be asked to do. . .[15]

And so, in the summer of 1903 the Nashville Bible School moved to its new location on Granny White Pike. When school opened that fall, classes met in two large brick buildings that had been erected during the summer In slightly over a decade the school had made it evident that it was here to stay.

---

[14]David Lipscomb, "Nashville Bible School," *Gospel Advocate*, Vol XLIII, No 23 (June 6, 1901), p 361
[15]David Lipscomb, "The Nashville Bible School," *Gospel Advocate*, Vol XLV, No 9 (February 26, 1903), p 136

Two ideas were prominent with the founders of the school: viz. the Bible should be uppermost in the course of studies, and the school did not exist exclusively to prepare young men to preach.

The Nashville Bible School originated in the twofold desire on the part of disciples of Christ to see schools in which children, while gaining an education to prepare them for the duties of life, will be also daily taught the Bible as the most important study of life and as the only rule of faith and life, excluding all additions and devices of human wisdom from the faith, work, and worship of the Christian. This purpose was set forth in the original subscriptions to build the school, in the following clause "The supreme purpose of the school shall be to teach the Bible as the revealed will of God to man and as the only and sufficient rule of faith and practice, and to train those who attend in a pure Bible Christianity, excluding from the faith all opinions and philosophies of men, and from the work and worship of the church of God all human inventions and devices Such other branches of learning may be added as will aid in the understanding and teaching of the Scriptures and will promote usefulness and good citizenship among men "

It was further set forth in the deed conveying the property on Spruce Street for the use of the school in the following clauses or statements: That the property shall be used for maintaining a school in which, in addition to other branches of learning, the Bible as the recorded will of God and the only standard of faith and practice in religion, excluding all human systems and opinions and all innovations, inventions and devices of men from the service and worship of God, shall be taught as a regular daily study to all who shall attend said school, and for no other purpose inconsistent with this object. This condition being herein inserted at the request of the founders of the proposed Bible School, the same is, hereby declared fundamental and shall adhere to the premises conveyed as an imperative restriction upon their use so long as the same shall be owned by said Bible School, or its trustees, and to any and all property which may be purchased with the proceeds of said premises in case of sale or reinvestment, as hereinafter provided. .   All trustees shall be members of the church of Christ, in full sympathy with the teachings set forth above, and willing to see that they are carried out. Any one failing to have these qualifications shall resign or be removed.[16]

Preachers, as a professional class of men, generally excited the contempt of many in those earlier years Allied with the professional status of the preacher was the opinion that no man was

[16]J. S Ward, "Nashville Bible School Notes," *Gospel Advocate*, Vol XLIV, No. 32 (August 7, 1902), p 505

qualified to preach who did not have a college education. David
Lipscomb himself did not share this feeling   He never wanted
to view himself as a preacher   Rather he thought of himself as
doing the work which he could do   As a Christian, he must do
all the good in life that it was possible   He expounded the word
because he could not be a Christian and fail to do so, but he had
no desire to preach a day longer than he could do good.   He re-
sented the popular insinuation that the study of the Bible was for
preachers to professionally qualify them, while others should remain ignorant of it   Shortly after the Civil War, a great interest
was displayed in educating preachers, and Lipscomb thought that
either consciously or unconsciously the impression was being made
that a man was not qualified to preach unless he had a college
education.

We certainly do not object to an education, but we protest
against the idea that no one but a college educated man is fitted
to preach the gospel.   The great qualification of the preacher is,
to thoroughly imbue his heart with the truths and spirit of the
Gospel, and then study how to impress them upon his fellow-men [17]

But the idea of the professional preacher was growing in the
world, and professionalized training was becoming prominent.   In
view of the rising drift in thought, F. D Srygley's lengthy comments are well worthy of consideration

An educated preacher a hundred years ago was simply a preacher
who had a classical education   There were few, if any, schools
then especially designed and operated to educate men for the
ministry as a profession, but within the last century schools have
been established by the various denominations to give men special
education as professional preachers.   An educated preacher now
means a preacher who has attended a school where men are
educated for the ministry as a profession   Graduation from such
a school is a passport to a position as a professional preacher in
any denomination, while the lack of such education and training
as these schools give puts consecrated men who know the truth
and preach it from a sense of duty in a spirit of self-denial at a
disadvantage in any denomination   The idea on which all such
schools are founded, and by which they exist, is that men who
are educated in them can preach better than men who have never
attended them   This creates a demand for preachers who have
attended such schools, and causes people in general and churches
in particular to underestimate preachers who have not taken the

---

[17]David Lipscomb, "Education of Preachers," *Gospel Advocate,* Vol IX,
No 8 (February 21, 1867), pp 157, 158

prescribed course in such institutions   Of course no man who is worthy to preach is unwilling to attempt it unless he feels that he is thoroughly furnished unto all good works and fully prepared and qualified to declare the whole counsel of God, and the people naturally prefer to hear men preach who are supposed to be best qualified and prepared for the ministry   If there is something in such schools which prepares and qualifies men to preach, and which cannot be found anywhere else, it is easy to see that such institutions have a patent on the ministry and a monopoly in the business Moreover, a man who is specially educated as a professional preacher is poorly prepared for any other business or occupation To try to support himself in any other way than by preaching is to forfeit all his special education and training for the ministry as a profession   It is as a doctor who gives his attention to another occupation than the practice of medicine after a special course in a medical college   This creates a class of dependent professional preachers who must have remunerative employment as preachers or come to want   When the supply of such preachers exceeds the demand, there is a glut in the ministry which cannot be relieved by opportunities for remunerative employment in other vocations, because the unemployed preachers are not qualified to engage in other occupations   Moreover, professional preachers feel that it is not in keeping with ministerial dignity to earn their bread in the sweat of their faces, and inasmuch as they have prepared themselves to preach and have made no preparation to do anything else, they consider the churches under obligation to support them in the ministry   Places must be found or created for them, and the scramble for position discredits religion in the eyes of the world   Within the last few years several secular papers and some religious papers have stated that there is now such a glut in the ministry, and have argued that schools ought not to educate so many preachers for the next few years till the situation is relieved   The burden of supporting so many professional preachers is heavy on the churches, and doubtful methods of raising money are resorted to, and inventive genius is exhausted in devising organizations and schemes to make places and create salaries for professional preachers   In this rush for places, the interest every school feels in its graduates and every man cherishes for his alma mater and fellow-students tends to clannishness in mutual efforts to promote a common interest in the distribution of patronage   Charges have been openly made on high authority in more than one denomination within the last few years that great theological schools in this way practically dominate the preachers and churches to the extent of their influence   The effect of it is to centralize in such schools what might be termed "the appointing power" over the ministry, especially in denominations which have a congregational form of church polity. Such schools, probably-without intending it, gradually be-come a kind of ministerial "pie counter," as politicians would- say, around which aspiring young men, with an eye to the main chance in a desirable profession, crowd for a chance at the crumbs which fall from the institutional table in the distribution of patronage in what Alexander Campbell aptly termed "the kingdom of the clergy." In politics all this would be called "a ring" or "a party machine," but in religion it is known by the softer name of "an educated ministry." Preachers who do not rank in this class are relegated to "our poor and country charges," if, indeed, they are not denied any recognition at all in the ministry.

The idea that men who graduate from schools designed and operated specially to educate preachers can preach better than men who have not taken the prescribed course in such schools turns the attention of the people from the Bible to the schools as the source of religious light. The philosophy of it is that something about Christianity can be learned in such schools which cannot be learned from the Bible without the help of the school. This weakens the confidence of the people in their ability to read and under-stand the Bible without the help of such schools. The effect of this is to discourage efforts among people who cannot attend such schools to study the Bible for themselves, form their own conclusions as to what it teaches, and preach the gospel exactly as it reads in the New Testament. Instead of robust individuality in Bible study and independent vigor in faith, people accept the doctrine promulgated from the schools, even though it is contrary to what seems to them to be the plain teaching of the Bible. They gradually come to have more confidence in the dictum of the schools than in their own understanding of the Bible. This gives the schools the power, and sometimes creates in them the dis-position and desire to "lord it over God's heritage."[18]

Reaction to the establishment of the Nashville Bible School was varied. J. W. McGarvey felt "cross" at Lipscomb for start-ing it, thinking it might be a formidable competitor of the College of The Bible. J. M. Barnes of Alabama and M. C. Kurfees of Kentucky failed to have much enthusiasm for it, both men, as Lipscomb put it, "think they are against" such schools. *The Christian-Evangelist,* traditionally unable to see a distinction be-tween the school and its Missionary Society, ironically reported that the Nashville Bible School had been started. Daniel Sommer coolly received the word that the School had begun, and tersely commented,

---

[18]F. D. Srygley, "no title," *Gospel Advocate,* Vol. XLI, No 7 (February 16, 1899), p. 97.

There is a Bible School in Nashville, Tenn, which we presume is doing a good work, but if the brethren who have it in charge ever call it a college, and give the pupils a regular collegiate course, and a diploma with titles, then we predict that it will be an institution of mischief. Collegism among disciples led to preacherism, and preacherism led to organism and societyism, and these led to worldliness in the church.[19]

On the whole, the successful establishment of the Nashville Bible School ignited a flaming desire for such schools over the entire brotherhood Colleges were springing up everywhere. At Bowling Green, Kentucky James A. Harding had established Potter Bible School at the instigation of C. C. Potter and wife. Four years later, J. N. Armstrong announced that he. A. D. Gardner, R. C. Bell, B. F. Rhodes, and R. N. Gardner would open a new school at Paragould, Arkansas to be known as the Southwestern Bible and Literary College. Six weeks after this announcement was made came another saying that the location had been changed to Odessa, Missouri forty miles east of Kansas City. About the same time Southwestern Christian College was born at Denton, Texas, and a little earlier, Gunter Bible College at Gunter, Texas. Lockney Christian College had been in Texas since 1894 A. B. Barrett received inspiration from Lipscomb and Harding to establish Childers' Classical Institute (now Abilene Christian College) in Abilene, Texas in 1906.

There were many other colleges established shortly before and after the turn of the century. The inspiration for most of this came directly or indirectly from Harding and Lipscomb, and the influence of the Nashville Bible School.

The reaction to the establishment of the Nashville Bible School was both positive and negative. The positive reaction is seen in the wave of schools and colleges later to be set up in the brotherhood. Of far greater significance is the negative reaction. Daniel Sommer, editor of the *Octographic Review,* was the epitome of this negativism.

Schools in which brethren taught the Bible were almost as old as the restoration movement itself. Alexander Campbell had taught "Buffalo Seminary" in his home and closed it only when he realized that the students were less interested in the Bible

---

[19]Daniel Sommer, "Notes and Annotations," *Octographic Review,* Vol. XXVI, No. 47 (November 21, 1893), p. 1.

than they were in getting an education in those early days. But his interest in establishing a college had never subsided, although it was delayed some by the establishment of Bacon College in Kentucky. Bethany College which he set up in 1841 was in a large measure the climax of a life-long dream, and into it he poured the best of his energies until his death.

The principle behind the Bible school was almost never discussed. It was generally assumed that the schools were acceptable, and there were almost no suggestions to the contrary. It was not until the proposal of the missionary society was before the brotherhood that people began to critically examine into basic principles involved in human institutions.

Alexander Campbell and a corps of younger preachers consisting of Isaac Errett, W. K. Pendleton, C. L. Loos, W. T. Moore, and D. S. Burnet satisfied their minds that human institutions, whatever their nature, were acceptable to the Lord. The church *universal*, not the church local, was divinely commissioned to evangelize the world, teach the Bible, and exercise benevolence in works of charity. Since God had not told the church what *methods* to use to do its work, any method the best wisdom of the church devised was permissible on the ground of expediency. And so, largely through the influence of Campbell and his younger corps of lieutenants, the missionary society was inaugurated So also were Bible Societies, Publication Societies, Educational Societies, and Bible Colleges. The church could establish, maintain, own and operate these human institutions. In doing so it was using a method which God had left the church at liberty to use. This was one school of thought.

These, however, of this school of thought recognized prominent dangers. Chief of these was that the child of their creation might become strong enough to become their master. The human institutions must be subservient to the church, not masters over it. The church must control the institution, not the institution the church. Some, fully cognizant of this danger, launched into the promotion of these institutions with the same disquietness of an individual nursing a baby tiger. There was always the question, when the monster would grow up, would it devour the person that fed it?

In the process of time their worst fears were realized. J. H.

Garrison and the *Christian-Evangelist* cried more and more for centralization. The General Convention should become the voice of the brotherhood and the *Christian-Evangelist,* the agent of that voice. The *Christian Standard* viewed this trend with alarm, and the result was—and is—everything but an open division in these ranks.

Meanwhile others could not accept the viewpoint of Campbell and his lieutenants. They could find no scriptural warrant for the church universal acting as the church universal in an organic sense to do anything. The formation of human institutions to do the work of the church was a human addition to a divine plan, an assumption of the prerogative of God in making laws for his people, besides being a threat to the local independence and autonomy of the individual congregation. On this basis Jacob Creath, Jr. and Tolbert Fanning waged a relentless war against the Society.

For a quarter of a century it did not occur to the opponents of the Missionary Society to measure their principles against the Colleges. So thoroughly was Tolbert Fanning settled that the college belonged to a different category that he failed to notice Isaac Errett's witticism when Errett declared he could not take the opponents of the Society seriously as long as they persisted in operating colleges in which the Bible was taught.

The whole question as to the principles involved in the Bible College was opened when the trouble at Kentucky University burst before the brotherhood in the fall of 1871. John F. Rowe openly asked, "Are Colleges A Blessing Or a Curse?" and concluded with some indefiniteness that they must be a curse. Ben Franklin declared that he had always assumed colleges were permissible without examining into them, but the affair at Kentucky University had caused him to see the dangers of such schools. The brief remainder of his life was spent in opposing colleges. Jacob Creath, Jr. likewise turned against them and became an outspoken critic. David Lipscomb likewise cocked an eyebrow in the direction of Kentucky University, but his criticisms were more tempered. Kentucky University taught him two great lessons. One he was never to forget, and the other, he found easy to forget. The chief objective in the College of The Bible was to train preachers. He became convicted that this was wrong.

"We think the most fatal mistake of Alexander Campbell's life," he wrote at the time, "and one that has done much and we fear will do much more to undo his life's work, was the establishment of a school to train and educate young preachers.[20] This lesson Lipscomb would never forget, and when he established the Nashville Bible School it must be understood that this school was not to exist "to train and educate young preachers."

Kentucky University also taught Lipscomb the lack of wisdom employed in richly endowing colleges. McGarvey, representing a conservative element, was turned out of the school, and the "progressives," as Lipscomb called them, took over. Thus, the endowment that had been years in being accumulated would be used to tear down the cause it was given to build up. So Lipscomb wrote,

Endowment funds so universally are thus perverted to pull down what they are intended to build up, that we can hardly hope for a change.

Great amounts of money have been donated to build up the Christian religion. The religion of our Saviour exists today in spite of the influences exerted through nine-tenths of the amount given to endow schools for teaching that religion.[21]

This lesson Lipscomb found it easy to forget after he had established a school of his own.

For nearly a decade during and after the troubles at Kentucky University brotherhood periodicals gave considerable attention to Colleges. Then for a score of years almost nothing was said on the subject. Discussion on the matter has followed pretty much of a pattern from that day to this.

David Lipscomb's views on teaching the Bible in schools followed those of Tolbert Fanning before him. No human institution had any right, as he viewed it, to exist to do the work God gave the church. This principle was clear in Fanning's mind The simple fact was that a school, as he ran it, and believed they ought to be run, did not exist to do the work God gave the church. The school to him was a "worldly" institution, not a religious. The Bible did not regulate those things on the worldly side of a

---

[20] David Lipscomb, "Schools for Preachers," *Gospel Advocate*, Vol. XVII, No 15 (April 8, 1875), p. 345

[21] David Lipscomb, "Kentucky University," *Gospel Advocate*, Vol. XV, No. 42 (October 23, 1873), p 998.

man. The Bible did not tell a man what kind of a house to build, what kind of a horse to ride, how to plow his ground, how to earn his livelihood. These belonged to what Fanning would call the "worldly" side of a man. The principles of Christ may in a general way guide and control this side, but no more   The Bible does not tell a man, he reasoned, whether he ought to earn his livelihood by farming, teaching school, practicing law, build houses, or run a bank. These belong to the "worldly" side of man's life. Yet, if a man did any of these, and if that man were a Christian, he could hardly be a Christian and fail to teach the Bible in conjunction with his work   If a farmer were a Christian, he would teach the Bible to those that came under his influence, if he were a banker, a lawyer, a doctor, or a school teacher, he would do the same   He could not be a Christian and do otherwise.

Lipscomb was frequently called up to distinguish between the school, the Gospel Advocate Company, and the Missionary Society. He had condemned the Society as being a human institution doing the work of the church   Was not the school a human institution doing the work of the church? Was not the Advocate Company a human institution doing the work of the church? But to Lipscomb there was a difference. The business of sending out and overseeing missionaries was a work which God committed to a church. No human organization could do this work without usurping authority. On the other hand, the work of teaching the Bible was a work for every Christian.

The school was but a means of educating children. Lipscomb failed to see that the Bible ever committed the work of educating to anybody except parents. Yet, when children spent several hours a week learning worldly knowledge and only one hour a week learning the Bible, the result was they received the impression that Bible knowledge was a matter of indifference. So he wrote:

When we relegate the study of the Book of God to an hour in a week, and then in a loose and careless way, and study other things every day in the week, the children cannot avoid the conclusion, the one is a matter of indifference compared with the other. . .

Our effort in the Bible School is, to give Bible teaching its true importance in education, to train children to be better, truer Christians   We are doing what we believe should be done in teaching every child, whether he intends to farm or merchandise, preach the gospel or practice medicine [22]

Early in 1891 Lipscomb found himself in a controversy with P W Harsh through the columns of the *Advocate* Harsh defended the use of missionary societies He places the societies on a par with the orphan school, the Gospel Advocate Company, and the Sunday School But again, Lipscomb denied that the orphan school or the Advocate Company were parallel to the missionary society. He wrote:

And whenever you will convince me that the school is usurping any function of the church of God, takes out of its hands or the hands of individual Christians, what God has committed to it. I henceforth will oppose all schools The orphan school is for the same end as Hamilton College, or any other school Its purpose is to educate girls for usefulness that they may be able to make a living in a creditable way While educating them, we try to make Christians out of them Just as it is the duty of the farmer to try to make Christians of every one under his influence . I have never found where the Bible committed to the church or to anybody but parents, the work of educating their children for making a living . . I fail to see one single point of likeness in the two institutions.[23]

James A. Harding saw eye to eye with Lipscomb on the subject of a Bible School. His ideas were forthcoming in a discussion of the subject with J M McCaleb in 1895 McCaleb was in Japan as a missionary at this time Aside from McCaleb, almost all the brethren in the Japanese mission at this time were behind the society. McCaleb, in an attempt to think his way through the issue carefully, wrote to Harding, asking the difference between the Bible School and the Society in principle To this, Harding replies:

The day the Bible School becomes an organized society for preaching the gospel, teaching the scriptures, or for any other purpose, that day I leave it The Bible School is a *school,* that is all. . .

May the richest blessings of God ever rest upon this work, and may He forbid that it should ever become a Society organized for the purpose of doing what He has committed to His church

---

[22]David Lipscomb, "Bible Schools," *Gospel Advocate,* Vol. XXXIV, No 26 (June 30, 1892), p 404

[23]David Lipscomb, "Missionary Societies." *Gospel Advocate,* Vol XXXIII, No 5 (February 4, 1891), p 70

No living man is more intensely opposed to such a thing than am I, not even Brother McCaleb himself [24]

The relationships between the *Gospel Advocate* and the *Octographic Review* had on the whole been pleasant since Daniel Sommer took over the latter paper as editor. A few times the truculent James A Harding thought he saw some peculiarities in Sommer, and readily pointed them out, but on the whole, while these brief skirmishes were fiery, they were good-naturedly taken by both men. In 1894 Daniel Sommer ran a series of articles in the *Review* by way of examining Lipscomb's book on "Civil Government," Sommer, of course, holding the opposite viewpoints Lipscomb thought Sommer misrepresented him, and so, wrote out his answers to Sommer's charges, sent them to the *Review* with the request they be printed Sommer refused and announced that the discussion was closed Thereafter, Lipscomb wrote, "It seemed to me his misrepresentations were intentional, and his refusal arose from fear of exposure before his readers I passed the matter over without mention, willing for him to do what good he could, satisfied we could not work together " Sommer thereafter insisted that Lipscomb's coolness toward him was occasioned because he [Sommer] had "felt called upon to expose his errors "

Lipscomb in the meantime persisted in his policy of ignoring Sommer. While other writers of the *Gospel Advocate* for the next few years felt occasionally called upon to debate with him, Lipscomb rarely did, "willing for him to do what good he could," but satisfied that he and Sommer could never work together.

In January, 1901, a Brother Young of Oklahoma Territory sent a clipping on "Marriage and Divorce" written by Daniel Sommer to the *Advocate* with the request Lipscomb examine it. Lipscomb did and wrote briefly his own comments Sommer replied with a violent attack on the use of Sunday School citing two cases where the literature was wrong. E A Elam, then a young man, was writing some of the literature. He had commented that on the triumphal entry of Jesus into Jerusalem, the Lord had ridden an untrained ass, but Sommer took exception insisting Jesus had straddled two asses at once Elam replied to this by a gentle article, intending to disarm Sommer's criticisms

---

[24] James A Harding, "A Friendly Criticism," *Gospel Advocate,* Vol XXXVII, No 41 (October 10, 1895), p 662

by kindness, but Sommer again replied comparing Elam to an assassin that sneaked up behind his back. Elam hardly knew what to make of it, but Lipscomb was thoroughly disgusted. "Does not this," he asked, "savor more of the bravado of the slums, than of the courtesy and graces of the Christian?" And again, Lipscomb repeated his intention of ignoring Sommer,

> I have no disposition to hinder Brother Sommer in doing all the good he can. But I am sure we cannot work together, with his present style; so in the future, as in the past, I shall let him do all the good he can, and I will go the way that seems best to me.[25]

Lipscomb summarized Sommer's attitude by saying that Sommer "seems to think it is discussion to dogmatically state his opinions, often crude ones, and then to abuse the person who dissents from him."

With personal feelings already at a breaking point between the *Gospel Advocate* and the *Octographic Review,* between Daniel Sommer and David Lipscomb, and with Bible schools sprouting rapidly over the brotherhood, Daniel Sommer now felt obliged to attack these schools. He began in the fall of 1901 by reprinting the old articles of B. F. Leonard (L. F. Bittle) that had appeared in the *American Christian Review* in 1873. By the next year, 1902, Sommer was ready for a full-scale war against colleges.

Daniel Sommer's opposition to Bible colleges dated back to at least twenty-five years before this Beginning in the October 29, 1878 issue of the *American Christian Review,* he presented a series of articles on "Educating Preachers" which were intended as an attack against Bible Colleges. From 1878 to 1902 he had presented occasional articles on this subject, but it was not until 1902 that he waged a bitter war against them.

When Sommer first renewed his attacks against Bible Schools early in 1902, James A. Harding was the first to take notice and seek to reply. For a considerable time, the main force of the discussion was centered between Harding and Sommer, the *Advocate,* as a general rule, maintaining its policy of ignoring Sommer. It will be of special interest to observe what Sommer's objections were, and the answers that were commonly given to them. On the ground that the Bible Schools were unscriptural

---

[25]David Lipscomb, "Our Reason for Our Course," *Gospel Advocate,* Vol XLIII, No 20 (May 16, 1901), p. 312

organizations, Sommer found many points of criticism against them. It cannot be denied, in all fairness to Sommer and to the facts involved, that on many points he was right—more correct than his enemies ever gave him credit for being. Yet, it was unfortunate that he ever went to such an extreme and became so dogmatic and unyielding on that extreme.

Sommer, in noticing the catalogue of the Potter Bible School during the summer of 1903, observed that the school was established as a "most appropriate monument" to the memory of a man, Brother Potter. Sommer then quoted scriptures such as Numbers 20: 10 and showed that it had always been a desire of man for self-glorification, but that it had never pleased God for man to do this. He leveled the charge against Bible schools that they are, essentially, institutions built up for the purpose of glorifying man.[26] A man's ego was much more highly honored if he can be recognized as the president of a college or university than if he is known simply as a preacher of the gospel. There was nothing of the pomp, the show, about the latter. Suffice it to say that there is probably more point to the objection than most men are honest enough to admit.

But in the main, Sommer leveled two charges against the schools. They were charged, first, with glorifying man and seeking the exaltation of man; and, secondly, that Bible Schools involved the mistake of the misappropriation of the Lord's money. He objected strongly to churches contributing from the treasury to this work, and he even thought that if men were giving all they could to the church to do the work of the Lord, they would not have enough left to make large gifts of money to a Bible School. If a man had five thousand dollars to give to a Bible School, it was, with Sommer, a good sign he has not been giving to the church "according to his ability," and the five thousand he gave to the Bible School was but the amount he kept back from the church.

In years to come Sommer was to accuse both Alexander Campbell and David Lipscomb of holding back from the church, of saving money that rightfully should belong to the Lord, and of using that to establish schools. But Sommer could never be made to see that this was an overstatement of the case. When,

---

[26]Daniel Sommer, "Educating Preachers," *Octographic Review*, Vol. XLVI, No. 31 (August 4, 1903), p. 1.

for example, Sommer purchased the *American Christian Review,* he promised to pay fifteen thousand dollars for it. Where was he to get this money? By his own reasoning it could be gotten only by his taking it from the Lord.

It is hard to escape the conclusion that Daniel Sommer on the one side and David Lipscomb or James A. Harding on the other were not closer together in their thinking than they admitted. In Sommer's articles of 1878 on "Educating Preachers" his major criticism is against raising up preachers as a special class and bestowing upon them special training. Ten years after this he wrote another article in which he said,

Public sentiment is generally in favor of colleges for educating preachers. As a result thereof it endangers the reputation of any one to express a sentiment in opposition thereto   Opposition to colleges in any department is supposed to result from aversion to education, and surely, it is thought, none but erratics or simpletons could be averse to educating the rising generation. But we respectfully claim that one may possess common sense in a respectable degree and yet oppose the building of colleges by the church of Christ for the purpose of educating men to proclaim the unsearchable riches of Christ. . .

Colleges for educating preachers have proved to be perverting schools among disciples of Christ   When the corner stone of Bethany College was laid, the foundation for another clergy was begun, and thus it was that a revolutionist establish the institution which tends to destroy his revolutionary work. . .[27]

Near the close of his life, Daniel Sommer wrote again,

When discussing the college question among disciples of Christ at Odessa, Mo , in 1907, I was challenged to state what kind of a school I would endorse. My prompt reply was—"An untitled school such as Buffaloe Seminary, which Alexander Campbell conducted for years before he seemed to have thought of Bethany College." Such a school did not graduate pupils, and thus did not confer on them any empty, pompous titles. To such a school pupils went to learn without any idea of degrees or titles of any kind   Any such schools could never have impoverished the brotherhood by using millions of money to pile up brick and mortar and secure furnishings [28]

Taken at their face value, it is difficult to find any difference in

---

[27]Daniel Sommer, "Colleges Again," *Octographic Review,* Vol XXXI, No 47 (November 22, 1888), p 1

[28]Daniel Sommer, " 'Disciples of Christ' Challenged !" *Apostolic Review,* Vol. LXXXI, Nos. 9, 10 (March 2, 1937), p 8

these thoughts and in those of David Lipscomb or James A. Harding. Neither man believed it was right for the church to own and operate schools, or to turn its work over to a human institution like the school They protested vigorously against schools existing to give special training to preachers to promote a class of clergymen upon the brotherhood. That it was wrong for the church to organize societies—whether missionary, Bible, Publication or Educational—these men believed. But that the individual Christian, in connection with his livelihood, could teach Bible to all who came under his influence, whether he intended to preach or not, Lipscomb or Harding both believed. From all appearances Sommer believed it too.

This made the enigma of Daniel Sommer which Harding found difficult to solve. Harding had been sparring with Sommer only about a year, when Sommer announced,

But from the first response to what I have written on subject to the last, that I recollect having seen, I have been charged with teaching that it is "wrong" to teach the Bible in connection with secular things, and that it is even "wicked" to do so. . .

In regard to the charge just quoted I state that it is utterly destitute of truth, at least so far as the *Review* is concerned . .[29]

In the summer of 1905 Sommer proceeded to put in bold type and run in weekly issues of the paper the exact position of the *Review* on Bible Schools. He wrote:

This journal favors and advocates all schools, colleges and universities, which do not oppose the Bible, nor disregard the physical health and mental temperament of their pupils, and it contends that the Bible, or certain parts of it, should be used as a text book in every school, college and university.

Then Sommer proceeded to say:

But this journal is set in opposition to the New Testament Church establishing schools, or colleges, or universities, from either wholly or partly secular, as institutions separate from the church, and with money which should be placed in the treasury of the church. Such an institution, even if wholly religious, is as much of an innovation as a man-made missionary society . .[30]

His announcement that he was not against the Bible being taught in secular institutions, but only against the church es-

---

[29]Daniel Sommer, "A Plain Statement and Challenge," *Octographic Review,* Vol XLVI, No 31 (August 4, 1903), p 1

[30]Daniel Sommer, "The *Review's* Position in Regard to Education and Colleges," *Octographic Review,* Vol. XLVIII, No 30 (July 25, 1905), p. 6.

tablishing such schools with funds which belong to the Lord, immediately surprised Harding. He had not so judged Sommer's beliefs. After reading Sommer's first announcement of his position on July 25, 1905, Harding replied:

So his announcement in his issue of July 25, that he favors its use in all schools, colleges and universities, came to me "like a clap of thunder from a clear sky." I am amazed to think how successfully he kept me in the dark about his true position in all these years. While I and others were "raking him fore and aft with shot and shell," for opposing the use of the Bible in schools that teach secular learning, he was actually burning with zeal for that very thing—more in favor of it than any of us, and we did not find it out till July 25, 1905.[31]

Periodically from 1906 to the present the brotherhood has not been allowed to forget this controversy. It is difficult to escape the conclusion that if men of like thought of David Sommer understood the true nature of the colleges, they would oppose them less. But personalities, sectional pride, and prejudice have played no small part in keeping the question alive, and until time produces a more perfect work, there is little promise of a permanent cessation of hostilities.

---

[31]James A. Harding, "Another Effort to Secure a Discussion of the Bible School Question," *Octographic Review*, Vol. XLVIII, No. 34 (August 22, 1905), p. 8.

Chapter XIX

AUSTIN McGARY

The fictitious Praxiteles Swan of the Methodist Episcopal Church, South, Captain of the Fifth Texas Regiment, Confederate States Provisional Army is a composite character created from the yarns and legends which Lt. Col. John W. Thomason, Jr. heard from the "old timers" during his boyhood days in Huntsville, Texas. *The Lone Star Preacher,* Thomason's life of Praxiteles Swan, reads like another *Seventy Years in Dixie.* Some of the tales, woven into the fabric of Swan's life, Thomason picked up from one of the most colorful preachers the church has known in the last century—Austin McGary of Texas.

What David Lipscomb was to the church of Christ in Tennessee Austin McGary was to the church in Texas. "A. McGary," wrote J. D. Tant, "did more to stem the tide of innovations the Christian Church was making in Texas than any other man."[1] Possessing a boldness born of sagacity, the truculent Austin McGary was a match for any occasion where fearless reproof was demanded. "To be great," said Emerson, "is to be misunderstood," and McGary was often misunderstood. Some considered him too extreme, too bold to have the meekness and humility required of a Christian. Generally, a personal acquaintance with McGary convinced even his enemies that he was meek, although they were not always convinced that he was not yet too extreme. Weighed from the standpoint of the total effect of his life, Austin McGary had had few peers in the church within the last century.

Much of the colorful story of Austin McGary goes back to the days before he became a Christian, and in some cases, is intimately linked with the history of early Texas. When the army of Mexican General Cos was driven from San Antonio late in 1835, General Santa Anna, with a much larger army, determined to attack the city early the next year. The result was that on March 6th, 1836 the Alamo fell. Garrisoned by 183 men, they died to the last man. Two weeks later Texas General Fannin and his army

---

[1] J C Tant, "Brother Tant Answers," *Apostolic Review,* Vol. LXXX, No. 26 (June 23, 1936), p 15.

of 371 men were captured. A week after this all were shot except
the twenty who escaped. Sam Houston, a Major-General under
Governor Henry Smith, in the Texas provisional government,
was elevated to a full General   Gathering a small but courageous
band of men, he faced General Santa Anna   It was a dark hour
in Texas history   Houston's small army was poorly equipped
and far outnumbered numerically   But the fate of Texas was
hanging upon it. Houston skillfully retreated before Santa Anna,
and received taunts and jeers from citizens of Texas as well as
his own soldiers. At the San Jacinto River, however, he suddenly turned, drove against his enemy and destroyed the Mexican
army. But, where was Santa Anna, the chief prize? That evening,
a tired, bedraggled Mexican was brought in by Texas soldiers,
who recognized him only as another Mexican prisoner   He might
have remained unknown except that his own soldiers gave him
away   That night, Santa Anna was placed under guard as a
prisoner near the quarters of General Sam Houston   The guard
who watched Santa Anna all that night, and who had fought so
valiantly in the decisive battle was Isaac McGary, the father of
Austin McGary.

Isaac McGary had immigrated to Texas from Ohio, had fought
against superior odds to help gain Texas freedom, and afterward,
entered into Texas politics   He was County Court Clerk of
Walker County, and Sheriff of Montgomery County. In 1858
he ran on the Sam Houston ticket for the State Legislature, but
was defeated by three votes   Since first coming to Texas, Isaac
McGary had been a votary at the shrine of General Sam Houston
Houston who had been inspired to an indomitable courage by a
similar devotion to his close friend, General Andrew Jackson,
was thoroughly capable of similarly inspiring others. It was
natural that Isaac McGary should pass his great devotion to
General Houston on down to his own son, Austin McGary.

Austin McGary's childhood was spent in Huntsville, Texas
which also was the home of Sam Houston   Here, as a boy before the Civil War, McGary played with Sam Houston's children
One Sunday afternoon the children were playing ball on a vacant
lot. A doctor, a bitter enemy of Sam Houston, was walking
down the street, and was met by Houston, coming from the other
direction. Houston courteously spoke, "How are you, sir?"

To which the doctor replied, "I don't speak to a d--- rascal."

"That is the difference between you and me, sir. I do," said Houston, and walked on

Austin McGary was born February 6, 1846 at Huntsville, in Walker County, Texas His mother died when he was but eight or nine years of age Educational opportunities were scant, but McGary attended McKenzie Institute, a Methodist school, in Clarksville, Texas, in Red River County The Civil War broke out when he was sixteen For a while Texas was uncertain on which side to plunge The Union made pleasing overtures to her, and Governor Sam Houston pleaded with the State to remain loyal to the Union. Despite this, the Southern sympathizers were strong enough to secede Houston himself refused to take the oath of allegiance to the new government, and accordingly, was deposed Meanwhile, Texas regiments mustered into service over the state

When the "Huntsville Grays" were organized in Madison County, Austin McGary, although barely sixteen, joined them. Sam Houston, Jr,. son of the veteran fighter, also joined up, although against his father's wishes Some of the young men went off to join the Army of The Confederacy Sam Houston, Jr was seriously wounded at the battle of Shiloh, and was officially listed as killed But, after the battle, he was found alive by a Union army doctor, and nourished back to health. Before the "Huntsville Grays" were scattered to join Texas regiments, they marched in review before General Houston As they marched, Houston called out,

"Eyes right!"

Then asked, "Do you see anything of the son of my friend the great anti-secessionist who has been so anxious for us to go to war to preserve the Union?"

The company answered, loudly, "No!"

Houston then called, "Eyes left!"

"Do you see anything of Sam Houston's son?"

The answer: "Aye!"

McGary was placed in the Hamilton Guards which were later connected with General J. B Head's Brigade. McGary saw no action in the war, but was kept in coast guard service in Texas and Louisiana until the conflict ended.

Texas suffered along with other southern states at the close of the war, but hardly as much as those on whose soil the struggle had been waged. Coming back from the war, McGary found that his father's horses had been commandeered for the use of the Union Cavalry garrisoned at Navasota. About everything on his father's homestead of any value was gone except a buckboard and a sorrel buggy horse. His father was leaving for a trip to Tennessee, so McGary and a companion, decided to jump in the back of the buckboard and go along. As they rode along a narrow lane, two Union Cavalrymen came riding to meet them, and commanded they go over, and let them pass. As the cavalrymen rode past, McGary noticed that on the horses' flank, above the U. S. brand, was his father's own brand. McGary and his companion grabbed rifles, commanded the soldiers to dismount, took their horses, and rode ahead toward Tennessee.

Years later, when mounting age tried to grapple with the more modern iron horse—the Model T Ford—McGary found that his experiences in the Confederacy came in handy. Riding on South Main Street in Houston, Texas, he was stopped by a traffic policeman who severely reprimanded him for running a red light

"What do you mean, running a red light and giving me a ticket?" he asked the policeman.

"You drove right through that red light," replied the officer, "and that's a very dangerous practice. I will have to give you a ticket for it."

"I don't know what you are talking about. What are red lights?" queried McGary.

"Don't sit in that Model T and tell me that as long as I have seen you driving around Houston, you don't know what red lights are. What is your name so I can make out a ticket?"

McGary insisted that he didn't know what a red light was, yet he had driven a Model T for several years without an accident. He had always driven carefully, and upon coming to a corner, if he saw the cars "bunched up," he would stop; when the way cleared, he would drive ahead.

The policeman insisted, "I can't accept that answer. Give me your name and address." McGary was tired arguing, and so informed him of his name and address.

The officer was shocked. "You mean you're Aus McGary?"

he inquired. "I can't give you a ticket. My father was in the Huntsville Grays, and he would turn over in his grave if he thought I had given a ticket to Aus McGary. You are the only man in the world whose statement I will accept when you say that in all the years you have been driving that you had not known that you were to stop for a red light."

At the close of the war, when McGary was twenty years of age, he married Miss Narcissus Jenkins of Grimes County, Texas, a girl that was four years younger than he. Two children were born to them—a boy and a girl. The girl died at the age of eleven. In January, 1872 his wife died, and three years later, McGary married Miss Lucie Kitrell, who bore him nine children Three of these died in infancy, but the others lived to adulthood When the second wife died on June 1, 1897, her dying request was that McGary devote his entire life preaching this gospel, for by this time, McGary had become an ardent proponent of the plea for the return to the ancient order. A year later, McGary married Miss Lillian Otey of Huntsville, Texas, a young lady he had known all her life. She still lives [1950] in old age in Houston, Texas, at the old McGary home, 1709 Yale Street.

After the war, McGary entered into politics. Texas was still working at reconstruction. The country was sparsely settled, and its wide-open plains were inviting to unlawful citizens of other states. But the name of Austin McGary was soon to become legendary with Texas outlaws, and a name to be feared

The election in Madison County, in 1872 was to be a decisive affair. Since the close of the war, the republicans or "radicals," as they were sometimes called, had politically controlled the County. McGary entered the race as candidate for sheriff on the Democratic ticket, but the election race was no tea party. The former sheriff was lax in enforcing the law. His brother-in-law was the biggest cow thief in the county, and preyed upon the herds of the ranchers in the county without fear of interruption. Ex-confederate soldiers, democrats to the last man, had become discouraged at the mishandling of justice, and were indifferent about voting McGary saw that his only chance to win was to muster up enough interest among these ex-soldiers to get them to vote. As election time drew near, it was evident he was having surprisingly good success. But another problem now faced him.

The Republicans, sensing they were about to lose the election, felt their only chance was to get the negroes, all ex-slaves of course, to vote. However, all over the South, the negro-vote, no matter on which side it was cast, was unwelcome. McGary could not have been a Texas Confederate soldier and not resent it

In nearby Hempstead, there was a man known widely by the distasteful sobriquet, as a "nigger voter." McGary and his supporters learned that this man was riding from Hempstead, and McGary determined to interrupt him. Saddling his horse, he rode southward out of town to meet him, and waited in a grove of trees until he saw him approach Rider and horse galloped by. McGary pulled out of the trees, and trotted up behind the man. When the man turned, he was looking down the barrel of McGary's gun. McGary spoke emphatically,

"You're the 'nigger voter' from Hempstead, and I want to talk to you about this election. We don't want any outsiders here, and I want you to go back peacefully."

The stranger insisted that he was going to ride ahead, but McGary's gun helped persuade him to return to the grove of trees. Taking a jug from his saddle horn, he handed it to the man, and said, "Now, let's take a drink before we start talking " The man demurred, but the menacing-looking six-gun prodded him ahead He took a swallow, vomited it out violently, and cried,

"That tastes like castor oil!"

"That's what it is," replied McGary, "and you're going to drink it all!"

The "nigger-voter" drank the jug of castor oil, and returned to Hempstead. The "niggers" did not vote, and Austin McGary won the election by only a slight **majority.**

During the two terms he served as sheriff, he had many hair-raising experiences against Texas outlaws. Once he disarmed and arrested John Wesley Hardin, "one of the coldest-blooded" gunmen in Texas history. Hardin had the record of killing twenty-seven men in his life-time. On another occasion McGary got the drop on a desperado, and had him standing with his hands in the air. Standing beside McGary were two of his younger deputies. The outlaw had two guns buckled on his hips. McGary told him he was coming after him, and that if he went for his guns, his deputies would shoot. As soon as McGary holstered his guns, the outlaw reached for his, and McGary's deputies shot him

In years to come, after McGary had settled down to preach the gospel, reports circulated that he had killed a man. Actually, McGary, with all of his experiences, never killed a single person, although on this occasion, his deputies, acting upon his orders, did shoot an outlaw.

Near the close of his second term as sheriff of Madison County, McGary resigned his office to take a position as conveying agent for the state penitentiary. His job was to go all over the state and get the condemned criminals and bring them back to the state prison This was far from a simple, monotonous job Texas then had few railroads. The plains were infested by wild indians and desperadoes. Often McGary would start across the plains with eight prisoners, and one companion. They would ride for days at a time without passing a white settlement or seeing another man than his little party. They would sleep at night on the plains, and cook their meals over an open fire. In two years of this service, McGary did not lose a single prisoner

It was in 1880 that Austin McGary resigned this work to return to Madison County to live After settling down he gave himself to some serious thinking He had thought little about religion, and had come to the conclusion that he was an infidel He determined, however, to give the whole subject a thorough and impartial investigation, and so began by making a critical study of the Campbell-Owen debate. During the summer of 1881, an English emigrant by the name of Harry Hamilton came to Madisonville, Texas, to preach on the principles of apostolic Christianity. McGary's sister, Mrs J. W Gillespie, heard Hamilton, was convinced, and obeyed the gospel. She urged her brother to go hear the preacher, so McGary went But his studies continued. It was December 24, 1881, that he was baptized into Christ

Now McGary plunged more deeply into a search of the Bible. As he had an opportunity he preached In 1883 he moved to Austin, Texas For several years he made this his home, living a little west of the town

As in politics so in preaching, McGary found his greatest felicity wherever the demand was most needed for a pugnacious style. He once received a letter from a young lady, a schoolteacher, who had recently moved to west Texas. She wrote saying that she longed to hear the gospel preached like her mother believed, and if McGary would come there and preach, she would pay his expenses. McGary wrote that other engagements prevented his going. Later, a meeting was cancelled, so he determined to go to the town Without writing the young lady he was coming, he drove his horse and buggy the distance, arriving on a Saturday morning. Philpot, a great Methodist evangelist, he found was in town, causing considerable excitement in a large tabernacle meeting. McGary retired at a hotel that night, expecting to attend the meeting the next morning.

Sunday morning he had overslept, and when he arrived at the tabernacle, the crowd had already assembled. McGary took a seat in the rear of the building. Philpot's speech made the "Campbellites" his target, and straight toward it he drove. He announced that down in Texas was a Campbellite preacher by the name of McGary that taught people had to be baptized in running water to be saved. When Philpot finished, McGary stood up, walked casually to the front, across in front of several preachers who sat on the platform behind him, took his place and spoke.

"I am a stranger in your town. There is nobody to introduce me, so I will introduce myself. I am A. McGary from Austin, Texas. I baptized the doctor that Mr. Philpot referred to, but I did not baptize him in running water. Philpot's information is wrong, and if I can get the tabernacle this afternoon, I will be glad to tell you the facts in the case."

The owner of the tabernacle called out that he could get it. Philpot went into a rage, and announced that the meeting was closed. But McGary preached that afternoon, and on for several days. He also baptized the young lady schoolteacher who had written him, although he learned several days later that she had joined the Methodists under Philpot's preaching before McGary arrived in town.

The most prominent characteristic of McGary was his courage. Fear had absolutely no part in his make-up. At Willis, Texas, near Houston, the Ku-Klux Klan became active after the Civil War, and McGary was widely recognized as a bitter enemy. He was warned to get out of Willis, but he ignored the warning, until a stranger from another town informed him that he would be

killed, and that people from another community would do it if
he did not move. McGary was puzzled for a moment what to do
He conceived a plan, and sent an old Negro to every street corner
in the town to shout at the top of his voice that McGary would
speak on a certain Sunday afternoon at a specified locality on the
subject of "Ku-Klux Klan."

The time arrived and the town was full of people McGary laid
serious charges before the Klan The Klan was unconstitutional
He related how they had taken an old preacher out of his house
at night and beaten him unmercifully McGary's language was
bitter in the extreme. He told them his door was unlocked at all
times; that they could come any time they choose, but they better
bring a wheelbarrow in which to haul their boys off. "I have a
gun and some of you know that I am handy with it," McGary
cried. The Ku-Klux Klan never bothered A. McGary.

But perhaps the crowning work of McGary's life was the establishing of the *Firm Foundation* at Austin, Texas. The name is
selected from the fact that Jesus is the Foundation upon which
His church is built; hence, the church has, in Christ, a *Firm
Foundation*. The paper, then a monthly, began publication the
first of September, 1884. It was not intended that it should be
projected for over a year, but in September, 1885, McGary announced that it would henceforth be a weekly. How long it should
run in the future was indefinite.

In announcing the launching of the paper, McGary wrote in
the first issue:

This pamphlet, *The Firm Foundation,* in its contemplated
monthly visitations, is respectfully, fraternally, and affectionately
dedicated to all that class of brethren who, believing that the New
Testament Scriptures are from God, to man, through His Son
Jesus the Christ, and who, regarding this book as an infallible
guide through this wilderness of sin to the promised haven of
safety beyond, are willing to turn their steps away from *all* human
systems, plans and *directions* into this *one* mapped out by he
apostles of our Lord.

. . . It goes forth to battle for the truth, ignoring the conven-
tionalists of so-called "polite society" preferring to call things by
their right names as did He who "spake as never man spoke."[2]

The avowed purpose of the establishment of the *Firm Founda-*

---

[2]A. McGary, "no title," *Firm Foundation,* Vol I, No 1 (September, 1884),
p 1.

tion was occasioned by McGary's growing alarm at the practice of some preachers of "shaking in the Baptists" The point, of course, was that the Baptists were baptized not "for," viz., "in order to" the remission of their sins, but because their sins had already been remitted The question was, when a Baptist decided to abandon the Baptist Church for apostolic Christianity, should he be rebaptized? McGary discussed the issue with everybody who would discuss it, but in those days he was very much in the minority Before long, he gained the reputation of making it a hobby, still he would not be discouraged The "Progressives" used it to his disadvantage.

W. H. Bagby, of Bryan, Texas, was a liberal and wrote the news of Texas for the *Christian Standard* He opens an attack on McGary.

Every phase of foolishness that ever sprang from the faithful soil of dwarfed and ignorant minds among us may be found in Texas, as I, at least, have never seen it elsewhere From the anti-society doctrine down to the rebaptism hobby, the contemptible foolishness of which English language has no word to express, we have everything No wonder that in many places we are regarded with contempt by intelligent and good people The whole body has to bear the reproach that belongs only to a few irresponsible hobbyists who are no more in sympathy with the feelings of God's word and the spirit of true Christianity than are the Holiness people Their leader enjoys the liberty of a man who carries in his pocket a letter of dismissal from the church in the community where he lives. . . . [2].

Concerning McGary's idea on Baptist baptism, Bagby writes

We know of no departure from the faith in modern times so hurtful to the cause of New Testament Christianity as this hobby which the *Firm Foundation* was established to advocate [3]

David Lipscomb and the *Gospel Advocate* were less concerned about it as an issue When Lipscomb was only fourteen years old, he was recovering from a spell of typhoid fever, when he sent for Tolbert Fanning to come and baptize him He had told no one about his intention When Fanning arrived, he asked the boy, David Lipscomb, why he wanted to be baptized, and Lipscomb's reply was, "to obey God" Forty years later Lipscomb wrote about it, still determined that he could not improve his reply With this statement Fanning baptized Lipscomb in a box

[2]W H Bagby, "Texas Tidings," *Christian Standard*, Vol XXI, No 8 (February 20, 1886), p 61

At the first gospel meeting Lipscomb ever conducted, a woman came forward to "unite with the disciples," having been a member of the Baptist Church Lipscomb inquired of her if she had been baptized to join the Baptist Church or for another reason. This was the question he generally asked in such cases She replied "My friends were not Baptists, and my preference was not to join that church, but they were the only people I knew that practiced what I believed the Lord required, so I united with them "

Jesse L Sewell happened to be passing through the community, and attended the meeting that night Lipscomb asked Sewell his opinion of whether the woman should be rebaptized Sewell answered, "it would be mockery for that woman to be rebaptized "[4] Lipscomb always thought so himself

But, here was the issue David Lipscomb believed that if an individual were baptized from the motive of wanting to obey God, that motive was acceptable whether the individual understood that baptism was in order to the remission of sins or not Austin McGary, on the other hand, denied this, insisting that obeying God "from the heart" required an accurate understanding of the purpose of baptism For more than fifteen years brethren discussed the issue in both the *Firm Foundation* and the *Gospel Advocate* Many doubtlessly tired of it, and some thought the difference in viewpoint was only slight indeed. J D Tant, who himself sympathized with McGary on the issue, once wisely wrote

> I often think of what a noted Texas preacher said to me some years ago that the best way to bring about an understanding between Lipscomb and McGary would be to work up a big meeting somewhere, select the two to hold it, and at the close of the meeting they would find they were so near in accord on almost all things that they would be ashamed to claim a difference   [5]

Nevertheless, McGary's insistence that it was wrong to "shake in the Baptists," a term he frequently used, gained for him the reputation of being an extremist When H F Williams paid a visit to Texas in 1894, and met McGary, he hardly knew what to expect

Here also I had the pleasure of meeting A McGary, of the

---

[4]David Lipscomb, "Queries," *Gospel Advocate*, Vol XXXIX, No 23 (June 10, 1897), p 355
[5]J D Tant, "Our Nashville Meetings—No 1," *Gospel Advocate*, Vol XLI, No 27 (June 6, 1899), p 427

Firm Foundation   I had heard much of him, and read from his
pen. My acquaintance with him was very pleasant   He is one
of the "rebaptism" folks   As I had met several of that tribe in
my travels, but had never heard one of them preach, I was interested to know how they preached   I heard Brother Mc one time
He was a plain, earnest, interesting talker, but it would surprise
some people in some places to hear that he just preached like
many other folks   If he has horns, I did not see them   I do not
think him overly sound   He said nothing about "rebaptism," and
I understand that he preaches many sermons without referring to
the "baptism of Baptists "   This was refreshing to me, as I had
understood that many of the *Foundation* folks took their text on
"baptism for the remission of sins," and seldom got further on
baptism than the talking of "Baptists on Baptist baptism "   It is
strange how much prejudice a little fire will kindle   ."[6]

Although McGary was a lover of music, and himself quite
talented as a "fiddler" [the instrument that played his kind of
music was a "fiddle," not a "violin"], he believed the use of the
instrument in the worship of God to be an innovation, corrupting
the simple pattern of New Testament worship. Likewise, he
believed societies to do the work of the church were wrong. Consequently, Austin McGary will always be remembered "primarily
for his firm and fearless stand against the wave of digression
that deluged the churches of Christ in Texas during the last
quarter of the nineteenth century "

In the early part of 1903 McGary moved to Los Angeles,
California where he published a paper called *The Lookout*   He
stayed there only a short time, and in June of that year moved
to Eugene, Oregon   The next year his health failed, so he
moved to Bryan, Texas   Nor did his health improve here   He
thought a higher climate would help, and so moved to Springdale,
Arkansas in the Ozarks   But this helped little   He decided
then, to return to his native state   Houston was now to be his
home

On February 6, 1926, Austin McGary passed his eightieth birthday   The inexorable demand of nature slowly reached out for
him, and, on June 15, 1928 he passed away at his home in Houston
His body was laid beside that of his mother in the cemetery at
Huntsville

---

[6]H F Williams, "Field Findings In Texas," *Gospel Advocate,* Vol
XXVI, No 1 (January 4, 1894), p 12

Chapter XX

TEXAS

One of the most thrilling chapters relating to the restoration movement could be written covering the church in Texas from the close of the Civil War to the turn of the twentieth century It would certainly include the lives of many noble preachers—Carroll Kendrick, John T. Poe, J. W Jackson, H. D Bantau, C M. Wilmeth, A J Clark, J D Tant, and Joe Warlick, to mention only a few Such a history would breathe the atmosphere of conflict, and could justly close with a crowning victory to the purity and simplicity of apostolic work and worship It cannot be expected that one chapter could serve any more than a prelude to such a gallant and glorious history

After the Civil War, a steady migration pushed into Texas from the east There is an indefiniteness about the cause Probably it was a combination of factors The restlessness of the human soul, inherently sure that the best is beyond one's reach, probably entered Cheap lands, with the possibility of grasping a fortune over-night, had something to do with the sky-rocketing growth in Texas population. With some, adventure and romance were attractive as there were indians and outlaws to fight. Earlier settlers had migrated to Texas, and had learned to love the state Their letters to relatives back east urged them out to the west, to the land of golden opportunity. In the sheer desolation of wide open plains, the matchless marvels of broad, yawning valleys, in the sacred dignity of gaunt, angular peaks, bursting suddenly upward from a wind-swept mesa of sand and cactus—the westerner learned to love these scenes Every Texan became a salesman, and with his broad arm. beckoned his friends westward.

Foremost among the immigrators to Texas were native Tennesseans. Their state, torn apart by the ravages of the Civil War, offered little inducement for them to stay Their economic system was poor, their slaves were free, and their property gutted by the merciless sword of Mars If start over they must, why not in a new place? So to Texas they went David Lipscomb, in

1872, paid an extended visit to the state. Twelve years later he returned, and was impressed by the way Tennesseans had filled Texas

Texas, within itself, is a nation in extent A constant stream of immigration from the older states is pouring into its borders It must soon be a nation in population and wealth It is strange how many Tennesseans are there. For some years after the formation of its government, nine-tenths of the members of its congresses and legislatures were Tennessee born, as were several of its first Presidents, Governors and Congressmen We have concluded that Tennessee has been the prolific spawning ground for the South and Southwest Many shoals have gone forth to people and subdued these regions A Tennessean may always feel at home in Texas.[1]

V. R Stapp wrote from Coleman City, Texas to the *American Christian Review* in the summer of 1879 that the tide of immigration was astonishing Almost half of the population in his own county, and in Runnels County, to the west, lived in camps

It was, of course, to be expected that in the migration westward many members of the church would be found. T. W. Caskey, the Mississippi "fightin' parson," left the ruins of his home east of the River and came to Texas after the Civil War. H. D. Bantau, a native Tennessean, moved in 1870 to Waco on the advice of his physician. He had been preaching at Weatherford eleven years when he died in 1888. E. J. Lampton moved from Illinois to Denton in 1877, where he found a small congregation. P. Minor, a carriage-maker, was preaching for it. In the fall of 1871, L. C Chisholm, a dentist by trade, took his brother with him, and left Tuscumbia, Alabama for Texas Many congregations in southwest Texas owe their origin to Chisholm's preaching About the same time, R. C Horn left Hartsville, Tennessee for Texas. C. M. ("Uncle Mac") Wilmeth graduated from Kentucky University in 1871, spent the summer preaching in middle Tennessee, and then moved to Texas in the fall. Wilmeth became one of the church's most noted preachers in Texas.

The list of names of pioneer preachers pushing westward after the war could be extended endlessly On they came, but their work in preaching the gospel was to be everything but soft. Railroad companies were only beginning to meet the challenge of the

---

[1]David Lipscomb, "A Trip to Texas," *Gospel Advocate*, Vol XXVII, No 4 (January 28, 1885), p 50

plains, and so preachers rode horseback or on stagecoachs for many miles to preach at distant appointments They would often sleep at night on the open, rattlesnake-infested prairies, and then with the coming of daylight, push on to a school-house, or old barn, and announce a gospel meeting was about to begin. For three years, 1887-1889, J. D Tant preached, being sent out by the brethren in Hamilton and Coryell County, Texas. He received five hundred dollars a year. His father, mother, sister and himself lived on two hundred dollars a year and spent the remainder in payments on their home. Pay amounted to very little—but so did expenses.

Typical of the experiences of these preachers were those of A. J Bush who came to southwest Texas after the war. The church in that part of the state was very weak; here and there were a very scattered brethren Bush got himself a "yellow-sided" Texas pony, put a saddle on him, picked up his Bible and hymn-book, and a few scattered pieces of clean linen and started out to preach He rode twenty miles to Goliad and preached, he rode another twenty to Popolota Creek and preached. Here he learned that Lagarto in Live Oak County needed a preacher, so he started there. On the way he got lost On Sunday morning he found himself nine miles from his appointment. He was told that he would find a Brother Stillwell, six miles on the way to Lagarto Stillwell was supposed to be a leading member of the little congregation.

Bush spurred his pony on and finally arrived at Stillwell's home. He noted that there were several men gathered around the home, all heavily armed with knives and guns. Bush inquired for Stillwell, found him, introduced himself, and then inquired what was happening Stillwell replied, "We are glad to see you; don't be alarmed at appearances; you go over to town, and the brethren will care for you. We have three or four Mexicans to hang, and then we will be ready for a meeting."

GROWTH IN TEXAS

One of the most intrepid preachers in east Texas after the war was John T Poe. Through his influence many congregations were established His naturally independent turn of mind can well be seen in his earlier religious experiences. Although reared in the Methodist Church, he was never satisfied that this was

according to New Testament teaching   But he had never heard
of any other kind of preaching, and so remained with the denomination   Poe was in the Confederacy during the Civil War.   In
1864 he was one day sitting in camp, reading his New Testament,
when he decided that he would be immersed the first time he had
the opportunity.   After the war, he moved back to his home in
Huntsville, Texas   The next Sunday after his return, he heard
J W D Creath preach at the Baptist Church   He and a brother-
in-law, H C. Wright informed Creath that they objected to many
teachings of the Baptist Church, but they wanted to be immersed—
to obey God   An old Colonel Rogers, a Baptist deacon, discussed
the unusual request, and, being thoroughly satisfied in his own
mind that these men would later agree with Baptist teaching,
acquiesced in the decision to baptize them.

Two years later, having learned of a people who were Christians
and Christians only, who took the Bible and the Bible only, Poe
"bade adieu to sectarian folly," and became a member of the
church of Christ in Huntsville.   He had no intention of preaching,
but at the urging of some members, decided to try once   He
prepared earnestly for a month, gathering scraps of quotations
from Beecher and others.   When he got up to deliver the sermon,
he spread papers out before him, and started   He noticed women
whispering to each other, and, fearing that had discovered his
secret that he had borrowed his sermon from others, he sat down
in confusion.   He was resolved never to preach again until an
old lady asked him to speak the next Sunday at her husband's
sawmill, and promised to take him out there and back in her
buggy   She told him not to "prepare" a sermon, but just get
up and tell the people what the Lord wanted them to know about
the plan of salvation   Poe obliged, and baptized two people at the
sawmill meeting.

The congregtaion at Huntsville, Texas had been established in
1860   When David Lipscomb visited Texas in 1872, he found
that this congregation had one hundred members, and that John
T. Poe was preaching for it quite regularly   Although Poe was
constantly and intrepidly fighting innovations, there were times
when his life's work was lost by the congregations accepting
these, and Poe had to begin again   There were strong congregations at Longview and Palestine, but both departed with innovations   In the summer of 1899 Poe sent out a call for help, got

some, went back to Longview, and held a meeting A small congregation of seven members was established Four years later, when it had only thirty members, the Longview church sent Poe to Palestine, Texas to re-establish the cause The old congregation now had J C. Mason, a Texas-Arkansas preacher of definite "Progressive coloring," who was preaching for this church Eighty-three year old. John F Taylor, who had once been an elder in the other congregation, but was driven out when the instrument was driven in, asked for the privilege of using the old meeting house for a meeting with Poe He was refused An old sister, Alice Brown, borrowed a tent from a Baptist preacher, and so in this, Poe began his meeting, to plant again the cause in Palestine, Texas

At Waco, the congregation was organized in 1870 with forty members Three years later it had a hundred members, but no meeting house J H Bantan, a district judge, from Huntsville, did frequent preaching here during the summers At Hamilton, the congregation was established on the second Lord's Day of April, 1876 Here, J D Tant did considerable preaching in his earlier days. Mrs Dillie Harris moved from Thyatira, Mississippi to Kyle, Texas around 1887. She put an item in the *Gospel Advocate*, asking someone to send a preacher there Her home congregation saw it, contacted John T Poe, and paid him forty dollars to establish a congregation At Marshall, Poe went in the summer of 1888, but the meeting closed in two days with a "dyed-in-the-wool digressive" elder protesting W. D Ingram reported to the *Christian Leader* in the summer of 1894 that there were four hundred members of the church in Van Zandt County, although there was considerable indifference

In Hood County, Thorp Springs became a radiating point for the churches in the early years following the war J A. Clark, a native Tennessean, had become a member of the church of Christ in Titus County, Texas as early as 1843 At the close of the war he had moved to Fort Worth to become the city's first postmaster Two years later he and his sons, Addison and Randolph, opened a college By 1873 in order to avoid the influences of an evil city, they had determined to move their college into the country J A Clark purchased a two-story building at Thorp Springs, and opened school that fall, September, 1873.

The school was known as "Add-Ran Male & Female College," but more popularly, as "Add-Ran College"

There is, and has been, a wide misunderstanding as to the source of the name. The general opinion is that it was taken from "Addison" and "Randolph," the two sons of J A Clark Aaron Prince Aten visited Texas in 1879, making Thorp Springs a stopping point on his itinerary In his report on his visit, he reported that the school was named for "Addison" and "Randolph," sons of J A Clark, and for this mistake, the elder Clark chastised him, saying,

He says, "It is locally known as Add-Ran College, the name being formed from the first syllables of the two names just mentioned" Here, again, the writer has affirmed without being fully posted At least, his statement is calculated to convey an idea that is not strictly true Did the writer know this college was named for one person alone? If he did not, he knew not how it got its name, and ought not to have undertaken to tell I can tell him, if to know will afford him any satisfaction, that the college was named for one who has for years lain buried in the graveyard at Fort Worth .   [2]

Clark made it clear that Add-Ran College was to have no endowment, was not to belong to the church, and yet would hold forth Christian principles "We have never asked," he once wrote, "an endowment from the brethren, nor have we asked them to take the college under their control as church property, believing that we could do better for the brotherhood with it as individual property." James L Thornberry expressed their point of view by writing,

A church had as well run a farm as a college The business of the church is to "edify itself, to shine as a light in a dark place, to hold forth the word of life to a dying and lost world" When the church perceives in the body gifted men, men of faith, humility and piety, whose sole desire is to preach, men who as the lamented R. Rice said, "can not help preaching," let the church aid such to educate themselves, send them to college and pay for it . . I am by no means opposed to colleges, and I am glad to see my Christian brethren conducting them, but let not the church be burdened with them, nor put in money there that ought to be used for other purposes Nor do I like a college whose ostensible purpose is preacher-making   Let God and the church make the preacher and the colleges the scholars.[3]

Thorp Springs, then, three miles west of Granberry, county seat of Hood County, a mile west of the Brazos River, having, in 1873, a population of less than six hundred, became a strong focal point for the influence of the principles of primitive Christianity.

Churches over Texas grew up by sacrifice, slow constant toil, and for the most part amid inward turmoil.   Nowhere was there more evidence of this than in the central and southern part of the state.   The church at Austin had dated from 1853 when Henry Thomas had moved there from Missouri.   Soon, forty members were organized, and the first meetings were held in a school house.   Soon afterward, it was meeting on Congress Avenue, in an old house it had bought from the Methodists   W. H. D. Carrington was the chief spirit in building up the congregation in those earlier years.   In 1879, W. E. Hall, a young man of only twenty-eight, came to Austin.   He was beset by constant criticism.   He, too, had a definite "progressive coloring," and the congregation was torn by dissension   John T Poe was certain that the church was killed by the "pastor mania"

When McGary came to Austin and saw the church beset with innovations, he rolled up his sleeves and went to work.   In opposing Hall's liberalism, McGary wrote articles and sent them to the *Advocate*.   He succeeded in getting Hall to leave Austin and head back for headquarters at St Louis, but that did not end the dissension.   McGary then asked for a letter from the congregation, and went outside the city, at a place called Pecan Springs to worship.

Around Austin, congregations were springing up like magic. At San Marcos in 1873 there were one hundred members meeting in a new house.   At Bethany, near Willis, in Montgomery County, was reported to be the strongest congregation numerically in southern Texas.   This was in 1886.   Small congregations were found at Goliath, Manahuella, Charco, and Harwood.   In March, 1882 L. C. Chisholm came to Goliath, a village of three or four thousand people   Goliath was the site of the massacre of General Fannin and his Texans by the Mexicans in 1833.   All but one of

---

[3]James L Thornberry, "Texas Letter," *American Christian Review*, Vol. XXII, No. 22 (May 27, 1879), p. 171

the American force had been slaughtered   This one to escape
was an old brother who attended church at Goliath, and who
was also a judge in the town   He escaped by playing dead, and
crawling away at night   At Uvalde, 95 miles west of San Antonio,
Chisholm came in January, 1882 to preach   This was a typical
western town, located in a stock-raising country   It had then a
population of only five hundred, and only a small congregation

At San Antonio as late as 1883 there were only a few brethren
meeting   Although the city had a population of forty-two thousand,
it was difficult to plant the church here   D. Pennington came
here to build up the church   He spent all of his money, got no
support, and left   W J Barbee went in 1886 and stayed one
year   When he left, he declared San Antonio to be the hardest
place he ever saw to establish the truth   David Lipscomb explained that the real difficulty at San Antonio lay in the fact that
the preachers who had gone there, and the few members to be
found, straddled the fence on the issues before the church until
few brethren were willing to support them

The church at Houston was slow getting planted   A E. Cloud,
a businessman and member of the church, earnestly requested
W F Barcus to conduct a meeting here   Barcus went in July,
1886, and afterward declared, correctly or incorrectly, that this
was the first time the gospel had ever been preached in Houston
We are inclined to the opinion that Barcus' statement was made
incorrectly for John T Poe declared that he and D Pennington
went to Houston early in 1876 and established the church in
the town   If so, it yet would seem evident that it functioned
very little in the coming years   At any rate, when General R M
Gano went here in the spring of 1888 to conduct a meeting, he
found a small congregation   His meeting resulted in ten additions
By the fall of 1904 one reads of a small congregation of twenty-
nine members meeting at Houston Avenue and Bingham Street

John T Poe was largely responsible for establishing the church
at Corsicana   In September, 1888 Poe went to the city at his
own expense to conduct the meeting   He rented the city hall,
paying a dollar a night for it   He ate his meals in a restaurant,
and again at his own expense   T F Driskill, a dentist and a
preacher, who lived in the city, aided him   The meeting lasted
ten days, and before it had ended, a congregation of sixty-two
members was organized.   Shortly after the congregation was

organized, B B Sanders, state evangelist for the Texas Christian Missionary Society, came to the town, introduced the organ, and divided the church Meanwhile, the brethren who worshipped as they had originally done before Sanders came, continued When R L. Whiteside left the Nashville Bible School to return to Texas, he went, in a few years, to Corsicana to live F W. Smith visited the city in the summer of 1903, and conducted a meeting for the church He wrote of Whiteside, "Brother Whiteside is a strong man, and will some day take his stand among the clearest reasoners in Texas "

When "Bold and Beseeching" W F Black went to Fort Worth in June, 1887 to conduct a meeting, he found that the congregation had the reputation of being the largest church among the brethren in the state The first preaching in the city was done in 1857 when B F Hall established a church of fifteen members When David Lipscomb visited Fort Worth in 1872, he estimated the population of the city at less than seven hundred This was at the time that J A Clark was anxious to move his school to the country to get away from the evil influences of a large city By 1889 the congregation had grown to number four hundred members That year it moved into a new building that cost ten thousand dollars, and was said to be the finest in the city That year also, scholarly J W Lowber was called to be the preacher

The attainments of the church became widely known, and the fact that it had the finest church building in Texas became equally as well known

I notice an account in the Texas Department of the *Guide* of May the 24th of the grand work that our esteemed Kentucky brother, J W Lowber, is doing at Fort Worth For the marvelous success of his work there, we feel truly and thankfully proud, but there are some things in the report of Brother Lowber's work to which I feel constrained to object While Paul doubtless saw many virtues in his brethren that were praiseworthy, he saw things that he could not praise and told them so In my judgment, if Paul were to write an epistle to the saints at Fort Worth, he would tell them that he praised their liberality, but as to the way they used it, he "praised them not " I refer to the cost of the interior finery of the house of worship One window cost the immense sum of five hundred dollars—quite enough to have built a new little house at some destitute point Why did they not pay about twenty five dollars for a window and send the four hundred and seventy five to some mission work? *Pride.*[4]

This original congregation by 1896 had grown to number eight hundred members, and was widely referred to as the Central Church. The brethren had two other congregations in town, although they were much smaller. Homer T. Wilson, the only located preacher in the town, was now preaching at the Central congregation J. D. Tant came to the city in the spring of 1896 and conducted a meeting on the south side of town with a small congregation Members of the Central Church had gone to a State Meeting in the central part of the state, and so could not support Tant's meeting The action was a straw to tell which way the wind was blowing.

James E Scobey came to Fort Worth in the spring of 1899 This small south side church had grown some. W. T. Kidwell now preached regularly for it Scobey could now declare that this was the only church in the city which "maintains the apostolic work and worship" Homer T. Wilson had led the Central Church into putting in the instrument. J. E McPherson, who succeeded Wilson, had the same policies. Wilson had taken another group and established what was called the "Second Christian Church."

In Dallas, a congregation was organized about 1855. At first its meetings were held in the Masonic Hall, then in the courthouse, then in the City Hall, and frequently afterward in other rented halls. After the Civil War, the congregation bought a lot and built a meeting house. This was the first church house of any description ever to be erected in Dallas The congregation gradually outgrew it. About 1885 a Brother Peak gave them a lot on the corner of Pearl and Bryan Streets, and here the church continued to meet General R M. Gano served as an elder for this congregation for over thirty years

After the Civil War, this congregation was known as the Commerce Street Church. Kirk Baxter, brother of William Baxter, biographer of Walter Scott, came to preach for the Commerce Street Church. At his instigation, Knowles Shaw, "the singing evangelist," came to conduct a meeting During this meeting, Baxter and Shaw introduced the organ and divided the church. It was immediately upon the close of this meeting that Shaw took

[4]John W Ligon, "Church Finery," *Gospel Advocate,* Vol. XXXI, No. 24 (June 12, 1889), p 380

the train for McKinney, Texas at which time occurred the train wreck that took his life.

The division at Commerce Street probably resulted in strengthening the Pearl and Bryan Street church   In 1884 "Weeping Joe" Harding held a lengthy meeting here   The congregation now had four hundred members   They employed Harding the next year to work in the county, establishing congregations. W H. Bagby reported to the *Christian Standard* in 1887 that in the county, about Dallas, there were eighteen or twenty congregations, many of which had been established by "Weeping Joe" Harding

After the war, T W Caskey settled in Dallas   Here, he spent most of his last years.   The truculent Caskey, like Joe S Warlick who followed him, held many a debate that strengthened the church greatly in that general area   From April 13-14, 1874 he held a debate in Fort Worth with a Methodist preacher by the name of Price, who was widely referred to as "the Campbellite killer of Texas."   Addison Clark, in describing Caskey at this time, says of him,

To those who have seen and heard him, I need not say that there is but one T W Caskey on this globe   A man more peculiarly *sui generis,* I never saw   I believe he told me he is 57 years old   Is 6 feet, 3½ inches high   Is dry and humorous in conversation.   I don't suppose he has shed a tear since his mother whipped him, and I doubt much whether he did then [5]

At both Denton and Sherman there were strong congregations very early   As early as 1877 Denton had a fine meeting house, but when H. F Williams visited here in 1894 there were omens of trouble ahead   Williams observed that "they nearly all spell it with a big D, which means *one* more of the denominations that afflict professed Christendom."

For several years following the Civil War the church at Sherman, Texas had met in the court house and in the Odd-Fellow's Hall   "Uncle Charlie" Carlton and B F Hall did the preaching In 1874 a new building was erected at the corner of Montgomery and Houston Streets   At this time the church had only forty or fifty members   The next year the congregation received its greatest boost   John S Sweeney debated Jacob Ditzler, the noted Methodist.   Shortly after the debate, Sweeney conducted

---

[5]A Clark, "The Caskey and Price Debate," *Gospel Advocate,* Vol XVI, No 19 (May 7, 1874), p 443

a meeting which closed February 19, 1876 that resulted in one hundred and twenty-four additions to the congregation   In 1894 T B Larimore held, what was perhaps his greatest meeting, at Sherman

At Weatherford there was a strong congregation   A lady by the name of Soward was largely instrumental in building up the church   H D Bantau preached here, so did John T Poe   J D Tant's mother lived here for a while, so Tant was frequently "in and out "   At Breckinridge, Addison Clark established a church of forty members in the summer of 1885   The city of Abilene was established about 1880   Three years later, it had a population of four thousand   That same year, 1883, T H Hughes came to the town and established a congregation of fifty members   There were then small churches at Anson, Buffalo Gap and Dead Man Valley, but Hughes found no preachers within a hundred miles

Professor Bruner, a teacher at Eureka College in Illinois, made a move to El Paso for his health around 1890   Three years later a small congregation was regularly meeting with Bruner doing most of the preaching

Texas gradually became dotted with congregations, although in many locations omens of impending strife were plainly visible   At Tioga and Collinsville were small churches   At Whitesboro Dr H H Talley, formerly of Petersburg, Tennessee, had established a small church, but when H F Williams visited here in 1892, he found an organ and a society, "a heap of church fussing," and little interest   At Mason a church was established in 1875   At Bryan, there was a church as early as 1869   Carrol Kendrick did some of his early Texas preaching here   The church was set up in Fayette County, at the town of Liberty before the war by a Colonel I H Moore, "a wicked outsider," who built the meeting house because he hated to see the church suffer persecution   Afterward, Moore became a faithful Christian   In August, 1885 a congregation was set up at Benjamin, Texas   The county judge, the sheriff, the trustee, the tax collector, the county treasurer, and the justice of the peace all belonged to the church   .

The struggle over the instrumental music and the missionary society was as inevitable in Texas as it had been in other places   The tide of immigration that swelled the state's population was

a heterogeneous group To no small extent this was true even
within the church From Tennessee had come a host of church
members who had been taught against these innovations in the
worship, and, upon their arrival in their new home, they were
thoroughly determined to build up churches where these innovations would be unknown There was one thing in their favor
Texas was a southern state, and, with the bitter prejudices that
lived on for awhile throughout the nation after the war, Texas
people found more affinity to‚ Tennessee people than those migrating
from the North The fact that the *Christian Standard* was
violently pro-northern made its reception somewhat slow in the
state The *Gospel Advocate* had been introduced before the war,
and was widely received

Still, as many congregations in other states back in the east
had introduced the organ, more frequently than not, with division
resulting, the same conflict was inevitable in Texas As a matter
of fact, definite signs had been pointing in that direction since
the war

Before the war, it was common for brethren to meet together
in what was often referred to as "Cooperation Meetings," "Consultation Meetings," and sometimes, "District Meetings" or "State
Meetings" depending upon their extent These comparatively
innocent meetings were nothing more than mass gatherings to
discuss problems relative to the advancement of the church Everybody was invited so there was no tendency of a segregation into
"clergy" or "laity," named or unnamed No influence toward
coercion was put toward any of the churches

Carrol Kendrick left his home of Kentucky in 1851 to move
to Texas In the west Kendrick became a most influential
preacher It was he who introduced "State Meetings" to Texas
churches These meetings were mass gatherings of brethren at
specific locations to discuss the work of the church It was not
a missionary society, although in these earlier years Kendrick
was not averse to societies Before the war, Kendrick and Tolbert
Fanning discussed these societies at great length through the
Gospel Advocate, Kendrick affirming their right to exist After
the war when David Lipscomb came prominently to the front in
the *Advocate,* Kendrick and Lipscomb had a great misunderstanding When Lipscomb visited Texas in 1872, he attended the
State Meeting held at Bryan, but was ignored and discourteously

treated by Kendrick   Afterwards, rumors of Kendrick's disapproval of Lipscomb reached the *Advocate* editor, and Lipscomb blazed forth with a sizzling chastening for Carrol Kendrick. Although afterward, Lipscomb regretted what he had done, the harm was done, and the personal feelings between Carrol Kendrick and David Lipscomb were never the most fraternal

Although in the last twelve to fifteen years of his life, Kendrick opposed the missionary society, for several years earlier he had spoken favorably of them   At the State Meeting held in Dallas in July, 1876 Kendrick spoke, favoring adopting a plan to do missionary work in Texas   T W Caskey openly objected on the ground that this "plan" was just another "Louisville Plan," "whitewashed over "   So the suggestion was killed

Nevertheless with the passing of years, and the growing influx of advocates of both the missionary society and the use of the instrument coming into Texas, the battle loomed more definitely upon the horizon   By 1885 advocates of the society hoped to get a missionary society started that year.   It was thought that the State Meeting in Sherman would be the ideal time to put across the proposal   At this meeting, W K Homan put forth the resolution to organize a Texas State Society   Thomas Moore, W. H Wright, R. C Horn, J. R Wilmeth, and C. M. Wilmeth fought the resolution down   J A Clark afterwards reported to the *Old Path Guide* that the opposers of the society were more interested in notoriety than in the cause of Christianity

But the fact that the advocates of the Society had failed this once, did not mean they were through   A J Bush proposed in the December 3, 1885 issue of the *Texas Christian* that the Texas State Missionary Society be organized at the close of the next Bible Institute to be held at Thorp Spring   This would be in early January   At this Bible Institute there were many lively discussions on "Church Organization," "Christian Liberty," and "The Pastorate And The Work of Evangelizing," but still, the missionary society idea was not able to be put across

Proponents of the society now looked forward to the next State Meeting to be held in July, 1886 at Austin   Early that year, W R McDaniel reported that the lowest estimate of the number of disciples in Texas was thirty thousand, and added, "there are more than three times seven thousand of these who will never board the progressive car "   Nevertheless, Chalmers McPherson made it clear that this time there would be a society organized, so sent out word that all who were opposed, please stay away from the meeting

According to plans, the State Meeting convened in Austin on July 7, 1886 at ten o'clock in the morning The sessions lasted for three days W K Homan, ardent proponent of the Society, was chairman A committee on resolutions was appointed which drew up seven resolutions favorable to the establishment of the Society A few opponents of the Society were present These included C M. Wilmeth of Dallas and General R M Gano; W H D Carrington, the man who led J D Tant to the truth, and Carrol Kendrick who by now was violently opposed to the Society J D. Tant was also present, but Tant was a young preacher, and confessed later that he came, not out of interest in the meeting, but rather to get himself a wife "He came, he saw, he conquered," and Tant went home with a wife

When it was announced in the meeting that the resolutions had been drawn up, it was suggested that the consideration of these be put off until the next day Opponents of the society had from some source gotten the impression that no attempt would be made to introduce the society, and so were surprised at the resolutions. The next day the resolutions were read one by one, and generally agreed upon down to number seven When the seventh resolution was read, Society advocates knew that this was the signal for the battle to begin Before a word could be said against the resolutions, "Uncle Charlie" Carlton, an advocate of the Society, jumped up and led in the singing of "All Hail The Power of Jesus' Name " C M. Wilmeth later wrote in the *Christian Preacher*, "They sang as lustily as niggers at a corn-shucking, while good men and women sat and wept." General Gano stood up and begged the brethren not to introduce the society, and when they persisted, he "went to the door and wept as a child " Later, Carroll Kendrick wrote,

In July, 1886, after an absence of nine years, I attended the State Meeting at Austin, Texas, because I was urged to do so, and because I saw from the papers, that an effort would probably be made at that meeting to form a Society, or, at least, to have the work take on more of the society form For over twenty years the meetings had done moderately well, and I was sure that such a move would cause a division and great harm. My objects were to prevent a division and encourage union and all the right ways of the Lord. I was not mistaken. The effort was made, and succeeded, after all we could do to prevent it. After the order of political management, a leading progressionist was put in the chair. He appointed his committees of his own class. The Committee on Ways and Means soon brought in their report for a Society; it was what we would, in other days, have called a *constitution*. A number of us told them plainly that we could not work on such a plan without being hypocrites, and that to urge it was to urge *division*—to *carry* it, to make a division We implored them most earnestly to desist, and to let us work on in harmony. They persisted. The vote was a tie, and the chairman decided for the division. . . This caused us to feel that they did not desire *harmony*—that they *desired* to get rid of us, so they could add innovations without opposition! This, I think, was fully proved. Certainly they could have had harmony had they desired it The rest of us, after they closed, called together the State Meeting, as formerly, and did what we could in the brief time we had. . .⁶

When it became evident that the Missionary Society would be launched, W. H. D. Carrington stood before the audience and asked that all who wanted to do missionary work on a scriptural basis to come to the basement. Carrington's intention, of course, was to have the work continue as it had been done. Beginning in 1867, it had been the practice of the churches to put the work each year under the elders of one Texas congregation. The work was under the Sherman church perhaps more than any other one congregation. Of this practice Kendrick wrote:

. . . The churches sent messengers, pledges, etc, and the meetings chose evangelists and a committee from among themselves to act for them from one meeting to the next. Each meeting determined the time and place for the next, and each meeting chose its own chairman, secretary, treasurer and evangelizing committee We had very little machinery about these meetings. We had out some years from twelve to eighteen evangelists, and never any trouble with them or their salaries. . .

I think we should never have had any serious difficulty among Texas preachers or churches, but preachers came from the East, and human organizations were urged to great disadvantage. To guard against these evils, and seeing we had example for it (Acts ii 27-30), we requested first the elders of the church at Austin to act as a receiving, managing and disbursing evangelizing committee. Afterward and for several years, the elders of the church at Sherman did all this, and the work went on increasingly

⁶C Kendrick, "Our Missionary Machinery—No III—Former and Present State Meetings," *Christian Leader*, Vol. II, No 42 (October 16, 1888), p 1

well. It was hindered some, and finally, two years ago, greatly interrupted by a human organization, in opposition to all our efforts. . .[7]

W. H. D. Carrington's suggestion for a meeting in the basement met with approval, and so several retired to hold a meeting of their own. Carrington was chosen chairman and I. D. Faut, secretary. There were two brief sessions—Friday evening and Saturday morning. The elders of the Pearl and Bryan Streets church in Dallas were to oversee the work for the next year. Meanwhile, the Society upstairs announced its intention of meeting with the Commerce Street church the next year in Dallas, so the State Meeting downstairs decided to meet at Pearl and Bryan Streets.

During the 1887 meetings, held at the same time in Dallas, committees representatives of each group, met back and forth, to discuss the possibility of harmony, but to no avail. The Society took steps to appoint a State Evangelist who had about the same authority as a Methodist presiding Bishop. Churches wanting "pastors" were encouraged to contact him, so he could look after the matter. Of course, a primary qualification of the State Evangelist had to be that he was not opposed to either the Missionary Society or the use of the instrument in worship. The State Society took steps at this meeting to form a stock company with which to publish a paper, called the *Christian Courier*. W. K. Homan was made editor. The *Christian Courier* for the next several years was the *Christian Standard* of Texas.

Opposition to the State Society came from various sources John T. Poe wrote in the *Advocate*

Recently, certain brethren have thought we were not progressing in the work as fast as we should, and assuming that there was lack of organization, system in missionary work, they have gone to work, and sent out agents on behalf of their plan, or system of work. A large portion of the brethren in Texas protested, that this is wrong, and refuse to work in the name of the Society organized at Austin last year, contending that the church alone, is God's missionary society, and that all must be done by the church, and thus done in the name of Christ.[8]

---

[7]C Kendrick, "Our Missionary Machinery, No. II," *Christian Leader*, Vol II, No 39 (September 25, 1888), p 1

[8]John T. Poe, "Two Sides to the Question," *Gospel Advocate*, Vol XXIX, No. 12, (March 23, 1887), p. 179

In the spring of 1887, J D Tant moved to Hamilton to work with this congregation   Tant was only twenty-six.   He had been under the influence of Carrington and that probably helped settle him against the Society   Concerning the church at Hamilton and the cause in Texas in general, Tant wrote:

And permit me to say the congregation at Hamilton is under a leadership that does not know what it is to stop and discuss the insufficiency of the Bible, for they do believe the Bible will furnish them to all good works .   They are men of too much intelligence to inquire after some organized state machinery under the name of the Society.[9]

In the same article Tant continued and wrote of the cause in general.

When I think of Dabney, Hansbrough, Durst, Burnett, Hawkins, Poe and many more of us who have left home and friends and gone through cold and rain, and have night after night slept upon the ground, whose covering was the sky, that we might preach the word, and have done more good for the cause of Christ than the little two by four society will do in a hundred years, (for when the money fails the society is going to fail also), and then when I hear those who claim to be our brethren put us down as anti-missionaries because we will not turn back from serving God that we might with them partake of the flesh pots of Egypt, it is enough to make us hang our heads in shame.[10]

The *Octographic Review* copied an article from the *Christian Messenger* from one who severely rebuked the Society in Texas.

The Society advocates and adherents have method in their madness.   One might think from hearing them say that "Just so the work is done it matters not to the *how*" they care very little about the way in which it is accomplished.   Really, one might suppose that they would hail him happy who preaches the primitive gospel on any plan.   But the leaders of the Society men in Texas have shown a different spirit.   They show very little sympathy for any preacher who does not follow after them, no matter how much he has labored or suffered for Christ.[11]

The history of the restoration movement has well shown that the Missionary Society and the instrumental music were inseparable twins   Like Mary's little lamb, wherever the one went, the

---

[9]J D Tant, "Notes from Hamilton, Texas," *Gospel Advocate,* Vol XXIX, No 20, (May 18, 1887), p. 307
[10]J D Tant, "Notes from Hamilton, Texas," *Gospel Advocate,* Vol XXIX, No 20, (May 18, 1887), p 307
[11]Anonymous, "The Society Spirit," *Octographic Review,* Vol XXI, No. 22, (May 31, 1888), p 1

other was sure to follow As early as 1873 Carrol Kendrick wrote, "We have no use for organs in our churches here *yet*. We have not got that far along in our progress" L. P. Phillips moved to Johnson County in October, 1876. Two years later he remarked that he had yet to see a preacher afflicted with the "organ mania." Instruments of music in the worship of the churches in Texas were few and far between before 1890. Not until the Texas Christian Missionary Society became firmly established did the churches begin to put these in on any large scale

At Denton the instrument was pushed into the church late in 1893. P B Hall who was present at the time wrote T. R Burnett of Dallas the following

Dear Brother Burnett .   I witnessed one of the saddest affairs last Lord's day that I ever witnessed in my life. The church at Denton has been in trouble for some time over the organ and other things, until a few weeks ago, when those in favor of the organ had a called meeting, with Brother W. L. Thurman for chairman, and withdrew from all the brethren who opposed them. Those who were excluded were the most faithful and devoted brethren in the church at Denton. Brother A Alsup had been employed by the elders of the church to labor for them, but those in favor of the organ were not satisfied to let him preach in the house. So when we met last Lord's day to hear Brother Alsup, they refused to let him preach in the house. Some of those in favor of the organ went so far as to say. "That a man who would not use the organ in worship was not fit to preach in any church in Texas" Now, they may talk about the inconsistency of making rebaptism a test of fellowship, but how does it look to make the using of an organ a test of fellowship? When the brethren were refused the use of the house, they bore it patiently, and I did not hear an unkind word from any of them. They turned then and asked them if they would take the house they had built with their own hands, turn them out of doors, and for all their labors give them not a cent. They made them no reply As the old gray-headed brethren arose and walked out of their own house, you know not how bad I felt Now, I have tried to keep from being prejudiced towards our progressive brethren, but I just know it is wrong to take a person's property without paying him for it .[12]

The church at Sherman had a bitter conflict over the instrument. Before Larimore's meeting of 1894 some attempted to

[12]P B Hall, "Denton, Texas," *Gospel Advocate*, Vol XXXVI, No 4 (January 25, 1894), p 61.

introduce the organ but failed.   After the meeting, it was put in, and the church divided.   At Longview, the church divided in 1895.   W. H. Wright of Dallas came down and helped the preacher, L. A. Dale put in the instrument, and about twenty-five or thirty left to start over again.   At Paris, the organ was put in in the spring of 1891, causing fifty-three members to separate and build again on a new platform.   B. B. Sanders came to Hamilton, Texas in December, 1893, introduced the organ, and divided the church.   The church at Commerce, Texas divided soon after the new building was completed in 1894.   R. G. Scott, an employee of the Cotton Belt Railroad, and a member of the church, moved to Commerce in August, 1900.   He received permission to use the building for a worship service at a time when the others were not in it.   This arrangement went well until they invited General Gano to conduct a meeting.   Gano was refused permission to preach in the building.   A turmoil resulted when an old sister, ready to demonstrate her loyalty, tore down the door with an axe to let the brethren in to worship.

In the summer of 1885 the church at Waxahachie put in the instrument.   Chalmer McPherson led the move, and Isaac M. Fuston opposed it.   At the sign of the first opposition, it was temporarily dropped.   But when brethren assembled on Sunday, October 4th, they found the organ in the church.   McPherson had secretly raised the money among those who favored it, and bought it.   His wife played it at the services.   The next Sunday, October 11, when the organ was used again, Fuston stood up and asked all who objected to it to meet him that afternoon at the building.   McPherson was present and tried to argue its scripturalness.   General confusion resulted, and the result was another division.

Slowly those who opposed the organ were losing patience. What could they do to stop this?   It was evident that they were losing valuable church property by these innovations.   What could be done?   Some were bold enough to suggest the answer.

We want to warn the brethren everywhere against those who divide the churches.   "Mark them that cause divisions," says the apostle, "and have no company with them."   It is the work of the Dallas committee through its agents to divide the churches and if possible drive out all not in favor of the human plan work, then possess themselves the church property.   Let the congregations look to this.   If they can succeed in driving out of the congregations—by the introduction of the organ or other means—all those who oppose the plan and its sectarian work, the church property will be left in their hand. This is no doubt their program. They have at least worked this way to the present [13]

Affairs then in Texas had entered this critical period. The introduction of the Society and the instrument caused several of the congregations to be lost to our brethren. There was a growing impatience. One can well see that sterner measures to counteract this influence were in the making.

[13]John T. Poe, "Among the Churches," *Gospel Advocate*, Vol XXXI, No. 31 (July 24, 1889), p 475

CHAPTER XXI

THE REALITY OF DIVISION

On Sunday, August 18, 1889, six thousand members of the church gathered in Shelby County, Illinois, at the site of the old Sand Creek congregation in a great mass-meeting. Since 1873 large masses of brethren had congregated at this site to enjoy a few days of fellowship, and to have opportunities of hearing prominent preachers. With the passing of years the general condition of the church had a tendency to reflect itself upon this gathering, so they came somberly together contemplating the rising threat of division within the church. On this particular Sunday in 1889 the taciturn audience listened for an hour and forty minutes while Daniel Sommer spoke on the condition of the church. Sommer charged the "innovators" with being responsible for all the division, discord, bitterness and strife within the church. He claimed that they had constantly asked these men *not* to push their innovations, but they had been refused. The missionary society and the instrumental music were being pushed into the churches, driving a wedge between brethren. What then, was to be done?

At this point in Sommer's sermon, P. D. Warren, one of the elders in the Sand Creek congregation arose and read what later came to be called the "Sand Creek Address And Declaration." Because of its great significance the document is given in whole here:

To All Those Whom It May Concern, Greeting

Brethren—You doubtless know that we, as disciples of Christ, with scarcely an exception, many long years ago took the position that in matters of doctrine and practice, religious, "Where the Bible speaks we speak, and where the Bible is silent we are silent." Further, we held that nothing should be taught, received or practiced, religiously, for which we could not produce a "Thus saith the Lord." And, doubtless, many of you also know that, as long as the above principles were constantly and faithfully observed, we were a prosperous and happy people. Then we were of one heart and of one soul; we lived in peace and prospered in the things pertaining to the kingdom of God and the name of our Lord Jesus Christ. Then what was written as doctrine and for practice was taught and observed by the disciples of Christ. And it may not be amiss in this connection to say that many—yes, very many—in the sectarian churches saw the beauty, consistency.

and the wonderful strength and harmony. in the plea as set forth by the disciples for the restoration of primitive or apostolic Christianity in spirit and in practice, and so came and united with us in the same great and godly work

It is, perhaps, needless for us to add, in this connection, that we, as a people, discarded all man-made laws, rules, disciplines and confessions of faith as means of governing the church We have always acknowledged, and do now acknowledge, the all-sufficiency of the Holy Scriptures to govern us as individuals and as congregations As an apostle has said, "All Scripture is given us by inspiration of God, and is profitable for doctrine, for reproof, for correction, for instruction in righteousness, that the man of God may be perfect, thoroughly furnished unto all good works "

And now, please to allow us to call attention to some painful facts and considerations There are among us those who do teach and practice things not taught or found in the New Testament, which have been received by many well-meaning disciples, but rejected by those more thoughtful, and in most instances better informed in the Scriptures, and who have repeatedly protested against this false teaching and those corrupt practices among the disciples Some of the things of which we hereby complain, and against which we protest, are the unlawful methods resorted to in order to raise or get money for religious purposes, viz that of the church holding festivals of various kinds, in the house of the Lord, or elsewhere, demanding that each participant shall pay a certain sum as an admittance fee, the use of instrumental music in the worship, the select choir, to the virtual, if not the real, abandonment of congregational singing. Likewise the man-made society for missionary work and the one-man, imported preacher pastor to feed and watch over the flock These, with many other objectionable and unauthorized things, are now taught and practiced in many of the congregations, and that to the great grief and mortification of some of the members of said congregations.

And now, brethren, you who teach such things and such like things, and those who practice the same, must certainly know that they are not only not in harmony with the gospel, but are in opposition thereto You surely will admit that it is safe, and only safe, to teach and practice what the divine record enjoins upon the disciples. To this none can reasonably object This is exactly what we want and for which we contend

And now we say that we beg of you that you turn away speedily and at once from such things, and remember that though we are the Lord's freemen, yet we are bound by the authority of our Lord Jesus Christ You know that it is by keeping his commandments, and not the commandments of men, that we have the assurance of his approval Therefore, brethren, without addressing you further by using other arguments, and without going further in detailing those unpleasant and, as we see them, vicious things, you must allow us, in kindness and in Christian courtesy, and at the same time with firmness, to declare that we cannot tolerate the things of which we complain, for if we do we are (in a measure, at least) blamable ourselves And let it be distinctly understood that this address and declaration is not made in any spirit of envy or hate or malice, or any such thing But we are only actuated from a sense of duty to ourselves and to all concerned, for we feel that the time has fully come when something of a more definite character ought to be known and recognized between the church and the world Especially is this apparent when we consider the scriptural teaching on the matters to which we have herein referred Such, for instance, is the following

"Be not conformed to this world, but be ye transformed by the renewing of your mind, that you may prove what is that good and acceptable and perfect will of God "

It is, therefore, with the view, if possible, of counteracting the usages and practices that have crept into the churches that this effort on the part of the congregations hereafter named is made And now, in closing up this address and declaration, we state that we are impelled from a sense of duty to say that all such as are guilty of teaching or allowing and practicing the many innovations and corruptions to which we have referred, after having had sufficient time for meditation and reflection, if they will not turn away from such abominations, that we can not and will not regard them as brethren

(Signed)

P P Warren
A J Nance
Daniel Baker
J K P Rose
James Warren
Officers of the Sand Creek Church
Randolph Miller
Charles Erwin
W K Baker
Wm Cozier
Officers of Liberty Church
Wm R. Storm,
Ash Grove Church
J. H Hagan,
Union Church
Isaac Walters,
Mode Church [1]

---

[1] P P Warren, "Sand Creek Address and Declaration," *Christian Leader,* Vol III, No 37 (September 10, 1889), p 2

To avoid, if possible, any misunderstanding, those responsible for the "Sand Creek Address And Declaration" made it clear that this mass-meeting was not a convention to be considered a representative body of the church of Christ. It was made plain that this document was an expression only of the will of the churches that were responsible for it, and that it was presented only after it was seen that there was no other solution.[2]

The reaction for the moment was hardly dramatic. The *Christian-Evangelist* and the *Christian Standard* gave it slight notice. Samuel Magee thought it was a "foolish" move, 'in that it would be the means of prejudicing the popular mind. The brethren, however, were fully serious. It was plainly evident that somebody meant to do something, but what? Alfred Ellmore looked at it in this light:

I have a long and thoughtful letter from Brother Rose, of Sand Creek, Ill., in which he urges that all who are sound in the gospel come out and take a stand against this mountain of "progression" lately heaped upon the apostolic teaching. He is anxious that the *Leader* come out in clear terms, and show where it stands. Now, it seems to me that the *Leader* is pronounced against *all* this ungodliness, and has been from its birth. But we should all remember that we can't build a house in a day. This leaven of unrighteousness has been twenty-five years in gathering its mass of corruption. And like the man of sin, whom it serves, it has come in the garb of righteousness, hence the deception. As every generation must learn largely by experience, we were not prepared to meet it. Good men have wept and prayed over the matter, hoping that it might be only a transient cloud, and would soon dissipate, but in this they were disappointed. Like Catholicism and Mormonism, and every other ism, it is growing, and will continue to grow, as an eating cancer, and unless we *cut it out* the body will be ruined.

I hear that Brother Herndon is not in sympathy with the "Sand Creek" move, but he is in favor of a complete separation. But it is a great undertaking to declare a full separation in this great body. And seeing the danger to which we are exposed, and the body, as such, declining to take action, have not the Sand Creek brethren done precisely what we say the whole body should have done? And in making the advance, have they not done what many of us think is right? As I have said before, there is one of several things we can do, viz:

1. Ask the "progressive" men to return to our original plea

---

[2] Daniel Sommer, "Address and Declaration," *Octographic Review*, Vol XXXII, No 36 (September 5, 1889), p 8

in all things, viz, speak when the Bible speaks, and be silent when the Bible is silent

2. The brethren who are yet loyal to this plea, leave it, and go with the party who declare us only a religious "movement"

3   Remain together as we are and go on in endless confusion and strife; or,

4. Separate and have peace.

Now, let every thoughtful, loyal praying man decide for himself, and so act   As to my own individual part, I have decided long ago, and intend to stand by my convictions and the word of God. . .[3]

However, if the "Sand Creek Address And Declaration" of 1889 failed to arouse the brotherhood, the one of 1892 made up for any lack   Whereas the former declaration set forth the belief that the "innovating brethren"—those who had added instrumental music and the missionary society—had departed from the gospel, and unless they surrendered these, they could not be considered as brethren, the declaration of 1892 now went a step further, strongly recommending that every church that bought property should put a clause in the deed declaring that no instrument of music or other innovations should ever be used on the premises.

This suggestion touched off a verbal warfare that had repercussions upon all the brotherhood, and became a subject of discussion in all of the papers   The *Christian-Evangelist* insisted that this was a new creed made binding upon the people, that Sommer was now using civil law to enforce his beliefs. Sommer denied it   As for the matter of using civil law in church matters, the deed itself was that   The clause in the deed was simply a declaration that the property would not be used for other purposes than that for which it had been purchased. Sommer observed that brethren were tired of building church houses, only to be driven from them when someone comes along to put in an organ with which they cannot conscientiously worship.

The *Christian Standard* was loud in its denunciation of the Sand Creek Declaration. It called it a new Confession of Faith and suggested that all adherents to this must separate themselves from other brethren where the organ is used and where the society

---

[3]A Ellmore, "Wheat and Chaff," *Christian Leader*, Vol III, No 51 (December 17, 1889), p 4

is involved   Daniel Sommer was openly accused of being a
schismatic and a church divider. The *Standard* wrote.

The churches should be on their guard   They should know
that Daniel Sommer has abandoned apostolic ground and is no
more identified with the Disciples of Christ than Sidney Rigdon [1]
The *Standard* of June 25, 1892, advised "without reservation"
that Sommer should not be used as a preacher because of his
tirades "against the progressive Christianity we teach "[5] Probably
nothing had so aroused the ire of the *Standard* in some time
The *Standard* declared it to be the duty of other papers, like the
Advocate and the *Leader,* to say whether or not they are behind
this Sand Creek Declaration.

The *Advocate* watches the proceedings with mixed feelings
Lipscomb was prone to look upon mass-meetings with disfavor
He had observed the general tendency of them to assume a legislative position over the churches and to be the voice of the
congregations.   As for putting a clause in the deed, Lipscomb
was not quite ready to go that far, although he saw nothing objectionable to the practice.   He merely chose to wait and hope
there was a better way   As for the *Standard's* challenge for the
Advocate to speak out, J C. McQuiddy wrote:

Well for our part, the *Advocate* needs no second call to express
its sentiments on this momentous matter   The Sand Creek
manifesto was manifest folly, and the *Advocate* emphatically
denies any sympathy with Sommerism—whatever that is—Sand
Creekism, Sand Lotism, Sans-culottism, Standardism or any
other partyism in religion.   The *Advocate* is for Christ and His
church (chosen ones) and is in ardent sympathy with all who
are drawing their life from Him who is the true vine   . It
is not trying to build a church on the teachings of the *Standard's*
Fathers, nor is it following anybody's Fathers [6]

Lipscomb strongly defended Sommer.   He showed that Sommer,
in opposing these innovations, was not going against the pioneers,
but the *Standard* was   When the *Standard* complained about di-

[4]Russell Errett, "A Divisive Work," *Christian Standard,* Vol XXVIII,
No 25 (June 18, 1892), p 521

[5]Russell Errett, "Daniel Sommer," *Christian Standard,* Vol XXVIII,
No. 26 (June 25, 1892), p 540

[6]J. C McQuiddy, "Miscellany," *Gospel Advocate,* Vol XXXIV, No
26 (June 30, 1892), p 408

vision, it should remember that the men who introduce these things are the ones causing division.[7]

The *Christian Messenger* of Dallas, Texas, after reading Errett's remarks against Sommer and division, regarded the *Standard's* remarks as altogether ridiculous, insisting it could point out churches all over the country which have been divided over the organ and the missionary society, and the *Standard* during that time had not become the least indignant. Was the *Standard* really concerned about division, or was it more concerned about protecting its innovations?

The core of Sommer's declaration was that churches should put the clause in the deed to protect the building. Brethren who had worked and put their money into a building would not be forced out when others brought in the innovations. As to the principle involved, John T. Hinds writes:

If those who desire to change the use of the house from the well-understood purpose would pay those who dissent the money they put in the building, it would not be dishonest. though it would not be commendable to thus destroy the peace and harmony of the church. But when, by majority vote, the organ is put in and the house taken without paying those who are forced to leave, it is no more honest than it would be for a majority of a business firm or corporation to take the business without paying those who must leave the firm. Many times churches would do better if all the members possessed more of the common honesty of business life.[8]

The attitude of the brethren who opposed the introduction of these innovations during these years may best be compared to the perturbation occurring at the outbreak of any holocaust. No one knew quite what to do. General bewilderment ensued. J. W. McGarvey believed that the tendency toward the use of the instrument was then a current fantasy that would soon run its course, and so wrote,

. . . the prevalent rage for instruments of music in our worship is a passion and a fashion of the hour, and that like all fashions, when it shall have endured for a time, it will pass away. As in the case of other fashions. too, its devotees are usually deaf to reason on the subject and rebellious against authority. This tide

---

[7]David Lipscomb, "Our Response," *Gospel Advocate*, Vol XXXIV, No 27 (July 7, 1892), p 429
[8]John T Hinds, "Hearing and Doing," *Christian Leader*, Vol. IX, No. 20 (May 14, 1895), p. 6.

of feeling will not be stemmed and turned back by reason and authority of Scripture, but, like all other movements of the kind, it will go on from bad to worse until its own excesses will breed disgust for it and bring about a reaction   Such at least, is my expectation; and therefore, having little confidence in human nature but great confidence in the final triumph of the truth as it is in Christ, I shall toil on hopefully as the Master of the vineyard seems to direct [9]

But McGarvey's prophecy itself proved to be only a vain speculation.   Others lived on in hope that something providential would hinder the pushing of the instruments of music into the worship, but finally, it became evident that more stringent course of action must be devised.   By 1895 T. R. Burnett of Dallas, author of "Burnett's Budget" was ready to declare.

This Budget becomes more and more convinced every day that it will become necessary to establish churches of the apostolic order in every town in the state where the so-called "Christian Church" now holds sway   The lawless determination of the society and organ people to rule or ruin every church with which they have connection, and either put in the unscriptural things, or put out the brethren who oppose them, makes this plainly evident The loyal brethren need not waste any valuable time waiting for a reformation, for there is none in prospect.   Ephraim is joined to his idols, and he would rather have his society and music idol than any kind of Christian union known to the Bible. Brethren, proceed to re-establish the ancient order of things, just as if there was never a Church of Christ in your town   Gather all the brethren together who love Bible order better than modern fads and foolishness, and start the work and worship of the church in the old apostolic way   Do not go to law over church property It is better to suffer wrong than to do wrong   Build a cheap and comfortable chapel, and improve it when you get able.   It is better to have one dozen true disciples in a cheap house than a thousand apostate pretenders in a palace who love modern innovations better than Bible truth.   The battles of this reformation have yet to be fought.[10]

Since the churches were locally governed, it was impossible for them to act in any concerted action by any authorative convention.   The problem of what to do about those who were adding these innovations had to narrow itself down to the action of in-

[9] J W McGarvey, "What Shall We Do About the Organ?" *Gospel Advocate*, Vol XXVIII, No 25 (June 23, 1886), p 386

[10] T R Burnett, "Burnett's Budget," *Gospel Advocate*, Vol XXXVII, No. 19 (May 9, 1895), p 291

dividuals and of single congregations   That extreme measures
would be taken at one time and lax measures at another seemed
inevitable   There was no convention or synod to dictate measures
to be taken, and so the reaction to the introduction of innovations
was different in different places   Some, realizing that no representative convention of the churches ever met to declare non-
fellowship with the "so-called Christian Churches," to use Burnett's
phrase, have denied that there is any real division today   This
thought would easily furnish occasion for an interesting little problem for those with the idle time to engage in it

As the reality of division becomes increasingly evident, it will
be of interest to trace the hopeless plight of the so-called "middle
ground" that arose in Kentucky following the Civil War   J W
McGarvey, Moses E Lard, W. H. Hopson, L. B. Wilkes, and
Robert Graham were leaders in this school of thought   Each
adherent maintained and defended the right of a missionary
society to do the work of the church, while at the same time, each
fought the instrument of music in the worship as an innovation
In the days following the war there were no more popular preachers in the church than these men

In 1866 the *Gospel Advocate* was revived at Nashville while
the same year the *Christian Standard* was born. The *Standard*
looked upon these men in Kentucky as entirely too conservative
while the *Advocate* thought of them as entirely too liberal   So
far as the *Advocate's* line of thought went, the missionary society
was an unscriptural, unauthorized aid to the *work* of the church,
and the use of the instrument was an unscriptural, unauthorized
aid to the *worship* of the church.   The principle in each case was
the same   The *Standard* vigorously promoted the society, and undoubtedly, had it not been for the *Christian Standard* in those
critical years, the Society would have died   The *Advocate* was
published too far south, was too small a periodical, and the bitter
feelings between North and South that prevailed, made it almost
a hopeless task for the *Advocate* to exert any great influence,
except in its own local sphere of influence.

Some realized this and felt that the most hopeful prospects
possible before them would lie in starting the *Apostolic Times*
Over thirty years later, when Lipscomb reviewed the starting of
the *Times,* and its history, he wrote of it saying,

. . . About twenty-five years ago J. W. McGarvey, Moses E. Lard, W H Hopson, L B. Wilkes, and Robert Graham started the *Apostolic Times* at Lexington, Ky It was an open secret. if secret at all, that they started it to oppose the influence of the *Standard.* Wilkes wrote he disliked to do anything that would injure the *Advocate,* but the *Advocate* was too far South to hold Northern Kentucky against the influence of the Standard; so they thought it essential to establish a paper in Lexington, in the heart of Kentucky, to check the influence of the *Standard* They thought the *Advocate* would be smothered out (and I thought so, too) and they would get a large patronage in the South, all Kentucky, Missouri and a fair share north of the Ohio River There was no special objection to the *Advocate* then, all of them opposed the organ, and their support of the societies was not hearty This is proved by the fact that when they did not succeed as they had hoped, McGarvey wrote me and offered, if we would combine and come to Lexington, Brother Sewell or I, as we thought best, could be managing editor The *Times* went into other hands. Allen had started the *Old Path Guide,* that seemed to prosper, and McGarvey went on it with him After Allen's death McGarvey and Kurfees wrote for the *Guide* Some of the owners sought to restrict Kurfees that he should not write on these subjects He refused to write unless he could be free to maintain the whole truth as he saw it. McGarvey stood with him. Both left the *Guide,* and McGarvey went to the *Standard,* the influence of which he started out to oppose; but he did not go free to discuss such questions as he thought the Bible and interests of truth required He submitted to have his hands tied, he submitted to the very restrictions on the *Standard* that he and Kurfees had refused to submit to on the *Guide* In the *Christian Evangelist,* last year, he said "I did my best by writing and speaking for about fifteen years to check the progress of the innovation (of instrumental music) among us, but when all the papers through whose columns I could hope to reach those who engaged in it were closed against the further discussion of the subject, and when the minds of those I could hope to convince were equally closed, I desisted, because I did not wish to whistle against the wind, especially when I had no whistle to whistle with " Which means the popular papers would not permit him to discuss questions he thought the truth of God demanded should be discussed He sticks to them, with his hands tied, and ridicules the *Advocate* because it is not as popular as the society and organ papers I said, "He sat on the hind step of the band wagon", to have completed the picture. I should have said, "with his hands tied " Brother McGarvey now says he will not leave a church for perverting one part of the service James says "Whosoever shall keep the whole law, and yet offend in one point, he is guilty of all." Certainly it is applicable in this case, if ever.[11]

Thus, the passing of years had wrought changes. By 1890 Lard, Graham, and Hopson were dead, and Wilkes because of old age was no longer active. McGarvey remained the sole survivor of the five earlier men. The *Apostolic Times* had seen its failing days. F. G. Allen had grasped it from possible oblivion and joined it with the *Old Path Guide*. Allen's death, however, in 1886, made its future still uncertain. For awhile, McGarvey and M. C. Kurfees tried to make it steer a conservative course, but Kurfees' conservativism became unbearable to the management and he had to retire. McGarvey resigned in 1889, taking "the last of the conservative element from the *Guide*." From here on, the *Guide* steered the same editorial course of the *Standard*.

After McGarvey ceased his editorial labors on the *Guide,* he turned his attention to writing for the *Christian Standard.* At first his articles combated the spirit of rationalism and higher criticism an interest in which was aroused in the brotherhood by the teachings of R. C. Cave. Although he still disagreed with the *Standard's* attitude toward instrumental music, McGarvey felt a closer affinity to the *Standard* than to the *Advocate.* The exact reason for this may be hard to say, but probably several entered in to it. For one thing the proximity of Lexington to Cincinnati had something to do with it. McGarvey was literally swallowed up by a people of the *Standard's* type of thinking. The *Advocate's* strict insistence that the missionary society was unscriptural aroused McGarvey's ire who always defended the society's right to exist. Then, too, Lipscomb himself had at times snubbed McGarvey's overtures of friendliness, and furthermore, had openly criticized McGarvey's course. All of these factors had a tendency to alienate McGarvey from the *Advocate,* and made him set out for himself a course which he pursued almost alone.

On March 1, 1901 McGarvey passed his seventy-second birthday. The last forty years of his life had been spent in connection with the College of The Bible and the Broadway Church at Lexington, Kentucky. In September, 1902 he passed the fiftieth anniversary of his preaching career. Thirty-two years he had

---

[11]David Lipscomb, "Brother McGarvey's Position, Again," *Gospel Advocate,* Vol XL, No 6 (February 10, 1898), p 88.

spent as an elder of the Broadway Church. All of this time he
had vigorously opposed the use of the instrument in the worship.
In 1883 when the rumor was circulated that McGarvey had
ceased his opposition to instrumental music, he wrote to Moses
Porter, an elder of the church at Lovington, Illinois, the following
postcard:

Dear Brother:
Yours of the 3d I answer at the earliest opportunity. I have
not withdrawn my opposition to the organ. I would not hold
membership with nor contract to preach for a church using one.
Its introduction against the conscientious protest of a minority is
high-handed wickedness, and can be prompted by no spirit but
that of the world and the flesh.[12]

When it became evident that the instrument of music was to
be an occasion of the disruption of fellowship in the church, many
looked to McGarvey to see his attitude. The terse answer of
the Lexington professor was, "I have never proposed to withdraw fellowship from brethren simply because of their use of
instrumental music in the worship."

Now the enigma of J. W. McGarvey became clearly evident.
On the one side McGarvey maintained his belief that the introduction of the instrument was "high handed wickedness"; on
the other, he would never withdraw fellowship from those who
used it. Again, McGarvey deplored the fact that Lipscomb,
Sewell, and James A. Harding bitterly opposed the Society; on
the other hand, McGarvey would never contract to preach at a
place where the organ was used. But still, it was plain that
"society churches" were the ones that planted the instrument.
Srygley was certainly right when he wrote,

Brother McGarvey ought to feel very grateful to David
Lipscomb, J. A. Harding, and the Gospel Advocate, if for no
other reason, because they are building up and maintaining
churches in which he can hold membership and for which he can
contract to preach, as he cannot do in the churches he himself
is helping organized effort to build up.[13]

Two months after McGarvey celebrated his fiftieth anniversary
of preaching the gospel, the Broadway Church announced that

---

[12]J. W. McGarvey, "Queries," *Gospel Advocate*, Vol. XXXIX, No 33
(August 19, 1897), p 518
[13]F. D. Srygley, "From the Papers," *Gospel Advocate*, Vol XXXIX, No
34 (August 26, 1897), p. 529

on Sunday, November 2, 1902 a vote would be taken on the use
of the instrument in that church.   McGarvey, knowing that the
predominence of feeling in the congregation favored the instrument, went to the preacher, Mark Collis, and asked for a letter
for his wife and himself.   The voting was deferred until Sunday,
November 23, at which time, by a count of 361 to 202, the church
voted in the organ.[14]   McGarvey took his letter, and he and his
wife went to the Chestnut Street Church.   I. B. Grubbs, who
had preceded him a few years before in going to this congregation, met McGarvey when the latter, on the third Lord's Day of
September, walked down the aisle to present himself and his
wife as members of this congregation.   Moved with deep feeling,
Grubbs remarked, "Brother McGarvey, we'd rather have you
than ten thousand aids to worship."[15]

Thus McGarvey was driven from one congregation to another
until his death, but it was hardly more than McGarvey himself
could expect   In the words of Jesse P. Sewell,

Professor McGarvey may speak out against the use of instrumental music in the worship, as he does, and say things
against it that those who refuse to use it would hardly say; but
what do the people who want the instrumental music care about
this thing so long as he gives his influence almost entirely (except
in his home congregation) to those who use it ?   Brother McGarvey
believes that instrumental music is wrong, and so teaches; still,
he gives his name and influence to a paper that advocates its use
and associates with churches that use it (except at home and possibly on a few other occasions)   So, while he believes and teaches
that the thing is wrong, there is not a church in the land that
uses it that will not today point to Brother McGarvey as "one
of the strong men on our side."   His influence goes with his fellowship, not with his faith and teaching.[16]

Thus McGarvey became the last of the vanguard of the "middle
ground" whose pretentious claims were a tower of strength after
the war.   This distinction although of dubious value the pertinacious McGarvey will always possess.

As two groups now emerged, a prominent question became

---

[14]Daniel Sommer, "Publisher's Notes," *Octographic Review,* Vol XLV,
No 49 (December 9, 1902), p 1

[15]W C Morro, *"Brother McGarvey,"* (St Louis, The Bethany Press,
1940), p 223.

[16]J P Sewell, "Wouldn't Stand for Organ," *Gospel Advocate,* Vol
XLIV, No 49 (December 4, 1902), p 771

"What Name Shall We Wear?" Barton W. Stone, perhaps following the suggestion of Rice Haggard, had insisted that we ought to be Christians and Christians only. Alexander Campbell, on the other hand, had positively expressed his preference for the term, Disciple, because it was used in the New Testament to refer to Christ's followers before the name Christian was given, and too, because a religious group in New England, Unitarian in religious beliefs, called themselves Christians, and Campbell did not want to prejudice the restoration movement by putting this dubious title upon them. At the time Stone, John T. Johnson and many others refused to be moved by Campbell's reasoning. Stone wrote in answer to Campbell:

You well knew the great attachment thousands of us had to the name *Christian,* and many believed from your writing that you had adopted it as the most appropriate name. You also knew that many could not conscientiously be called *Disciples,* as a family name. You knew your two warmest friends, J. T. Johnson and myself, rejected the title of our Hymn Book, because it was called the Disciples' Hymn Book. Brother Campbell, ought you not to have respected the feelings of so many, who united their energies with *yours* in promoting the common cause? The reasons given by you for rejecting the name *Christian,* because you were anticipated by a people in the East and in some parts of our country, who are Unitarians, and who do not baptize for the remission of sins, nor break the loaf every first day, are the things so objectionable, and objected to by all, whom I have heard speak on the subject.[17]

Stemming from Campbell's influence came an element who strongly favored calling the church the "Disciples of Christ Church." The title "Christian Church" was perhaps most frequently used, and for many years, except on a few occasions, was very little questioned. Still the title "church of Christ" had nothing to be said against it being the most defensible title of it. The lucent pen of Ben Franklin wrote:

Those who are aiming to be simply *people of God* have nothing to do with *naming themselves,* or *choosing what name they shall wear.* They should speak of themselves in the style of scripture precisely That is, they should speak of themselves as the Lord speaks of them . The Lord did not select a name and call them by that name *exclusively* Nor did the apostles, or

---

[17]Barton W Stone, "Communication," *Millennial Harbinger,* New Series, Vol. IV, No. 1 (January, 1940), p 21.

followers of Christ, select and adopt any one designation *exclusively*. . . . No matter whether it was intended as a reproach, by those who first applied it, or not, it is no reproach to be *called a Christian,* much less to *be a Christian.* . . . But if the whole church existed some ten years before any were *called Christians,* and the whole New Testament written, with the name but *three times in it,* it is clear that it was by no means *exclusively* used to designate the first disciples or followers of Christ.

. . . In nine cases out of ten we will be perfectly understood by saying "the church," "the body," or the "kingdom."   There is no necessity for lugging in such terms as "Christian Church," "Disciples' Church" or "Disciple Church."   This is as ridiculous as "Disciple Preacher."   If we have simply *the mind* of the Lord, we can express ourselves *in the words* of the Lord.[18]

W. K. Pendleton disagreed with Alexander Campbell on the name.   Admitting there were four terms common to the primitive church (viz., (1) disciples, (2) saints, (3) believers, and (4) brethren), Pendleton found no reason to adopt the title "Disciples of Christ," as the exclusive title.   On this appellation Pendleton said: ". . . We cannot concede that it should be adopted by us as the specific name by which we would be called."   The term, thought Pendleton, was "too vague and indefinite to answer the demands of a significant and definite name."   However, for individuals to refer to themselves as Christians, thought Pendleton, is at once "sufficiently definite and comprehensive for a significant and adequate name."   As to calling the church "The Christian Church," Pendleton wrote:

Since the public name of the disciples is Christians, are we warranted in calling the church, which is composed of Christians, "the Christian Church"?   We judge not.   Such an expression is nowhere found in the language of the New Testament.   We have "The Church of God," "The Churches of God," and "The Churches of Christ," but nowhere Christian Church or Churches.[19]

By the decade of the 1890's considerable agitation over the name was now coming up.   Among the more liberal element the "Disciples of Christ," as a designation, became more popular.   But, was it to distinguish a new denomination?   President McDiarmid of Bethany College writes in the *Christian Standard* on this usage.

---

[18]Ben Franklin, "What Name Shall We Wear?" *American Christian Review,* Vol XIV, No. 26 (June 27, 1871), p 204.

[19]W K Pendleton, "What Shall We Be Called?" *Millennial Harbinger,* Vol XXXVIII, No. 9 (September, 1867), pp. 498-505.

F. D. Srygley copies McDiarmid's statements and adds some thoughts of his own. McDiarmid writes:

How shall one religious body distinguish itself in literature from other religious bodies *without either using an unscriptural term, or using a scriptural term unscripturally?* *This thing cannot be done.* And all for the reason that the divisions that make the distinguishing names necessary are themselves unscriptural But we *have* these divisions, and while they exist we must find some terms that will distinguish them.

F. D. Srygley commented:

This is a distinct admission that the religious body which he designates Disciples of Christ is itself an unscriptural body As long as an unscriptural body exists the world must have, and will have, some name to designate it, of course. In such a case it is courteous and proper to use such name to designate it as those who compose the body select for themselves. But what authority, according to the New Testament, has President McDiarmid or any other Christian to belong to such an unscriptural body? Does he seriously think the New Testament authorizes him to belong to a body which cannot be designated without using either an unscriptural term, or using a scriptural term unscripturally. and all for the reason that the body itself is unscriptural?[20]

Bethany College, in those days, was publishing a student paper called the "Bethany Guardian" An item in the paper suggested that Alexander Campbell had belonged to the "Disciples of Christ Church." C. L. Loos cared very little for such designations and so replied to this statement by saying:

No, Alexander Campbell never belonged to the Disciples' Church. There was, to the best of my knowledge, no such church in his day. Yet I ought, perhaps, not to assert this too positively. There may have been in A Campbell's time, in some remote backwoods corner of the land, where schools were poor, where the sun rises late and sets early, a Disciples' Church. If so, it must have lived in great isolation, for at Bethany, where I lived almost an entire generation, we never heard of a people or a congregation with such a name. . . . The Disciple Church is a thing of later times, born of an ignorance of the elementary New Testament teaching of our better days, of a sad lack of sound grammatical teaching in English, and, above all, of a disposition to yield to the pressure for a denominational name. so that we might be like other people.[21]

---

[20] F D Srygley, "From the Papers," *Gospel Advocate*, Vol XXXVIII, No 1 (January 2, 1896), p 2

[21] F. D Srygley, "From the Papers," *Gospel Advocate*, Vol. XXXVIII, No. 16 (April 16, 1896), p. 241.

But W K Pendleton has shown great acumen by writing:

> The *quality* of the members of a church may be Christian, and
> Christian Church expresses this thought; but when the purpose
> is to state the possessor and head of the church—that is, the
> relation of founder and proprietor—we say "church of Christ"
> It is very plain to me, therefore, why the Holy Spirit never used
> the phrase "Christian Church." The grand idea is not in it.
> Brethren, is not this another striking example of how dangerous
> it is to depart from the rule of calling Bible things by Bible names?
> There is a mighty difference between the "church of Christ" and
> the "Christian Church" Let us be careful to mark it.[22]

The prophecy of Moses E. Lard, that "expediency may well be
the rock on which this reformation will go to ruin," was proving
remarkably accurate. Every addition to the work and worship
of the New Testament Church was excused on the ground of
"expediency" How long the church might have continued without disruption had nothing but the missionary society been involved is difficult to say. It is certain that the Missionary Society
did not present the impetus to division that the instrument did.
Individuals could have attended worship services, and otherwise
worshiped acceptably, even though there were differences. of
whether the church should support the society. Those who conscientiously believed the instrument a sinful addition to the worship could not have gone to the service where it was used, and
worshiped with it, without directly violating their own consciences
Therefore, once the instrument was introduced, they, believing
as they did that its use was sinful, had little other choice than to
leave, and band together and worship without it

This problem being settled in the individuals' minds, there came
now other problems   Could this band of people who came together determined to worship without the instrument and the
former group that worshiped with it continue in fellowship? Considered from a practical standpoint, this was impossible   That
body of people who refused the worship with the instrument soon
found that if they allowed preachers who favored the instrument
to come in, that in time it was a reoccurrence of the old trouble,
a division within the congregation   To prevent this constantly
recurring division they were forced to use those public teachers
who did not believe in the use of the instrument, and, also, teach

---

[22]W K Pendleton, "Christian Church or Church of Christ," *Christian
Standard*, Vol. XI, No. 18 (April 29, 1876), p 140.

the flock against it. Thus, from the practical standpoint there was no other step to take.

In taking this drastic step, which was clearly unavoidable, they must now meet the accusations of proponents of the instrument, viz , that they were making the instrument a test of fellowship, and were, therefore, causing division. Actually, of course, these lines of fellowship were definitely drawn by both sides. Advocates of the instrument were as consistent in their refusal to use preachers who would preach *against* the instrument as those opposed to the instrument were in their refusal to use preachers who would preach *for* it

Basically, the action is to be understood only in the light of the real issue involved. On the one side, the following statement from W K Homan in the *Christian Courier* expresses the viewpoint of advocates of the instrument:

One who admits that the New Testament is silent as to the use of an organ as an aid to the worship of God in song, and yet refuses Christian recognition and fellowship to Christians who exercise the liberty that God has left them to use such aid, is guilty of flagrant sectarianism in attempting to make a law for God's people where God has made none, and is a divider of the Body of Christ . . .

This sentiment was expressed hundreds of times in different words by the numerous advocates of the instrument. It was precisely the argument of J Carroll Stark to Joe S Warlick. God had not said, "Thou shalt not use instrumental music in the worship." Since God had made no law against it, the use of it is a violation of no law of God, and is, therefore, not sinful But opponents of the instrument regarded this as a dodge of the basic issue. God had not said, "Thou shalt not count beads as an act of worship." If someone introduced the counting of beads, as Catholics practice it, as an act of worship, would any person objecting be the cause of division? The principle could be applied in a thousand such cases. To adopt that as a principle of restoring the New Testament church is suicidal, for it would, as McGarvey pointed out, open the floodgates to an endless number of unscriptural practices.

The basic issue lay, not merely in an innocent-looking thing like an instrument, but in a principle beneath it. Moses E. Lard forceably put it:

The question of instrumental music in churches of Christ involves a great and sacred principle. But for this, the subject is not worthy of one thought at the hands of the child of God. That principle is the right of man to introduce innovations into the prescribed worship of God   This right we utterly deny.   The advocates of instrumental music affirm it.   This makes the issue. As sure as the Bible is a divine book, we are right and they are wrong.   Time and facts will prove the truth of this.   The churches of Christ will be wrecked the day the adverse side triumphs, and I live in fear that it will do it.   Our brethren are now freely introducing melodeons in their Sunday schools.   This is the first step to the act, I fear   As soon as the children of these schools go into the church, in goes the instrument with them.   Mark this.

And so, by 1906, the work of division had taken its full course. The "Christian Churches" or "Disciples of Christ," as they preferred to be called, took their instruments and their missionary society and walked a new course   The battles had been long, treacherous, costly and bitter   Many brethren, still licking their wounds, looked to the future to start all over again.

CHAPTER XXII

HORIZONS OF DESTINY

Nearly half a century has passed since J. W. Shepherd compiled and submitted the first religious census on the numerical strength of the churches. With the year 1906, the date of that census, the scope of these volumes closes But, before drawing the curtain across this study a final word should be said about the various congregations of the church of Christ—their problems, past and present, and the destiny awaiting them.

When the innovations began to be introduced into the work and worship of the church a century ago, strong opposition resulted. With the passing of a few years some, even of the more intrepid opposers, sensing that these were going to be popular despite their opposition, relaxed and joined the popular movement. Others, however, with more trenchant consciences found it impossible to yield. Driven from their former places of worship, they were forced to start all over. Since they were in the minority, the majority forged ahead. The churches of Christ at the present time are realizing an astonishing growth, but this has not always been true. It would be vain—not to mention untruthful—to deny that there have not been problems internally that have delayed this growth. It is toward some of these problems that we now turn our attention.

EXTREMES

Certainly one of the major concerns of the church has been presented by the extremists who have frequently arisen. The sincerity of this class is hardly open to question, but that the total effect of their influence has been a retarding influence is equally undeniable. These extremes owe their origin to a jealous concern over the full import of Thomas Campbell's famous motto, "Where the Bible speaks, we speak; where the Bible is silent, we are silent." Since the Bible is silent, they reasoned, about the Sunday School, the use of literature, etc., these cannot be allowed. Thus, the extremes were created.

The Sunday School. The prime objection to the Sunday School was expressed in the words of Lydia L. Bowman in the *Christian Leader* in 1890 when she wrote:

There are many advocates of the Sunday School, but surely these have not seen the evils of this institution as they now exist. In the first place, there is no authority for it in the word of God, and those who plead that it is essential to the growth of the church must admit that God overlooked a very important item in the plan of salvation, and man, being wiser than God, has supplied the deficiency with a Sunday School. . . .[1]

Thus, the very existence of the Sunday School has far-reaching implications, according to one extreme view. But it is obvious that the very ambiguity of the term, Sunday School, is one cause of the discussion that has centered around it. David Lipscomb wrote: ". . . A Sunday School as a distinct organization or under the direction of or composing a part of any organization except the simple churches of Christ, is open to all the objections laid against the missionary society." If the Sunday School be organized as a separate organization from the church to do the work of the church, it differs, according to Lipscomb, in no major principle from the missionary society. But, if the term, "Sunday School," connotes this, it need not necessarily be so. Lipscomb wrote:

To have clear conceptions, let us go back a little. The only manifestation or development of the church on earth is the local congregation. The church cannot be approached save in and through the local congregation. It cannot act save in and through the local congregation. The local congregation can act as a whole or through its individual members. Just as the human body to which the spirit likens it, can act as a whole or through the individual members. The idea of a church on earth, save as it manifests itself in the individual congregations and through its members as parts of this body, is contrary to every presentation of the church in the Bible.

Now any Sunday School other than the local church through its members, or individual Christians, directed by its elders. teaching the word of God to those who assemble to be taught, is wrong It is the duty of the elders to direct in this teaching and to control and guide the Sunday School as much as it is their duty to direct the Lord's day worship It is simply the church doing the work committed to it. No officer, no organization outside of the regular

[1]Lydia L Bowman, "The Sunday-school," *Christian Leader,* Vol IV, No 24 (June 17, 1890), p 1

organization and officers of the church is needed or is allowable
Any association with any society outside of the church is sinful.
I do not mean the elders are to do all the teaching in the Sunday
School, any more than they ought to do all the reading, exhortation,
thanksgiving at the worship. But they should direct it all and see
it is properly done. The only allowable Sunday school is the
teaching of the word of God in classes under the direction of the
elders of the church, or by individual Christians. A separation
of the Sunday School into an organization distinct from the church
and the teaching done in it, without the superintendence of the
elders, is the source through which many of the corruptions work
into the church of God.

With this understanding of a Sunday School there is no principle in common between it and the missionary society. The one
is the church in a perfectly scriptural manner doing the work God
has laid upon it, without any organism outside of or separate from
the church and without any unscriptural organisms in the church
The society is a distinct organism from the church doing the work
God committed to the church. It takes the work from the officers
of the church, and gives it to officers of its own body and all the
evil before mentioned, necessarily grows out of this perversion of
the order of God. . . .[2]

And so, with David Lipscomb the principle to be followed was,
". . . whatever can be used to enable a man to do more of the
service of God or to do it better without entering into or modifying
that service or without adding to or taking from the appointments
or institutions of God, is an allowable expedient. Whatever modifies or changes, adds to or takes from the services and appointments of God is sinful."[3]

It is right for the church to study the Bible when it comes together to worship; it is wrong·for it not to. The segregation into
classes according to age or knowledge attained is but a convenient
arrangement to do the thing God requires—study the Bible. So,
E. G. Sewell wrote:

. . . But while God has thus required his people to know and
to do his will, he has not fixed the time and place where the reading
and studying shall be done; whether alone, in the family when all
are together, at prayer meeting in the week, or in the meeting on
the first day of the week. This part of it is left to our wisdom.
The Lord requires that we shall study, shall know his will, but

---

[2]David Lipscomb, "Is It An Unauthorized Practice?" *Gospel Advocate.*
Vol XXXI, No 5 (January 30, 1889), p 70

[3]David Lipscomb, "Is It An Unauthorized Practice," *Gospel Advocate,*
Vol XXXI, No. 5 (January 30, 1889), p 70

the precise time, place and circumstances under which the reading shall be done are not given. It is certainly right for a man to sit down alone every day at some hour that may suit his other engagements, and read the word of God. It is unquestionably right for a husband and father to read the word of God to his family, and thus teach them the will of the Lord while he himself is studying, for he is required to bring up his children in the nurture and admonition of the Lord. It would certainly be right for a man to sit down in the morning when he first rises from sleep, and read a few chapters of the word of God, and thus begin the duties of the day with a lesson in God's word. And yet there is just as much authority for several members to sit together when assembled on the first day of the week and read and study a chapter of the Lord's word as for one to sit alone and do it on that day or any other. That we must study and learn the Lord's will is positively required. But as to when and where we shall do the studying is not fixed. This is left to our discretion. . . . Some of the strongest churches, and most thoroughly enlightened members we know, are those that have Bible classes on Lord's day, and read, investigate, and talk over a chapter or more each Lord's day, and that do not allow anything they control to keep them from it. Yes, there is just as much authority for the Bible class on Lord's day as there is to sit down and read a chapter alone at home. No one needs be afraid of starting an innovation in the church by having a Bible class in it. Nay, verily, have more of them, and study the lessons more at home.

The Bible class is simply a help in doing a thing which the Lord has commanded to be done, but has not prescribed the precise manner in which it shall be done. God has required Christians to meet together on the first day of the week to break bread, but does not tell how they shall travel to get together. This is left to them. They walk, ride on a wagon, horseback, in a buggy, or on a train. But come together they must, or they will not obey the Lord. But that one that walks to the place can worship God just as well when he gets there as the one who came horseback or on a train. The whole manner of getting there is left to man's choice. But he that willingly fails to go sets at naught the authority of God and endangers his soul's salvation. . . .[4]

Literature. Closely allied to the extreme of the Sunday School was the contention that the use of the literature in the Sunday School was a sinful practice. It is difficult for one to escape the conclusion that the origin of this extreme lay in jealousy over commercial interests between publishing concerns. The *American*

---

[4] E G Sewell, "Shall We Have Bible Classes?" *Gospel Advocate,* Vol. XXVIII, No 32 (August 11, 1886), p. 497.

Christian Review, while under the editorship of John F. Rowe, complained of the *Christian Standard* that one of the departures it fostered was the use of lesson leaves. The *Standard* was shrewd enough to single out this extreme and make capital of it.

Actually, of course, the use of literature was a very innocent practice. Extremists showed the utmost folly in comparing it to the creeds of denominationalism. Lesson leaves represented no more than a *written* method of teaching, whereas public preaching was *oral.* No more authority was attached to it than was attached to oral declamation.

The Preacher. Extremists have generally made a field day of the preacher—his work, his pay, and in fact with nearly every phase of his life.

The problem of "located preachers" came in for the usual critical examination. One extreme begets another, and so it is here. D. S. Burnet fathered the idea of making the preacher the "pastor" of a congregation. In Bible times it is generally understood that the term bishop and the term pastor referred to the same function—that of overseeing the flock. This function belonged to the elders of the New Testament church. By the time of the Civil War, it was becoming an increased practice in the church of placing a preacher in "charge" of a congregation, and giving to him the title "pastor." Usually the responsibility of overseeing the flock belonged almost exclusively to him.

This tendency very correctly came under the critical eye of many brethren. But in their application of a remedy, many concluded that a "located preacher" was to be tabooed. The idea was slow taking hold that a preacher might possibly establish himself in a certain geographical area for a lengthy period of time and preach the gospel under the oversight of a scriptural set of elders without assuming the function of those elders. The failure to sense this possibility greatly deterred the forward progress of the churches for many years.

Still connected with the preacher was the problem of his pay. In the earlier days Alexander Campbell preached without receiving financial remuneration for it. There were two reasons for this. The first reason was that Campbell did not have to be paid From the farm which he received from his father-in-law Campbell managed to make considerable money, so that when he died he was a relatively wealthy man. The second reason for taking no money

showed the sagacity of the Bethany sage. Leaders in any movement are subjects of considerable criticism, and by his refusal to
take money for his religious work, Alexander Campbell was never
criticized for leading a religious reformation as a means of making
money. Likewise, David Lipscomb seldom accepted pay for his
preaching It was not because he believed this wrong, but only
that he made a sufficient living from secular work that he did not
need it.

The economic condition of the country, particularly in the
South, reflected itself upon this whole problem. After the war,
people had no money, and nearly everyone was in exactly the same
condition If preachers had refused to preach because there was
no money in it, few communities would have had any preaching.
Consequently, that preacher was looked down upon who would
refuse to take the gospel to the poor. The poor were far more
prevalent than usual. A cardinal virtue of the preacher was his
willingness to preach where he would receive little or no pay
Most preachers, then, were farmers, doctors, teachers, or merchants They made their living in this way that they might preach
the gospel free of charge.

In the course of time churches began to expect to receive all
preaching without paying the preacher. If, in a few cases, they
could get Alexander Campbell to preach for nothing, they could
hardly see why they should pay another preacher with less ability
than Campbell. As economic conditions bettered themselves in
the country, church members had more money, but they still
wanted their preaching for nothing. No one can read the files of
the *Gospel Advocate* from the close of the Civil War until after
the turn of the century without noting the swinging of the pendulum on this subject At first, every encouragement was given
for preachers to earn their living at a secular work and preach the
gospel free of charge. It was a case of necessity. By 1901 and
after, E. A Elam felt frequently called upon to censure the selfishness of churches who refused to pay their preachers anything adequate for their labors. When John Augustus Williams, biographer
for "Racoon" John Smith, wrote his reminiscenses of the restoration, he could not fail to notice this attitude He wrote:

As for the churches, though they were zealous enough for the
ancient faith, they had not yet been fully trained in the ancient
work. They had been quick to learn from Mr Campbell the evils

of a hireling spirit in the ministry, and they curiously reasoned among themselves that if it is wrong to work for hire in the Lord's vineyard, it is equally wrong to pay hire to those who labor. The gospel, many thought, should be freely dispensed, and as freely enjoyed Hence it was, in those early days, that so many earnest preachers were doctors, or farmers, or schoolteachers, or merchants, or dentists, or even phrenologists, or, in fact, anything by which they might, like Paul, earn an honest support while preaching the Word . . [5]

But the pendulum was slow in swinging Any preacher who undertook to teach the congregation out of its selfishness, and to stress their duty to support their laborers, immediately ran the risk of severe criticism for preaching for money. Many were silent, preferring insufficient support to the criticism that they were preaching for money.

Acts 2 42 Another problem closely allied with those of the preacher was the "order of worship." The originator of this extreme was Alfred Ellmore. Ellmore, born near Elnora, Indiana (then called "Owl Prairie," after an Indian chief by the name of Owl), was reared south of Frankfort, Indiana. About 1886 he moved to Covington, Indiana, from whence radiated his ideas Ellmore, despite the fact that he promoted an extreme position on the "order of worship," was one of the most tireless gospel preachers in the church of his day, and one of the most devoted to Christ. It is one of the tragedies of promoting extreme positions that in future years one's good points are forgotten in the objections raised against his extremes.

The point in his position was that Acts 2: 42 furnished a divine pattern of worship. This affirmation arose chiefly as an answer to those promoting "innovations." As the use of the instrument came to be more widely advocated, objectors raised the point that it was a human addition to a divine pattern. This was in turn met by a fervent denial that there was no divine pattern laid down for us in the New Testament And to meet this, Alfred Ellmore conceived of the idea that Acts 2: 42 was the divine pattern of worship. He said:

Within the last seventy-five years, Acts 2: 42 has been quoted perhaps ten thousand times as describing the order of the worship of the first church, and yet, in about nine thousand nine hundred

[5]John Aug Williams, "Reminiscences—VII," *Christian Leader*, Vol. XII, No 9 (March 1, 1898), p 2

and ninety and nine and a half times, the advocates have failed to adopt this order. I have often heard of men carrying dark lanterns, but I am inclined to think that nothing is so dark as the man who is religiously blind. Fifty years hence, children in the gospel will wonder at our stupidity in not being able to see the harmony of the order of the worship in the Jewish temple and that of the Church of Christ.

And upon this divine order I comment again. Let the bishops go up into the stand: one read and another offer the opening prayer. (1) Then, under the supervision of the bishops, let a half-dozen occupy five minutes each in the lesson, which was announced the Lord's Day before teaching (2) Take up the fellowship. And I would be understood here as teaching that they should *take up the fellowship,* and not do something else in the place of it. (3) Break the loaf. (4) The prayers. Let from two to five offer prayers of two to three minutes each time. Now, if Acts 2: 42 is the divine model, then nothing else is. And I insist that we wheel into line at once. Professing to be apostolic, let us be apostolic. . . .[6]

Ellmore was vociferous in insisting that all the churches adopt this "divine model." "Why continue in that hireling-pastor-every-Sunday system?" he once asked. If it be inquired, if Acts 2: 42 is intended to be the "divine model," why does it exclude singing, Ellmore's reply was that it was implied in the "teaching."

Ellmore's known love for the truth and knowledge of the Scriptures gave a ready impetus to the spreading of these ideas. Churches grew up, particularly around Ellmore's home in Indiana, thoroughly imbibed with this point of view, and have in some cases remained so unto this day. This extreme very early became planted in Indianapolis The ancient order was first preached in the city in 1833. After the Civil War, the original congregation, called the Central Church, put in the instrument of music. It was about 1878. A group refused to worship with the instrument and left. Leader in the group was Dr. Joshua Webb, the man who converted S. K. Hoshour from the Lutherans. The little church met on Mulberry Street in a house built on the property of Dr. Webb. No preacher was allowed to preach at the morning worship. Each man read a scripture and "exhorted" as far as time permitted. The evening service, if any, was given to evangelistic type of worship with the preacher, if any, preaching.

A Ellmore, "Wheat and Chaff," *Christian Leader,* Vol. II, No 9 (February 28, 1888), p 5

It can be safely said of all of these extremes that they represent only a small minority in the churches of Christ today. Here and there are geographical areas where pockets of extremist-colored congregations are found, but this is not generally characteristic of the church. Consequently, members of the church seldom fail to feel some chagrin when one of these extremes is held up as being representative of the church when this is far from the case. The extremes actually owe their origin to a reaction against the introduction of "innovations," and to genuine desire to be wholly acceptable to God.

MISSIONS

Because many brethren objected to the missionary society, they were accused of not believing in cooperation, having no love for lost souls, and generally, of having no interest in mission work. While this may have been true in some instances, it was far from being predominantly the case. Most of those who objected to the society were busily engaged in establishing churches throughout the nation. Their work was less glamorous, received less publicity, and the preachers themselves received far less money. But they did considerable mission work.

While Tolbert Fanning was objecting to the Society, the church established at Franklin College was sending J. J. Trott to the Cherokee Indians in Arkansas. Later, when the Cherokees were pushed further west into Oklahoma Territory, the churches were not lax in preaching the gospel to them. R. W. Officer, supported by the Gainesville, Texas, congregation, began work among these Indians about 1880 Two years later, the church at Paris, Texas, undertook this mission work, sending Officer among the Indians. In 1888 there were over fifty-six thousand Indians in "Indian Territory" divided among the Choctaws, Cherokees, Creeks, Chickasaws, and Seminoles. That year there were about nine hundred members of the church of Christ among the number, mostly the converts of R. W. Officer. Among the converts was H. C. Collier, a full-blooded Cherokee, who was instrumental in establishing a church at Muskegee, a town one hundred miles north of Atoka, Officer's headquarters.

Foreign missionary work received little concern from the churches of Christ until after 1880 That year, Jules DeLaunay went to Paris, France, to establish a congregation. At his death about fifteen years later, he had a congregation of four hundred people worshiping after the pattern of New Testament teaching DeLaunay, reared a Roman Catholic, was educated in Rome After becoming a Jesuit priest, the Roman Catholic Board of Foreign Missions was preparing to send him to China. Once, while walking in the catacombs of Rome with two friends, De-Launay was struck with the idea that the religion of the early martyrs was that of the New Testament, not of the papacy. His friends told him not to say that publicly or he would disappear. Soon after he came to America, he heard for the first time the preaching of the apostolic gospel, and espoused the cause of New Testament Christianity.

During the summer of 1889, three congregations in Nashville undertook to send Azariah Paul to Armenia. Paul, born near Harpoot in eastern Asia Minor in the ancient province of Cappodicia, came to the College of the Bible in 1884. During the summers he was in school, he preached for a colony of Armenians at Worcester, Massachusetts. The Nashville churches banded together to send him to Turkey. The Turkey mission, however, closed in only a few years with the untimely death of Paul.

Perhaps the most publicized foreign mission work the church undertook was in Japan in 1892. Early the year before, W. K. Azbill of Indianapolis proposed a Japanese mission and asked for several volunteers. Major repercussions were started in the Society. The General Society, fearing it would lose some of its support by the congregations giving to the Azbill mission, notified Azbill that he could expect no help from them. and asked him to raise his money from churches other than "society churches." Young J. M. McCaleb, reared in Hickman County, Tennessee, and educated at the College of the Bible at Lexington, counseled with David Lipscomb about going. Lipscomb encouraged him and was a great help in raising his support from Tennessee churches. The first of March, 1892, Azbill and McCaleb, with five others in their party, started for Japan.

Mission work among the churches of Christ, and especially foreign mission work, has subjected itself to considerable criticism. Foreign missionaries, so to speak, live in glass bowls, and are, therefore, open to the scrutiny of all. The Japanese mission, at first, was subjected to servere criticism. It was complained that Azbill was a "Society Man." Actually, while Azbill was hardly as opposed to the Society as some brethren, yet he did not solicit funds from it When The Society offered him money, he was inclined to take it, which was the occasion for a difference between McCaleb and Azbill. Others complained of the Azbill mission that it was getting too much money, forcing the preachers at home to have less.

Foreign mission work has been received by churches of Christ with varying degrees of enthusiasm. Criticism of this type of work has generally followed a set pattern.

1 It is suggested that there is so much mission work to do at home that this ought to be done first.

2 The foreign missionaries themselves are criticized for desiring too much the glamor and publicity of the thing. If five people are baptized in Russia, news is spread all over the religious periodicals, but five baptisms in Kentucky may hardly find space in a news report.

3. Foreign missionaries are criticized for taking "sight-seeing trips" at the expense of the church. They must ride airplanes, go first-class on ships, or ride pullman on the train whereas the preachers who stay at home cannot afford such "luxuries"

4. The results achieved in the foreign field on a per dollar basis hardly measure up to that received at home. Hence, it is argued that foreign mission work is too expensive for what it costs.

Other criticisms, growing out of particular circumstances, generally follow this set pattern. Suffice it to say, those aspiring to foreign mission work have become more cognizant of these criticisms and have been wise enough to try to avoid them.

PRESENT-DAY PROBLEMS

Suggestions have been made as to some of the problems that faced the church in the past We turn our attention now to some of the more modern problems facing the church.

The problem of fellowship. The matter of drawing lines of fellowship against individuals in the New Testament Church was an act of the most serious import. It was done generally as a last resort after all other efforts to correct the incorrigible had failed. Still, when being exercised it was done reluctantly and regretfully and with the hope that it would correct the error of the individual.

The problem of who to fellowship remains acute in the churches of Christ today. The action of brethren has had a tendency toward two extremes. On the one side, there is a laxity of drawing lines of fellowship against the disorderly, while on the other, the practice of disfellowshipping individuals is promiscuously used by a clique in power, generally spearheaded by the preacher, as a whip to keep the flock in line. Both extremes are revolting to individuals having a desire to pattern after the New Testament order.

How much error must one imbibe before the church disfellowships him? This problem was faced by David Lipscomb many years ago. Lipscomb believed that it was sinful for a Christian to participate in warfare, and to participate in civil government. The next question was, Would he disfellowship those who did? Consequently, when R C. Horn asked Lipscomb how far a man may go in sin without being withdrawn from, Lipscomb replied:

We are not much of a believer in capital punishment either in church or state. We are never willing to give a man up finally, until we believe he has committed the sin unto death. So long as a man really desires to do right. to serve the Lord, to obey His commands, we cannot withdraw from him. We are willing to accept him as a brother, no matter how ignorant he may be, or how far short the perfect standard his life may fall from this ignorance. We do not mean either to intimate that we are willing to compromise or to hold in abeyance one single truth of God's holy writ, from any motive of policy or expediency. We will maintain the truth, press the truth upon him, compromise not one word or iota of that truth, yet forbear with the ignorance, the weakness of our brother who is anxious but not yet able to see the truth. I feel sure, if I am faithful, and he willing to learn the truth, he will come to the full measure of my knowledge. Why should I not, when I fall so far short of the perfect knowledge myself? How do I know that the line beyond which ignorance damns, is behind me, not before me? If I have no forbearance with his ignorance, how can I expect God to forbear with mine?

What is needed is patient instruction and discipline in the church, instead of withdrawal from the weak Final withdrawal is the end of discipline. I have no doubt it is much too often hastily resorted to, without previous instruction and discipline. . . To withdraw from and turn over to Satan, is just the opposite of discipline. It should be resorted to only when all discipline has wholly failed. So long then as a man exhibits a teachable disposition, is willing to hear, to learn and obey the truth of God, I care not how far he may be, how ignorant he is, I am willing to recognize him as a brother. No matter how wise or how near the truth or how moral a man may be, if he sets up a standard of his own or another and is not willing to learn of God, take his law and obey him, then I can withdraw from him Not until he is beyond the reach of all instruction, expostulation or exhortation would I then surrender him.[7]

Colleges There is so much pride in the human heart that it is very often difficult to learn from one's enemies. The question of the Bible College has already been discussed, and will not be repeated here. The oft-repeated statement of Sommer's that the colleges were the beginning points of all digression probably would not bear up under more thorough investigation. As L. F. Bittle pointed out as early as 1873 in his letters to Jacob Creath, it had rather been the tendency of colleges to fall in line behind the popular sides of issues in the brotherhood. Colleges, as a general rule, will as a matter of policy pursue for a time a midway "safe" course until it is known which side will be the most popular, and then will jump with full force on that side. Colleges, as a general rule, have not fostered the thinking of brethren on certain issues, but rather have reflected the opinion of the majority after the issues have arisen. Consciously or unconsciously, this has been the tendency. The reason is clear colleges must have money to operate and if they get too unpopular, they will not have enough funds to run.

The charge, therefore, that the Bible schools have been the cause of digression is a generalization of very little historical accuracy. Rather, just the opposite is true. The chief forces of opinion and policy in the brotherhood have always been the brotherhood publications. Here the issues are discussed. Here the merits of any issue are weighed. Here the opinions are finally fixed. Churches all over the nation reflect the attitudes and opinions of the papers that are most read. The churches in the North where the *Octographic Review* was read came to be modeled after the policies and views of that paper, just as churches in the South came to be modeled after the views expressed in the *Advocate*. Digression began in the restoration movement not with colleges but with papers, which is to say with influential editors and writers. It was not until after they had swung the opinions of the brotherhood into one line or another that the

[7]David Lipscomb, "Queries on Civil Government," *Gospel Advocate,* Vol XVII, No 17 (April 22, 1875), pp 399, 400

colleges began to take up the issues and become champions of them. The popular side in the restoration was swung after the *Standard* and the *Evangelist*. After they set the pattern of thought, the colleges, one by one, fell in line behind them.

The outlook for the future of the church is far from being dark and the subject-matter is not all distasteful. There is little question that the church is now enjoying one of its greatest surges of growth New congregations, though in some cases yet small, are springing up in cities and towns like magic Churches more and more are arising from the decadence of indifference to be filled with strong missionary zeal. Individual congregations are awakening to their possibilities and are putting forth strenuous efforts to convert the lost in their own community

The coming generation of gospel preachers is in some respects one of the most optimistic signs in the church. They are, on the whole, young men of talent and sincere love for the truth. Many have gone to higher universities and are proving themselves capable of understanding and meeting the mightiest thrusts of liberalism and modernism Grounded in the truth that they love so well, they are extending whole-heartedly the warm hand of sincere love to each other, so that the absence of jealousy and suspicion is noticeable.

So also is the interest in Christian education an encouraging sign With the passing of each year one finds additional plans being made to establish a school in which the Bible may be taught as well as other subjects. It is to be hoped that in a few more years there will be hundreds of schools dotting the nation—schools in every city and town where boys and girls can be taught to love God from the moment they enter school until they graduate from college. While, as has been noted, there are always problems, God-fearing men will find the solution.

The wide interest in foreign mission work it is hoped will not prove to be only a current fad. Despite its culpable points, it is good to see the gospel preached successfully and correctly in foreign lands.

Likewise is it encouraging to witness the extreme positions that formerly faced the church gradually fading away, and a vigorous program of launching the truth daily planned.

But there has never been a time when the church did not have problems. After the present generation is dead, there will still be others. But, whatever their nature, there are principles that will guide the church on safe ground if the church but remembers them. In the light of this we can think of no words to serve as a more fitting close for this volume than those spoken by F. G. Allen a few years before his death.

While we remain true to the principles on which we started out, there is no earthly power that can impede our progress. But the day we leave these walls and go out to take counsel with the world, will mark the day of our decline. We have nothing to fear from without. Our only danger lies in the direction of indifference and compromise. While we are true to God in the maintainence of these principles, the divine blessing will be upon our work. But should they ever be surrendered, ruin will as certainly follow as that the Bible is true [8]

[8] F G Allen, "It Came to Pass," *Gospel Advocate,* Vol XXXVIII, No 4 (January 23, 1896). p 54

INDEX

465

CPSIA information can be obtained at www.ICGtesting.com
Printed in the USA
BVOW02*0135060315

390528BV00003B/15/P